W9-CQO-729

THE WRITER'S HANDBOOK

The Writer's Handbook

Edited by A. S. BURACK
Editor, *The Writer*

Publishers   THE WRITER, INC.   Boston

Copyright © 1978

by

THE WRITER, INC.

"The Theory of the Silver Bullet," by Leonard S. Bernstein.
Copyright © 1977 by Leonard S. Bernstein.

"Writing Poetry for Children," by Myra Cohn Livingston.
Copyright © 1977 by Myra Cohn Livingston.

All rights reserved including the right to
reproduce this book or parts thereof in any form
Library of Congress Catalog Card Number: 36-28596

ISBN: 0-87116-111-7

Printed in the United States of America

FOREWORD

In the many years since the publication of the first edition of *The Writer's Handbook,* there have been marked changes in writing techniques, as well as in market requirements and in types of magazines and book publishers open to free-lance writers. The chapters that have been included in the successive editions have reflected these changes, as have the annual revisions in more than 2,500 markets for manuscripts that comprise Part IV of this volume.

The present edition is a complete revision, the first in several years, with sixty-five of the 100 chapters included here for the first time. The section that opens the book, *Background for Writers,* offers inspiration and advice on how to approach the creative writer's world. Part II deals with the specific techniques that have been successfully used by outstanding writers to achieve publication in the fields of fiction, nonfiction, poetry, and juvenile writing, and in such specialized fields as playwriting, television, science fiction, trade journals, religious publications, fillers and short items, and humor. Finally, Part III offers detailed information on literary agents, the new copyright law, pen names, the editorial process, and manuscript preparation. The lists in Part IV provide up-to-date names and addresses of magazines and book publishers, editors and their manuscript requirements, including length, type of material wanted, and payment rates.

My special thanks to the authors of the chapters in this new edition of *The Writer's Handbook,* which I hope will be a continuing source of instruction and inspiration for beginning and experienced writers.

A. S. BURACK

CONTENTS

PART I—BACKGROUND FOR WRITERS

PART II—HOW TO WRITE: Techniques

FICTION

Nonfiction

Poetry

PART III—THE EDITORIAL AND BUSINESS SIDE

PART IV—THE WRITER'S MARKETS

WHERE TO SELL

PART I

BACKGROUND FOR WRITERS

1

MAKING THE MOST OF YOUR TALENT

By Marjorie Holmes

I WONDER if teachers, particularly good English teachers, realize the profound impact they may have on developing talent? My teacher was Dewey Deal, slim, blonde, with her hair in a silken bun and a voice that was like rich velvet. I had her in eighth grade, and then by a remarkable stroke of fortune, for freshman English in college. It was there she wrote the following words on a notebook. Words that were often to keep me going during periods of discouragement; words that were to influence my writing itself:

You must make the most of your talent—you have been endowed with so much. I can feel joy with these paragraphs, I can feel sorrow, I am moved by their imagery. I know that if you want to badly enough you can write beautiful things for people who crave beautiful things. There is a duty!

There is a duty. . . .
Talent is a gift. You had nothing to do with receiving yours, nor I with receiving mine. But each of us has everything to do with what becomes of that talent. I am firmly convinced that each of us is given his talent for a reason; and that having talent, any talent, but particularly one for writing, imposes two responsibilities.

First: It must not go to waste.
There is a parable in the Bible about a master who distributed talents among his servants to see what they could accomplish with them. And those who put their talents to work were rewarded. But there was one who was skeptical or maybe just lazy; instead of investing his talent he buried it in the ground. So it was taken away and given to somebody else.

And he was miserable. The Bible doesn't say so, but he was.

I know. Because surely the most miserable people a professional

3

writer encounters are those who speak of past glories, the promise, the prizes won; and who now are haunted by the knowledge that they have buried a precious talent. No matter how they try to escape such nagging accusations—through activity with children, in churches, coffee klatches, work, politics—they will not be still. Would-be writers send hand-wringing letters to "luckier" writers, listing excuses, begging for the kind of help no outsider can give. Because the trouble lies inside.

What is the true cause when talent is thwarted? I think it's primarily a lack of that sense of responsibility or duty. Too often talent is regarded as a mere adornment, something with which to amuse yourself and dazzle your friends. That's how it seems when one is very young. I used to write long continued stories which the kids passed around in school (ending when the tablet paper ran out). I dashed off poems dedicated to everybody in sight and read aloud on all possible occasions. I even wrote my own declamatory pieces. And it was all part of a heady show-off syndrome.

Yet deep beneath all this ran a fierce compulsion: I *had* to write. Even minus an audience, into a vast notebook, late at night, I had to write. And what clinched this compulsion for me and turned it into a profession were the words: "There is a duty."

People who fail to follow up their own bright promise seem to lack this compulsion. Or, if they have it at first, they cut it off when it begins to hurt (and it hurts, oh, how it hurts), or when it becomes hard work resulting only in a rain of rejection slips and bitter disappointments. How much easier to regard your talent not simply as essential if awesome equipment for an important calling, but as an ornament to be tossed in a drawer. You know it's there, your pretty little talent, and you can always dust if off and don it if you wish—when you're "inspired." Or to delight admiring friends. "She writes," they say of you, and you prove it by doing witty newsletters for your organizations, or composing the club show.

Yet how brief is the sweet satisfaction. You know, deep in your guts you know, you can and should be doing so much more. And the sense of guilt and failure intensifies when one day the drawer is opened to find the talent has lost its luster, or even vanished altogether.

The list of excuses for wasted talent is endless. Illness, economics, responsibilities to family, friends, the church, the community. They confront each of us every day the minute we open our eyes. The person without a sense of obligation to his own talent promptly takes his pick. The person whose talent is a serious responsibility, however, appraises this obstacle course and figures out priorities.

When people ask how I've done it—raised four children while writing hundreds of magazine pieces and seventeen books—I tell them: "I'm disciplined and I'm organized."

Back in college, I had come to realize that the only way I would accomplish anything was to finish *something* ... no matter how boring or bad—just finish it and get on to something else. I had entered a contest for the best essay on nutrition. If there was anything that bored me at that time, it was nutrition, and having to do the research for it was hell. But, having signed the entry blank and started, I forced myself to trudge to the library and cull the (to me then) miserable facts and write about them. Before I was half through I had lost interest even in the prize of fifty much-needed dollars. Yet, I pushed grimly on to the bitter end—and felt such a moment of triumph when I finished! Even though the essay was absolutely awful, and there was no hope of my winning a prize, I realized deep in my psyche that I had taken one sure step on the road to self-discipline.

Later, when we so desperately needed money during the Depression, it was much easier to attack all sorts of projects (limericks, contests, trade journal ideas, interviews, etc.) with the prospect of making a buck. And though only a few of these produced, at least each one that was actually stamped and fed into the mail enhanced and strengthened that inner conviction. I could and would finish what I started. And among all the things finished and started, *some* would be worthwhile.

How was I able to do this? My teacher's words, framed over my desk, often goaded me on: *"If you want to badly enough, you can...!"*

One method is to make lists of projects, putting large and small ones on the same list. Take the idea in which you've already invested the most time and energy, and finish it! Once you get into it again, the original excitement will return. The creative process, rekindled by actual work, does wonderful things. Film strip, play, novel, TV series

—whatever—go back to it thinking, "How great. Look how much I've already done!" And finish it.

Refuse to get diverted by anything else until you put your manuscript in the mail.

Meanwhile, carefully and lovingly write down the plans, projects, peripheral ideas that come.

This means stopping your main project for a few minutes to jot the idea down. Maybe waking up in the middle of the night and writing more thoughts about the same idea. Or more new ideas, because ideas travel in flocks. I pin some of these to the curtains as reminders. "Don't forget me!" they say. And the very fact that they are there awaiting their turn urges you on faster toward finishing what is in the typewriter.

Keep file folders filled with material that pertains to them. Write an occasional sentence or paragraph that seems just right. But don't be seduced by the siren voice that will keep you from *at least four hours of daily progress on what you have begun.*

Here's the secret: Having a weekly plan of achievement helps. In those days when I was freelancing so widely the fact that I *had* a goal to aim at greased the wheels. I was working toward something definite. When new ideas came soaring in, beating and clamoring for my attention, I could say, "Yes, yes, you're lovely. I'll grab you right now, but you'll have to wait your turn."

The wonderful part of all this was that I always had so many manuscripts in the mail. I remembered the advice of a college mentor who said, "Nothing ever sold in a desk drawer." Once a manuscript was in the mail, the greater the odds in my favor; there was something to hope for. Though lots of things came back, eventually, *most* found a home somewhere. Sometimes I had to revise between submissions, which meant taking a few days or even a whole week to do a rewrite. But that was even more satisfying, because of the sense of direction.

Of course I didn't sell everything I wrote. Sometimes, heartbreakingly, my manuscripts failed after editors ordered rewrites. (Some of my very best are still in my files.) And I didn't finish *every*thing I started. Some things I had the good sense to abandon. But when I did so, it was with the satisfying feeling that it was not because I lacked the will power to finish. I had developed enough judgment to realize what was valuable and what a waste of time.

I wrote in the inspirational field from the beginning. I found that facts bored me, and research took too much time away from home and typewriter. For me it was easier and more fulfilling to write creative articles born out of my own experience or observation, personal discoveries or formulas for living. And whether torn out of the very pit of suffering, or sprung from an incessant love affair with life, all were upbeat, constructive.

I believe the writer's second responsibility is this: *to use his or her talent for good.* Not necessarily to preach or exhort or reform, but to affirm life rather than debase it, to inspire and help and encourage.... *"You can write beautiful things for people who crave beautiful things...."* Despite the sex and cynicism and materialism that seem so common, and the avalanche of products that pander to a lust for the perverse, the ugly, and the decadent, there is still a vast hunger for things of the spirit, beautiful things. And the writer who is able to nourish and fill that hunger is beginning to reap incredible and long overdue rewards.

The success of religious and inspirational books in the past few years has become the phenomenon of the publishing industry. Books of prayers and meditations, conspicuous by their absence on most best-seller lists, actually sold circles around many of the titles that did appear there.

Nobody, however, could be more surprised than I at turning out to be a "religious writer." I never even considered myself an especially religious person, although I recognized the Creator as the source of all creative talent, and was immensely grateful for mine. I also felt God was an unseen companion who understood me far better than I could understand myself, and to whom I could pour out everything, from the sublime to the ridiculous. Now and then, just as a change of pace in my newspaper column, I would publish one of my informal conversational prayers ("Psalm for Scrubbing a Floor," "Prayer for Peeling a Potato"). Invariably reader response was so great it came to the attention of Doubleday, who'd already published *Love and Laughter,* a collection of my columns. It was decided that when I'd put enough of these prayers together, they might make a book.

No one expected much of it, least of all me. So all of us were astounded at the immediate success of *I've Got to Talk to Some-body, God* (which has sold a million copies in hardcover, counting book clubs, and is approaching its second million in paperback); its sequel, *Who Am I, God?, How Can I Find You, God?* and the book of prayers for girls, *Nobody Else Will Listen,* are catching up to it, while my novel, *Two from Galilee,* is approaching *its* first million in hardcover and its second million in paperback.

Now that we've "let it all hang out" in literature, I doubt if we'll ever go back. Obscenity, pornography, violence and books of artistic merit filled with scenes of raw, explicit sex will continue to pour from presses as long as there is a market for them. But I find it hearten-ing that so many people are reaching out for something else. Not pieties and preachments; not writing that simply shuts its eyes and pretends there is no evil or sorrow in the world. But rather writing that shows the basic goodness and decency of human beings despite their trials; that celebrates compassion and love and wonder and all the other things that make life worthwhile.

There will always be writers willing to aim at the lowest common denominator of taste. Some of them are poor writers, of course; but sadly, a number of them are good, maybe even potentially great, writers. And to me, this abuse of talent is far worse than not using it at all. Anyone who *reads* knows that writing has a powerful effect on behavior. And you can't have it both ways: If books can do good in the world—teach, inspire, change things for the better—then books can also damage and destroy.

Are you making the most of your talent? Only you can decide: Are you using it? And what are you using it *for?*

2

GENIUS AND THE CRAFTSMAN

By Kaatje Hurlbut

ONCE on the edge of a woods at twilight I came upon a small peach tree in flower. I stayed there watching until the light was gone. I saw nothing of the tree's origin, nothing of the might which had forced open a pit you could break your teeth on, and nothing of the principle which held it separate from the oaks and the grasses. All that appeared to me was a profound and eerie grace.

So it is with the reader who comes upon an outstanding story: spellbound, he takes it to his heart, no questions asked.

But even the beginning writer knows there is more to a story's life than the body of words which carries it into the world, and that it does not begin with writing, but with conception in the dark of the mind.

It is not necessary to understand the creative function in order to produce original work. Centuries of art, philosophy and science have emerged from the minds of people who may not even have suspected the inner process. It seems to me, however, that at least a degree of understanding of the creative event increases our wisdom in dealing with the emerging story by making us aware of two things.

The first is that genius is not the exclusive property of the master craftsman: it is the creative function of the human mind. There is no mastery without it, and there is no person without it, however undeveloped it may be. Mastery is genius afoot. It is genius cultivated, developed, and exercised. Your genius works at the level of origins; its business is to create; it is the creator of your story.

Second: the body of words which carries your story into the world is the work of the craftsman, and the craftsman's labor is as conscious, as canny, and as practical as that of the bricklayer. While genius is a natural part of our mental equipment, like perception, memory, and imagination, craftsmanship is not. It must be learned.

9

It is learned by practice, and by practice it is mastered. If the stories that rise within us are to emerge and flourish, each must be provided with a strong, handsome body of words, and only sound craftsmanship can provide this.

How is a story conceived? It is said that we write from the first twenty years of our lives, perhaps from the first five; it may depend on the individual, as so much does in writing. In any case, the lucid impressions of childhood and early youth, more or less unconditioned, unexplained, unchecked, lie in the memory, live and timeless. Enigma, wonder, fear, rapture, grandeur, and trivia in every degree and combination, these early impressions throb and wait—for what? Completion of some kind? For recognition of their own peculiar truth? It would seem their wounds want lancing; their secret knowledge wants telling; the discoveries would be shared, and woes admitted, and the airy tracery of beauty given form.

Thus variously laden we move through life, and now and then an experience, often slight, pierces the memory and seizes upon one of those live, expectant impressions of long ago, and a quickening takes place.

This happens to everyone and more often than is known. But there are times when it happens to the creative writer and causes him to catch his breath because he knows that the seed of a story has quickened and has begun a life of its own.

Like any seed, the seed of a story has its own principle of growth which employs a process of intelligent selection, drawing from the unconscious mind's vast treasury of experience what it needs to fulfill its inherent form: there come together people and their ways, with weather and times and places, and the souls of things. In short, there is produced a world, complete with stars and stumbling blocks.

Thus "made in secret and curiously wrought in the lowest parts of the earth," the story expands and rises, unhurried, until at last it presents itself to the conscious mind. Here at the threshold, vibrant with expectation, it awaits its body of words.

Genius, the creative function, has done its work. And only now does the craftsman, the deliverer, begin his.

A story rarely, if ever, presents itself as a whole. Robert Frost said that he never knew where a poem was going when he began it. Until I am almost upon it in a first draft, I do not know a story's end, or even its point; and there are times when only after two, three or more drafts will the story come clearly into focus.

Years ago in the early dawn of an October morning, I watched the tiny Sputnik cut its brief arc across the sky. Sometime later, a story I knew to be gathering and rising presented itself: An old man who had spent a lonely life in the depths of the city retired to a house on a cove near the sea. Overwhelmed by the beauty of the cove and the kindness of his neighbors, he began to know the desperation of those whose lives are almost over, and who, for one reason or another, have never given, or even shared, anything.

Knowing only this, I moved swiftly into the first draft and wrote: "The people of Pomeroy's Cove gave Mr. Paradee the sky. They gave it all to him, from dawn to dawn—with thunderheads and flights of geese and the red moon rising"*

What was I doing? I wrote of a curious gift; there were more curious gifts to come. I moved into the sky; later I would head toward celestial traffic. I marveled, when I reached the end, that I had not known the whole story from the first paragraph: every word pointed the way. But not knowing, why did I begin to write? What was I doing?

I was fulfilling two of the craftsman's three functions: *trust,* and the second: *write.* I was trusting in the inevitability of the story's intelligence, its truth, whatever it might be; I was trusting in its completeness, its form, whenever it might emerge. By writing, I was allowing it, inviting it to emerge: I was providing its vehicle. For how else could it emerge?

Trust your genius: it is your creative function and its business is to create. Because it works at the level of origins, the story it creates is original; it is yours alone. No one else can know it or write it. That is a story's value, and its only value. Respect your creative function; rely on it to be intelligent: it is not a thing of random impulse, but a working principle. Trust it, be glad about it, and use it. That is the secret of cultivating it, and the beginning of true ability.

Trust and write. Write your story when you begin to feel its insistent pulse. If you don't know it all, write as much as you know;

---

*"A Passage from the Stars," (*Saturday Evening Post,* 1961). Also appeared in *7th Annual of the Year's Best SF,* Edited by Judith Merrill (Simon & Schuster).

work receptively and patiently, and it will all come to you presently. If you can't write well, write the best you can, always the best, with all the intelligence and clarity you can command at the moment. If you do that, and persist in it, you will improve steadily. The reason for this is that earnest work literally generates intelligence. Consistent practice generates skill. And to generate skill is the craftsman's third function.

Give every story, every letter, every entry in your daily journal, if you keep one, the best writing of which you are capable. Write well. Write skillfully. Write beautifully, or write superbly, if you can. Be watchful and objective about what goes down on paper. Anything less than the degree of excellence of which you are capable at any given time is not craftsmanship. It is dabbling.

The beginning writer saves time and effort by being prompt and businesslike about finding a method of work which suits him. Look into methods. We know writing cannot be taught, that it can only be learned. But common sense, the canny handmaid of genius, tells us that practicing writers, like practicing plumbers, politicians and goldsmiths, who get the job done day in and day out, know what they are talking about when they talk about work. Read them and listen to them, and you will recognize in their working habits many tendencies and impulses of your own. You will see that they are not your private vagaries, but in many cases unique and vital aspects of the writing temperament, things in your favor that can work for you.

I wrote four hours a day for ten years before I was published. Working without teachers or books on writing, I was a long time discovering a method of work. Years later when a very fine teacher remarked: "You know, a good story is not written, but rewritten," I replied somewhat wistfully: "Yes, I know. I wish someone had told me that long ago."

My way of dealing with a story is simple and it works. When a story presents itself and I catch a glimpse of what I have, I capture it in a swift, skeletal draft. Presently, perhaps the next day, I rewrite from the beginning, inevitably adding more, filling out, and always treating the story as a whole. I continue to rewrite at intervals, letting it cool in between times, and rewrite as many times as needed until the words seem to fit the story smoothly and comfortably, always trying for a wording that clings as wet silk clings, and always reaching for that mastery which can fashion a body of words that is no more than a filament.

There is magic in intention. When you work with the intention of excellence, no matter how hard you work, it is never drudgery. No matter how far short of the mark you fall, it is never failure— unless, of course, you are willing to stop there. Rewriting in this way is not a chore, but an adventure in skill.

When you treat the story as a live, intelligent whole, rewriting is dynamic because three things happen:

First: you gain a complete knowledge of the story. You can scarcely believe how little you know of your story in a first or second draft until you reach the fourth or fifth. Layer upon layer reveals itself; small things, at first unnoticed, expand in importance; areas of vagueness or confusion become sharp and clear. Things which slip past the eye in rereading leap at you and demand attention. Such expert knowledge of this one story gives you control; and control allows you to do your best writing on that story because you know what you are doing. To know one story thoroughly prepares you for your knowledge of the next: you won't puzzle and perhaps despair over a first draft, assuming that, with all its imperfections, its haziness and poor writing, it is the best you can do. You will rewrite with confidence, knowing the story will certainly improve.

Second: you gain a facility which no other exercise, no book, no teacher, however knowledgeable, can possibly give you. In dealing again and again with the same story problems and the same writing problems, you learn to do things efficiently; you learn new ways and, most important, you learn *your* way. Rereading tends to condone errors in writing; rewriting tends to reveal them. Self-conscious flamboyance shows up for what it is; what you considered a clever understatement is often revealed as an evasion of something difficult to state, but which is vital to the story and worthy of clarity. Your judgment and sensitivity sharpen as you are forced to face, word by deadly word, the ill-written, ungainly passages. You cannot improve one sentence, one paragraph without improving your skill. You begin to see that mastery is no pipe dream, but a possibility.

Third: rewriting is rewriting, and writing is a writer's work. Reading, attending classes, talking to working writers are all helpful activities, but only if you work at writing. Rewriting provides steady work with a distinct purpose, and that purpose provides an ever-present reward: continually improving skill. Work of this kind is habit-forming, and there is nothing known to man that stimulates genius like the habit of work.

Never impose a limit on your ability, and never allow anyone else to. When working with the intention of excellence becomes a habit with you, you will understand that the masterpiece is not a mystery and not an accident, but that it is the by-product of a way of life.

3

SHOULD I BE A WRITER?

By Joe Gores

I MAKE my living writing, not talking, but like most professionals I am periodically asked to speak about my craft. Certain questions always pop up in the cat-and-mouse sessions which follow. Since they seem to reflect genuine concerns of beginning writers, and since I presume my answers reflect the attitudes of the average pro, I list herewith a few exchanges of possible value.

I have a good job, but I have always wanted to write. Should I be a writer?

I believe it's more a question of *must* you be a writer. It chooses you, not the other way around. Keep your job and write in your spare time until you find out whether you can make it or not. Try to avoid professions which leave your creative faculties dulled at the end of the day, such as teaching, writing for a newspaper, or doing ad agency copy. Writing is not a "second profession"—it demands as much time as you can give it, preferably a lifetime. Nor is professional writing therapy, an outlet for creative energies, or a hobby. Dorothy Parker once wryly commented, after mentioning certain writing-is-fun writers, "And there was that poor sucker Flaubert, rolling around on his floor for three days looking for the right word."

The day before I graduated from Notre Dame, I asked my creative writing teacher, Richard Sullivan, whether I should be a writer. I have never forgotten his answer. "It's very easy, Joe," he said. "Go to a big city and get a little room with a table and a chair in it. Put your typewriter on the table and your backside on the chair, and start typing. When you stand up ten years later, you'll be a writer."

I am interested in the creation of literature, so why should I have to demean my art by writing for money?

Don't knock it until you've tried it. And who told you writing is an art? It's a craft. Unless you are making a living from your writing, or are trying to, you are just kidding yourself. Ernest Hemingway stated, "I write hardcover books for money." William Faulkner often said that when he got a letter he turned the envelope upside down and shook it. If a check fell out, he read the letter.

I find it unusually interesting that the proliferation of university and foundation grants-in-aid to writers has not produced anyone with the enduring stature of a Hemingway or a Faulkner. Writing is grueling work, and most of us would rather make excuses than stories. But when your food and rent come out of the typewriter, you tend to give it regular exercise. I doubt if most non-professionals have any idea of the amount of work a pro regularly turns out. In a typical year, for example, I have written three novels, two screenplays, a nonfiction book proposal (fifty pages and a detailed outline), and several short stories and articles: two thousand typed manuscript pages, including revision drafts. And I am light years away from being the most prolific pro around.

Geoffrey Household, British master of suspense, put it this way:

> If you cannot live by your writing, the translation into words of your own manner of thinking cannot be effective, for your whole aim and object is to be so completely good that the maximum number of people, whether they approve or not, will have to pay money to read you. The market is the ultimate test for the craftsman. That it should also be the first and only test for the hack is unimportant.

Isn't professional writing merely hack writing anyway?

All hacks are by necessity professionals, but not all professionals are hacks. The hack works *only* for money, invariably subordinating artistic considerations to the buck. The professional can take on almost any writing chore, as long as he involves himself in the project and does the best job he can, without descending to mere hack work. Our business is to write, exactly as a bricklayer's business is to lay bricks. I have yet to hear someone accuse a bricklayer of being a hack because he laid bricks for a sewage disposal plant

instead of waiting around (while his family starved) to lay bricks
for a cathedral.

How long will it take me to become a professional writer?

If we assume a modicum of talent and a lot of drive (ten percent
ability, ninety percent determination, according to W. Somerset
Maugham), Professor Sullivan's figure is about right: ten years to
learn the craft well enough (and to make a sufficient percentage of
your living from it) to consider yourself a professional. You never
stop learning, of course. Nothing you will ever write will be quite
as good as it *could* be. Faulkner once said of the writer in relation
to his work, "Once he matched the work to the image, the dream,
nothing would remain but to . . . jump off the other side of the
pinnacle of perfection into suicide."

Can you break it down into dollars and cents?

When I began selling, I made a penny per hour at the typewriter.
It took me four years, averaging three hundred rejection slips a
year, to make my first story sale. During the next six years, my
writing income averaged $354.50 a year. If you can live on that,
hop to it. I'd guess that the pro with those necessary ten or fifteen
years behind him will be making between $5,000 and $15,000 a
year, with the norm between $7,000 and $12,000.

Will writers' courses help me become a good writer?

No. Writing will help you become a good writer. The single most
important thing for a writer is to write. The second is to rewrite.
Writers' courses *do* make the beginning or amateur writer write and
provide him with criticism of his work.

One of the big arguments advanced for such courses is that they
help dispel the loneliness. If you can't stand being alone, find
another line of work. Punch tickets in the subway or something.
Nobody can write it for you, nobody can help you write it (my cat
tries, he sleeps on my desk as I work and talks over plots with
me). Being solitary is not being lonely. Watching a host of heroes
and villains and lovers and haters emerge from the typewriter is
not being lonely. Working on a novel the other day, I had to sit by
in astonishment while a couple of guys I've written about in short

stories for years got into a devil of a row. I had no idea they were going to do that. I'd always thought of them as close friends.

Write. And write, write, write. And submit. Take your lumps and your rejection slips. When your work gets good enough, you will start getting the occasional editorial reaction along with the printed confetti, and you will be on your way.

How can I determine the correct markets for my material?

Use common sense, first of all. In *Playboy*, Jack and Jill don't go up the hill *just* to fetch a pail of water; in *Good Housekeeping*, the heroine does not smoke pot and have a live-in boyfriend. *Read the magazines*. And I mean read (or skim) *everything* in them, especially the advertising. Reading the ads will help you judge whether your work is calculated to grab the reader of that particular magazine.

Novelists should read a lot of novels, especially those from the current lists of publishers they favor. If the publishers' editorial tastes vary wildly from your own, start considering a different publishing house. And do not be discouraged when, after all of this, the inevitable rejection slips pile up. Even some major best sellers have collected a dozen or more rejections before a publisher finally took them.

As a beginner, should I stick to shorts or try the novel?

Each form has much to offer. The short story usually deals with a single incident or point in time which radically and instantly changes the protagonist's life. The short is the great teacher, forcing you to be parsimonious with words, to write compelling and revealing dialogue, and to be selective in your use of description.

The novel usually is marked by the impact of time on its characters, and shows gradual significant change or development in them —a war, say, rather than a single battle. Unlike the short story, the novel forgives many errors, but you have to *write* the darned thing. Pages and pages, thousands and thousands of words, weeks, months, sometimes years, with no money coming in and little assurance of any even when it is finished. You have to stick to the novel, yet most amateurs remain amateurs precisely because they *don't* have sticking power. They'd rather play golf.

Whatever you write, be aware of the market. In the thirties, a

10,000-word short story was acceptable; by the fifties the optimum word length had dropped to 5,000 words. Today it's about 3,500; we live in a faster age. Novels should range between 55,000 and 85,000 words, with 60,000 to 70,000 optimum. Too short, the reader feels cheated; too long, the printing costs become prohibitive. Herman Wouk and Harold Robbins write 900-page books which sell for $10.00; you and I don't. Why? For the moment, at least, we aren't going to sell like Wouk or Robbins.

Do I need an agent?

No. Beginning writers not only don't need an agent, most of them aren't going to get one, not a reputable agent. Why *should* he take you on? Ten percent of almost nothing leads to forced sales of his office furniture. He wants writers who not only can sell, but who also can *produce*, can meet deadlines, can absorb criticism, can function, in short, in a professional manner.

Contrary to popular belief, an agent is not going to sell your book any faster than you are, not if it is a salable book. If it isn't, he's not going to sell it at all. Editors buy books, not somebody's boyish good looks. It is after you are offered a contract that you need an agent, and you can then probably get a reputable one.

He will know why clauses can be blue-penciled from the standard contract, he knows where to look for foreign, movie, and condensation sales that form such a vital part of a book's income. It is the *selling* writer—and above all the professional writer—who needs an agent.

One final point: the author/agent relationship is a delicate one, a sexless marriage. There must be mutual trust and a give-and-take in which both are comfortable. A bad or untrustworthy or dishonest agent is a thousand times worse than no agent at all, because he can, quite literally, destroy you as a writer.

Does it help your sales to know editors?

Knowing editors helps you find out what sort of material is in current demand. And if a book or article is to be farmed out, editors will naturally turn to professionals with whose work they are familiar and who they know will produce to deadline.

But even if you've never sold anything in your life, the editor is not The Enemy. He is not some alien creature standing between you and success. Editors are skillful intermediaries between writers interested in artistic creation, and publishing houses interested in making a profit from selling books. Of course, there are lousy editors, but there are plenty of lousy writers, too.

A *good* editor is a joy forever, able to make a sick story well. I remember Lee Wright of Random House once saying to me, during a head-knocking session over a proposed novel, "Remember, Joe, the most useful word in a writer's vocabulary is 'meanwhile.' " This is a profound insight into the art of storytelling: try it sometime when you're bogged down in a plot line.

It is easy to get to know editor . Submit salable material to them. But don't count on a first-name basis to insure sales. You're only as good as the work in hand; the fact that they buy from you this month doesn't mean they'll buy next month. Or buy a bad book or story. Or take something unsuited to their market.

Knowing editors is not the way to success as a writer. Nor is having an agent. Success does not come from slanting your material to a market, or from sitting around chanting "literature" like one of the seven names of God. Success does not even come from smoking a briar pipe and wearing a Harris tweed with leather patches on the elbows.

Success as a writer comes from writing—constantly, compulsively, in a word, professionally. Writing is communication, and writing is a craft. In any craft, practice is the only means to success. From practice comes the technical mastery which must be assumed before profound (or, indeed, light) fiction can be written. Technical mastery frees your creative intuition from worry about words, lets it create from raw sensory data and what French philosopher Jacques Maritain has called the "pre-conscious intellect," a new entity which readers will recognize as more real than reality itself.

This is what writing is all about. And this is what writing *has* been all about, ever since man first learned to tell his stories on the walls of his caves instead of just talking about them.

4

AIM FOR THE HEART

By Paul Gallico

If I wished to write a novel for my own edification, which really is just another way of saying for my own vanity—most of those books that writers are always telling you they are going to write someday just for themselves are indicative of narcissism—I suppose I could delve backwards into what was actually a reasonably happy childhood and find dark moments of anguish or self-induced terrors. I could manage to exploit weaknesses of my elders, sexual experiments, and produce an adequate panopticon of unpleasant subsidiary characters who frightened, harassed or disliked me at one time or another, or made me aware of my inadequacies, to be able to come up with a fair facsimile of what seems to be the modern novel and the aim of the young writer. It might even draw me one of those two-column, analytical reviews, or unwarranted praise.

But if I wanted to write a novel that would sell, I would sit down at my desk and try to think of some human and likable characters, for whose makeup I would borrow here and there from the personalities of people I had met—men, women and children—and I would then attempt to invent a situation that would try them almost beyond endurance.

I would endeavor to make you care deeply about these people, and hence I would have to care deeply about them myself first. In each one I would have to find some echoing chord of my own being: the kind of person I am, the kind of things I like, my fears, my hopes, so that these would be recognizable as genuine fears and hopes, the longings and appetites and the ambitions that might be found in any of us.

I would give these people spiritual strength coupled with near fatal flaws, good luck and bad, and a meed of cowardice, but a greater gift of courage. In the course of the trials I would prepare for them, they would have need for all of these things and love besides—love in the sense that it is the one emotion capable of mounting guard over our natures. I would wish you to feel at one with someone, if not with several of the people in this book, to the point where you entered into their adventures and lost yourself in them. And I would try to tell my story and their story, and vicariously your story, in such a way that once you began, once you had recognized yourself in either the characters or the situation, you would not be able to put it down.

I would want to tell you the story of people under adversity who struggled and won or lost, according to their capabilities, but without too great an emphasis on victory, so that those who lost might even be thought to have won something beyond those who seemed to triumph.

It would be a story of man against nature, or man against man; man the supreme being on earth, or man the infinitesimal speck. But a story it would be, with a beginning, a middle and an end, and at that end, after you had followed with me the travail and strivings of these persons, I would hope that I would leave you not quite the same as you had been before you started. That is the kind of book I would try to write, if I wanted it to sell.

"Wanted to sell"—or just "sell" alone—has a harsh sound and some of the stink of the market place.

Yet to sell is what the honest writer wants to do, to sell to earn a living to feed his family, or even for the pure satisfaction of selling, of having written something good enough to cause the largest number of people to reach into their pockets and give over money they have earned, for the privilege of spending some hours alone with characters and narrative that the writer has created.

The highest form of flattery comes not from the reviewer, however erudite or complimentary he or she may be, but from the man or woman unknown to you who enters a bookshop, finds and fingers a copy, tests a page or, listening to the bookseller tell what it is about, says, "I think I'll have that one," and produces his wallet.

It is possible, I know, to do this today in many other ways—by writing the kind of obscenity one only used to see on privy walls; by lifting the lid on human sewage pits and letting the reader look within at the horrors; by rewriting some well-known human folly or personal disaster into fiction form. But the great storytellers of the past never needed these, nor will the great storytellers of the future. To sell, it is only necessary to capture the human imagination and touch the human heart.

Fashions in fiction come and go, but the storyteller will never go out of date. I remember when I was a young man and sold my first stories to *The Post,* I was summoned for a visit with its great Editor, George Horace Lorimer. Several of these were sports stories, and Mr. Lorimer said that the magazine had a great need for these and hoped that I would fill it. And I remember remarking, even through my awe of the great man, that I wanted to play Hamlet. He eyed me and said, "And what form does your Hamlet take?"

I said, "Stories with a d-d-different b-background, sir, not just sports—newspapers, circuses, other things. . . ."

When I had finished stammering, he said quietly, "Young man, I'll tell you something. I don't care what background you decide to use, just don't forget to tell me a story."

Around ancient campfires, or at court, the jester with the dirty joke could make them laugh for a few moments, but it was the story-teller who had his listeners spellbound, whether he twanged his lyre in song or spoke in poetry or prose of heroes who overcame great odds, and of lovers whom not even death could part.

The anti-hero is the prototype of despair. The hero flings aloft the banner of hope. The storybook ending isn't life, but life often enough provides the storybook ending to make it worthwhile to tell about. If we thought that there was nothing but misery, degradation and darkness and above all perpetual defeat, what would be the use of trying to feed or clothe ourselves, raise children, and put a penny by to purchase a book to refresh one's spirit and fortify one's hopes?

It isn't easy and everyone can't do it, but everyone can try. Tell a story in which you believe, about people with whom you sympathize or admire. Tell it simply and enthrallingly, and the pile of your books on the bookstore counter will melt away like the snows in spring. Aim for the heart.

5

THE GOLD MINE OF EXPERIENCE

By Carol R. Brink

EVERYONE, whether he writes it or not, has a novel in him, for no life is so completely dull and uneventful that it will not make a story. But we all know the one-novel writer, who, when he has told what happened to him, has exhausted his little vein of gold and can produce no more.

The trick of longevity in writing is to begin laying up riches in childhood and never to cease learning and experiencing and storing away, so that the older the writer becomes, the richer the hidden mine will be. The next trick is to learn how to bring out a very little bit of gold at a time and spin and beat and carve it into something precious. The person who can do this will not be a one-novel author, but can continue to create as long as his mind remains clear and he has the gumption to use a typewriter.

What have I already stored up? It is a good question for any writer to ask himself. He should take stock of his mind and see what it will yield. If he learned in childhood to use his senses and observe the world around him, he was fortunate. A lonely or unhappy childhood may be the greatest blessing for a writer. If it does not make a criminal of him, it may make him a genius. Many of us who fall between the two extremes learned in childhood to amuse ourselves by observing and storing away details that the happy and extroverted child often misses.

Early in my life I had to face family tragedy, and later I had many lonely hours to fill. For the most part I was not unhappy, and I spent hours on horseback, looking and learning. So now for much of my writing I go back to the small Idaho town where I knew every weed and wild flower, every turn of season, the smell of dusty clover, the distant chime of church bells and the chanting of the meadowlarks on fence posts in the wheat fields. I was acquainted with the sad or noble or funny people, and, if I did not know their stories, I made the stories up myself. The richest veins of my gold mine of experience come from this childhood of silent observation. I continually go back to it.

But suppose that the writer has missed this background of childhood experience—how can he compensate? The answer is that he must set out consciously to acquire what he might have come by unconsciously as a child. It is never too late to learn to use the senses.

I remember hearing one of my college teachers say that many people go through life without seeing the world around them. "How ridiculous," I thought. "Unless he is blind, everyone can see what is around him." But the idea nagged at me, and I began for the first time consciously to make use of my senses. I remember walking home after class and noticing *consciously* the smell of wet lumber, the feel of gravel under my feet, the clear look of the mountains after rain. Observation is an acquired taste, but it can grow into a passion.

The more the writer stores away in the cells of memory, the more wealth he can pull out and use some day when he is sitting at a desk in a small room with a blank page of paper before him. The details, with which he surrounds his characters and rounds out his plot, leaven his story and make it come alive for his reader.

Thomas Wolfe, in *Look Homeward, Angel,* has a long passage which is merely a catalogue of smells. But close your eyes and let yourself go with him: "... the exciting smell of chalk and varnished desks; the smell of heavy bread sandwiches of cold fried meat and butter; the smell of new leather in a saddler's shop, or of a warm leather chair; of honey and of unground coffee; of barrelled sweetpickles and cheese and all the fragrant compost of the grocers'...." *Compost!* What a wonderful word to use in this connection! But we don't care to write so lavishly these days. What we aim for now is more compact writing, the spare, the lean, the elegant. We are content to leave the catalogues and rivers of sensation to Wolfe and Walt Whitman. Yet the writer must never miss an opportunity to appeal, however briefly, to his reader's senses, so that the reader may experience vicariously the sensations which the writer has stored up for him.

Selection of material is another thing that the writer must practice both consciously and unconsciously. If we were to put down every sensation that we experience and every action that we perform in a single day, the account might run into volumes. Yet tomorrow we will remember only a few major happenings, and by next week we will certainly not remember what we had for dinner nor how many times we cleaned our teeth. Mercifully, our memories are the first unconscious selectors that save our minds from needless clutter. Sometimes our memories are very cunning and adroit selectors.

Years ago when my husband and I traveled a good deal in Europe, we kept a joint diary. For one week my husband would write in it and the next week I would do the recording. This diary has been very useful to me many times when I wanted to recall a foreign setting. One day we were driving in the French Alps and we lost our way on a mountain road. Seeing a peasant across a field, my husband stopped the car and ran across to ask directions. The man was harvesting the linden blossoms which he would dry and later brew into *tilleul,* a kind of herb tea that the French used to consider good for all the little ills of children and old people. The linden blossoms are very fragrant, and the tree he worked on was full of bees. The man gave my husband clear directions for getting back on the main road. Then he said in French, "Wait. Give me your hat." Wondering, my husband held the hat out to him, and the peasant heaped it full of linden blossoms.

Many years later I thought that I would make a poem out of this event, calling it *International Incident.* In order to refresh my mind, and perhaps glean other details than I remembered, I hunted up the old diary and turned to the proper date. But I could find there only the mileage we had made, the hotel where we had stayed, a description of a town hall and a cathedral, and what we had eaten for dinner. In that case, my careful notes were of no use to me, yet unconsciously my memory had chosen to keep the one significant event of a day that is now lost in the past. So we have this wonderful built-in selector in our minds.

Diary entries are chiefly interesting as factual sources. We rarely entered conversations or detailed experiences, but I often found that brief entries could later be expanded into scenes in books. For instance two events that concerned our children, Nora and David, were entered in the diary for May 27, 1933.

We visited the Chateau of Kerjean, quite a charming old place, built partly for pleasure and partly as a strong fortress. Nora lost her doll, Maggie, on the floor of a dark defensive tower where we had to feel our way along, and there was great consternation until she was recovered.

On the same day there is another entry:

We arrived at Morlaix about six o'clock and found that the town is having a 15 day commercial celebration and is quite animated! We had a special dinner at the hotel and were given numbers in a tombola, the prizes being a dish of cooked carp and a bottle of champagne. David won the fish, but the waiter gave us a bottle of champagne also. Great celebration!

These two small events, enlarged by memory and imagination, grew into major chapters in a book for children, called *Family Sabbatical* (Viking Press, 1956). In the chapter called "The Last Castle," young readers still suffer with the little girl who loses her doll in the dungeon of an old castle and does not recover it until the end of the book; and in the chapter called "Numero 54," they laugh over the fish and the bottle of champagne and how the mother made three hilarious children get into bed before they were allowed to sample the funny-tasting drink.

The writer must also use conscious selection in choosing material. Sometimes I think that the difference between good and bad writing depends entirely on the wisdom the author has used in selecting his material. Out of all the possibilities in the world, he has selected these characters, these events, these charmed words, and in the end he is either a good writer or a poor one. More than likely, it is the richness of his own experience that will tip the scale in favor of good writing.

We must open our senses to the mood of a new place. Change can stimulate the sensibilities, and I find myself most creative at the turn of the season or when seeing new places or meeting new people. It is not always about the new places or the new people that I want to write, but they may remind me of something in my past, and, when I am in Europe, I may want to write about Idaho, and, when I am in America, I think back to Europe with creative nostalgia.

Now that I travel less than I once did, I get great pleasure out of using foreign settings that I once knew and loved. *The Bellini Look* (Bantam, 1976), the first paperback original that I have ever done, is an imaginative and rather fantastic story, but it has great reality for me because it is set in an old Venetian palace turned into a *pensione* for artists where we once stayed. I had a good time writing the novel because I had lived in this *palazzo,* and I was delighted to return to it in imagination. It was fun to people it with characters that I had known elsewhere. The old Scottish spinster was a real person who had stayed at the *palazzo* when we did. I intended her to be one of the main characters, but gradually she receded as I was writing, and the tall, boyish Australian Major, whom we had met on shipboard, and the two mousey little English ladies, who had been with us on a Greek cruise, grew in importance as the story grew. Now I am beginning to write a story set in Brittany, because it will give me pleasure to go back to a travel experience that I once enjoyed.

The best fiction writing, it seems to me, arises out of the emotions. Most of my books, both for adults and children, start with a *feeling* for a person or a place. Plot comes harder for me, and it has to grow naturally out of the emotional feeling for the people or the place. I like my characters to grow and change as the book progresses. The plot may well be only a series of events that change the characters for better or for worse. In at least two of my adult novels, *Strangers in the Forest* and *Stopover,* the same series of events makes some characters grow and others shrivel, but no one is quite the same at the end of the book as he was at the beginning.

Conscious experience includes listening to the rhythms of speech and learning how people talk in ordinary conversation. When I wrote *Caddie Woodlawn,* I found myself imitating the cadences of my grandmother's speech. She was a marvelous storyteller, and I had loved the stories of her pioneer childhood so much when I was small that I heard her own words and phrases as I wrote. I knew what kind of slang the children had used and the Irish brogue of the hired man and girl. I knew how her Boston mother and her English father should express themselves. When the book came out, my grandmother said to me, "But, Kit, you never knew my father and mother. How could you draw them just as they were?"

"Why, Gram," I replied, "you *told* me."

Dialect is a dangerous temptation to the writer. A little of it goes a long way and it often sets up a barrier between the reader and the writer. When I wrote my favorite adult novel, *Snow in the River*

(Macmillan 1964), I was faced with the problem of reproducing the speech of three young men from Scotland. The story is based on the lives of my father and his two brothers. I knew intimately the warm, burr and quirky turn of their Scottish dialect, but it was tedious and almost impossible to reproduce. I did not want it to come between my readers and their pleasure in knowing my characters. So the problem was to try to suggest it without laying it on too thickly.

"I'm sorry, Doug," said Willie humbly. "I was only tryin' to have a bit of fun. It's no' so easy to come by a wee bit of fun these days. But happen I worked too hard at it."

I hoped that just so much dialect would suggest the character without bewildering the reader.

Conversation should always be lively and interesting, and it should unobtrusively explain a situation or a character, or advance the plot, but do not try to reproduce ordinary conversation verbatim. Selection is the keynote. Let the characters reveal themselves, but never let them become tiresome. When you feel bored with your writing, your reader is going to feel twice as bored in reading what you have written. Get up then and feed the cat or walk around the block or take a hot bath. If you have established good writing habits, you will soon want to go back to your desk, reread the last few pages, erase the dull part, and go on. If necessary just leave a blank line and proceed to the part that interests you. There is great virtue in the blank line. You need not say, "Day followed day" or "Came the dawn"; you just skip along to something more interesting, and your reader will be right with you instead of asleep in his chair.

I have learned that a wealth of conscious experience not only makes a good writer, but it makes a sympathetic reader. What you have fully experienced will enrich your writing, and what you have fully imagined will enrich your living.

6

A WORKSHOP TRIO

By Paul Darcy Boles

"THE THINGS for which we visit a man," wrote Thoreau, "were done alone in the dark and the cold."

I think a lot about those good words whenever I serve as a workshop leader in fiction, at one writers conference or another. And I think about William Saroyan's honest statement about courses in how to write. "Useless, utterly useless."

Both Thoreau and Saroyan are right.

Good writing—or creation of any kind—does take place out of a kind of pain. From the dark and the cold. The writer must fly blind before he comes into the morning. There's no trick or gimmick or instrument that can take the place of talent. And talent itself needs a special spark no teacher can quicken unless it's there to start with. Still, a published writer, flying blind himself, "winging it," as they say, with full regard for the sensibility, sensitivity, and talent of the beginning writer who sits down with him and waits for his Word— such a published writer can—now and then—at least start to help.

Which explains why writers conferences aren't a waste of human spirit.

Last summer I was on the staff of one of the smaller writers conferences. It was well run and intimate, and the participants were hard working. Like all real workshops, it didn't pretend to give any courses in how to write. It was a burning glass focused on the samples the students had submitted to get into the workshop. It was a buoyant and free-swinging and healthy experience for the tough-minded and the tender-skinned alike. The workshop leaders learned from it. So did those who attended it in the mood to learn.

A solid workshop always brings this sense of progress and even sometimes of exaltation. There are others, of course—fashionable conferences, social-club conferences. For serious writers, it's better to avoid that kind and fly straight to Acapulco.

The true workshop tries to shoot the moon. It even tackles the giant job of trying to let the beginning or struggling writer find out who he is, or she is, so he or she can start writing out of that discovery, and stop faking around.

In what follows, I'm summing up the work of three unpublished writers, and the writers themselves, as I went over the work and talked to the writers in private conferences.

I'm changing their names, as well as some of the elements of their characters and the shape of their work. I'm giving a distillation of them and of their problems and letting these stand as representative of all the other students. In other words, I'm taking the fiction writer's license of turning fact into something truer than truth.

1. *Ringo.* Six feet four, tawny, crag-faced, quiet-eyed. Moves like a hungry lion. He has submitted sixty pages of a novel. I've read them a couple of weeks before the workshop started—just as I've read the pre-screened fiction of all the other people who made it to my class. Ringo grew up in a mining family in West Virginia. His father worked underground and retired without a pension when black-lung got to him. Ringo mined for four years before he got out.

He has a real storyteller's swing. He writes with a ballad-singer's ear and eye for the right sound and the deft detail. He makes me see the dark hills and hear the night wind move around the scarred, raped earth. He makes me feel the unkillable generations who have stuck to this land that was theirs to begin with, the ropy strength of their legends, their laughter, their violent deep loves, their endurance. He's a writer born and bred. For him, plot should be only a light saddle on an able horse. But Ringo has saddled himself with about a ton of junk, and he can hardly come to a trot under the weight of it.

Somewhere—from Spillane or television or any of the million variations of rot in between—he's picked up the notion that native poetry has to be hyped up with heroic super-feats and constructed so that great batches of cement sex, and action, of the sort J. B. Priestley calls *Admass,* keep getting in the way. Instead of the natural love-making that comes to a man and a woman as inevitably—and fiercely —as laurel budding on a mountain in springtime, he drags in all this silly and dead matter, because he thinks he has to hold the reader

by artificial means. Or, anyhow, by means alien to his own soul.
He is a man standing in a blazing wild garden and making, clum-
sily, an artificial rose.

He's proud of it, just because it came hard to his hands.

We talk a long time. I show him what I think he ought to be
proud of. And what he ought to throw out with yesterday's bath-
water. And why. He agrees to stop forcing the work, to let it spin
out of him as a spider spins a web over an old mine shaft. To let
plot grow from character, to avoid the hypodermic needle of what—
no matter how valid it may seem to the born hacks who write it and
the poor in spirit who lap it up—will always be alien to his gift. He
will never need to assume the mantle of the Twentieth Century Rover
Boys in the mountains. He needs to be Ringo—speaking, singing,
telling the story for his people.

2. *Marjorie.* Bright, small, witty. Divorced once, remarried once,
two children. An admirer of Saki, Ronald Firbank, Max Beerbohm.
And, inevitably, Dorothy Parker.

She has two short stories on hand. The first is whetted to a keen
point with the sting where it should be, in the tail. Her talent for
dialogue is rare. She doesn't write what people think they say. She
writes what they do say. Her people reveal themselves from left field,
and all at once there they are, in nice devastating dishabille. So far
so enjoyable. But they are people who live without air. They stifle
everything around them with their wit. By the middle of the second
page the reader feels they were knitted, not born. They are surrounded by nothing but the paper on which Marjorie has trapped
them. All her excellence shines behind cotton wool. She hears wonderfully—but she hasn't taken the trouble to see.

The second story is as crisp as the first, as tight and controlled,
with sweet and graceful transitions; and reading it is like being locked
in a chromium-lined vault. At any rate, this is so until page nine—
when all at once, in about three sentences, one of the people is
beautifully, succinctly described. And the whole page leaps alive. I
sit up straight and jab my finger at this miracle. And Marjorie says,
"Oh, that's what I always want to do—tell just a little of what they
look like, what they're wearing, where they are, and what they're

eating or drinking. But I don't, because a short story isn't supposed to waste words.''

I point out—not so gently—that the shortest story in the world
takes place in both time and space. That people come in all sizes and
most colors and that often their noses, eyes, legs, hands, mouths,
hair, feet, and the clothing covering the rest of them are all we have
to go by for direction-signs to what they are. That while character
is inherent in action and sometimes even more so in speech, mood
itself—made out of place, smell, all the tactile senses—is always there
around us. That even now, as we sit in the lounge of the conference
center, life stirs beside us, its sound and scent, its walls and chairs,
its window-glimpses of July grass under the hot sun. And that with
her command of quick, accurate description and summation of
mood, she can with comparative ease surround her stories with a
little breathable air. A certain essential balance has been cut out of
her stories with a much too sharp knife, except for those life-
saving lines. Fiction may well be a mirror in the roadway, I say—but
it is also a mirror in which the discerning eye sees all it can. It may
distort or condense for effect, but even if it concentrates on a butterfly, it tries to see the *whole* butterfly.

She says, "I've been writing around a blind spot."
As I said, Marjorie is small, witty—and bright.

3. *Jake.* In his twenties. Extremely earnest—somewhat solemn,
I'm afraid, in addition to being serious—bespectacled, going for his
degree in psychology. Fascinated by fiction. An avid pursuer of
various theories about fiction. In brief, a seeker after pigeonholes,
but I hope not a dilettante.

He is here on the visible evidence of one short story. It is a fat one
about thirty pages long. And wonderfully typed with neat wide
margins and no strikeovers and a doughty black ribbon.

It is also in ·essence a fair and very bold transcript with all the
words changed for the worse, of F. Scott Fitzgerald's "The Rich
Boy." I liked it better the first time. One of the people in it retains
the name of Anson, the central character of the original opus. So I
ask Jake how long it is since he's read *All the Sad Young Men,* the
Fitzgerald short story collection in which it was published.

He doesn't blush or shy around. "A month ago," he says. "I'm like Robert Louis Stevenson. As he was when he started out. I'm playing the sedulous ape."

I tell him that's all right as far as it goes. But that I can hardly begin to comment on work that's consciously imitative. And that Stevenson grew out of apishness, developing his own style, which was more distinctive than even his moustache, at a very early age. I ask him if he has anything else handy so we won't fiddle away his time. Meaning mine as well as his. After all he's been very vocal during my discussions with the morning class, and I want to go on seeing him get his workshop's worth. He nods. And digs into a pocket and gives me half a page. "I wrote that this morning. It's about my young sister. She died this spring."

Here are ten lines—not a poem, but deeply poetic in intent. He's written about his sister's auburn hair as it glowed one evening in the tiny light of a firefly she held cupped in her hand. It is honest and wonderful writing straight from the agonized spirit, and its words ring with truth and rightness.

Suddenly in Walt Whitman's words "there is commerce between us." His time is not idle. Neither is mine. When we stop talking some time later, he has understood that he has to start out from here. He knows as well that there always comes a time—at any age— when a writer starts out. Up to then, the writing has been done in the real dark, tentatively or theoretically; the start has been no start at all, merely a wish to be a writer without the wish to write. Now it will still be dark and often cold on the brightest and warmest day. But there will be this direction, this signal, this glint of the presence of a lighthouse. And this inward heat of purpose along with the light of need.

I believe this is what writers workshops are all about.

7

BEGINNINGS

By Sylvia Rothchild

WHENEVER an article, story, or novel of mine is published, I almost invariably am asked to talk at literary forums, clubs, or other groups about new books, writing, or the pains and pleasures of my own creative and working processes.

One morning after I spoke in a small New England town, I was awakened by the telephone. . . .

"Excuse me for calling so early," said a young woman's voice, "but I have been up all night because of you. You reminded me of all the things I meant to do and didn't, and there are some questions I must ask you."

I rubbed the sleep out of my eyes and waited for her to ask.

"First of all," she said, "you made it seem that it is necessary to be alone to be creative. I have never done anything all by myself. Is it really necessary to work alone?"

I didn't know what to tell her. Writing for me was a way of finding and expressing myself and that had to be done alone, without help, by me.

"How do you know when you begin that you can do it?" she asked.

"You don't," I answered. "You begin to see *if* you can do it."

"How long does it take to get over the feeling you may make a fool of yourself?" she asked doggedly.

"I don't know," I admitted. "I've never gotten over it."

"Why then do you continue?" she asked, still hoping for a reasonable answer. I could tell her only that I was more frightened of losing that fragile self than of feeling like a fool. I heard a long sigh and a silence before she said, "Thank you very much. Goodbye!"

No one had ever asked me those questions. Usually women asked me how to begin, as if it were harder to begin than continue. Unfor-

35

tunately, I couldn't remember how I began. Before I could read or write I was telling stories. I can remember sitting on the steps of a Brooklyn tenement on summer nights with a circle of listeners. As soon as I could read, I recognized myself as a writer. I didn't know what that meant or whether anything would come of it but I knew that the books in the library were written by people who had something in common with me.

I wrote my first story between the lines of a second-grade reader. I can still remember the red-faced screaming teacher who caught me scribbling in a holy school book and denounced me as a defacer of public property. Luckily, she read the scribbles before erasing them and found them precocious. After a long harangue with the principal, I was skipped to the next grade, not sure, however, whether I was being promoted or banished.

When I was eleven I had my first story in the school magazine. Another trauma! It was written on the brown paper of my grammar book. "Listen when I speak," shrieked my English teacher. "Do not write while I am talking!" She grabbed the book from my hands and, sure that I was sending improper notes somewhere, read the story on the cover. Later, she asked me to rewrite it neatly on lined paper so she could use it in the magazine she edited.

Writing, from the beginning, was a secret stolen pleasure, an act of defiance, an invitation to punishment. At thirteen I would take a flashlight and an old copy book to the bed I shared with my sister and wake in the middle of the night to scribble my secrets. We were a family of five living in three rooms without doors. The only way to be alone was to be awake when everyone slept. At sixteen, I would go to bed at nine, sleep until twelve, and then stay awake till three, writing in privacy. We had by then acquired an extra room, and I could sneak out of the bedroom I shared with my two sisters and turn on the light in the kitchen without waking anyone.

My room of my own was in my head and there was no door to lock. I majored in science in college so that I could make my own living. When I married at twenty-one, I didn't tell my husband I was a secret writer. I was not proud of my stories and had no wish to share them with him, especially since he figured in many of them. The diary I kept after our marriage was stilted and dishonest because he could see it. He had no reason to suspect me.

Later, when I told him, he thought of my writing as a harmless hobby, not as a hopeless passion, a chronic fever, a compulsion neither he nor I could control. The years of waiting, of storing and saving had left me with a lot of material squirreled away and a kind of pressure on the brain to use it. I itched with impatience to take the risks and made a pact with myself that I would write regularly for five years. If by the end of that time nothing was published, I would give up, or try to. I didn't tell my husband my plans. I was too afraid of failing, too worried about seeming foolish, too concerned that he would discourage me or find my ambition threatening. I kept my own council. A woman who wants everything learns early to be foxy. There was no feminist movement in the forties to help. I had never met a woman who shared my drive to find and use my self.

Oddly enough, having a baby saved me. For the first time I was free to be at home during the day, to use my time as I pleased. My infant daughter took only a fraction of my time. Our small apartment in Back Bay, Boston, could be put in order in an hour. We were new to Boston, and I did not have a friend to distract me. The exhilaration that came with the freedom to write in daylight was extraordinary. I was twenty-five years old, and no part of me was being wasted. The nights belonged to my husband. The days were my daughter's and mine. I could feel myself expanding, unfolding, becoming what I could be. The days were divided by my responsibilities, but I felt whole, powered by some magic source of energy that put ideas in my head and milk in my breasts. I was that bottomless fabled pitcher that filled as fast as it emptied.

The cobwebs I had been spinning in my head took their first awkward shapes as stories. I sent the first to *The New Yorker*. It came back without comment. The second earned a letter of encouragement from Elliot Cohen, then editor of *Commentary*. The third, after many revisions, was published, two years after I began to begin.

In the next ten years, I had three more children, published ten stories, six articles, eighty book reviews and a biography for juveniles. I began a novel. One of the children died soon after birth and taught me about mortality. Many more stories were written than published. I learned about risks and rejection.

When asked my occupation, I said I was a writer. We left Boston for the freedom and isolation of exurbia. Though my husband drove to his laboratory in Boston every day, I imagined that we lived like a family of hibernating bears in the woods. Most of my day was spent on the chores all housewives and mothers have to do but that didn't seem to change my image of myself. My papers and books rested on a wobbly shelf over the kitchen radiator. I found it easier to read and write standing with my children playing underfoot. They seemed to need me less if I didn't sit down. I found a special wavelength in myself where it was possible to concentrate under the sound of their voices and the noises of their games. They seemed content to have me as an available presence. I learned to hear only the sounds of danger. It was a feat to keep two or three pages in my head like a rabbit under a hat, to be able to turn off the washing machine, stir the soup, comfort a crying child, answer the phone without losing my place. It was a trick like juggling, walking a tight-rope or balancing plates. Though an inefficient way to write, it was an efficient way to live. "When one succeeds in one's foolishness, it seems like wisdom," was one of my mother's maxims. To survive, I needed to succeed.

Our children grew up with a writing mother but did not think it extraordinary. They thought mothers came equipped with typewriters as well as vacuum cleaners and ironing boards. When visiting their friends, they would look for the "typing place," expecting to find everywhere a forbidden shelf of books and papers.

My husband, however, was torn between pride and ambivalence. He was pleased to be told that his wife was a promising writer but not prepared for the possibility that her work would interfere with his life. It was perfectly acceptable in the late forties for a woman to work while her husband went to graduate school and to teach school before her children were born or after they left home. A woman who was ambitious about a career for herself when she had young children to look after was considered negligent, eccentric and unfeminine. Unable to believe that I was ambitious for myself as well as responsive to him and our children, my husband held as long as he could the illusion that marriage had made us one. He expected the lines of separation and private striving to blur and was confused to find that I was not losing my identity like a good wife, but strengthening it. Every published piece provided the energy to continue my struggle to become a separate creative person. Every crumb of praise and recognition helped me survive. While trying to explain myself to my husband, I began to see that his resistance and the hostility of relatives and acquaintances also added fuel to my fire.

I lived from page to page without plans for the future. My ambition was simply to continue in spite of the relatives who did not see why I worked so hard for so little pay, the neighbors who did not want me to put them into my stories, my children who needed daily reassurance that they were more important to me than anything else, and the older women who would invite me to speak at their meetings but scold me for not being at home, taking care of my family.

I felt as if I were wandering alone in uncharted territory. *The Second Sex* was of no help to me. Simone de Beauvoir fascinated me, but we had too little in common. I wanted to change my marriage, not abandon it. Mothering children came as naturally to me as thinking. I saw no reason to choose between one part of my nature and another and saw something obtuse in de Beauvoir's assumption that femininity was largely a masculine conspiracy.

My husband, meanwhile, also lacked models. He responded to my wish for help with the children and time for myself but resented what seemed to him to be an insatiable need. "How much time do you need to finish?" he asked reasonably—and did not want to hear that I needed as much time as it would take. He felt rejected if I came to bed late or left it early to finish a manuscript with a deadline, and he did not think it amiss to turn down the heat in winter to freeze me back to his side. Sundays, holidays, and vacations created problems because he would be free of his work when I was not free of mine. We bargained and compromised, stretched each other's tolerance for accommodation, but not to the point of breaking. We valued each other's affection in spite of the struggles. I wanted the freedom that came from respect and understanding, not from divorce or separation, which seemed more like another problem than a solution.

I graduated from my radiator shelf to a small partitioned alcove off our bedroom. Though it became harder as the years went by to concentrate without removing myself from interruptions, I was able to keep a short story or article in my head for weeks, mentally writing and rewriting before I sat down at the typewriter. Working on a biography and/or a novel was much more frustrating. I could not keep a hundred pages in my head while doing other things. Perhaps it was no accident that the biography, *Keys to a Magic Door,* was completed while I was in the hospital recovering from pneumonia. My novel *Sunshine and Salt* was put in its final form from my hospital bed after I'd had a hysterectomy. A summer at the MacDowell Colony would no doubt have been more agreeable.

Ten years later, safe in a room of my own in an empty house, I can look back with astonishment at the grotesque early struggles for time, space and acceptance. The inner freedom, taken under the pressure of a need for self-determination, is now matched by the heady freedom of the ex-mother of ex-children. The respect and understanding from a once-ambivalent and threatened husband make those early contentious years seem like another incarnation, from some dim, distant past. My struggle for liberation that seemed eccentric and unfeminine in the early fifties is conventional and conservative compared to the demands of contemporary radical feminists.

Discovering and developing a sense of self that is a source of creative energy still seems a private, personal, and solitary preoccupation. I would like to believe that a benign and supportive environment is better than a hostile and destructive one. The early years of writing as an act of resistance taught me the value of conflict, the need to take risks to achieve a sense of worth. The freedom *given* to me always seemed compromising. It was as if slavery can be imposed from outside, and freedom begins within with the capacity to struggle against values that are arbitrarily imposed.

I first began thinking about the wish to be free to be myself without any awareness of the women who were my models. Their life styles were so different from mine that I didn't notice the drive we had in common. My need to believe that I had invented myself from my own specifications was hard to reconcile with the likelihood that I had connections to my mother and grandmother.

My grandmother used her freedom to leave the country in which she was born. In America, however, she continued living in her own culture which she thought superior to that of her neighbors. She dressed according to her own fashion without concern for the taste of other people, prepared the foods that pleased her, adhered to religious customs that her neighbors had never heard of, and set an example of non-conformity. My mother lived between two cultures, picking and choosing, judging, evaluating the ingredients for a life different from her parents. My first lesson was that there were choices to be made and that one learned best from one's neighbor what not to do. I was taught early to admire strong capable women and to laugh at silly girls. Two women who could not read or write English let me know that there was a marvelous and mysterious world open to readers and writers.

Watching them take as much freedom as they could handle gave me the courage to do the same. That may be as much as any woman can hope for in any generation.

8

THE CREATIVE CYCLE

By Sue Grafton

SOMETIMES I think it might have been helpful if someone long ago had told me that writing was part of a creative cycle, that it was more than an activity that I might do or not do, depending upon the mood I was in. For years I wrote without any sense of what was happening to me, without any sense that I was, willy-nilly, repeating the same sequence of interior events, time and time again, whether I was writing short stories, articles, television scripts, or screenplays. Now as a creative writing teacher, it has occurred to me that others might benefit from a description of the creative process, as I perceive it; that certain comfort may be drawn from the realization that we are all caught up in the same recurring stages. There is a cycle that I think can be broken down into ten steps: URGE, INSPIRATION, RESEARCH, FIRST DRAFT, REVISION, COMPLETION, SUBMISSION, ELATION, SECOND THOUGHTS, DORMANCY.

The creative urge

First of all, there is the urge to create, a need that comes to us in some formless state—the impulse, the itch, something stirring within that will not quite give us peace. We simply want to write. That urge sends us to creative writing classes, makes us scribble on the back of envelopes, or drives us to the typewriter day after day, even when our minds are blank. In this first phase, I try to be patient, wanting to write but often without a subject, content, or form. I just know it's time to write.

During this period I read feverishly: I go through newspapers, clipping items that strike my fancy—human-interest stories, current events. I read books, old issues of magazines. (I have fifty back copies of *The Writer* that I read again and again, as though they might have magical properties.) I comb library shelves, read fiction, history—everything. I feel restless and discontented, searching for a project, considering every possibility. I have some idea of where I want to go and what kind of piece I want to do, but I may not have the remotest notion what it will actually be. I go through my files and reread the bits and fragments I've jotted down in my notebook from time to time.

Inspiration

Eventually there is that spark—that wonderful flash—aha!—that mental leap, however brief, in which my mind darts out like a frog's tongue taking a fly on the wing. Oddly enough, this is often the shortest phase I will go through. It's the hardest to come by, the most irrational, the least predictable—impossible to command. If the spark of inspiration doesn't come, I begin anyway on something. I may haul out an old piece and revise it, or take a story or article to see if I can revamp it for another market. I may just arbitrarily choose an idea that I've been toying with for some time and begin to work on it. I've even found it helpful, when I'm stuck, and inspiration is in short supply, to go back through my rejection slips. Often I discover that a publisher or an editor has expressed an interest in some manuscript in a slightly different form or with a different approach. Sometimes I find that in my initial reaction to the rejection itself, I completely missed the attached message: "Try us again," or "Resubmit if you revise this piece."

Inspiration is like an electric shock—jolting and unexpected, sometimes surprising in its source. Anything can inspire us to do a story, or novel, or play. Usually the idea first occurs in a fragile, undeveloped state, but it is an idea, nevertheless, that fires me for the moment. I feel myself respond instantly to the possibilities, excited, anxious, full of hope. Sometimes the idea comes out in one piece, full-blown, with all of its particulars, and only a few incidentals to be filled in. If the notion is incomplete, I can at least capture the essence of it in outline or paragraph form. I do find it essential, at this point, to sketch in as much as I know, mapping out the rough terrain even though some areas might be left blank.

Research

Now the research begins. I may have an idea, yes, but I'm not always sure it will work. Perhaps the crux of the story has to do with someone's profession (a doctor, a detective, a chemist, a thief), or an avocation such as rockclimbing, spelunking, weaving, antiques, or a geographical area which I'm not acquainted with—something, at any rate, which is crucial to the story's credibility. I might need a clearer sense of how my main characters would think or feel. I might need to see the place where he/she lives. I might have a vague sense that a plot can be laid out as planned, but I might lack documentation or authority for some of the story's claims. I might want to deal with a period of history that I don't know well.

I try to determine exactly what information I'm going to need before I write, and then I try to determine the possible source. I go to the library and check out books on the subject. I take the telephone book, which is a wonderful reference source. I call up everyone I think might be remotely helpful. Most of the people are very friendly and very helpful indeed. Sometimes my questions are very specific, and I can get the answers in a few minutes chatting on the phone. On other occasions, I make an appointment at a time convenient to my "source." People have been exceedingly generous with their time, but I make it a point to do my homework so I don't talk to them cold.

Often in the course of these informal interviews, whether I conduct them by phone or in person, I am given enough information—stories, personal experiences, incidents—for another entire story or article. If the information I want is specific, I take notes. Otherwise, I simply sit and ask questions, listening carefully, absorbing attitudes and gestures, the sense of place, the look and feel of the location or job. I listen to past history, dreams, ambitions, complaints, all of the nuances that are conveyed by tone and emphasis. I try to be as candid as I can. A couple of weeks ago, for instance, I was working on a treatment for a screenplay, a thriller, and I needed information about a gun. I took out the telephone book and looked in the yellow pages under "Guns and Gunsmiths," and dialed a gun shop.

"Uh, hello," I said. "I'm a free-lance writer, and I'm working on a script and need to know about a gun. I've got it in my head that this guy is using a .44 magnum, but I don't even know what that is. . . . I saw *Dirty Harry*, but that's about the extent of it. . . ."

I got exactly the information I needed in two minutes flat. I ended up using a .357 magnum, a Ruger, which sounded classier to me than some old Smith and Wesson. I still haven't the faintest idea what a .357 Ruger is, but I really don't need to either, since it was simply something I referred to in passing. (If I'm ever pinned down, I can at least refer my critic to the same gun shop I called. The name of the guy I spoke to was Bill.)

First draft

There are occasions, of course, when the research itself makes it plain that a story won't work. Either I'm operating under misconceptions or my mental information is out of date. Whatever the reason, there are some projects that don't survive to this point. Those that do push me into the next phase. Writing.

I return to my typewriter. And I sit. And sometimes I sit some more. I have everything in my head. My story, by now, has usually developed to some extent from its fragmentary inception. Now I have to decide how to begin—my strategy, my approach. Do I start with dialogue? Action? A character sketch? Do I begin at the beginning of my imagined tale and move forward in an orderly fashion, or would it be best in this case to begin at the end and tell everything in retrospect? Most of the time the idea itself will dictate how and where to start. With a short story or novel, the choices are varied. I am interested in setting a tone, establishing a "voice," a stance from which the tale can be smoothly and credibly told.

Sometimes, I go through a couple of false starts before I really get underway. If I'm lucky, I strike exactly the right note, and I'm off. My objective at this point is to get the raw story down on paper, moving quickly from beginning to middle to end, to give me a true picture of the whole and how each piece fits. I can discover subtleties of character, the richness of minor events that contribute to the verity of the tale. I uncover. I impose. I invent.

I conjure up everything I know, every story ever told to me, everyone I've ever met, selecting, rejecting, fleshing out the bare bones, filling gaps and holes. What's said? What's done? What information has to be laid in at this point so that the reader understands what's going on? What do I say now? What do I withhold? Hundreds and hundreds of choices have to be made. Sometimes, the simplest stop me dead for days. Names, for instance. I have trouble writing a piece until I know the names of my characters. I get out the telephone book again, the dictionary, too. I check through "Common English Given Names" for just the right sound, just the right combination that makes a made-up name sound real. Or maybe the names tumble out all at once, and I have to stop to think about some minor piece of action, something that appears to be insignificant at first glance but which stops me, nevertheless, and will not let me proceed until we come to terms. Hundreds and hundreds of questions surface. Some I can answer. Some I dismiss.

I tend in this phase to get somewhat manic, in part because I become so truly obsessed. I think about the piece all the time, dream about it, wake feeling anxious to get back to the typewriter, impatient to be done. I go at it again and again and again until it's done. Fini. First draft at last. In the case of a novel, this process might take months, even years. For a short story, sometimes, blessedly, two days or even one. Whatever the time span, it is the easiest part of the cycle in some ways. It is hard work but it's exhilarating. My aim is to get it all out, not to let any one portion stand in my way. No writing of the first page over and over again. No getting hung up on chapter one. I move at a relentless pace, and when I reach the end, I sit back, panting. I stack up the papers on my desk. I walk away. I do errands, sit-ups, anything. I don't dare look at the piece. I can't stand to see it. I might go to a movie, read a book, call a friend, have a drink — anything to create distance between myself and my current torment.

Revision

Eventually, I go back to page one and begin to read. I try to make my mind a blank, to look at the piece as though it were new and I were an objective, neutral observer taking it up for the first time. Where I spot ragged sentences, unevenness, I make a mark or a note in the margin. Where I see holes in the structure or places that need further work, I make circles or red marks, some indication for me that this is a passage that needs my close attention. Where I can edit or delete, I do so. If dialogue seems awkward, I make a pencil note, crossing out a line, adding words in the pitiful squeezed-up spaces between the lines, hoping that I can remember later what I meant to include. I go through it once then, reworking the sections that need redoing. I let it sit. I go through it again. And perhaps a third time.

Completion

I begin to type clean copy. I am, at this stage, a true perfectionist. I will type a page over and over again until it looks right to me. Sometimes I alter the paragraphing or the punctuation. I keep the dictionary close, the thesaurus open. Whereas before I allowed myself to play fast and loose, now I am meticulous, demanding, exact. I work the manuscript over and over again until it seems perfect to me. Literally perfect. Every single line and every word are as I meant them to be. When I finish the clean copy, I let the piece sit again and then I read it through.

Submission

And then I send the manuscript on its way. This is a critical point, it's not enough to sweat and labor and produce; it is also essential to subject a manuscript to public view, to the open market. Beginning writers are not always ready for this, and it's important for them to understand this point. "Young" writers must learn to wait before submitting their work, setting a piece aside for a time, allowing an interval for reflection, for comment or advice from others, for feedback of some kind. I think it is dangerous for new writers to compete too soon. On the other hand, every writer has to learn to be tough, to take rejection, to accept criticism or momentary defeat. If I submit a manuscript, I must accept the fact that I might end up with countless rejection slips.

In the back of my mind there runs a saying that may seem grim, but it's true all the same: "No one asked me to be a writer. No one cares if I quit." My writing is something I choose ... that chooses *me* ... and I will go on. The fate of one manuscript will never defeat me. I will be resilient, roll with the punches, bend with the wind— clichés perhaps, but sustaining to me, anyway.

For the intermediate to advanced writer, the time comes when the manuscript must be sent to a publisher, to a magazine editor, an agent, or a producer. If it comes back the first time, it must be sent out again ... and again ... and again. If I am sure where a manuscript should go, I send it there first. Otherwise, I consult market lists, working out a plan. "I'll try it here first, then here, then here; then I'll try this place, then that, and so on down the list."

Elation

The process does not end when the manuscript is sent out. At this point there is a wonderful glow, that incredible sense of satisfaction. I've done what I set out to do. It's finished. I've pushed and prodded and nibbled an idea from beginning to end. I'm a genius, a master. I'm relieved, amazed, exhausted.

Second thoughts

Usually after the first glow wears off, I go into a slump. I realize, looking back, that I didn't *really* do what I set out to do. The story isn't nearly as rich or as smooth or as subtle or as eloquent as I had first thought. The characters seem flat and stale. The dialogue, which I thought was so witty, now seems trite. The passages that I thought were profound seem derivative instead. All of my dreams of instant fame fade. I'm embarrassed that I've even had the nerve to put the manuscript in the mail. Now that it's on its way, or on the desk of an editor, I feel restless and pessimistic. Having spent my internal resources, I feel a sense of emptiness. I'm convinced that I'll probably never write again.

After a time, my sense of humor returns. Imagining that I'm *that* bad is almost as egotistical as imagining that I'm that good. I remember that I've been through this before, and I know that the low spirits won't be permanent. But in some odd way, it's essential to me to go through this, a humbling process that helps me keep my head straight. After the exaltation of writing, I need the negative reaction, too. It keeps me realistic about myself and what I do. It gives me some perspective on where I am and where I want to go. My mood lightens and for a time, I'm content. I *have* finished a piece, for good or for ill. No matter how good or how bad it seems, it is done. I've survived as a writer. I've grown. I've tried something new, and the experience itself has been worthwhile.

Dormancy

Now I go into my dormant phase, during which I turn my attention elsewhere. I feel used up, my creative energies burned out. I catch up on all the chores which I neglected in my manic phase. I clean my desk; I make a file and put everything connected with the manuscript into it: routine outline, first draft, a copy of the finished piece. I label it and close the file drawer. I call up the people I didn't dare talk to when I was feeling superior or depressed. I read. I jog. I meditate. I restore my life to its former state of grace.

And then one day the whole cycle begins again. I feel the urge, that itch. I know that I want to write something, but I don't always know what. There are subtle variations each time around, depending on the work or idea. Sometimes, the first draft comes easily and the revisions are minimal, a gift. Sometimes, a piece requires no research, and sometimes the research takes five times longer than the writing phase. Sometimes when a piece is finished I feel very good—not up, not down, but well-satisfied, a pro. The point is that inevitably I must work my way through each phase of the cycle. I often think that I'm caught against my will, acting out the stages of the writing cycle as I go through life itself: ashes to ashes, dust to dust, dying, being born again. There is a certain mystical element. For me, now, nearing the end of this piece, I know that my "work" is nearly done. I will reach the "end," submit, and move on ... delighted or discontent. I will replenish my mental stores and then set out again, back to square one, caught up again in the same cycle that, in truth, I've never left. Be brave, I tell myself. Take heart, I say. The worst is not over, and the best is yet to come.

9

SIX MOST-ASKED QUESTIONS ON WRITING

By Samm Sinclair Baker

THROUGH years of teaching nonfiction and fiction writing, I have compiled the six questions most asked by aspiring writers. The same queries recurred every time I talked with one or more beginners. I have answered their questions for them, and for you now, from what I have learned in writing twenty-five nonfiction and fiction books, and innumerable articles and stories.

I'm really answering the self who sat as a student yearning to sell his first story or article not too many years ago. I'm still seeking answers. I'll never stop—neither should you. Here we go:

1. How can I become a selling writer?

You cannot "think" about writing, or waste time "making plans" to write, or make some excuse leading to "I'll start writing it tomorrow." No matter what, you have to write, to put those words visually on paper, whatever the subject.

Here's my method: No matter how reluctant I may feel, I roll an empty sheet into my typewriter, or grab a big pad and write by hand. (To say "I need a typewriter to work," or "I can only write by hand" is a cop-out.) I force myself to put down words and sentences, however dull they may seem. I keep pushing, I keep going. By the bottom of the page, I'm started—I'm moving.

I keep filling up pages. In an hour or so I'll usually begin making real headway with my first draft. If not, after a few pages, I go back to reading from the beginning what I've written, either correcting or rewriting—or I start over. What I find, and what you will discover, is that by using this method of attack, you have written, and you are writing more. That's the best way I know to release all kinds of writer's block, once you have completed your preliminary planning. If you don't produce pages, you're not a writer, are you?

50

When I complete the story or article or chapter, I start rereading and rewriting again, then I retype the work. I put the manuscript away for at least a week and turn to my next project. At the end of a week or longer, I read the pages afresh. Usually I see many things that seemed right when I wrote them but are now revealed as clearly wrong. I rewrite them, removing the confusion, dullness, or lack of clarity that would have kept the piece from selling.

Ask yourself right now, "Do I rewrite enough?" A young beginning writer sipped a drink on our porch and wailed, "I'm going crazy ... I rewrote my story three times and, by God, that's it, I've had it!" I showed her the first chapter of my twenty-sixth book-in-progress. "Look at those lines crossed out, words inserted, scribbled sentences running around all four sides of the page. I can't believe it ..." I replied, "That's only my sixth rewrite—I have a long way to go until it's satisfactory."

Prolific John Creasey, who wrote hundreds of mystery novels and stories, told me that he used the put-away, rewrite system. He would make himself begin a story or book by writing a sentence, any sentence, such as "The red-faced man was obviously drunk." Then he would follow with another sentence and another, and he would keep filling up pages.

When he finished writing and rewriting, he would file away the manuscript for three months while he started another. Then he would return to the manuscript, this time with an objective eye. Then he would cut, clarify, add, and enrich the story until he had it right, made it salable.

Another point to keep in mind—you must write enough, story after story, piece after piece, and on and on. How much is "enough"? When you make a sale. That's not a glib answer; it's a reality. It took me years, reams of writing, and many hundreds of printed rejection slips before I made my first sale. Recently, I reread some of my previously rejected efforts, now saw their flaws, and realized that by writing enough I had finally achieved work of sufficient vitality and interest to satisfy editors and readers.

Now and only now, years later, could I assess what I had done wrong. I was able to rewrite some earlier pieces and sell them. Writing is a personal craft. You can learn how to write well enough to sell, but only by writing—enough.

2. Where can I find subjects that sell?

Whether you are writing fiction or nonfiction, pick subjects that will be primarily of interest to editors and readers, not just yourself.

Timely subjects: Not long ago, after a controversial living room discussion about unmarried people living together (you have certainly argued about that!), I said to a friend who was frustrated about trying to sell an article, "Why don't you write about the pros and cons of 'living together'?" *Idea!* She presented a comprehensive outline to the editors at a national magazine; they bought it, commenting, "Good! It's a topic people are thinking and arguing about."

Personal experiences: A friend who tried to grow a vegetable garden and succeeded only in raising the biggest tomato borers in his area remarked, "Hell, people take gardening too seriously." His eyes lit up suddenly—*idea!* He wrote a humorous piece about his bumbling and failures and sent it to the gardening editor of the Sunday *New York Times*. She agreed that it was time for a light touch, and bought it. How about a story or article, comic or tragic, on your personal experience? Almost anything can be made interesting; I used my early textile factory background as the setting for an acclaimed mystery story.

News items: A young woman in one of my classes read a newspaper item about a girl who graduated from high school with honors, even though she had no use of her arms, was half deaf, could see only dimly. *Idea!* The writer in search of an idea secured an interview and wrote the story which became her first magazine sale. Now she is adapting the basic material for a novel.

Unusual occurrences: Years back when I was beginning and was an adman, a stenographer typed a letter for my signature. Checking it, I saw that instead of typing "this," her fingertips had struck one key to the left of each letter and typed "rgua." *Idea!* I wrote a short story in which a woman dying of a bullet wound typed faintly: "weux." That revealed to a detective the name of the murderer (figure it out yourself). An editor bought it and asked for more stories.

Salable ideas are all around you—if you will look for them, recognize and use them.

3. How can I find the right market?

Match the timely, personal-experience, and offbeat ideas with markets that feature similar themes and subjects. When I heard about an unusual case involving skin cancer, I wrote and sold it to a health magazine after it was turned down by four general women's magazines. If I had bothered to analyze the market beforehand, I would have saved time, rejection pain, and stamps.

Watch "market needs" in *The Writer,* newsletters, clues in newspapers and other media, and those that come word-of-mouth. I read a magazine interview with a national magazine editor who complained about the lack of short humorous submissions. Watching television that night, I laughed about a TV commercial so mawkish that it became hilarious. Recalling the interview, I sent that editor a burlesque of TV commercials; she bought it.

A current best seller is a dictionary of CB language. The frenzied market was wide open—any of us could have researched and written the book; some alert opportunist did.

The markets are there—you must watch, analyze, pinpoint, fire, with a much better chance to score than shooting haphazardly.

4. How can I get my writing read by editors?

Editors are not gods, they are people and readers themselves. Your writing must interest them as individuals before you can reach their readers. Heed the sage old advice: to catch fish use the bait that fish like, not what you like. As an instance, I decided that I would aim to write a salable story for *McCall's.* I bought the current issue, read and analyzed the four short stories and pinpointed two "musts" to get my story read by an editor:

(a) Each story compressed into the first paragraph a problem to hook the reader (and editor). The first story placed a couple married nine years, with two children, at the start of their summer vacation: "Summer always puts a strain on our marriage . . ." Reader wonders, what strain this time? Will the marriage and family survive?

The second story revealed a series of deaths in a large family, "almost epidemic." Why all the deaths? Who is next? The third story concerned a New England "monogamous village," where divorce and adultery were "unheard of," but where two married people were in love with others. What catastrophe would result for them and their families? The fourth story involved a husband who wanted a child, and a wife who didn't. Baby born. Wife antagonistic to newcomer. Will she overcome her hostility? How?

(b) The stories all centered on marriage and family problems, some romance. Clearly, for *McCall's* (and other women's service magazines publishing fiction), I'd have the best chance to get my story read if I wrote about marriage, family, romance—and I had better present an intriguing human problem in the first paragraph.

The same basic rules apply in getting a nonfiction piece read by an editor. Concentrate on subjects commonly treated in the publication, such as marriage, family, and romance in the women's service category. Then hook the editor in the first line or two of your piece, or with a well-baited, comprehensive query letter. What do I mean by "comprehensive"? My query letter to the editor of *The Writer* for the article on which this chapter is based is a specific example.

The core of my letter ran only a little more than a half page. My first paragraph was very much like the first paragraph of this piece. Then I listed the six questions, stated that my answers would apply to both fiction and nonfiction, and closed with my suggested title. From that brief outline, the editor had a clear idea of just what the piece would encompass and illuminate; he made some suggestions about points that might be included in the answers, and gave me the go-ahead.

Note this fact carefully: Before writing the query letter, I made notes over a period of several weeks until the total idea solidified for me. It took me hours to work out the questions in simplest, most compact form. Only then did I compose and send the query letter. Most beginning writers I talk with admit that they get an idea, put it into letter form hastily, leaving it to the editor to flesh it out or read between the lines. Editors are too busy and impatient to do that work for you. Don't make that mistake.

5. How can I keep rejections from getting me down?

If you follow the advice in the preceding answers, you are likely to get fewer rejections. However, you had better understand that you will get some rejections all your writing (and selling) life. Yes, I have written best-selling books, but I still get rejections—understandably.

Realize that editors may reject your story or article not because of its quality or appeal, but for other sound reasons: They don't want a story or article with that background and content because they have published a similar one recently; or they don't consider the subject timely or fresh—"it's not for our readers"; or they have overbought at the time your brainchild arrived; or a particular editor hates dogs, and your piece concerns dogs.

Dashiell Hammett told me that the editor of a top magazine rejected one of his stories with a tropical setting. Months later Hammett resubmitted the same manuscript and it was accepted enthusiastically. Told what had happened, the editor admitted, "I don't remember the story, but I guess it arrived when we had just published some stories with similar backgrounds, and I was fed up with the tropics."

When I wrote *The Doctor's Quick Weight Loss Diet* with Dr. Stillman, all my publishers who wanted books from me did not want a diet book: "People aren't buying diet books." Sixteen rejections later it was purchased and became the best-selling diet book of all time. Does that make you feel better? The knowledge sustains me every time a book proposal is rejected, to this day—and tomorrow, I'm sure. What's my reaction when I'm hit with a rejection? *I go on writing.* You, too.

Here's a lifesaver I recommend strongly to you: Keep a number of manuscripts and/or proposals circulating at the same time, on different subjects. If one is rejected, the others are still alive, and so is hope. Keep writing, keep submitting, and you may be rejected without becoming hopelessly dejected. I have had three book proposals circulating at a time; if one is rejected, the other two will serve as a buffer and sustaining hope. Inevitably the day comes when the letter or call arrives: "We like your manuscript and are accepting it."

6. How can I get an agent?

Don't waste your time, effort, and stamps in trying to get an agent until you are selling enough to justify an agent's time and effort. That's necessarily blunt; figure it out in dollars and cents: An agent gets 10 percent of what you sell, not what you write. If it takes an agent six months to sell one of your stories for $500, he collects only

$50. That doesn't come anywhere near paying for his office over-head, employees' costly time, office supplies, phone calls, mailing costs, and so on.

Furthermore, an agent has no magic wand which will wave and sell an unwanted manuscript. The agent needs proof from your own record that you write salable work, and that you write enough on a regular basis to keep producing sales which make it profitable for him or her to represent you.

Practically every selling author I know has followed the do-it-yourself, prove-yourself route. On my own, using the mail (as you are doing), I sold over twenty stories, articles, and two books before I sought and teamed up with an agent. What's more, lots of pro-fessional writers don't use an agent and don't want one; they believe that they do as well or better on their own, especially in selling to magazines.

Think about the agent/writer situation sensibly, objectively. To blame your failures on not being represented by an agent is wasteful self-delusion.

*   *   *

These answers necessarily hit high spots briefly. They are not every-body's answers but they have worked effectively and keep working for me. They have worked for many aspiring writers I've told them to. They can work for you—if you will work.

A bonus suggestion: Don't lock yourself in as either a fiction or nonfiction writer exclusively. More and more successful novelists and authors of short stories also write nonfiction, and vice versa. The number includes James Michener, Truman Capote, John Hersey, many more. If you are adamant about limiting yourself to one form, O.K. You are an individual; make your own decisions about all my suggestions.

Years ago when I was a young radio director, Fredric March appeared as a guest. He asked me, "How should I play this part?" I gulped. "You're such a great star, Mr. March, do it the way you feel it." He glared at me, "Are you the director?" Meekly, "Yes." "Then, damn it," he roared, "*direct!*"

My exhortation to you is similar. Above all else, if you are to be a selling writer—*write!* Sure success to you.

10

THE BATTLE OF FICTION AND NON-FICTION

By Elizabeth Janeway

WHY has non-fiction become so much more popular than fiction? Why is non-fiction so much more widely read? Except for phenomena like *Love Story*, it is generally true that non-fiction sells much better than fiction. Why?

This is an interesting topic, and because it is germane to our present social situation, it is a trend you can expect to continue, rather than just a fashion of a few years. A basic reason is that fiction is much harder for people to follow than non-fiction.

Fiction, you see, is not about facts, but about relationships. In that sense, it's like algebra instead of arithmetic. Fiction isn't a straightforward statement; it's a comment on something the author believes the reader knows something about already. But today in a very heterogeneous society like ours, it's rare for people to have the sort of common background of assumption which permits fiction to speak movingly, evocatively and clearly to its audience.

As everyone knows, our society is shifting; it's much more mobile than in the nineteenth century when there was a common, bourgeois, middle-class sense of relationships—of the world being more or less the same, of standards being more or less accepted within it. This is not so today. Consequently, it is much, much, harder to write the sort of book which assumes that the reader will feel as the writer does about a given personal relationship, a given moral situation.

People are much more isolated—and that includes emotional isolation. We tend to find it harder to feel our way into other people's emotions because they are more various and less familiar. People come from other parts of the world. The reading audience now comes from many, many more different kinds of childhood than potential readers in 1850 or 1870.

For this audience non-fiction spells things out. You know how children ask you to tell them a story and want to know if it's true. And by that they don't mean is it fictionally true, is it true to a level of plausible emotion? They mean, did it really happen? Non-fiction is able to answer, yes, it did happen; or else, at least, to *pretend* that it did happen.

Of course, as we all know, history is often rewritten from generation to generation, as historical attitudes and views on life change, but historiographers and their readers still assume the facts they are discussing are the same. It takes a fairly sophisticated critic to realize how emphasis and interpretation change our map of the world—or (as I suggest in my book *Man's World, Woman's Place*) how they rework our "social mythology."

But fiction, unlike history or biography, openly and overtly requires from the reader some prior knowledge of the way life works, some sense of what's plausible and possible. Fiction—and, of course, I am talking about good fiction—demands that a society should seem to be knowable to the audience living within it. The writer and the reader have to agree that they are talking about the same facts and the same rules. We have a very bad situation for agreement today, not only because fiction writers are isolated from their possible readers, but also because social change takes place so fast. This is one place where the generation gap is wide indeed, for young people and their parents seldom read the same writers.

Fiction is about personal relationships. These relationships must seem to the readers out there to carry the same moral overtones that the author feels as being present and significant in them. But since so much of the common background of social and emotional and cultural experience has vanished, this similarity of response can't be taken for granted. Take an obvious example. One hundred years ago it was a tragedy if an unmarried girl had a baby. An author writing about such a situation could assume that this is what his readers would also feel. They might sympathize with her and they might feel that her plight was unjust, but they would feel, nonetheless, that it was a tragic situation. Today this isn't true. Our moral judgments have shifted and become much more diverse, and fluid.

An author can still set up a situation that involves the girl, her lover, the man she might have married and didn't, the child, the parents, the whole village, but his readers won't react in a predictable way. Some people will say, "Right on," and others will say, "What about the population explosion?" Some people will say her parents are callous pigs, and the tragedy lies in their anger with the girl. In short, there will be all kinds of reactions to the situation, and not just one you can count on.

In other words, the symbols and the meanings which are the tools of fictional communication have ceased to carry a significance which will be commonly agreed upon. Fiction is becoming an archaic and special language. It is no longer a *lingua franca* that everyone can understand. I don't, myself, think that fiction will die out; but it will have to change.

Meanwhile, non-fiction reaches the readers, but, again, the writer can't take this for granted. This book of mine, *Man's World, Woman's Place*, is the first long work of non-fiction I have written and, in doing it, I had to learn quite new techniques. One of the things I discovered was that I had to know who my audience was. I had to think consciously about whom I was writing for. In fiction, I always assumed that I was writing for people who would understand me because we shared the same assumptions about the world.

In more stable times, when people have a better idea of what's going on around them, they turn to fiction for an interpretation; whereas, in times like these, people turn to non-fiction just to find out what's going on. When people lived in tiny communities and knew each other extremely well, and could tease each other, and joke about relationships, you had communication by poetry. You didn't have to set up inter-personal relationships. You could assume that everyone knew what you meant if you wrote in lyrical form. Fiction and poetry both demand an intimate knowledge and a shared experience, based on the size and intimacy of the community, and on the rate of social change.

Fiction should be about recognizable people. That, to me, makes it very difficult to read certain writers who are enjoyed by other people. For instance, I'm not very fond of Kurt Vonnegut and Joseph Heller, writers who are difficult for me to read because their characters too often fall toward stereotypes and toward a kind of allegorical presentation of themselves in what seems to me a flat situation. A situation where right and wrong are too easily determined.

I find this unexciting and lacking in tension. I understand why writers do this: they are looking for the moral agreement that I spoke of earlier. We can no longer expect it when we're talking about an unmarried girl having a baby. But it's assumed that we will all agree that war is hell, and we shouldn't have bombed Dresden and all Air Force generals were nitwits, etc., etc.

To people my age, this is dull partly because it is hellishly oversimplified. Also, being oversimplified it seems to us false in many respects. Vonnegut and Heller and many of their followers are like Irving Berlin—they can only compose in the key of C. Berlin has had a special keyboard made that transposes his key of C tunes into B minor or F sharp for him. I wish allegorically inclined writers could do this too, and have their stereotyped situations enriched by doubt and diversity.

I suspect that another effect on fiction that we're experiencing comes out of television. McLuhan, though out of fashion today, is perfectly right about his basic premise: what is important about television is not just what it says but—much more—how it says it, how it picks up experience and processes it and passes it to the viewer.

Television speeds up the processes of life. You look at the tube long enough and you'll begin to believe that every problem can be resolved in a time span of half an hour or, at most, an hour. Leonard Woolf writes in his marvelous autobiography that when he gave up his job as editor of *The New Statesman* he found a heavenly relief. *The New Statesman* is a weekly, and he'd begun to count everything in the world, political processes, news events, human life in seven-day spans. In television everything happens, reaches a climax and is resolved in an hour at most. Of course, art and fiction compress experience, but that is not the effect that television gives.

It's difficult to know what's going to come from television. I can't be completely hopeless about it because there's a great deal of talent there. But again, I think factual documentaries are at present a good deal better than the fiction shown. When you really had some plausible and complicated fiction shown, as in *The Forsyte Saga,* you found the television audience very much moved and involved.

Now, it's certainly true that anyone my age has seen film turn into an art form in the past thirty or forty years. Perhaps television will too. As yet it hasn't achieved a depth of experience which permits art to grow, permits diversity, suspense, surprise. Art needs this richness of possibility to hold its audience. When it doesn't exist, the creator too often falls back on seeking to grab hold of the audience by a shock effect. But shock effects wear off. They can't be used too often because you begin wondering what else for an encore.

It's interesting today to see how many writers want to grab the reader via sex; and of course it works—for a while. But sex novels defeat themselves in the end, because they cease to be novels. They reach for the reader at the level of involvement which produces heavy breathing; and Janeway's law on critical appreciation declares that heavy breathing breaks down the brain cells.

In other words, personal involvement at this level wipes out critical ability. Instead of understanding the word through art, the reader experiences sensations. Now it happens to be psychologically true that the more you want something, the less you can tell how good it is until you've had it.

The remarks on this situation by a great author of former times sum it up pretty well:

> The expense of spirit in a waste of shame
> Is lust in action; and till action, lust
> Is perjur'd, murd'rous, bloody, full of blame.
> Mad in pursuit, and in possession so;
> Had, having and in quest to have, extreme;
> A bliss in proof—and prov'd, a very woe;
> Before, a joy propos'd; behind, a dream.

Which brings us directly to the question of pornography and censorship. I'd better begin by saying that I'm totally opposed to any kind of censorship from anyone: from the local police chief, from the courts—which means that I support the publication of pornography, including hard-core pornography. But I warn you not to get pornography mixed up with literature, which it isn't.

It's more like "How to Fix the TV" and "Everything You Always Wanted to Know About Air Conditioning, Hair Setting, or Septic Tank Repair." It aims at hard breathing and no thinking at all. It is a substitute for action, not a comment on it.

Pornography purports to be fiction, but it really isn't about personal relationships, and relationships are the stuff of fiction. Pornography is only about relationships within the self. It is deeply narcissistic and claustrophobic. So, though I support the publication of pornography for those who want it, I can't call it literature.

Part of the confusion about pornography arises from the fact that literature can be written and art created around pornographic situations. But this requires the introduction of human relationships into the closed world of pornography. Henry Miller is a good example. In his books, we find recognizable human beings who are caught in pornographic situations which become both comic and tragic because the characters know they are trapped, and their emotions are moving and effective. In such scenes, publication of pornography has opened the door to a wider area of consideration for fiction. To this extent literature itself may be said to have profited by it.

I have cited this example both because it is so common today and because it illustrates clearly how writing may extend its range. Humanity suffers when there are areas of experience and emotion which cannot be discussed, which are cut off by barricades of taboo. Such hidden, denied emotions are the breeding ground of neurosis, fear and compulsion. For the artist, there should be nothing human that is alien. Part of his job, his obligation, is to show his audience the reality of other people's experience. And so, the wider the range of life that can be used as material for art, the better for all of us, readers and writers alike.

11

FOLLOWING ONE'S INSTINCTS

By E. B. White

STUART LITTLE, himself quite a traveler, came into being as the result of a journey I once made. In the late Twenties, I took a train to Virginia, got out, walked up and down in the Shenandoah Valley in the beautiful springtime, then returned to New York by rail. While asleep in an upper berth, I dreamed of a small character who had the features of a mouse, was nicely dressed, courageous, and questing. When I woke up, being a journalist and thankful for small favors, I made a few notes about this mouse-child—the only fictional figure ever to have honored and disturbed my sleep.

I had eighteen nephews and nieces. As a young bachelor-uncle I used to be asked now and then to tell a story. At this task I was terrible. Whole minutes would go by while I tried to think of something. In self-protection I decided to arm myself with a yarn or two, and for this I went straight to my dream-mouse. I named him Stuart and wrote a couple of episodes about his life. I kept these stories in a desk drawer and would pull them out and read them on demand. As the years went by, I added to the tale. Book publication never crossed my mind. These were the golden days before television, when children got their entertainment not by twisting a dial but by twisting an elder's arm.

In 1938, having decided to quit New York, I began tidying up what I called my "affairs." One of these was the Stuart Little adventures, now grown to perhaps a dozen episodes. At the suggestion of my wife, I carried them to a publisher (not Harper) and left them, to see whether they might be acceptable if expanded. The answer came back No, and I left for Maine, taking my rejected child along.

Seven years later, in the winter of 1944–45, I returned to New

© 1966 by The New York Times Company. Reprinted by permission of the author and *The New York Times*.

York to spend a few months in a furnished apartment and do some work for *The New Yorker*. I was almost sure I was about to die, my head felt so queer. With death at hand, I cast about to discover what I could do to ease the lot of my poor widow, and again my thoughts strayed to Stuart Little. My editor at Harper's, Eugene Saxton, had been urging me to finish the narrative, and I determined to put it off no longer. Mornings I sat at a top-floor window looking out into West 11th Street and there I completed the story. I turned it in to Harper and then took a train for San Francisco, to join Stettinius, Molotov, Lawrence Spivak, and that crowd, for the formation of the U.N. Another springtime, another journey!

Harper accepted the book, and Stuart was off at last, after a pardonable delay of some fifteen years. Garth Williams was brought into the enterprise and began turning out the drawings that were to give shape to my diminutive hero.

A few weeks later, back home in Maine, a letter arrived for me from Anne Carroll Moore, children's librarian emeritus of the New York Public Library. Her letter was long, friendly, urgent, and thoroughly surprising. She said she had read proofs of my forthcoming book called *Stuart Little* and she strongly advised me to withdraw it. She said, as I recall the letter, that the book was non-affirmative, inconclusive, unfit for children, and would harm its author if published. These were strong words, and I was grateful to Miss Moore for having taken the trouble to write them. I thought the matter over, however, and decided that as long as the book satisfied me, I wasn't going to let an expert talk me out of it. It is unnerving to be told you're bad for children; but I detected in Miss Moore's letter an assumption that there are rules governing the writing of juvenile literature—rules as inflexible as the rules for lawn tennis. And this I was not sure of. I had followed my instincts in writing about Stuart, and following one's instincts seemed to be the way a writer should operate. I was shook up by the letter but was not deflected.

Stuart was published in October, and other surprises were in store for me. Miss Moore's successor at the Library had some misgivings of her own about the book, and Stuart met with a cool reception. He got into the shelves of the Library all right, but I think he had to gnaw his way in. The press, to my astonishment, treated the book almost as though it were adult fiction. The daily *Times* gave it a full-scale review by Charles Poore, who praised it. Malcolm Cowley, in the Sunday *Times,* said it was a good book but disappointing— should have been better. This exactly expressed my own feelings about it.

A couple of days after the book appeared, Harold Ross, my boss at *The New Yorker,* stopped in at my office. His briefcase was slung over his shoulder on a walking stick and he looked unhappy. "Saw your book, White," he growled. "You made one serious mistake."

"What was that?" I asked.

"Why the mouse," he shouted. "You said he was born. Goddamn it, White, you should have had him adopted." The word "adopted" boomed forth loud enough to be heard all down the corridor. I had great respect for Ross's ability to spot trouble in a piece of writing, and I began to feel uneasy. After he left the room I sat for a long while wondering whether Miss Moore had not been right after all. Finally I remembered that Harold Ross was not at home in the world of make-believe, he was strictly for the world of 43rd Street, and this cheered me and revived my spirits.

My next encounter was with Edmund Wilson, who stopped me in the hall. "Hello, hello," he said, in his wonderfully high and thrilling voice that sounds like a coaching horn. "I read that book of yours. I found the first page quite amusing, about the mouse, you know. But I was disappointed that you didn't develop the theme more in the manner of Kafka."

I thanked Edmund and wandered back to my room to chuckle at the infinite variety of *The New Yorker;* the editor who could spot a dubious verb at forty paces, the critic who was saddened because my innocent tale of the quest for beauty failed to carry the overtones of monstrosity. What a magazine. There's never been anything like it.

Despite the rough time the author was having, Stuart himself seemed to be doing all right. The book drew generally favorable reviews, and by October 24th Harper had sold 42,000 copies.

The next thing that happened was that three fellows turned up claiming that *their* name was Stuart Little, and what was I going to do about that? One of them told me he had begun work on a children's story; the hero was a rat, and the rat's name was E. B. White. I never learned how far he got with this splendid project, but I know he phoned Ursula Nordstrom at Harper's to alert her.

The real returns came when letters began arriving. **Some were** from children. Some were from teachers. They expressed pleasure, along with a fairly steady stream of abuse about the book's ending, which fails to tell whether Stuart found the bird. The letters have not stopped coming. Of the many thousands I've received, only two, I believe, questioned the odd fact of Stuart's arrival in this world and the propriety of an American family's having a boy that looked like a mouse. After twenty years, I am beginning to relax.

I learned two things from the experience of writing *Stuart Little:* that a writer's own nose is his best guide, and that children can sail easily over the fence that separates reality from make-believe. They go over it like little springboks. A fence that can throw a librarian is as nothing to a child.

12

STANDING IN THE WINGS

By Julia Cunningham

WHEN I was recently asked, "What is the creative process?" an image immediately rose in my mind. It was a stage, empty and waiting, at that moment, for me. I was standing in the wings, watching for the first entrance of the first character (as I had for so many years as a writer), both welcoming and dreading the first cue that would begin the book, the commitment, the overwhelming responsibility to be honest. I was once more involved in what I like to call the second reality.

There are, in my thinking, two realities: the first need not be described. It is where we all live, where the oatmeal cools on the kitchen table, where night sometimes descends at noon, where buttered popcorn is to some a vintage food, where the roof shelters space and serenity or dust, hunger and desperation. It is where we wake and sleep, however and wherever.

But the second reality is another landscape altogether. It shares in the first and is furnished by its observations, feelings, and learning. But one passes through a kind of gate into a country where the imagination is completely alive, where the attic of the unconscious is released into words. All the stored trunks and boxes fly open. The old letters scatter in the air and find their voices. The remembering of an ancient terror may form the villainy of a devil in human clothing, or a moment of grace, of loving someone, may become the base for a story of passion and compassion. All is ready, free to move, to run, to love, to strike. And this second world is always present. One needs only to wait in a kind of concentrated quiet to enter it.

Upon my imaginary stage come the people we call characters. The tree house, the castle, the fetid cellar, the hut, the cave have no meaning without them. They are all of us, but newly translated, transformed, given their own lives by the writer's invitation to them to come into being. They lead you, follow you, haunt you, occasionally club you to death, keep you a hundred years in a dungeon. They love, hate, torment, and amuse. Most important of all, I belong to them first and before all else and all others. And, great friends that they are, they belong to me.

There exists a mutual seesaw of trust and friendship between them and me. And the keystone is sincerity. We must as writers be as clear and honest as possible. Falsify the accent of a French mouse, carelessly describe the light-footedness of a heavyweight, forget that Emily Batsford gets indigestion from eating raw onions, and the characters will turn their backs on you, leave you very lonely indeed in front of a silent typewriter. We need not love the evil characters, but we must understand them; we are there to record, not to judge. All the time there will be a deep, almost subterranean bond between writer and characters. They will be loyal, but only if I am. They will act with conviction and style and proceed convincingly to their natural or unnatural ending.

I suppose there are as many definitions of what a writer is as there are writers, but, aside from the instinctive drive, unconsciously present, to me a writer is a person of certain habits, and the first of these is the ability to listen. It's as though we had three ears instead of two. We may be crouched in grief or aching in the ribs with laughter, but that third ear is recording the moment. And at the same time, the mind is storing each detail in a vast attic where nothing is ever lost or forgotten, but perhaps unused. The simplest place to see this habit in action is at a party of more than three people. It is impossible to resist the role of eavesdropper. I have an actress friend, a master eavesdropper, who can hear and remember three conversations going on simultaneously. I hear only my own and one other.

Another useful habit is looking. All of this sounds so obvious — listening and looking — but perhaps the difference between the ordinary participation of all people and the writer is a matter of intensity. You see and hear not only for yourself, but for your writer self. In some ways, this sounds like intrusive rag-picking, and maybe it is, but it remains irresistible.

Still another good habit is daydreaming. This may seem to some to be an alibi for laziness, but it isn't. It is creating without recording. If you are or want to be a writer, don't allow any criticism of this occupation to diminish its place in your life. Take to the hills (or to another room) where you won't be observed, or go wandering anywhere, at any time, with anyone.

Awareness of smell and taste is also on my list of worthwhile habits. I think that sometimes these two senses are neglected in books, especially books for children in middle grades. Yet, these two senses are often the most evocative of mood and feeling. And a smell does not always have to evoke a rose. A stable, a cow pasture, acrid smoke from burning cloth, sweat — there are thousands of smells — can express what nothing else can. Someone once asked me what France smelled like. I happily rummaged in my memories of streets and alleys and churches and crowds and came up with three major sources: animal, architectural, and human, meaning drains, damp stones, and wine.

All these habits contribute to that fateful moment when the first sentence is put down on paper, and maybe they can be headed by the word *attention* — attention to everything that passes, that happens, that makes for terror, joy, sorrow, humor—that same kind of intense attention that a very young child gives to whatever is suddenly new.

I had intended here not to mention the habit of imagination because it must be active inside the writer all the time. But then it occurred to me that this imagination can also be expanded. It can become freer and freer, if unrepressed, until there is nothing that doesn't stimulate it and no distance it cannot travel. For the purpose of a story, imagination has to be grounded in reality (even a dragon must be made plausible), but the habit of giving the imagination wings can be achieved by encourging short flights to become longer ones.

The last habit is discipline—sitting down and doing—which can make a very minor talent show results that an undisciplined near-genius will never know. Just plain grubbing has inchwormed many writers to success.

The setting of a story should at least be mentioned here, though I am guilty, sometimes under disguises, of returning my characters to the landscape I love best—France. These fictional creations of mine seem to prefer acting out their adventures there—a place that has a magic that just makes me happy. But I believe that settings in general are more than the boundaries of a country and are truly inhabited by the writer. In my book *Onion Journey,* where the indoor scene was a very poor room with not much more than two beds, a table, a chair for Gilly and another for his grandmother, that setting became so real to me, I could taste the half-filled crock of apple butter in the almost empty cupboard, though it never appeared in the story. And the not quite tight window frames that allowed little slivers of wind to enter the room and cut across my own cheeks as I was writing.

I don't know where the props come from—memory, probably. Long after I had written *Dorp Dead,* I recognized the tower where Gilly retreated to be with himself as a ruined tower I had found long ago when I was walking up a grassy hill in France. I was seeking shelter from the cold (it was autumn) and a place to eat my enormous French sandwich; more than that, I needed to shut out my own loneliness. Again, the terraced orchard I used in *The Treasure Is the Rose* was the rear, walled garden of a chateau. But these are afterthoughts, "after-memories." I am very grateful that they rise up out of the half-forgotten at the very instant their appearance is vital to the story I am writing.

Now for plots. I make a very complete outline of each chapter before I begin to write a book. There are certain ingredients I believe necessary. There has to be conflict, a building to a climax, excitement of one kind or another, and that most difficult of all elements, a satisfying conclusion. Also, to me there has to be contrast in the scenes as they happen. After violence or high tragedy, I am aware of the need, however brief, of a kind of quiet, a release from the preceding tension. It strengthens the next blow of the hammer. Humor can accomplish this, if you can pull it off. I also try to let the characters play their parts in relative importance to their roles, to give each one a fair share, while I attempt always to control their tendency to lead the writer down deserted roads that never lead back to the main direction of the story. But so much arrives unexpectedly. While writing *Dorp Dead* in a small garage room that was filled with leaf shadows and silence, I came to the part where Gilly is looking for the dog and, instead, sees a trail of blood across the kitchen floor. This was an utter surprise to me and it frightened me so that I had to stop right there and rush out.

Style, it seems to me, is the outcome of work. It grows as the writer grows and quite without urging or instruction. I have been told that my style varies a little with each book, but I am not aware of this. In *Dorp Dead,* I admit to having purposely had Gilly tell his story his way, and, in another book, to having the naive American rat in France use his own rather slang-filled language. But after that, they chose their own rhythms of speech, of telling, and I simply tried to keep my ear true to their individual pitch.

A writer friend once said that to her a really fine story was like a balloon, suspended lightly in air by its own inner breath, holding perfect shape. This has meant a geat deal to me through the years. I can feel its rightness even when my own balloon sometimes leaks into lopsidedness.

I've been standing in the wings for quite a while. A moment ago, the stage was empty because I was thinking of letting impressions and shadows and moods of new characters arrive to fill it. But now, to end, let me step down and offer what to me is a superb gift—something that the great artist Georges Rouault wrote in a letter, expressing his experience with the whole wonderful mystery at the base of any art—inspiration:

I saw what I had seen before, but the form of it and the harmony were new.... A gypsy caravan halted at the side of the road, a weary old horse nibbling stunted grasses, an old clown patching his costume—the contrast, in fact, between the brilliance and scintillation of laughter and the intense sadness of life itself, that was how it began. Then I enlarged it all. I saw quite clearly that the clown was myself, us, all of us, almost. The gaudy, spangled dress was what life gives us. We all wear spangled dress of some sort, but if someone catches us with the spangles off, as I caught that old clown, oh! the infinite pity of it. I have made the mistake (if it is a mistake; certainly it causes me suffering beyond description) of never allowing people to keep their spangles on. King or Emperor, it's all the same. I want to see through to his soul, and the more the world thinks of him, the more I fear for that soul.

There is one last element that perhaps should be left to speak from between the lines, silently, but without which all the words, all the work, all the talent are as nothing, and that element is love.

13

CREATIVE TRUST

By John D. MacDonald

The writer and the reader are involved in a creative relationship. The writer must provide the materials with which the reader will construct bright pictures in his head. The reader will use those materials as a partial guide and will finish the pictures with the stuff from his own life experience.

I do not intend to patronize the reader with this analogy: The writer is like a person trying to entertain a listless child on a rainy afternoon.

You set up a card table, and you lay out pieces of cardboard, construction paper, scissors, paste, crayons. You draw a rectangle and you construct a very colorful little fowl and stick it in the foreground, and you say, "This is a chicken." You cut out a red square and put it in the background and say, "This is a barn." You construct a bright yellow truck and put it in the background on the other side of the frame and say, "This is a speeding truck. Is the chicken going to get out of the way in time? Now you finish the picture."

If the child has become involved, he will get into the whole cut-and-paste thing, adding trees, a house, a fence, a roof on the barn. He will crayon a road from the truck to the chicken. You didn't say a word about trees, fences, houses, cows, roofs. The kid puts them in because he knows they are the furniture of farms. He is joining in the creative act, enhancing the tensions of the story by adding his uniquely personal concepts of the items you did not mention, but which have to be there.

Or the child could cross the room, turn a dial and see detailed pictures on the television tube. What are the ways you can lose him?

You can lose him by putting in too much of the scene. That turns him into a spectator. "This is a chicken. This is a fence. This is an apple tree. This is a tractor." He knows those things have to be there. He yawns. And pretty soon, while you are cutting and pasting and explaining, you hear the gunfire of an old western.

You can lose him by putting in too little. "This is a chicken," you say, and leave him to his own devices. Maybe he will put the chicken in a forest, or in a supermarket. Maybe the child will invent the onrushing truck, or a chicken hawk. Too much choice is as boring as too little. Attention is diffused, undirected.

You can put in the appropriate amount of detail and still lose him by the way you treat the chicken, the truck, and the barn. Each must have presence. Each must be unique. *The* chicken. Not *a* chicken. He is eleven weeks old. He is a rooster named Melvin who stands proud and glossy in the sunlight, but tends to be nervous, insecure and hesitant. His legs are exceptionally long, and in full flight he has a stride you wouldn't believe.

If you cannot make the chicken, the truck, and the barn totally specific, then it is as if you were using dingy gray paper for those three ingredients, and the child will not want to use his own bright treasure to complete the picture you have begun.

We are analogizing here the semantics of image, of course. The pace and tension and readability of fiction are as dependent upon your control and understanding of these phenomena as they are upon story structure and characterization.

Here is a sample: The air conditioning unit in the motel room had a final fraction of its name left, an "aire" in silver plastic, so loose that when it resonated to the coughing thud of the compressor, it would blur. A rusty water stain on the green wall under the unit was shaped like the bottom half of Texas. From the stained grid, the air conditioner exhaled its stale and icy breath into the room, redolent of chemicals and of someone burning garbage far, far away.

Have you not already constructed the rest of the motel room? Can you not see and describe the bed, the carpeting, the shower? O.K., if you see them already, I need not describe them for you. If I try to do so, I become a bore. And the pictures you have composed in your head are more vivid than the ones I would try to describe.

No two readers will see exactly the same motel room. No two children will construct the same farm. But the exercise of the need to create gives both ownership and involvement to the motel room and the farm, to the air conditioner and to the chicken and to their environments.

Sometimes, of course, it is useful to go into exhaustive detail. That is when a different end is sought. In one of the Franny and Zooey stories, Salinger describes the contents of a medicine cabinet shelf by shelf in such infinite detail that finally a curious monumentality is achieved, reminiscent somehow of that iron sculpture by David Smith called "The Letter."

Here is a sample of what happens when you cut the images out of gray paper: "The air conditioning unit in the motel room window was old and somewhat noisy."

See? Because the air conditioning unit has lost its specificity, its unique and solitary identity, the room has blurred also. You cannot see it as clearly. It is less real.

AND WHEN THE ENVIRONMENT IS LESS REAL, THE PEOPLE YOU PUT INTO THAT ENVIRONMENT BECOME LESS BELIEVABLE, AND LESS INTERESTING.

I hate to come across a whole sentence in caps when I am reading something. But here, it is of such importance, and so frequently misunderstood and neglected, I inflict caps upon you with no apology. The environment can seem real only when the reader has helped construct it. Then he has an ownership share in it. If the air conditioner is unique, then the room is unique, and the person in it is real.

What item to pick? There is no rule. Sometimes you can use a little sprinkling of realities, a listing of little items which make a room unique among all rooms in the world: A long living room with one long wall painted the hard blue of Alpine sky and kept clear of prints and paintings, with a carved blonde behemoth piano, its German knees half-bent under its oaken weight, and with a white Parsons table covered by a vivid collection of French glass paperweights.

I trust the reader to finish the rest of that room in his head, without making any conscious effort to do so. The furnishings will be appropriate to his past observations.

How to make an object unique? (Or where do I find the colored paper for the rooster?) Vocabulary is one half the game, and that can come only from constant, omnivorous reading, beginning very early in life. If you do not have that background, forget all about trying to write fiction. You'll save yourself brutal disappointment. The second half of the game is input. All the receptors must be wide open. You must go through the world at all times looking at the things around you. Texture, shape, style, color, pattern, movement. You must be alert to the smell, taste, sound of everything you see, and alert to the relationships between the aspects of objects, and of people. Tricks and traits and habits, deceptive and revelatory.

There are people who have eyes and cannot see. I have driven friends through country they have never seen before and have had them pay only the most cursory attention to the look of the world. Trees are trees, houses are houses, hills are hills—to them. Their inputs are all turned inward, the receptors concerned only with Self. Self is to them the only reality, the only uniqueness. Jung defines these people in terms of the "I" and the "Not I." The "I" person conceives of the world as being a stage setting for Self, to the point where he cannot believe other people are truly alive and active when they are not sharing that stage with Self. Thus nothing is real unless it has a direct and specific bearing on Self.

The writer must be a Not-I, a person who can see the independence of all realities and know that the validity of object or person can be appraised and used by different people in different ways. The writer must be the observer, the questioner. And that is why the writer should be wary of adopting planned eccentricities of appearance and behavior, since, by making himself the observed rather than the observer, he dwarfs the volume of input he must have to keep his work fresh.

Now we will assume you have the vocabulary, the trait of constant observation plus retention of the telling detail. And at this moment—if I am not taking too much credit—you have a new appraisal of the creative relationship of writer and reader. You want to begin to use it.

The most instructive thing you can do is to go back over past work, published or unpublished, and find the places where you described something at length, in an effort to make it unique and special, but somehow you did not bring it off. (I do this with my own work oftener than you might suppose.)

Now take out the subjective words. For example, I did not label the air conditioner as old, or noisy, or battered, or cheap. Those are evaluations the reader should make. Tell how a thing looks, not your evaluation of what it is from the way it looks. Do not say a man looks seedy. That is a judgment, not a description. All over the world, millions of men look seedy, each one in his own fashion. Describe a cracked lens on his glasses, a bow fixed with stained tape, tufts of hair growing out of his nostrils, an odor of old laundry.

This is a man. His name is Melvin. You built him out of scraps of bright construction paper and put him in front of the yellow oncoming truck.

The semantics of image is a special discipline. Through it you achieve a reality which not only makes the people more real, it makes the situation believable, and compounds the tension.

If a vague gray truck hits a vague gray man, his blood on gray pavement will be without color or meaning.

When a real yellow truck hits Melvin, man or rooster, we feel that mortal thud deep in some visceral place where dwells our knowledge of our own oncoming death.

You have taken the judgment words out of old descriptions and replaced them with the objective words of true description. You have taken out the things the reader can be trusted to construct for himself.

Read it over. Is there too much left, or too little? When in doubt, opt for less rather than more.

We all know about the clumsiness the beginning writer shows when he tries to move his people around, how he gets them into motion without meaning. We all did it in the beginning. Tom is in an office on one side of the city, and Mary is in an apartment on the other side. So we walked him into the elevator, out through the foyer, into a cab, all the way across town, into another foyer, up in the elevator, down the corridor to Mary's door. Because it was motion without meaning, we tried desperately to create interest with some kind of ongoing interior monologue. Later we learned that as soon as the decision to go see Mary comes to Tom, we need merely skip three spaces and have him knocking at Mary's door. The reader knows how people get across cities, and get in and out of buildings. The reader will make the instantaneous jump.

So it is with description. The reader knows a great deal. He has taste and wisdom, or he wouldn't be reading. Give him some of the vivid and specific details which you see, and you can trust him to build all the rest of the environment. Having built it himself, he will be that much more involved in what is happening, and he will cherish and relish you the more for having trusted him to share in the creative act of telling a story.

14

THE THEORY OF THE SILVER BULLET

By Leonard S. Bernstein

OUT of the legends of the Old West, passed down from father to son, comes the tale of the silver bullet. That there was a hero, so magnificent, so pure, and so inviolate, that he could only be brought down by a single silver bullet.

So the outlaws plotted and schemed, and finally fashioned this bullet of pure silver, and waited and waited for their one chance. The chance came, the bullet was fired, and it missed, of course. There was no second chance, and the outlaws, having spent months preparing for the moment, slunk away, defeated forever.

So the theory of the silver bullet means one chance, one glorious chance at success—never to come again.

It is this theory that governs the beginning writer.

The hero? Why, the hero is the editor of *Redbook* or *The New Yorker,* sitting somewhere on his (or her) white horse, godlike and untouchable. And the silver bullet? That is the one great short story, torn from the heart, shaped and worked over, until it becomes the very essence of the writer, the very cornerstone of his identity. The divine silver bullet is fired at the hero, and the writer *knows* that it can't miss, because it is his soul that he surrenders. At the very least, it will come back with a glowing statement of apology. "A major work of fiction—overstocked at present—try again soon."

Yes, it misses, and returns with the inevitable printed card; it is not a manuscript returned but a whole personal thing. The writer slinks off, defeated forever, and the story goes in the bottom drawer, never again to see the light of day.

I prefer the buckshot theory.

The buckshot theory argues that if you fill your rifle with shot and spray that shot all over the place, you have to hit something. Translated, it means that if you write ten articles and get them onto the desks of ten different editors, you have ten shots at the target. Which means that even if your marksmanship is not world-class caliber, one of your shots is likely to hit the mark. (It does not mean that you should send the same article to ten different magazines. That *does* multiply your chances, but it is not appreciated by the larger body of editors.)

The buckshot theory also argues that much of being published—assuming that the writing is competent—is having your story on the right desk on the right day. It certainly argues that manuscripts buried in the bottom drawers of America have very little chance at all.

Acceptability is not an absolute quality. It depends on the needs of the magazine, the mood of the editor, and—who knows?—what the weather outside is like. Acceptability is in the eye of the beholder, which is why stories and articles have been known to be rejected fifteen or twenty times and then to be accepted by such magazines as *Redbook* or *Ladies' Home Journal.*

Let us assume that your story is whimsical, and the editor has just emerged from a conference where it was pointed out that the last three issues of the magazine seemed a trifle stiff. She returns to her desk wondering where are the humor writers of yesterday? Why doesn't anyone submit whimsy any more?

Now it happens that there are seventy-four manuscripts piled on her desk, but it also happens that this time yours is on top. She turns to the first paragraph—why, it's kind of clever. Where has this writer been all these years?

I'll tell you where the writer has been—in the rejection pile. Because if the story was not right on top, or if she had read it after three other whimsical pieces, or if she was rushed or irritated, or if she was thinking, we've been running too much humor—the manuscript wouldn't seem so clever after all.

The buckshot theory goes on to state that there are probably seventy-four editors who might consider your piece, and each one has a stack seventy-four manuscripts high. If you get your buckshot into seventy-four piles, one of the shots will be on top. Of course another shot will not be on top, but it may be on top tomorrow. And still another shot may be near the bottom, but the editor will love it anyway.

A beginning writer will often say, "*Redbook* has just returned my story with a printed rejection slip. What do I do now?"

The implication is that she might go on a hunger strike or perhaps look over the edge of a very high cliff.

I'm exaggerating a little. More likely, the writer will say that the story has been rejected by *Redbook, Good Housekeeping, Cosmopolitan, Esquire* and *The New Yorker,* and she wonders what to do *now*? This implies that she has suffered more humiliation than she should have a right to expect.

"How about the quarterlies?" I ask. "How about *Partisan Review, Prairie Schooner, Colorado Quarterly*?"

But she is genuinely wounded, and all because the story is her silver bullet. It will take some doing to convert her to the buckshot theory. And the buckshot theory is so inelegant. What writers want to think of their stories and articles as just so much buckshot? After all, this is literature we are involved in—this isn't commerce! Better to think of our stories as silver bullets—messages from the heart. Well, better to *think* of them as silver bullets perhaps, but better to handle them as buckshot. Buckshot hits. Silver bullets miss.

Getting published is not like getting married. Nobody promised you romance. So if your masterwork is yellowing in the bottom drawer, and if you are yellowing, because, after all, how can you write when your greatest story has been rejected by five major markets, try to look at it this way: How can it get accepted if nobody is looking at it?

The editors of America—however you may imagine them—are not like the Lone Ranger on a white stallion. They are intelligent and competent, but they are neither sacred nor saintly. Like most of us, they spill coffee on their desks, miss deadlines, and worry about their jobs.

Editors are more like a flock of geese, flying all over the literary horizon. One of your shots will hit. One of them is going to like your story.

PART II

HOW TO WRITE: TECHNIQUES

15

WHAT MAKES A FICTION WRITER?

BY B. J. CHUTE

THE other day, an interviewer asked me, "What makes a fiction writer?" and I could only answer, "I have no idea." It is a time-honored and shopworn question, and there are as many answers to it as there are writers, because all writers are different.

The interviewer, being neither time-honored nor shopworn but, on the contrary, young and lively, changed her question to "What makes *you* a fiction writer?" I felt I could answer that question reasonably well, and I did so by offering such (time-honored and shopworn) reasons as a natural bent for storytelling, a life-long habit of reading, a love of words, and all the etcetera of halfway answers which I hope were useful to her but which really did not satisfy me.

Thinking now about her question, I have been turning it over and over in my mind until I arrived, like Alice, at my looking-glass desti-nation by walking away from it. I do not believe I know what makes me a fiction writer, but I do believe that there are four qualities with-out which one cannot write fiction at all.

The first, of course, is *imagination.* Imagination is as necessary to a novelist or short-story writer as the spinning of webs is to a spider and just as mysterious. It defies analysis (either one is a spider, or one isn't), and it has been quite properly called "the creative impulse." It has also been called the Muse, and, when the Muse vanishes, that yawning void she leaves behind her is known as "writer's block."

Imagination cannot be created, but it can be fostered, and this fostering is part of the writer's duty. It is not enough to congratulate oneself on having been gifted (lovely word!) with imagination, though it is certainly a major cause for rejoicing. The imagination, like the intellect, has to be used, and a creative writer ought to exercise it all the time. There is no idea, however insignificant or vague it may be, that the imagination cannot touch to new beginnings, turning it around and around in different lights, playing with it, *listening* to it. One of the most marvelous things about spiders (and writers) is the way they will launch themselves into space on a filament so infinitely slender as to be nearly invisible, and, lo, there is suddenly a bridge flung over the chasm, across which any fly (or any reader) can walk with perfect confidence.

The second quality I believe to be essential for writing fiction is *empathy,* which the dictionary properly defines as "mental entering into the feeling or spirit of a person or thing." As with imagination, one is to a degree born with empathy; but, like imagination, it can be fostered. Writers of fiction write from inside themselves, but they also write from inside other people, and, again, this is a kind of gift. It is what produces strong and believable characterization. *Madame Bovary* was written from the inside out. Flaubert seems to know not only the passion, the boredom, the despair and the terrible loneliness of that pitiful woman, but he also seems to know the most trivial light or shadow that falls across her mind. Imagination could create her, and her world, and the people around her, but it is Flaubert's empathy that makes his unhappy Emma not just credible but totally real. This is Melville's "subterranean miner that works in us all," and, although we cannot expect to be Melvilles or Flauberts, we can mine what we have. And if we do that, with honesty and intensity, who knows what lode of treasure we may strike?

The third quality is *style.* In its simplest form, style in writing can be defined as the way in which a thing is said. It is a much abused word, and it sometimes seems to me that it is woefully misunderstood by writers and readers alike. Style does not exist apart from the story, and, if five people tell an identical story, each one will tell it in a different style. The best style will produce the best story, and the listeners will turn to it even if they do not know why they turn. Style is a great preservative of writing, and no writer ought ever to think that a really good style is beyond his reach. But many writers do think so, and too many settle for second best when, in fact, they ought to be working all the time against any such preposterous limitation of their own capacities.

Once I ran across a description of style as applied to architecture, which is just as true of writing—"What is style? Clear thinking, really; the ability to use your head before you do anything with your hands." Sloppy thinking will produce sloppy style, and I am certain there is not a writer among us who has not stared hopelessly at the written page which reflects the muddy results. What to do? Go back, of course. Find out what you are trying to say, and, having found it, select the words that will make the reader see what you are seeing. Selection is vital to style. Because English is an incredibly rich language, there are many bad ways of saying something, and many good ways, but there is usually only one right way. This right way will be the writer's *own* way—in short, his style, or what Proust called "the underlying tune" which distinguishes one writer from another. This should represent the very best the writer has to offer. "Second best" will not do.

Take, as an example, a description from Nathaniel Hawthorne. He is introducing a minister, and all he wishes to say about him is that he is a serious person, wears a beard, and is dressed in the kind of dark clothes and tall hat that would have been affected by a clergyman of his time. There are perhaps a hundred ways of putting all these details together so that the reader can visualize the character sharply, and most such descriptions would probably take a paragraph, certainly several sentences. Hawthorne does it in seven words; his minister is "grave, bearded, sable-cloaked and steeple-crowned."

This is perfectly beautiful writing, and it is as exact as it is beautiful. The picture is instantaneous and vivid, and the tone is faultless. I do not know whether Hawthorne got those seven words right the first time, or whether he labored over them in rewrite after rewrite. Even successive drafts of his manuscript would tell us nothing, because the majority of a writer's work goes on in his mind. What matters is that every word in Hawthorne's description is the right one: *grave,* with its sonorous double meaning; *bearded,* just the simple piece of information to balance the poetic images that follow; *sable-cloaked,* concealing, mysterious, and darker than darkness itself; and, finally, the triumph of *steeple-crowned,* which makes us see not only the minister in his tall hat, but Church, Authority and Heaven as well.

It is true that the average writer is not a Nathaniel Hawthorne, but it is also true that none of these seven words is in the least obscure or recondite or self-conscious; each one would be available to any writer who was craftsman enough to persist in finding it. If a writer is willing to work all the time and in everything he writes to achieve the best style of which he is capable, the words will be there for him as they were for Hawthorne.

And this brings us, inevitably, to the fourth quality, which is *patience.*

Patience in a writer is many things, but most of all, I think, it is characterized by concern for the words on the page. The aim of this concern is "to see the thing and throw the loop of creation around it," as Joyce Cary said. (And notice how riveting the phrasing of that statement is; there's style for you!) What Cary calls "the thing" is the idea, the initial impulse, the product of imagination and empathy. The "loop of creation" is the finding of the right words that will make it possible for the reader to share the writer's special vision, and such words can be very evasive, very slow to come.

At rare and wonderful intervals, the stars in their courses do seem to join together, and the writer finds himself writing so effortlessly and with such precision that it almost seems as if he were taking dictation. These are the best of times, but they are certainly not ordinary. In ordinary times, the words on the page are merely adequate: they move the story along; the second draft will be easier; experience lends hopefulness. The worst of times are when the words will not come at all, and the writer feels as if he were floundering in a swamp or gasping for air in a desert. This can be really frightening, and it is here—in swamp or desert—that the quality of patience will spell the difference between disaster and survival.

In the dictionary, the second definition for the word *patience* is "calmness in waiting." I like this definition very much indeed, because there is a steadiness about it and a good deal of faith, and any writer needs both.

When the final draft of a manuscript is on paper, the words are all that really matter. Money, status, and fame are by-products; nice to have, but nothing permanent. If that statement seems idealistic, of course it is. It is meant to be. To call upon the dictionary once more, idealism is "the cherishing or pursuing of ideals, as for attainment." For the writer of fiction, the pursuit is through imagination and empathy, the cherishing is through style, and the attainment is through patience.

Excellence is simply idealism in action, and so high an aim is bound to fall short of the mark many times. I call to your attention the words of John Adams, written in February of 1776—"We cannot ensure success, but we can deserve it."

16

HOW TO WRITE A NOVEL

By Morris L. West

YOU buy two reams — one thousand pages — of blank paper. You sit down, and you write one complete page every day for one year. At the end of that time, you have a book — good, bad or indifferent! You also have a wastebasket full of rejected pages.

The prescription sounds simple. In practice it is very difficult because it demands industry and continuity. Besides, like a sentence of death, the mere act of writing concentrates the mind most wondrously.

In a longish life as a professional writer, I have heard a thousand masterpieces talked out over bars, restaurant tables and love seats. I have never seen one of them in print. Books must be written, not talked.

Writing is like making love. You have to practice to be good at it. Like the best love-making, it has to be done in private and with great consideration for your partner in the enterprise, who in this case is the reader.

A novel is a story. It is a story about people. People live and die in a dimension of space and time. People have a past, a present and some promise of a future.

If you want to be a novelist you have to know people. You have to know the dimensions in which they have lived, do live, or may live. Again it sounds like an elementary proposition. But, try writing a novel without adequate preparation, and you will find that the people of your dreams have no bones to hold them up. The country in which they live is vague and featureless; and the time dimension is an evanescent moment.

To tell a story you need an audience. Have you ever tried talking to a blank wall? Have you ever tried writing a letter to a nonexistent lover? Both experiences are extremely frustrating. Every act of communication presupposes a communicator and an audience, whether the audience be actual or putative. If you want an audience, you have to have enough art to be able to command its attention for a single instant, which is the beginning of your story, and hold it thereafter for the duration of your narrative.

It's a kind of social contract. One doesn't pay $10.00 for a book in order to be bored. One pays for the classic experience of being purged by pity, terror, laughter and vicarious living and loving.

Do you want examples? Go back to the fairy tales of your childhood: "Once upon a time there were three bears who lived in a little house in the forest...." Go back to the Bible: "One day Saul was sitting in his house, spear in hand, with the evil spirit upon him, and David was playing the harp before him. He tried to pin David to the wall and David escaped from his presence whilst the spear stuck in the wall...."

Are you interested? Of course you are. Do you want to continue? Of course you do. Child or adult, you are instantly involved. The personages are real and vivid. The time, the place, the action are instantly defined. Disbelief is suspended. You cry to know what happened next.

What happens next constitutes the plot and the theme of the novel. For me, the theme always develops before the plot. The plot is the framework within which the theme is exposed and expounded. For example, in *The Shoes of the Fisherman* I tried to understand how the world might look through the eye of a loving creator; a single unified purview of the constant struggle between good and evil. The plot grew out of the theme. The Pope claims to be the vicar of Christ on earth. In theory, at least, from the moment he is elected, he must look upon the world with the loving and caring eye of the creator. But a Pope is only human; he is limited by the historic circumstance and by his own personality. How, therefore, will he comport himself?

I began *The Ambassador* in a different fashion. I knew a great deal about the circumstances that led to the assassination of President Diem and his family in South Vietnam. I knew of the American involvement in the assassination. I knew many of the political complexities involved. I asked myself how would I, a supposedly moral man, act if I were asked directly or indirectly to sign a death warrant?

The Salamander was a different case again. I had lived a long time in Italy. I had developed a profound love/hate relationship with the country, its culture, and its passionate people. I decided that I wanted to express this relationship in the form of a novel. I decided first to write an historical novel — the story of one Italian, born in 1900, who had survived the First World War, the Fascist period, and the Second World War, to become a leading industrialist.

I made four attempts at this historical treatment. I wrote nearly a hundred thousand words and threw most of them away. The theme was very clear to me. I knew everything I wanted to say. However, I had chosen the wrong vehicle through which to say it. I discovered that I was not an historical novelist. I am a novelist of the immediate drama. I had to construct my plot in the now. I had to begin with a trigger incident in the present, with characters existing in the present, and show the past through their eyes.

The experience was a salutary one: I had finally discovered the "why" and the "how" of what previously had been a purely instinctive method of working.

The "why" was essentially simple. I am a man, deeply involved in the business of living. I am hungry for all sorts of experiences. I cannot live at secondhand; therefore I cannot write at secondhand. I must write now about things which I know now, feel now, suffer now, enjoy now.

The "how" also became very clear. I must begin in a single moment of potential drama. I must be able to state this moment wholly and completely in a single sentence or, at most, a single paragraph. *The Devil's Advocate* begins with such a sentence: "It was his profession to prepare other men for death. It shocked him to be so unready for his own." The opening of *The Shoes of the Fisherman* was even shorter: "The Pope was dead." *Summer of the Red Wolf* begins: "Suddenly I was sick of the savagery of the world." *The Ambassador* commences: "As a diplomat I have a good record. In his valedictory letter the President called it, 'a distinguished and meritorious career, the sum of whose service represents a great profit to the United States of America.'"

Until this opening statement is made, I cannot begin the book, no matter how clear the rest of it is in my mind. Once the statement is made, the book proceeds by a logical process based on one question, "What if...?"

Think about this for a moment. It is the end of the day. You are leaving the office as usual. A number of choices are open to you: You can turn right and go downtown to catch the subway; you can turn left and walk half a block uptown to the neighborhood bar; you can cross the street to buy an evening newspaper; you can go back into your office to pick up a file which you have forgotten. Each of these choices will have a different consequence for the narrative.

Back in your office, you will find an ambitious colleague ransacking your filing cabinet. In the neighborhood bar, you will find an attractive woman with whom you may be tempted to start a love affair. On the subway, you may be mugged or you may be conned into a bad business deal. As you cross the street to buy a newspaper, you may be run down by a car. Whichever course you choose, you are committed to it for the rest of your story.

All of which brings me to the *selective process* of the novelist. You can't tell or show everything within the compass of a book. If you try to tell or show everything, your reader will die of boredom before the end of the first page. You must, therefore, ask yourself what is the core of the matter you wish to communicate to your reader? Having decided on the core of the matter, all that you tell him must relate to it and illustrate it more and more vividly.

Example: A story from the Hindu epic, *The Ramayana*. Rama and his two brothers were trained in archery by a great master. One day the master said to them:

"You are now ready to be tested as marksmen."

He took them to a clearing in the forest and showed them a tall tree upon one of whose branches was a beautiful colored bird. To the first brother he said:

"Stand to the mark, take aim and, before you fire, tell me what you see."

The first brother said:

"I see the tree and the bird."

The master said:

"Stand down."

The second brother stood to the mark, took aim and said:

"I see the bird on the branch."

The master said:

"Stand down."

Then Rama stood to the mark and took aim. The master asked:

"What do you see, Rama?"

Rama answered:

"I see the blue feathers on the neck of the bird."

Twentieth-century readers are assaulted at every hour of the day and night by audio impressions, visual impressions, subliminal solicitations. They see everything, hear everything. They perceive too much, reflect too little, and their imaginations become atrophied for want to use. It is a test of our skills that we, with nothing more strident than black print on white paper, can force them to concentrate on the blue feathers on the neck of the bird, and yet be aware, without our telling, of the myriad wonders of the surrounding forest.

17

A NOVELIST'S IDENTITY CRISIS

By Helen Van Slyke

IN SEPTEMBER, Doubleday published my sixth novel, titled *Always Is Not Forever,* the story of a young woman who marries a concert pianist, one of a family of eccentric, selfish, talented musical geniuses.

Unless this book is the exception which proves the rule, I will be barraged by the same questions which have hounded me after every book: "How do you know so much about mother and child relationships? Were you married to a man like that? What parts of the book are autobiographical? Did you draw on real people and experiences?"

The answers, as in the past, will be mixed.

I know about mother/child relationships from *having* a mother and *being* a child, not the other way around.

No, I was not married to a man like that.

And I've not lived the heroine's life.

Do I draw on real people and experiences? Of course, but only in the sense of having lived long enough to have known a great many people, heard so many stranger-than-fiction real-life stories, read about daily problems and joys, soaked up the feelings of others, combined them with philosophy of my own and overlaid the whole with vivid imagination and a love of yarn-spinning.

My "success" as a contemporary novelist lies in two overworked words: *identity* and *empathy*. The readers who ask the above questions seem to feel that I have lived through some or all of the situations I invent. And, more important, they are amazed that in the pages of my books they come upon familiar emotions and recognizable reactions expressed by the characters. Their conclusion is that since one can "write only about what one knows" I must certainly have experienced the feelings of the people who populate my novels. Otherwise, how could I convincingly portray the hurts and happiness of the central and peripheral figures?

The multi-faceted answer is that of course one writes best about what one knows, but what is it one knows? In my case it's people. Real, vulnerable, quite ordinary people. I write about them and readers relate to them, seeing them in the context of their own lives or in the experiences of those they've known.

People are my joy, my interest, my constant source of inspiration. Female people, usually, because I understand my own sex better than the other one. But male people, too, because men also can rejoice and be wounded and aspire and succeed or fail. Dealing with people, in a very personal way, has enabled me to produce stories about the day-to-day existence of believable human beings.

A few examples: Elizabeth Quigly, the heroine of *The Heart Listens,* is the kind of strong, generous, slightly flawed woman most of us have encountered and admired.

But I did not have to *be* Elizabeth to know how she would react to an unfaithful husband, to reverses in fortune, to a trio of children so disparate she could have, in her words, "picked them up on three different street corners."

I did not have to *be* a mulatto, as Toni Jenkins of *The Mixed Blessing* is, to understand the torment of a young woman born of a racially mixed marriage.

I did not have to *be* a widow in Cleveland to share the confusion and sadness and disorientation of forty-seven-year-old Sheila Callahan in *The Best Place To Be.*

And so on.

I can and do draw on the little I know about human nature, about the way people react to stress or happiness. In the course of selling more than four million copies of my books, I have answered hundreds of letters from readers and spoken to thousands of others at luncheons and seminars and meetings across the country. More than ever, I am convinced that the "ordinary" man or woman is the backbone of the faithful reading public. The wish to understand and identify with the characters in a novel is a strong motivation. The ability to relate to the fictional "friends" in a book is the key to pleasing a public which many writers dismiss as dull and uninteresting.

These people are anything *but.* They are articulate, sentimental, compassionate, understanding. Because they see in the imaginary characters a reflection of things they understand.

For some time I have been crusading for the emergence of the "old-fashioned, modern novel." The nineteen seventies is a time of return to the verities after a decade of books about far-out, neurotic, narcissistic, oversexed, drug-addicted people who are the lunatic fringe of our society. These "heroes and heroines" are incomprehensible to most people whose lives are not rampant with erotic adventures. The "constant reader" — if I may believe what I read and hear from him or her — is one who wishes to get involved in a book, to discover with pleasure that it has a plot, including a beginning, a middle and an end! These readers, of both sexes and all ages, rejoice in reading about people they can understand and — I repeat — with whom they can identify.

Surprising? Not really. We are all more at ease with the familiar, more comfortable with the understandable. Novelists who set out merely to shock or horrify or disgust may have great success with one best seller. But if one is writing for a living, looking at one's work realistically as a full-time job, my belief is that a sense of caring and concern is a more solid foundation on which to build an enduring readership. And a more rewarding one, as well. How fulfilling is the friendliness of one's readers! What pleasure in letters which almost invariably begin, "I've never written to an author before, but I just had to tell you...." And then go on to say that they cried for Elizabeth or understood Toni or lived through Sheila's widowhood. How rewarding to meet a sixteen-year-old girl at an autographing session who confides that you've "introduced her to reading...!" Or to meet a matron who confesses that she "nearly left Elizabeth Quigly off her Christmas card list...." Or try to convince a young woman that you did not really know *her* mother when you were writing about a character's parent. How rich and satisfying to know you've reached people in their hearts by the simple device of relating a story that is comprehensible within the realm of their own experience.

I think this is not a special skill or a device on the part of the author. It is a genuine interest in people and a reaffirmation of the power of storytelling as it's been practiced since the days of the caveman around his fire. I am not sure that everyone can *write* a book, but I am convinced that everyone's life would *make* a book. All one has to do is learn to listen and absorb, to hear the underlying meaning behind the simple story, to recognize the pride and pathos that exist in every life.

To the genuine horror of my Doubleday editor, I often refer to my books as "soap operas between covers." In doing so, I do not put down either my writing or the TV serials. I believe they have a common bond, which is that both portray a "slice of life" as most people know it. Like the daytime heroines of the daily "soaps," women in my books become real to those who follow them through the pages. So real, in fact, that when I wrote *The Mixed Blessing,* using the same characters as in *The Heart Listens,* I was inundated by letters from outraged readers complaining that I did not exactly follow events in the first book. They were quite right. I had taken poetic license in *The Mixed Blessing,* altering some situations, never dreaming that readers would remember tiny details from the previous novel. I was hard put to explain why I had made these changes in the sequel. (Actually, I thought it would not be read as a sequel, but as a new story unto itself. In fact, it was billed as a "semi-sequel," whatever that means!) In any case, the indignation was both flattering and upsetting. Flattering to know that readers remembered so well the events of an earlier book; upsetting to realize that if I received a hundred or so letters of protest from the hardcover, I might receive thousands when the paperback of *The Mixed Blessing* appeared! The editor of Popular Library quickly suggested that we correct the errors before the paperback appeared, and this we did, revising more than sixty references to make the follow-up story conform to the novel which preceded it.

All of which only proves that the people I write about become comrades instead of characters. They exist for my readers, and like the cast of a "soap," they must not be tampered with by their creator!

Indeed, I have learned not to underestimate the interested and watchful eye of the novel-lover. Just this week I received a to-the-point note from a reader of *The Heart Listens.* It went something like this:

Dear Mrs. Van Slyke,
   On page 209 you say that Barney Nash was killed in the war in France.
   On page 256, he declines an invitation to Ann's wedding.
   Obviously for the reason listed above!
                                        Sincerely....

To which I replied,

Dear Mrs. Blank,
   Your eyes are sharper than mine, my editor's and professional readers of manuscripts and galleys. You are so right. Oops!
                                        Sincerely,
                                        Helen Van Slyke

18

A CASE OF SLANDER

BY JOANNE GREENBERG

I ONCE wrote a story about an old woman whose life showed both great force and great fastidiousness. She died when she tripped on a loose edge of stair carpet and fell the length of the stairs to lie broken at the bottom while the telephone (it was good news) rang on unanswered. I wrote the starting down, the trip, the fall. But my old lady did not lie still. She got up, dusted herself off and addressed me: "I won't have this! I didn't die this way at all! You have spent no small space explaining how fastidious I was, and then you kill me on a loose carpet, the hallmark, if I may say so, of an improperly run home. Now if you will sit still and listen, I will tell you what really happened.

"I am a meticulous woman, as you spent pages confirming. I was upstairs where you had me arranging the little pin boxes and dresser things on the top of the dresser. Beautifully written, that description — it showed me, rather than just telling about me. I heard the phone just as you said. I started down the stairs, but as I was going down I saw in my mind the serenity and order of the room I had left. But something was wrong. I saw then what I must have half noticed but left unattended, that the dresser scarf was uneven and, if left as it was, its weight on the wrong side would drag the light glass and china whatnots over. I saw the ruin of it, the broken glass on my smooth, waxed floor. I began to turn, to go upstairs and straighten the scarf but of course the phone was ringing, and it rang again. Now, you know that no American lets a phone ring. It was in turning and then turning again that I had a little vertigo and lost my balance and fell. I'm sure that your sympathy for me is real and that you wouldn't consciously slander me with that insult about the loose carpet."
With that she disposed herself neatly at the bottom of the stairs and died.

A character's independence is good evidence of the "reality" of his characterization. For this reason, while I make fairly detailed outlines of my plot in a novel, I often change them as the characters take over the reality of the story for themselves.

This connects to what I see as one of the basic causes of writer's block. If the structure of a work of fiction is poor or the characters have no life or validity, the work will get more difficult to write in a very specific way. It will become harder to concentrate because there is something wrong with the reality in which the writer is trying to concentrate. Poor writing is easy to see — lapses in mood or tone come clear on the fourth or fifth reading or in letting the work rest for a while and then looking at it again with a coldly objective eye; but poor structure masquerades as a dozen other faults, and poor characterization looks and sounds like dull plotting. This is one reason why the characters in most adventure fiction are so flat. The adventure writer's concern is usually plot only. If you find that your characters are influencing your plot, you will know that they are probably alive and well.

Seen in this way, writer's block is a useful part of what a writer goes through to do his work. Writer's block is the writer's own inner resource trying to tell him something.

One of my students in a short seminar I once gave told me that she desperately wanted to be a writer. She had begun to practice various bizarre habits to "gain the experiences" she wanted to write about. She was very serious about this and mentioned a trip I had made to Sweden as an example of my "getting experience." I told her I wouldn't dare to write about that trip or about Swedish characters after a ten-day jaunt, as "experiential" as it all was. She was disappointed in me because I hadn't forced more reward out of my foreign travel.

I think the problem with this is a misunderstanding of the word "experience." I see an experience as something which touches a person's inner life: It is not only joining the Penitentes or starring in nude movies, but what actually happens in the inner lives of the people who do these things which makes the events "experiences," and more than a movable background against which stick figures are posed.

One of my favorite novels shows this strength brilliantly. It is Chaim Bermant's *Diary of an Old Man*. There are few people in this novel, and the main character is an old man who seldom goes farther than a block from his apartment. In his circumscribed world with few contacts, and a small physical and even smaller financial resource that is all too quickly spent, the little events of the day loom large; the small pleasures are carefully husbanded, the setbacks can be horrifying tragedies. The hero, and he is a hero, does not see himself as a figure larger than life. To the reader the old man's small losses strike with terrible power. What are his "experiences"? A favorite radio program looked forward to all week; the death of an acquaintance, which narrows the world by a third; a power failure; a glass of hot tea on a cold day.

I told my student that her running around from job to job and sleeping around from man to man was taking time and energy from her real business as a writer, which was to work at her craft with what had been given her. She became very impatient with that advice and told me to get lost. She is now writing poetry and publishing it in one of the less particular underground magazines. They too easily allow her any self-indulgent habit she wants because she will pour out "experiences."

For more evidence of what I think a novelist's work is about, read *Augustus,* by John Williams. Octavian (Augustus) has a fascinating life full of adventures, wars, intrigues and travel, but Williams never allows his generous, intelligent, practical hero to break out of the bounds of his own personality as Williams sees it, to exult in the wars or the glory. Williams as a writer is very careful to honor his characters; they in turn honor the plot.

Sometimes a structural problem can masquerade as poor character development. If there are so many flashbacks and jumps ahead that we don't know who is who or what is presently happening, the characters may lose themselves, and the reader's sense of their growth will be forfeited.

My first book was a novel called *The King's Persons.* It was a novel about the York Massacre of 1190, and in order to write it, I studied very hard in medieval poetry, music, art, medicine, metallurgy, etc., etc. Most of the technological information I had was never used except as mistakes I did not make (e.g., referring to peaches, chimneys, distilling of whiskey, use of yeast, sugar, etc.). But the poetry that rang in my head from the eleven-hundreds gave to the prose of the book a long, lyrical line with what was, in 1190, a fashionable amount of alliteration. I wanted the prose surrounding my people to have a flavor of the times in which they were living. When my third novel, *The Monday Voices,* came out, some readers said they were disappointed because I had "lost" my lyrical poetic style. The subject of *The Monday Voices* was the work and reality of a State Rehabilitation counselor in a modern, moderately large city, where caseloads are overfull and the clients delinquents, misfits, and losers of various kinds. It would have been ludicrous to surround modern, urban characters with a biblical, alliterative, medieval style unless some special symbolic meaning was intended. Or unless one is writing humor. Although there are always symbolic overtones in what one hopes to write about people and their predicaments, I think these things are part of the resonance of a book and should be suggested, not stated.

A character may stand as a symbol for something else, but he should be, first and foremost, himself. If I can do Uncle Louis well enough, the part of him which is Everyman will make itself felt without my having to labor the point.

The most aggravating example of the failure of this I find in James Agee's brilliant, flawed book, *Let Us Now Praise Famous Men.* In it, Agee takes us to the rural South of the thirties. We meet the people, eat the food, wear the clothes of his tenant farmers. He can tell us exactly where the body aches after a day in the cotton fields, what kinds of choices the farmer's wife has with 39¢ in her hand and the family's clothes in tatters. The sounds, smells, tactile feel of things have seldom been so deeply or richly conveyed. And then — in part three, Agee decides to bring out his heavy artillery. He wants to show us where this tenant farmer stands in the Universe. He wants to Link Him to Mankind. *All* of it. Back through time. The Stars. Karl Marx, Gandhi, John Jacob Astor. The brilliantly aware novelist-reporter degenerates for a longish section into a self-conscious, self-indulgent, sophomoric, and windy philosopher. This is all the more galling because he has interrupted his own work of power, grace, detail and exquisite honesty and a quiet, deeply felt, moving indictment of poverty to give us this windy nonsense.

Writing, for me, is a voyage of discovery, as I think reading ought to be. Perhaps what I have said here makes it seem that I am hard to please, but that isn't true. Give me characters who have dimension and depth and are respected by their authors, and I'll follow them anywhere. It isn't all the excitement in *Huckleberry Finn* that makes me love the book, but Huckleberry himself. Thomas Williams's masterful short stories make very special truths arise from people who are not special at all and have no built-in claims on our sympathies. Yet through the characters we know enough about them and we know them deeply enough to care very much about them. It then becomes less important whether his endings are happy or sad, or his plotting includes lots of action or not. The endings are right because the characters, like a certain little old lady of my acquaintance, see to it that they are.

19

ORDINARY THOUGHTS ON THE WRITING OF A NOVEL

By Judith Guest

OVER painters, writers have this advantage, that they are allowed the luxury of dreaming on paper, of going off on mystery trips, philosophical binges, lost weekends of self-indulgence, all because of that ultimate in security blankets, the comfortable, if sometimes elusive, Final Draft. For this writers are punished — as painters are not — by being expected to articulate exactly what it *is* that they *do* all day. But I doubt that it's any easier for a writer to explain a piece of writing (does he even *know*?) than it is for an artist to explain a painting; to ask is to invite deceit, for writers are people, after all, and people are not always honest. Or consistent with themselves. Or aware, for that matter. I've been asked many times how many hours a day I write. Sometimes I say five or six; other times two or three. Or eight or ten. Depending on how many it was last week, or how many it *felt like,* or how fired up I was at the time, or how guilty about goofing off yesterday. Thus, the spirit of communication notwithstanding, it takes an incredible lack of common sense to do what I'm doing, which is attempting to explain how I wrote my novel, *Ordinary People.*

It began the way all of my writing begins — in the middle. I have an unreasoning fear of outlines. I can't use them. Having been absent in junior high the week we learned how to make outlines has nothing to do with it. More to do with it is that any sort of advance organization — specifically chapter outlining and plot ordering — makes me feel as if the thing has already been written. Writing is an experience in revelation for the writer as well as for the reader. Characters develop, the story unfolds, and one aspect advances another in a kind of footrace. If I knew each thought, word, and deed of the characters before I started, I wouldn't have the interest or the need to write it all down. I hope this doesn't sound mystical; I'm not trying for that. I'm also not saying that I had absolutely no idea where I was going, or with whom, when I began. I had certain characters in mind; namely, a boy. His parents. His psychiatrist. An admired older brother, who was dead. I had some ideas for certain scenes — sessions with the psychiatrist; arguments between mother and father, and mother and son; a love scene; a scene of reconciliation. I also thought I had a beginning and an end, but neither of them survived the final draft.

Mostly what I had were questions: how does someone who has gone the radical route of attempted suicide come back from such a step? How does he live a normal life, and how does it affect those closest to him? Suppose I were to take these characters through this specific circumstance — what will happen?

In addition, I had a couple of personal goals. The first was to finish *something* — to work through the inevitable boredom, the frustration, and the fear of inadequacy (unique to me, I had always assumed), to the completion of a project. I have always had great trouble finishing things. *Ordinary People* began as three separate short stories, none of which was completed. The first of these took place on the family's annual Florida vacation shortly after the death of the older son. Written from the point of view of Conrad, the second son, it was a series of surrealistic conversations with Buck, his brother, who the reader does not realize is dead until nearly the end of the story. The second was written from the point of view of Cal Jarrett, the father, exploring his feelings during a visit to the mental hospital where he was forced to commit his son as a result of the suicide attempt. The third, an extended scene of dialogue between Conrad and his psychiatrist, appears almost intact in the novel. I used bits and pieces of narrative from the second story, and about ten lines of dialogue from the first, and that's all.

So I wrote sixty pages of material and netted about fifteen for the book. But I didn't feel the time put in on these stories was wasted at all; it was a form of research. I wanted to know how everybody felt, and it seemed that the only way I could know it was to write it. Anyway, the more the material is worked, the tighter it gets, the more precise its wording, and the closer to the writer's original intent. At least that's how I feel about my writing — and editing is the sort of job that one gets better at the more one does it.

When I edited what I'd written, I always made sure there was a sufficient lapse of time between the writing of it, and the revision. I don't edit scenes that are still smoking in my hands; I have to acquire some distance. For me, the longer it sits — a day, a week, or a month — the better I am able to see the good points of it — and the flaws.

These three separate perspectives covering essentially the same ground made me realize that I hadn't yet said all that I wanted to on the subject; also, that I had to write the story from a dual point of view.

Working through the mind of Conrad, I had the feeling that the story written solely from his point of view would soon become whiny and self-serving. He needed someone to help him, someone who could bring a degree of maturity and insight to the problems. I chose his father, but, as I began writing chapters from these two alternating viewpoints, I discovered something: the chapters written from Conrad's point of view were all about Conrad. The chapters written from the point of view of Cal, the father, were about Cal's feelings — about Conrad. Again, too one-sided. In order for Cal to come off as a real person, a *character,* not just a *narrator,* he would have to have a life of his own, with thoughts and feelings and ideas separate and distinct from those of his son. As soon as I made this decision, the story got off the ground and began to take shape as a novel. This decision wasn't made until I was a year and some two hundred accumulated pages into the work, and it was two more years before I was able to finish it.

The other goal I had was to tell a story with as much truth and feeling as I could, without allowing it to sound like a sentimental soap opera. Life, being in essence a soap opera, doesn't set much of an example here. If I believe in any rule of writing, I guess it's the old *show-don't-tell.* Somehow, the emotional impact of a scene does seem stronger to the degree that the reader is allowed to interpret it on his own, without benefit of stage direction from the nervous author. In *Ordinary People,* a scene occurs in which Conrad overhears his teammates discussing him in the locker room, after which he informs the coach that he no longer wants to swim for the team. What I wanted the reader to feel in this scene was first, the hurt Conrad experiences at the blunt, callous remarks tossed around in the room; and second, a subtler hurt as his best friend, Lazenby, ineffectually defends him from the attack. It is obvious to him that Lazenby has also lost faith. In addition, I wanted the reader to be better informed than Conrad; I felt the scene would have more strength if Conrad refused to acknowledge to himself that he had been hurt at all. Thus, he listens without reaction "...stands outside the open door,

smoothing his hand along the polished wood frame, slowly, slowly.''
And, later: ''. . .more laughter, and he does not wait to hear the rest, but
turns abruptly, heading back up the stairs. Nothing touches him on the
way, not even the air in the hallway.''

Another technique is to let the emotional weight of a scene rest on the
dialogue, whenever possible. This is the easy way to avoid over-
interpretation, which seems to be what turns a scene from *sympathetic*
into *sentimental.* The following is an excerpt from a session between
Conrad and his psychiatrist, Dr. Berger:

"I didn't say I never feel things. I feel things."
"When?"
"Sometimes."
"You gonna give me the famine, wars, violence-in-the-streets business again?"
He doesn't answer.
"Come on, kiddo, I'm doing all the work here. I thought you told me you
didn't like to play games."
"I don't. I'm not. I don't know what you want."
"Then I'll tell you. I want you to leave 'I don't know' out there on the table
with the magazines, okay?"
"And what if I don't have an answer? You want me to make one up?"
"Yeah, that'd be nice. Make me one up right now, about how you've turned
yourself inside out and the overwhelming evidence is that there are no feelings in
there, no-how."
"I said I have feelings."
Berger sighs. "Now you have 'em, now you don't. Get it together, Jarrett."
"Why are you hassling me? Why are you trying to get me mad?"
"Are you mad?"
"No!"

Sometimes it is tempting to interpret, but any directions I use, such as
''he says angrily'' or ''he replies calmly,'' are, upon editing, seen as the
intrusions they are, and I then leave them out.

Deciding which scenes to present ''live'' and which to summarize is a
matter of personal preference and judgment. It's difficult to explain how
such a judgment is reached. Generally, if I have enough interest in a
scene to write it in the first place, and if I like it after it's written, I
assume the reader will feel the same.

My choice of present tense for the narration was made in the early
stages of the novel's inception. For some reason, the sense of immediacy
that I wanted only came when I was working in the present tense. Again,
this seems a matter of personal taste, because the novel I am presently

working on works fine in the past tense, and I feel no loss of immediacy when using it.

As for length, I wrote on *Ordinary People* until I felt the story was finished. Some luck is involved here, I think. Sometimes a story will outlast its author's interest in it, and the reader is left with a sense of overhearing the author thinking, "Oh, hell, I'm sick of these people, and I want out *now.*" I hoped that this wouldn't happen to me, and it didn't. However, I doubt that the writer has much control over this.

Having come this far, I may as well step over the line into Hard-Core Advice: first, I don't read many how-to books or articles. Mostly they seem to tell you what you can't do, and the truth is you can do whatever you want, as long as you make it work. For myself, I've always found the how-to article more intimidating than helpful (so much for the time we've all invested here). However, I *do* read other things. I'm a fiction addict. I read as much as I write. I try to read only good authors, and not bad ones. (No need for any Zen descriptions of which is which. Everyone recognizes quality; nobody can define it.) Reading bad authors is depressing; they make one aware of how fine the line is between garbage and quality. Reading good authors is exhilarating. And encouraging. The medium is words. One has only to put good words together in good order to produce quality. When I read authors I love, I see these words that they use — the same ones I use — and I tell myself that my work isn't that far away.

Second, I take myself seriously as a writer. That is, I write what I want to write. Not what I think is timely, or in vogue, or what will sell. I didn't write *Ordinary People* in order to sell it; I wrote it to try to please myself. If it should turn out that it pleases others, that's a terrific bonus, but it wouldn't be the reason that I continue to write.

20

KEEP THE READER GUESSING
TILL THE END

By Richard Martin Stern

THE late Agatha Christie is alleged to have said that putting together a mystery novel was somewhat like putting together a salad: every now and again the ingredients came out in just the proper proportions.

Perhaps because we are always looking for support for our own views, I find in this concept more than a hint of improvisation and even uncertainty, and I am tempted to rise and cry, "Hear! Hear!"

I have been told that there are those who know precisely where a story is going and how it is going to get there before they ever put a word on paper. I genuflect in their direction, and continue in my own uncertain way.

Every writer is frequently asked how he begins a story and what he has in mind in the way of characters, setting, story line, ending. And I have an idea that every writer, if he chose, could answer those questions truthfully in a different way.

At the first Crime Writers International Congress in London in the fall of 1975, I was on a panel with Dick Francis moderating, and Eric Ambler, Gavin Lyall, and Stanley Ellin as the other guests. In the course of the discussion, it became evident that while we all agreed that stories have beginnings, middles, and ends; that the narrative art consists of making the reader turn the page; that although misdirection is allowed, even encouraged, a writer must not lie to his reader; that character development is of primary importance; that stories are made, not born; and so on through the storytellers' list of for-motherhood-and-against-sin axioms — we also agreed that each of us went about his work in a different way.

But we did have one characteristic in common. To a greater or a lesser degree, each of us moves along in a story with a sense of uncertainty, prepared for surprises, I think right to the end a little hesitant to say even to ourselves, "This is exactly how it is going to be." Perhaps I am inferring too much from the discussion, but that is the way it sounded to me, and certainly that is the way it is *for* me.

I dislike the word "inspiration." It smacks of the supernatural. Instead, I prefer the concept a writing friend gave me once, that of a little man buried deep in my mind who is actually writing the story, whose insistence on sometimes mysterious and apparently extraneous ploys I ignore at my peril. He seems to know where we are going, even if I do not. Does that seem strange?

Then consider: I opened my novel *Power* with a man being shot to death in a mountain meadow. Somehow the scene seemed the right opening, although I was prepared to change it if it turned out to be extraneous.

But the fact was that I did not know exactly who that man was, or precisely what part he was going to play in the story, until I was halfway through the book, and until I reached that point, although I was tempted many times to scrap that opening scene because it seemed to have no purpose, I did not because the feeling was too strong that the man's death was going to play an important part — as it did. The little man down in my subconscious knew what he was about all along.

This is admittedly an extreme instance, but it is illustrative.

Now none of this is to say that I have no idea where I am going when I begin a story, that I simply close my eyes and go into a trance and let my subconscious do all the work. It isn't quite that easy.

Before I begin I know a great deal more about my characters, for example, than ever goes down on paper — although I will admit that every now and again I find myself altering a character during the writing of a story because my original view of him, or her, was too limiting, or not as interesting as I would like; or because a plot change which has just occurred to me (and I wonder why I didn't think of it before) simply does not fit in with the character as I have presented him. Then it is back to the business of rewrite to take care of Emerson's "hobgoblin of little minds," consistency. Two steps forward, one step back.

This kind of nonsense could be avoided, I am sure, *if* I knew down to the last detail before I began just how the story was going to be set up and told. As you may have gathered, I do not.

There are probably a number of reasons for my ignorance, but to me the basic reason has to do with the quality which might be called "freshness." It is for that same reason that I refuse to discuss a story I am working on lest my enthusiasm be dulled by talk, and the characters, situation, and conflict all seem stale when I actually sit down to write about them. I marvel, for example, that an actor night after night can speak the same lines with enough feeling to arouse emotional response in his audience.

You may wonder, then, what about rewriting material that is already on paper? To me, that is a different thing entirely, and I am not sure I can explain the difference other than by saying that the changes involved in rewriting are also fresh, not withered by over-familiarity.

What I want before I sit down to begin a story — and I am referring to *any* story, from a short-short to a 300,000-word novel — is a certain grasp of the major characters, the basic situation, the conflicts, and some of the scenes, perhaps even to complete some of the lines of dialogue, and, most important of all, enthusiasm.

In *The Tower,* for example, I was enthusiastic about the situation of a great building catching fire on its dedication day and trapping a number of persons high above the reach of immediate rescue. I knew the main character, the young assistant architect, who would direct rescue attempts from the ground; I could already see a few physical scenes having to do with the building's destruction; and I had fairly well in mind some of the other characters, their conflicts, and their places in the story.

What I did not have was the means of giving that young assistant architect a real stake in the story. He was on the ground, in no danger, and the whole thing wasn't his fault anyway, so, in effect, what the hell?

But my feeling, irresistible, was: get on with it, start telling the story, and it will work itself out. And it did. Along about page 75, the little man let me see what he had in mind:

What about forged change orders authorizing the hanky-panky in the building's construction that was causing the developing catastrophe — with the assistant architect's name on them? By God, then he would be involved, wouldn't he?

What if it meant going back to the first scene in which the assistant architect appeared to introduce copies of the change orders? Easy enough, and even better than if I had done the scene that way in the beginning because now, after 75 pages, I knew with more certainty how that first scene had to be done. It all fell into place.

The point I am making is that by and large when I begin a story, I am embarking on a journey into a largely uncharted land, prepared for all manner of surprises and wonders and inevitably some why-didn't-I-think-of-that-before? recriminations, and the resultant need for rewrite.

Worse, from the meticulous outliner's point of view, except in a short-short, I rarely know the ending before I come to that last wonderful downhill slope that leads to the final page.

Should this character die or live? Should this man and woman walk off into the sunset hand in hand, or should one of them walk away without even looking back? Is the quest to be ended, or should it be made clear that like the search for the Holy Grail there is no end? How much do I spell out, and how much leave to the reader's imaginative preference? What will be the most dramatic, and satisfying, way to wind this up?

The answers to questions like these must come out of the story itself, of course; they cannot be dragged in on the last few pages and be expected to stand unsupported. And here I return to the concept of that little man in my subconscious, who is really writing the tale. He has known all along, and made his guidance felt, and if he and I have worked together as we should, then the ending becomes clear and understandable, even inevitable.

Listen to your subconscious, or that small voice, or whatever you choose to call it. Play the dual roles you must play, that of the writer *and* of the reader, and ask yourself if the story *feels* right, or does it, like a badly told joke, leave you cold and unsatisfied when you read it? Does this scene you have just written leave you with a nagging doubt that like a misspelled word it somehow isn't right, or with a sneaking feeling that it doesn't quite fit? Maybe your subconscious is trying to tell you something, and you had damn well better listen.

Remember that, aside from the basic axioms, there are no hard-and-fast rules that apply to every writer. Find your own way. Then judge your own work as you would have it judged. Is it honest, is it credible, does it all hang together, and above all is it interesting?

Because it makes no difference whether you started with a meticulous outline or only a vague idea, it is the finished product that matters, and unless that finished product satisfies you, *and* the little man who looks over your shoulder, it is not going to satisfy anyone else either.

21

PEOPLE, NOT PLOT

By Jean Rikhoff

ONE OF the most common misunderstandings of beginning writers is that plot is the most important element a writer must invent and organize to get his book under way. In my experience as a novelist working with creative writing classes and workshops, I continually find beginning writers laboriously constructing great weighty structures of plot on which they intend to erect their novels. Often pages and pages of notes, elaborate outlines, constant worry over incidental incidents and trivial turns of the story usurp vital energy needed for planning elsewhere, erode the writer's confidence in completing the project, and bog the writer down in useless detail. The book is finally abandoned, an object of despair and disgust because "the plot wouldn't work out right."

First, let me say that in my experience with writing six novels, *no* plot ever works out the way a writer first thinks it is going to. If it does, something is probably radically wrong. More likely than not, the writer is manipulating characters to make them fit into preconceived schemes, forcing the characters to behave in unlikely ways, or to go through contrived situations in spite of a character's "natural" inclinations to behave in a completely different way. Often, characters are forced to behave unnaturally in order to obey an author's original outline.

Dynamic characters take on a life of their own — what most writers vaguely (but accurately) describe as "running away with the author." That is, as a character begins to emerge and develop, he takes on a life of his own; he becomes larger than the sum of his parts and assumes, like most of the people we know around us, complexities and inconsistencies that are difficult to pin down. In other words, the character does not fit into the neat plot outline that the writer has originally drawn up.

Characters in fictional works are usually divided into two classifications: round and flat. A round character is one who acts from a whole set of motivating forces rather than from one simple, easily discernible one.

He pushes the action along — creates it, changes it, shapes it, and, even when seemingly immobilized by it, seizes on his powerlessness to try to show us how forces outside ourselves often paralyze us by events too strong to control. Nevertheless, even at a time like that, a round character struggles against his fate so that he still is, in a sense, "acting."

One of the key ways of detecting a strong character is by the fact that he is capable of surprising the reader. He probably not only surprises the reader but also most certainly surprises the writer who, in wishing to push him to conform to some given situation, finds the character a stubborn, balky figure, one who says petulantly from the paper, "But I wouldn't act like that!" If the writer forces him, that character turns from someone "real" to someone *un*complex, and — worst of all — dull. Very likely the character who is made to conform, for purposes of the plot, to what he wouldn't do "on his own" goes from being a round, dynamic, complex, three-dimensional character to a flat, cardboard, one-dimensional figure whose actions are completely predictable. Such characters are often referred to as "sign-carrying characters," meaning that they might just as well come on carrying a sign that signifies how they will *always* react under any given situation. They can never surprise us because for all eternity their responses will be the same — one of Greed or Lust or Miserliness, or whatever single "humour" the author has originally assigned to the character. (There is, alas, no such single characteristic signifying The Hero or The Heroine; heroes and heroines are always a bewildering variety of divergent motivations.) A book filled with cardboard characters is a flat book; flat books very often can be traced to overelaborate structuring in the initial stages of plotting, or — more simply — to overplotting.

People, of course, are what create most of our problems. There are great natural catastrophes that rearrange (or wipe out) our lives — earthquakes, typhoons, hurricanes, floods, and so forth. But in the mainstream of everyday life it is the interaction of people on one another that really shapes the true concerns of our lives. The main events of our inner lives are those carved by other human beings; thus, it is natural that our curiosity about motives and drives in other people should be bottomless. We assume the more we understand about other people the more we can understand what is happening to us.

But those around us move in a haze of complexity, duplicity, and difficulties. We seem unable to pinpoint why they behave the way they do. We ponder and question and analyze endlessly; yet answers elude us. No one ever knows precisely why another human being acts the way he does — not in real life. But in fiction there is a set situation, one that is not fluid and changing but one that can be reassessed over and over. The same people say exactly the same things, they reenact the same situations, they behave from the same motives, they pursue exactly the same actions: We can go back again and again to reexamine the same unchanged scene fixed on the printed page. Moments are captured and crystallized, and that seeming permanence permits us to believe that in these instances the world is knowable. We know the people of fiction, then, far better than we know "real" people.

A short story usually deals with a single incident in which all the strands and twists of plot relate to one incident that shows some character crisis of a central major figure. There is usually only one central character, as opposed to several major figures who populate a novel, because of the limitations of space — for, in Poe's famous dictum, the short story is one that can be read at a single sitting. Since there is a time limitation in the short story, the writer only has time to develop one well-rounded character.

The short story character, then, may seem more a reflection of his actions than the figures in a novel. In a short story, a single action may be of prime importance because it is a symbol of the character's reaction to a crisis. At the most, the action can be only a series of short incidents which reveal the personality of the protagonist. Plot and character most often merge in the short story because of space limitations, but in the large, sprawling novel, with its ability to span longer periods of time, interweave subplots, and introduce many fully developed characters, the restrictions of plot and character in relation to one another are not so rigid. The people in the short story may have a good deal of their complex nature sacrificed to the needs of developing the story. We are more likely, in many cases, to remember the plot of a short story than of a novel — the famous "The Lady or The Tiger?", O. Henry's "Gift of the Magi," Henry James's "The Real Thing," Joseph Conrad's "An Outpost of Civilization," Fitzgerald's "The Diamond as Big as the Ritz."

The larger canvas of the novel makes characters far more memorable than action. To name a few — Dostoevski's Raskolnikov, from *Crime and Punishment;* the Joad family, from *The Grapes of Wrath;* Squire Western, from *Tom Jones; The Return of the Native*'s fiery Eustacia Vye; the romantic Heathcliff and Cathy, from *Wuthering Heights;* or in more modern times, Joseph Heller's famous World War II hero, Yossarian, in *Catch-22;* Saul Bellow's modern picaresque figure, Augie March; the great central protagonist of Doris Lessing's twentieth-century exploration of political involvement, Martha Quest.

It is true of course that the earlier novels of the eighteenth and nineteenth century were more plot-oriented than people-directed: One thinks in particular of Dickens, Thackeray, Mark Twain, but even in these cases the people remain more vivid than the various incidents of the plot — Dickens's Miss Havisham, David Copperfield, Tiny Tim, Scrooge, Mr. Micawber, Dorrit; the unforgettable Becky Sharp of Thackeray's *Vanity Fair;* Twain's Tom Sawyer, Huckleberry Finn, Becky Thatcher. Even in those novels which at first seem plot-directed, the characters remain more permanently engraved upon the mind than the incidents from the story.

Why should this be so? I believe because essentially the story is a form of the anecdote, the novel, a number of very elaborate and extended anecdotes. In the telling of an incident or anecdote, the reader's main concern is centered in the mystery of "what will happen." There is a question as to how everything will work out. Suspense is the key to our pleasure. But once we know what has happened, there is no more suspense, and hence there is no sense of urgency for us to pursue the end of the sequence of events again. We already have the knowledge we need to tell us how things will work out. Thus the inevitable storyteller's opening question, "Have you heard the one about...?" or the ubiquitous question, "Did I tell you about...?" These are ways of finding out whether the listener knows the mystery already or not. If he knows, there is no need to go through the events again — what is often called "the story."

But plots are more than "stories." Stories are merely a frame of events strung together; they lack the cause-and-effect sequence and significance of a plot. Hence the usual example of the difference between a story and a plot is that a story is "The king died and then the queen died," while a plot says, "The king died and then the queen died of grief." The "of grief" explains the action; it sets up a cause-and-effect relationship for why the queen died.

Now if it is true that round characters run away with the story, what we are essentially saying is that strong, dynamic characters develop in the course of the novel and come to control and direct some of the action — what the bewildered writer has been trying to describe when he says "the characters just sort of ran away with me." If this is going to happen — and one certainly hopes it does or there isn't going to be much life in the book — then obviously even the most carefully constructed plot outline for a novel isn't going to be of great use, once the writer gets into the book. Of course, the writer must have some kind of plan, but there is a danger in an overelaborate outline that sacrifices all for the skeleton of the story; it is the problem of overplotting.

Rather than spending long hours grinding out plots, then, the beginning novelist would do much better to concentrate his efforts on formulating the kind of people he wants to write about, to setting up his cast of characters. It is odd, but in general the easiest people to write about are the ones we truly dislike. Hate seems to generate stronger and longer emotions than love; in other words, villains are easier to come by than heroes. Most writers have "pet peeves" or "pet peeve people." They begin with letting people they like or dislike wander through their heads, meeting, coming into conflict, trying to work out their problems (this is really, in a sense, plotting). It is often said that the three basic components of conflict are (1) man against nature, (2) man against other men (or another man), (3) man against himself; and that the truly great novel makes use of all three of these. As soon as strong figures begin to come up against one another, or themselves, there is the nucleus of a novel; the plot seems in some mysterious way to take care of itself once the characters are clear.

Henry James had notebooks full of half-finished stories that he heard at parties and jotted down in the hope of expanding them into either story or novel. But James was never interested in the story *per se;* his overwhelming passion was to find out why people in these incidents acted the way they did. James's "stories" are merely vehicles for a deep exploration of character. While anecdotes or stories, then, may suggest the nucleus of a work of art, they are not the prime movers. Something more is needed to fuel the imagination; a story of itself is a dead piece of machinery without the characters to put it in motion.

Hence, the novelist is one in perpetual search for the great memorable characters who have been lifted out of fiction as if they were real people and incorporated into our vocabularies as symbols of recurring patterns of behavior in people — Mrs. Malaprop, Oedipus, Electra come from plays, but we find their counterparts popping up in fiction. We think of Uriah Heep rubbing his hands in greed and Madame Bovary wistfully whiling away the time in romantic daydreams that have no chance to be fulfilled in reality; we remember the great detectives — Dashiell Hammett's Sam Spade, Erle Stanley Gardner's Perry Mason, Agatha Christie's Hercule Poirot and Miss Marple, Raymond Chandler's Philip Marlowe, the marvelous Ellery Queen; and we think of the memorable children of literature — little Eva and Rebecca of Sunnybrook Farm, Nancy Drew and Judy Bolton and Little Nell; and even the animals — Rosinante, Black Beauty, The Red Pony. They all seem more alive and vivid than the people who move around us daily and whom, presumably, we know almost as well as ourselves.

The truth is that the people of fiction are in many ways closer to knowing than the real people with whom we pass our lives, one of the ironical paradoxes that dot discussions of literature and life. What makes this so is that the artist has fixed the people of fiction in that time and place to which we may *objectively* return again and again to analyze and to comprehend them. These people cannot slip into new lives and new projections of their personalities that make mock of all we have previously assumed about them. We can dissect the dissident and varying reasons people in novels behave the way they do, and though we may never finally grasp *the* reason or find *one* answer, we can discover *some* of the final reasons and say, "Yes, that is certainly the reason he behaved that way..." or "Yes, she would never have...if...." As many critics have pointed out, this is, in the end, what the novelist is engaged in: separating out of all the data that barrages us some few coherent, comprehensible streams, so that for a moment the reader (the writer) can say, "Ah, yes, I see....That is what it is all about. That is the way it is."

It is people, not plot, who show us this. It is therefore essential for fiction writers, especially novelists, to create unforgettable characters before fussing and fretting about plot. Certain directions only the characters themselves can point; in the others the author helps to point the compass, but he is not always in complete command of where he will wind up.

Every small thing he knows about the character before he begins to write is of primary importance, *every*thing. Even a name can be of paramount importance in fixing a character in a reader's mind. I don't know whether the story is apocryphal or not, but it doesn't really matter so far as our point is concerned. I have always heard that Margaret Mitchell first called her great character Scarlett O'Hara Pansy. Now Pansy is just not Scarlett — we all know that. And knowing that tells us a great deal about how we bring characters in fiction into being.

22

LEAVING THE READER SATISFIED

By Phyllis A. Whitney

THE conclusion of any piece of fiction is as important, if not more important, than the opening. True, if we lack a good opening, the reader will probably never reach the end of the story, but if we don't provide an ending that will seem right, our story or novel will bring no satisfaction to the reader. The best way to build success as a writer is to develop a following of satisfied readers who will come back for more of your written words.

"Satisfied" doesn't necessarily mean "happy." The reader must feel that the ending of a story or novel grows naturally from the events that have been evolving and from the particular characters he has been reading about.

I've noticed in my writing classes that very young writers tend to kill off their characters at the end of a story, while older writers prefer to keep them alive. Perhaps this is more a commentary on age than on art. Either way can be right, provided the reader feels that the ending is justified and grows logically from what has gone before. "Grows logically" is the key phrase. Gratuitously unhappy endings — chosen because the writer believes they are more "artistic" — never satisfy.

Before going on with our discussion, a word about the examples I'll be using in this chapter. Some of them will be drawn from books for young people, because I know this field so well. But whether you write adult or juvenile fiction, there is no difference in the techniques of telling a good story and interesting a reader.

In old books on writing technique, there was a type of story known as "the biter bit." Here, the main character is so thoroughly unpleasant that readers follow him eagerly to the end in order to see him get the awful punishment that is coming to him. The ending can thus be tragic and satisfying at the same time.

(At this point, permit me a Victorian aside: Dear Reader, please allow me to use the pronoun "him" instead of the awkward and self-conscious "him or her" that is being nervously interposed these days. Until someone comes up with a usable pronoun to cover both, may we follow the more customary convention that implies that "she" is included in "he.")

To resume... There is another kind of punishment story besides the one in which the main character seems to be asking to be punished. This second type may bring the reader deep regret, even to tears, yet it leaves him with a feeling of rightness at the end.

A good example of this is Kin Platt's gripping young adult novel, *Head Man.* The boy in the story, a member of a Los Angeles street gang, is picked up and sent for two years to a rehabilitation camp in California. There he begins to make it toward a better sort of life, and we become so emotionally involved in following his story that we plug for him all the way. When he is on the outside again, the good effects of the camp, the counseling of men who have become his friends, stay with him for a while. He almost makes it. The choice is his. He weakens, chooses the wrong course, and meets a brutal death at the end of the book. The reader feels devastated. Yet we know that this ending is right. He *had* a choice. And in this case it is a more effective ending because of the punch it delivers than it would have been had the boy been "saved."

Another "sad" ending occurs in Norma Mazer's sensitive young adult novel, *A Figure of Speech.* The girl in this story opposes the intention of her family to send a beloved grandfather to an old people's home. Her efforts to prevent this lead to a touching but unsentimentalized story. The old man dies at the end — a tragedy that needn't have happened. But because of the young woman's own clear and honest vision, we are left with a clearer vision of old people and their treatment than we had before reading the book. There is satisfaction as well as regret in the ending, because she *tried,* when others did not. She has grown as a human being.

A totally different sort of ending is suitable in a good tale of action and adventure, in which disappointment is seldom allowable. An excellent example of this may be found in a marvelous novel for young people — *Snowbound,* by Harry Mazer (husband of Norma Mazer).

In *Snowbound* a boy and a girl who heartily dislike each other are trapped in a car in a blizzard and must stay alive until rescued. This is breathless reading, as both must use ingenuity to help each other and themselves. The faults and strengths of each character surface under these primitive conditions, and by the time they are rescued they have learned respect for each other and for themselves. No other ending but rescue is possible, and it is enormously satisfying to have these two people come through their terrible ordeal. They *deserve* to win.

That is one of the measuring sticks one can apply to an ending. In most cases, what happens to the main character or characters should be deserved because it has been earned. When that is the case, reader satisfaction is guaranteed. The boy in *Head Man* made the wrong choice, and though the ending is grim, he could have escaped by earning a different ending. The young reader is poignantly aware of this and, perhaps, carries the lesson over into his own life.

Scarlett O'Hara in *Gone With the Wind* gets exactly what she deserves in the course of the novel. She deserves to save Tara, because that is the one thing she has always worked for unselfishly and wholeheartedly. But she also deserves to lose Rhett Butler at the end.

On the other hand, Norma Mazer's young heroine in *A Figure of Speech* deserves to save her grandfather, but fails because reality defeats her. There is sadness and grief in the ending, yet the book is entirely satisfying. The reader is forced to admit sadly that the world is like that — and perhaps he is prompted to try to change what is wrong.

Sometimes the criterion for the ending must be found in what we are trying to say to the reader. In the examples I've given, there may be greater satisfaction in an "unhappy" ending because of the painful truth that has been revealed.

I am reminded of two film versions of the same story — *That Hamilton Woman,* produced by Alexander Korda in 1941, starring Laurence Olivier and Vivien Leigh; and *The Nelson Affair,* produced by Hal Wallis, starring Glenda Jackson and Peter Finch. In the first, the true-to-life ending seems shocking and wrong. In the second, it feels right. They are totally different in treatment. My favorite is the lovely, romantic, earlier version in which Emma Hamilton is portrayed as a beautiful and gracious woman who has risen above her rough beginnings to become Lord Nelson's love and very much a lady. The film and the acting are perfect in their romantic way, until the end when we see Emma in prison, having been picked up as a drunken slut on the street.

Even though we have been warned in the prologue that this is coming, it is a shock, because the character as portrayed has never seemed to deserve such an ending. It doesn't seem justified by the character's actions as revealed to us. In the second, less romanticized Hal Wallis production, Emma is capable of being rough and crude, given to disgracing herself on various occasions. Despite her love for Nelson, she is often tipsy, and the same ending as in the first picture comes as no surprise. It is what she has been heading for and probably deserves. For me, the Korda film thus seems flawed in its ending.

A few months ago, I heard Joshua Logan interviewed on television. He told of a conversation he'd had with Maxwell Anderson about Anderson's successful plays. Was there some one thing, Logan asked him, that had served him above all else, one bit of advice he could give to young playwrights? Anderson advised that the main character must learn something *about himself* before the end of the play, and that this must be something that would *change his life forever*. Only then would an audience feel satisfied enough to make the play a success. Logan asked why there must be such satisfaction, and Anderson said, "... because otherwise they walk out of the theater."

Such change is equally important in a short story or novel. The most satisfying endings always involve change. If the main character remains the same at the end as he was at the beginning, he hasn't gone anywhere. He needs to change — either to grow or to deteriorate. Which brings us to the come-to-realize ending.

Because the come-to-realize ending, in which the main character sees the error of his ways and changes (grows), can so easily fail, it has often been frowned upon by editors. However, it can be one of the most useful and satisfying endings, once we understand the technique of using it. To be used properly, there must be three steps:

1. Character becomes aware of how wrong he has been because something *happens* to shock him into realization.

2. He thinks about this, and tries to understand, to recognize and accept that he was wrong.

3. He proves *through action* that he has changed.

If you omit any one of these three simple steps, the ending will fail. Under Step 1, you can't have your character merely *told* in an undramatic way that he is wrong. It may be that someone has tried to tell him all through the story, and he hasn't believed or listened. Telling isn't strong enough unless it comes through dramatic action.

Once the shock that wakes him up has been administered, there should be a pause — a quieter moment in which he considers what has happened and makes the change-over in his own mind. Omit this pause, and the change won't be convincing. If you end the story at this point, however, it will sink, and the reader will be left unbelieving.

So there must be a third step. Now the character must *prove* that he has changed. It is the omission of this step that most often causes editors to condemn this type of story. Now the character must take some positive course of action to show that he has changed. Only then can the ending be completely satisfying to the reader — who will only be convinced by action. Words and thoughts are not sufficient proof.

To use an example from my own writing, where, in retrospect, I think the ending could have been improved, let's look at my novel *Spindrift*. I had written the ending twice, and finally let the third version go into print. After publication, a number of readers told me that they didn't entirely believe in the ending, even though they liked the rest of the book. I now know what was wrong: I had left out a step.

The heroine of *Spindrift* has spent most of the book falling out of love with her husband (for reasons she thinks justifiable), and being attracted to another man. There was no difficulty about waking her up to the truth of the situation and letting her come-to-realize how wrong she had been. The man she was attracted to is the villain, who holds her in a dangerous situation at the end of the story and is threatening her life. There is plenty of dramatic action to change her mind. The second step is taken care of when she realizes that her husband is a far stronger and more worthy person than she has lately given him credit for being. She knows that she still loves him.

Events move furiously toward the end, with her husband rescuing her against odds from the other man. The third step is missing. All the protagonist does to prove that she has changed is to fling her arms about her husband at the end, the equivalent of walking happily into the sunset. The reader is left questioning. Will she be satisfied? How do we *know* she has changed? How do we know that her husband will now hold her love? She hasn't proved a thing. And I think that particular ending is weak because I didn't heed my own rules. What the main character does to prove change doesn't have to be something tremendously dramatic. It can be a very simple thing the character does. I'm sure that if I had "come to realize" myself what I was doing, I would have sought out some earlier element in the story that could have been used to give the heroine a bit of convincing action to prove to the reader that she had really changed.

The type of ending you prefer to write will, of course, grow from your own nature and life experience. I have always believed in fighting no matter what the odds. It isn't my nature to be easily defeated, and I am always optimistic, so my heroines put up a very good fight. My role is that of an entertainer, and thus my endings are always upbeat — though, I hope, not unrealistic.

There are a few other things to be said about fiction endings. Certainly the conclusion should surprise. If the reader guesses all along exactly what is going to happen, we fail. I don't mean the old-fashioned O. Henry twist, but nevertheless something unexpected. Part of the fun (and reading should first of all be entertainment) is not being able to tell how the story will come out. That doesn't hold for mysteries alone. Every story should keep the reader guessing and anticipating. If we can't stay one step ahead and furnish surprise, we will leave a so-what reader to put aside our books and never remember our names.

Another thing that the author must take care of is picking up any loose ends. This becomes particularly difficult in the mystery novel, where there can be all sorts of unanswered questions in the reader's mind. So much that is complex has gone before that a great deal of explanation may be needed. When I read a mystery or suspense novel in which the writer goes on and on *after the story is over,* I am bored. This type of explanatory ending (at great length) used to be more common than it is now, but I still see it from the hands of writers who should know better. We must work in as much explanation ahead of time as possible. Often this can be done just before the climax scene, when the reader is willing to stand still for a moment because he knows excitement is coming. The idea is to explain as much as possible well in advance, yet still hold out something that the reader is eager to know. You don't give up this tidbit of answer until the last page. Last paragraph is even better, but seldom possible.

One more word — and it is one that returns us to the opening and the very backbone of our story: The main character must have a strong desire for something he wants tremendously. (Weak *want,* weak *story.*) It will be something he wants enough to give him drive and purpose and goal all the way through. In the end, he will either get what he desires, or lose it — depending mainly on what he deserves. When you come to the ending, don't overlook that purpose, which must be attained or be lost in the last pages. If you keep in mind where you are going with this from the very beginning, you will be likely to leave a satisfied reader at the end of your novel or short story.

Which brings us to an ending here and now. *My* purpose and desire were to tell you what I know about endings. I hope I can leave you satisfied.

23

SECOND TIME AROUND

By The Gordons

THE OTHER day we took inventory to find out what we had done right and what wrong in forty years of writing. It was the old game of what we would do differently if we were starting out all over again.

We were surprised and sometimes shocked. In hindsight, it would seem we should have been a little brighter. But we will get to that shortly.

During those forty years, we have written everything from five-dollar newspaper fillers to screenplays for which we were paid scandalous sums. We have pounded typewriters in dark closets of tiny apartments and in wind-swept garages with black widow spiders lurking in shadowy corners. We have sat sweat-drenched in shorts in hot desert country and caught colds in rooms we couldn't afford to heat adequately.

We were poor, but the wondrous part was that we didn't know it, so we had a ball. It was all a prelude to later years when we have lived beyond any dreams we ever had.

All the years have been exciting, frustrating, excruciating, and often maddening. There were times when we rocketed off for the moon on $100-checks that were a fortune to a couple with a gallon of gasoline in the car and two bucks tucked away — and times when the checks didn't come and we hid out from friends so we wouldn't have to answer embarrassing questions.

What would we do differently? First and foremost, we would keep notebooks. In the beginning, we thought the idea foolish, even though we knew that the great writers of the past had jotted down descriptions and impressions of people and events, bright bits of dialogue, flashes of apt phrasing, anything and everything that came to mind. Maybe, we told ourselves, when you're old and doddering, you need to write it all down. But we were young, had photographic memories that had got us through the university, and, we thought, had no need of props. We had it all stored up here, see. Well, in time, we awakened with a shock to the truth; photographs fade and the memory is a leaky old bag of wind.

Among other things, we wish back then we had scratched notes about our Aunt Hattie of South Bend who called automobiles, carriages and rigs, and garages, shacks. She was a delightful anachronism. Think what a gold mine we would have had today. Whatever became of that photographic memory?

People don't realize as they see things happen that even random scribblings about those events will years later help them reconstruct an era long forgotten. We can read about events in the newspapers of the period, but seldom do we gain a feeling for the people, an insight into what they were thinking and how they were reacting.

Eventually, we started tossing notes into file folders. Now we have headings that read: "Things That Irritate People," "Unusual Characters," "Teen-Age Dialogue and Attitudes," "Problems — Couples in Their Thirties," "Descriptive Phrases," "Dated Talk," "Plot Ideas," etc. We have one labeled simply "Japanese," that contains letters from a Tokyo friend. She writes flawless English but doesn't put the words and phrases together the way Americans do.

Another is titled: "D.C.," the name of our cat, the prototype for *That Darn Cat*. The other day one of us said, "That cat can hear a nose wrinkling," and we wrote it on a memo sheet and dropped it into the file. We're not ashamed of the fact we play Boswell to a cat, not with all the vittles he buys us.

These are not neat, efficient files. They contain torn scratch sheets, matchbook covers, menus, etc., any scrap of paper that was handy at the time. We've discovered that we can forget an amusing phrase or descriptive bit merely by walking out of a restaurant to a car. To keep our files orderly would take us full time and serve no purpose.

When we started *Catnapped!,* a sequel to *That Darn Cat,* we got out the teen-age dialogue file, the D.C. one, the "Mrs. Macdougall" one (the nosy neighbor next door), and a few others. For *Ordeal,* our suspense novel set in Arizona's Navajo country, we reached back many years to find a yellowing file on old desert prospectors, three files on the Navajos that we had been filling for ten years, and one on strip coal mining that we started a couple of years ago with nothing specific in mind. The subject sounded like something we might one day use. Of course, we have scores of files that we may never look into. (We also have a twenty-foot storeroom!)

Our next most grievous error was that we never did any practice writing. That is, we wrote only when we had an article or story on the schedule. We guess we were too practical minded. We couldn't bear to waste time or paper.

If we were starting over, we would write some every day, even when we were not on a project. We would write about someone we had seen the day before, or a walk we had taken, or what the cat did. We believe a writer needs this practice, the same as a pianist or ballet dancer. It develops a facility with words and an awareness of life about us. One day recently, we wrote a page about a woodpecker that seemed intent on chopping down a walnut tree, a few lines about a teen-age friend who had been over the night before, and three pages about our 93-year-old cousin who had talked freely about her "exit" from this world.

And that brings us to another point. We would be more observant of people and places. We would watch for mannerisms or ways of saying something, all those little touches that give realism to an article or story. Some people are instinctively observant. However, we who are not can train ourselves. We can say when we wake up in the morning, "Now, for heaven's sake, try to remember today to look *at* people instead of looking *through* them." And listen to them. Do not be too eager to dominate the conversation. Finally, we've learned that when we do all the talking, we aren't adding anything to our background as writers. But when we just sit back and let someone ramble on, it's amazing what we can pick up. It's amazing, too, how a few questions or the show of a little interest will open up friends and acquaintances.

In time we realized that being observant produces remarkable results; observation allied with perception can multiply results a hundredfold. For instance, after talking with a troubled friend, we may sit down that night and discuss between ourselves just what makes her tick, why she handled the problem the way she did. Did she solve it through emotion or reasoning or a combination? How did others enter in? And the person doesn't have to be an unusual character or the problem a major one.

We should note, too, that looking back, we wish we had read more and gone to more movies and stage shows. They do more than just keep us aware of the passing scene. Subconsciously — we call it "osmosis" — we pick up and assimilate plotting and characterization and the handling of situations. And in our brains there's a fantastic computer that now and then will pull something out that we desperately need.

Take *Ordeal,* for example. Originally, we had a story that wandered all over the place, a chase plot. But it didn't seem to work. It was clumsy. Still we persisted. Chase scenes are among the oldest in fiction, and we told ourselves we could bring it off if we worked enough on it. Then from far out of our past, back to our college days, the computer tossed out the teachings of a Greek playwright. He maintained that a story nailed down to one setting worked better than one that rambled geographically. So we tried corraling much of the action in *Ordeal.* We maneuvered the basic plot so that the characters were brought together one stormy night at a prehistoric cliffhouse in a remote canyon.

In our early professional years, we should have overcome our dread of rejection, this mailbox syndrome that affects most writers. We can remember when the postman's walk sent shivers of fear up and down our spines. It became a daily trauma. We should have given ourselves a few stern lectures — to the effect that writing is as much salesmanship as creative effort, and anytime you go to the marketplace, you have to expect rejections. It doesn't matter whether the product is a new car, a house, a cosmetic, a magazine article or a novel.

Never should we take rejection as a personal matter. We should think of ourselves as the Avon lady. If we knock on a certain number of doors and have a good product to sell, we will find a buyer. We should have told ourselves that no one sells everything he offers, not a stockbroker, not a realtor, not the girl behind the jewelry showcase. The point of this syndrome for writers, of course, is that they are offering something they created, unlike most other salespersons, and rejection of the product becomes rejection of the author personally. Yet the professional must separate his two identities, that of the creative person and the Avon lady.

We should hasten to add that by salesmanship we mean studying the markets before rushing to the post office, and asking ourselves why an editor would want to buy what we are proposing to offer. We should do this before we write a single line. By salesmanship, we mean, too, being persistent, keeping a piece moving when we have confidence in it.

Most authors are sensitive beings. They must be to understand and empathize with the people they create. And because we are sensitive, we are easily hurt. Still, we have to train ourselves to put aside our sensitivity as writers when we set about to market our wares.

So now we have taken inventory of the years, and the word "inventory" reminds us of what we should have started doing at the very outset. Taking inventory. Sitting down every few months to talk over our goals. Are we writing what we want to? Are we keeping up with the constant flux in life styles? Have we fallen into a rut?

Maybe we are writing articles when we want to do fiction. That was our situation once. We were earning a good income doing articles, but we had a longing, for no reason that we remember, to become storytellers. One day we said, "Let's try a suspense yarn." Did we have the talent and the craftsmanship for it? We didn't know, but we would gamble. We believe that at times a writer must change pace. He must take risks, the same as artists, movie makers, sculptors, and others in creative fields. Our decision that day led to nineteen novels.

About the time we turned to fiction writing, we stumbled onto the idea of taking regular inventories, the same as businessmen do. Twice this paid off handsomely: On one occasion, we decided to switch our plots to what we call a "novel of continuing suspense," a story in which a person finds herself/himself in a dangerous situation, and the risk to life progresses as the story progresses. We made the change because it was far easier to film such stories than those that called for extensive explanation following the climax. Stories of deduction, for example, are difficult to film. Usually they are talkative, and the unraveling of what happened calls for a chart and a scorekeeper.

Another time, we decided to gamble on a humorous yarn set around our big, black cat, D.C., who is now fifteen, badly needs a girdle, but still fights off all invaders of our property. We had never tried humor before, and it was as much a long shot as if we had bet on an old nag at Santa Anita. But it was something we wanted to do, just for the fun of it. The result has been that the cat now maintains us in a style to which we never before had been accustomed.

So every six months without fail we sit down to inventory ourselves.

We were slow learners, but we think in the beginning we did do a few things right. We worked hard, sometimes long after midnight, sometimes before dawn. We wanted to become good craftsmen. We recognized we might never develop into truly fine writers, in the sense of creating beautiful word imagery, but we might just possibly become good storytellers. We saw ourselves in the marketplace of a thousand years ago, weaving tales and holding spellbound the ragtags crowded about us.

Forty years are many in any field — and there's no denying the despair at times, the rough going — but they've been exciting years, skateboarding all around, and we wouldn't trade them for all the oil in the Middle East.

We haven't made Mt. Everest. We never will. But we're trying.

24

THE ANCESTRY OF YOUR CHARACTERS

By Shelby Hearon

A YOUNG newswoman who sat interviewing me over coffee told her own life story of a mother overeducated for her household, a demanding great-aunt in her nineties, a grandfather stuck in a three-car town. Unknowingly, the journalist proved more effectively than my answers that we are all defined by whom we come from.

Too often in writing fiction, bent upon telling what happened in the plot, we forget that even the most sensational news story of would-be assassins delves into the early years, the parents, and the influences on those making the headlines. For all of us want to understand why that person is who she is and why she did what she did.

Just as in the journalism world there is a time to look into the past of the newsmaker, so in fiction going back to the early family of your character adds the necessary dimension of reality. For it is only in the light of these beginnings that your story is convincing to the reader.

Why does a man — craving sweets — pass up a box of Godiva chocolates he is offered at the office, forgo a quick Hershey bar at lunch, and then consume, while no one is watching, half of a stale chocolate layer cake his mother had set out to throw away? Or why does a woman, raised to believe herself a dutiful daughter, a Christian, and a successful breadwinner, limit her friendships to those women who cannot challenge her and those men who do not excite her? Suppose you have invented a fat mother who is not content until everyone in her household is as fat as she; suppose a jogging father who drives his body as if whipping a winded horse. The reader must be shown what happens to that fat woman's daughter, that runner's son, as well as who made them what they are today. No amount of exposition about a character's childhood is as telling as one such scene. No comment on eating problems is as revealing as the image of a grandmother in her bedroom slippers serving canned peas for supper every night of the week.

All families have such events, and the beginnings of fictional lives must be constructed from just such small specifics of ordinary days. The problem for the writer becomes how to show enough of these concrete touches from your characters' families to make their adult actions believable. In the best-selling novel *Looking for Mr. Goodbar,* the factual account of the heroine's death, following a pickup in a singles bar, which could have been sensational or pathetic, was made extremely moving and almost inevitable, by the long careful detailing of where the woman came from, of her parents and their neglect, her sisters and their ambivalence toward her.

For her, as for each of us, from the earliest impress of loving arms or their absence, there are a few important kin whose influence forms us. My father had a grandmother who rocked back and forth, snapping green beans, her small feet barely touching the floor. So real was this woman in the legend of his life, that I can shut my eyes and see her as if I had known her myself.

Many times these vital relatives are part of an unwitting conspiracy by parents to make their children "take after" those who have come before. "He is the spitting image of my dad; look at those ears." "She takes after that wild Nettie and has since the day she was born." "Every time he opens his mouth I can hear my late husband's voice; it's like living with a ghost." The influence on each of us as a child of being inhabited by past lives, of being both oneself and an aunt, say, whom we never knew but are molded to resemble, makes the rest of our lives an effort to duplicate or deny the pressure of these instructions. It is necessary in such cases to show the reader not only the person whose prior existence has influenced what is expected of our character, but also what part of this relative has been adopted and what rejected by the character in the novel.

For example, in one of the families in the book I am working on, all the daughters named Sarah are expected to be loving; without exception they are remembered as biscuit-making, sachet-smelling gentlewomen. And because it has been declared so in advance, this is exactly what each Sarah in turn becomes. Had one of these been the heroine of my book, I would have thought it essential to portray a girl fighting against such an ordained image, refusing the model pressed upon her. It would have been central to my story to show the conflicts her resistance created throughout the network of the Family.

Most such past generations of family can only be suggested to the reader. Although in the front of Russian novels, as well as in many much-loved family chronicles like *The Forsyte Saga,* there is a complex and lengthy family tree, on one branch of which the characters sit, most authors do not provide this. But it must always be clear in our own minds. In my current story on three generations of two Texas families, I know the river-running ancestors of the East Texas man as well as the Georgia and South Carolina kin of the Houston woman. I have to — for the inflections, priorities and fates of these past kin who are not mentioned in the story color the lives of those who are.

To show your particular family in the wider setting of how it views and is viewed by the outside world, make the reader part of the town or neighborhood or even the feud your fictional family is involved in. In my last novel, I needed a lowland town, laid back from the Gulf of Mexico, on a railroad and a river. The emotional town I was creating was the small (pop. 2000) Kentucky town of my own childhood, but for the book it needed to be translated into a Texas setting. (I had decided on the name Dimple, only to find in the *Almanac* that there already was a Dimple, Texas.) Sally, then, my fictional location, was a composite of several towns in a network of small truck-farming communities which bore girls' names, like brief romances met and left in the night. Once I had seen this real area and caught the distant salt air, changes took place in my characters. Because of the nearness of Corpus Christi, the passing of the trains, the drying up of oil wells, the influence of weather on crops, my character's father grew more stooped with his bad back, and his wife became more of a social climber, in her effort to escape the town.

A similar thing happened after I had imagined a setting in East Texas in which a major character was raised. When I walked through the actual land and smelled the pines, and was shadowed and dwarfed by the overwhelming hardwood forests, my boy's parents changed from having spent their lives enclosed in such trees. The father saw the practice of law as cutting through a thicket of brush; the mother became so obsessed with politics, as a way to control the sawmills, that her zeal descended to her granddaughter.

Families also mark us on a deeper level. The anthropologist Jules Henry, who studied a series of middle class families in their homes, showed how in each case certain predominant scenes are played over and over. We acknowledge this, when, glib from popular psychology, we talk about the "games people play" or the "scripts people read." (At my house it is: "Don't ask me; it's your movie.")

Happy families are not all alike. Like unhappy ones, each is a distinct blend of the repeated signals and taboos from its past and each fills its young with this overwhelming legacy from those who went before. All of us, and our characters as well, grow up in the midst of the particular messages, undercurrents, hurts, pleasures, rooms, streets, meals, voices, touch of the inescapable place which was *home*.

In this sense, the family's primary setting remains its myth about itself. This means the echo your character carries throughout her or his life: "In our family we have certain standards, Billy"; "Nice girls don't get involved with their kind, Mabel." Your reader needs to hear that same voice and to see its influence when the character is away from home and interacting at last in the situations which are the plot of your story.

At that point, it is, after all, a simple matter of watching what happens. As I told my journalist friend when she asked, "How do you invent a character?" — if a woman has that mother, that demanding great-aunt and that forgotten father, the author doesn't have to create her. For the family already has.

25

FINDING THE RIGHT SHAPE FOR YOUR STORY

By Gail Godwin

For every story there are many potential shapes. The ideal shape allows the story to be most fully itself, reveal its deepest intricacies, and stretch itself to the very borders of its best possibilities. Many promising stories have been cramped and stunted and killed by being forced into premature or inappropriate shapes.

By shape I mean the pattern through which the story finds itself in a finished form. I mean the way in which the writer makes a space for what he wants to say. Is the story told as a joke or a sermon? As if it all happened a long time ago in a distant land, or so immediately that it is as if someone is thinking aloud? Is it long, short, connected, broken? One fluid sweep, or nervous stops and starts? In dialogue? Diary form? Confession? Reminiscence? A story "framed" by a story someone else is telling?

There are countless shapes to choose from. Like clothes, they go in and out of fashion. In Jane Austen's day, the epistolary shape was "in," and she first tried to make *Sense and Sensibility* an exchange of letters between two sisters. But the sisters had to be together; therefore the letters had to go. Fictional shapes tend to mirror the age. In the eighteenth century, travel was difficult: people wrote twenty- and thirty-page letters instead. It is not surprising that in our decade, a very fashionable story shape is the fragmented one: the tale told in chunky blocks of prose, with "headings" like an official report; many events erupting in very little space, with "blanks" to indicate transition, passage of time.

I can't get into a story seriously until I reach that point at which I feel I am moving within its shape. This may take months, years. The material, however urgent it is, just has to wait. Then there are the other, rarer times when the shape emerges simultaneously with the idea. From the start it is a perfect marriage. And, very recently, after waiting a full fourteen months, during which I wrote at least the same number of false starts, I understood that my psyche had to be tricked into writing the story (a complicated one, involving disturbing personal circumstances). One day I sat down and told myself: "I will not write this story. I will only allow myself to write *about the story I want to write.*" I wrote very fast, notes to myself about how I would pace this story, what the problems were (technical and personal), and when I came to a description of someone, I just typed rapidly: *physical description of Catherine,* or *physical description of Rudy.*

About halfway through — no, before that — I realized that this very form, "notes for a story," was the form I had needed all along to contain my story! Which was the story of a writer, a woman who makes everything into fiction almost as soon as it happens, dealing with materials so close and dangerous, she cannot fully assimilate them.

But this shape would be pretentious for other stories. I may use the "trick" of it to get going again, but I must be wary of imposing it upon a future story just because it once worked perfectly.

The following process is more typical of the way I work. I say "I." That is too glib. So many influences, mysterious connections, chance happenings, go into the shaping of a story. And, too, I believe that the writer's unconscious works always within his conscious craft. Sometimes it slows him down, even blocks him; other times it wrests his material right out of his hands and produces unexpected results. My own happiest results have been those stories in which the Uncontrolled gave energy and magic to the part I could control; when the Unknown surfaced, suddenly, beautifully, after I had labored over the proper words, the "spell" that would release it.

I want to talk about a story called "False Lights" (*Esquire,* January, 1975). The germ of that story came out of a conversation with a woman. She told me her husband's ex-wife had written her a letter which spelled out, in much detail, the diet he must follow if he was to live long.

Even as she was telling me this, the writer-part had already separated from the friend-part and was thinking: "Hm-m-m. A story which would be the correspondence between two women who have been married to the same man." Originally, I conceived a rather brittle, cynical story: the wives were bitchy, they had much fun in the letters at the expense of the husband they had shared.

I filed the item away in a "non-urgent" part of my writer's brain. At the time, I was trying to begin a novel (always an ordeal because of the commitment it means: two or more years of staying interested in the same idea). It was the beginning of summer and I went away on vacation to Cape Hatteras, North Carolina, one of the loveliest and wildest areas left on the East Coast. I walked a lot and grew very excited about the new novel (which was later abandoned). I passed some elegant old beach houses along the sound: two and three stories, with Victorian porches and cupolas, some dating back more than a hundred years. "I want to have a party in one of those old houses in my new novel," I thought. And I had much fun imagining that party, the rooms of the house, the wind blowing the upstairs curtains of a bedroom. The house would be the summer cottage of a southern judge in his sixties who had just taken a very young bride. . . I knew that, too.

June 18. I was back from vacation, alone in the country, relaxed, and at one with the unfolding summer. It was my birthday. "I think I will begin a story as a present to myself," I said. "Maybe that one about the two wives writing letters."

I sat down and wrote the ex-wife's letter (checking out details in nutritionist Adele Davis's books). Then I had the young wife (very young and innocent, not like the friend who had told me the anecdote, more like the young bride I imagined on my beach walks) write a return letter. It was very humble and polite, thanking the old wife, reassuring her that the diet would be observed.

Fresh from Hatteras, I couldn't resist letting my young bride live on the secluded little island of Ocracoke with her new husband. I decided to make him a successful writer, whose books were alternate fictions about his past and his ex-wife as a young girl who had saved his life during the war. There were things I wanted to say about the process of writing, and I could put them into his mouth.

Then I had my young bride (I named her Violet) write a second letter to the ex-wife on the evening of the same day she's mailed the first. This letter began telling the ex-wife all the things Violet wished she had said in the first: how she thought about her quite a lot, wished they could all be happy, wondered what marriage would be like in a hundred years, etc.

"This letter is getting a little long," I thought (typing the sixteenth page). But my Violet had so much to say! She was pouring out her heart to this woman she had never met. Very sincerely she was revealing her thoughts about love, marriage, people who write fiction about their lives, what life would be like in a hundred years, eccentric characters she had met in her solitary beach walks while her husband was writing...She even wrote to the ex-wife about a party she had gone to, in an old beach house in Hatteras, owned by a judge and his new young wife, and about how the two of them, Violet and Nancy, had gone upstairs and had a heart-to-heart talk about what it was like to be married to men who had already spent half their lives with someone else.

In the writing of this story, one character had become so appealing, had so thrust herself upon my sympathies, that her own needs dictated the shape of the story. The letters became a mere device which had led me into the real story which was, of course, Violet's, and her "fancies," as the ex-wife calls them in the very brief, cold letter which ends the piece.

I used to think writers were in control of their stories. Now I have come to the conclusion that the process of one story is a vast and mysterious network of influences. What if I had not chanced to go to Cape Hatteras on my vacation? What if I had been in a cynical and bitter mood on June 18, instead of a sun-filled and loving mood? What if my friend had not told me about that letter? So many what ifs!

I used to begrudge the fact that the story I proposed to write and the story I finally wrote were never the same. Now I am beginning to understand. My task is simple. "Try to be one of the people on whom nothing is lost," urged Henry James. I try. I listen more than I used to. I force myself to be more adventurous, take more unknown journeys into new places (both outer and inner). Anecdotes, experiences, gossip, dreams...I try to be open to them all. But I am beginning to know that, ultimately, my material chooses me. Then I must help it find the shape in which it can best reveal the secrets which it is bursting to tell.

26

HOW TO BE AN EXPERT ON ANYTHING

By Frank G. Slaughter

THE NOVELIST who chooses to tell a story against a technical or historical background quickly discovers that he must be something of a magician; he must create the illusion of having wide knowledge of a subject, without spending the years of study necessary to become an expert. Fortunately, if the novelist is a skilled storyteller, creating the illusion of expertness is not really very difficult; properly handled, a little knowledge can be made to go a long way. Moreover, simply by using the very latest scientific information, the fiction writer may often give the impression of outexperting the experts.

My own educational background includes a college major in chemistry and biology, an M.D. degree, plus Fellowship in the American College of Surgeons, Diplomate of the American Board of Surgery and twelve years of private and military practice, before laying down the scalpel in favor of the pen. In 1957 I wrote a definitive article for *Scientific American* on heart surgery up to that time; yet years later when I decided to write about heart transplant in my novel *Surgeon's Choice,* I had to stand at the shoulder of a colleague in the operating room for eight hours during open-heart surgery to familiarize myself with a technique that had not existed in 1957. I spent only three hours observing the use of the hyperbaric pressure chamber at Duke Medical Center, but my fictional presentations gave the illusion that I was completely up to date in all phases of medicine, an obvious impossibility.

In preparing to write my novel, *Plague Ship,* I spent roughly twelve hours with a textbook on epidemiology and another six with a text on microbiology, subjects I hadn't studied for almost fifty years. With the information newly gained, however, I was able to dramatize the steps by which my epidemiologist hero finally controlled a plague caused by a five-thousand-year-old organism accidentally released from a sealed burial tomb in the Peruvian Andes. He did it by a mutation of the deadly bacterium in a form that would cause an immunity to the organism when injected as a vaccine, yet not cause the disease.

Doctors' Wives came about when a newspaper account led me to read an article titled "Psychiatric Illness in the Physician's Wife," a report of fifty cases treated in a famous psychiatric clinic. For my novel, I simply created five female characters, all wives of doctors in a university clinic, and transposed a set of emotional symptoms and problems for each woman from the actual article. In the opening scene, the wife of a faculty member is shot and killed by her husband after he discovers her *flagrante delicto* with the husband of one of the five. The dramatic problem for me was how to keep the wives from learning the identity of the wounded doctor, who had a bullet in his heart. I accomplished this by dramatizing the rather simple surgical procedure involved (removing a bullet from the heart), against a running account of the shock, fear, and guilt as it developed in each major character, a process that occupied 91 pages of the story, until the wives learned which one was in immediate danger of becoming a widow. Here a minimum of medical information, revealed while the operation continued, established the technical background and also delineated sharply the problems of the major characters and their reactions to the crisis.

Handling geographic backgrounds is perhaps the easiest problem for the regularly producing novelist, but visits to exotic regions, although enjoyable, are not always necessary. For example, the early chapters of *Plague Ship* take place in the valley of the Santa River, some ten thousand feet up in the Peruvian Andes and almost directly opposite the seaport city of Chimbote on the Pacific coast. A single chapter in each of three travel books gave me all the colorful descriptive material I needed to set a half dozen important early scenes in the lovely high valley. A large-scale nautical chart that cost only $1.50 also located accurately the very dock in the harbor of Chimbote where the hospital ship featured in much of the story was moored. It also supplied a backdrop for the dramatic scene in which the natives, convinced that the plague unloosed by an archaeologist when he opened a sealed cave-tomb was a curse, cut the ship's moorings, allowing the current to carry the crippled vessel (where most of the action takes place) into the open Pacific. Presto! I became an authority on the Peruvian Andes and docking facilities at an obscure Peruvian port, without having been closer to them than Miami.

After writing thirty-two historical novels, I still find the background research for each one of them the most fascinating part of my work; yet here the less experienced novelist can easily get into trouble. The problem arises when the background study becomes so interesting that you are loath to undertake the drudgery of daily writing. Through long experience, I have found that once your story germ bursts "full-panoplied" from the brow of whatever your muse — and if you want to succeed nowadays, it had better be Venus! — research and writing had best go along together.

Take time to read a few good general studies of the selected period, but start actual production as soon thereafter as possible. At least half, and probably more, of your story incidents are not going to involve any historical or even background material at all. They are merely dramatic episodes that either move the story or enhance characterization. When you do come to an incident requiring a specific background, a day at the library should give you the necessary information. Also, while it is pleasant to have history buffs acclaim your thoroughness, the majority of readers of popular fiction will be quite satisfied if you are accurate, which I always try to be. To achieve this, shortcuts can be used effectively, as witness the following example.

The Stonewall Brigade (published in 1975) is the story of General Thomas J. (Stonewall) Jackson's part in the American Civil War, along with the five Virginia regiments making up the most famous military unit in that tragic conflict. In writing about the first battle fought under Jackson's command, even though it was a small engagement confined largely to a churchyard at a place called Falling Waters just south of the Potomac, I wanted to create the illusion that I had an encyclopedic knowledge of Confederate weaponry.

Fortunately, only a few hundred troops took part in the battle, and one artillery piece. That was established at the start as one of Jackson's favorite cannon, a Parrott gun with a brass-bound barrel that, though accurate, was also somewhat dangerous because of its tendency to explode. Moreover, the cannon was being handled by Jackson's chief of artillery and former pastor, an Episcopal clergyman, the Reverend Major W.N. Pendleton, whose son, Alexander, was also Jackson's chief aide.

It was easy for me to establish that the outer covering of the cannon barrel was brass by mentioning that a waterproof sheet was drawn over it to shield the metal from reflecting the sun and thus warning the enemy of the ambush planned by the wily Jackson. Since Confederate troops carried every weapon from squirrel rifles to muskets used in the Revolution, it was much simpler to describe the Enfield rifle that was the standard weapon of the Northern troops, particularly since detailed information on the rifle was easily available. Moreover, when the unsuspecting Union troops appeared in the churchyard, I promptly seized that unusual opportunity to create the illusion of expert knowledge by having Jackson's young aide exclaim: "That's a fifteen-shot repeating Henry rifle the sergeant's carrying. You can load one on Sunday and fire it the rest of the week." To which Jackson replied: "He's worth ten soldiers in the open."

Young Pendleton next removed from his saddle a "Sharps carbine," glancing "at the fulminate cap which, when struck with the hammer as the weapon was fired, would ignite the powder charge and send the bullet hurtling toward its target.... The puff of smoke from the gas leak at the breech, as the power was ignited — a characteristic of all Sharps — momentarily obscured the target." And a sentence or two later, when the cannon was fired, the Reverend Pendleton "jerked the lanyard of the three-inch rifled Parrott gun."

Note that in the first real battle fought under Jackson's command, three weapons have been described, and the superiority of the North in arming its troops, a major factor in the Confederate defeat, has been clearly shown. And all this, too, has been accomplished in less than a page of descriptive writing, interspersed frequently with bits of action, such as the humorous reference to the Henry rifle being loaded on Sunday and firing the rest of the week. Moreover, Jackson's own demeanor during the brief battle — as he waited to see, literally, the whites of the enemy's eyes before giving the order to fire — tells more about his character than pages of expository writing, which would be likely to interrupt the reader's interest in the narrative and lose him or her forever.

These tricks, which I have developed during my years of becoming a professional writer, may not be immediately obvious to the tyro, but once alerted to them, you too can become an "expert" — with just a little trying.

27

FROM "MOVIES" TO "TALKIES"

By Margaret Edwards

PERHAPS *great* fiction can break all the rules, but *good* fiction must follow most of them. I am going to assume here that my readers are interested in learning to write good fiction, in the hope that great fiction will follow. I've discovered certain rules that help in writing dialogue, and I want to explain what I believe these rules to be.

Much has been written about the importance of the writer's "ear" for dialogue. You might assume that all you must do is go out into the world and listen to people talk. An accurate memory for speech—its inflections, vocabularies, dialects, phrasings — all of this is certainly valuable. But if it were crucial, a good tape recorder would be all you would need. The fact is that most people seem to know well enough how and what others say. We quote each other all the time, orally, as we converse. In my opinion an "ear" is not such a rare talent. However, what is invaluable, and utterly necessary for a fiction writer to develop, is a sense of how dialogue meshes with characters and action.

If you create a story that introduces characters and progresses, let's say, for seven pages without any dialogue, this can mean that you haven't yet trusted your characters enough to let them speak. If they act silently or if all their speech is presented as part of the narrative, you risk having characters not fully developed, either in your imagination or in what you have written. I plan to conjure up here a hypothetical piece of fiction as an example. Let's assume that within a story that involves Tom, Dick, and Harry, the theme and plot require a scene in which two of the men wake the third:

Tom and Dick, laughing together, walked back into the house and there caught sight of Harry, who had fallen asleep on the sofa. He was sleeping so soundly that he did not wake even when they approached him and cracked jokes about him.

Tom pretended to be Maureen, Harry's girlfriend, by raising the pitch of his voice and mimicking her.
Dick, who had decided they shouldn't wake Harry, told Tom to give up pestering him and to come along to the kitchen for breakfast.

This is a scene devoid of dialogue. All of the action, as it's presented above, remains in the narrative. This is legitimate and acceptable; however, actual speech from the characters might very economically reveal what could be interesting or even essential for us to know—it could tell us, for example, what sort of girl Maureen is, how she talks, and at the very least, how Tom *believes* she talks and what he feels about her and Harry. These bits of characterization are left out completely because Tom isn't permitted his own words. Also, we learn only that Tom and Dick "cracked jokes" about Harry. But what sort of jokes? Derisive? Friendly? Dialogue could recreate them.

Good dialogue furthers action and characterization. Poor dialogue distracts from the action and mars characterization. Good dialogue, first of all, must be based on realistic speech. Suppose Dick, whom, let's say, we know to be a gruff, unpretentious character, were to say on seeing Harry, "Well, whom do I spy here? A comrade fallen? A *bon vivant* who's a bit less *bon* than usual?" Such a speech, though it furthers the action, would mar the characterization of Dick because it is not true to his voice. The vocabulary and phrasing are not what we associate with a plain-speaking person.

Suppose, on the other hand, you knew just how Dick would talk and you inserted what he said into the narrative in this manner:

Tom and Dick, laughing together, walked back into the house and there caught sight of Harry, who had fallen asleep on the sofa.
Dick was surprised. "Hey, look at this!" he said. "Here's Harry asleep on the sofa. He couldn't even make it up to bed."

It's true that Dick would speak this way. In fact, this is realistic speech and cannot be faulted on that score. It is still not wholly successful dialogue, however, because some of it repeats rather than furthers the action. Look at the above scene closely. We should drop the interpretive aside, "Dick was surprised," because his very words, " 'Hey, look at this!' " and their exclamation point, indicate surprise. We should also delete " 'Here's Harry asleep on the sofa,' " not because Dick wouldn't say such a thing (he probably would), but because it tells us what we already know. If we edit the dialogue in this manner, we get down to something that moves much more quickly:

Tom and Dick, laughing together, walked back into the house and there caught sight of Harry, who had fallen asleep on the sofa.
"Hey, look at this!" said Dick. "He couldn't even make it up to bed."

Or we might do it this way, making other corrections to obliterate the faults:

Tom and Dick, laughing together, walked back into the house and through the livingroom.
"Hey, look at this!" said Dick. "Here's Harry asleep on the sofa. He couldn't even make it up to bed."

There's been a slight shift of emphasis, but both scenes move fast. Both capture Dick's true speaking voice. And both not only reveal in part Dick's attitude toward Harry, but also suggest the action of the previous night.

In creating any scene, remain aware of how the reader will interpret the action. If we had left out "Here's Harry asleep on the sofa" from that second example, we would have created a scene in which what Tom and Dick saw was not clear. Dick's remark, "Couldn't even make it up to bed," would have been very ambiguous to a reader. Keep in mind that you want the reader to be intrigued, never confused. Make sure that dialogue does not subvert essential description. Just as it is annoying or boring in real life to hear people talking about something you don't fully comprehend, the same is true in fiction.

It is very difficult to create the sort of "overheard" dialogue—what I sometimes call "keyhole" dialogue—that makes the reader willing to be perfectly attentive, "listening," while waiting for the meaning to be revealed. Yet this is the ploy of some fiction. Occasionally stories or sections of novels open by presenting the reader with a dialogue stripped of its context. Even the identities of the speakers can be omitted, at least at first. Let's go back to our example and change it so that it begins:

"Hey, what's this?"
"It's Harry."
"He asleep?"
"Looks dead to the world."

"What's he doing down here on the sofa? I mean, isn't that just like him? He couldn't even make it up to bed."

"Well, he's getting to be an old man. Aren't you, Harry? Aren't you? Hey! Harry!"

"Hell, don't wake him up. He's probably got a bad headache. He'll feel it soon enough."

"Like you and me."

"Yeah. Like us."

Here we don't know Tom or Dick. We do know, by means of the punctuation, that the speakers alternate. It could be an advantage for the purposes of the story to omit Tom and Dick in this manner. For one thing, written thus, the visual focus is Harry. We, like the unidentified speakers, see Harry and react only to him. We are no longer watching Tom and Dick as well. But this means we are also *confined* to Harry; and since Harry is a sleeping man, he's not visually very exciting. He must wake up and speak fairly soon or the scene will become tedious.

Just as in our own lives we have a limited tolerance for not knowing what's going on, we have a limited tolerance for the same in fiction. Let's let our example, from its start, read as follows:

"Hey, what's this?"

"Oh, no. Just look at him."

"He's asleep, isn't he?"

"Yep. He's dead to the world."

"But what's Harry doing down here? He shouldn't be here. He's supposed to be sleeping upstairs."

"Well, he's getting old. Aren't you, Harry? Hey!"

"Don't do that. Let him sleep. I could use some sleep myself."

"So could I."

Here the dialogue is realistic. The action moves quickly. But this won't do at all. The problem is that in this instance Harry could be a pet cat.

If you let dialogue substitute for narrative, you must be sure the dialogue informs the reader of the relevant facts. This can be difficult. Suppose you want to describe Harry physically so that the reader will know just what he looks like. It's almost impossible to put such description into the dialogue.

"Hey, what's this?" said Dick.

"It's Harry. He's fast asleep, lying prone on this sofa with one arm dangling to the floor and his mouth open."

"And his hair looks as if he's been standing in a high wind, doesn't it—not to mention that he's unshaven and his clothes are beer-soaked."
"He stinks, too."
"Sure does."

Anyone can tell at once that this dialogue is wrong. Two people standing together and looking at a third do not describe what they see to each other. This means that the description of Harry in most of its particulars will have to be dropped altogether or placed in narrative. Traditional narrative will require that the speakers be identified. If we decide to revise the passage to include a description of Harry, this might be the result:

"Hey, what's this?"
Tom looked. "It's Harry."
The two approached the sofa so as to see more clearly the man lying there. He lay prone, unmoving, with one arm dangling to the floor. His head rested on a cushion at an uncomfortable angle. His mouth was open.
"He asleep?" said Dick.
Tom nodded. "Dead to the world."
The man named Harry did not stir at these voices but remained asleep. His hair was as tangled as if he had been standing in a high wind. His face was unshaven and beer had been spilled on his clothes.
Dick drew back. "Whew! He stinks."
"Sure does," said Tom.

Dialogue must try to avoid digression from the point. Sometimes fictional characters, just like any of us and our friends, will talk too much. It is one thing to create a character who's expansive, loquacious, and something of a bore. It is another to let a character yak on and on. You may find that once you get a character to talk, he won't shut up. You'll slow down the action if you can't resist tossing into dialogue your elaborate social theories or "inspired" details, which may be very interesting but are digressions within the context. For instance, if Tom here suddenly describes in detail how he, like Harry, sleeps with his mouth open and that this causes his wife to complain that he gargles in her ear, this may be amusing, and it may also reveal Tom's marital status and sleeping habits, but it does not belong in this dialogue which has as its theme poor Harry and the wild party of the night before.

There are other rules that aid in shaping dialogue and paring it down to what is essential for the story. One rule is this: eliminate the use of colorful verbs and adverbs when presenting the speech of your characters. For example, suppose we had written our dialogue with descriptive language:

"Hey, what's this?" questioned Dick curiously.
"It's Harry," Tom answered.

The substitution of "questioned Dick" for "said Dick," has the effect of repeating the obvious. (" 'Hey, what's this?' " is undeniably a question.) And because people who ask questions can be assumed to do so out of curiosity, "curiously" should be eliminated as redundant. My rule is this: always use "said" unless you must characterize the action further by telling *how* something is being said. In other words, if we choose to emphasize that Dick doesn't want to wake Harry, we could write: " 'Hey, what's this?' Dick whispered."

It's best to remember that *what* is said in any page of dialogue is at least three times as important as *how* it is said. The phrasing of a statement and its punctuation will usually provide clues as to the tone of voice of the speaker. Be sure you refrain from supplying "stage directions" that do not match the character's spoken words. For example, this wouldn't be convincing:

"Rouse yourself from that sofa and come have breakfast with us!" shouted Tom.

No one shouts a full, complex sentence. This is more likely:

"Hey!" Tom shouted. "Wake up! Have some breakfast!"

You may feel reluctant to follow a rule that tells you to employ the verb "to say" when denoting speakers and to avoid all the other verbs except in special cases. Won't each page of dialogue fill up with "he said" and "she said" in tiresome repetition? This might happen if it weren't for a useful trick of punctuation that allows a writer to assign an individual paragraph to a character whenever that character speaks. Notice that in all of the examples I have given thus far, I indent to indicate a change of speaker. It follows that if I do not write out "Tom said" or "said Tom," but allow Tom an action in the same paragraph, the reader will not be confused as to the fact it's Tom who's speaking. Observe:

"Yooo-hooo!" Tom pitched his voice high, imitating a woman. "Ooooo Harrikins!" He sounded remarkably like Maureen, Harry's fiance. "Haa-ree, sweetie? What haa-ppened?"

Dick shook his head. "Don't do that. Cut it out."

"Did you get an eeensie weensie bit inebriated?" Tom's voice was a quavering falsetto.

"Come on!" Dick was laughing in spite of himself. "Maureen never uses a five-syllable word—and I'm hungry, even if you're not."

Nowhere in the above example is there a "Tom said" or "Dick said," and yet, the assignment of speech to both speakers is perfectly clear.

Generally, dialogue must never be used in predictable interchanges that hinder the main action. In the first of our quoted examples — "Tom and Dick, laughing together, walked back into the house" — expanding "laughing together" into a full exchange of dialogue with witty jokes would halt these two characters on the threshold and prevent their going into the room where the third is sprawled on the sofa. "Laughing together" is all that's needed to let readers know that Tom and Dick are friends. Therefore, it will not be surprising when they join forces to continue their fun by teasing Harry.

Dialogue is an important fictional technique. Perhaps the rules I've set out here will encourage you to use it more often and more successfully. It would be absurd to make the generalization that fiction without dialogue is inferior to fiction with it. But I don't think it is wrong to consider dialogue an *advance* in the technique of fiction writing. Just as films progressed from "movies" to "talkies," so fiction has increasingly added verbal sound tracks to narratives. Fictional characters, just like the old-time movie stars, may have trouble evolving from silent ballet to conversation. But the best ones can make the switch, and it's worth their trouble.

28

ANGLE OF VISION

By Rosellen Brown

I'm in the middle of it again, this minute. I feel as though I'm sending this dispatch fresh from the front, though just this week I think I've begun to see my way out. My reward for having finished my last book and turning to my next, my current, my probable, is this nerve-racking limbo in which everything's begun but nothing's *happening.* (A fine reward, I find myself thinking each time, and wish I'd never finished, or better yet, that I could be revising something, since revision is the safest point from which to view a poem, a story, a novel: the hard work's done; you're busy enough to feel positively virtuous, and yet it's easy. Revision is tightening the screws, planing the edges.)

But now I am trying to find my way into a new novel, and for more than a month all I've done is walk the edges of an unmeasured field, a wild place I've come upon with excitement but whose size I can only guess at roughly, whose density I can barely imagine. What grows there? And is it worth the scratch-marks and the aching feet?

Only take the metaphor a step farther and you come to the peculiarly difficult part. The mysterious field I wake up to these mornings is an imaginary one, of course, mine to create as I want to. But its imperatives are very real to me. I believe there are particularities and limitations in this landscape, whether it exists yet or not, just as the wood-carver would tell you he can see the figure hidden deep within the branch he's chosen. He is only drawing it out, he will insist; he is not making it but setting it free.

I am in the period now when talking about my novel is far easier than sitting down to it each day. Talk, after all, has no shape. Suppose I approach the novel from the point of view of character: My central figure, Laura, will be a quadriplegic, a woman paralyzed from the neck down as the result of an accident. The story is about her and her husband Dan. Or, I can change the focus and say it is going to be a novel about a marriage under tremendous stress, at the flashpoint. Hard edges from all directions loom up for my characters to trip over and emerge from, bleeding, healing. The book will be short, I know; intense, I hope, rather than comprehensive; full of domestic detail, yet, if I can manage it, not trivial. Somewhere in it I shall ask such petty questions as "What is important? Past, present, future? Credit, blame? Comfort, pleasure, or freedom from pain? What might have been? What is?" Until I've finished the book, these are boring, bony, even nervy questions. Looking at these questions set down like this assures me that writers are arrogant optimists to dare concoct such agendas for themselves. (And having completed a book once does not make it any easier to believe you'll manage anything coherent again.)

All that's left to do is to write it.

Consider my brief summary of the story of Laura and Dan. How many choices have to be made by the end of the first page, if not the opening paragraph? (And bear in mind the hardest lesson, which I learned midway through my first novel: Basic choices, especially in a long form like the novel, are almost irreparable. Each major change disrupts a complicated whole in which every part depends on every other. A friend of mine says that rearranging a novel is like moving an elephant: Push one side and the tail flops down; run around and jack up the tail, and the trunk is dragging; rescue the trunk...so on and on.)

The story sounds simple, but there are a dozen potential novels in those few sentences of description, and they are vastly different from one another. Which one I decide to write will depend not only on what I want to say, or which character demands most loudly to be granted flesh and bone and voice, but also—realistically—which novel I feel capable of writing.

There is the story of the woman Laura. But from whom do we hear it? Told by an omniscient narrator, whose intimate comprehension of her feelings is conveniently boundless? Or by an onlooker who enters the story as a participant and stands close enough to guess at her states of mind? Or should it be told by Laura, the maimed woman? If so, to whom is she telling it? This frequently neglected question brings in its wake a battery of subtler questions: Is there an actual listener to this story? Or are we overhearing a story told to no one in particular?

Subtler still, the question—always in need of an answer, even if the author never realizes it has been asked—how near are we to the speaker? How broad, for one thing, is the historic scope of the novel or short story? Is it going to be intensely compressed, from the first word, or will there be an expanse in which these characters play out their roles as small figures in a social context which ultimately dwarfs them? How much time will pass—days, years, generations? And will the author's tone—whatever his choice of viewpoint—be ironic? Straightforward? Will the writer insist on seeing these characters under the unsparing eye of eternity, or will he take a more limited, forgiving, neighborly look at them? Will he be arch, judging, approving, awed? Ambivalent, even-handed, neutral? (Is there such a thing as neutrality in such matters?)

Let me open two books at random from my cluttered desktop. Here are the opening few sentences of Susan Fromberg Schaeffer's *Falling:*

It was a time of inexplicably happy marriages. Elizabeth's grandparents had arrived penniless; their first wealth was their children.

Consider the complexity of that second sentence: the cunning with which Ms. Schaeffer sketches in her historical perspective, yet lets us know that this is, at some point, going to be Elizabeth's story. Elizabeth is immediately seen as one fruit (whatever kind she may turn out to be) on the family tree.

Then again, here are the first few sentences of a novel of equal, though very different, complexity, whose immediacy is signaled instantly. Theodore Weesner's *The Car Thief* begins:

Again today Alex Housman drove the Buick Riviera. The Buick, coppertone, white sidewalls, was the model of the year, a '59, although the 1960 models were already out.

We have the year, the event, a loving attention to the distinctions between cars, all without preliminaries, in the matter-of-fact voice that will continue unswervingly through the book.

From the very first words of these novels the reader stands at a different distance from each character, Elizabeth and Alex. Neither book is written in the first person, yet we feel ourselves as close as possible to the center of Alex's consciousness. The sentences are short, unmetaphoric; the author makes himself transparent—he is only reporting a state of mind, not commenting on it. Comment, opinion, an historic perspective, or Alex's feelings would put us far outside them. Yet that perspective is precisely the one Schaeffer needs to provide background for her Elizabeth, who will turn out to be alive and depressed today in the America her grandparents sailed to with such hope.

Visual artists use the concept of "vanishing point" to convey this in spatial terms: Where—at what distance back from the subject—would the viewer of this scene be presumed to be standing to see it in this perspective? And then there are the paintings, the novels, even an occasional story, with multiple vanishing points; in and out they drag us, through the remote to the intimate and back again. Actually, *Falling* does that, with formal separation into Parts. After the Prologue, with its happy marriages seen from a distance, we are plunged into the middle of a more intimate but less promising situation:

> After Mark finished shaving, he came out to look for Elizabeth; she was lying under her crescent shaped stained glass window, curled up, muscleless.

The focus has changed.

I try for a kind of openness at the early stages in my writing, try even for a kind of irresponsibility that will invite all ideas, all approaches, and entertain them with equal seriousness, until some drop away as foolish or beyond my scope, and others hold their ground. Sometimes I even go to sleep as a convenient escape from uncertainty.

Quite frequently, I manage to wake up to clarity, to a problem solved, or a new beginning. It's not a restful kind of sleep, but what serendipity it is, what a reward, to put the seal of your deepest imagination on your conscious life; to turn the matter over to a less inhibited self to outwit your preconceptions, to untie the knots and make unpredictable associations! Psychiatrists speak of the uniquely accessible part of an artist's mind as the "preconscious." Less dignified about the matter, I think of it as my "semiconscious." I know it's infinitely more interesting and flexible than I am.

It was no surprise to me, therefore, to discover after I thought I'd been through all the alternatives for my novel that I didn't really want to tell the story from Laura's point of view at all, but from Dan's. It was like breaking a code. The feeling of certainty, the key-in-lock fit of such a decision is nearly sensual for me, a shot of Adrenalin, an immediate surge of usable energy. I can't guarantee I've hit the best way to tell my story—give me a few weeks and I'll know a little bit better. All I can attest to is that this choice frees me to say a hundred things, whereas, before I made that decision, I was tongue-tied.

Think, I told myself when the idea occurred to me, how much more dramatic leverage there will be if I show Laura from the vantage point of the man who loves her, or who once did, deeply, and is in terror that he may not continue to love her as she is now. I can suggest her feelings of anger and impotence (which are after all not hard to imagine), and leave the action of the book to Dan—the only person who can still act and move outside the tight frame of the crippled woman's cramped space.

And so to the next choice—the tone, the sound, the color of the writing: to take sides or to stay neutral? Can I counteract, as I think I must, the sentimentality engendered by Laura's helplessness? Will the writing be hot, cold? Spare, wordy? Straightforward, elaborate? Colloquial, formal? Every word, every bit of syntax I set down must be consistent. Once I've begun, I am stuck with my materials; they can't be exchanged when I feel the need for another perspective (unless I'm careful to work out the terms of a new consistency). This, I should say, is the place where the inexperienced writer gives himself away most often: Having selected an angle of vision, he cannot keep it; or having failed to select one, he is off to a wobbly start, and the whole way through speaks like a ventriloquist in whatever voice happens to come out of the dummy at hand.

These questions are as crucial to stories as they are to the novel. It's distressingly easy to show how banal a story can sound until the right, the dominant angle of vision has been hammered out. I enjoy telling writing classes that I never know what I know until I discover how I know it. If they doubt me, I show them any one of too many examples of failed vision, and then, if I'm lucky, the result of that vision when it's finally taken fire.

There is a story of mine which has an intensity and compression I fought hard for. I ended with a not-quite-realistic heightening of language that makes it a pleasure to read to audiences, who hear it, they tell me, as a poem. I had a friend whose young husband died;

only then did she discover (or did *I* discover?) that he had been a heroin adict. She—her situation—some indefinable combination of the two—were unrelentingly interesting to me, though I had no desire to write realistically about either my friend or her situation (nor, had I been that literal minded, did I know enough about them to do so). I still have the first draft of my story, "A Letter to Ismael in the Grave." It is unreadably boring: "First I was going to tell this as if it were somebody else talking. It would have been dramatic, a good gimmick. The husband of a dying woman or a new widow. But that's not true, it's only me. . . ." I tried again: "I dream them. They walk toward each other in a slow gavotte, through the tangle of sun and the slats of the El." I tried addressing my character as "you" but I felt as if I were giving her orders. Finally, I hit on a poeticized language which seemed to capture the drama that might have been taking place invisibly, beyond real words, in some part of my character's mind.

A human voice is a sound you can identify at a hundred yards, by vocabulary, timbre and inflection. Having found that voice, and in this case the daring to make metaphors, some earthy, some literary, as though they were ordinary language which needed neither explanation nor apology, I was on my way:

Somebody once told me I didn't have welfare mothers' eyes. I.I.I.I.I. As white is supposed to be made up of all the colors, "I" is made up of all the words you can possibly say all running together in a circle very fast. It is red and shiny and purple and sweet. A mouthful of I-berries.

The rest was easy because it was natural: I had only to listen to this woman speak—and she never deviated from the rules she'd laid down implicitly in her very first paragraph. (For me one of the delights of first-person writing is that those limits and possibilities are clear; they are things a given person will and likely will not say. These individual but not arbitrary laws of speech that my characters adhere to are infinitely easier for *me* in turn to maintain than those of a third-person narrator for whom, verbally, the sky's the only limit.)

The "vanishing points" in my other stories have varied tremendously. My first novel, *The Autobiography of My Mother,* is a kind of argument between mother and daughter, who alternate chapters in voices one would not be likely to confuse. What an exercise in vocabulary, in sentence structure, in the construction of whole styles of reasoning and metaphor the book turned out to be! I could hear those distinct timbres of voice in my sleep. There would literally have been no book without the differences in voice, because each embodies a contrast in temperament, a separate person.

To be truly free to choose from this variety of voices and opening gambits, one has to have a certain versatility. *How in the world do you do a flashback when the story's already in the past tense?* There's a question I came up against, and couldn't imagine why I'd never noticed. I admit to doing a sort of primitive, ad hoc kind of research when such a question presents itself: flip through a lot of books with childish curiosity, nourishing myself rather vaguely on others' solutions. Which is not to say that what I find I use in any recognizable form; only that I get a sense of the range of techniques available.

The prerequisite for versatility is the sheer technical competence to pull off nearly anything. This is journeyman competence, necessary but not sufficient, and as in all crafts, it comes with experience. Few are given a gift of language so inclusive that it makes all styles possible. Some writers try to break out of a narrow and predictable range, while others make it their specialty and perfect their single note.

I myself want to have the armament of voices and perspectives to be able to choose the most appropriate for any theme or character or situation I may choose to write about. The New Hampshire neighbors I most deeply respect are the farmers and artisans, because they keep near their right hand, always, their tools and their willingness to improvise. If the right tool is lacking, they are never daunted. They'll fiddle and glue, borrow and bend, till they've made the tool they need to do the job. That's the kind of writer I'd like to be.

29

RISKS AND REWARDS
IN WRITING THE SAGA

By Susan Howatch

When I last saw my editor I speculated that the next book I wrote would be short—"like a miniature," I added, exhausted, after having just completed a third saga of a quarter of a million words. Without looking up from his broiled shrimp, my editor murmured politely: "I think you paint better on a large canvas."

Since in my less exhausted moments I do enjoy writing sagas, I was more than willing to believe him, and no doubt there are numerous other writers who share my preference for the large canvas. Yet perhaps they are hesitating before embarking on such a lengthy project. What are the hazards of saga-writing? What are the rewards? What *is* a saga? Recently, I have been asked all these questions, and although I can only attempt answers based on my personal experience, I hope they may be useful to other writers who have a long story to tell.

The word "saga" is used today to describe a story which spans several generations. My two sagas, *Penmarric* and *Cashelmara,* both have Gothic and historical elements, but they differ from the Gothic and historical novels I wrote earlier not only in their length, but because they are primarily concerned with the development of a group of characters over more than thirty years. Much can happen in three decades, and the inevitable profusion of incident presents special problems for the saga writer, since he has so much more material to assemble than has the author of a regular-length novel.

However, the point about the saga is that it *is* a novel. It should be a coherent unity, not an unmarshaled mass of narrative, and to achieve coherence it is important to be concise. "What fun it must be to write a long book!" someone commented before he had read *Penmarric.* "In a saga you can ramble and digress!" He was amazed when I told him I had spent five years trying to tell my story in the shortest possible way. It is *because* of the saga's length that any leisurely digression becomes a dangerous self-indulgence. The reader has to be lured on, not merely to page two hundred and fifty, but to page six hundred and beyond. So before embarking on that delectable scene that you've been promising yourself for six months, you should always pause to consider if it's truly relevant to the plot.

The corollary of the rule "No rambling" is the rule that the saga must have a beginning, a middle, and an end. It is not a "continuing story," a soap opera in which a group of characters jog along in accordance with the weekly whim of the scriptwriter. Again, because of the length of the story, plot and construction are as important as a concise narrative.

Penmarric and *Cashelmara* are both based on historical facts, so in a sense my plots have been ready-made, yet I have still had to interpret those facts, update them to modern times and shape them into a cohesive whole. In *Cashelmara* (set in nineteenth-century Ireland, but, in fact, a study of three of the Plantagenet kings of England), my problem was to decide where to begin. I wanted to write about the marriage of Edward II and Isabelle of France (Patrick and Sarah in the book), yet I came to realize it was impossible to achieve this satisfactorily until I had explained Patrick's past to the reader. To present him as he was at the time of his marriage, a good-natured but essentially weak young man involved in a latent homosexual relationship with his best friend, would have been to present him not only as unsympathetic, but as incomprehensible. I decided the reader had to understand Patrick. Why *was* he getting married? The answer to that question led me back to his stepmother Marguerite, who had her own reasons for wanting him to marry, and on considering Marguerite, I was led still further back to her husband Edward, Patrick's father.

Having realized I should begin not with Patrick and Sarah but with Edward and Marguerite, I then saw that Patrick and Sarah formed only the middle segment of a conflict resolved in the third generation by their elder son, and it was not until I had grasped the plot in its entirety that I was able to see the unifying thread which ran from the beginning to the end: inevitability. In a fatal crescendo which had begun with an old man's marriage to a young girl, the principal characters had traveled inexorably down the road to murder, revenge and retribution. There was also a second unifying thread: irony. These characters had been convinced throughout that they were acting for the best, and once I realized this, I was able to sum up the book's theme in a single sentence: "The road to hell is paved with good intentions."

Themes are important. As a saga writer, you cannot rely on the panoramic sweep of your epic to make such a basic requirement as theme unnecessary, for without a theme—as without a tightly constructed plot—you are in the realm of soap opera. Some writers think of their theme first and build both plot and characters around it; but since my characters always come first, I have to help the theme emerge from their actions.

However, before you can play midwife you have to find the baby! I can remember floundering in the early drafts of *Penmarric,* while I wondered not only how to find the theme, but what I could do with it when I found it.

In *Cashelmara,* as I've explained, I found the theme buried in the plot. In *Penmarric* I found it in the characters. I asked myself: what do these people show? And at last I knew them well enough to see the answer. *Penmarric* touched several themes—the disintegration of an old social order, the cruelties of the class system—but primarily it was a study of hypocrisy. For example, Philip, who prided himself on his passion for truth, found that by his own actions he had entwined himself in a web of lies; he was leading a double life, in much the same manner as the father whom he had so loudly condemned.

Once I discovered that the main characters all illustrated the saying, "He that is without sin among you, let him first cast a stone...," I was able to make sure that this theme was present, if only by implication, in each of the book's five parts. Then, I named these parts after the changing sources of the hypocrisy. Philip's section clearly demanded the label, "Truth and Falsehood."

Of course there's no need to hit the reader over the head with the theme on every page; a saga isn't a moral tract. But if the theme can be surreptitiously suggested to the reader in the manner of a subliminal message, he will probably find the story more satisfying than if the theme had remained buried deep in the text.

Having dealt with theme, construction, and style, I would sum up by saying that the hazards of saga-writing lie in thinking you can be less disciplined than you would be if you were writing a regular-length novel. Possibly you need to be even more disciplined—and you also need patience and stamina! *Cashelmara* and my saga *The Rich Are Different* each took two-and-a-half years, five drafts and considerable research but—and here are the rewards of saga-writing—the satisfaction of being able to explore characters in such depth is enormous. A span of thirty years enables you to follow characters if not from the cradle to the grave, at least from immaturity to maturity. With the challenge of charting their psychological development comes the challenge of knitting their lives into the historical background to give the saga its "epic" effect. Ideally the characters should be people of their times to the extent that the era is no mere backdrop but an unobtrusive additional character permeating every turn of the story.

Before I could start *The Rich Are Different,* I had to decide where and when the story was to be set. I already had the people; as in my two previous sagas, I had borrowed them from history. I now needed an eighteen-year span of time which would show the story to its best advantage, and I finally decided that the period between the World Wars would offer the most scope to my characters. "But why 1922?" asked a friend, astonished after hearing the starting date of the book, "What happened then?" The answer was: not much. "But think what happened in 1929," I said. By that time, my characters had strong roots on Wall Street.

Obviously, the right historical setting can add an extra dimension to the story, and with a saga, I believe in aiming for the multi-dimensional effect. A painting means little if the paint is just color on a flat surface, and it's because I aim for varied perspectives in my sagas that I use the multi-narrator technique. *Penmarric* is told by a succession of five narrators, *Cashelmara* by six, and their changing viewpoints form a mosaic that enables the reader to see different interpretations of character and different aspects of the plot. For me this technique is one of the rewards of saga-writing, since it gives me the opportunity to project myself fully into half a dozen different minds; but of course every saga is different, and the writer must tell his story in the style he feels is best.

My final plea to this writer who hankers for the large canvas would be: Don't be afraid to start! It *is* terrifying to think of tackling all those characters who are probably still strangers, but the only way to know them better is to set out to meet them. When I begin my first draft, my characters are mere nodding acquaintances, and I'm a foreigner in their country. But two-and-a-half years later, when I finish the final draft, those characters are as real to me as my own family, and their world is as familiar as the view from my window when I look up from my desk after typing THE END.

30

ABOUT THAT NOVEL

By Evan Hunter

STARTING: If you haven't got an idea for one, forget it. If you haven't got an idea you want to express on paper, in words, forget it. If you prefer putting paint on canvas, or rolls on your pianola or in your oven, forget it. You're going to be with this novel for a long, long time, so you'd better have *thought* about it before you start writing it. When it's ready to be written, you'll know. You'll know because you can't get it out of your mind. It'll be with you literally day and night. You'll even *dream* about it, but don't get up and rush to your typewriter. Go back to sleep. Only in movies do writers get up in the middle of the night with an inspiration. The time to go to the typewriter is when you're fresh and ready to do battle. There *will* be a battle, no question, a siege that will seemingly go on forever. So sit down, make yourself comfortable, and begin.

No outline at first, except the loose one in your head, draped casually around the idea. The thing you are trying to find is the voice. This is the single most important thing in any novel. The voice. How it will *sound*. Who is telling the story? Why is he telling it? If you're sixty years old and writing in the first person singular about a sixteen-year-old high school student, beware of the voice. It may be your own, and that is wrong. If you're writing in the third person, you can change the *tone* of the voice each time you switch to another character, but the *voice* itself must remain consistent throughout. The voice is your style. Except in my mystery series, I try to change my style to suit the subject matter of any novel I'm writing. I've come a hundred pages into a novel using the wrong voice, and I've thrown those pages away and started a new search for the right voice. Don't worry about spending days or weeks trying to find a voice. It will be time well spent. You'll know when you hit upon it. Things will suddenly *feel* right.

Once you've found the voice, write your first chapter or your first scene. Test the water. Does it still feel right? Good. *Now* make your outline. First of all, determine how long the book will be. The average mystery novel runs about 200 pages in manuscript, but a straight novel can be something as slim as *Love Story* or as thick as *Gone With the Wind.* You are the only person who knows in advance what your story is about. You are the only one who can figure how many pages you will need to tell this story. Take out your calculator. Are you writing a 300-page novel? O.K., how many chapters will you need? The length of each chapter will be determined by how much you have to *say* in that chapter. If you're depicting the Battle of Waterloo, it might be a trifle difficult to compress it into ten pages. If you're writing about a man putting out the garbage, you probably have only a scene, and you'll need additional scenes to make a full chapter.

Outline the novel in your own way, never mind freshman high-school English courses. I've outlined a forty-page chapter with just the words "Father-son confrontation." The outline is you, talking to yourself on paper. Get friendly with yourself. Tell yourself what you, as the writer, want to accomplish in any given chapter. "O.K., now we want a big explosion in the garage, and we want to see all these goddamn flames, and smell the smoke, and we want neighbors running over with garden hoses. Bring the little girl in at the end of the scene, shocked by what she's done." Got it? *Talk* to yourself. You don't have to outline the whole book. Just take the outline as far as your invention will carry it. Later, when you've written all the chapters you've already outlined, you can make another outline of the *next* several chapters. If a chapter is needed between something that has happened before and something that will happen later, and you don't know what to put between those two slices of bread, just type in the words, SCENE MISSING. You'll come back to it later. You're going to be here awhile.

MOVING: Set yourself a definite goal each day. Tack it on the wall. Ten pages? Five pages? Two pages? Two paragraphs? It doesn't matter. *Set* the goal, make it realistic, and *meet* it. If you're writing a planned 400-page novel, it will seem impossible ever to get it finished.

400 pages may be a year away. But your daily goal is here and now, and it's important to set·that goal and meet it so that you'll have a sense of immediate reward. At the end of each week, on your calendar, jot down the number of pages you've already written. Store your kernels. Watch the cache grow. Keep the thing moving. If it bogs down, if you're supposed to write a tender love scene and you've just had a fight with your accountant, put the anger to good use. Jump ahead and write the Battle of Waterloo chapter. *Don't stop writing!* It's easier to go fishing or skiing—but sit at that damn typewriter, and look at the four walls all day long if you have to. There is nothing more boring than looking at the walls. Eventually, if only to relieve the boredom, and because you've made a deal with yourself not to get out of that chair, you'll start writing again. At the end of the day, read over what you've written. If you think it's lousy, don't throw it away. Read it again in the morning. If it still looks lousy, do it over again. Or if it's still bothering you, and you don't know why, move on. Keep it *moving*. The nice thing about writing, unlike public speaking, is that you can correct all your mistakes later.

CHANGING: The only true creative aspect of writing is the first draft. That's when it's coming straight from your head and your heart, a direct tapping of the unconscious. The rest is donkey work. It is, however, donkey work that must be done. Whether you rewrite as you go along—taking that bad chapter from the night before and putting it through the machine again from the top—or whether you rewrite everything only after you've completed the book, you *must* rewrite. But be careful. You can hone and polish something until it glows like a diamond, but you may end up with something hard and glittering and totally without the interior spark that was the result of your first commitment to paper. You're only a virgin once, but try to bring to each rereading of your own material the same innocence you brought to it the first time around. You will be rereading it *twenty* times before you're finished. Each time, ask yourself what you intended. Do you want me to cry when I read this scene? Well, are *you* crying? If you're not, why aren't you? Find out why you aren't. Did someone say something that broke the mood of the scene? Is that field of daffodils too cheerful for the tone of the scene? Has your heroine stamped her foot when she should be tearing out her hair? Work it, rework it. When you yourself begin crying, you've got it.

ENDING: How do you know when you're finished? You're finished when you're satisfied. If a scene is right the first time around, leave it alone. Tell yourself, "Terrific, pal," and leave it alone. You'll know you're getting to the end because you'll suddenly slow down. When that happens, set smaller goals for yourself. Instead of those five pages today, make it three. Your pace is slower because you don't want to let go of this thing. You've been living together for a long, long time, you've let this smelly beast into your tent, and you've grown to love it, and now you're reluctant to have it gallop out over the sands and out of your life forever. The temptation is to keep it with you forever, constantly bathe it and scent it, groom it and curry it, tweeze its lashes and tie a bow on its tail. *Recognize* the temptation and recognize too that everything eventually grows up and leaves home. When you've done the best you can possibly do at this time (there *will* be other books, you know) put it in a box, give it a farewell kiss, and send it out into that great big hostile world.

SENDING: Where do you send it? Be exceedingly careful in choosing your agent or your publisher. Don't send the book to anyone who charges a fee for reading it or publishing it. In the real world of publishing, people pay *you* for your work. The Society of Authors' Representatives (if you decide to go the agent route) will send you on request a list of reputable agents in the United States. The address is 101 Park Avenue, New York, New York 10017. Just write and ask, enclosing a self-addressed, stamped envelope. If you decide to submit your manuscript directly to a publisher instead, a long list of publishers looking for various kinds of novels appears in *The Writer* Magazine, or in the market list in Part IV of this volume. Although some book publishers today have given up reading unsolicited manuscripts, many others still maintain reading staffs, and their sole purpose is to search for publishing possibilities. Send the novel manuscript out. One publisher at a time. Multiple submissions are frowned upon except when an agent is conducting a huge auction, and then the publishers are made aware beforehand that the book is being submitted simultaneously all over the field. Choose a publisher who has previously published your sort of book. Don't shotgun it around blindly. If your novel espouses atheism, don't send it to a religious publisher.

WAITING: So now your monster is out roaming the countryside, trying to earn a living. No, there it is in the mailbox. Damn thing. Wish you hadn't given it life at all. Tear open the package. Nice little noncommittal note. Thanks a lot, but no thanks. Despair. Chin up, kiddo, send it out again. But here it is *back* again. And *again.* And *yet* again. Plenty of publishers in the world, just keep trying. Pack it, send it, wait again. Why? Why wait? Why set up a vigil at the mailbox? Why hang around the post office looking like someone on the Wanted posters? You should be *thinking* instead. You should be mulling a new idea. *Don't* wait. What you *should* be doing is—

STARTING: If you haven't got an idea for one, forget it. If you haven't got an idea you want to express on paper, in words, forget it. If you prefer putting paint on canvas, or rolls on your pianola or in your oven, forget it. You're going to be with this novel for a long, long time, so you'd better have *thought* about it before you start writing it. When it's ready to be written, you'll know.

Write it.

31

VISUALIZING FICTION ON PAPER

By Dorothy Uhnak

WRITING began so far back in childhood that I literally cannot remember a time when I was *not* writing. I spent fourteen years of my adult life as a police officer in New York City. During all that time, I wrote continually, drawing on everything around me: the unique, exciting situations, the deadly boredom, the brutality, sadness, pain, humor (often macabre), the courage, cowardice, intelligence, stupidity, greed, anger, danger, and intense loyalty which characterize the working life of a police officer.

I was a capable police officer: I was promoted three times and awarded medals twice. I worked hard, was dedicated and earnest and concerned. Yet all the time, the writer in me was compiling events, feelings, atmosphere, emotions, situations for future use. *Policewoman*, semi-autobiographical, semi-fictional, was published during my tenure as a police officer and was my first attempt to set forth some things I had observed, learned, experienced, been a part of.

My first novel, *The Bait,* was published after I resigned from police work in order to devote myself more fully to writing and to continue my education. It was awarded the Edgar for the Best First Mystery of 1968, which I felt was somewhat ironic, for I never considered myself a "mystery writer." People are my main concern as a writer, and the task I set myself is to dig into the "mystery" of human behavior in given circumstances.

I have used the police world in all my books to date in order to explore certain events occurring between people, rather than to tell a "cop story" per se.

The Bait dealt with a sex murderer. On a deeper level, it explored the tormented world of a tragically demented man and his impact on a bright, sensitive young policewoman.

The Witness, second in my trilogy set in the Manhattan District Attorney's Squad, was a straightforward story about black organized crime and corruption. It was also a story about youthful idealism, hopes and energies that were misused and betrayed. It was part of the education-in-life of young Detective Christie Opara.

The Ledger, third in the trilogy, could be described as the story of the beautiful mistress of a crime lord. It was also a character study of two apparently opposite young women: one the worldly mistress, the other the idealistic Christie Opara. It was a probing of the painful, hidden truths each girl had to face about herself.

When I undertook my latest novel, *Law and Order,* I realized it was a radical departure from anything I had previously attempted. It was to span three generations, through four decades which have seen more social, political, moral upheaval than most of the rest of our history all put together. For one solid year, I did nothing but research. I probed back more than a hundred years to gain a fuller understanding of the immigrants who came to populate New York City, to lead and dominate not only the Police Department but the political and religious structure of the city for so many years. While the main characters are Irish, I also had to study all the important ethnic groups who comprise New York, to understand their aspirations, backgrounds, influences, self-image. I immersed myself in reading and discussion not only about politics, religious and ethnic history and folklore, but in economics and the effects of the Great Depression, World War II, the post-war world, the Korean War, Vietnam, the youth movement, generation gap, emergence of the drug culture.

I spent three weeks in Ireland wandering at random through that lovely tortured country: spoke to people, listened to them, read as much Irish writing as I could absorb until I could *feel* the rhythm of Irish thought and emotion. I allowed myself to get caught up and carried by the Irish idiom.

My characters grew out of the research. Certain strong characters began to dominate the other members of their family. And it was a "family" that grew into the story. They were at the hub and center of all the changing times of their city and their world. Through the three generations of O'Malleys, my aim was to present some of the social and moral questions with which we are confronted today, in the seventies. My hero, Brian O'Malley, is first introduced as a young, inexperienced boy of eighteen, faced with the sudden responsibility of caring for his mother, grandmother, brothers and sisters at the violent death of his policeman-father. The book ends when Brian is a fifty-two-year-old Deputy Chief Inspector in the New York City Police Department, dealing as best he can with forces of corruption, coming to terms with his own policeman son, a Vietnam veteran, trying to live in a rapidly changing and always puzzling world.

One of the most exciting things about writing *Law and Order* was when the characters "took off" on their own. This hasn't happened to me as a writer very often. It is a rare, exciting, heady, exhilarating experience and occurs only when the characters are so well known, so well loved, that they can be trusted to act and react instinctively true to themselves.

The worst moment came when the manuscript was totally completed—all polished and ready to be set in galleys. I experienced the most dreadful sense of loss imaginable. All those warm, exciting, wildly active, strong and familiar people with whom I had shared my life for so long were suddenly taken from me, to be thrust out into the large and critical world.

The solution to this feeling of loss, for me at any rate, was to let a little time go by, enjoy the fruits of my labor, involve myself in other facets of the work, i.e., promotion and publicity—to relax, enjoy, take a deep breath, and begin the whole process all over again.

It must be admitted that no matter how many books I've written, how many characters created and lived with and let go, when I put the blank white paper in my machine, it is no easier for me to begin the written word than it ever has been. Publicity tours and best-seller lists, and book club and movie and TV sales are all very exciting and rewarding and lucrative. However, at the beginning of the day I am a pauper before the blank white paper. The trick is, I guess, just to keep at it from ground zero and to build on it during each session at the machine. Happily, it has started again for me; tentatively, fragilely, hopefully, I've begun a new book. Thankfully.

Since I've always been curious about other writers' work habits,

I will set down some of my own with hopes that my example will warn others to adopt other methods. Sometimes I wonder how in the world I've ever accomplished *any* body of work: I never seem to do all those things I'm positive a writer *should* do.

I've never kept notebooks filled with valuable phrases, impressions, observations. Oh, I've stacks of notebooks of all kinds— spiral ones with businesslike brown covers and spiral ones with pretty flowers on the cover. Somber little black looseleaf notebooks that fit into the palm of my hand and large ones that fill up my lap. They are all filled with empty pages, because I've never really known what to put in them. Once or twice, I've jotted down phrases which I conjured in the middle of the night, or en route somewhere on the subway, but somehow that never seemed pertinent to anything, and I spent too much time wondering what in the world I had in mind when I wrote them down in the first place. There are also pencil sketches of advertisements and some interesting doodles, not one of which is helpful.

A long time ago, I came to a strange conclusion relative to me and note-taking. Mysteriously, it has worked for me, but I do not recommend it to anyone else, merely report on it. If the thought, impression, idea, phrase, situation, or whatever is important enough for me to remember and use somewhere in my writing, I will retain it in cell x-y-or-z of my brain. If it isn't worth using, I will forget it. I don't remember how many flashing, brilliant thoughts might have been retained had they been jotted down. I do know that many conversations between characters in my stories give me a strong sense of *déjà vu*, because they were carried on in my head at some unconnected time in the past.

Another thing I don't do and feel I should: I don't have any work schedule. I mean, *I don't have any work schedule at all.* For a person who spent so many years in a structured work-situation, this leaves much room for feelings of guilt. I know I *should* sit at the machine and accomplish at least *that* much work each day, but I don't. I frankly don't know *when* I work. Sometimes, I leap out of bed at six in the morning, jump into my clothes, gulp my cup of tea and hammer out scene after scene after scene. Then, for days at a time, I avoid the top floor, which is where I work. At about three in the afternoon, the urge might hit again, and I hammer away at the next scene. I will point out that no matter how remiss I am about regulating my work schedule, at least this much is structured: I work a scene through, beginning to end, whether it runs for four pages or forty, whether it takes twenty-three minutes or six hours. Maybe it's those six-hour binges that get the job done for me.

In between actually sitting and pounding the keys, the story does go on inside my head, regardless of what else I am, physically, doing. I rake the leaves, play with the dogs, feed the cats, forget to defrost the supper, stare at daytime television (which is a horrible admission, I realize). The saving grace is that the story process continues, sometimes in some subterranean, unknown manner, because solutions to story problems sometimes take place when least expected. For example: in the shower, riding in a car at night, folding laundry, dusting the furniture, painting a wall.

When I'm well into a manuscript—in fact, during all stages of the manuscript—I rarely if ever rewrite. Probably because I wait so long before actually sitting down to the task, forming sentences in the air before I form them on paper, by the time I actually *do* sit down to work (whenever that is!), the phrases are ready and generally come out the way I want them to. Not always, but more often than not.

Generally, I am amazed at the way the pages of a manuscript pile up, given a particular period of time, because although I complain continuously about working too hard, when it's all over, I have very little remembrance of having worked *at all*.

Given one magic wish as a writer, I would want to be gifted with some kind of power to transform the scene in my head immediately into a bound, printed form without the ever-present struggle to find the words to frame and form the thought. My constant struggle as a writer is to zero in on the exact words that will enable my reader to see, feel, experience a particular scene with as much concern and intensity as I experience while visualizing and writing it.

I don't know what advice to offer young writers. I'm not even sure anyone should presume to offer any advice beyond that one tormenting, beautiful, obvious, obscure, demanding, torturous ecstasy: WRITE. Don't talk about it, whine about it, rap about it, agonize over it, dissect, analyze, study or anything else: Just do it. WRITE.

32

WRITING THE SUSPENSE-ADVENTURE NOVEL

By Clive Cussler

I HATE to write.

Quite frankly, I see nothing blasphemous in admitting it. There are thousands of writers who find scribbling words on paper a colossal drag. Writing is a damned tough way to make a buck, at least to most people. I seethe internally when I hear or read about those Pollyannas who merrily peck away at their typewriters, whistling while they create, morning, noon and night, tossing off 20,000 words between coffee breaks.

I hate them, too.

On a good day of total effort, beginning at nine o'clock and ending at five (an old routine carried over from my advertising agency days), I'm lucky if I turn out four finished pages or 1,000 words. And then I have to take a long walk, indulge in a martini and take a snooze prior to dinner, before I'm mentally rejuvenated enough to return to the land of the living.

When I finally type THE END to a novel, the clouds part and the sun bursts through, flowers blossom across the land, angels sing along to harp music, and I deflate like an old balloon whose elastic is shot.

Therefore, because writing is so exhausting, to me at any rate, I plan and research each project thoroughly before hitting the proper keys to spell out CHAPTER ONE. My problem is that I can visualize my characters, backgrounds, and events as though I were standing in the middle of the action, so the difficult part is turning all these wonderful sights and sounds into mere words that place the reader amid the action, too.

To me the readers come above all else. I look upon them as guests who have gone out of their way to spend time and expense to indulge in whatever small enjoyment I can provide. My particular genre is suspense-adventure, so in order to get off the mark quickly, I must find a concept that grabs the reader's fancy before he turns past the title page. Within the realm of adventure there are thousands of subjects and tales that have great appeal. One of the trends in fashion at present is for novelists to write fiction based loosely on a non-fiction event. This often revolves around a "what if" principle. For instance, one day I asked myself, what if they raise the *Titanic*? The next question that entered my mind was why? Obviously the cost of salvaging the great liner from two and one-half miles down in the abysmal depths would be enormous. What reason would justify the effort and expense? Out of this pre-examination a plot was born.

Without a concept hook to hang your plot on, you have nothing. The swashbuckler of yesterday who chopped up the moustached villains and did little else but carry the insipid heroine off into the sunset at the finish won't cut the mustard today. The idea of having a blimp bomb the Superbowl as in *Black Sunday* was a good hook for a "what if" adventure. *Airport* and of course *Jaws* are other successful stories that embraced this principle.

More than ever, the reader who shells out for your novel is looking for an escape. It's a fact of life, that if you don't aim your talents at the market, you won't sell. If the reader isn't presold by an author's past reputation, or by word-of-mouth recommendation, or a blitz publicity campaign, he has no other reason to select your masterpiece except for one hell of an intriguing concept.

Assuming that you have the story the world is waiting to devour, you should now turn your energies to the next step in the adventure novel—structure.

Gotcha! I'll bet you thought I was going to say plot or perhaps characterization. Not so. Next to a mind-boggling concept, structure is the most important foundation for a novel. Whether you intend to write it in the first person or the third is elementary. You should take the path that makes you comfortable. First person allows you to probe the hero or heroine's mind in depth; you see only what they see. The third-person narration, on the other hand, gives a wider range of freedom to travel into areas the first person cannot follow. Seeing the action from the central character's eyes limits the writer to what I call the "Formula-A Structure." You travel with the narrator from pro-logue to epilogue, seeing only what he sees. This is a common practice among new writers because of its basic simplicity.

However, I do not mean to suggest that Formula A is mundane. Hardly. It has been used with great success by writers since man first scratched in the sand. The classical love stories, mysteries and, yes, horror stories, too, have taken advantage of its storytelling smoothness. Formula A also makes for a tight tale that involves the readers as closely in the action as though they were the parrot on Long John Silver's shoulder.

For writers who turn on to intricate plotting and a cast of hundreds, Formula B is the only way to fly. Here the third-person viewpoint throws open the floodgates of creativity, and you can pull the reader through a labyrinth of subplots, "sideplots," and "twistplots." You have the opportunity of setting the scene in a jet over the Arctic in one chapter and suddenly switching to a camel caravan crossing the Sahara in the next.

Leon Uris, Robert Ludlum, and Harry Patterson alias Jack Higgins are all masters of the complex structure. Instead of studying flowery prose and in-depth characterization as most writers are prone to do, you should examine quite closely the organization and precision the authors mentioned above weave throughout their stories. Harold Robbins, for example, used the epilogue as the prologue in *The Adventurers,* and then went on to slip his hero deftly in and out of first- and third-person narration.

Do you intend to utilize the advantages of a prologue to set up future conflicts? Will you need an epilogue to tie the ends together? Have you the guts to combine several plots into one? Have you considered dividing your novel into different parts? This is what we mean by structure.

There are no hard-and-fast rules for structuring the modern adventure novel. In Formula A, you must keep your hero believable and the action moving to keep readers turning the pages. With Formula B, the trick is to keep them second guessing and so involved with who's-doing-what-to-whom they can't put the book down. This is achieved by alternating your characters and their personal conflicts so that in the beginning there seems to be no comprehensible connection. Then as the plot unfolds, they're all irresistibly drawn together into an ever-heightening climax. I call this threading the needle. You've got to sew all your characters into the same pocket and thereby give your reader a satisfying conclusion.

A satisfying conclusion can never be stressed too strongly. How many books have you read that began like gangbusters and then fell to pieces in the end? The sad result is that you forget them damned quickly while a tale that has a smash ending stays with you.

All too often a writer will sit down with a blockbuster concept and barrel through the first half of the story only to fall off a cliff because he had no idea where he was going in the first place. You have to know what you're aiming at in the last chapter and then backtrack and work toward it. That's why planning your structure is so important. Creative blueprinting can't turn a bad book into a good one, but it sure helps.

When it comes to plotting, so much has been written by renowned authorities of mystery and adventure writing, I see no reason simply to repeat most of their well-known rules. I plot as I go. Many novelists write an outline that has almost as many pages as their ultimate book. Others knock out a brief synopsis. Again, do what is comfortable. If you have to plot out every move your characters make, so be it. Just make sure there is a plausible purpose behind their machinations. A good reader can smell a phony plot a block away.

In modern adventure writing, the trend seems to be to sacrifice great gobs of character-probing in favor of fast-paced action. Sad to say, most critics are still hung up on finely tuned character definition. but then critics only concern themselves with how well a book is written. The guy who actually lays down the cash for it is more interested in how well it reads.

Alistair MacLean, perhaps one of the finest adventure writers of the last several decades, favors rapid pace over character psychiatry. His people are sharply defined in their looks and mannerisms and come across very well, without pages of historical background.

The hero in my series is usually described through the eyes of other characters. These observations, usually in small doses, occur only when they appropriately add to a particular scene or action.

They don't make good heroes these days. The anti-hero seems to be currently in vogue, especially in detective and spy novels. But pure adventure is something else again. A Casper Milquetoast just won't do. Men readers want to identify with the shrewd, devil-may-care hero who surmounts every obstacle put up by the opposition and emerges victorious in the end. Likewise, women, in spite of the current hoopla about equality, still secretly yearn for the rugged he-man to sweep them off their feet. If you doubt this last statement, simply take a look at the staggering sales figures of the romantic novels by Rosemary Rogers and several other astute women writers.

In most dramatic genres, the reader likes to identify with the characters and to experience what they see and feel. In adventure, the reader runs along the sidelines, cheering everyone on—a prime reason for your characters to be bigger than life, but still believable. That's what's called walking the tightrope. On one hand, you run the risk of making some characters too ordinary. On the other, you don't dare allow them to become comic book Supermen or Wonderwomen.

If your hero must save the world, at least let him act human while he goes about it. He should still put his pants on one leg at a time, sneeze occasionally, blow his nose, and feel the urge to go to the bathroom. What man can identify with another who does none of these? Same with women. I like my girls to zing in a few four-letter words when they're angry or frustrated. Show me one who doesn't at least say "Damn!" after ramming a painted toenail through a pair of new pantyhose.

There is an old saying in the advertising business: "See what your competitors are doing, then do just the opposite." That's the whole idea of writing a book: You're telling a story no one else has told before.

When I decided to develop a series hero, I looked around the field and studied everyone from Sherlock Holmes to James Bond to Travis McGee. I figured the last thing the adventure arena needed was another private detective, spy or CIA agent. So I created a guy by the name of Dirk Pitt who is the Special Projects Director for NUMA (the National Underwater & Marine Agency). Fortunately, I stumbled onto a good thing. The mysteries that can be expanded upon in and around water are as boundless as the oceans themselves. I might mention that I chose the name Pitt partly because it is one syllable, thus making it easy to say, "Pitt did this, and Pitt did that," etc.

My final suggestion relates to what I said earlier about treating the reader as an honored guest. Every so often I'll stop and ask myself, what would the reader like to see at this particular moment in the story? Then I'll try my best to give it to him. I figure that since my reader paid good money or took the time and trouble to check out my efforts from the library, the least I can do is place his interests above mine.

I don't cotton to writers who engrave on marble what *they* think should be read. My work is geared strictly to provide a few hours of enjoyable escape. I don't believe in imparting personal philosophy, social commentary, or hidden meanings between the lines. Some writers prefer to be called novelists, some storytellers, others spokesmen for the masses.

Me: I'm an entertainer, no more, no less.

33

EXPERIMENTING WITH PERSPECTIVE

By Barbara Rohde

WHENEVER I tell someone I am working on a story and he asks the inevitable, "What's it about?" I find myself pausing before I answer. I can't decide whether to answer in terms of the events of the story ("Well, it's about this family on a summer vacation in Europe, and their little boy who has a stuffed cat he is always losing...") or to answer in terms of its meaning (Well, it's about the relentlessness of time and how people deal with that.")

I suppose I should always give both answers, since what makes a story is the coming together of events and meaning. The reason that similar events can have a multiplicity of meanings is a question of perspective. We learn early in our attempts at fiction that a story is not merely a chronology—this happened and then this happened and then this happened—that the meaning of a story depends upon how these events are seen and understood, first of all by the writer, then by the characters within the story, ultimately by the reader.

If I tell you I am writing a scene involving the death of one of my characters, for example, I have not really told you very much. (Our response to the death of Cordelia in *King Lear* is vastly different from our response to the death of the third corpse in an Agatha Christie mystery or the death of the giant in *Jack and the Beanstalk*.) It is the structure I give to my story that will, I hope, reveal the meaning of that death and determine whether the reader will view it with pity and terror, with deep compassion, with relief, or triumph or dismay or merely with an intellectual curiosity about "whodunit."

Thus the power of any story depends upon two things: upon the nature of the writer's vision (whether he sees certain things with more clarity, with a newness, with a depth or breadth beyond the ordinary) and upon his skill in structuring the story so that the reader will share that vision, will see the events in the same way and thus respond to them as the writer did in the creative impulse that evoked the story.

A number of technical skills are involved in the success of that sharing—the selection of descriptive detail, the ability to write dialogue that enables the reader to hear the characters come alive in dramatic scenes, the sense of how much weight to give to different aspects of the story in order to prepare the reader for the climactic insight, and so on. But one of the more important technical skills that I think writers need constantly to experiment with and think about is the use of "perspective"—the question of where you would like your reader to stand to view the events of the story.

Perspective is a common enough term in art classes, even for the very young. I think I was in sixth grade when I first learned some of the techniques of perspective in drawing. It was like a new toy. I filled page after page with telephone poles disappearing into the distance, cups and plates and glasses seen from various angles of vision, or scenes of city street corners, all the lines of the many-storied buildings converging on the horizon at the edges of my paper.

It was then, I suppose, that I first became dimly aware of the difference between "seeing" and "knowing." I *knew* that the top of the cup was a round circle; yet if I placed the cup on the table, a foot or so in front of me, I *saw* the opening as an elipse. The only way I could make my seeing and my knowing come together was to stand over the cup and look directly into it, but then, if I drew what I saw, no one could recognize it as a cup. It looked more like the beginning of a cartoon profile, the handle/nose jutting jauntily into space.

Nowadays I use this example when one of my more literal-minded friends tries to convince me that fiction is not true. I try to explain that often the only way I can make her see the same truth that I see is to create an image that she can look at and respond to, rather than to present her with some abstraction, a statistic or a measurement, that she would call a "fact."

It was long after the sixth grade that I learned that *perspective* comes from the Latin meaning "to see through." That delighted me, as discovering the origin of a word often delights me, and it also evoked images of ways and instruments of "seeing through"— windows and skylights, microscopes and telescopes, keyholes and peepholes and fissures in walls. I began to recognize perspective as a way of helping the viewer to see more clearly and to see more certainly the reality you hope he will see. It is an instrument of focus.

I had been writing short stories for some time before I began to distinguish the questions of perspective that were involved in what I was doing. I had, of course, heard about "point of view"—those categories of first person, omniscient observer, dramatic objective, stream of consciousness, and so on. But, though textbooks and lectures described various points of view, that didn't help me understand what they were for, didn't make me realize the difference that angle and distance could make in the way events were seen in a story, just as they make a difference in the way images are seen on a sketch pad. The descriptions also seemed to imply that the "point of view" involved was the writer's, though obviously the writer, as creator, is always omniscient. It is the reader's point of view that is at issue. The question is how much the writer wants the reader to see and from what distance and at what time and through whose eyes—where he wants the reader to stand to witness the events of the story. It also seemed to me that discussions of point of view rarely discussed the fact that in fiction there is a temporal as well as a spatial dimension.

Let me explain. When we talk about point of view in fiction, we are first of all recognizing the importance of the place the reader is standing in space to view the events. (Is he inside the mind of one of the characters and what is that mind like? or is he standing godlike above the entire scene, or over to one side, away from the heart of things, emotionally uninvolved, an objective witness?) But it is equally important where the reader stands in terms of time. Are the events of the story occurring as the narrator is telling it? Did they occur in the immediate past? The distant past? What has happened in the interval between the occurrence of the events and the telling of the story? What new knowledge does the narrator or the reader have that will change his perception of the events?

The story of Cinderella becomes a radically different story, if, instead of being told at the time of the wedding ("and so they were married") with a brief nod toward the future ("and they lived happily ever after"), it is told two months after the wedding, when Cinderella has discovered the prince is as much of a tyrant as the stepmother and she has merely exchanged one form of bondage for another; or if it is told seven years after the wedding when Cinderella decides that she married the prince merely to escape an intolerable home life and it is the court musician whom she truly loves; or if it is told sixty years after the wedding, at the end of a long and rich married life, on the occasion of the funeral of the prince. If you add to these temporal variations the infinite number of spatial perspectives (the story told through the eyes of an ugly stepsister we sympathize with, for example), the variety of stories within one story becomes almost endless.

There are two aspects of perspective that seem to me particularly important to consider: the question of "distance" and the question of "multiplicity of vision."

The reader's understanding of and emotional involvement with the events of the story depend to a large extent on how close he is to them. When I taught a class in fiction writing a few years ago, I found one of the commonest errors among beginners to be a failure to bring the reader close enough. Frequently, a story would be written without a single dramatic scene to create immediacy. One always had the sense of looking at the action through the wrong end of a telescope. The reader could not hear what was being said, or see the expressions on the faces, or have an inkling of what went on inside the minds. Even the descriptions of setting were slightly out of focus. The reader could tell he was at a beach. There were sun and sand and water, but he could not see clearly enough to tell whether the beach was on the coast of Maine or the coast of Georgia or the coast of Italy.

On the other hand, much of my own experimentation with perspective grew out of a realization that something about a story wasn't working, and what wasn't working had something to do with the fact that I was having the reader stand *too close* to the center of the story. It is easy when writing about children, as I often do, to sound sentimental. It is easy when writing in the first person, as I often do, to sound rather silly if one is writing of romance or heroism or virtue. Here's an example:

"Whenever a friend of mine nods toward a couple we both know and whispers, 'I wonder what he sees in her,' I secretly rejoice in the certainty that no one has ever wondered that about Paul. It is obvious why Paul loves me. My physical beauty is evident at a glance, and at the inevitable second and third glances as well. And after only five minutes with me, total strangers are struck by my wit and intelligence and by the unusual generosity of my nature. They look at Paul with envy and awe.''

I had to experiment with distancing, occasionally by changing from the first person to an objective point of view, more often by telling the story, still in the first person, but through the eyes of a person less directly involved with the events. Often I distance with time. (We allow old people the privilege of telling their tales of valor and love, and do not think them silly, unless they are silly old people.) Sometimes I distance by tone or by the attitude of the narrator toward his part in the story. (One can play the comic hero more easily than the noble one.) Occasionally I risk the closeness by exaggerating the closeness, finding that the reader is able to accept wisdom or beauty in the narrator if the flaws and faults and foibles are also visible.

When I mention multiplicity of vision, I refer to the marvelous fact that writers can have their readers stand in more than one place to view the events. We are familiar with those classic tellings of the same story by different characters, like *Rashomon* or Lawrence Durrell's *Alexandria Quartet*. But even the familiar childhood reminiscence is of this nature; the innocence of the child's perspective is poised against the experience of the adult. My own experimentation with the double voice of the childhood reminiscence resulted in my first published story, ''Even the Devil Gets Lonesome,'' which appeared in *Redbook* some twelve years ago. In this story of the relationships of three children during a summer vacation, the events are given immediacy and life by being presented in dramatic scenes—at the moment the child is experiencing them. Yet the reader is aware that the person remembering the story is an adult and thus the reader accepts the more complex structural style, the reflective tone, the adult images and allusions.

Frequently the double voice is itself a factor in the meaning of the story, in the complexity of the way the reader views the events. There is the voice of the child (or of the innocent or inexperienced) saying, ''This is what I saw and what I felt,'' and there is the older voice, the voice of experience and knowledge, adding, ''Now I understand why it seemed so important.'' One of the most skillful and moving examples of the use of this double perspective to convey meaning is Hortense

Calisher's beautiful short story, "The Nightclub in the Woods." The main events of the story take place eighteen years before the telling of the story, but it requires those eighteen years, and the gradual "distance that seeps between people, even while they live and lie together as close as knives," to enable the narrator to understand the meaning of those events.

As writers, I suppose most of the time we are calling to our readers, "Oh, look, look. Come see." But it is not enough to call to them. We have to call them to the particular window, to find the crack in the wall for them, to create the mountain we want them to climb. For a reader to share your knowledge, he must look through the spectacles you hand him. That is what I mean by perspective.

34

USE THREEFOLD MAGIC

By Jean Z. Owen

A number of years ago I wrote a multiple-plot novelette that dealt with the problems of four women who, for one hour, were caught between floors in a department-store elevator. When I had it finished I took it to my friend.

She frowned as she read it.

"There's something not quite right about it," she told me. "The plot and characterization are sound enough, but there seems to be a lack of balance in the story that I find irritating. Perhaps you are trying to juggle too many major characters. Do you suppose you could eliminate one of them?"

I was aghast. Couldn't she see that the story needed all four of the problems if it were to say all I meant it to convey? I was positive that the deletion she suggested would ruin the story; I felt my opinion was vindicated when the story—just as it was—promptly sold to a top slick magazine, and then to television and to a number of foreign markets.

Several years went by, and I thought no more about it until the story finally appeared as an hour-long television drama. I had no part in the adaptation, and as I watched the play, I was astonished to observe that although the cast had been cut from four to three major characters, the play seemed complete and well-rounded. I went to my files and dug out the yellowing carbon of the story and read it with fresh perspective. Now—belatedly—I could perceive the lack of balance that had disturbed my critic. I recalled, too, that the magazine novelette, *A Letter to Five Wives,* had appeared on the screen as *A Letter to Three Wives,* and that *Four Secrets* had been changed to *Three Secrets.* Other motion picture titles came to mind—*The Three Faces of Eve, Three Smart Girls, Three Coins in a Fountain,* and many more.

It dawned on me, too, that I had begun to sell nonfiction pieces only after I learned that the most effective means of presenting factual material is via the classic threefold method—1) tell them what you're *going* to tell them, 2) *tell* them, 3) tell them what you *told* them.

The more I thought about it, the more convinced I became that a writer must pay attention to the Number Three. I don't know *why* this should be so. Some persons think it has a religious basis, while others point to mythology and to the Greek triads. Numerologists have their own explanation. I am inclined to suspect it may be a carry-over from our nursery-rhyme days when we learned to react emotionally to the vicissitudes of the three bears, the three little kittens, the three blind mice, the three little pigs, the three Billy Goats Gruff, the three little fishies, and Wynken, Blynken, and Nod.

I do not wish to imply, of course, that all stories can be forced into a three-sided mold. But I have found that in my own stories and in manuscripts other writers have asked me to evaluate the use of tricornered characterization frequently provides the solution to a stubborn problem of roughness or imbalance.

Once I became aware of the Number Three, I discovered that it can help a writer in many ways. Take the matter of *plants,* for instance. Just as language experts assure you that you can make any new word a permanent part of your vocabulary merely by using it three times, a triple repetition will firmly convey any information you wish your reader to retain.

Suppose, for example, that the climax of your story is going to involve the collapse of a bridge. Even a beginning writer knows that if you toss this at the reader "cold," with no preliminary build-up, you will have the word "coincidental" tossed right back at you. So you painstakingly plant the fact, early in the story, that the bridge may go down. And the best way to do it to make it seem a logical, inevitable part of the story (and a suspense-building factor, as well!) is to mention it three times, from three different viewpoints:

1) Your hero drives across the bridge and notices that it creaks and sways *dangerously* in the wind.

2) An old-timer remembers a storm of 1890 when the old bridge—sturdier, by cracky, than this newfangled flimsy one—washed away as if it had been made of matchsticks.

3) A fortuneteller warns of approaching peril; her crystal ball has revealed a glimpse of people falling into water from a collapsing structure.

This is an oversimplified example, of course. Most of the stories for today's market require less obvious repetition. A plant must be handled so subtly, so artfully, that the reader is not consciously aware of the fact that important information is being accented. The best way to find out how skillfully it can be accomplished is to read again some of the recent stories you have enjoyed. Look for the triple plants—they will be there!

The same principle holds true of characterization. If you describe Ellen, your heroine, as having *shy* brown eyes—if you have some other character mention the fact that it's a shame Ellen *can't seem to mix with people* as easily as her sister Kate—if you show Ellen *flushing with embarrassment as she makes a casual remark*—your reader will thereafter see Ellen as a quiet, retiring, indrawn young woman. If you belabor the point by excessive use of such phrases as "she said timidly" and "she glanced up shyly," the story will seem overdrawn and amateurish. Merely make certain that everything Ellen *says* and *does* and *feels* lies within the framework of a timid personality; your reader will automatically supply most of the stage directions far more effectively than you could possibly depict them.

Another area in which Number Three can help you is in smoothing out jarring sentences and rough paragraphs. There is a natural, euphonic cadence to three modifying words or three descriptive phrases that makes for a smooth, even flow. See what happens if you try adding to, or taking away from these examples: *Blood, sweat, and tears. Of the people, by the people, for the people. Three cheers for the red, white, and blue. Bell, book, and candle. Tom, Dick, and Harry. Morning, noon, and night. Tall, dark, and handsome. Love, honor, and cherish. Healthy, wealthy, and wise. We're having fun-fun-fun! See no evil, hear no evil, speak no evil. Faith, hope, and charity. Gold, frankincense, and myrrh.*

Very likely you have been utilizing three-word or three-phrase descriptions without realizing it. Just for fun sometime, hunt up the rough copy of one of your old stories—or, for that matter, take a look at the story or article you are working on right now. Find one of the paragraphs that sounded uneven, harsh, and amateurish as you first wrote it. So you wrote it again . . . and again and again. And finally, after switching sentences around, putting a phrase in here, pulling a word out there, you could get on with the story, secure in the knowledge that the difficult portion now has a polished "feel" to it. Look at it again; I'll give you odds that you'll discover much of the smoothness resulted primarily from using sequences of three words or three phrases.

(Notice the above paragraph. *Uneven, harsh, and amateurish. Again . . . and again and again. Switching . . . putting . . . pulling.*)

Perhaps the greatest asset Number Three gives a story is a natural, built-in suspense mechanism, free for the writer's taking, simply because in our culture we are geared to react with an automatic "This is *it*" feeling when we reach number three. Three strikes and you're out. One-two-three-*go!* The third time's the charm. Three on a match and evil will befall. Trouble comes in threes. A *three*-time loser is sentenced to life imprisonment.

When we wanted to prove to the world that our space program was something to be reckoned with, we sent John Glenn around for three orbits. Playgoers sit contentedly through Acts I and II, knowing that Act III will give them the same kind of emotional payoff that kindergarten children expect from the *third* wish the fairy queen has granted the poor woodcutter. And next time someone says to you, "Have you heard the one about—?" I'll give you odds that the punch line of the joke will directly follow two build-up lines.

For a writer, the awareness of the fact that the reader's *feeling of expectation* will automatically reach its highest pitch at the third climax of the story is like knowing that one's house is electrically wired. When the occasion calls for it, all you need to do is to plug in your story and the vitalizing current goes to work for you.

Again—an oversimplified example: Your hero wants to get the girl; he tries—and fails. He tries another approach—and fails again, more abjectly than before. So, from the depths, he rises to make a third attempt and *this* time . . . ! If he were successful on the second attempt, it would give the reader the same thudding sensation you get when you lift your foot to step up, only to find you've already reached the top of the stairs. Success on the *fourth* effort is very likely to make the reader bored and impatient. Three—and *only* three—climaxes give the reader his expected quota of emotional impact.

To those of you who protest, "But that's *formula* and I thought formula stories were *out!*", I can only refer you to the best of the non-formula stories that are being printed. For although *story formula* may be discarded, *story form* remains constant, and any fiction, whatever its type, is only as good as the emotional response it draws from the reader. If you will study the markets you will observe that the one-two-three-*payoff* principle works just as strongly in the artistic as it does in the strictly commercial story. The difference lies only in the subtlety of its presentation.

Why is Number Three so important? I haven't the faintest idea. I don't understand the principle of electrical refrigeration, either, but a few moments ago, as the California sun beat down on our house, I pushed the button that turns on our air conditioner—and I strongly suspect that the breezes now wafting through my study are just as cool as they would be if I had a degree in electrical engineering.

Think about Number Three. Note how often it appears in our culture—how frequently it is reflected in the work of writers you would like to emulate. It's only a minor bit of technique, perhaps—but for the writer who seriously seeks to perfect his craftsmanship it can be another tool that can help him create effectively.

35

ROUTINES AND RULES FOR THE
POLICE PROCEDURAL

By Lillian O'Donnell

Why a police procedural? Because the cops are the pros. That's why.

We live in an age of professionalism. To be an an amateur denotes incompetence. Crime is rampant in our society; whether it is organized with the soulless efficiency of a major corporation or random, spontaneous violence, it has become arrogant. It doesn't hide. It walks boldly and openly down our streets, performs its bestialities in daylight before the horrified gaze of a so-called law-abiding citizenry too terrified to lift a hand. The amateur sleuth, no matter how talented, hasn't got a chance against it. The private detective doesn't have the tools. It takes ten, twenty, fifty police officers to shake down a neighborhood for the mosaic bits that, pieced together, make up a single clue in a case of homicide or a big heist. They are backed up by a network of experts in ballistics, fingerprinting, photography, explosives. Forensic medicine is no longer a matter of a few test tubes and a Bunsen burner. Blood tests, body secretion tests, voice spectography require sophisticated lab equipment running into the thousands and hundreds of thousands of dollars.

So unless you want to write a mystery about a murder committed during a house party snowbound in the mountains, or on an island with the ferry service knocked out, your hero, if he's going to have any legitimate chance of solving the crime, had better be a pro. In other words—a cop.

He could be a retired cop, of course; or have a friend, a very close friend, in the department, but if you ask me, that's a cop-out.

Even though your hero is a working cop, does that mean you have to write a procedural? Procedurals can be dull, and their heroes even duller. Think back and try to recall a hero of a police procedural. Pretty hard, isn't it? Heroes of procedurals tend to merge into their own background.

Now try to recall protagonists of the other kind of mystery fiction. One after another, they leap to the mind along with all their glorious idiosyncracies: Sherlock Holmes—a dozen titillating characteristics instantly occur; Hercule Poirot—he becomes so real that his death was reported on the front page of *The New York Times* (we should all create such a character!); Nero Wolfe—with his orchids, his rigid routine, his gourmet taste buds. The average person in the street would recognize them instantly and knows more about them than he does about his next-door neighbor. But does he remember any of the cases with which these distinctive characters were associated? Do you? Probably some will come to mind if you think hard enough, because the writers backed up their creations with good, strong plot material, but it's the central figure that makes the whole memorable.

In the end it's the character that counts. But you can't put Lord Peter Wimsey or Miss Marple into a squad room. Then how are you going to make your police officer exciting? Well, you start out by making him real.

If the officer is human, if the reader recognizes him (or her) as a person, and he deals with the situations that confront him according to his own nature, the excitement is bound to follow. All of us, no matter what our jobs or professions, are involved with the "business" of living. We spend eight hours working and eight hours sleeping, but how about the other eight? One hour to get up, wash, grab breakfast before going to work. Half an hour to get there? The same at the other end of the day. A couple of hours for lunch and dinner. That's five out of the precious eight, and we haven't even mentioned doing the laundry, going for the papers, paying the bills. A detective, no matter how dedicated, is chained to that routine like the rest of us. Remembering that is a start toward making him or her real. What he does with the leftover two to three hours—read a book, go jogging, make love—will serve to individualize him.

There's no doubt that the major segment of everyone's day is the eight-hour working period, and of course it's the eight hours the professional detective spends doing the job of tracking down criminals that you're mainly concerned with. Is he doing it by the book? Then you'd better know what that entails. It entails procedure. Crimes are solved by routine. The TV shows skip the long hours spent on a stakeout and depict only the drama of the final minutes. You can, too, of course. Maybe your hero is a maverick, a Serpico? He ignores procedure; he flouts authority. As a writer, you have to know the rules before you dare turn your back on them. On the other hand, are readers really interested in the details of arraignment, say? Do they care about the searching, mugging, fingerprinting, etc., of a suspect? Yes, if you tell them the suspect's reaction to the humiliation of it. Yes, if you tell them how the arresting officer feels about it. Yes, if you care. And if you get the details right, you may surprise yourself and find that you do care—very much. Then the fascination of the procedural begins.

All good mysteries are rooted within the frame of their own time. Consider the history of the mystery story from Wilkie Collins's *The Moonstone* and Edgar Allan Poe's "The Murders in the Rue Morgue" through to the present: It is evident that the mystery not only "holds the mirror up to nature," but to its period as well as any good work of so-called legitimate fiction. How much more a police procedural! This is not the place to go into the history of law enforcement, but it doesn't take a student of the subject to appreciate how far we've come since the birth of the Sûreté in 1810; the thief-takers and Bow Street runners that were the antecedents of New Scotland Yard; our own Pinkerton national detective agency (motto, "We Never Sleep") to our present highly complex and much diversified law enforcement agencies.

To begin with, police departments are not uniform. Procedures vary from city to city; we won't even get into what they are in the small towns and villages. Police officers work around the clock; that would at least seem a safe assumption. It is. The duty is divided into three shifts: eight A.M. to four P.M.; four P.M. to midnight, and midnight to eight A.M. But in some cities, the officer works the same shift permanently. In others, he changes every few months. In New York the "swing" is every week. New York policemen like it that way. Different methods are espoused by different cities. For instance, I read just the other day that Los Angeles has a Hypnosis Squad. It has been found that under hypnosis a witness can often be helped to remember details of a crime that in his conscious condition he is not even aware of knowing. "Mesmerizing a consenting witness" the *Time*

Magazine article called it. Last year fourteen L.A.P.D. officers were trained in the technique. It is the only such squad in the country. If your story is laid in New York, don't have a Hypnosis Squad on it.

Watch the changes. The major procedural change and one which has affected every law enforcement agency in the nation is the "Miranda warning."* Almost everyone is familiar with it and takes it for granted, but not so long ago it was a shocking innovation.

It's the local changes that are the tricky ones. I don't know about the other police departments because I find my hands quite full enough with the New York Police Department. There has been lately and continues to be a drastic reconstruction in the department in New York, particularly in the detective division. Detectives used to work out of the precinct on every type of crime. If a homicide occurred, someone came from Homicide North or South, moved into the precinct, and worked with the local officer. No more. Now there is only a token force of detectives in each precinct; the majority has been divided into specialized squads: Homicide and Assault, Burglary and Pickpocket; Organized Crime Control; Tactical Patrol Force; and on and on. Only a skeleton crew of detectives now work the graveyard shift, on the theory that little investigative work can be done during that period and only a few men are required to answer the actual calls.

With the city's financial problems, the department is trying hard to cut down on overtime. This has resulted in the "pass along" system. It's exactly what the name suggests. It used to be that when a detective working on a case got a hot lead he continued on with it despite the fact that his tour of duty was over. No more. Now the detective "passes along" the information he has garnered to the officer on the next shift. He follows up. Most officers deplore the procedure, and since I have a high admiration for New York policemen on the whole, I believe their dislike is not merely on account of the loss of the extra pay but because the second detective perforce doesn't have the same

---

*Basically, the *Miranda warning* is a statement of a person's rights with regard to interrogation by police. The police officer is required to recite these rights to the suspect *always* when placing him under arrest; when the suspect is in custody, in the station house or the squad car: that the subject has the right to remain silent; that he is entitled to consult a lawyer, and if he cannot afford a lawyer, one will be provided for him free of charge. Also of importance in the warning is that if the suspect does answer questions, what he says can and will be used against him in court.—*Ed.*

feel or instinct for the case, and has priorities of his own as well. Something is lost in the transfer. Not only are momentum and "feel" lost, but also a sense of responsibility for the case and a pride of accomplishment in solving it. The detective is reduced from being a skilled artisan to being a person on the assembly line.

Watch this kind of change. Keep up to date. Make sure that if you talk about the D.A.'s Homicide Bureau, it still exists. Has the Special Division Unit which includes the helicopter squad and the mounted patrol been phased out? Don't send anyone up in a 'copter till you make sure.

In my own instance, I started with a pro—Lieutenant James Felix of Homicide North (that gives you an idea how far back I go). All I wanted was for him to know his job, but police detectives don't work alone. Jim Felix had men and women under him and above him. They began to take shape. I began to know them and like them. Each one in turn had his or her book, but "the lieut" remained throughout in major or minor capacity as required. I chose the detective to fit the crime. My novel, *The Face of the Crime,* dealt with the murder of a movie star trying for a comeback. My detective was a recent recruit, young, impressionable, and half in love with the dead actress. When I became personally incensed over the epidemic of obscene telephone calls to lonely women, I decided that the story begged for the empathy of a woman to investigate, and Norah Mulcahaney appeared.

Norah came as a rookie working out of the women's pool. That was in *The Phone Calls*—five years and five books ago. The women's pool has long since been abolished and women officers now work out of the precinct like the men. In my *Don't Wear Your Wedding Ring,* Norah made detective and worked out of Homicide North. Now she works out of Assault and Homicide, Fourth Division, headquarters on West 82nd Street. In *Leisure Dying,* she's a sergeant forming and heading her own Senior Citizens Squad. Such a unit is operating in the Bronx and was specifically singled out for praise by the Mayor.

The ground rules may seem a maze, rigid and confining, but I find them stimulating. How much can you tamper with them? How much leeway can you give yourself? Well, as far as I know, there are no female detectives working Homicide. Only Norah. So far.

I expect reality to catch up with the fiction any day.

As of early 1978, every area of the Detective Division of New York City has women assigned to it.

36

TOUCHING THE HEART OF YOUR READER

By Catherine Cookson

IF YOU have it in mind to enter this trade of writing there are one or two precautions you must take. You must first of all make up your mind to turn deaf ears to all those well-wishers who tell you that the markets are swamped already and that there isn't a hope in hell for newcomers; or that—take their word for it—there's no money in this game. Far better settle for a steady wage and pension.

Then, they will warn you that if you are foolhardy enough to want to suffer and you send your efforts to one of "those" agents, he'll take ten per cent of any advance royalties you are likely to receive. But, if you should ever manage to get into the paperback racket, your hardbound publisher will nab fifty per cent without blinking. And when finally they remind you with relish of what the tax man will take off the remainder, you must smile, just smile, that's all.

Oh, and I mustn't forget to tell you about the frustrated writer who'll inform you that, having received forty rejection slips in one year (and mind you, the stories were first-class; all his family and friends said so), he gave up writing . . . It was either that or suicide.

Finally, finally, steel yourself to look that other dear friend straight in the eye when he casually remarks that without a suitable education, by which he means university, your chance of landing on the literary planet is on a par with that of your being selected to orbit the moon. . . .

Early in my career, one of my manuscripts was returned without a covering letter, but written across the back page in red ink were the words: "Strongly advise author not to take up writing as a career." I cried my eyes out and stopped writing for a fortnight.

Then I said to myself, "What do they know? They have never lived in the northeast of England; they don't know that when I was a girl I was surrounded by famous characters. Why, there was a famous character in every house in our street." At that time, most of these characters would have been on the dole, and all the cupboards very often bare, but yet, for me, every household held a famous character.

Then there were the tragedies that occurred in each house, and the humor that helped to overcome them; and the neighborliness, and the spite and vindictiveness, and the narrowness, and the bigotry. But above all, there was the hope—the hope that something would turn up; the hope that, come the New Year, things would be brighter; the hope that their babies would never have to experience the same hardships they did, the hope that one in the family might even go to "college," better still, go to America and make his fortune.

I left the northeast of England when I was twenty-two. I took only one suitcase with me, but a great deal of mental luggage. Into my subconscious, I had packed all those important people. And there they stayed until I was forty years old, when my world exploded in a breakdown and out they poured, and their emergence wiped off the map all the refined, gentlemanly characters on whom I had wasted years.

In my early twenties when I was striving to educate myself, I had taken for my mentor Lord Chesterfield, through his *Letters to his Son,* and naturally he influenced my writing. This was a big mistake, for what knowledge, real knowledge, had I of 18th century ladies and gentlemen, so called? It wasn't until I realized that I had brought with me from my early environment all the material I would ever need for my stories that I wrote my first novel—and real story, and so came into my own.

There are clever people who can read a bit of history, look up a few maps, then write a knowledgeable story around the data. But there is so often something lacking in such writing. If you want to touch the heart of a reader, and I think this should be the aim of the writer, then write about the kind of people you know from the inside, whether your acquaintance with them was in the slums, in the middle class, or in a stately home, because then, and only then, will you get heart into your work. And that is what the reader wants, that is what holds the reader, that is what makes one reader say to another those beautiful words: "I couldn't put it down."

Some writers bamboozle you with highfalutin screed, as do some reviewers with their reviews on what they consider the writer intended to convey, and in the main what they both succeed in doing is to irritate the reader. It is what I call ego-writing, for both writer and reviewer have enjoyed expressing themselves.

Until you have tried it, you will not believe that the simplest language is the hardest to write.

After all, what are we writing about? Mostly two things, a male and a female, and how they react on each other in their set environment. It is my belief that it isn't the human being acting on the environment that makes the story; it is the environment acting on the human being.

Take a man and a woman into an operating room and cut them up. Whether they be black, brown, or yellow, apart from slight differences in height and breadth or because of deformities, the bone structure, the muscle pattern, the brain size of all males will be similar, and so will those of the females. Now go back in time and take two males, identical twins. Separate them, sending one to be reared in the slums of a big city, the other into the well-ordered routine and luxury of a mansion set in an estate. Jump twenty years, then look them up. One has had all the opportunities in life, the other none. All right, the very fact of his having the background of the slums might be the urge for him to strive to get out of it and to do something with his life. Here, heredity might be playing a part, telling him that he's a misfit; yet, should he achieve success, say become a millionaire, as has happened, will he be able to forget his early environment? No, never.

This early environment is the most important thing in a man's life. No matter what happens in the after years, this sticks with him. He may be able to obliterate it for a while, but as the years mount up it will return, until, in his old age, sitting in his mansion, he is back mentally in the slums.

Equally, the other twin, although brought up in luxury, might just as conceivably be ending his days in poverty; or, if we don't want to fall as low as that, in mediocre living. And with time to think. What is he thinking about? Again, mostly of his early environment.

To my mind it is the environment that is the important factor in the story. Set your environment, and the characters will fit into it.

In the course of writing each book—after some initial uneasiness —I have a feeling of deep involvement, deep excitement. And always this:

Every character in the story becomes real to me; there they all are, moving about in my head, and if I show one acting out of character in relation to his environment, he rebels. Just before I finish the book, I get worked up, tense, wondering how it is going to turn out. Will others see it as I see it?

At one time, I used to think that what I was about to produce was, if not unique, then entirely original. I imagined that nobody else could have thought up such a plot, such experiences, such characters, but in writing subsequent novels, I learned my mistake. I know now that very likely at the precise moment I get this brilliant idea for a new story, there are perhaps a dozen other writers thinking along the same lines.

This was proved to me some years ago when I thought I would write a story about a dustman, a South Shields dustman. I wrote my novel, and the week it was published so was another book about another dustman. The only difference was that my dustman was inarticulate, while the other was a man who could discourse on theories of this, that, and the other. And yet both stories grew from a similar idea.

I no longer worry that this kind of thing will happen, for I have learned that it is how one deals with the idea that counts. The beginnings may be very much alike, but the development and final form of each novel are different.

There was another thing I had to come to grips with, and that was being dubbed a regional novelist. When this term was first applied to me, I didn't like it. It was no consolation to know that Hardy, Bennett, and others had the same tag. I thought, I can write about any place I put my mind to—just give me the idea, and I'll be away. I was proved wrong, and it happened in this way.

I was coming down the High Street when I was accosted by a lady. I had never seen her before, nor have I seen her since, but she came at me, finger pointing, and in what would be called a stage duchess voice she said, "Mrs. Cookson, the regional novelist! Ha! I've read your books, but I've been made to wonder why you must always write about the northeast of England. Can't you write about any other place? You reside in Hastings—can't you write a story about this town? There are so many wonderful things that have happened here. There was the discovery of the caves, the smugglers, not forgetting 1066. Can't you write about any other place but the northeast?"

It's funny how you can come to hate somebody in two minutes dead flat.

Nevertheless, I determined to show that lady. . . . I would write a story about Hastings, and I would center it around the fishing fleet. And so I did my homework, and one day I started my story on Hastings. Six months later I stopped writing my book on Hastings because I knew, I knew that the only thing in that story that had any guts was the fish.

It was then I recognized that what they said was true: Like it or not, I was a regional writer.

I have written over fifty books and have acquired a certain technique. I have learned, and I'm still learning my craft, but I don't think I would have got as far as this had I not done a brave thing, in fact the only consciously brave thing I've done in my life.

It concerns my second novel. This book took a year to write in longhand, and the publisher accepted it, but in his letter to me he said these words: "It isn't as good as your first, but we'll do the best we can with it for you."

The best they could with it for me!

I sat down and did some hard thinking. I was forty-two years of age. I had arrived where I was under my own steam, I knew no one in the literary world—still don't; the only help I'd ever had had been from my husband. This sentence of the publishers had a touch of condescension about it: they were going to do the best they could for something of an inferior quality which I had landed them with. Well, was I going to let it go through?"

In blood I wrote to them, saying, "Send it back."

And again I cried my eyes out.

But from then on I determined that each book I wrote—and I

was going to write dozens, God sparing me—must in some way be an improvement on the one before, whether it be in construction, humor, the portrayal of reality, or, I should like to add, homespun philosophy.

I don't mind admitting now that I have eight similar rejects up in the attic; three the result of my having fallen between two stools. This can happen when you are also writing under a pseudonym, as I have done. The work I do under my own name I consider novels, as opposed to the romances I do under my pseudonym, Catherine Marchant.

I'm often asked, "How do you write? Have you set times? How do you get your plots? What sparks off the first idea?" Well, as to how I write, I now dictate my stories onto tape. This came about after I developed a frozen shoulder, caused through years of scribbling every spare minute of the day, and often far into the night. I have never had a set time for writing, and I am of the firm belief that writers, especially beginners, should make a practice of writing some part of every day, if it's only one sentence.

The germ of a story is often dug up from my subconscious. My mind is like an incubator; everything I've put into it has hatched. A small incident that happened in my youth might reveal itself, but clothed now in the slumbered growth of years; and here I will have the nucleus of another story.

One thing I am no good at, and that is doing a synopsis. If I were to show an editor a synopsis of any story of mine, I'm sure he would say there was nothing in it. And so I rarely write down anything, except names, ages, and dates. When I have gathered all the characters together, I take them to the pictures. This can happen in the middle of the night, when I see everything in film form. I play all the parts, I talk all the dialogue. By the time I get the characters onto the tape, the story line may have changed somewhat but the substance is there. My Catherine Cookson stories develop from environment and character, not from plot. Not so my Catherine Marchant romances.

I like to get down a story while it is, as I call it, hot, everything vibrating inside me. I sometimes sit for as long as six to eight hours at the tape, stopping only for coffee or a snack. As the tapes are finished, my secretary takes them down in the rough.

The telling of the story is pleasure; what follows is grind. I might go through the rough, correcting it, four times before it again goes to my secretary. When she finally brings it back to me, pure and unsullied, I let it lie for a few days, and then I start on it again. If I have to alter more than two or three words on a page, I have that page retyped. And at this stage I can return as many as a hundred pages. I know that a clean script won't help a bad story, but I've heard of untidy scripts causing editors to overlook a good one.

Have I said anything that might be of help to a new writer? I don't know. All I know is if you want to write, you'll write.

37

WRITING FROM RESEARCH

By David Westheimer

For many years, George Williams, a professor of English at Rice University, would tell his student writers, "Write about what you know."

I was one of those students thirty-seven years ago, and I still think his advice was excellent, certainly for beginning writers. A new writer has enough problems grappling with a project as large as a novel, without suffering the labor and insecurity of working with unfamiliar material. It is so much simpler to draw the material from your own background and ideas and concentrate on getting your characters developed and your story told.

But, if you have a theme so compelling to you that you simply must develop it in a novel, and that theme requires research, then research you must. If Margaret Mitchell had been put off by the amount of research necessary to do a book set in the Civil War era, we would not have *Gone with the Wind*.

Even if you are writing about what you know, it may still require a certain amount of research. My first novel, *Summer on the Water*, was set in an area I knew well, the little bayshore communities not far from Houston, Texas. But I realized I did not know enough about this setting to capture it fully in fiction. I went to some of the places I thought I knew well to refresh my memory. I looked at things through the eyes of a prospective novelist rather than of a casual visitor and discovered much that was significant in the light of fiction but which I had overlooked when I was visiting for recreation. This was research in every sense, even though this setting was one I had known since childhood. (I even looked at the area from the air, but how many fledgling writers have a brother-in-law who is a licensed private pilot and will take them up for nothing?)

You're writing something based on your own youth or childhood and set right in your own hometown, and what do you need with research? Can you really remember what was on the corner of Travis and Lamar fifteen or twenty years ago, or what an ice cream cone or a pair of Keds cost then, or what the hit song was in July of a certain year? Such little details may be useful to your story, and you'll have to look them up somewhere. That's research. If you haven't realized such little details are useful, think about it now. Ordinary facts such as those can contribute a strong sense of place and time and often react with the personal recollections of the reader to enhance the effect of your narrative.

I've mentioned two major disadvantages of writing from research —the amount of work and time involved and the insecurity of dealing with unfamiliar material. There are also advantages: You broaden your range of subject matter, you have the use of material with which to enrich your narrative, and you engage your reader's interest in what you have to say apart from, and in addition to, the story you're telling. You learn things from your research, and your reader learns them from your novel—the reader unaware and painlessly so if you use your material correctly.

Where do you find research materials? The most accessible and, unless you live in a small town, richest source is usually the public library. It has shelf after shelf of books all indexed by subject, one of which may be yours. It has encyclopedias and reference works, bound magazines and journals, often files of major newspapers. When you do research from a book, be sure to check the bibliography. It almost invariably will lead you to other works on your subject or related ones. Do not overlook the periodical files. Periodicals publish a lot of material that never finds its way into hardcovers. Periodicals, too, have subject-matter indexes.

If you live in a university town, get to know its school library. On some subjects a university library may have better research sources than the public library. If non-students are not permitted access to the stacks, it is likely you may be able to get a library card by paying a small annual fee.

Newspaper files are invaluable sources of the details of daily life and of history in the making. If the library does not have bound files of back issues, your local paper should at least have its own files. The repository of a newspaper's files was once called the morgue. Now I think it's called the library. By either name, it is usually open to the average citizen and almost certainly to a writer doing research. Just tell the librarian who you are and why you want to use the files, and you'll have no problem. Nowadays the back issues are generally on microfilm. The library will have a microfilm reader. If you don't know how to operate the machine, the librarian will show you. Never, never clip anything from a paper's bound files.

The Library of Congress and the National Archives in Washington have, of course, an immense range of books, photographs, and documents. You can get a certain amount of information by mail, including some microfilm or page copies, but really to dig into their resources, it's better to go there.

You can get information on a lot of different subjects from government agencies. Some of it is free. Some pamphlets and brochures may require a small fee. You can get long lists of available publications, including expensive hardcover books, from the Government Printing Office, Washington, D.C. 20402. Or you can write a specific department of government, say Defense, Interior or Agriculture, for information in their purview.

You can get information from industry. Want to know how an oil refinery operates? Write the public relations department of any major oil company. If you're persuasive enough and/or they're on the ball enough, you'll get an answer. This is generally true of any firm large enough to employ a public relations staff or have a company library.

There's information to be had from your local government and business firms, as well. The Chamber of Commerce is often a good place to begin a search for information. The local police department and crime lab can fill you in on crime and punishment; someone in the mayor's office can tell you how a city is run or where to find out exactly what happens after a fire alarm goes off.

People are an inexhaustible source of information. People with special knowledge, such as college professors, old-timers or your family doctor, or people in trades who can tell you how to repair or sabotage a truck, build a house or dig a well. (I made extensive use of truckers and mechanics in research for my last novel, *The Olmec Head*.) Don't be afraid to ask. They can only say no but will usually say yes when they learn you're writing a book. For *The Olmec Head*, among the many things I learned from truckers were fuel consumption, fuel capacities, load limits, cruising speeds, descriptions of equipment, truckers' jargon. A dispatcher who helped me told me that the load I was hauling would put the gross weight over the Texas limit of 78,000 pounds if transported by the usual tractor-trailer rig. But, he added, if I used a "ragtop" trailer, it would get the weight down below the maximum allowed. So I used that little detail in the novel: "That means our rig can't weigh more than thirty thousand pounds empty," Bell said. "The people renting it to you can tell you the weight. Get a ragtop trailer. That's one with a fabric cover instead of a solid top. It's lighter." (*The Olmec Head*, p. 235.)

As the above demonstrates, some informants may get involved in your project and volunteer information you did not have enough knowledge of the subject to ask about. (The mechanic who told me what could cause a diesel truck to run poorly without actually stopping it, later told me after reading the book I could have done a much better job than I did in switching a heavy load from one truck to another.)

As for researching a physical setting, the best thing to do is visit the area, study it, take pictures to use later to refresh your memory. If you can't get there, you'll have to read about it. For foreign locations, travel agencies, tourist bureaus and consulates can usually provide illustrated brochures. I used a lot of such materials for areas of Italy I did not know in writing *Von Ryan's Express*. One of the travel brochures I got from the Italian consulate mentioned the fact that a spire in Modena was visible for many miles. In the novel, the train bearing Colonel Ryan and his fellow POWs was approaching Modena at dawn. This is how I used that bit of seemingly insignificant information in the book. Ryan had to finish killing off the German guards before they reached the next town. He was not sure just when that would be. And then, "Far up ahead a slender column glistened like a white thread dangling from the rim of the sky." Ryan now knew they were getting close to Modena.

How much research do you do? For something based on your own background, probably not much. Just enough to confirm your recollections or to provide information you could not have known about. That big fire downtown was in 1953, not 1954. The President of the United States came to your town in 1948, but you didn't know that because at the time you were too young to be aware of it. Or one of your characters works in a bottling plant. You've never been in a bottling plant. Now is the time to visit one.

For work, based chiefly on research, a historical novel, for example, or a story about prospecting for gold in Brazil when you haven't even any gold in your teeth and have never been farther than the county seat, of course you must do a whole lot of research. Just remember to steep yourself in it, not drown yourself. Some writers get so involved in their subject that they research endlessly and never do get around to writing the book. Or they wear themselves out with the research and haven't the energy or will to do any writing. Either way, the book never gets written. Also, there is a tendency to continue the research beyond the point where you have enough material, simply because you feel too insecure about actually writing the book. You have to start writing, insecurities and all. If you find you don't know enough about your subject after all and were right to feel insecure, call a brief halt to your writing and do some more research. Now, however, you may find you know exactly what information you lack and can go directly to a source instead of following a lot of blind trails.

Never let research become an excuse not to sit down and write instead of a means to an end. I know "writers" who are not only unpublished but also unwritten because of that.

When you've got all this research material, how do you use it? *Sparingly*. Don't give your reader gobs of undigested information, or even crumbs of facts, merely for the sake of using something you're pleased with yourself for having learned. Your research material should enhance the narrative, or make it move, or make it more real, or reveal something about your characters and their times or life styles. Often a few significant details will suffice to establish an entire era or place or way of life.

By selecting your details carefully you can avoid bogging your story down and telling your reader more than he wants to know, and you can still create the illusion that you know everything worth knowing about your subject.

I once read an otherwise good novel about a World War II bomber pilot by a man who knew nothing of pilots or bombers except what he had learned from research. Which was a great deal—and which he found it necessary to share. He told everything he had learned about how to run through the checklist, start the engines, taxi, take off and get into formation. And it was dull, dull, dull, stopping his story in its tracks. A writer more discriminating in his use of research material would have mentioned only the most significant details of the procedures, those the reader might be expected to find interesting, and written a much shorter and far more exciting scene.

What I wish to stress is, do not use material just because you know it, or because it was so much trouble to obtain. In writing *Lighter Than a Feather,* a novel about what might have happened if the U.S. had invaded Japan instead of using the atom bomb, I sometimes spent weeks trying to obtain documents I'd heard about, and then when I had them, I realized there was nothing in them worth using in the story. When this happens, there is a tendency to force some of the material into your story just because it was hard to come by. It is a tendency that must be resisted.

Naturally, there was an enormous amount of information I could use in the many U.S. and Japanese documents I amassed in my *Feather* research. Tides and weather conditions in the invasion areas on specific dates, for example, and the location and composition of U.S. and Japanese units, descriptions of U.S. and Japanese tanks and weapons, the training of Japanese civilian "volunteer" forces, the way Japanese soldiers addressed their superiors, what Japanese soldiers ate, why Japanese soldiers did not surrender, how much Japanese soldiers of all ranks were paid. These are but a few samples chosen at random. I used literally thousands of bits of information because *Feather* depended so heavily on research. To sum up:

Try to write about what you know.

If you must write on subjects or backgrounds you don't know, do your homework thoroughly and utilize all available sources.

Don't spend so much time and energy on research that you never get around to writing your novel.

Use your material sparingly; don't smother your reader or your novel with masses of raw information.

Try for the significant detail, the one that will engage the reader's interest, add to your story and give the impression you could say a great deal more on the subject if you wished.

38

MULTIPLY BY TWO

By Doris Betts

In my story-writing classes, I can almost predict the content of a first student story. Paragraph one will describe the morning sky, and establish the weather through ten adjectives and adverbs about the condition of that firmament. In paragraph two, we will see the exterior of some building, then pan like a slow camera through an upstairs window and focus on a ringing alarm clock. A hand will reach from under the covers and turn off the jangle. Note that a *hand* will do this. In amateur stories whole human beings rarely function, but disembodied hands, feet, and eyes swarm in midair like insects.

Now a man will get slowly out of bed, and for several long sentences his left foot and then his right foot will carry him into the bathroom where we will have some mention of the "cool tile." As he examines himself in the mirror, the reader will receive his physical appearance plus his full narrated biography, and while *hands* shave his *face,* will be introduced also to his sad memories and sensitive thoughts. By page four, shaven, he will walk to his bedroom window, examine that familiar sky, and will think one profound page, gradually getting around to some dilemma, which will then be explored by flashback. If he happens to own a dog, things get worse. He will explain that dilemma to Fido in lengthy speeches. Fido will wag his tail sympathetically, and so forth.

When I complain to students that nothing is really happening, they are artistically outraged. "Aha! You want me to write pulp plot stories!" To the contrary, my interest is in the literary story which has descended from Chekhov, Joyce, Mansfield, Hemingway, and Katherine Anne Porter. Here, as in *True Confessions,* a story is about meaningful events. Distinctions of "good" and "bad" applied to literary or slick stories are not very useful. It works better to talk about simple or complex stories, in the same way one describes simple or complex biological organisms. The mockingbird, for example, is simply doing more things with life than the amoeba is able to do.

Once that old bugaboo is out of the way, we can direct attention to the material in this typical amateur beginning for a short story. What is taking place? If the reader closes his eyes to visualize events, he will be able to see no more than a turned-off alarm clock and some short whiskers. The writer's clue may lie in the verbs he has chosen to use. In a static, nothing-happening story, these are usually forms of *to be* (he *was*) or weak verbs in which action is either minimal or boring. (He looked, walked, glanced, put, smiled, frowned, thought, remembered, saw, turned, etc.) A character alone, thinking, is not a visualized event, but only a snapshot of a still-featured man lost in thought, raising his eyebrows occasionally. And unless the character is as complex as Hamlet, the writer had better avoid soliloquies.

This is what led us to the dictum for beginning fiction writers: Multiply by two. Start the story with two people on the scene, or bring in a second character before more than five sentences have elapsed. Yes, this produces at first a great many "There-was-a-knock-on-the-door" stories, but at least we are into the area of conflict and interaction, and subtlety will come.

Anyone interested in writing fiction will benefit by reading a book published in the late twenties but still appropriate, *Aspects of the Novel*, by E. M. Forster. Here, Forster points out that there are only five universal human experiences. All men are born, but this is hearsay experience. We do not remember it ourselves, and doctors and mothers must tell us about it secondhand. All men must die, but we have not experienced this yet and can only anticipate its mystery. The corpse has left us no direct testimony. All men sleep about eight hours a day, but although Freud has given us insight into dreaming, there is a limited amount of fiction spent on the act of sleep itself. All men eat about two more hours a day, but how much time in a novel or story is spent on this activity? It is used for social events, for busy scenes, for revelations about fam-

ilies or small communities. This leaves the writer, Forster said, with
the fifth universal activity to which men devote the remaining fourteen hours of every day—relationships with other people. So no
wonder the writer is tirelessly preoccupied with relations between
human beings, through which he may also portray conflicts with
self, society, and perhaps God.

Whether students aspire to writing slick, pulp, or literary fiction,
we ask them to write dramatic scenes in which two characters will
participate. We ask to know where we are—rapidly—and to have
some tension exist between these characters. Perhaps one is angry
at the other, or wants something, or is trying to get the better of the
other. Their dialogue and activity will carry the story forward
through an event and an interaction. If a flashback occurs through
the viewpoint of one of these characters, it will be "triggered" by
something legitimate in the scene—something done or said. None
of this gazing at the stormy sky and remembering a sweet day in
May twenty years before.

The word "drama" comes from a Greek root which means "doing." Once two people are in a scene, the verbs will begin to "do"
something and we can move to the second dictum of short story
writing, "Show me, don't tell me." In fiction, interpretation and
mood must be sunk below the surface of events, where they will
permeate action like a visible stain. A sentence like "Mary was
happy," which explains a state of mind, will be revised to "Mary
ran laughing up the stairs." The happiness has become implicit in
something Mary did, and we have—as our grandfathers used to say
—killed two birds with one stone.

The focus on event, as it sinks meaning inside activity, will inevitably shorten stories and make them more dense and compact.
Chekhov said in a letter to his brother, "I can speak briefly on long
subjects." Never has there been a better definition of what a short
story can do. The well-chosen event is, itself, a comment on life.
Someone once said the short story writer would do well to adopt as
his motto the one used by the Bank of England: *Never explain,
never apologize.*

Having two people in a scene brings up automatically other writing techniques such as point of view. So long as the story is ram-

bling along in the author's tone of voice, the author will assume it is focused and unified. After all, this is the way we are accustomed to hearing stories. Somebody relates what happened and nudges us in the ribs to make certain we get the point.

But questions of choice and perspective appear when two characters exist on the same page. Whose story is it? Which of the two is the more important? On whom will the full effect of these events fall? Through which character should the story be told? If Character A is chosen, Character B may not ramble off into his flashback; was the flashback really essential to the story? Is there a third character? What is his relationship to the first two? Like painters, we must decide on a background and foreground, where we will make our picture more vivid and where we will let the less significant recede. As the story is revised and begins to have shape and direction, the writer has a better basis for asking himself the two chief questions used in revising: Do I need it? Does it work? Even if he has written three pages in which his character is taking a long and thoughtful walk in the woods and remembering his old love affair, he may find that the story does not really begin until the character returns to town again and meets his old love with a baby on her hip.

The main value of insisting that a beginning writer "multiply by two," however, is that this alone will help him define for himself what a short story is. It is not the mental experience of a character. It does not take place within a human skull, and attempts to make it do so will only give the reader claustrophobia. One may not begin with a plot and then manufacture characters to act it out; one may create two characters who—by their own natures—will exude disagreements and plots.

Look back at some of the stories in your drawer which were turned down by magazines. How many of them start with a description of the sky? How many make use of dramatic scenes? (The average published short story has five dramatic scenes, in which something takes place *between* characters.) How many of them contain long passages where your main character is all alone, recalling an event which took place before the story actually began?

Multiply by two. Try rewriting the story so the meaningful event takes place—not in the past—but in the story's "now" time, before the reader's eye, with more than one human being on the scene. Often a good idea can be rescued when two characters act it out, and one character stops thinking-it-out.

39

BUILDING TENSION IN
THE SHORT STORY

By Joyce Carol Oates

THE most important aspect of writing is characterization—does a character come alive, is he memorable in some way? But the means of disclosing character is also important, for if a story lacks a strong narrative line, an editor or reader might not be patient enough to discover even the most stunning of fictional characters.

Novels are complex matters; the density of interest has to go up and down. Short stories, however, are generally based on one gradual upward swing toward a climax or "epiphany"—moment of recognition. A good chapter in a novel should probably be based on the same rhythmic structure as a short story. The novel, of course, can be leisurely while the average short story must be economical. Certain modern stories are so economical that single words or phrases are used to reveal the story's meaning—for instance, John Collier's "The Chaser," which ends with the words "au revoir" and not "goodbye."

While I think the best kind of contemporary story is much more rich and complex and daring than the Chekhovian-type stories so fashionable a few decades ago, still the writer must be careful to limit the range of his "secondary" material—descriptions, background. If he succeeds in winning the reader's attention by dramatic means, then the more important aspects of his story will be appreciated. We have all written wonderful little stories that are "hidden" somewhere in overlong, awkward, unsatisfactory masses of words.

Here are two examples of short story beginnings, each leading into a different kind of story:

1) "Let me tell you something about the Busbys," the old gentleman said to me. "The Busbys don't wash themselves—not adequately. And especially not as they grow older."

2) Just around the turn, the road was alive. First to assault the eye was a profusion of heads, black-haired, bobbing, and a number of straw hats that looked oddly professional—

The stories following these beginnings are to be found in *Prize Stories 1965: The O. Henry Awards*, edited by Richard Poirier and William Abrahams. The first story, "There," by Peter Taylor, invites the reader to listen in on a confidential, gossipy conversation: the words "Let me tell you" are intriguing enough, but the surprise comes in the second line. And we are introduced to a strange little town, "There," where each family seems to have a peculiar trait all its own—not washing properly, eating too much, narrow-minded complacency—and dying. Peter Taylor, the author of many excellent short stories of a rich, complex type, builds tension in a highly refined manner. We listen in on this old man's monologue, amused by his portraits of people back "there," and gradually we become emotionally involved in the pathos of his love for a girl who belonged to a family with a secret common trait—and then we find out, along with the narrator, that this common trait is dying. The girl has died young; the lover, now an aged man, has married someone else; there is no tragedy here, everything is muted and understated. But the story is unforgettable because Taylor has built so very gradually and unobtrusively the tension that arises out of the girl's impending death. Everything is past tense, but vitally alive.

The second beginning is from a story of mine, "First Views of the Enemy." Beginning with a near-accident, this story relies on tension building up within the main character's mind. A bus carrying migrant fruit pickers has broken down at the roadside, and when a young mother with her child drives by, one of the Mexican children darts in front of the car to frighten her. The tension between the young, American, rather materialistic woman and the socially-marginal people is the theme of this story. The woman arrives home safely, but she carries the image of this "enemy" with her into her expensive home, which now seems to her vulnerable. Her realization that she could lose everything she owns drives her to an orgy of selfishness as she locks things up, closes her drapes, even picks her most beautiful flowers and forces food upon her child. The tension is psychological, not active; the "enemy" does not appear after the first encounter. We see that the true "enemy" is the woman's hysterical selfishness, which she is forcing upon her child also.

Franz Kafka's classic, "The Metamorphosis," begins like this:

> As Gregor Samsa awoke one morning from uneasy dreams he found himself transformed in his bed into a gigantic insect.

Incredible, of course. Unbelievable. But Kafka's mild-mannered prose proceeds on as if an event of no great dimensions has taken place. You, the reader, find out about Gregor's metamorphosis at the same time he does. You are surprised, yes, but so is Gregor—a quite ordinary young man, devoted to his family and his work. This surrealistic story is much more "realistic" in its ability to convince and emotionally involve than most slick fiction with its easily-recognizable people. But Kafka thrives on tension. He builds it from his first sentence on. Kafka is always asking, "What happens next?" and then he asks, "After that, what happens?" Like Simenon, he drives his characters to extremes and tests them. "The Metamorphosis" is beautifully constructed in three sections, each dealing with the tense relationship between the stricken Gregor and his family, until Gregor dies in order to release his loved ones. Tension is achieved on the literal level—what is going to happen to the insect-man?—and on the symbolic level—what will be the outcome of the "love" between members of a family when one of them is mysteriously stricken and is no longer "human"?

These three stories, widely differing in technique, build up tension through an accumulation of detail. If violence erupts in fiction, it should be the outcome of tension; it should not come first, nor should it be accidental. Action stories are of interest to certain audiences, but quality stories usually refine action onto a psychological level. There is "action"—movement—but it takes place in a person's mind or in a conversation. If someone finally kills someone else, it is simply the climax of a rhythmic building of tension that lasts long enough to be convincing but is short enough to be interesting.

Remember that tension created for its own sake is cheap; no one will read your story more than once. The tension is part of your technique but technique is only a means to an end; it is never the end itself. That is why the French "new novel" is so boring—it has no capacity to move us—while older, stormy works like *Wuthering*

Heights (which could only be "camp" to today's *avant-garde*) will be interesting to all imaginable future generations. I think the stress placed today on technique is misleading. A writer should imagine his scenes dramatically, as if they were to take place on the stage. There, empty, wordy passages are found out at once. It isn't "words" or "style" that make a scene, but the content behind the words, and the increase of tension as characters come into conflict with one another. "Words" themselves are relatively unimportant, since there are countless ways of saying the same thing.

A final suggestion: be daring, take on anything. Don't labor over little cameo works in which every word is to be perfect. Technique holds a reader from sentence to sentence, but only content will stay in his mind.

40

THE NEW MYSTERY

By Joseph Hansen

THE way to write a mystery novel is to have a dead character and an assortment of living characters who might have killed him. That's all there is to it. No form is simpler. Nothing is easier to write. But from the evidence nothing is harder to write well. For every good mystery there are twenty bad ones.

What is usually wrong with the bad ones is that they aren't life-like. Even those not wholly bad are likely to be lifelike only up to the solution of the crime. Then the writer betrays his book by asking the reader to accept an impossible killer. Why does this happen? Why do writers, some of them professionals with long lists of titles to their credit, so often wind their books up lamely?

Because you can't give the reader the strongest suspect and not disappoint him. You have to give him a suspect he didn't suspect. It's a basic rule, the heartbeat of the classic mystery form. But failure to do so is also what wrecks so many mysteries.

There's no reason this should be so. Every suspect ought to be strong. Naturally, motive one or two may be more urgent than motive three. But if each motive is legitimate and is ingrained in the character whom it drives, then there can't be any letdown for the reader when the killer with motive three turns out to be the guilty one. So why is it that this is where most mysteries fall down?

Because the writer has put plot before people. Yes, the plot of a mystery has to be strong. But this means only that the characters must be even stronger. Both must be true to life. But any plot is likely to be tidier than life. If it weren't, we wouldn't read it. Characters, on the other hand, needn't be tidy; if they are to seem real, they won't be tidy.

With real people in a strong plot, a detective story can become more than that—it can become a real novel. The need for story is as basic to humans as the need for love. Most straight novelists these days forget this. But most detective story writers make as bad a mistake—they forget that story isn't everything.

My most nagging fear as a writer is that my readers will be bored. That's the best reason I can give for writing mysteries. Like every writer of fiction, I'm interested in people and the way they interact, the way they cope with life and with each other, with birth and death, hunger and fear, love and lust, rage and cowardice and courage, logic and impulse, money and the lack of money. And the thousand ills that flesh is heir to.

And in the novel with the strongest story line—the detective novel—I see the chance to deal with these things and still keep the reader turning the pages to find out what's going to happen next, how it's all going to turn out. Whodunit is a device I use to keep the reader's eyes fixed on the words and what I mean by the words.

In the case of my novel, *Death Claims,* I wanted to say some things about how in our society a catastrophic illness can take away everything a man possesses, about how the collapse of an industry can set a craftsman adrift without any way to make a living, about how the needs of an ailing wife can turn a scrupulous scholar to forgery, and how drug addiction can drive a formerly decent man to blackmail and theft. And in that book, as in the one that proceded it, *Fadeout,* I wanted to talk about the homosexual, how he manages or fails to manage in a society that treats his existence as, at best, a sick joke.

To look without flinching at real problems, hard problems, is as much the right of the mystery writer as of the writer of books without killings and clues. Readers of mysteries are for the most part brainy people. They like puzzles with substance. Poor mysteries fail them because in poor mysteries the characters are mere functions. The writer's purpose isn't large enough or near enough to life. The mystery that is also a good novel is peopled by men and women, not functions.

And men and women are restless, dissatisfied with themselves and others, are lonely sometimes and sometimes wish for loneliness. They lose and regret their losses. They hope and as they age know their hopes to be futile. They spend themselves unwisely, make mistakes, drink too much, waste time, speak too soon, judge too harshly; they grieve and suffer pain. Put such people in a mystery and it will transcend its plot, however crafty.

Such people have weight and shape and meaning. The writer using them will avoid the weakness of which the detective novel in general is rightly accused—of having nothing to say, of being trivial, a waste of time. When the reader of a mystery filled with people who seem real to him closes the book, he ought to say and feel, "That's sad." Because murder among real people is sad.

It involves—not just police officers and pathologists, judges, lawyers and juries, but mothers and fathers, husbands and wives, lovers, sisters, brothers, friends, children, business associates. It involves the end not just of a life but of the part the dead one played in countless lives.

If the mystery is to be a real novel, then the end has to be as much question as answer. Because this is the function of real literature—to ask questions. A novel is usually bad and unreal to the extent that it offers solutions. Life is never so simple as in slick fiction. Life is much more apt to be a hopeless tangle as in *The Brothers Karamazov*—which is not only one of the best novels ever written but is a mystery novel.

That the mystery novel has to climax with a solution to the murder is true. But that this solves anything in the larger human sense for the characters involved, if those characters are written faithful to life, is untrue. A sudden death by violence and the sudden end of the road for the killer—these alike will breed more problems than they solve. And the reader will come away from the book with a sharpened awareness of human frailty and vulnerability.

He's less apt to do this if the characters are from a world too remote from his own. If the writer picks characters out of the familiar life most of us are trying and failing to live from day to day —those "lives of quiet desperation" of which Thoreau spoke—then I think his book has a chance. Yes, the beautiful people suffer. The rich, as Hemingway said to Fitzgerald, are different from the rest of us only in that they have more money. And, I suppose, the poor in that they have less. But extremes are shaky ground for realistic

fiction. The danger is of writing—to paraphrase Rust Hills' definition of the difference between bad and good fiction—daydreams
instead of nightmares.

In *Death Claims,* my insurance investigator protagonist comments to a friend, "Repeated encounters with nice, normal, everyday people who kill each other for money can wear a man down
after a couple of decades." And I think that's central—a man or
woman dead, who could have been a man or woman we know, and
killed by someone who turns out to be not only true to his own
character in that last desperate gesture, but also could be someone
we know. So that the tragedy is not only the dead's and his execu-
tioner's but ours, in that we shared their lives.

If as much truth, clear-eyed, steadfast and loving, can be
brought to the characters in the mystery as in the novel without
crime, then maybe the mystery can move out of its literary ghetto.
There was a time when all novels were popular novels—the time
of Dickens, Thackeray, George Eliot, best sellers, all of them. Then,
at the turn of the century came the concept of the literary novel,
lifting away from the common reader. It's a false and pernicious
distinction. There are only two kinds of novel—the good and the
bad.

But there is no reason except failure of nerve and imagination
why the detective novel, the mystery novel, can't join, in far larger
numbers than those already there, the ranks of the good. There is
every reason, I think, for the young writer today who wants a future outside university libraries and reviews in literary quarterlies
to try writing mysteries. It's a chance to say what you honestly feel
about the human predicament and still hold your reader with a
compelling plot.

There are added advantages. Out of twenty-odd-thousand new
hardcover titles published in the U.S. every year, only a scant three
hundred are whodunits—and the bulk of these are written overseas, mostly in Britain. There is room on publishers' lists for more
mysteries. There is a steady, year-in-and-year-out public for this
kind of book. The pay is not fantastic but it is decent if what you
write is above average. And beyond the hardcover, which may sell
only three or four thousand copies, is the paperback sale that gen-

erally follows a first-rate hardcover, and sales overseas where they are hungry for good thrillers, *romans policiers, Detektivgeschichten.*

But your greatest satisfaction will, of course, come from reaching readers with your vision of the world, your insights into what human beings and the life they live are all about.

41

SUSPENSE: RULES AND NON-RULES

By Patricia Highsmith

"Too much thought is bad for the soul, for art, and for crime. It is also a sign of middle age. . . ."

Patrick Hamilton wrote this in one of his novels about Gorse, a real-life criminal who started early and successfully, but later began to plan a bit. It was his doom.

I wrote Hamilton's words down in the back of my notebook, where I keep other people's remarks that I wish I had made myself. I do not set much store by logic, no doubt because nature did not give me much. Novels are products of emotion, and to my illogical mind Hamilton's statement seems doubly true, because a suspense writer must be at the same time an artist and a criminal. It is probably better to be young for this. Middle age does bring thought, alas, and looking before leaping. Not much can be done about middle age, but thinking and logic should be discouraged, except in minutiae of the plot: e.g., would X really have had time to wipe up the blood, make a telephone call, and get all the way from Hoboken to Grand Central in seven minutes?

People who don't write often ask writers where they get their ideas from, not knowing that writers get them out of thin air a good part of the time, and at other times from incidents so trivial and fleeting that the incident, or face, or phrase can hardly be recaptured and repeated as an answer as to where their novel came from. Is this logical? Of course not. The unconscious mind takes the germ of an idea and develops it, but usually this happens only when a writer has tried hard, and logically, to develop it himself. After he has given it up for a few hours, getting nowhere, a great advancement of the plot will pop into his head. I have been waked up in the night sometimes by a plot advancement or a solution of a problem that I had not even been dreaming about. Everyone functions like this to some extent, and it is what people mean when they say, "I don't want to make up my mind today, I'd better sleep on it."

I like a wild coincidence in a plot—as in *The Blunderer*, in which I had Walter guess the murderer (Kimmel) and his method of killing his wife, then attempt the same kind of attack upon his own wife, or rather contemplate it, because to give the plot a further twist, I had him not carry it out. His wife committed suicide. It looked like murder. And the similarity of the circumstances to Kimmel's tragedy exposed the guilt of Kimmel. *The Blunderer* has been made into a French film, *The Murderer*.

Wild implausibilities I highly recommend, too. My most celebrated —thanks to Alfred Hitchcock—is *Strangers on a Train*, which might be described as a series of almost incredible events. They were a little too incredible for the scriptwriters of the film (they cut out the second murder), just as the story, when presented as half the written novel and a synopsis of the remainder, was too incredible for six publishing houses which turned me down. They thought it could not be made convincing. The novel when finished was accepted by the next publisher I showed it to, Harper's, which shows the power of persuasion of illogical prose.

And I like harebrained schemes that must forever waver on the brink of discovery, as in *The Talented Mr. Ripley* (later the film *Purple Noon*), in which Ripley impersonates the man he has killed, though he does not look enough like him to pass for him among even his casual acquaintances. By an act of even greater audacity at the end of the book, Ripley allays any suspicion of himself, acquires his victim's income for life, and gets away with it all. Of course they couldn't have him get away with it either on television or on the screen, but the novel won a prize from the Mystery Writers of America in 1956 and in 1957 the Grand Prix de Littérature Policière in France.

Young writers often worry about pace and atmosphere. Pace is no problem if one has a story. If I find my pace slowing, it is because the story is vague in my mind and I am muddling about, getting stuck on details and overdescribing. A writer should be quite sure of his story for at least thirty pages to come, and as for myself, I like to rush ahead—in a way, as if I were narrating a story to someone and talking a little too fast. Some writers, I know, like to plan very carefully, make outlines before they begin, and I do not mean to say here how writers should write, I am only saying the way I prefer to write and probably the only way I can write. My headlong method often necessitates heavy revision and major changes and then a new plunge. But often it comes off, too, as it did in *The Talented Mr. Ripley,* certainly the fastest book I ever wrote (five months) and consequently the fastest of all my books to read. When I begin a book, I have no more than sixty pages clearly in mind, often much less, but I have an idea of the effect I want to create—tragedy, success, a sense of being hopelessly trapped, as in *This Sweet Sickness,* a plodding gloom, as in *The Blunderer.* And I do know what the end will be, therefore. After a few pages (it ought to be before the first line) the characters are alive and move, they have directions in which they move, or they have directions that circumstances prevent them from taking. Anyway, one has a dynamic situation, and from then on—certainly by page sixty—the book seems to write itself. When writers look through one of their printed books, see all the twists and turns, the speculations of harassed characters and their possible lines of action (all brilliantly set forth, of course, like spokes radiating from a wheel hub), surely many must say to themselves, "I don't remember thinking all that out in such detail. My goodness, I don't even remember writing it." This has already happened to me on looking through my book, *The Two Faces of January,* which I wrote only a few years ago.

Atmosphere? I am grateful to reviewers for saying that my books have it, but it is another thing I have never given any thought to until now. And it seems to me that laboring it, like laboring anything in a creative work, is fatal. If I have any suggestion as to the building of atmosphere, it is to let the characters react to whatever environment they are in. Thus one presents a setting through the senses (how does it smell, what color is it, how does the color strike the person looking at it?) and also reveals a great deal, effortlessly, about the character perceiving it. A formal garden in Italy may delight a spinster schoolteacher; she may want to sit for hours on a cold stone bench reading her favorite poems in it; it may make a young American football player want to scream, tear out the hedges with his bare hands, or at any rate get out of it as fast as possible. Either reaction gives "atmosphere." A melancholic scene, mist on a deserted beach at night, may please another character who (for some reason) has certain associations with such a place. Characters' reactions produce atmosphere more vividly than solid paragraphs of prose about places—though even solid paragraphs can be relieved and made more alive by one small "he felt . . ." in regard to colors, sounds and smells.

I disapprove of the word "discipline" in regard to writing—that is, in the grim way in which it is generally used. A young writer looks, I imagine (I once did), with wide-eyed and respectful bewilderment at the well-meaning teacher who advises him to get it and keep it, for without it he can do nothing. No wonder the young person does not understand—not completely, because he probably already has the makings of this severe and abstract thing called discipline. Writing is a way of life, and what teachers mean by discipline is the habit and necessity of writing. Discipline never made a writer. Discipline is for the armed forces. And I think distractions and non-writing never unmade a writer, because a real writer will chuck his obligations, shed them somehow, and get away by himself and write. Writing is a way of organizing experience, or of organizing something imagined, of making something perfect and beautiful—even something as small as one sentence—in a world that can be at times chaotic, wretched, ugly and upsetting.

The habit of writing often begins in adolescence, sometimes even earlier. In adolescence, when emotion is intense, when many emotions bring tears, and the teen-ager picks up a pencil or a pen and writes a poem or a paragraph about it, and feels better—that's the beginning of writing. And all art comes from the prolongation of this childlike intensity, which many people lose even at puberty. When writing becomes a habit and a necessity, the writer need never give a thought to discipline, because writing is a pleasure. Then friends and relatives will say, "Ah, what discipline!" on seeing the writer at work, not realizing that it would take more discipline than they dream of for him to spend the next few hours in their company. After a good day's work, when one is feeling rather godlike, it is a different matter, a writer looks on the human race with a new joy, and feels like saying even to the Fuller Brush man, "Come in! Got time to sit down for a few minutes?" Discipline may be needed later when a writer has to cut forty pages from a manuscript he already considers cut, for instance, or his editor tells him to get rid of his favorite minor character because he doesn't advance the plot.

Life can also be chaotic at forty, of course, and a writer can feel he is written out, that he has nothing to say—at least not at the moment. I have just had a letter from a writer friend saying this, that he's written out, and so forth. He hasn't been writing very long at fiction (he was formerly a newspaperman), and he has also rather recently been married, and his wife has had a baby. He writes that he is getting tired of little marital tiffs—among other things—but mostly he writes about not being able to get settled in the book he is trying to start. I suggested to him that his problem might be the sense of loss-of-importance of what he wants to write—a ghastly condition that can easily come when one is faced with marital tiffs, household bills, a sick child, a weekend shattered by a visit from the in-laws, or, above all, by lack of privacy. It is astounding how after days of being with people—sometimes out of necessity, social or economic—a good and exciting idea becomes pale and wan, vague, and not worth writing. It is just as outstanding and thrilling when, after a day or so of solitude, silence, daydreaming and loafing, the same idea comes alive again, beautiful and bright like a wilted plant that has been given a good soaking in the rain.

It takes a few years to learn this. It takes a lot of skill and scheming, make-believe and trickery, to preserve one's enthusiasm through the hideous periods of reality, of people, of obligations, of non-privacy. It is sometimes necessary to avoid thinking about one's story in the midst of people, because it can be crushed like a violet—a violet tossed on a subway platform in the rush hour. I so often think of young writers everywhere who are not able to have, yet, that most expensive commodity in the world—aloneness. I think of young writers who get married thinking that their wives will be so cooperative about their weekend stints at the typewriter, of writers whose wives are cooperative and who themselves are jangled by obligations that will not let their minds be at peace, or by interruptions their wives are not militant enough to prevent. The greatest service a wife can render her writer husband is not typing his manuscripts for him, but keeping people away from him. Of course, a husband might do the same, if his wife is the writer.

How to make psychopathic types attractive? I would suggest mak-

ing them young, perhaps even rather handsome, tidy in their dress
(heavens, what a picture of impropriety we could conjure up by remarking quietly that our psychopathic hero was wont to be untidy in
his dress), or give them a nice trait or two, like being generous, or
kind to old ladies and animals. A sense of humor is also of tremendous help. This, perhaps, does not always work. Tom Ripley was
nice looking, though his face was thoroughly forgettable; he was
tidy; he had a sense of humor, and many readers liked him; yet
others said they disliked him, with an "Ugh-h!" and a shudder. But
the likers and dislikers kept turning the pages, the dislikers with an
attitude of "Good Lord, what's he going to do *next?*" What writer
could ask for more? And I also feel sure it would be possible to write
a book with an untidy, fat, sloppy psychopath as hero, if one only
gave him enough fascinating and audacious things to do. His more
repellent qualities might have to be introduced gradually, but if you
introduce him in some kind of action, the reader will be drawn along.
Good action and a good story are irresistible.

Of all my published books, two, I think, are decidedly dull. They
are *A Game for the Living* and *The Cry of the Owl.* In the first, a
psychopathic murderer-hero is missing; in fact the murderer is off-
scene, unknown, so it becomes a mystery whodunit in a way—definitely not my forte. In *Owl,* the hero is too square, becoming a sitting
duck for the more evil characters, a passive bore. In both, I tried to
do something different from what I had been doing, but left out some
elements vital for me: surprise, speed of action, coincidence, and the
stretching of the reader's credulity—which I ordinarily do to excess
and without scruple. The result was mediocrity. It would be easy for
me to keep on writing stories with heroes like Bruno of *Strangers on
a Train* and Ripley, but it would also be cowardly and unenterpris-
ing. My conclusion is that it is well for a writer to realize what he can
do best: a frightened heroine, a mad hero, a chase; and what emotional elements he does best: anxiety, the destructiveness that is associated with the criminal mind, the playing off of good against evil
—and use them as the strong points of his story. I believe that any
story, about anything, in the suspense category, can be told using
some of the writer's stronger points, if he takes the trouble to find
out first what his strong points are. I did not in these two dull books,
and it was unforgivable of me.

42

THE WILLING SUSPENSION OF DISBELIEF

By Elizabeth Peters

ALTHOUGH Coleridge coined the useful phrase, "the willing suspension of disbelief," it has been the goal of storytellers since the pre-literate dawn of time and of writers since fiction began. Writers of suspense fiction particularly depend upon this gesture of good will on the part of the reader, but successful achievement of that goal depends upon the writer as well as the reader. Presumably, the reader of thrillers or novels of suspense starts each book in the proper mood of suspended disbelief, but he cannot sustain this mood if the author taxes his intelligence too much. How, then, does the writer of suspense fiction create an aura of plausibility which will allow readers to accept his creation, "for the moment," as Coleridge adds?

The so-called Gothic novel is a sub-category of the novel of suspense. In most cases, the term "Gothic" is a misnomer, for the romantic, "damsel-in-distress" thrillers which publishers label "modern Gothics" are not Gothics at all. Their ancestors are not Mrs. Ann Radcliffe's *The Mysteries of Udolpho* or Horace Walpole's *The Castle of Otranto,* but Wilkie Collins' *The Moonstone* and Charlotte Brontë's *Jane Eyre.* The true Gothic novel requires an atmosphere of brooding supernatural horror and a setting that includes ruined castles and desolate moors. I don't consider my books to be true Gothics, but it would be pedantic of me to object to the term, which is certainly more succinct than more accurate designations. I may then be forgiven if I refer henceforth to this form of fiction as "Gothic."

The most important thing for a writer of Gothics to recognize is that the genre is inherently incredible, almost as unlikely as a fantasy novel. Personally, I find it as easy to believe in the green Mar-

228

tians of Barsoom as I do in the adventures of Gothic heroines. Some writers of Gothics seem to feel that because their plots are fantastic, they need not be logical. The converse is true. The more fantastic the plot, the more important are those factors that invite belief, or, at least, the suspension of disbelief.

What are these factors? Some may be seen in the three elements of plot, character and setting.

The pot of a Gothic novel must be tight, consistent, and logical —within the given framework. Like the fantasy novel, which starts with a single fantastic premise, the Gothic begins with what I like to call an "initiating coincidence." The heroine happens to over-hear a conversation between two people who are planning a mur-der; or she happens to accept a job as governess in an isolated household whose inhabitants all suffer from severe neuroses. None of these situations is very likely, but we can admit one such for-tuitous occurrence in order to get our plot moving. From that point on, however—no coincidences, no lucky accidents. If the hero is walking down Main Street at the moment when the heroine, cor-nered by the villain, screams for help, the hero must have a reason for being on Main Street at that vital moment. It will not suffice to explain that he keeps in shape by jogging down Main Street every fine afternoon. If the heroine is to be rescued—and Gothic heroines always are—the rescuer must be brought to the spot by hard work and/or logical deductions.

Plausibility of character is as important as consistency of plot. The two are related, of course. A stupid heroine's foolish behavior can lead to plot complications. Indeed, the plots of the poorer Gothics seem to depend wholly on the heroine's incredible naïveté, as she falls into one pitfall after another. But it is difficult for the reader to identify, or even sympathize, with heroines of such consummate imbecility. Admittedly, Gothic heroines have a pro-pensity for getting into trouble. It is one of the important elements of the Gothic plot, but it can also be one of the great weaknesses of the genre. Critics justifiably jeer at the dim-witted girls who take nocturnal strolls around grim old mansions. If you must get your heroine out of her nice, safe, locked room in the middle of the night, after two murders have already been committed, do give her a good reason for leaving that security. (I cannot think of anything that would induce me to leave my room under those circumstances, except perhaps the voices of my children screaming for help.) Your heroine must have an equally pressing motive. Better yet, have her stay in her room and get into trouble in some less conventional manner. And no mysterious notes asking for a midnight rendezvous in the castle crypt, please. Critics sneer at that one, too. A heroine ought to have sufficient intelligence to check with the hero to make sure he actually sent the note before she ventures into a crypt.

The characters of Gothic novels are not profound or complex; in two-hundred-odd pages we do not have space for such luxuries, since we must spend a good deal of verbiage on plot and atmosphere. But if our characters are cardboard, they need not be absurd. They must not exhibit flagrant personality aberrations, or behave so idiotically that the reader begins to hope they will be murdered in the crypt, as they deserve to be.

Of course, the more fully developed and realistic your characters, the more plausible their actions will seem. One of the classics in the field, Daphne du Maurier's *Rebecca*, has a heroine who has always exasperated me by her timidity and docility; but she is believable, because she behaves in a way that is consistent with her background and her personality.

Atmosphere and setting are particularly important to thrillers of this type, and the same rule applies: the more unusual or exotic the setting, the harder you must work to give it an appearance of authenticity. In these days of jets and travel books, Samarkand is no more exotic than Paris or Rome. But you must make sure that your descriptions of these cities are accurate, and that you include enough details to convince the reader of the reality of the setting in which your heroine's wild adventures are to take place. I do not subscribe to the theory that a writer can write only about things he or she has personally experienced. I have personally visited all the cities and countries I have used in my books; but I could not have written about them without the aid of maps, photographs, and detailed notes taken on the spot. Perhaps a conscientious writer can do this with a city he or she has never seen—but it will require a great deal of work.

The rule holds even when you are inventing a setting. In one of my books, the action takes place in Rothenburg, a small German town I know fairly well, but for various reasons I decided to add an imaginary castle to that city instead of using an existing structure. I did almost as much research on the castle as I did on the city, reading about medieval castles and Franconian architecture, so that the description of my imaginary castle would agree with details of real structures of that period. If your characters do a lot of running around, draw floor plans. Readers love to spot discrepancies, and will write irritated letters if you have your heroine descend a staircase where no staircase can conceivably exist.

One useful trick to make sure that the reader will accept your devices of plot or of setting is to prepare him for them well in advance. A strategically located doorway, through which the hero gains entrance to the conference room—a secret passage whereby your characters can escape when danger threatens—these, and other devices, will seem more plausible if they are mentioned before you actually need them. Again, the more unusual the prop, the more carefully you must explain its presence. A secret passage in a medieval castle needs only a sentence or two of description, since the reader knows that medieval castles abound in such conveniences. A secret passage in a modern split-level house requires considerable explanation—and perhaps a brief character sketch of the eccentric individual who had it built.

Plot props require the same advance preparation. If the heroine's knowledge of Urdu is going to save her from a fate worse than death, or expose the master criminal, you must tell the reader early in the book that she is an expert in this abstruse language. If you do not, she will resemble Superwoman when she comes up with the information. And for pity's sake, if she or the hero is to be an expert in ichthyology or Egyptology, learn something about those subjects before you talk about them. I was once put off an otherwise readable Gothic because it involved a reincarnated Egyptian princess named Cha-cha-boom, or something equally absurd. No reincarnated Egyptian, fake or genuine, would have such a name, and the repetition of the inane syllables grated on me so strongly that I never finished the book. The author could easily have found an authentic ancient Egyptian name in the encyclopedia. I remember another book I never finished reading because the villain, a German sea captain, kept shouting "Grüss Gott!" in frenzied moments. If you do not know that "Grüss Gott" is a friendly greeting in southern Germany, have your villain stick to English.

You may think that few readers have much knowledge of Egyptology or other abstruse subjects. This would be a dangerous assumption. Archaeology is a popular field, and for some odd reason, which I mean to investigate one day, archaeology buffs seem to be especially addicted to thrillers. But that is not the important thing. The important thing is that plausibility depends upon the accumulation of consistent, accurate details. They really do add verisimilitude to an otherwise bald and unconvincing narrative. The reader may not consciously note all your errors; but a series of careless inconsistencies will tax the reader's willingness to accept your imaginary world, and a single glaring error may be enough to snap that fragile thread on which the suspension of disbelief depends.

Of course, you are bound to slip up occasionally, no matter how conscientiously you research your book. As I work through revision after revision, I come across howlers I can't believe I missed the first and second times. To my chagrin, a few of them escape me even in the third and fourth revisions and get into print, despite the additional efforts of my intelligent editors. In one of my books, written under another name, an integral plot prop was an old family Bible. Long after the book was published, a reader wrote to me inquiring how the Bible happened to survive the conflagration that had destroyed the equally ancient family mansion and most of its contents. "I can imagine several possible solutions," she added charitably, "but I do think you ought to have *told* us."

She was absolutely correct. I should have told her. And I would have done so, if I had noticed the discrepancy. However, errors of this sort are not in the same category as careless mistakes or poorly developed characters. An occasional gap in the plot or an error of fact will not be serious if the rest of the plot is as tight as you can make it, and if the other facts have been checked and rechecked.

I could go on, giving examples of the basic rule, but if you read many Gothics, you will spot plenty of other cases, of success and of failure. Of course there are some writers who seem to be able to break all the rules and get away with it. Don't bother writing to tell me about them. I know about them. I only wish I knew how they do it.

43

PEOPLE AT WORK—FICTION BONUS

BY PEGGY SIMSON CURRY

SUCCESSFUL short stories have distinction. They have a special something—a kind of flavor. Where does the writer find the source of that flavor? Many times it grows from a blending of characters and background—*job background.* The work people do determines to a great extent their status as human beings. A man's work colors his speech, presents him with challenges and conflicts, and often gives an overall tone or atmosphere to his life. The conditions of his work may affect his relationship with family and friends. It may encompass his hopes and fears.

Although all the stories we write do not need emphasis on job background, this area is one that should be noted. It may offer opportunities when we most need them. When you are hard put to develop the initial spark into a completed story, remember that the occupation of your protagonist sets a natural stage, a background against which things may happen. Action is inevitable.

Much of the fiction I have published has been firmly rooted in job background. And there is an added element in such stories: they offer the reader *information* along with *entertainment.* Such information is an interesting addition to adult fiction. It can be significant in juvenile fiction.

"Gypsy Trainer," a juvenile story of mine, was published in the March 1974 issue of *Boys' Life.* In September, 1974, it was reprinted in *Hub Rail,* The Standardbred Journal, an adult magazine read by professionals in the field of harness racing.

In the past I had written harness-racing stories for adult readers. One of them sold to Walt Disney Studios. I thought I had exhausted that background, but on a trip to central Illinois, I went to a farm where pacers and trotters were raised and trained. As usual, I was looking around and listening to the talk that went on in the stable. A horse had a sore on his leg. It wasn't healing, although an expensive veterinary had been treating it.

"What they need is an old gypsy trainer," one of the men muttered. "He'd fix that. He'd stand that horse in river mud."

Gypsy trainer! In all my reading and interviewing about harness racing, I had never found a gypsy trainer. I began to ask questions: Did gypsy trainers still exist? What did they do? What were they like? Could they really heal sores in mud?

My questions were quickly answered. And yes, it was sometimes possible to heal a sore by "standing the horse in mud." Protagonist, plot, climax, atmosphere, interesting information—I got it all in less than an hour there in the stable.

My hero, a boy, would run away from an orphanage, take up with an old gypsy trainer "who believed in all sorts of far-out things: colts foaled in the full moon could pace faster, river mud would heal sores on horses that nothing else could heal; horses were smarter than humans and sometimes they talked to you. . . ."

Conflict? The boy becomes a gypsy trainer himself, gets qualified to drive, has his "colors." The boy goes to work for a famous owner and driver, but he has to take a job as a lowly swipe—chore boy around the stables. He finds a mare with the heart of a champion but she has a sore above a front hoof that won't heal. The impatient owner is ready to get rid of her, sell her to the "killers" from Chicago. The boy can't stand having her turned into dog food and glue. He says he will not only heal her, but also qualify her to pace in the great Illinois Stake Race at the state fair. To do this he must race her in the country fair races before the state fair. He challenges the owner; in the mare's first race he will race her against the owner's favorite.

This story, strengthened by all the color and detail of the harness racing background, practically wrote itself. Only one problem developed: The ending was flat. The boy had won that first race, defeated the famous owner-driver and his equally famous horse. Things had gone too well for him—from the successful mud treatment to the winning of the race. I changed the ending paragraphs to include this material:

I got off the sulky and walked unsteadily to her head and put my arms around her and laid my cheek against that hot, wet, black neck. I don't know how I happened to look down but I did. And I saw she held up that front hoof and blood was oozing down over it. I knew then she'd never go on to race for the championship at the great Illinois Stake. It would take two or three months to heal that hoof again—and maybe it would never be healed for always. I'd worked her too hard or maybe there wouldn't be blood on her now...I dropped down there in the dust of the track and took that hoof in my hands. I began to cry....

The famous driver consoles and congratulates the boy. He asks him to come home and bring the mare home where they can care for her. The orphan has, at last, found a home and the mare is safe from the killers. Whether she will ever race again is left to the reader's imagination.

Job background—harness racing—gave me everything I could possibly need for this story. Even the names of my characters were chosen to fit the background. Nicknames are popular in the harness-racing world. My hero is named Coonhound Johnny—he "liked to prowl around at night and pet the horses." The famous driver is known around the race tracks as "The Duke."

The dialogue in the story is true to the background. In a moment of angry confrontation The Duke tells the boy, "I aim to drive to win. That means driving rough if I have to." The phrase "drive to win" is typical track talk.

The *flavor* of the harness-racing busines permeates the story. And I, as well as the readers, learned something—there are gypsy trainers, those wandering men with mythical and mystical beliefs who drift from county fair to county fair, entering broken-down horses, second-rate pacers and trotters in "overnight events." And although they lack money to own farms or expensive horses, their lives are interesting, fascinating.

Let's move on to another job situation. Three years ago I stopped with some friends at a place known as "the fossil diggings." They were intent on finding a fossil. I sat in the sagebrush—hot, thirsty, tired, and bored. A man in a truck drove up. He turned out to be an expert on fossils and fossil digging. He showed my friends how to dig, where to dig, talking as he worked. "Them beautiful little fish in the shale, been there so long," he said. "Kinda like poetry."

By then I was writing as fast as I could in my notebook. Four hours later I was sunburned, hungry and happy. I knew a lot about fossil hunting—as a hobby and a business. I had plenty of job background for a story, and I had an idea for a poem. I wrote the poem when I got home, and it was soon published. I filed my notes on the fossil digging. Then, not long ago, I wanted to do another story for the young readers of *Boys' Life,* but my mind was a blank. I took out my notes on the fossils.

Why not put my leading character, a boy, in the hot, dry fossil beds in Wyoming? Give him motivation for being there, problems to solve —and bring in a man like the expert I had met to play a part in the boy's problems. Conflict? The boy could be bitter because after his father's death his mother married again—a man he didn't like, a man who interfered with the boy's dream of bringing his mother West. The dream might be one his father had often talked about—a ranch and cattle near sheltering mountains. But the boy can't find a job when he gets to Wyoming, and hears that some people make money digging fossils and selling them.

I made my hero bitter, independent, a loner. He doesn't have any luck until the expert comes along and helps him. A climax occurs when "claim-jumpers" try to take over the boy's diggings—a thing that happened once in a while at the fossil beds. The boy finds he can't fight the claim-jumpers. They beat him up, but other people come to his rescue, people he doesn't even know. He finds out people need one another; he's no longer a loner. And the fossil expert convinces him that he has no right to decide what his mother wants to do with her life—and maybe his stepfather isn't such a bad guy after all.

The hot, dry prairie atmosphere—so much like my hero's mood—is part of the fossil-bed background. All the descriptive passages were in my notes. All the *information* was there to be introduced in the older man's dialogue while he helped the boy dig fossils. The story sold at once, and when the reader finishes with it, he will know a lot about fossil hunting as well as human nature.

A third example of a story inspired by background on the job was also published in *Boys' Life* (September 1974). I was visiting a friend who owned a country store. I had been there many times but never thought of writing a story with that setting. A high school boy was working for her. Talking with him, I learned that he wanted to be a stock-car driver, to drive in stock-car races.

His old stripped-down stock car—which kept him broke—was parked near the store. In a lull between customers, he took me out to see it, explaining all its features—no glass in the windows, roll bars on the sides and ceiling, wide tires, over ten years old, with original engine and transmission. He told me he was trying to save money to buy a new crash helmet.

Why not combine the two occupational backgrounds, stock-car racing and working in a country store? Had the store ever been robbed? It had. Suppose the boy is in disrepute with the stingy woman who owns the country store, because he is overgenerous with customers and always borrowing on his wages to improve his stock car? He might even get fired on the day he returns from having a day off—a time in which he bought a new red, white and blue crash helmet. (Red, white and blue because his stingy boss might respond to patriotism; she runs up the flag every morning and takes it down each night because the country post office is located in the store.) That day, when the boy gets his long-wanted crash helmet and is fired, the store is robbed. The boy takes after the robber's car in his stock car and pursues him on a dangerous country road that curves up a steep slope. The robber goes over the edge, boy recovers the money, etc.

Dialogue? It was all there in my listening to store talk between the boy and customers. Description? All I had to do was look around and select a few outstanding details distinctive to the old store, the prairie around it, and the stock car. How to get information about the stock car across to the reader? The boy can pass it on in tight dialogue to his boss when she condescends to go out and look at his "junk heap." Even the two cats, named Golden Boy and Batishka, might be worked into the plot.

"Trial Run"—complete with the two cats—came alive very quickly when I got to the typewriter. The background of the boy's work, the store, and the information concerning stock-car racing combined to make it possible for me to produce an interesting story.

One last example of job background as a help in creating fiction is my *Boys' Life* story, "In the Silence," which won the Gold Spur Award for short fiction of the American West given by Western Writers of America. (In 1973 it was reprinted in a textbook published by Houghton Mifflin.) This story had its roots deep in all the details, the hazards, the psychological strain of herding sheep alone on a mountaintop. The time was early 1900—before herders had radios, trucks, frequent visitors in their canvas-domed wagons. Job background then had significant *psychological* effects.

My material for this came from an interview with a rancher who had herded sheep "in the silence" of a mountaintop when he was only thirteen years of age. I had the notes for several years before I wrote the story. But the conditions of that job—the tent living, the night fires to keep away the coyotes, the wild horses in search of salt, the frightening loneliness and silence—all these were as alive as when he had first told me about them.

Until I put my leading character to work on that job, I had no ideas for the story. The problems, the atmosphere, the texture of the story grew from the ramifications of herding sheep.

Looking back to stories published in the past, I note how many of them drew heavily on job background for their color, characterization—all those little touches of authentic dialogue, descriptive passages, elements of plot. The same thing is true of my novels, where the blend of characters and job background is the stage and support for the whole work. A variety of occupations has been explored in these published pages: herring fishing, oil field work of many kinds, trapping, hunting, harvesting hay, breaking horses, punching cows, driving pacers and trotters, rodeoing, raising cattle, running a girls' dormitory, saddle-making, clerking in a store, fortune-telling. There are many more.

Ideas, initial sparks that touch off the creative fires, come from all sorts of things. Regardless of what it is that stirs our imagination, the people we put on paper are all-important. They begin to function when we can visualize them making a living—and a life.

It's time for me to write another short story. In one of my files I have notes on cutter-racing in Jackson Hole—chariot racing on runners over frozen ground. Or what about a boy among the mayonnaise jars in a supermarket? And there are my neighbors—an electrician, a baker, a garage owner, a jeweler (diamonds aren't always a girl's best friend), a school teacher, a nurse, a banker, a man who owns a furniture store.

You can't think of anything to write about? Put your people to work—and let them work for you.

44

WRITING THE CONFESSION STORY TODAY

By Norma Stoyenoff

IF YOU'VE checked out your neighborhood newsstand lately, or stopped in front of the magazine rack at the supermarket, you might have begun to suspect there are far fewer confession magazines being published today.

O.K., so you never really yearned to write for *Ranch Romances* or *True Medic* anyway; but you did think that maybe someday you'd give *True Story* a try. Especially since your latest piece of fiction came zinging back from *Good Housekeeping*. Of course, now, with all the heightened competition, is it really worth your time and stamps?

There *is* more competition in the confession market these days, just as there is in all fields of writing. But what you need to keep in mind is that the remaining magazines still need a steady supply of good stories to fill those pages. Come up with the right stories, and the editors will be more than happy to mail you the checks.

What kinds of stories are they looking for? Love stories, naturally. And teen-age stories. But also light, humorous stories; serious, "problem" ones; and even stories with a holiday theme. They don't have to *be* true, but they do have to *seem* true, and be written in the first person. (Female narrators are the most popular with the editors, but I've never failed to sell one of my male-narrator stories. Sometimes it just takes a little longer.) The teasing cover blurbs aside, many of the stories aren't too different from what you might find in this month's *Good Housekeeping* or *Redbook*. Strange as it may sound, a story I'd written with the teen-age religious market in mind took very little rewriting to sell to *True Story*. And "What Happened to Yesterday?" (*True Story*, January 1975) had its beginnings years ago in a story I had hoped to sell to *Woman's Day*, but with this one an almost complete face-lift was in order, not so much because of the change in destination, but because of the change in times. Since I'd written that first version, women's lib had come along, and this story of a mother who reluctantly comes to terms with her changing life-style when her last child is married had to be affected by it.

This brings up another point: Editors want stories that are timely, stories that reflect our present attitudes and mores. Many human problems, of course, have been plaguing us since the year one, and will probably continue to plague us right into the twenty-first century and beyond; but even these universal troubles should be presented in the context of today's world.

Through changes in social mores, advanced technology, or medical breakthroughs, problems that were once shattering have become less serious than they once were and should probably be scratched from your list of story ideas. But in confessions as in life, when one door closes, another door opens. A narrator agonizing over an unwanted pregnancy would have rough going with the editors in these days of birth control pills and legalized abortion; but what about the girl who's always dreamed of giving birth to her own baby, yet falls in love with a man who's had a vasectomy? Does she love him enough to give up her dream of having a family? Or do they decide to gamble on an operation to restore his fertility? Before, or after, they marry?

Look around. Listen to the people standing next to you on the elevator, or sitting in the next booth at McDonald's. Read your daily newspaper. Not just the front page, but "Dear Abby" and the medical question-and-answer columns. There are ideas for good stories everywhere.

I once accidentally solved a story problem while I was leafing through our local television program guide. I'd been making notes, off and on, for a story about a young husband who bought a motorcycle to ride back and forth to work, and the terror his wife felt each time he revved up to start down the driveway. But somehow my notes refused to turn into a living, breathing story for me. Until I happened to pick up that program guide.

In it, there was a brief, off-hand mention of a former TV series called *Then Came Bronson*. So what? I'd never seen it. I didn't watch much television anyway. I was just about to flip the page when something stopped me. The main character in *Bronson*, it said in the very next line, had ridden off to meet his weekly adventures on a motorcycle. A *motorcycle*. Something in my mind went "click," and my writer's antennae began to quiver. Suddenly I could actually *see* my young husband glued to the TV set, watching that program each and every Wednesday, riding right with Bronson as he took each curve. And his wife? Well, Vicki started talking, and I had to grab a piece of paper and start scribbling fast to get it all down. First of all, she had plenty to say about the TV program that started all of her trouble:

Have you ever wished every tube or transistor in your television set would just suddenly go *p-f-f-f-t*? I mean when it's not even football season or Miss America pageant time?

Well, I couldn't help wishing some kind of catastrophe would strike our TV, because it was responsible for the biggest trouble Ron and I ever had come between us in our six years of marriage. Because of that darn box sitting in the corner of our living room, I felt I was faced with the prospect of becoming either a divorcee or a widow.

The whole thing started a few years back when I was about four months pregnant with our third baby, Lorie Ann. That was when Ron first tuned in to a TV series called *Then Came Bronson.* Maybe you remember it. I don't think it lasted more than a season or two, but even when it was taken off, I had no cause for rejoicing—because by then the damage had already been done.

Bronson, in case you've forgotten, wasn't a TV cowboy or a trench-coated private eye. He was, my husband would tell you, the rider of the greatest thing on two wheels—a motorcycle. At nine o'clock every Wednesday night, Bronson and that blasted machine of his would come roaring into our living room. And from the minute the opening scene flashed on, until Bronson and his cycle faded off into the wild blue yonder, Ron wouldn't take his eyes off that screen. I mean, even if I wasn't pregnant and if I'd taken off all my clothes and paraded in front of him in my lace bikini panties and bra, he probably would have just yelled, "You're blocking the picture!"

The tone of the story was set. Now I could round out Ron's character a little more. I decided that, until *Bronson,* his one consuming passion had been buying, restoring, and then selling antique cars. How would Vicki, who had been indulgently tolerant of his tinkering with old cars in the safety of their garage-turned-workshop, react when she sees him scanning the newspaper ads headed not *Antique Cars,* but *Motorcycles*?

"Ron—" I began hesitantly. "You're not really thinking of—"

He looked around at me sheepishly. 'What, Vic? Oh, you mean this? No, of course not. What would I do with a motorcycle anyway?"

"You'd have to put on a buddy seat to hold me and the kids," I joked, even though something way deep inside me was sending out warning signals a mile a minute. "I don't think they make them big enough for pregnant ladies, do they?"

He laughed. Then his face turned serious. "But you know, Vic, it would be a good way to get back and forth to work. Then you could use the station wagon whenever you wanted—"

"There's nowhere I need to go that I can't walk," I cut in quickly. "Everything's nearby. That's why we bought this house, remember?"

But Ron didn't even seem to hear me. "Chuck Sprague rides his to the plant every day. Says he'd never go back to a car."

"Chuck Sprague is single!"

"What's that got to do with riding a motorcycle to work?"

"Everything, as if you didn't know, Ronald Carlton! You have two kids in there sleeping and another one on the way and—"

"*Victoria,*" Ron interrupted in his now-see-here tone. "I have never been irresponsible or neglected you or my family, have I?"

"Not so far," I retorted. "And you don't have to shout. But I'd call thinking about riding one of those—those *things*—pretty darn irresponsible!"

"Why?"

"They're dangerous, that's why!"

"Not if you know how to handle them! Not if you dress right and you—"

"And they have a bad image! All those gangs having brawls all the time and trying to blow each other up!"

"Vicki, I'm not talking about joining a gang! I'm not talking about blowing anybody up! All I'm talking about is getting a little kick out of my daily trip to work, instead of being stuck behind a wheel in the bumper-to-bumper line every lousy morning!"

"Oh, so it's kicks you're after!" I stormed. "How much of a kick do you think I get out of doing the washing and the ironing—"

"So if you're jealous, I'll get you a cycle, too!"

"Then you've made up your mind to really go through with this dumb idea?"

"Yeah, I guess I have!"

This story was bought by *True Confessions* ("The Guy on the Slightly Used Honda," May 1974). But maybe it would still be languishing as a jumble of notes in my file if I hadn't been thinking "story ideas" all the time, if I hadn't been receptive to finding an idea in an unlikely place.

The confession editors don't demand soaring prose, but what they do expect is good, clear writing—no muddled flashbacks or sloppy transitions, and plenty of dialogue. And, if you want to avoid getting that hefty manila envelope back in the mail, *accuracy.* If you use a regional background to add extra punch to your story, make certain that you check the details. Don't make the mistake of having one of your characters lean against a live oak tree if your story is set in Nebraska.

Medical details, too, should be checked and double-checked. If the child in your story has leukemia, what are the symptoms? Do you know the type of tests that may be administered by the doctor? The possible treatment? Since so many of my stories involve some medical problem, along with my bulging file of newspaper and magazine clippings, I've found it helpful to keep an up-to-date copy of a good, home medical guide right next to my dictionary.

Sometimes the medical problem is incidental to the main theme of the story. For instance, although I have never written a story *about* hemophilia, I *have* written and sold a story about a divorced mother with a son who happened to have this blood disorder; and although the hemophilia per se is not the main problem of the story, it does add to the the mother's dilemma in trying to decide whether or not to let her son risk establishing contact with the father who earlier rejected him. And in another story of mine, "The Curse I Passed on to My Son" (*Real Confessions,* September 1976), although the young wife becomes almost blinded by a sudden attack of acute glaucoma, the real blindness she suffers from is not seeing her husband for the loving man he is, until it's almost too late.

In other cases the medical problem *is* the story, as in "The Gift of Love," purchased by *True Story.* The male narrator in this one is sterile because of a childhood bout with rheumatic fever, but he decides to give his wife the gift of a child through artificial insemination. Or in "Our Son Was Supercharged" (*Secret Romances,* May 1975), which explores the problem of hyperkinetic children.

Editors, as I've mentioned before, are more likely to look kindly on your manuscript if you let your characters tell most of the story in their own words.

If the story you're working on seems hopeless, with poor characterization and not much plot, the best way to save it may be by paying more attention to your dialogue. Good dialogue is bound to move your story forward, and at the same time give your readers a glimpse of your characters' unique way of looking at life. In my story "Bed Drifter" (*Secret Romances,* December 1972), I needed to have Jack Duncan move in with the narrator, Linny McAllister, but I wasn't sure quite how to bring this about. Finally, I did it this way:

I could hardly bear to look at him as he came toward me, but as he got to the top step I saw that he was grinning at me. "Ma'am," he said with an exaggerated drawl, "you got any room for a boarder? Just wasn't satisfied no longer at Mrs. Carmichael's place. Packed up my gear and cleared out. Now if you want, I can just bed down in a corner on the porch here. Might get chilly, of course, but—"

I laughed. "Jack, what are you talking about?"

"About moving in with you," he said, his tone serious now. "Linny, maybe you haven't been listening, but I've been telling you these last two weeks that it's not safe, you being here all alone."

"But—"

"Afraid the neighbors will talk? There aren't any, Linny. At least, not close enough to notice." He stood looking at me for a minute before he said, "Look, you planning to let me in before I catch pneumonia out here or not?"

Jack carried in his duffel bag and his guitar while I looked around for something to give him to eat...

Here's another example, from "I Still Couldn't Forget His Touch" (*Revealing Romances,* November 1971). I could have had the narrator, Lila, describe her husband as a cautious, careful man, but I think this bit of dialogue does it better and, at the same time, hints at the conflict to come:

"You know, Ken," I heard Jess break in, "maybe Lila and Frank might want to put a little money in with us. After all, it's not like we'd be letting strangers in on it. They're family."

"Come to think of it, they might be interested," he agreed. Turning to Frank, he said, "What about it? Would you be willing to gamble a little? The stakes are pretty high."

Frank was lighting his pipe. "I'm not much of a gambling man," he openly admitted.

Ken answered, "I'd think a farmer would have to be. Planting a field of wheat or corn is a gamble, isn't it?"

"I suppose so," Frank said slowly. "But it's the only kind of risk I've ever taken."

Maybe that's what's wrong with us, I thought. Maybe a little gamble is what we need right now, and the money was in the bank.

"Frank," I said then, "we shouldn't close our minds to an offer like this, should we?"

"The only investment I've got my mind on is that piece of land," he answered.

Readers—and editors—of confession magazines like happy endings. At the conclusion of every story there must be that ray of hope that lets the reader know that although the narrator may have had a miserable childhood, an unfortunate marriage, a wrong attitude, things *will* be better tomorrow. But this happy ending can never be tacked on; it must evolve out of the story itself. The narrator can't just sit back and hope for the best; she or he must take definite steps to insure that the future will be better than the past, and that the story doesn't end too soon.

For my story, "Don't Talk to Me About Women's Lib" (*True Romance,* September 1976), after my truck driver-narrator makes a telephone call which reunites him with his runaway wife, the ending I first wrote seemed a natural:

> I took a deep breath. "You got two little tykes still to liberate, honey—you're gonna have to show them the way. Hey," I gripped the phone, "you think one of them might turn out to be a trucker?"
> She started crying then.
> All of a sudden I knew everything was going to be okay.
> On my way back from the phone I stopped at the juke box. I was looking for something by Johnny Cash, when I noticed that Reddy dame's latest. I hesitated for a minute, then I gave a shrug and pushed in my quarter.
> I still didn't like her, I thought as I sat down opposite Bev and took a swig of my coffee that by now was stone cold. And I still didn't like women's lib, either. But—I took another swallow of my coffee—maybe I'd learn, maybe I'd learn....

The editor of *True Romance* felt that the ending left the future too uncertain. She asked for a revised ending, which turned out like this:

> All of a sudden I knew everything was going to be okay. I mean, I've been married to Marie long enough to know that she only cries after a fight's all over—when she's ready to kiss and make up.
> I had to clear my own throat a couple times and my voice sounded pretty gruff when I managed to say, "Hey, baby—your old man here still loves you, you know?"
> There was silence on the other end of the line for a minute and I could just picture Marie looking frantically around for a kleenex. Finally she said softly, "I love you, too, you big lug, even if you have been a—a stubborn male chauvinist."
> "Hey," I shot back, "this is one male chauvinist who's learned a helluva lot about doing dishes, and I bet I can vacuum a rug and clean the bathroom better than you. I can even fry some pretty good chicken."
> "Care to prove it?"
> "Like when?"
> "Like tomorrow."
> The next night when I got home from my run, there was Marie at the door waiting. Supper was all set on the table, too.
> "What gives?" I asked as I gave her about the tenth kiss. "I thought I was scheduled to do the honors tonight."
> "You'll get your chance, don't worry." She took a deep breath. "I've decided to take some night-school courses in selling real estate."
> I knew she was watching me for my reaction.

I just grinned back at her and said, "Guess I might need to brush up on a few more recipes, huh?"

The real-estate courses are turning out to be tougher than Marie expected, but she's so enthusiastic that I think she's going to do a really great job of selling houses once she gets her license. We've all had to pitch in and help out around here—even four-year-old Kimmie. But it's not hurting the girls any, and when I see Marie going off to class, or studying her books, I suddenly realize she's liberated me, too—I don't worry so much any more about the future, about me getting hurt or sick or maybe even killed. I know Marie will be able to take care of herself and our girls, if she ever has to. She won't be left stranded, the way Bev Crawford was, and that's a mighty big weight off my mind.

The editor liked the new ending and bought the manuscript.

So, give the editors a story about life today, told by the people involved in living it, and wrap it all up nicely at the end. And even though it may be more challenging to make a sale these days, sometime soon you'll go to your mailbox and you'll find the same thing I just did—a check.

It's a good feeling.

45

THE USES AND ABUSES OF DIALOGUE

By Bill Pronzini

PERHAPS the most important technique a fiction writer must master in order to achieve any degree of lasting success in today's highly competitive magazine and book markets is the art of writing believable and appropriate dialogue. Without that mastery, he is foundering in heavy seas, and, like as not, he'll go down and fail to come up again.

Many beginning writers tend to de-emphasize the importance of dialogue. They believe that narrative is the key to salability, and hence, to success. But, in my opinion, the argument that characterization, mood, and plot line should be set forth primarily in expository passages in which the author alone does the talking is not valid. The characters themselves *must* have a voice—a strong voice. They have to corroborate the author's statements about them, about their qualities, temperament, eccentricities, etc.; they have to reflect and intensify the established mood in their spoken words as well as by their actions; they have to advance and reaffirm and assist in clearly establishing the plot line by what they say and how and why they say it. In short, and in a very literal sense, if the characters aren't able to speak for themselves—if the reader can't believe them simply on the basis of what they *say* —then the author has failed to do his job properly.

The best-selling novelists in all fields—for example, mystery-suspense, science fiction, westerns, mainstream—are to a man (or woman) highly capable practitioners of the art of dialogue. Prime examples are found in the mystery-suspense genre, into which perhaps 75% of my own writing output is channeled. Evan Hunter, whom most everyone knows is also Ed McBain of 87th Precinct fame, is perhaps the best writer of realistic dialogue. You can learn almost everything that needs to be learned about composing believable, moving, suitable colloquy from reading and studying his work. Chandler and Hammett and Erle Stanley Gardner became giants because all were able to write superb fictional conversation. Other contemporary craftsmen who come to mind are Donald Westlake, John D. MacDonald, Thomas B. Dewey, and Ross Macdonald.

The following ideas have for some time governed my own writing of dialogue. They certainly aren't intended to be hard-and-fast rules, for they are what works best for one *individual* author, but I hope that in some small way they might prove helpful to beginning writers.

There are, basically speaking, two schools in the writing of dialogue. One is the "short dialogue" school; the other is the "exposition dialogue" school (some writers, though I'm sure not many, believe in a composite of both—and all writers, of necessity, are members of both schools at times—but as a general rule you can place any author into one or the other category merely by examining his work). Both schools are perfectly tenable, and have their distinct advantages, but I belong—heart and soul—to the "short dialogue" school.

This is to say that I believe conversation in a fictional endeavor should be short and crisp between speakers whenever possible. When you consider it, this is normally the way you and I converse with friends, relatives, business associates every day of our lives. When an individual asks a question, it is most often a single, brief question; and having asked his single, brief question, he will usually wait for an answer before asking another question or continuing on to something else. And the answer, more often than not, will be as succinct as the question—a single, concise sentence, or perhaps two concise sentences. For example:

"Where were you?"
"At the park."
"Which one?"
"Oak Hill."
"What were you doing there?"
"I went to find Jack."
"Did you find him?"
"No. He'd already gone home."

A brief answer follows a brief question, a simple corroboration or negation follows a simple statement. This kind of dialogue flows quite nicely, for both the reader and the writer. And the reader is not overloaded with ideas, questions, or factual material presented in blocks. There is time for him to assimilate each detail before going on to the next.

Unless a writer is accomplished technically, expository dialogue (in which each speaker is given several sentences, some of which may take on the characteristics of straight narrative, before he relinquishes the floor to the next speaker) can be very difficult to write. The progression has to be planned *ahead* of time, rather than allowing questions, answers, statements to flow naturally from one speaker to the next and back again. Of course, there are times when I'm forced to write expository dialogue—these are unavoidable, especially when unraveling a complicated plot—but I've found that people simply do not, on the average, speak in intricate, verbose sentences and paragraphs. Most individuals run out of ideas (if not inclination) after three successive statements and wait to be led on by someone else's comments.

People generally speak idiomatically. All of us utter clichés, overwork certain words, use double negatives, preface ten sentences in a row with the word *well*, swear, and pretend that we've forgotten every grammatical axiom we ever knew. We seem to have an affinity for words and phrases like *sure, uh-huh, right, well, O.K., listen, look, why not?, all right, yeah, huh, oh, ah, um-m, hm-m,* etc. Should fiction be any different?

I am not advocating that every character's dialogue should be idiomatic or exhibit all of these features, or that these speech traits should be used indiscriminately. But a sprinkling of them will make any piece of dialogue seem more real, less stilted and contrived. The following example, while perhaps *too* idiomatic, will serve to illustrate my point:

"Listen, let's go to a movie."
"Why not?"
"Which one you want to see?"
"Oh, I don't care."
"How about John Wayne?"
"Yeah, he's good, all right."

"Or maybe Rod Steiger."
"Sure."
"Well, which one?"
"It makes no difference to me."

You *can* go overboard with this kind of thing, especially if you follow the methods of some writers to reveal lack of intelligence and/or education, and of other writers hung up on backwoods dialect. These are the authors who write phonetically, combine words and phrases, drop g's, and so on—perpetrators of the *gonna, wanna, c'mon, whyain'tcha, yer, ya, lessee, whazzat, whozzit, dunno, comin', goin',* etc., school.

While fictional characters should be made to speak as realistically as possible, there are limits. A reader can grow very weary of page after page of lousy English, and if he is forced continually to decipher elided words and phonetic spellings, he can very easily lose the flow of the story. And, ironically, this kind of writing does not establish lack of intelligence or lack of education—nor is it particularly representative of the backwoods. I've known educated men who went around saying "gonna" and "wanna" and dropped their g's; and I've known some "down-home" types who spoke clear, grammatical English.

Writers who persist blithely in this sort of thing are largely responsible for fictional stereotypes: a back-country sheriff saying ponderously, "Wal, Sam, them there fellas ain't goin' ta get away, I'm tellin' ya that"; a criminal raised in a slum district saying out of the side of his mouth, "Less'n ya want dat dere cement overcoat, bud, ya'll keep yer yap buttoned up, see?"

Careful, sparse usage of such devices is permissible, of course, but there are simply better ways of accomplishing the same purpose. To show that a character is uneducated or unintelligent, for example, the author can give him a limited vocabulary, have him repeat favorite words or phrases, or stumble over words of more than one or two syllables and seem not to understand words and phrases whose meanings should be apparent—and so on. In this way, stereotyping is eliminated and, at the same time, character is effectively revealed.

Slang and dialect should be employed by the fiction writer to achieve realism as long as he keeps three things in mind: 1) Don't use slang that is out of character (i.e., having a sheltered spinster say, "He's groovy" or "She's up tight" or "They're really cool"). 2) Don't overuse dialect or slang; there's nothing more irritating to a reader than to be confronted by one slang expression after another, especially unfamiliar ones. 3) Don't use slang expressions or jargon that is likely to go out of date. What is an "in" phrase today may become passé tomorrow. If a supposedly hip character uses slang which is obsolete and the reader is more hip than the author, the author is in trouble.

Dialogue, as I mentioned earlier, must be an integral part of a story. Dialogue which does not move the story along, or add to the mood of the story, or have an easily definable reason for being there at all (such as to establish important characterization), should be considered superfluous and therefore cut.

As a means of telling the story itself—moving it from Point A to Point B to Point C—dialogue is invaluable. In many instances, when the author has a choice of writing a scene in narrative or in dialogue, he would do well to choose the latter. Conversation is a superb way to build tension and suspense between two or more characters—and, at the same time, to build tension and suspense for the reader. Character A speaks, and the effect of his words on Character B is reflected in B's response as well as in B's actions. The effect of B's response on A is then reflected in A's subsequent response as well as in A's subsequent actions. The impact is therefore *doubled*. That is why scenes with more than one individual can be (if the conversation is skillfully handled) much more exciting, can move much more swiftly, than scenes involving only a single character and his actions, or two or more characters who do not exchange words and their actions. And that is why stories and novels using well-written dialogue can be more exciting, more rapidly paced, than stories and novels written primarily in narration.

Without conversation that flows smoothly, a story can noticeably drag; it can lose some or all of its impact on the reader; it can be divested of mood, characterization, even plausibility. If the dialogue is stilted, illogical, overwritten, patronizing, condescending or consistently inappropriate or unsuited to setting and situation, it does not matter how well the plot or the narrative is constructed;

chances are that the story or the novel will not sell "as is" in to-day's market.

There is nothing wrong with the word "said." Some writers, especially beginners, seem to spend more time thinking up synonyms for that perfectly good word than they do in plotting their stories or novels. There is no good reason for this. Words are *spoken;* they are not *ejaculated, flung, rasped, gurgled, expostulated, hissed, grated, sneered, predicated, heaved, gulped, vociferated, wheezed, blatted, pontificated, croaked, bubbled, fumed, proclaimed,* or *asserted.* Indiscriminate use of such substitutes can weaken otherwise acceptable dialogue, and make a scene less than effective—perhaps even ludicrous.

Certain *said*-substitutes may be used now and then to avoid constant repetition. Such words as: *agreed, admitted, replied, answered, asked, muttered, whispered, shouted, told* (him, her or it), etc., are all excellent synonyms. But in two out of three instances, a simple "said" is sufficient.

Some writers seem to feel the need to use *said*-substitutes to convey manner or emotion. All a writer needs to do to show that a character does more than simply "say" something is to add an appropriate adverb after the word *said* (or *asked* or *answered,* etc.); *slowly, warily, evenly, happily, cheerfully, argumentatively, solicitously,* and so on.

One thing to keep in mind, however, is that no one makes a statement or asks a question with particular inflection or emotion or purpose *every time.* Most often, we simply make statements and ask questions. Adverbs are fine as long as they're used sparingly, and when genuinely necessary.

To illustrate the foregoing, I offer the following two passages of dialogue. Which would you consider the most effective?

"Where's the money, Harry?" Jack asked.
"I don't know," Harry said.
"You stole it, didn't you?"
"No."
"Don't lie to me," Jack said.
"I'm not lying!"
"I can always tell when a man is lying," Jack said coldly.

Or

"Where's the money, Harry?" Jack hissed.
"I don't know," Harry ejaculated.
"You stole it, didn't you?"
"No."
"Don't lie to me," Jack blatted.
"I'm not lying!"
"I can always tell when a man is lying," Jack iced out.

Almost any kind of fiction can be effectively written if the dialogue is properly constructed and used. The best sex scene and the best tender love scene I have ever read were both done entirely through dialogue. There were no graphic bits of narrative in the former, and no "shining eyes of love, and palpitating heartbeats" in the latter. Both were memorable—real—because all the elements of humanism and emotion were inherent in the words which were spoken by the characters.

Mastery of the art of dialogue truly *can* make the difference between sales and rejection slips.

46

POINT OF VIEW: EXPERIMENT IN LIVING

By Marjorie Franco

A few years ago I walked into a New York office, gave my name to the receptionist and sat down. The receptionist, a young girl, turned to me and inquired, "Are you an actress?" "No," I said, disappointing her, "I'm a fiction writer." I had the feeling she wanted me to be an actress—it's more glamorous, I suppose—and to make amends I said, "Inside many a writer lives an actor." Nodding agreeably, but clearly dissatisfied, the girl returned to her work. Had she been interested I could have explained that writing, like acting, is an experiment in living, and that the writer (and the actor), by lifting himself out of his own particular life, looks at life from another point of view.

What is point of view, and what does it have to do with writing, or acting, or the persons behind either of these creative arts? The dictionary says point of view is a "position from which something is considered or evaluated." All right; that seems clear. The writer takes up a position from which to tell a story. What position? A reader might say, "That's simple; he tells a story in either the first or third person." It might seem simple, but for the writer it is not.

There are at least six third-person viewpoints and five first-person viewpoints, some rarely used. To discuss all of these or to discuss technique without a story to hang it on can be confusing. Even though the writer has an intellectual mastery of viewpoint techniques, he may not create a good viewpoint character. Writers learn by doing. Did Chekhov sit down and ask himself, "Should I adopt the position of concealed narrator and third-person protagonist narrator restricted, or what?" Or did he simply write "The Kiss"?

This is not to say that it is unimportant to learn technique, for a writer needs to learn as much as he can about the tools of his craft. But tools are only a means to something more, and a preoccupation with them can lead to mechanical writing. Viewpoint, then, is not a matter of manipulation, of attaching oneself, willy-nilly, to a position, to a character, and then telling the story through that character's mind and feelings. Viewpoint is organic, and writers have in common with the actor the method to make it work.

An actor trained in the Stanislavski method knows the psychology of his character; he knows *how* he does things because first he knows *why*. The actor tries to put himself in his character's place, to enter his world, live his life, master his actions, his thoughts and feelings. His truth. It is not enough merely to think of an emotion. Abstract emotions don't come across, or they fall into clichés. It is better to imagine what a character might think or do in a *certain situation*. Then the emotion comes of itself.

A writer uses a similar method of organic viewpoint. He puts himself in his character's place, enters his world, indeed creates his world, suffers his pains and celebrates his joys. If a writer has never laughed or cried at his typewriter, then I doubt if he has ever been deeply inside a character.

Before a writer takes up a viewpoint position he might do well to consider his own temperament and personality and the limitations these impose on his choices. Fiction is personal, as personal as the writer's imagination and emotional experience. New writers are often told, "Write what you know." I would broaden that by saying, "Write what you know emotionally." Love, hate, anger, joy, fear—these are universal. They become unique when they are connected to experience. Our emotional experiences are stored within us. Filtered through memory and a well-developed imagination, they can be called up, made fresh and organized into the work at hand. Creative imagination is the writer's valuable gift, and even though it is somewhat limited by his experience, within that sphere of experience it is unlimited in variety and combination. Hopefully the writer is always enlarging his sphere, adding to his storehouse with outward experience in reality.

Out of the sphere of my emotional experience I wrote "The Poet of Evolution Avenue" (*Redbook*), the story of a young wife and mother who was, also, a bad poet. She believed her creative gift was being hampered by the intrusion of her family. She had neither the time nor the privacy to write a real poem. Time and privacy are practically forced on her in the form of a vacation alone in her father's California apartment, but it isn't until she is ready to go home that she is able to write a real poem, and then only because she doesn't want to go home empty-handed.

This story is based on the old Ivory Tower idea: a poet is more productive when isolated from the world. My poet discovered that she had been making excuses for herself, that her world was her stimulus, and that she had trouble producing poetry without it.

The idea for that story came out of my own emotional experience. Some years earlier I had gone to California to be near my father while he was in the hospital undergoing surgery. For three weeks I lived alone in his apartment, a large, tight-security building in which I rarely saw the other residents. I had brought my typewriter, thinking I would turn out a volume or two between hospital visits. It didn't work. I was accustomed to working with people around. Interruptions. Interruptions can be marvelous. They take the place of pacing, a necessary activity of some writers. I learned that I am not an Ivory Tower writer, ideal as that may seem; I need the stimulus of family and friends.

Every writer has his own voice, and it is up to him to find it and use it with authority. That voice comes through as male or female, child or adult, humorous or serious, but behind it, within it, is the author's brooding presence, his vision of life. He describes the world from his point of view. He is on intimate terms with his viewpoint characters. Henry James could imagine what his focal character (he is never named) in *The Aspern Papers* might think and do when he is forced to admit to the woman who loves him that he has been using her for his personal gain. But I doubt if James could have lived inside Bigger, as Richard Wright did in *Native Son*, and chased and killed the huge rat in a Chicago tenement. Who is to say one view is better or worse than another? Each is different, unique.

Recognizing his limitations, an author adopts a viewpoint position he can understand emotionally as well as intellectually. My story, "Miss Dillon's Secret" (*Redbook*), is about a teacher. I have never been a teacher, but teaching is within the sphere of my emotional experience. I have been a student, of course, and my husband, now a principal, was once a teacher. His experiences have rubbed off on me. I believe that a natural teacher is born, not made, that the qualities in such a person work together to make learning exciting. The title character in my story, Miss Dillon, is drawn from a real person, an experienced teacher whose students come back to visit her with their husbands and wives and children and grandchildren.

I adopted the viewpoint position of a young teacher who had worked with Miss Dillon. There were more decisions for me to make. Will I place myself inside or outside the viewpoint character? And how far inside or outside? This can be a difficult choice, for each character has its own limitations, and the author, to keep his voice appropriate to the viewpoint, puts limits on his "knowledge" accordingly. He seems to know less than he does. Consider, for example, Hemingway's camera-eye view which limits his "knowledge" to what can be seen from the outside. Or, at the other extreme, Joyce's deep internalizing, which limits him in the other direction.

For my viewpoint character I adopted a position somewhere in between. With the story told in the third person, my character's problems are external, but her discovery of Miss Dillon's secret is internal, brought about by an emotional experience with one of her former students.

We might ask ourselves certain questions concerning viewpoint: 1) Who will be the narrator? author, in first or third person? character, in first person? or nobody (omniscient narrator)? 2) From what angle does the narrator tell the story? Above, center, front, periphery, shifting? 3) Where does the author place the reader? Near, far, shifting?

Sometimes an author adopts a viewpoint position instinctively, and all goes well. The voice flows from a stable position. At other times an author finds himself tangled in clumsy sentences and tedious explanations, surrendering his surprises too early, battling predictability, placing his best scenes offstage. When this happens, the problem could very well be the viewpoint he chose. He may be looking from the wrong angle. Usually I can tell by the way it "feels" if I'm in a good or poor viewpoint. But not always. Four years ago I wrote a short story called "The Boy Who Cooked." **The** title character, Benny, was the antagonist, and the viewpoint character was a woman protagonist whose name changed with each of the many versions I wrote. I couldn't sell the story. But I continued writing it, on and off, for four years, always keeping the boy, but frequently changing the characters around him, including the viewpoint character. The total number of pages devoted to that story runs into several hundred, which is some indication of my devotion to a character. But finally I gave up and put the story away.

Meanwhile, I had written and sold a story called, "No Such Thing as a Happy Marriage" (*Redbook*), in which the viewpoint character was a wife and mother named Jenny. Six months after that story was published, my editor, in a letter to me, mentioned Benny, the boy who cooked. Even before I had finished reading the letter, Benny, like Lazarus, rose from the dead. Why couldn't I write a new story for Benny? And why couldn't I surround him with the same cast of characters I had used in "No Such Thing as a Happy Marriage," with Jenny as the viewpoint character? I could, and I did. This time the viewpoint felt right; the voice flowed clearly from a stable position, and I wrote the story in a matter of hours. After four years of roaming through my typewriter, Benny had found his place, and his story, "The Boy Who Cooked," was published in *Redbook*.

The author's attitude toward a character (and his desire to create a similar attitude in the reader) can help determine the angle from which he views him. If the character is obviously sympathetic, the reader will identify. With some characters, however, the reader may feel only a tentative sympathy, until he is shocked into understanding by some revelation which allows him to feel complete sympathy. Sometimes, reader and character start out with a great distance between them. Perhaps their worlds are totally different. The author gradually pulls the reader into the character's world, and the reader ends by feeling sympathy. (I have this experience, as a reader, when I read Jean Genêt, for example.) A difficult relationship for an author to achieve is one in which the reader is forced to identify, perhaps unconsciously, with a character he dislikes. He is left wondering what there was about the story that fascinated him. What he may not realize is that, being human, we all

have our share of unattractive qualities, and seeing them in someone else stirs our recognition. Playwright Harold Pinter frequently
achieves this kind of relationship.

In my story, "An Uncompromising Girl" (*Redbook*), my aim
was for tentative sympathy and eventual complete sympathy. As
the author (concealed narrator), I speak in the third person
through the focal character. The channels of information between
author and reader are a combination of the author's words,
thoughts, and perceptions, and the character's words, actions,
thoughts, perceptions and feelings. I used the angle of the character attempting to see herself from the outside, but erring in her
vision—a position which placed limits on my "knowledge" of the
character.

Earlier I spoke of the writer's voice, which I related to his vision
of life and which includes his entire personality. Now, to that voice
I would add two more voices: the story voice, which is the pace,
the music, the tone of the story; and the voice of the viewpoint
character, since it is through his eyes that we see everything that
happens. Actually, it is impossible to separate all these voices, fused
as they are into a creation that has passed through a maturing
process in the author's mind and found its way to the page, either in
harmony or dissonance. But for the sake of clarity, let us for a
moment consider the voice of the viewpoint character.

If a story is told in the first person through a character (and not
the author), then that character's voice is ever-present, and the
writer, like the method actor, must know the character's every
thought, act, feeling and desire. He must know his truth, his conscious and unconscious life, what he wants, or thinks he wants, and
the difference between the two. My story "Don't Call Me Darling"
(*Redbook*), was written from such a viewpoint. I had to know my
character's attitude toward herself as a woman pursuing a career.
I had to know how she felt about women's rights in general. And
how she felt about friendship and human communication. I had to
understand her intellect, her ambitions, her habits, and her insights. When she spoke, she revealed herself as a careful individual, and this voice had to remain consistent throughout the story,
even though some of her attitudes were undergoing a change.

When an author knows the details of action and speech in a

character, he is in control of his material. He can become more familiar with his character by spending time with him, engaging him in conversation or argument, as if he were a living entity. He may even want to get up from his typewriter to act out a detail, a gesture, or an entire scene, in order to visualize it more clearly in his mind. Creating characters, seeing them come to life, is an exciting experience.

The entire experience of a story, from start to finish—and it may cover a period of several years—is an exciting one, in spite of the hard work, frustration and failures. Not a small portion of that excitement lies in the discoveries that are made, for in any work of creative imagination one looks for insights. What does the story have to say? Does it reinforce a shallow view of life? Or does it open up new insights for the viewpoint character? When I write a story about a character who seems very real to me, am I not at the same time making a discovery about myself? Writing, like acting, is an experiment in living. It is looking at life from another viewpoint. And life can be exciting wherever it is lived, or re-created— on the stage, or on the page.

47

THE LIFE AND DEPTH OF STORY CHARACTERS

By Adele Glimm

My daughter's English teacher, teaching the short story, told her students that an author first decides on the theme for his story, then searches for characters who will illustrate the theme. My daughter, who knows about writers and writing from the inside, disagreed. She said: "The first thing you think of is a character."

I would only amend this to: the first thing is, you are possessed by a character. A character happens to you. In my case, a still unwritten story steals into my mind in the form of an image of the main character in a crucial scene. One minute I may have had no story in mind, and the next minute a character has appeared in my head and another story exists, at least in its essence.

Ideally, a printed story should steal into the reader's mind in a similar fashion. The main character, living and breathing, is suddenly part of the reader's consciousness, a being complete with family and friends, life situation, unique personality and interests, and a problem. This character will occupy the reader's mind and emotions for the reading time of the story and, I always hope, beyond that.

What transforms my initial image of my protagonist into the character the reader is engaged with on the page? An amazing amount of hard work, of course, but chiefly my concern for the character. The act of writing a story is an act of caring and closeness. While I am writing a story, the main character is closer to me and has more of my attention than anyone I encounter in the real world. My character needs me in order to breathe. I need him in order to be myself, that is, a writer. It's a kind of desperate joining forces for survival. For me it is impossible to dislike a principal character, though I can see his faults as I can see my own faults or those of people I love. This is not because I've created this individual, for it's easy enough to dislike my own *minor* characters. But the hero of a story, like a child one is raising, must be loved in order to live a healthy life.

My own favorite among my published stories, "Child of the Heart" (*Good Housekeeping,* November 1973), opens this way:

> Karen Bayley was always nervous on the days the social worker was due to visit. Waiting at home made it worse, so she spent the morning pushing her adopted son, Paul, around the city in his stroller.

As you can see, in the first two sentences in which we meet her, Karen already has a problem, a family situation, and a setting. When I first thought of Karen, I envisioned the young, intelligent mother of an adopted baby waiting anxiously in a city apartment for a visit from the social worker, an older, self-assured woman who seems to have so much power over the heroine's life. At that point I didn't know what would happen to Karen, that is, what the story's plot or theme would be. Rather, I was obsessed with Karen as a person, with her state of mind and her emotions. I wanted to stick close to her awhile and leave her free to pursue her goals and hope she learned something valuable about life. Here is what Karen has learned by the end of the story:

> Paul would not belong to her, not even after the judge had made his decision. When the last paper was signed Paul would still be free, and in time he would make his own choices and his own mistakes. When the social worker had lost her power and been shown the door for the last time, other dangers would still threaten them.

No requirement for successful story writing is more important than the need for the protagonist to be someone with whom the reader can identify. (I've learned this from more editors' rejections than I care to remember.) This does *not* mean that the character must be a bland and average example of the life situation he or she represents. I tend to load my characters with individual quirks and interests, often more than the storyline requires. I think such details make characters real to readers very quickly and are worth the space they take. Let's consider Amy Snyder, the young heroine of a story called "A Day To Be Cherished" (*Good Housekeeping,* April 1974), which is actually a short short, where every word counts. Amy lives alone in San Francisco and has just met Josh, a man she may fall in love with:

Amy said that she was from Milwaukee and that she worked as a bilingual secretary for a shipping firm because her grandparents had spoken German to her before she was old enough to realize anybody was teaching her anything.

Often, adding a seemingly unimportant detail about a character's past serves to make the character convincing in the present and to make her a sympathetic person to the reader. The character then seems to move through more dimensions. Such information serves to relate the character to the future as well. I like to picture Amy, long married to Josh, baking German Christmas cookies with her kids. Beyond Karen's immediate problem with the adoption and the social worker lies the day when she will once again teach poetry to college students.

You can tell by now that to me *who* a character is matters more than what happens to him. I like to think of the reader as knowing my characters well enough to guess what they would do and feel in a plot situation other than the one unfolding in this story.

But it would be fatal to downgrade the question of plot. Like the main character, it helps if the main plot or problem is identifiable for the reader. But in creating plot I feel I can move farther away from reality, from the average everyday world, than in creating protagonists. A character's problem can often be a common problem for the reader but may be heightened, translated into an unusual form. For example, many mothers of first babies feel insecure in their new role. Karen's situation as a mother whose baby's adoption is not yet final presents the reader with an extreme form of a problem which she may be living through herself or may remember.

In "A Woman's Heart" (*Good Housekeeping,* May 1973), the heroine, Celia Watson, has the following problem. Thirteen years ago she quarreled with her father, a tempestuous show business type, over her marriage to Steve:

Steve was too ordinary to satisfy my father, who was an actor. He was disappointed in Steve, and he said so right out. He'd always wanted me to marry an actor or a film director or maybe an opera singer. Sometimes I thought that even the flame swallower in a circus would not have been too exotic a son-in-law for him, provided the flame swallower had style and dedication and a true love of show business.

Celia hasn't seen or heard from her father since. Now he returns for a visit and reconciliation and Celia is torn between the need to heal the rift between them and her resentment of the unsettling effect he produces on her serene family life.

Few people have experienced thirteen-year total breaks with their parents (though since this story appeared, more and more people confide to me some personal history of this sort!). But many young adults live through long years of difficult, rebellious relations with their parents until, like Celia at the story's end, they mature enough to coexist confidently with their own parents.

Celia's story deals with still another common problem, that of parent-child bitterness caused by a conflict between conventional versus bohemian or hip life styles. Only here it is the child who is conventional, the parent free and adventurous. This story has been reprinted in four foreign countries, so I suppose it strikes familiar emotional chords for many people.

Plot requires action, and I used to work unnecessarily hard thinking up fresh action for each scene of a story. I've come to realize that readers feel more comfortable and secure with repeated scenes, what we might call patterns of action. Most of us would find it too great a strain to wake up each morning to a world that was different from the day before. A reader following the action of a story is like someone experiencing a world. I think repeated action, like repeated phrases in music, anchors the reader and enables him to relax and give in to the emotional effect of the story.

However, there should be tension between repeated events and surprise events, between the reader's comfort while reading and his sense of shock or revelation when the story presents him with a new experience. In the story about Karen, the social worker's usual visits are described as being identical. But in the crucial visit, all the expected details are turned upside down, and the waiting and anxiety turn out to be related to the social worker's *own* role as a mother (her son has been arrested), not to Karen's role as the mother of her adopted son Paul.

What of the role played by minor characters in stories, those characters I said earlier I was capable of disliking? I find that the function of many of my supporting characters is to give good advice which the heroine ignores, or bad advice which she can argue against or which may lead her astray for a time. Supporting characters often represent character types opposite to the heroine. Karen's neighbor, Dinah, is an easy-going mother in contrast to Karen. Dinah says:

> "Relax, Karen. You and I are like two artists who paint in different styles, only with us it's different styles in motherhood, you know? I think you should stop trying to protect Paul from the whole world."
> I can't afford to stop, Karen thought.

Dinah already knows something Karen is suffering in order to learn: a mother's care does only so much for a child.

Nancy Saret, in "If I Could Tell You" (*Good Housekeeping,* May 1974), has a daughter who badly needs guidance on individuality versus conformity in female-male relationships. Nancy thinks women should be themselves. But her old friend Madeline is visiting during the crisis, and Madeline believes women do best to transform themselves into what men seem to expect them to be. Here the heroine's value system is challenged. She has something to work against. By the way, supporting characters should rarely open their mouths except to say something that is relevant to the main character's problem.

Once you've created a compelling main character, the reader is going to feel attached to the character, even if their relationship has only lasted for seven or seventeen pages. The reader must feel satisfied and not abandoned at the story's close. I often give the reader some point in the character's immediate future to think about, to hold onto, something to help the reader keep the character with her, preferably in her heart as well as her head, when there are no more words on the page.

A good way to do this is to leave the character about to do something. Karen is about to welcome her husband home from work and tell him of her strange experience that day. Celia is thinking ahead to the frequent happy visits from her father in the future. Characters don't have to be deprived of the life you've worked so hard to breathe into them, just because our story now is ended.

48

YOU CAN GET THERE FROM HERE

By Eileen Jensen

WRITING, like making love, is more fun when you know what you're doing. Editors keep telling me, a working writer, that my short story transitions are good. In looking through my story files to find transitions from my published work to illustrate this article, I was surprised to discover that I was using good transitions ten years ago. I can't brag about it, however, because in the beginning I honestly didn't know what I was doing. What came naturally to the young writer has become conscious craftsmanship. It's a lot more fun now.

What makes a good transition?

A good transition has thrust. It shoves your story forward like a booster rocket tilting a spaceship. Well-timed and carefully triggered, it will put your story into orbit.

Every story has its own pace. Some glide. Others race. A few seem to hop along, grinning. The best transitions are smooth. They do not jar the reader. Transitions, like cosmetics, are most successful when you are unaware of their presence. I believe any intelligent writer can learn to write good, quick, viable transitions. Two things are required: you must pay attention, and you must practice.

For the most part, I use three kinds of transitions in my short stories. I think of them as TIME transitions, ECHO transitions and LEAPFROG transitions.

TIME transitions are the easiest. They also are the most obvious, and you must be careful not to make them dull.

ECHO transitions are more interesting. They link one part of a story to the next part by repeating a certain word or activity or thought on the far side of the transition.

LEAPFROG transitions set up a scene, and skip over it, landing on the next lilypad. This is a tricky transition, but it is lively and interesting and forces your reader to participate in the action.

266

The TIME transition keeps your reader chronologically oriented. He knows where he is because he has been there before. The story is moving in intervals of time which he understands and relates to. Saturday night means something to everyone. Sunday morning is a different day, indeed. Monday morning? Ouch!

The Time transition becomes art when it is used in a story where time itself (meaning time-passing) is important. Time passes at two levels in such a story. A good example from my own published short stories is "The Loveliest Grapevines in Cleveland" (*Woman's Day*).

This is a story about children growing up in today's migrant culture. I related it through the planting, cultivation, harvest and distillation of one crop of grapes. Time was vital to the story in every way. The family was always moving. It was important to keep track of the ages of the growing children, the number of times the family moved, the length of time it takes a young grapevine to grow and bear fruit, and how long it takes to make wine. Even the passing seasons were important to this particular little story. The children, the grapevines, and the story matured together, going from one transition to the next through time within the story. I planned it that way. The mother in the grapevine story is the star. She's a loving gardener. Susie, the nine-year-old younger daughter, is the narrator. Early on I set the reader to thinking about time:

Last year for Mother's Day, Daddy gave her a riding mower . . .

This mother holds the family together in spite of constant relocation. She does it by cultivating a loving relationship as carefully as she husbands the grapevines. I don't say this in so many words (it's fatal to preach), but I plant the idea in almost every Time transition throughout the story:

When we move to a new house, my mother makes us feel it's home. The first thing she does is plant flowers . . .

I take the time to show the mother doing that. Then—

We've lived in Cleveland for three whole years now. I know Mother cringes at the thought of ever leaving our big old white house on this half-acre . . .

And then I flash back, moving the story backwards with a Time transition.

The week we moved in, an old man in the neighborhood brought us a wooden churn as a housewarming gift . . .

And forward—

She planted a willow whip that first year. It's taller than my sister Lissa now. It casts a shade. Buddha could sit under that tree . . .

The mother plants the grapevines.

The next year they didn't look a whole lot better . . .

The mother teaches her girls about life through the example of the vines.

Suddenly, our willow was taller. Buddha could stand under that tree. Our grapevines, three years old now, began to look great . . .

The harvest is near, and the pace quickens. The skilled writer will go to shorter sentences now. Transitions will speed up.

In June we knew we were going to have a crop . . .
In July robins perched on the trellises and eyed the green fruit . . .
In August, the grapes turned from green to bronze to velvety blue . . .
It was the first Wednesday in September, and school started the next week . . .

They make the wine. They wait two months. They bottle it. Eight bottles.

Mother said we would open it for Christmas. Let's see, if we open one bottle a year at Christmas, it will last until I'm eighteen. That's not bad.

Even at the end, you see, I am pushing the reader ahead of time, pointing him into the future.

That may be the most time-oriented story I ever have written. And yet, my files reveal that as far back as October 1959 *McCall's* published my story, "Some Day He'll Come Along," an equally time-conscious tale. In those days I wrote stories in the way some people play the piano—by ear. I knew when it sounded right. Now, so many years later, I can read music—and even compose a bit.

In "Some Day He'll Come Along," I took a romantic girl from the age of twelve through marriage and childbirth at age twenty-seven. She was searching for the one man she would love. The transitions are similar, if somewhat less skilled, than those in the grapevines story.

During her senior year . . .
It began to look as if she'd have to find him in college . . .
The next day he told her he was going into the army after college . . .
After college, her parents sent her abroad . . .
She was twenty-four when she married Howard . . .
Amy worked hard at being Mrs. Howard Garvin . . .
She began to wear maternity clothes . . .
She was twenty-seven when their child was born . . .

Surely any beginning writer can do as much. Or more.

ECHO transitions are the swift ones, extremely valuable in the short-short story. Take "Seasons of the Heart" (*Good Housekeeping*). It is a time-oriented story—but a short one—and transitions must be lightning quick. The narrative is related through gardening metaphors again. (I'm a gardener, and I am sensitive to the parallels between plant life and human existence.) I chose Echo transitions for sheer speed.

This is a story about Meg, a pretty young widow trying to adjust to the untimely death of her husband. When the story opens, Meg is pregnant. She and her husband Tony buy a small apple tree to plant in the backyard of their new house. They plant it while Diana, the disillusioned divorcée next door, watches cynically. Tony boasts—

"My son will play in the shade of this tree."
"If it lives," Diana says.
The tree lived, but Tony died—killed in a speedboat accident.

The echoing word "live" is the trigger to the quick transition. There is life here—going, coming, snuffed out. The transition is accomplished within the space of six words.

Later in the story as Meg struggles to adjust, Diana ridicules the young widow.

Meg burst into tears.
It was the last time she cried. In January, she brushed up on her shorthand and took a part-time job.

The Echo in the transition is the word "tears" as related to "cried."

I doubled the effect in that same paragraph when Meg reveals that she is taking

". . . temporary office work. A Skelly girl. It isn't much money, but you meet such interesting typewriters." She also met men, but they were either married or bachelors with dependent mothers, or ex-wives to whom they owed alimony and child support.

The Echo word is "meet." I take her from her first job through a series of men, and do it with one transitional echoing word.

And note that it's also a LEAPFROG transition as well. Meg meets and passes several men within that one transition.

I leapfrog again in the transition in which she accepts a glamorous date with her sophisticated boss who wines and dines her and invites her up to his apartment to see his stamp collection:

"He didn't even have a stamp!" Meg reported indignantly to Diana the next morning.

The transition is both Echo (stamp) and Leapfrog, because we jump over the seduction scene in the man's apartment. The reader knows exactly how that encounter went. We don't need to document it.

Warning: you must not leapfrog any scene which is out of the ordinary and different from the usual encounter. If it's vital, write it! If it's valuable only in passing, leapfrog it.

You can take giant leaps. Imagine this one:

Debbie lay awake all night, thinking of Jim.
Jim lay awake, too—in another woman's arms.

I recall one of my early stories in which I described a lovers' quarrel which broke up an engaged couple. It took place before a dancing party.

They didn't make it to the altar.
They didn't even make it to the dance.

By now you should recognize and identify the transitional technique in the quarrel. It's both Echo (didn't make it) and Leapfrog (skip the dance scene).

When you are reading, watch for transitions. Learn to identify them. Be conscious of the writer's craftsmanship. When you begin to notice and recognize what is going on, you will begin to use good transitions in your own writing.

49

WRITING THE MYSTERY SHORT STORY

By Edward D. Hoch

WHEN I was first beginning to write, a well-known mystery novelist advised me to forget about short stories and concentrate on novels. "Why waste a good plot idea on a short story?" he argued.

I've now been publishing short stories for eighteen years, with a total of close to 400 in all, and I don't feel that I've ever wasted a plot. In fact, I sometimes think that the plot devices used in my occasional novels might have been put to more effective use in a shorter length.

But the difference between novels and short stories is much greater than mere length or payment alone. Graham Greene, a writer I greatly admire, wrote recently that in spending some years writing a novel, "the author is not the same man at the end of the book as he was at the beginning." For this reason, he views short stories as a form of escape for him, "escape from having to live with another character for years on end, picking up his jealousies, his meanness, his dishonest tricks of thought, his betrayals."

The economics of modern mystery novel writing generally preclude an author's spending more than a few months on its composition, and yet he can still suffer from the sort of problem Greene mentions. If a story is to have any sort of unity, there should be a unity to the author's mood while he is about the business of writing it. This unity, obviously, is more easily achieved in a short story.

Basically, that is why I prefer writing short stories to writing novels, and here is how I go about it. If my remarks are directed mainly toward the mystery short story, it is because this genre has been the most successful for me. But they're just as applicable to science fiction, adventure, or any short story where the emphasis is on plot.

I suppose the ideal short story should be written, as John O'Hara wrote many of his, in one sitting. I have achieved this ideal occasionally with short-shorts, but never with anything longer. The technique I use most often is to plot out the story in great detail in my mind before starting to write it. I do not use written outlines for my short stories, though an outline of sorts exists in my mind before the first words go down on paper.

I begin sometimes with a character, or an unusual setting, or a plot twist that has occurred to me. Often I have started with nothing more than an unusual, provocative title—only to have an editor change the title after the story was sold. At times, when a new plot does not come full-bodied to mind, I will often try to combine two or three separate elements from my notes. Thus, I combined a newspaper article on a shooting at a wedding reception with a magazine article on a new Hollywood technique for faking bullet wounds. By the time I'd worked out a way of combining the two, I had my plot for "The Leopold Locked Room," a story published in *Ellery Queen's Mystery Magazine,* and later dramatized on television's *McMillan and Wife* (NBC-TV).

A personal experience of mine—a trip to a hospital emergency ward for treatment of a gashed forehead—afforded a plot which virtually wrote itself in my mind while the doctor was stitching up my wound. The story, "Emergency," was published by *Alfred Hitchcock's Mystery Magazine.*

By its very nature, a detective story—and to some extent, a crime story—must have a beginning and an ending. While a mainstream short story might well be started without its author's knowing quite where he's headed, this is virtually impossible in the detective short story. On the few occasions when I've started with only the beginning of a plot in mind, I've generally had to rewrite that beginning completely by the time I reached the end. For me, at least, it's much easier to have the story plotted out in my mind before the writing starts.

Certainly, this does not mean that every detail, every clue, every encounter, must be thought out in advance. Much of the fun of writing (and it *is* fun most of the time) comes from creating little plot twists as you go along—extra pluses that help make each story something special.

I'm often asked by beginning writers if they should concentrate on short stories as I have done through much of my career till now. Frankly, the markets are few, and the pay in most instances is not especially high. But once an author has published a number of stories, there are many secondary sources of income: anthology appearances, foreign sales, television adaptations, movie options. With luck you might even find a publisher willing to gamble on a collection of your stories.

The key to all this, of course, is to be prolific. I now publish about thirty stories a year in a variety of magazines and original anthologies. Almost all are mysteries, or science fiction stories with a strong mystery element. For those who wonder how it's possible to come up with thirty separate plot ideas in a year's time, I can give a fairly simple answer: *create series characters*.

These characters can be detectives or criminals, but it's important that they grow and develop with each story, that they become familiar to the magazine's regular readers. The first story I ever published concerned a mystic detective named Simon Ark who went on to appear in twenty-seven stories during the years that followed. At the present writing, six of my series characters appear regularly in the pages of *Ellery Queen's Mystery Magazine,* a publication especially amenable to the series format.

There are two prime reasons why a short story author (or any author) should try to develop series characters. The first is the obvious economic one. An editor who has already purchased a story about a given character is a ready market for a second or third story about the same character. But perhaps more important, a series character gives the writer a starting place, a familiar viewpoint that can be a big part of the story.

Sometimes, a plot will come to mind simply if you put your familiar series character in an unfamiliar setting or have him meet a strong or unusual protagonist. Especially effective in adding depth to your continuing character is the gimmick of having the crime he's investigating somehow involve his personal life. In this way, my series detective, Captain Leopold, uncovered a forgotten murder when he was invited to a reunion of his old high school class. This story, "Reunion," grew out of my own class reunion and has been widely reprinted since its original publication in *The Saint Mystery Magazine* back in December 1964.

The best detective stories naturally depend upon a surprise solution or unexpected twist at the end. Ideally, this should be saved for the last possible moment—even the last sentence of the story. This last sentence can be used effectively to reveal the murderer's identity or to deliver a shock of the sort the reader will remember, as in my story, "The Oblong Room" (which won an Edgar from the Mystery Writers of America).

In some cases where post-revelation explanations are in order, the story must continue for a page or so after the killer is revealed. It is important in such instances to avoid dullness in your explanations. Break up the paragraphs with questions from other characters, and if possible, still save some especially clever clue or twist for the last line. It will send the reader away satisfied.

In a series detective story, it is usually best to use some secondary character to serve as a "Watson" of sorts. If you use a series criminal, where no formal detection is called for, it is possible for him to be more of a loner. But we've come a long way from those days when the Watson was typed as a bumbling friend or stupid policeman. Today, he can be almost as smart as the protagonist. He may be the detective's friend or co-worker, or even a superior to whom our hero must report periodically. (This last is especially effective in spy stories.) With an eye on possible television sales, you might even want a pretty girl cast in this secondary role, with or without romantic interest in the detective.

Much of what I've said about series detectives applies equally to the short story or the novel, of course. The major difference is that character development in a series of short stories can come over a period of several episodes. Interest is built as readers learn a little bit more each time about the detective, his past life and personal quirks.

Occasionally, if one story in a series proves especially successful because of plot or setting, the author can return to something similar in a later episode using some of the same characters. Thus, my series spy Rand in "The Spy and the Nile Mermaid" (*Ellery Queen's Mystery Magazine*) journeyed to Egypt, where he shared an adventure with a girl named Leila Gaad. The encounter proved so successful that Rand has returned to Egypt for two further adventures, creating a series within a series.

But one important thing to remember with a series character is that the reader must not be cheated. Each story must stand on its own feet as a story. Such a caution is even more important when writing a non-series story. You must give the reader some reason for an emotion at the finish—whether that emotion be pleasure or sorrow or even anger at having been tricked.

I'm often asked how much rewriting is necessary, and my reply is that it depends upon the individual story. I've sold good stories without changing a word, and I've sold equally good stories after laboring over them for weeks, writing three or four drafts. In most cases I rewrite only portions of the story, to insert some extra clue or description or bit of characterization. On the whole, a mystery short story usually requires far less rewriting and revision than would a novel, and not simply because it's shorter. The story is short, yes, but the creative time span is also short. There is a unit of time and purpose.

To paraphrase Graham Greene, if you write short stories, you're usually the same person at the end of a short story as you were at the beginning.

50

BACKGROUND—THE MOST IMPORTANT CHARACTER

By Elisabeth Ogilvie

Novelists have always been intrigued and inspired by the power of environment to influence human lives. Since we're all readers, I don't have to list even a half dozen classic examples; you can name ten in as many minutes. And they all observe the rule for the background novel; whatever the situation may be, the cause, the working out, and the final effect are influenced by the milieu in which the characters experience their jealousy, hatred, love, adultery, greed, or sacrifice.

The word "background," in itself as flat as a backdrop on a stage, is a misnomer for the environment in which we live our lives. We are what we are because of it; if we are completely at home in it, we are shaped to it, but if we fight it, it becomes an impersonal yet hostile force that shapes us in another way. Or we have a love-hate relationship with it: we can't live with it and we can't live away from it, and that turns us into ambivalent creatures, never at home anywhere, always eaten with homesickness for we don't know what.

You have *your* background, which you know in every detail because you've been born to it, or else you've come to it with fresh and excited eyes, seeing things which the native doesn't even notice anymore. It can be a corrupt and fascinating old city in Europe, or a suburb full of status-seekers; or you may have a useful knowledge of steel mills, ranch empires, ocean liners, or research laboratories. Whatever and wherever the territory, as a writer you contemplate its citizens and its effect upon their personal lives. If there is an impressive physical setting to be described, so much the better. You are rich beyond the dreams of avarice, and you are going to spill these riches out on paper.

Now, where to begin, and how to get it all down on paper? You're not only spendthrift, you're like the enthusiastic new painter who wants to get every last twig of that enchanting scene onto canvas, not knowing that to leave out some of it is to strengthen the rest.

Or, you have people and their fundamental problems in human relations, and you want to use a rich and unique setting which you know well, but your problem isn't that of disciplining a mass of material, but of how to use it at all.

The rule in both cases is as essential and simple for you as it was for Emily Brontë, Thomas Hardy, and Mark Twain. In the novel of background, events must happen *because* of the background. Ask yourself this: Are these people acting the way they are because they live in a certain place, under certain conditions? Or could they be found anywhere? Could the whole action be picked up and set down somewhere else? If you say *yes* to these questions, you are not using your background correctly.

I write about fishing and lobstering people along the coast of Maine, more specifically about two islands. I live on one, which I used in my novels, *The Witch Door* and *There May Be Heaven*. The other is Bennett's Island which I used in my *Tide* trilogy, and in *The Dawning of the Day, The Seasons Hereafter,* and several juvenile novels. This island, twenty-five miles out in the Gulf of Maine, rugged and magnificent, turned me into a writer at the age of fifteen because I had to express my passionate emotions about it in some way. I still haven't finished exploring all the aspects of its disturbing influence on human beings.

Here is a world of stunning beauty and often of stunning brutality. Here are men making their living in an intensely physical way, on terms of truce with the elements. The women live accordingly. (Ask yourself, in what ways are the people in my setting different from other people? To what unique situations must they react in their daily lives?) The suburban woman whose husband is late getting home knows he has probably been caught in traffic on the freeway. The fisherman's wife, who may read the same magazines and whose children may be watching the same thing on TV as the children two hundred miles away in Newton, Massachusetts, knows that when *her* husband is overdue, his engine could be broken down and he may be drifting out there in the dusk, or he has lost his course in a surprise snow squall and piled his boat on a ledge. He may already be dead. She says nothing to the children, but lets out a long breath when she looks out at the harbor for the twentieth time and sees a moving light at his mooring.

In *The Seasons Hereafter,* as in the *Tide* books, I kept the strong rhythms of life beating like a counterpoint to a woman's private experience by the use of a few simple devices. To say that description and local color are combined with action may sound too simple:

> She got frantically out of bed and saw Western Harbor Point and the breakwater washed bronze and rose with the sunrise. A boat was going out by the breakwater, and the man was putting on his oilclothes, now and then touching the wheel.

Vanessa is frantic with her own confusion, yet life goes on, there is a clear sunrise and the boats are going out. The harbor is the heart of the place, it dominates her. She keeps coming back to it:

> The changeable harbor seemed curiously empty and lifeless this morning in spite of the skiffs at the moorings and the gulls picking through the fresh wet weed on the ledges. It was as if an invisible tide had gone out with the men and wouldn't return until they did.

In a quick sketch you get the look and feel of a fisherman's harbor when the boats are out.

They go out, they come in, no matter what happens to her. She has been waiting all day for her lover, "watching *White Lady* ride into the harbor on towering seas; Steve Bennett's *Philippa* rolled deep on one side, and Nils Sorensen came in behind, easing his boat when she slid downhill on the smoking green slopes. Charles rounded the breakwater after him, sinking out of sight in the trough. . . . When the family came in, it was an armada." This is the family whom she resents and tries to despise.

Walking to the store, what does Vanessa see that the farm or city woman doesn't see? "Seine dories newly painted buff and blue at the edge of the coarse grass, a graveyard of old hulls rotting beside a little pond." She smells a whiff of bait and wet lobster traps brought in to dry out. She recognizes the sound of trapnails being driven into a lath, oarlocks, an engine being tried out. And there are always the gulls that haunt the place like its familiar spirits. Vanessa is concentrating intensely on herself, yet you and she are forever conscious of messages from the outside.

"When she came into the house, Barry had been in and gone out again. His dinner box was on the table, and his rubber boots stood against the wall. He had cooked some lobsters and eaten a couple; the shells were in a sink." She takes two lobsters for herself, "breaking them open with quick professional twists of her hands and getting the meat out in big pink and white chunks."

The dinner box, the rubber boots, the fresh lobster bring Barry's work into the room; implicit are the long hours on the water in the rolling boat. The way Van handles the lobsters shows another of the small but significant differences that give validity to her and her background.

A child's accident can be of any kind, anywhere. Make the bad fall or burn something that could only have happened *here*. Don't miss any chance to strengthen the sense of apartness. A child in *Seasons* sees a starfish from a wharf, goes down over the ledges to get it, slips on wet rockweed, and falls in. Vanessa goes down a steep ladder to get him. Just as she casually handles lobsters live or dead, and can stuff salt herring into a baitbag, she is used to ladders at low tide. The suburban wife doesn't quiver at the thought of city traffic or the farmer's wife at helping a cow to calve.

In *The Seasons Hereafter,* the love affair begins and is carried on in secrecy only because it happens where it does. In the first confrontation, the man appears suddenly at Van's door looking for her husband to help him seine herring. In five minutes, simply because Owen Bennett heard herring "puddling" in the harbor, his and Vanessa's lives are changed, and they will never be the same again.

Because he is a lobsterman, it is perfectly legitimate for him to hire her to knit trapheads for him. This is a tiresome job many men don't want to do or have the time to do. It is a dying skill, and the person who can knit (actually *net*) can always be sure of work. When he brings her the twine and meshboards, the businesslike meeting is as intimate an encounter as exchanged glances over cocktails or dancing together at a party:

As he started to give her instructions for the heads, she said, "Wait a minute, I'd better write everything down." But she could find neither pencil nor paper, and she got very hot and her eyes stung. "Oh, damn it," she wailed softly, pawing without sense at magazines, and he called to her, "Never mind, I've got something in my pocket." . . . He was sitting at the table writing on the back of an envelope. She stood looking at the bulk of his shoulders and the back of his neck, at the way the wiry black hair grew down on it and at a small puckered scar, a white seam against the burnt-dark skin. She lit a cigarette after several futile attempts to scratch a match because her hand was unsteady.

They discuss technical details. Then, when he is about to leave, he tells her, apparently off-hand, that he'll be going around the shore in a dory looking for traps of his washed ashore:

> "This morning I saw three down in Ship Cove."
> "I'll bet your youngsters will enjoy going with you."
> "I'm not taking them. They'll still be in school."
> "Oh." The syllable floated between them, a leaf or a feather. . . .

As simply as this, the appointment is made; they can meet in a lonely cove because the island has so many such coves, and because he has a legitimate excuse to be out there at midday. She of course can take long walks without question. On an island with no automobiles, people still walk for recreation.

The nylon trapheads become a sexual symbol.

> Soon they would be handled with careless expertise by those brown hands with the long thumbs which she could see so clearly as they wrote, gestured, lit a cigarette, and held out the meshboards.

The trapheads represent the way of life which has thrown these two together, and something more subtle. This is something his wife can't do. What other need can't she fill for him?

The familiar situation in which secret lovers are crowded in with other people and must hide their feelings can also contribute to authenticity. In this case, it's a severe gale when the men stay up all night to watch the boats. Van is upset at being in close quarters with Owen, her husband, and another couple. What makes it more agonizing is that Owen ignores her:

> The scene around the table lacerated her nerves, yet she could not bear to go away from that oblivious black head. He could at least look in my direction once, it's his trapheads ruining my hands. . . . I wish all their damn boats would

come ashore at once. Then you'd see some hopping and swearing. And I'd sit here and laugh. I'd laugh myself sick and never stop. She drove the needle hard through the loop and gave a vicious pull.

Just when she thinks she can stand no more, a boat is driven ashore, and the men fly out in a grand scramble of oilskins and rubber boots. She is saved by one of this salt-water world's particular disasters.

Another appointment is made, this time almost within earshot of his children, the girl knitting baitbags for pocket money, the boy gathering ballast rocks to help his father: a tiny design to help bring out the whole pattern of the fabric.

This date is for a weekend. The island makes such occasions for lovers, because there are twenty-five miles of water between it and the nearest dentist, doctor, lawyer, or income tax official. A couple of errands that could be done in one morning by a mainlander take up two or three days for the islander.

These lovers, each with a different errand (Van's is false), travel across the bay at the same time, speaking to each other only casually. On the mainland they meet again, they go away, and because they are what they are, they seek another island. The stolen time is spent in a place of great beauty, no sordid hideout, and they are bemused and betrayed into believing for the first time that they can have a life together. In this spot between sun and sea, where he could go on being the fisherman and the islander that he was born, everything seems possible.

At home, waiting for the time to make a move, she rows across the harbor to relieve tension, as a mainland woman might get in her car and go somewhere. She thinks, "Anyone could row all around Jessup's Island in a few hours. I would like a little dory like the one we went out there in." She sees herself watching for Owen's boat to come up the thoroughfare on that far coast; she sees herself painting buoys while he builds traps. She is always true to her background, even in her dreams.

And at the end, who is to say whether his wife holds Owen or Bennett's Island does? Vanessa doesn't know.

When you are planning your story, take into account the hazards, the rewards, the triumphs and terrors of the world you are trying to create. What in his professional life makes a rancher, a doctor, or a schoolteacher happy? What depresses him or, worse, terrifies him? The fire in *The Seasons Hereafter* doesn't ruin everyone, as it could have done with the right wind blowing, and the fire department twenty-five miles across the bay, but it is a catalyst for Vanessa and a disaster for squalid little Gina, whose struggles run parallel with Van's. The two of them are, each in her own way, victims of the most important character in the novel—the island.

The island has made its people what they are. It imposes a peculiar discipline on them, and they must obey if they are to survive and prosper. It exercises a Lorelei charm on men like Barry, stronger than his rage at Van's betrayal.

Here's a final sympathetic word if you're afraid of swamping hard-boiled editors with masses of descriptive matter, but can't hold back. *Don't*. Put it all in that first draft; go madly poetical with description, or splash it on like thick paint. Don't refine as you go. Don't try to understate. Be free-swinging and uninhibited. But come back to it sternly a month later with a handful of sharp pencils, and *cut*. The essence will be there.

Without false emphasis but with a sure knowledge of your background and a meticulous attention to detail—from the games of children to the adults' tragedies, whether on a city block or a Maine island—you can make your reader *see, smell, hear,* and *feel* its presence below, above, and behind everything else.

51

FOUR TESTS FOR A PARAGRAPH

By John Ball

VERY early in the career of every aspiring author there needs to be a clear understanding that the golden words do not come on the first pass. There is a continuing need for careful reworking, revising and polishing if a salable piece of fiction is to result.

There are some writers, particularly those with newspaper training, who can do a moderately good job in first draft and who have been published in that form. For a fast-breaking news story this technique is acceptable when employed by a competent professional, but only a low-grade hack would turn out books, feature articles, or other forms of supposedly serious writing on a once-through-the-typewriter basis. In the days of the pulps when rates were often a half cent a word, no one who was attempting to survive by selling to those markets could afford to spend much time in polishing his copy. Under those circumstances a lot of first-draft manuscripts got into print and for the most part the editors who bought them got what they paid for. Now the marketplace has changed considerably, publishing costs have gone way up, and a better-quality product is demanded almost everywhere.

When a quarterback puts the ball in the air, he is aiming for his own man, but if he makes a mistake, or the intended receiver does, a game can turn around in seconds. There is no way to recall the play unless an official throws a penalty flag. But if the author writes a bad sentence, paragraph, chapter, or whatever, he has the invaluable opportunity to correct it before it gets off his desk. If he doesn't make full use of this rare privilege, then he's an amateur and very likely to remain one indefinitely.

The need for careful revision, rewriting, and editing has been pointed out so many times there is no need to labor the point here. However, the awareness of the need to revise doesn't always imply the knowledge of how to do it. I once knew a lady in Philadelphia who meticulously rewrote everything she produced, sometimes several times, and none of the revisions that I saw was any better than the original. Redoing per se is not enough. The fact that the same material has been completely rewritten does not automatically mean that is has been substantially improved. The new version could well be worse. The basic requirement here is knowing how to revise.

Many people are sensitive to the idea of cuts. When they have put something together with thought and care, they don't want someone else to start chopping it to pieces. Also, there are many readers who rebel against abridged versions and condensations done "to speed up the action of the story." However, if a housewife has prepared an elaborate dinner for guests, and everything has turned out splendidly until she discovers that she has hopelessly burnt the peas, if she has a brain in her head those peas will not be served, even if they would have been rather nice with the lamb.

Similarly, no competent author will serve up even as much as a sentence to his editor if it tends to detract from the remainder of his literary effort. A cute turn of phrase is no excuse for including something that doesn't otherwise belong. Professionalism consists in part in knowing what belongs and what does not.

One method that works is to review completed first-draft copy on a paragraph-by-paragraph basis. Reading each paragraph over to see how it "sounds" is not enough—each one should be required to pass at least one of four basic tests:

1. *Does the paragraph advance the basic action of the story?*
This is a relatively easy question to answer. If the paragraph contains a viable part of the progression of the plot, some action that must take place, then it passes the test. It also passes if it contains some information that the reader must have. If it does not, then the next question follows:

2. *Does it genuinely contribute to an understanding of the people involved?*
Personally, I do not believe in characters in a story. A character is a contrived thing, frequently with a limp or a scar on his cheek. I do strongly believe in people and prefer to write about them. If the questioned paragraph gives a clearer insight into one or more of the

people involved, it passes. If it does not, then the third question should be asked:

3. *Does the paragraph intensify or make more real the background against which the story is being told?*

This particular test is a little less easy, because there is a tendency to accept rather empty description as fitting the requirement. Saying that the sun is glinting off the water as the waves roll gently against the beach doesn't convey too much. Is it hot or cold? Is the air still or stirring? Is the place isolated or swarming with tourists? Is it clean and fresh, or pocked by litter? What time of day is it? If the paragraph helps the reader to see and experience the background, then it's doing a job. To offer experience it must be three-dimensional, just as the people on the scene cannot be puppets. If the reader isn't put into the picture, if he can't feel the sand with his own feet, then the paragraph fails and the final test is in order.

4. *Does it contribute to the mood of the story and add to the feeling that the reader is to experience?*

This is a very important test, as mood has a great deal to do with the success or failure of a literary property. It is always there, sometimes very passively and sometimes downstage center, as in the opening chapters of *Dracula*. Gothics depend heavily on mood. So do most other examples of storytelling. Sometimes, like expensive perfume, a sparing use of mood is best, but it must be a controlled factor. The author, of course, does the controlling. If the paragraph does genuinely define, deepen, or intensify the mood at that point in the story, it is earning its keep, and passes.

Asking these four questions is actually a very simple matter. It is not much more difficult than looking at a small round object lying on the ground and deciding whether or not it is a coin. With a little practice, it becomes all but automatic.

If a paragraph cannot successfully pass at least one of the four criteria that have just been listed, then there is only one answer: *out.* It does not matter if it contains beautiful language, poetic inspiration, marvelous word rhythm, or similar virtues. Take it out—and prove that you are a professional. It is almost as dangerous to fall in love with a literary passage as it is to become enamored of a particular stock and refuse to sell it when the time is right. Both failings can be expensive.

Like a number of other technical devices, this one works only if the person using it is genuinely objective and doesn't try to rationalize. There is, unfortunately, a certain group of writers who cannot resist the magic of their own words. Once they have written something, it is engraved on the book of time, and there it must remain—they think. If this makes them happy, well and good, but there is a greater happiness and self-satisfaction in getting published. The two do not go together.

This is so because the editors who are in the market for fiction want to buy material that is going to return a profit, directly or otherwise. There are times when something is published for prestige purposes, just as recording companies will occasionally put out a new recording of less popular chamber music in order to maintain stature, but this is coming in through the back door and isn't recommended. It's a poor bet at the very best.

Breaking into the writing business, or advancing within it, calls for constant decisions concerning what to write, how much research is necessary, what viewpoints to take, what length to aim for, and what revisions of the first draft will contribute to the quality of the finished product. In this area, particularly in writing as compared with other professions, discipline is essential.

The four tests of a paragraph just cited represent a form of discipline which, if followed, will help to increase the quality and marketability of a literary property.

52

KEEPING THE READER BREATHLESS

By Anne Chamberlain

The art of writing the suspense story must surely be one of the most harrowing and exhausting of all literary pursuits. More than with any other fiction, it involves a taut physical process, whereby the author strives to keep the reader in a state of compulsive anxiety (eased by occasional restorative pauses) from the beginning to the end. Whether he is aiming for 1,000 or 60,000 words, the writer must engender in himself a nervous tension even more consuming than that which he demands of the reader. How else can the writer identify with his characters, sustain the mood, control and direct that elusive sense of timing which is the key ingredient of his narrative? Unless he, too, is all but literally on the edge of his seat, ready to jump at the first unexpected noise, aware—as he writes—of dark shadows in other rooms and footsteps beyond the windows—he cannot hope to transmit through words that fearful anticipation of what might happen, what might not.

For it is anticipation of danger, not necessarily realization, that propels this type of fiction. In this, the form differs from its cousin, the detective mystery, in which the unexpected violence is committed (often more than once) and the perpetrator is eventually exposed. While the suspense story usually deals with physical peril, it promises nothing. The murderer may not strike; if he does, he may walk nameless and still threatening off the last page. Or the danger may turn out to be a tormented fantasy of the protagonist. But, actual or imagined, it must—sooner or later—become terrifying to at least one character, hence to the reader.

How to make terror believable? We have all, at certain unforgettable times, experienced it. Yet it is a nightmarish emotion that, even in factual recollection, remains difficult to describe. It is apt to spring from a bizarre situation, also extraordinary enough to defy credibility. The suspense writer's first problem is to convince himself not that the story can happen (he knows that anything is possible), but that, on paper, he can make it engrossingly real.

For the evocation of extreme fear, the writer must understand it. And, for understanding, he must sympathize, he must readily be able to perceive and describe the odd and often hysterical reactions of the frightened person. Although the story itself may be completely contrived, a pure figment of an artful plotter's imagination, the emotion that powers it must be deeply familiar. So the writer may ask himself what, of all potentially fearful moments in his memory, observation, in listening and reading and watching, has strongly stirred him, clung to his mind, lurked hauntingly in his heart?

Ideas are numberless. Which are the writer's own? The late night walk through lonely streets, with the soft steps following? The anonymous phone calls, the unsigned letter, the distorted face pressed against the window? The slow-growing realization that, while the author is away, a stranger has broken into his apartment and is prowling around? What to one may seem minor distractions can, to another, be the spur for a short story or a novel. Out of the wealth of material, he picks the situation or character (or both) that, before he hits the typewriter, gives him chills.

Consider the apartment prowler, who (for now, and for this writer's convenience) invaded the home of a young woman. Her name is Maureen. She is twenty-two, confident, casually flirtatious, not easily scared; she will be our protagonist. The prowler has been there and gone when Maureen hurries into her living room; he had left his message. Puzzled, she stares at the bottle of wine, the two crystal glasses, the tall candles in star-shaped copper holders, neatly arranged on her coffee table. She giggles. Someone's being cute. Ron? She shakes her head, not like him. Mr. Selgund, her boss? They're not on a first-name basis, but he gives her brooding looks. Toad? Real name Strode, but "Toad" is what they call him and he deserves it and, yes, come to think of those bulging eyes and that hangdog sidling walk and the way he licks his lips when she teases him, could be! At which thought she laughs outright. Then she notices the paper, folded and tucked partly under the ashtray. She reads it. She stops giggling.

Since the situation plays so strong a part in this fictional form, it is tempting to overlook the importance of characterization. Yet, for the very reason that the story is farfetched, the participants must be that much more vividly portrayed. The flirtatious Maureen cannot be painted in shallow colors; if she is dull, who cares what happens to her? Her foolish vanity, her girlish verve, the loneliness and insecurity that underlie her need to attract even the repulsive males in her vicinity (perhaps especially them) need perceptive delineation.

The note? It is a rhyme, printed with what looks like deliberate clumsiness, in thick black pencil (from the office?):

> We shall have wine by candlelight
> And I shall watch you move
> Like a silver shadow in the dark—
> My one, my final. . . .

She crumples the paper. "Nut!" she exclaims. And, with absurd indignation, "Why didn't he finish it?" Laughs again, but nervously, and her thoughts dart once more to Toad. Well, she hadn't meant any harm, had truly thought she'd please him, a bit of attention now and then, who else would give him a second look, poor creep? And the girls, especially Sue, needed a lift that time of the morning, also sometimes late afternoon; it had come to be a kind of office ritual. "Watch me turn on Toad," she'd whisper to Sue at the water cooler, and then slowly stroll near his desk and slowly, ever so innocently, brush against him. "Not speaking to me today, Toad?" She purrs, sees him lower his head, lick dry lips; the girls can hardly control their snickers. She leans closer, "Like this sweater, Toad? I wore it especially for you." It's worth the price of admission to see the sweat pop out on his forehead and on the backs of his big hairy hands, and now he can hardly sit still. He looks as if he'd like to crawl under the desk and hide; he mumbles something. "To-o-a-d, you call that *speaking*?" She flicks a strand of his pale hair and strolls away. Poor creep, she'd only meant to give him a little thrill. . . . But was it Toad who had been in her apartment? And how, however did he get in? And when?

The suspense writer is a legitimate magician; his is the craft of honest legerdemain, in which the audience knows that it is being fooled and appreciates the performer's dexterity. He should have dozens of little tricks up his sleeve, none of which need detract from the story's essential integrity. And the deft employment of a selected few of these sleights-of-hand can greatly enhance that breathless quality that itself is a form of magic. The "had I but known" device is one that can be used to provide an enticing narrative hook at the beginning and can be used again, sparingly, at other intervals. There are many variations of this.

An opening paragraph to my story about Maureen could run, "Had Maureen but known, that first day, who left the candles, the wine, and the strange note, she might have behaved differently. She might have been truly kind; she might have spoken frankly, fairly. Would this have changed what happened? On later days, she wondered."

Another device involves a series of small clues, not properly noted by the heroine, but clear to the reader, who soon wants to shout warnings: "Watch out! Don't you see?"

Next morning, in the sunlit office, Maureen avoids Toad; he appears oblivious to her. She can't resist confiding her experience to Sue, and before long, with rapid desk-to-desk whispering, all the girls know. It is generally decided that Toad couldn't have been the prowler; he's not subtle or imaginative enough. "Go turn him on," Sue suggests, "see what he does; we'll watch." Maureen ambles over to his desk; he lifts his head and innocently faces her. "Hi, Maureen," he huskily mutters. Friendliest he's ever been! He couldn't be the guilty one; if he were, he'd at least perspire. Our heroine is vaguely reassured. The wise reader moans: "*Why* is he suddenly more confident? Watch out, Maureen!"

Artful use of sensory detail, careful exposition of setting, and hints of significant contributing circumstances are important. Possible ways that the intruder could get into her apartment, and how (since he works in the office) he would manage this on company time should be clarified. Ground this out-of-the-world story as much as space and pace permit.

Maureen has her lock changed; the prowler visits again, and this time she notices that a window has been gently forced open. On the table are two more glasses, candles, another bottle, this one half-emptied. The note resumes the rhyme where it left off:

> LOVE
> And you shall hear the words I've kept
> In silence all this while.
> Beloved, I don't think you'll laugh
> I doubt that you will....

The suspense story (including the novel) usually covers a short span of time. The obvious reason is that the writer cannot hope to keep the reader in such tension over a prolonged period; one can hold one's breath for only a while, and—after those respites offered in every such story—will return only so often to the state of delectable anxiety that suspense at its best creates. Because the narrative's immediate action is of brief duration, the suspense writer frequently employs flashbacks for the rounding out of characters and the filling in of background.

For example: After the prowler's second visit, Maureen is truly frightened. Transfixed, clutching the scrap of paper with the verse, she stares out the window and wonders, "Why me? However did I get into this?" And rushing into her memory may be her mother's worried scolding when as a child Maureen had gotten into trouble: "However did you get into this, darling? Whatever did you *do*?" A long-ago scene, characterizing the pretty self-centered child, and perhaps a shambling schoolboy version of Toad. However, indeed, Maureen? But in her carryings-on in the office, she'd asked for trouble again and again, all the time telling herself that she just felt sorry for the poor creep, that she only wanted to give him a thrill. Who else would make the effort? She hurls the note into the wastebasket. There and there and that to you! But what can she do now?

Interweaving action with flashback, building Maureen's present peril on the strong foundation of her past, the story moves to its final terrifying crisis. She comes home late (she wouldn't miss her bowling, no matter what), she's had the windows secured, she's talked to the police and been told that he was probably just a crank but to be careful, she is singing as she waltzes into the apartment. Freezes. The same setting, but the bottle is nearly empty, the candles are burned down. Slowly, as though hypnotized, she approaches the table, picks up the note:

SMILE
Now will accept my ardent lips
Will taste my hungry breath,
If I command, you'll lift your glass
And drink a toast to. . . .

"Oh, no!" she cries aloud. Oh no, within her heart. Behind her, a footstep.

What happens to Maureen, to Toad, to all of them—men, women, children, who run and worry, chase and are chased through suspense stories? I, for one, like to know the last sentence of a suspense story I'm working on before I write the first. It is the lantern hovering at the end of the zig-zag path; it will light my way when it gets dark. But, before I start that first sentence, before I'm willing to undertake the myriad, haunting adventures in the land of fear, I must care enough to become, in the course of writing, the panicky girl in the story, and also—when necessary—to become the tormented intruder, and each and every character who emerges on the scene. Finally, throughout the long (but so short) journey, as the author, I must myself be in almost breathless and rapturous suspense.

53

STORY PLOTS AND THEMES

By Marlene Fanta Shyer

In my "Hopeless" file, I've accumulated at least a dozen clinkers, stories that have flopped here and abroad and represent more than a year's work which will never see print. I keep them for sentimental reasons; these are the efforts that carried me from the Bridge of Sighs to the Bridge of Sales; they've taught me how to sell, if not how to write.

Before I unburden myself with one more word of self-pity about how long it took and how difficult it was to get there, let me stress that there would have been no transition without persistence. In the years preceding my first sale, I gave up writing a half dozen times, the result of overdoses of failure, but each time I crept back. Persistence is to selling what will power is to diets; only one writer I've ever heard of sold a first story to the slicks, and she admitted that the next twenty were rejected! So endure the rebuffs, tolerate the rejections and faithfully read the stories that the slick magazines have chosen instead of yours. Like dieting, it becomes easier with time.

Watch a pattern emerge. Some things are *in* at the slicks and some are *out*. To mitigate the frustration of your apprenticeship I've capsuled some bylaws that distinguish the commercial from the *non*, and include as case studies some of my hopeless cases, hopeless characters and hopeless themes to illustrate where I went wrong—as well as a few that made the grade.

Next to giving up smoking and learning to address your mother-in-law as "Mom", it seems to me the hardest hurdle in a writer's life is learning what makes a good plot.

I've written enough stories to know how to put together a hero and heroine and make it all come out all right in the end, but after all these years I still get the shudders when I sit down in front of a naked piece of paper with not an idea in my head. Where, I ask myself, are all these other authors coming up with the sort of clever and complicated story convolutions that add up to a check? I stare at the paper, secure in the knowledge that I'm a published writer with a strong will and a dandy style. So why haven't I got anything to say?

One reason is that every plot has to go steady with a theme. It took me a mountain of rejections to make this discovery. Nobody thought to warn me. Actually, I don't think I ever really knew what a theme was. Now, after a lot of wasted postage and a few years of crushed hopes, I know. A theme is the answer to the question that is raised when your story is finished: What does it all prove?

Pull your story together and let it *say* something, and you're in. For example, if, in your story, your daredevil hero gets hit by a street-cleaning truck, he must learn something in the end. If he learns to beware of street-cleaning trucks, that's no theme. If, on the other hand, he learns that he must temper his incaution because his life is valuable not only to himself but to others (like a good little wife and apple-cheeked children you've introduced earlier), *that* could be a theme.

Themes must be positive or forget the whole thing. If you take a jaundiced-eye view of humanity in real life, reform fast or go unsold. The slicks are not convinced that life is a drag; they want to hear about generosity, love and the bluebird of happiness—preferably subtly.

Don't spell it out in black and white, if grey and white will do nicely. The reader is getting wiser and likes to use a little imagination, like putting his own egg in the cake mix. Go easy on the "I suddenly realized" department. Dialogue can be more effective than narrative.

When I began I wrote delightful stories with beginnings, middle, and ends, full of wit and sprightly characters. I have these stories and enjoy a laugh over them now and then. They are themeless orphans and might have sold to the *Woman's Home Companion* in the forties, when fiction was not so serious. For now, they score minus ten with every editor. One of these, "Daddy's Girl," concerned a lively girl who disobeyed her father and ultimately fell in love with the man she rebelled against because he was her father's choice. Theme? Obey your father. But no one has to be told that!

A story in *Good Housekeeping,* "Life and Love Upstairs," probably less witty than "Daddy's Girl," brought me a large check. The plot is simple: A young family is badgered by the lady downstairs, who vociferously objects to the noise of their lives being lived above. The simple theme: The young must come to understand and to tolerate the forms of loneliness of those who are old and alone.

The theme is the stuff of which the story is made and is as important nowadays as the paper on which it appears. It must have a basic truth, perhaps even a message. It does not have to be spelled out at the end like an essay on ethics, but even a witty story should be sewed together with one serious thread.

"First Smile," quite a funny story I wrote and sold to a Canadian magazine, concerned the disastrous results when a brand-new mother is faced with her overly helpful mother and mother-in-law, who come to assist with the new arrival. The story was light from beginning to end, but the new baby's first smile brought in the happy ending, complete with theme: becoming a grandmother is every bit as difficult as becoming a mother.

So now you know you've got to have a theme as well as a plot and here you are, face-to-face with your Smith-Corona, without a thought in your head. In answer to the question, "Which came first —the plot or the theme?" I start with the chicken, the meat, the plot, usually. When I've worked out some characters and action, I ask myself what it all means. Often I sit shrugging my shoulders over this problem for days. It often doesn't mean a thing.

For example: I thought up the beginnings of a very tidy plot about a girl in a country hospital (*Good Housekeeping,* "Rx: One Mended Heart") and a boy in the next room. The rollicking possibilities seemed fine: an escalating romance in an offbeat setting peppered with bumbling doctors and erratic plumbing.

But what about the egg, the theme? In other words, so what? I wasn't going to touch the typewriter until I'd nailed the answer. Finally, little by little I began to build. Suppose this girl hated the country, had just come up to visit, had broken her leg and was now stuck in this rustic wasteland? I elaborated on this; I gave her a solid city past, a job, and an urban beau. Here she was, lying in the hospital and feeling desolate.

The boy in the next room also had a past, and a fiancée who coincidentally wanted him to move to the city.

Now I brought the boy and the girl together through the machinations of a country hospital telephone operator, and they fell in love. In the end, the girl is convinced that country life is exciting and wonderful. Note the formation of theme with plot. The theme: Happiness is where the heart is.

Where did I get my idea for a country hospital in the first place? I don't have a little notebook full of spontaneous jottings. I carry my ideas in my head and wait for them to pop up at propitious moments. Sometimes they do and sometimes they don't; one needs patience.

Not the kind of patience that means you go out on the town instead of sitting at the typewriter. I mean the kind required for sitting somewhere quiet and really trying to build a story from scratch.

I don't mean a whole story. It doesn't have to jell from A to Z before you begin, unless you're the fastidious outline type. It seems to me that some of my best stories begin with a vague outline, a theme, and a firm idea of the end. As I work, new ideas pop unexpectedly into my head. Suddenly, the story begins to zip along in its own clever way, independent as a ouija board. The outcome often surprises me. Occasionally even the theme is changed. Often the firm ending is not the one I originally had in mind. This writer's serendipity is one of the great pleasures of writing.

The country hospital idea came, as it happens, from nowhere. I've never been in one, I've never seen one. I made it up. That's really my job, as a writer. Often I have help; I get an idea from something real, something that's actually happened. Slick fiction should mirror ordinary life, so I try to garner everyday things from people's conversations, the very things they wouldn't report to a writer.

For example, my last few published stories dealt with 1) a pair of neighbors, grown very close, who are now to be separated; 2) a husband who is promoted and can't seem to cope with success; 3) a mother, laid low by a brief illness, who finds no one can substitute mother-love; 4) a gloomy, rainy Sunday that helps a young wife to realize how lucky she is to have a family.

All these plots are based on the most mundane, day-to-day experiences, easy for the reader to recognize as real, incorporating pleasant characters with which the reader can identify.

I listen, I observe and I think. Then I stick a few things together, change the end, revise, cut, and I'm all set. Easy, isn't it?

That part of a plot which is pivotal in a story, I have dubbed the "hinge": the point toward which the characters must move all along, the point in a plot once known as the climax. Climax, nowadays, is too strong a word for this pivot; it can consist of a word or a look, instead of a war or a first kiss, but it changes the direction of the story and the writer must have established this point before his fingers first touch the typewriter. He must have planned it with utmost strategy, sneaking in forecasts of it almost from the beginning.

My clinker, "Christmas Incident," ran as follows: Joe's daughter had alienated him by a forced marriage to a man of whom Daddy doesn't approve. Joe is lonely and bitter, but on Christmas Day, he decides he must accept his daughter's invitation to visit her and her new baby. On the way to his daughter's house, Joe drives past a frozen lake and notices some children trying out their Christmas ice-skates. The hinge: Just as he passes, a young girl ventures too far and falls through thin ice. The water is not deep, and she is quickly hauled out, but the moment of fear has shifted Joe's sentiments. He is reminded of his own daughter in childhood, the fragility of their present relationship and immediately realizes how precious she actually still is to him. With this fresh viewpoint, he continues to his daughter's, determined now to accept his son-in-law and make peace with his daughter.

This hinge is marred with the anathema of coincidence and is therefore unacceptable. It strains the reader's credibility to believe that Joe just happened by as someone was about to be drowned; it does not stem logically, in A-B-C order, from the structure of the plot. It is a trick, and sounds as if it had been stuck in as an afterthought.

An example of a thoroughbred hinge appeared in *Redbook*, in my story, "The Difficult Part." The story concerned a mother who was told that her young son had musical talent. Without consulting him, she forced piano lessons on the boy, and despite his lack of interest, she made arrangements with his teacher to have him appear at a students' recital. The hinge follows naturally: The boy, frightened and a poor beginner, plays some wrong notes and runs off stage in a panic. His humiliation changes the focus. His mother realizes that "children do not always fit into the tuxedos their parents weave for them in their imaginations."

Here is the natural outcome of a logical hinge that does not depend on chance or coincidence. The reader, finishing the story, might say, "I could have guessed that would have happened," without actually having more than a clue and certainly without making the story predictable.

Whitewash the heroine—and that goes for the hero as well. The editors of the women's magazines are unified in demanding a protagonist with whom the reader can identify. This does not mean Pollyanna and Little Orphan Annie rolled into one, but it does mean, *no big vices!* She never embezzles, gossips or has dirty fingernails, and if she has a questionable past, it wasn't her fault. She's allowed little shortcomings and may be given to shyness or absent-mindedness or disorderly ways, but she is Virtue Personified, like you. That goes for her husband, too, and all those people near and dear to her with whom she's going to mingle in her plot. Not too much unpleasantness anywhere, please, as there was in my ill-fated story, "New Boy."

Strictly speaking, the protagonist of this story, one I considered excellent before it came back and back and back, was a sensitive boy. He adored his dear and loving parents who were, unfortunately, jewel thieves. If the readership of *Good Housekeeping* were composed of gun molls, this would have gone over big; unfortunately in this case, the readers of women's slicks are ladies between the ages of eighteen and forty, and for all practical purposes, they do not steal. They prefer to identify with paragons rather than felons.

And "New Boy" taught me something even more important: aim for non-fiction fiction. Avoid, like rejection slips, the incredible. The response that the writer must aim for is, "This is real. It's just like what happened to me last year!" or perhaps, could happen tomorrow. Jewel thieves don't happen to anyone, but car mishaps do, as in my *Good Housekeeping* story, "All My Own":

A young wife wants a second car for her own use. Husband says no but finally relents long enough to buy, reluctantly, an old heap from a used car dealer. These things happen every day. The hinge: the car, containing our *pleasant* heroine and three children, stalls and dies in the middle of a traffic tie-up leading to a huge department store parking lot. Please note: The car does not explode or hiss fire or lose a couple of wheels. These things *could* happen, but the slicks are not interested in improbable catastrophes. They want everyday occurrences. Whose battery, after all, hasn't gone dead at some time or other? In short, the trick is to be original—in an *ordinary* way!

Of all the mistakes my clinkers made, lack of action is the most deadly. Narrative, like aspirin, is only effective in small doses, except, perhaps, in *The New Yorker*. If you aim for the slicks, make the story move—no—jump from scene to scene. Jump into the dialogue at the beginning, if possible; if not, keep your introduction short because it will amuse only you and those who love you enough to be bored by overdoses of your descriptions of the mountain flowers that grew on the west side of your heroine's house. A successful writer I know once told me that she plans her stories like scenes in a play. Put your reader into a time and place immediately and avoid heavy details that can flower through dialogue. In a story I wrote recently, for example:

> Cass fumbled with the wrapping paper; I saw Dickie strain forward.
> "A muff! A muff! Cass cried, stuffing both hands into the white fur. "Thank you, Grandma!"

This is the rewrite of the original:

> Cass fumbled with the wrapping paper; I saw Dickie strain forward. She peered into the box, then pulled out a white fur muff. "Thank you, Grandma."

A slight difference, perhaps just a shade. But the rewritten paragraph jumps!

Unlike the slice-of-life fragments that are characteristic of small quarterlies, unlike the offbeat pieces that are occasionally seen now in such magazines as *Playboy,* the current high-paying slick market is oriented toward the sort of story which can best be described as optimistic. The jaundiced eye does not go over well here, and defeatist themes are generally unpopular. (There are exceptions.) This does not mean that you must tack a happy ending on everything; still, if things don't work out for the heroine at the finish, try for a ray of hope, at least. The experience you have put her through must have taught her a lesson or given her some insight, and at the end, things should be looking up.

Another criterion high on the editor's list is the predictability of the plot. If he can guess how it's going to end much before it does, you'll get the story back; the days of boy-meets-girl, loses girl, gets girl are over. And fantasy, slapstick, and farce went out with the mustache. The it-could-really-happen is very much *in*.

That goes for dialogue, double. No rhetoric, please. Characters must talk, not give Gettysburg Addresses. And, the briefer the better; it is amazing how many redundancies crop up in monologues, my own in particular. In real life, people tend to be repetitive; they don't dare to in fiction; still, they must sound real. "No!" is as effective as "No! No! No!" so learn to cut, even if it brings tears to your creative eyes.

And learn to stay on the track. Beware of those tempting extraneous details that derail your theme. Those beautifully written paragraphs about the heroine's life at the Sorbonne will have to go, unless they have a direct bearing on her situation right now. This is both the challenge and the limitation of writing for the slicks; plot first, style second. Don't let your own talent carry you away.

While you're cutting, be suspicious of double and triple adjectives. Sometimes they can't be helped, but consider trimming "She looked into a cold, flat, grey sky" to "She looked into a slate sky," and congratulate yourself on your economy.

Never, however, strain for an analogy or overdo a metaphor. This kind of overwriting is the mark of the neophyte.

Ready to begin? Of course you are. It's the middle of the story that sends the writer running, defeated, from the typewriter. The I-can't-go-on plateau is as common as a cold. Remember persistence? It's the only remedy.

54

TICKET TO TIMBUKTU

By Norah Lofts

THIS article is not directed at the well-to-do, or the footloose, or written for anyone whose imagination can only be sparked off by something that his physical eyes have seen. I am writing it specifically for people who are bound to a job, or to a family, or even to a wheelchair and have an impulse to tell a tale set against a background with which they are unfamiliar. Such people are often inhibited because they have been overexposed to the theory that one can only write about what one knows at firsthand, and are a little too ready to believe that only Mr. X, who has spent a lot of time and a lot of money in Timbuktu, can possibly use it as a setting. This simply isn't true. Given the story, enough curiosity and determination, enough time and enough exercise of what Wordsworth called "that inward eye", you can, without losing a day at the office, without being unfaithful to the kitchen sink, write your book about Timbuktu; and presently people will write to you and say, "When were you there? I lived there for twenty years and, believe me, your book made me positively homesick."

So far as I know, nobody has yet come up with any real evidence that Shakespeare was ever in Denmark or Venice or Padua. There is a strong likelihood that he was hobbled in London, earning his bread, saving his money for his old age, and keeping his eyes and ears open. In the Thames-side taverns, he probably talked to sailors who had visited far places; and it is true that his audience was less critical and less well-informed than ours. To balance this, we have wider resources: all those books by Mr. X, accurate maps, pictures, films, television documentaries.

The thing is not to be timid. Maugham once said—I can't give the actual words, but this is the gist—you don't go out and find stories, stories come and find you. A story about Timbuktu may have found *you,* seemingly the least likely person to write it, tethered as you are by all these Lilliputian strings, some so frail as the question, "But what will happen to my dog?" The thing is that this story has found *you.* You are the one to do it. Stories are wiser in their generation.

Another thing is not to think for a moment that to write about a far place without seeing it is easy. The material has to be found, studied and checked with more care than is required when you write of what you know. Two accounts of the same place may vary wildly; then you must find two more, find, if possible, someone who has been there and is willing to talk. Quite recently I met, on a train journey, a woman who had spent twenty-six years behind the Iron Curtain; she was talkative and fair-minded, and told me many things, both good and bad, about the regime. I was all ears, though at the time I had no intention of using anything she told me; but later on, two stories found me and I wrote them; both have been published and so far I have had no complaints. And if you are by this time thinking that nobody would bother to correct a blatantly ignorant writer, think again. The world is full of frustrated schoolteachers who are, like God, "extreme to mark what is done amiss." Ironically enough, the harshest reprimand I ever invited, and a well-deserved one, came after I had written something that I really did know about—or thought I did. Born and reared a Methodist, I thought I was safe with a Methodist hymn, quoted it without checking, and presently was slapped down in a letter from Malaya.

I know that the method I advocate and practice is often denigrated by the term "armchair traveling." I contend that the armchair traveler is a far more cerebral creature than the man on the spot whose mind is subject to physical concerns: will his money last out, has the last train gone, what was in that queer-looking dish that now lies so uneasily in his stomach, could that really be a bedbug? It is all too possible to look upon the Bridge of Sighs or the Leaning Tower and to be preoccupied with the site of the nearest lavatory. The books of genuine travelers often reflect this physical preoccupation which the reader can afford to skip or minimize. I remember one travel book through which the sentences, "We harnessed the yak," and "We unharnessed the yak," ran as recurrent themes. I had no responsibility for the animal and, after noting that in this particular place the yak is a form of transport, could afford to concentrate upon the scenery.

There is this, also, to be considered: If armchair traveling were not a pretty adequate substitute for firsthand experience, how would historical writers fare? So little of the physical past remains, and most of what remains has changed so much, that an effort of imagination is required to give even a glimpse of what it formerly was.

Once, in the company of a member of the you-must-go-and-see school, I traveled all the way to Spain to see a certain palace. There were bits of ruined wall, shoulder high in places, but the site was a pleasure garden, full of people, noisy with children, bright with kiosks selling ice cream. True, we stood on the spot where something had actually taken place, there was that satisfaction; but there was little to be learned, the atmosphere was wrong. For me, at least, a contemporary description, a picture, even the words "a castle in Spain," would have been much more productive.

I sorely disappointed—and this I regret—the kind person who took me to Rome and said, as proudly as though he had just built it, "There is the Colosseum!" I said, "I know. It is exactly as I imagined it." That was true, in a way, yet profoundly untrue in another, because in my imagination the marble facing had still been in place, and the seats had been filled with avid spectators, the gladiators' quarters occupied, the lions complaining of hunger.

I have to confess that when the time came for me to abandon armchair traveling for the other kind, my immediate reaction to any place was—I have been here before, and it was better then.

And to clinch this argument, let us think for a moment about my own home town. It grew up around a great Benedictine Abbey, the second largest north of the Rhine. St. Edmund, King and Martyr, was enshrined here, kings patronized and endowed it, it was a place of pilgrimage. Somewhere, sometime a story concerning its two most famous Abbots, Baldwin and Sampson, or its best known scribe, Jocelyn de Brakelond, may find somebody behind a desk or a counter or a cooking stove in Oklahoma. This chosen person may be one of the go-take-a-look practitioners. He will come to Bury St. Edmund's, which is well worth a visit, and he will receive a warm welcome. With his own eyes he will see the Abbey Gate, a Norman tower, two splendid churches which were once chapels to the Abbey and survived the Dissolution as parish churches and have been practically rebuilt in the intervening years; and he will find a public pleasure ground with lumps of grey ruin here and there. He will see only one thing which conveys the size and magnificence of the Abbey in its prime and that is a picture which hangs inside the Abbey Gate. This picture is a reconstruction, based upon actual measurements and upon contemporary or near-contemporary documents. From that picture the traveler will learn something that his own eye, however imaginative, could hardly have told him as he stared at the flowerbeds, the tennis courts and bowling green—that the buildings still standing are, compared to the Great Abbey Church, as a matchbox is to a two-floored house. In fact, with this picture and a few books, this would-be writer has a far more certain entry to the Abbey as Brakelond knew it than his actual visit could confer.

This is an age of realism; there may be some danger that the imagination, underexercised, will take the way of the appendix and end with nothing but a nuisance value. Publishers delight in announcing on a book's jacket that Mr. X spent four years in Timbuktu and that the book was ten years in preparation; they feel that this adds to its worth. If Mr. X has done a sound job, his book has worth, not least to those of us who need the information he imparts. But this kind of approach, used often enough, tends to make the writer who is unable to travel feel inferior, incapable of writing about anything but his own backyard. And this may mean a loss to the reading public, for a book's most real and lasting value is the pleasure that it affords to the reader. Remember this and be bold.

As a postscript this may sound frivolous, which is a pity, for everything I have so far written has been sincere and borne out by my own experience. But if, having studied books and maps and pictures, talked to people and done all that you can to provide your story with an authentic background, you still feel hesitant about launching it upon a critical world, call your place Gimbuktu; the story will not suffer; the initiate will know what you mean, and you are insured against any small slip or omission. Trollope did it: there is no English county called Barsetshire.

55

THAT ALL-IMPORTANT REWRITE

By Lois Duncan

A FEW years ago, to my great surprise, I was invited to teach a course in Magazine Writing at the University of New Mexico. I say "surprise"; actually, a better word is "amazement." Not only had I no teaching experience, but I was not a college graduate.

"There's only one way I can approach this," I finally decided. "It must be on the basis of practical experience." Although I was education-poor, I had been writing for magazines since the age of thirteen. I would provide a course that would resemble as closely as possible the situation my students would encounter in the outside world.

When the first set of assignments was turned in, I wrote critical comments on them and handed them back for the first rewrite.

"Rewrite!" a wide-eyed coed gasped in bewilderment. "But you haven't even graded them!"

"How can I grade them," I asked, "when you haven't even finished writing them?"

"*Mine* is finished," she snorted, glancing about at her classmates for support. "A paper doesn't have to be perfect to get a B or a C."

I drew myself up into what I hoped was a professional stance and delivered my first lecture:

"There is no such thing as a B or a C in Magazine Writing. Your article is either salable or it isn't. A halfway good manuscript is as much a failure as one that is completely awful. Neither of them is going to make it in the market."

Well, I've mellowed a bit since that first traumatic semester. I've accepted the fact that there *are* B and C students whose major interest is in some field other than writing, and I grade for effort and attitude as well as production. I now accept papers that come in

306

past deadlines (if a good excuse is offered), I'll take a handwritten first draft from a non-typist, and I've adjusted to the inevitability that no matter with what dignity I begin the term as "Ms. Duncan," I'm going to finish it as "Lois."

The issue I have not given in on is the rewrite. That is too important. My students write their articles—and write them a second time—and a third—and a sixth—and a tenth, if necessary, until both they and I consider them truly salable. Then, like releasing birds for flight, we send them into the market.

And in many cases, they fly! That's the thing that has so far kept me from being tarred and feathered. Class sales, over the past couple of years, have been made to such varied publications as *True, Holiday, Saga, Home Life, Junior Scholastic, The Denver Free Press, Catholic Digest, American Girl, New Mexico Magazine* and *St. Anthony Messenger*. In one semester alone—seventeen students, some of whom had never written before—made over two thousand dollars.

What exactly is a rewrite, and why is it so important?

To begin with, I think it is necessary to rewrite in order to allow the first draft to be spontaneous. Writing habits vary from person to person, but my own technique is to follow a general outline and pound out the first draft of my story at top speed without giving a thought to detail. I compare it to the way an athlete approaches a high jump. There's no time for him to think about being beautiful; the thing he is trying to accomplish is to pick up enough speed to sail over the bar. If he stops to worry about whether his position is graceful and who may be watching from the stands and whether his hair is staying in place, he never gets his feet off the ground.

My first drafts are a mess, and I wouldn't ever want anybody to see one. If, when I die, there should be a first draft lying on my desk (and there probably will be, because there always is), I want it burned unread. All I hope to do with a first draft is to give my story shape and movement. I find this especially necessary when writing at length. With a novel, for instance, it's easy to find yourself with a string of compartment-like chapters, each an entity in itself, instead of one great sweeping whole. By keeping a fast pace without pausing to search for the perfect way of saying things, I find I am better able to achieve a sense of continuity.

There are, of course, successful writers who do not work this way. There are some, I've heard—I can't say that I've ever actually met one—who write with such precision that their original wording cannot be improved upon. Their first copies are their final ones; no rewrites are necessary. Such writers do exist, but I cannot believe that there are many.

In one of my recent classes, there was one particular student who was the bane of my existence. He was also a delight. He was bright, funny, talented and so prolific that stories of all types—mysteries, juveniles, romances, psychological thrillers—came reeling out of his typewriter at the rate of several per week. Then he put them into envelopes and sent them away.

"Here's a copy of my new story," he would say, handing me a carbon. "I wrote it yesterday."

"Where," I would ask him, already sure of the answer, "is the original?"

"On its way to *Playboy*." Then, seeing my expression, he would smile ingratiatingly. "I know you want us to rewrite, but I just don't like to work that way. When I've finished something, I'm through with it. I want to get started on something else."

Which is understandable. But, did it work? Did his stories sell? No, they didn't, and they *should* have. For he had talent and sensitivity and drive, all the elements necessary for a successful professional. But he was releasing his birds with their wings still imperfect, with their tails trailing in long drooping arches behind them and their feathers of uneven lengths. He would not admit that this was the reason they didn't reach the treetops.

"It's the editors," he'd mutter. "They don't even look at the work of newcomers. They have their stable of regulars, and they won't buy from anyone else."

But these regulars were once newcomers. There are people breaking into the top magazines every day. I'd be willing to bet that they're not breaking in with their first drafts.

When my rough draft is finished, I usually stick it away in a drawer for a couple of days until I can read it over objectively. Then I ask myself a list of questions:

Is this story shaped right? Does it build to make its point? Is the hook interesting enough to intrigue the reader? Is there a smooth transition between this hook and the body of the article? Am I making all the points I want to make in the right order? Have I put in excess material that does not contribute? Does my climax come too abruptly so that I need more buildup? Do I wait too long so that my reader is worn out before he reaches it? Do I hit my climax hard enough to make it worth the reader's effort to get there? Do I wind things up neatly so that the reader is left with a feeling of satisfaction?

You may have noticed that I have been using the words "story" and "article" interchangeably. This is because these same questions apply to both fiction and articles. The basics of construction in writing are as constant as the basics in any other kind of creative building. Whether you're making a stabile or a coffee table, you have to get it in balance, or it's going to fall over.

When this rewrite is done, I again give it a rest period. The next time round is the one in which I try to make it beautiful. Now the questions I ask myself concern smoothness and polish:

Are the anecdotes appropriate and well-handled? Is the dialogue natural? Does my story read easily with neither choppy paragraphs nor long unbroken ones? Have I used the best words possible to express my meanings? Have I used a favorite word too often? Am I overworking my adjectives and adverbs? Are there spots where I have been too wordy? Are my sentences grammatically correct and in a style in keeping with the sort of piece I am writing? How is my spelling?

All in all—is this the best, most polished job I am capable of doing? Am I proud of the result? Is there any way that I can improve upon it?

These same questions are the ones I force upon my students. I have a pile of their manuscripts here on my desk now. As I write, I can glance over and see some of the notes I have attached to them:

"Andre—Exciting story, but I feel you've rushed your climax. You work for fifteen pages to get us into the big scene in the ballroom, and then you zip us through it in a page and a half. Can you make it longer and stronger—hit it harder—make it go 'bam!' instead of 'poof'?"

"Stephani—Lovely writing. Almost like poetry. But the girl's dialogue seems stilted to me. Would she really speak that way? Read it aloud to yourself and see what you think."

"Kevin—Incredible! You're the last person in the world I thought would come through with a confession story. You've caught the style well, but I think you need to do something to make your heroine more sympathetic. Can you enlarge your flashback to show more of her last marriage? If your readers understand her better, they'll be able to forgive her sins more easily."

"Jean—You'll have to do some heavy cutting if you're thinking of trying this on *Good Housekeeping*. Their short-shorts run closer to 1200 words than 2500. And do you realize that you've used the word 'very' three times in one paragraph?"

I wish I could say that Magazine Writing is the most popular course the University of New Mexico offers. It isn't, and I know it. There are students who drop it, and I cannot blame them; there are certainly easier ways to pick up three credits. There are some who suffer through it, moaning and grumbling with impatience and frustration.

But there are others, too, people like Tony, a young married veteran, whose twenty hours of classes were supplemented by his job in a supermarket. He turned up in the morning with circles under his eyes, but he never missed a class or a deadline.

At the end of the semester there was a note attached to his final manuscript:

"I want to thank you for forcing me into something I never believed I could achieve—self-discipline. This article is now the best I am able to write."

Two months later he phoned me. I was not at home at the time, but he left a message with my daughter. On its first time out his article had been accepted by *Argosy*.

56

WRITING DIALOGUE

BY JOHN SAYLES

MY WRITING is very character-oriented, and one of the best ways to learn about people, to make judgments on them, is to listen to what they say and how they say it. I worked in a factory once where almost everyone but me spoke Italian. I could figure out some of the power relationships between people and some broad traits of temperament, but at the end of my stay I didn't know what any of them were really like, what they thought or cared about. The few bilingual people at the factory tried to fill me in on everybody's personalities, but I hated to have to take their word for it. A writer who gives no concrete evidence of character (and dialogue is some of the best evidence) is asking the reader to take his word for it.

My book *Union Dues* involves dozens of people living through the social upheaval of the late sixties, people from very different camps, some of them at war with each other. They are all Americans, but the polarization of each side has shaped their thinking, their speech, into sub-dialects that might as well be foreign languages to the other group. I try to present each camp in its own words and attitudes, to make clear the basic humanity of all the parties at the same time that I make clear why they are at each other's throats. It's as if the writer and reader were in a room full of people violently screaming their different opinions at each other all at once. And like a sound mixer in a recording studio, I isolate each voice so the reader can listen to it alone, and make a judgment voice by voice till all sides are considered.

Life is not a story. To write is to see the enlightening metaphor in life, to arrange it in a way that makes it clearer and more entertaining. I would apply that to fiction dialogue itself. Recording life's dialogue verbatim is to put the reader back in the shouting room. The Watergate tapes were most effective in an edited form—newsmen did an author's job in selecting which bits out of the hours and hours of White House conversation would best present the key plot evidence and the essential attitudes of Nixon and his inner circle. What follow are some of the technical means I use to shape my characters' dialogue better to reveal them to the reader.

I use mostly "naturalistic" dialogue—something you might say or hear on the street. It is best for what I write, but not the only form of dialogue that can be effective. Writers as diverse as William Faulkner, Grace Paley, and Donald Barthelme often work in dialogue you'd never hear in ordinary conversation but is perfect for the tone and intent of their stories.

In naturalistic dialogue much is said about "having an ear." It is possible to have a tin ear for everyday speech, and naturalism might be a bad road for you to follow. I always read my dialogue out loud, give it what actors call a "cold reading," without dramatics or a great deal of inflection. Typewritten words have a lot of power, they look very official and convincing even though you know you just made them up. Your ear may catch what your eye is fooled by.

People rarely speak exactly like each other, and your characters shouldn't either. An exercise: take three or four characters from one of your stories and write a first-person account by each of them of the same event. It should make you more aware of how their thought processes and speaking styles should differ.

Be aware of what purpose you want dialect to serve if you use it. It is a relative thing; southern writers don't distort southern characters' speech nearly as much as northern writers do. Dialect immediately puts your reader in the position of an outsider, saying "Look at the way they talk." Dialect is also inherently comic; pushed to extremes it will make caricatures of its speakers. Dickens' minor characters and villains are allowed all kinds of thick dialects and speech pathologies, while his main sympathetic characters talk fairly straight. Comic effect tends to wear down if sustained for long periods, which can be useful or detrimental. Nigger Jim in *Huckleberry Finn* starts as sort of a minstrel-show figure, but later when Twain wants his full humanity to come through, we are used to his speech, and it is no longer so comic.

Dialect is a certain amount of *work* for the reader to figure out. Try to make the work as simple and pleasant as possible. I try to suggest dialect, not reproduce it phonetically. For the West Virginia accents in

Union Dues I had to concentrate on certain word usage patterns common among coal miners, especially their use of verb tense.

"There's good reason for that. Layoffs is layoffs. We don't tell the company how to run their business, they don't tell us how to run our union. They either got the work for people or they don't."

"And when they don't get called back, like that last bunch, they gonna find they been dropped out from the union? Seems like we're all of us in the same danger."

"Now those were bad members, Clete, they gone out and joined up with these dogholes we been tryin to close down. Spect the union to keep men that go right ahead, buck headquarters like they done? You should be glad them deadbeats were cut off, it bein *your* dues that kept them floatin."

This speech style is unusual but not so difficult that you'll need it translated. If well used, dialect can help root a character in place and life-station, and help distinguish him from the other speakers in the story.

Rhythm applies to the individual speaker's style and to the pace of the story. People speak in different tempos, breathe more or less in phrasing a sentence, put their sentences together simply or in a more complex way:

"...and so what you probably have to accept is the existence of an im*med*iate base, the people in the real world who will support pretty much everything you do, the aux*il*iary base, those who can be rallied to certain actions such as anti-war or specific union fights, and the pros*pec*tive base, the people who can only be expected to join us once the big-picture revolution is well underway. So..."

Or—

"Tired, did you say? Depressed? Overweight? Got that rundown feeling? Miles to go before you sleep? Friends and neighbors, I got just the thing for you, a miracle of modern pharmacology! Vim and vigor, zip and zest, bright eyes and bushy tails—all these can be *yours*, neighbor, relief is just a swallow away!"

The first speaker is a super-intellectual radical from *Union Dues,* the second a speed-tripping truck driver from my story, "I-80 Nebraska." The rhythm of their sentences tells us as much about them as the content. Individuals' speaking rhythms change with their situation, too. Only James Bond can remain dryly witty with the world crashing about his ears.

"I-80" is a story written almost entirely in dialogue, the disembodied talk of truckers over their CB radios. There is little but their voices to control the tempo of the action:

"Who?"
"Ryder P. Moses! Where you been, trucker?"
"Ryder—!"
"—crazy—"
"—weird—"
"—P.—!"
"—dangerous—"
"—probly a cop—"
"—Moses!"
"He's out there tonight!"

Just the look of this on the page gives a feeling of speed, of forward movement, excitement. If you picked it out of the static of your short-wave set, you'd stay tuned to hear what happened next. Conversely, a huge uninterrupted block of dialogue from a character gives the reader time to examine the content of the speech more closely. If you can control the rhythm of your dialogue, of your story, you can better hold the reader where you want him, make him want to listen to you.

In Hemingway's fiction, dialogue is stripped to its essentials, giving it a Biblical quality that is finally not naturalistic. His dialogue all has fairly equal weight because it is all essential. A different technique presents a fuller range of dialogue, but controls the emphasis so the essential stands out, much the way a sound-engineer balances tracks on a record or a cameraman changes focus within a movie-shot. It is a question of the weight you want the reader to give any particular sentence. For instance, a sentence standing alone on the page carries more weight than one floating in the middle of a paragraph.

"I was born here," he said. "Just a little after my family come from Arkansas. My mother was eight months and counting when they piled everything on the Ford and started west. Nineteen-thirty-one.
"Somebody told 'em they could eat in California."

Even the placement of quotation marks can alter the emphasis of a word or phrase within a sentence.

"Dawminic," said Vinnie, "you're a dangerous man."

Here "dangerous" is given extra weight by being set off, just like the little pause a comedian gives before his punch-line.

The relationship between dialogue and straight prose is also important for emphasis. The movie *Citizen Kane* opens with a series of silent images of Kane's great mansion, then a shot of the man himself toppling to the floor alone in his room, his face huge and distorted in the foreground, uttering the single word "Rosebud." The series of silent pictures, equivalent to straight-prose description in a book, gives a tremendous emphasis to that first word. In the next scene, the disembodied voices of a roomful of newsmen repeat it over and over in their chatter—already "Rosebud" is losing its emphasis, is being engulfed by a dozen different readings and interpretations. Not only should you control what you let your readers overhear; you should control what they hear most clearly.

Dialogue can be one of the most effective ways to reveal your characters to the reader. What I've given here are a few technical means of using dialogue to bring something across better, more clearly. They won't make anything live if there isn't life in it, just as mixing all the chemicals found in a human being won't make a man or a woman.

Writing, storytelling, is only another aspect of talking to people. Dialogue, people talking to each other, is only one aspect of writing.

57

STYLE AND THE FICTION WRITER

By Mary Wallace

SOMEONE—I wish I could remember who—once said that he could no more define a gentleman than a terrier could define a rat, but that just as a terrier knows a rat when it sees one, so he knows a gentleman. For most of us, that's how it is with Style.

A veil of mystery surrounds this word; or seems to. Actually only part of the veil is mystery; the rest is misunderstanding, which springs from a tendency to stress the importance of individual style above style in its broader sense. By this imbalance, beginning writers are led to believe they must adopt an individual style; something that will set their writing apart; something extra, like hot fudge topping on the ice cream or mushrooms in the gravy. But individual style—the manner of expression characteristic of a particular writer—though indeed something extra, is not something to be adopted. It develops from the writer's own personality, from every thought and feeling he has ever had, from his whole attitude toward the world about him, and, to some extent, from everything absorbed in years of reading. In short, *it is the writer.* Consequently, there is no need to worry about it, or even to think about it, for it is bound to make its own way to the surface in good time.

On the other hand, there is a very real need to think about style in its broad sense—those features of literary composition which belong to form and expression rather than to the substance of the thought or matter expressed.

That is a dictionary definition, and of course correct as far as it goes. But in the actual writing there can be no such division; form and substance must be one, as inseparable as body and soul. It may be true of a song that "As long as a tune has a right good swing, it doesn't much matter what words you sing," but never make the mistake of thinking that anything comparable can be said of writing—

316

that as long as the substance is there, any words will do. They won't. The words we use and the way we use them determine the strength or weakness, the brilliance or dullness, of what we write. It is form—*the adaptation of the expression to the idea*—that conveys the substance. A poorly worded thought is not communicated. A poorly presented character does not come alive. A poorly expressed emotion leaves the reader untouched.

But even to think of form as a vehicle is not enough. It is much more than that. It is the means by which the substance is made identifiable. Consider, for a moment, a diamond and a piece of graphite. Both are pure carbon; the difference lies in the internal arrangement of the atoms. Well, words are the atoms of writing; and since we all use (or have available) the same words—all the words in the English language—the difference between good and poor writing must lie in the arrangement of our words. Not entirely, for there are other factors, including the substance itself and the sincerity or insincerity of the writer, but the way in which words are put together is the secret and the only mystery of style.

For help and guidance the beginning fiction writer turns to the short stories or novels of writers successful in those fields. This seems the logical place to turn; and in regard to structure, dialogue, character portrayal, plot development, quite possibly help will be found there. But in regard to style, it is not the best place to turn; first, because of the temptation to imitate, and imitation is a trap; second, because character and story tend to overshadow the actual words used—as they should. I have often been asked what novels by other novelists helped me most. None. I was helped most by the "familiar essayists," from Sir Thomas Browne on up to E.B. White; and I would urge any beginning writer of fiction to make the acquaintance of those masters of style. If those of past centuries seem too far away to be "relevant," then at least read those of the twentieth century, being sure not to overlook Logan Pearsall Smith's *Trivia* and *More Trivia*, two small volumes of which it has been said that "their happy audacity is not more remarkable than the consummate felicity of their expression."

Any approach to style must necessarily be over a roadway solidly paved with the rules of grammar and the principles of composition. But to know the rules, to be able to write sentences that are grammatically correct, is only a first step. The *art* of writing goes beyond the rules into an area where nothing is fixed and absolute; where we must find our way by instinct, by ear, by some subtle awareness of what makes one word or group of words better than another for the expression of what we want to say. Still, since we write in sentences, mastery of the sentence has to be our first goal; and since it is not too much to say that the advantageous or disadvantageous positioning of *one word* can mean the difference between clarity and obscurity, effectiveness and ineffectiveness, to aim at that goal is to set our sights high.

So let's be sure we know just what a sentence is. It is a group of words expressing a *single complete* thought. It must contain, explicitly or implicitly, at least one independent predication. It is a unit, a constituent part of a larger whole, a thread in a pattern, and as such it must pass a double test: how well does it express the thought, and how well does it fit into the pattern?

There is no easy formula to follow. The structure of sentences may vary greatly, and there is no arbitrary limit to their length. In modern writing, simplicity is favored over complexity, and probably it is best—safest, at any rate—to use sentences of moderate length, except when short or long ones are needed for some special purpose.

Very short sentences are useful for emphasis or some other desired effect; but there is a risk, for if the effect is not achieved, a string of short sentences will sound crude or childish. Here is a paragraph from Ernest Hemingway's famous short story, "The Killers":

Outside it was getting dark. The street light came on outside the window. The two men at the counter read the menu. From the other end of the counter Nick Adams watched them. He had been talking to George when they came in.

Well, Hemingway could put it across; but a beginner would be ill advised to write in this manner.

The long sentence, too, has its special uses. If the thought is complex, the sentence may have to be equally so, for there should be no break in the continuity of the thought. For emphasis, for building up a mood, for revealing the way in which a character's mind works, a long sentence can be very effective. But again there is a risk: The effect is lost if the reader becomes lost along the way. Here is one of mine:

As in sleep a dream comes, seeming to cover hours, days, even years, yet in truth occupying only the space of a thought as it comes and goes, so in that moment of closing his eyes he had a dream-vision, in which he saw himself standing on the center section of a bridge, of which the part that he had just come over, and the part that he had yet to cross, had been swept away, leaving him stranded, cut off from all the rest of the living world; and all around, as far as the eye could see, was nothing but a desolate gray waste, like the sand-flats and salt-water marshes over which he had driven with Paul one day last winter, on a trip to a coastal town. (*Reason for Gladness,* Funk & Wagnalls)

This is a single thought; division into three or four shorter sentences would therefore be structurally wrong. Beyond that, the length contributes to the dream impression described at the start—the few seconds that seem like years. (Incidentally, with more care, this could have been a better sentence. "Of which" follows too closely upon "in which," and "as far as the eye could see"—a cliché—should have been omitted.)

Then there is the fractional sentence, incomplete in itself but nevertheless expressing a complete thought. This one should be used sparingly, for it must *instantly* suggest the parts needed to make it complete. If it meets that condition, either alone or in its context, then any fraction of a sentence—a subordinate clause, a phrase, even a single word—may stand as a sentence. An extreme example can be found at the start of *Reason for Gladness.* The first sentence, which is also the first paragraph, consists of two words, "Home today." The second sentence—and second paragraph—supplies only one additional detail, "Home today at half-past one." It is not until the third paragraph is reached that the context supplies the missing words needed to make the first two sentences complete. This can scarcely be called "instant," and can be defended only on the grounds that all the familiar connotations of the word "home" come immediately to mind, suggesting any number of complete sentences, though admittedly not "instantly"—"Anne would be going home from the hospital today at half-past one." The purpose was to emphasize "home" and all it connotes. But the writer took great liberty—even greater with the paragraph than with the sentence.

In creative writing, most rules are regarded as flexible, and may—knowingly but never *un*knowingly—be bent or stretched to suit the writer's purpose. The word, the sentence, the paragraph, all have as their primary function the creation of a mood or an impression. They must suggest far more than they actually say, for it is by the power of suggestion that they stimulate the imagination or stir the emotions of the reader.

What is a paragraph? Not merely a break on the page. Like the sentence it is a unit, usually a composite unit, that carries the reader one step forward on a course well laid out by the writer. If it is made up of several sentences, bear in mind that these must be *related* sentences, and that only those details which contribute to one central impression should be included. But there's more to it than that: there's the manner in which the details are arranged. Monotony of construction should be avoided. The sentences that make up a paragraph should vary in length, form, and sound; should be euphonious; and should not start in the same manner or with the same word, unless the writer is purposely using repetition as a means of emphasis.

Repetition is a hazardous device. It can be very dull. It can also be very effective, but only if the writer and the reader hear the same drummer. For better or for worse, in *Blue Meadow* (published by Morrow) I have several paragraphs in which a number of consecutive sentences start with the same word or words. In three or four of these, the repeated word is the name of a character. In another place, I start six sentences intentionally with "She had." Here, in its entirety, is another example of deliberate repetition:

Love was summer sunlight. Love was the fragrance of earth and leaves; the songs of birds; the wind in the trees. Love was a cresting wave, like the sea surf when it rises in an arched wall of green shadow and sunlit foam....

It may be interesting to note that these three sentences, though each begins in the same way, vary in length, and that with the increase in length there is increase in *forward movement,* as comparisons progress from stillness, to sound and motion, to the suggested power of the wave.

Perhaps all this can be called hair-splitting. Perhaps the fine points can be waved aside as nothing more than a bag of tricks. If a writer has a good story to tell, won't the words flow out under their own power and fall naturally into place? Don't count on it. Sometimes words do flow easily, and we all would like to think that when they have flowed easily they have flowed well. Once in a while this is so; but, unhappily, all too often it is not. Never send a manuscript off to an editor until you read and reread it. Revise. Rearrange. And be sure to read it aloud, because the ear will often catch what the eye misses —the unnecessary word, the awkward phrase, the unintended repetition, the pronoun that has lost touch with its antecedent. Examine every sentence for smoothness, coherence, clarity. Keep the reader's comfort in mind. Remember that easy writing usually makes hard reading. Don't be afraid that too much polishing will destroy the spontaneity of what you have written. There is no such thing as too much polishing. The author of *Trivia,* Logan Pearsall Smith, has this to say about it in his Preface:

"You must beware of thinking too much about Style," said my kindly adviser, "or you will become like those fastidious people who polish and polish until there is nothing left."

"Then there really are such people?" I asked eagerly. But the well-informed lady could give me no precise information about them.

I often hear of them in this tantalizing manner, and perhaps one day I shall have the luck to come across them.

And now, to end with a word about endings. Much advice is given about the start of a story, the need to capture the reader's interest with the first line or two. The ending is no less important. A good beginning increases the chances of a story's being read; a good ending, its chances of being remembered. Not knowing when to stop is a common fault; but even if a stop is made at the right point, simply to stop is not enough. There must be an *ending,* something that acts as a fixative.

More than forty years ago I read *The Forsyte Saga.* I still remember the closing line—"He might wish and wish and never get it—the beauty and the loving in the world"—and how sorry it made me feel for Soames. Everything the reader has learned about Soames in the three books of the *Saga* is condensed in that single line. There is nothing remarkable about the words themselves; they are simple and ordinary words. The poignancy is in the way they are put together—yet it seems an entirely simple and ordinary way.

That is the mystery. And that is Style.

58

WHEN YOU NEED A NONFICTION IDEA

By Max Gunther

"WHERE do you get all your ideas?" This question has been thrown at me often in two decades of free-lance nonfiction writing, but until recently I wasn't very good at answering it. I could only mumble, "Oh, ideas just pop into my head. Who knows where an idea comes from?"

Today I think I have some more specific and satisfactory answers to offer. After finishing my fourteenth book some months ago, I decided to let my typewriter cool for a month or so. One thing I hoped to do in this restful time, if I could, was analyze the operation of my own brain and maybe organize it better. I asked myself: Where have your best ideas come from? If you want a hot book or article idea next year or in 1985, where will you start looking?

I went back through my files to 1956, the year I sold my first free-lance effort to the old *Saturday Evening Post,* and tried to reconstruct the births and maturings of my favorite ideas. I couldn't remember every idea's beginning, but many came back to me with startling clarity. Whenever memory allowed, I jotted down what I was doing at the time the idea came to me, what the source was, what state of alertness or curiosity made me think, "Aha! Idea!" I've now put together a short list of rules that I will impose on myself when I next need an idea. Instead of waiting for ideas to come from nowhere, a nonfiction writer should:

1. *Talk to people.* Go out of your way to find them. Go to parties even though you hate parties. Go to school board meetings. Join bridge clubs. Sell greeting cards door-to-door. Talk to people who sit next to you on trains and planes, in diners, on park benches. Do anything that will get you into communication with other men and women.

Solitude is useful sometimes during the actual writing process, but as a means of generating ideas, it seems valueless. I honestly can't recall a single good idea that ever came to me while I was simply sitting or ambling around alone, staring into space.

Some of my most profitable ideas have sprung from conversations with other people. A remark by an acoustical engineer led to an article on the science of sound, which I sold to *Playboy*. A rambling talk with a television sales executive sowed the seed of a three-part *TV Guide* report on TV's problems with sex. A fellow I met casually started me on a mental journey that ended as *Instant Millionaires,* a Playboy Press book.

2. *Read newspapers hungrily.* Radio and TV news reports aren't nearly detailed enough. Only a newspaper can give you the depth, the background, the odd sidelights that can trigger a salable idea. A non-fiction writer should read at least one good, solid metropolitan paper every day, from front page to back, including obituaries and shipping news, and other material that might seem to be of only narrow interest.

A *New York Times* obit of an industrial inventor led me to the first article I ever sold to *True,* back in 1958. Over the next twelve years I was to sell well over a hundred more pieces to *True*—and, needless to say, I still read obits. Similarly, I plow through the *Times*'s food-and-fashion page and its national weather column every day, though neither section contains much that interests me personally. In the fashion section one day, I read an offhand reference that blossomed into a *Ladies' Home Journal* story on runaway wives, and an equally casual remark in the weather column became a *True* piece on scientific attempts to control weather.

3. *Read magazines* — not just those that attract you personally or those you hope to write for, but also the unfamiliar ones, the obscure ones, the ones that operate beyond your normal range of interests. By buying or scrounging an unfamiliar magazine and finding out what its editors and writers are thinking about these days, you can trigger fresh thoughts in your own head.

I don't normally read magazines that deal with money and investment, but one day on an airplane I borrowed a Wall Street trade journal from the fellow sitting next to me. Its letters-to-the-editor column contained a humorous note about a goofy new way to predict what the stock market will do, and a month later I sold *Playboy* a piece on oddball market-playing techniques. Similarly, I'm not a coin collector, but a magazine devoted to the hobby once gave me an idea for an article about gold, which I sold to *True.*

4. *Never scorn an idea because it is "publicity."* Nearly every big and medium-sized company, college, hospital and government agency has a publicity chief, usually called the news director or public relations director. This man's or woman's job is to get the organization favorably mentioned in the press. It is considered chic in some writers' circles to sneer at publicity people, on the ground that everything they say is self-serving. This attitude seems fairly dumb to me. Publicity may be self-serving, but it can also be interesting.

If you are an idea-hunting nonfiction writer, you should get to know the publicists in companies and institutions near you. They will gladly mail you news of their organizations and work. Listen to them with care; they may provide you with an idea for an article or a book.

A publicity man working for Johnson Wax, makers also of an insect repellent, gave me the idea for a *Travel & Leisure* story on mosquitoes. A college publicity woman planted the seed of a *Playboy* piece on the annual national campus manhunt in which businesses try to grab the brightest graduates. These publicists dealt with me because they hoped to get the product or college mentioned in print (which, in fact, happened). If I had refused to listen to them, I would have lost two sound ideas, not to mention two pleasantly hefty checks.

5. *Browse in books that aren't meant for browsing.* Spend an hour or two thumbing through some fact book like *The World Almanac* or an encyclopedia yearbook. Those columns of dry facts and figures look pretty dull to most people, but not to a writer hunting ideas. In these volumes you will find a wealth of information, greatly condensed, on what people are doing and thinking in the world today. Any of those statistics could sow the seed of an article or even book idea. An equally useful kind of browsing can be done in the yellow pages of any city phone book. The thousands of products and services

that are offered for sale there tell much about our society and its problems and dreams.

Leafing through a fact book in the library one morning, I was captivated by an odd little set of statistics dealing with highway accidents. According to these figures, there are more accidents on an average Saturday than on any weekday. This peculiar fact simmered in my head for a long time and finally led me to write a book. *The Weekenders,* published by Lippincott, studied what Americans do on weekends and why.

Many of my ideas have come from phone books. Thumbing through the yellow pages once in the mid-1960s, I saw a pest-control company's ad. This item became a *True* article on the centuries-long war of man against rat. About ten years later, in 1974, a rodenticide ad in another phone book made me think it was time to take a fresh look at the same subject. This new piece sold to *Today's Health.*

6. *Mine your own experiences.* You have done and are doing many things in your life that may seem dull and routinely familiar to you, but these same things may be interesting, even fascinating, to other people who aren't living with them every day. Your problem: if something seems mundane to you, how do you alert yourself to the possibility that the world might want to read about it?

We get back to what I said before about talking to everybody in sight. Your primary purpose in all these conversations is to be a listener, but a secondary purpose is to test other people's reactions to what is in your head. If you find people asking alert, interested questions about something you've said or done, ask yourself whether you've stumbled onto a potential nonfiction idea.

I lived with a good idea for fifteen years, never seeing it, until somebody else pointed it out to me. The somebody else was my wife. I had spent much of my spare time in those fifteen years trying to build a squirrel-proof bird feeder that really worked. One evening, after my umpteenth design had proved a failure, my wife and I spent an entertaining hour recalling all the other failures. Suddenly she said, "Why don't you preserve all this for posterity? Write an article about it!" She was right, of course. The thought had never occurred to me because squirrels and bird feeders had become too familiar to me, too much a part of my daily life. I sold the story, along with some pen-and-ink sketches, to *Travel & Leisure.*

Another salable idea, an article on office romances, stayed undiscovered by me in the same way for a long time, until a conversation with another person woke me up. For years a good friend of mine, a married man, had been carrying on a love affair with an unmarried woman in his office. The situation was giving him a lot of pain, and once in a while he would tell me about his feelings of guilt and helplessness. At a cocktail party one weekend, talking with a woman who had been involved in a similar experience, I tried to explain some theories about emotional bonds between men and women who work together. She looked at me archly and said, "You're writing an article about this, aren't you?" I hadn't been, but I knew instantly that I should have been. *Good Housekeeping* bought it.

59

THE PERSONAL ARTICLE

By Elsa Russell

AN OLD Tin-Pan-Alley formula for writing hit songs runs, "Keep it simple, keep it sexy, keep it sad." Not entirely applicable to the personal article, you'll agree. But not too far off either. Some personal articles *are* "sexy," some are "sad"—and some are funny, bright, brash, winsome, wry, angry, fearful, tearful, hopeful, rude. In other words, the personal article is *you,* what you want to say, a point you want to make, a funny/sad/harrowing experience you've had, a belief you hold, a memory you treasure.

True, you can keep yourself "out of the picture" in some cases, be objective, state your facts, back them up, then step aside, but, as novelist Arthur Hailey points out, "A writer must always be prepared to expose something of himself—his inclinations, weaknesses, frustrations."

Increasingly popular in these days of "personal journalism" and what Tom Wolfe calls the "Me Decade," a quality personal article is far more than a "confession" piece, a top-of-the-head ramble, a preachy collection of listen-to-me platitudes. Amateur writers, reading a Joan Mills lament for her childhood in recent *Reader's Digest*s or a Jean Kerr romp in the daisies, reach out for the form ("Hey, this is for me. No research!") and deluge magazines with cute-little-me-in-a-kitchen-apron pieces or with what editors call "sound-offs"— uninspired, unsupported, unexamined opinions on everything from teen-age hang-ups to the cost of living to retirement villages (all, by the way, too *broad* in scope).

Well, how *does* one avoid the lackluster subject, the sweeping generalizations, the ambling treatment? Best advice as always is to *read.* See how the pros like Joan Mills do it in their "personal articles" in popular magazines like *Reader's Digest.* (A pro now, Joan Mills—housewife, mother, sparetime writer—was "discovered" a few years ago when a *Digest* editor spotted her column in *The Berkshire Eagle*. He liked her warm, human approach to everyday topics.) See how she and other writers proceed to (a) find an "angle," (b) narrow the focus, (c) hone an idea to its sharpest edge.

Examine *your* idea in these terms, turn it over, trip it up, ask it questions, try a dozen angles for size. When you have it, you'll know. Emerson says, "A man should learn to detect and watch that gleam of light that flashes from within." (The old light bulb!)

And how does one find good subjects in the first place? The possibilities are endless. Look around you. What amuses you? What bugs you? What experience sets you apart? What do you feel strongly about? What memory haunts you? Marjorie Holmes, who's been prolific in this field for 25 years, says her "life will never be long enough" to write all the articles she has ideas for! For convenience, let's group the article possibilities into five categories and look at some examples:

1) *Narrative, Personal Experience.* Dramatic—man and girl, climbing, are trapped on a ledge for three days. He tells the story. An old Montana cowboy sends us (the *Digest*) a scrawled, illiterate but poignant account of a colt he once "broke" and learned to love. "The Day I Met Midnight" wins a First Person Award. An about-to-divorce couple find each other again when he takes her to his boyhood home.

2) *Memory, Recall, Nostalgia.* This overlaps the above. "Come Back, Come Back," Marjorie Holmes's lovely memory of going home for her mother's funeral to a town that "puts its arms around you when a parent dies." "What Was It Like to Kiss Clark Gable?" by Mary Astor (no fun at all it seems—too many lights, camera-angles, boxes to stand on!).

3) *Humor, Gripes, Everyday Frustrations.* A *New York Times* piece, "Dad Against the World" (Father was a *terrible* driver). "Chicken of the Sky," hilarious account of a trembling air-traveler who sinks his nails into the upholstery on takeoff, watches the wings ("Fire!"), eventually swaggers off. Columnist Virginia Payette's story

of her troubles with Gimbel's. She's "still waiting for Mr. McNally to call back."

4) *Opinion, Belief, Take a Stand.* (But don't preach.) The titles speak for themselves—"They're Ruining Easter," "A Mother Speaks Out," "The Rudest Store in New York." Or you can knock down an accepted shibboleth: "College—Who Needs It?," "Myth of the Perfect Parent," "Why Mother's Day?"

5) *Profile, Tribute to Someone.* Though his father couldn't read or write, he could "gently prune a fruit tree or wrestle an ornery mule"; by such touches the author, Calvin Worthington, brings a good man to life in "My Father's Hands." A violinist recalls playing for Toscanini. A writer pays tribute to his high-school English teacher.

And countless others. The very personal ("Living With Fear," "Our Last Child"), the subjective, "impressionistic," the mood piece (hard to bring off).

Your subject is on target, your focus is clear, you've done your homework—knocked on a few doors, blocked out the piece, lined up your arguments, collected your supporting data (examples, anecdotes, quotes, statistics). "No research" did someone say? Well, hardly...

But your finest efforts will be wasted if the piece isn't read, if its title is blah, its blurb dull, its lead heavy. "Reception by the reader is the aim and goal of all writing," says novelist Taylor Caldwell (and she should know!). The "hook," then, as we writers have been told *ad infinitum,* is what pulls them in, turns them on, sells the piece. Consider the "come-ons" briefly:

Titles. Look again at the many lively ones mentioned above. Do they intrigue you? I particularly like the play-on-words (pun) title: "The Grand Sham" (TV game shows), "Trouble on the Double" (twins), "The Crating Game" (moving day), and titles that proclaim "Soddenly It's Spring" or "Winter Leaves Me Cold."

I like titles that play on or borrow from other well-known titles or phrases: Judith Viorst on her three sons, "Little Boy Blues," Richard Bode's "My Son the Carpenter," Willie Morris on his Southern grandmother, "Weep No More My Lady." I like unexpected titles:

"A Planeload of Babies," "Eat Your Weeds!" (backyard plants), "Whatever Became of the Girl I Married?" I like the alliterative title of the Broadway musical, *Bubbling Brown Sugar*.

Blurbs. The little phrase or quip that follows (or precedes) the title, the second beckoning finger (often a sentence from the body of the article). Usually left to the editors (bless 'em) to compose or find, a blurb may just as well accompany your piece and be as good as you can make it. (Who knows, it may catch the eye of a tired editor yawning over a pile of submissions!) Here's a long one from Karen Walker's "A Planeload of Babies":

War makes death and orphans. Stewardesses make coffee, tea and martinis. And never the twain shall meet—at least, hardly ever.
On April 5, 1975, just before Saigon's fall, the effects of war came aboard a soft-carpeted, gaily-painted 747 jetliner more accustomed to chattering tourists. That day, 409 Vietnamese children came limping, crawling, screaming through the airplane doors.

One from Joseph Blank's "Two Seconds to Live":

Suddenly, young Ron Gillis was being pulled, inexorably, toward the whirling blades of the sawmill's chipper.

A short one: "Love can come in many disguises" (Erma Bombeck's "Some Day I'll Tell My Children").

Leads. If it catches the reader's attention and honestly leads into your story, it's good. A Hal Borland nature piece in preparation needed a lively lead. The first try:

It is best to live in a land of four seasons. I have this to say firmly every March because then come days I would gladly forfeit...just too warm or cold, wet or dry, the year round.

But we fiddled with it and further on, found another paragraph. Better lead?

March is a tomboy with tousled hair, a mischievous smile, mud on her shoes and a laugh in her voice. March is a sleet storm the day after you find the first violet. March is boys playing marbles and girls playing jacks. But most of all—here in New England anyhow—March is a promise.

Some pieces demand a straightforward lead. "You are there" in the opening scene of Jerome Kelley's "Pied Piper of 'A' Company":

My story begins in a Marine Corps recruiting office...a few days after Pearl Harbor. The square-jawed sergeant sat behind his scarred wooden desk tapping with his pencil as he looked me up and down.

I like the "disarming" lead. Here's how Judith Viorst gets into "Little Boy Blues":

I am a neat and cautious person, pained by dirt and disorder, the sound of loud voices, the sight of fresh blood. My athletic skills can be summarized in six words: I can float on my back...
I was clearly meant to be the mother of girls—dainty, well-mannered, ungrubby little girls for whom I could buy velvet dresses and dolls with soft, curly hair. So how did I ever wind up with three wriggly, blood-dripping, loud-mouthed, fresh, fierce little boys?

Ultimately, as all of the above has shown, what separates the men from the boys in writing is *technique—how* you develop your arguments, make your points. In the body of your piece you'll call upon a dozen devices, all based on the adage, "Show, don't tell." Here are three of them:

Anecdotes. Those little stories that say it all for you. A well-known one to show Lincoln's magnanimity:

When a friend reported to Lincoln that, even as a Cabinet member, Stanton called the President a fool, Lincoln calmly replied: "Did he call me that? Well, I reckon it must be true then, for Stanton is generally right."...Lincoln later appointed him Secretary of War because he saw Stanton as the best man for the place.

Sara Stutz, writing about "infant intervention" programs, uses a case history:

At nine months, Christy was hospitalized with malnutrition and other evidences of parental neglect. She was unresponsive and slow for her age. Now, enrolled in the Developmentally Delayed Infant Education Project at the Nisonger Center in Columbus, Ohio, she is, at 13 months, feeding herself, crawling, and trying to talk. It looks as if Christy is going to catch up.

In "The Myth of the Perfect Parent" Carole Klein makes a point about teachers:

A teacher's capacity to bruise often exceeds a parent's capacity to heal. For instance, impressively bright Robert comes home from first grade in humiliation, painfully sharing his "stupidness" over not being able to tie his shoes. His lack of small-muscle control (that six-year-olds are "supposed" to have) had led his teacher to deride Robert publicly for his failure.

"Who cares about such a silly thing?" Robert's mother says gaily. "I promise you by the time you go to college, you'll know how to tie your shoes."

Robert tries a smile, but in that moment, in his weakened self-regard, he suspects that he will *never* be smart enough to go to college.

For all but the narrative/personal experience and the mood piece, the anecdote, used judiciously, will prove your best friend.

Quotes. Too many writers, especially in "opinion" pieces, tend to say it all themselves. Deadly. Your readers will be much more likely to go along with you if you bring up your ammunition: *sprinkle* your piece with quotes, slip in statistics.

Clarence Hall, writing on "magnanimity," lets C.P. Snow define it for him: "a virtue which at any level sweetens life"; Jean George, seeking information on "Indian summer," consults a naturalist. "It has no particular duration," he tells her. "It may last as long as 50 days or as briefly as one." William Ellis, writing on "inner conversations," quotes his landlady: "Once a day before everyone gets home I have a ten-minute chat with myself." Your source may be an "authority," a next-door neighbor, your husband, the milkman.

Statistics. Figures can be dangerous, but handled carefully, they do lend support. A Daniel Sugarman article on marriage starts: "This year over a million couples will officially register their discontent by signing a divorce decree. Other unknown millions will remain committed to an empty shell of marriage." Lee Foster, telling how it is to live on a "kidney machine," says, "In 1964 fewer than 300 Americans were receiving dialysis. Now there are about 25,000 of us in the United States."

Again, it's not so much *what* you say as *how* you say it. It's "style." The writer who has mastered the use of the *specific,* the bold metaphor, the clever quip, the poignant phrase, the ringing word, has it made. As J. M. Barrie once said, defining a woman's charm, "If you don't have it, it doesn't much matter what else you have."

Here's a delightful Jim Bishop paragraph embodying metaphor, imagery and a sly twinkle:

Spring is a tease. She's a lady who kicks the bedspread of snow off a little at a time. Sometimes abruptly, she pulls it back up again. She cannot be entreated, coaxed or commanded. When, at last, she is ready, spring appears—the youngest and most beautiful of the seasons. The beautiful have a right to be late.

Later, he says, "It's muddy water hugging a curb, an insolent wind tugging at hemlines." Marjorie Holmes, back in her home town after many years: "Every walk and bench is a silent shout of memory." And "We spent days breaking up her home. Boxing up memories." A student describing a tenement window: "Bedclothes hung to air, tattered signals of distress...."

Don't be afraid of exaggeration. Viorst: "If there's thin ice, my boys will skate on it, if there's a deadly drop between two roofs, they'll jump it." Or slang: "As far as my own hang-ups go, that's another can of worms." Or fun: "I may look like a senior citizen but there's a romantic bobby-soxer frisking around inside."

Again, I particularly like a twist on a well-known expression or current custom: "One thing my W-2 form will never show is the intangible..." "In a pillow talk with my husband the other night..." "Let them look to the motes in their own eyes..." "How do I measure our love—let me count the ways..."

A final tip: don't meander, *write tight*. Author Robert Crichton once said, "Establish a momentum, let your sentences acquire a stride."

Could we perhaps sum up everything we've been saying in another slogan: "Keep it moving, make it sparkle, make it *sing*!"

Then, having done all this, how can you miss?

60

TITLES THAT TALK

By Mort Weisinger

WHAT'S in a name? Contrary to Shakespeare's rationale, a lousy title doesn't smell sweet; it stinks. It will handicap the author and frequently turn off the editor. On the other hand, a catchy, clever title is the greatest asset for the beginning writer as well as the professional. It's like a bright neon sign blinking "Read me! Read me!"

Is there an unsold article filed away in your cabinet? Did it ever occur to you that it failed to score because of an insipid, trite title? Perhaps you can find a happy editorial home for this orphan script by renaming it. I think I can prove to you that the title's the thing. So, if you can forgive my immodest name-dropping, let me share with you some of the arts of nonfiction name-calling, as I have learned them over the years. Whether you write fillers or features, my techniques may prove helpful.

High on my preferred list is what I call the "blue chip" title. This is the use of an arresting superlative to establish that your subject material is unique, in a class by itself, and an exclusive property. Few editors can resist this package.

Let me back this up with some case histories. When I did an as-told-to story by a victim of multiple sclerosis for *The Saturday Evening Post,* I called it: "I've Got the World's Most Mysterious Disease." When they ran it, it was the sole cover line for that issue. Similarly, when I profiled Robert Redmond, the official White House gardener, for the same magazine, my man gained stature because I titled the piece: "He's the First Florist of the Land."

My article about a 12-year-old genius who was a sophomore at Yale sold when I called it: "Meet the Highest I.Q. in America." (My original working title had been "High Chair Einstein.") My story about what happens to college graduates who win Phi Beta Kappa keys appeared in *Cosmopolitan* with the title "America's Smartest

334

Set." *True* succumbed to my superlative gambit by accepting "The Oddest Bets in History." *Argosy* was an easy market for "World's Greatest Sideshow."

I had a marathon honeymoon with the old *Coronet*, when it had a massive circulation and paid $650 an article, with a succession of these *ne plus ultra* tags: "World's Most Charming Business" (about the charm bracelet industry)..."Your Fabulous Frankfurter" (about the history of the hot dog)..."Super Store for Shoppers" (about a unique emporium).

The very first article I ever wrote centered around the Inquiring Photographer for the New York *Daily News.* It told of his brashness in accosting strangers and asking them such personal questions as: "Why didn't you shave today?"..."Are you a natural blonde?"... "What do you do if your husband snores?" A national magazine bought it from the slush pile. After I had become a regular contributor to that magazine, the editor invited me to lunch. Talking about that first article, he reminisced.

"When it arrived, it went right into our slush pile," he told me. "But the title was so provocative, the reader pulled it out and passed it upstairs."

What was this blessed title I had instinctively selected which started me off in the nonfiction business? It was: "America's Nosiest Man."

The *Reader's Digest* is also receptive to superlative titles. Not only did they purchase reprint rights to "America's Nosiest Man," but they took my article on Tiffany's jewelry store when I called it "There's Only One Tiffany's!"

I have found that another winner in the name game is the interrogatory title. The typewriter's question mark looks like an inverted hook, and it has enabled me to hook dozens of editors. I stumbled on this artifice during World War II, when I was in the Army and used to listen to Tokyo Rose's broadcast propaganda in the Pacific theater. She inspired an article, "Who Is Tokyo Rose?", which sold to the *Toronto Star Weekly,* and another question-titled article on bills of large denominations sold to *Cosmopolitan* under the title, "Can You Cash a $10,000 Bill?"

Several articles with my inquisitive titles sold to a major Sunday magazine supplement. For example: "Will Your Son Be a Chip Off the Old Block?"..."Should You Fight a Traffic Ticket?"..."Will

Your Car Be Stolen Tomorrow?'' Apparently, this hook still works. *Parade,* which is distributed in 108 cities and has the largest circulation of any magazine in America—18 million—also favors quizzical headlines. It featured my article, ''Is Astrology a Multi-Million-Dollar Hoax?'' on a recent cover. I repeated there soon after with another title in this genre: ''Your Fingerprints on File—Good or Bad?''

Also strategic in title treatment is to use captions which are in the active voice. Such angling will make your article sound urgent, timely, hot off the press. When I profiled a sound engineer who collected old wax cylinders which carried the recorded voices of history's greats, I called it: ''Listen! Mark Twain Speaking!'' and sold it pronto to the *Satevepost.* They also bought my account of the curator of the world's greatest coin collection when I titled it, ''The Man Who Takes Wooden Nickels.''

You'll find the active voice in the common denominator in these five pieces I wrote for the *Reader's Digest*: ''Look What They're Doing with Cameras''...''He Finds Jobs for Ex-Convicts''... ''Nobody Reads the Directions''...''He Knows How to Interest People''...''They're Out to Get Your Money.'' (This last was an article about the various incentives banks employ to lure depositors' accounts.)

Many of my titles for *Parade* are in the active voice. Some recent examples: ''The Bodyguard Business Is Booming''...''The Strange Things That Can Happen When You Travel''...''America's Employees Are Stealing Their Companies Blind.''

Included in my repertoire is the ''think negative'' headline. Judging from my experience, its effect is to make the editor think positive about your submission. For example, ''What You Don't Know about Beauty Contests'' found a home at *Pageant.* ''Don't Panic Over Polio'' clicked at *Parents'.* The title of my exposé of crooked veterinarians, ''The Patient Can't Talk,'' won prominent display on the cover of a recent *Parade.* The same publication also featured my article, ''Men—Don't Be Ashamed to Cry.'' A solidly researched article about famous beauties of history titled, ''Be Glad You're Not Beautiful,'' proved a natural for *Ladies' Home Journal.* And slated for *Reader's Digest* is a drama in real life about an ordeal my wife and I experienced when we thought our son had perished in a plane crash in Russia. The harrowing experience we underwent trying to contact U.S.S.R. officials will run under the title: "Moscow Doesn't Answer."

What is the appeal of these negative titles? Dr. Andrew Collister, a leading Long Island psychologist, offers this analysis: "Words like 'not,' 'never,' 'don't,' and other expressions of denial have a shock value and, in a title, serve as a red traffic light which jars the reader and grabs his attention. Obviously, the author of the Ten Commandments must have been aware of this nuance, and that may be why he used so many 'Thou shalt nots.' "

Also in my grab bag of title tricks is the digital come-on, which consists of titles like "Ten Tested Tips for Staying Thin," "Twelve Ways to Cut Fuel Costs," etc. Everybody loves the numbers game. There was Dumas with *The Three Musketeers,* Dickens with *A Tale of Two Cities,* and Verne with *Around the World in Eighty Days.* The old pros knew what they were doing by invoking the numerology mystique in their titles.

To cash in on this value, when I did a nostalgia piece on the late master of makeup, Lon Chaney, for *True,* I called it "The Man of 1,000 Faces." When Herb Mayes was editor of *Cosmopolitan,* he gave me a bonus for my article, "Twenty-five Ways to Win a Bet." An article on the famous newsstand in Times Square, where papers from out of town are sold, lent itself to the title, "400 Main Streets in Manhattan," and sold to *Cue.* And when I wrote an in-depth psychological piece as to why people keep diaries, I placed it with *Family Circle* embroidered with an eight-digit title: "20,000,000 Private Lives."

About eighteen years ago, I had an idea for an article about free goodies available from the government, private industry, public relations firms, etc. Items like free maps, posters, games, kits, puzzles, samples, stamps, films and manuals. After I'd completed my research I had a file two feet high. The article I had intended to write was to have been called "Every Day Can Be Christmas." Then it occurred to me that I had enough material to expand the project into a paperback.

I called Oscar Dystel, president of Bantam Books, for whom I had written when he was editor of *Coronet, Parents'* and *Collier's,* and told him my idea.

"What's your title?" he asked.

At that moment inspiration struck and I responded: "I'm thinking of calling it '1,001 Valuable Things You Can Get Free.' "

Dystel's reaction was instantaneous. "You know that Bantam is strictly a reprint house and never publishes originals," he said. "However, I'm going to call an emergency meeting of our board of directors so that we can make your book an exception. I'll have a contract for you in forty-eight hours."

The rest is publishing history. My book became Bantam's first original, has gone into nine editions, forty-one printings, sold over three million copies, and has earned me over $300,000. And everyone in the trade agrees it was the "1,001" handle that did it. I shudder to think what might have been the book's fate if I had stuck with my original title.

The pun, says the literary establishment, is the lowest form of humor. However, when used adroitly in the title, puns have invariably brought me fan mail from editors instead of pan mail. This category is always hot. Some years ago, I sold an article to a mass magazine about the world's top autograph collector, entitled, "Big Name Hunter." And puns still work: Only last year I punned my way into an issue of *Signature* with a featured piece dubbed, "Astrology—Hit or Myth?"

Other such lowbrow appellations helped me sell articles to top national magazines. For example, when comedian Red Buttons had a popular weekly television show, I sold my interview with him labeled, "Everybody's Seeing Red." The profile I did on industry's top consultant, titled, "He Pleases the Public's Palate," was quickly placed. And when I did a personality story on Joseph Nathan Kane, author of the voluminous reference book, *Famous First Facts,* which is in every library of the world, how could I resist not giving it the pun treatment by calling it: "The Man Who Knows Everything First." It was right on for the *Reader's Digest.*

Nor did I find an unwelcome mat at the sedate *Saturday Evening Post* for my penchant for playing with words. When I gave them a story about the bizarre problems encountered by the Bronx Zoo's head keeper in feeding his aardvark-to-zebra menagerie, with trepidation I titled it: "He Serves Zoo-Plate Specials." They loved it. So naturally, for an encore, I did a piece for them about an eager-beaver female summons-server and captioned it: "She Always Gets Her Man." It brought me a check.

Two other viable words in title-craft are "how" and "you."

"How" semaphores inside information or expertise. I've sold dozens of "how" articles, ranging from "How to Keep a Friend" to *Better Homes & Gardens,* to "How to Stump an Expert" to *Pageant.* Rare is the cover which doesn't carry the ubiquitous "You" in at least one of its cover titles. The word "You" always works because it insures reader identification. I've milked this fail-safe pronoun to death. Examples: "When the Tax Collector Calls You In" (*Esquire*), "Before You Get Hooked on Astrology" (*Seventeen*).

When you combine "you" and "how" in the same title, it's almost invariably a winner. *Parade* featured my exposé, "How Magicians Fool You." One particular article I did for *Today's Health* combined *three* title gimmicks—"how," "you" and the question mark. The piece was called: "Do You Know How to Stay Alive?"

How many times have you seen the word "secret" on a magazine cover? "The Secret Sinatra Can't Forget," "Greta Garbo's Secret Hideaway"—I could cite endless other examples. This proliferation is no accident. Editors have long ago discovered that a big "box-office" magnet on a cover is the word "secret." It's a surefire circulation booster.

I discovered this gold mine myself years ago when I was the first editor of *Superman* and found that when I used "secret" in a title on the comic book cover—"The Secret of Superman's Fortress," or "Superman's Secret Enemy"—newsstand sales would zoom. And over the years, hitching onto this magic word whenever possible in a title has proved quite rewarding. My article "Can You Keep a Secret?" scored at *Redbook,* and *Lady's Circle* recently bought a piece from me called "Secrets about Men That Will Surprise You." One article of mine, called "How Secrets Leak Out in Washington," was published in a national magazine and read into the *Congressional Record.*

The opening article in the January 1975 issue of *Today's Health,* "The Secret Diet That Saved My Chubby Hubby," was written by my wife, Thelma Weisinger, an R.N. with a strong nutrition background. Her article told how she succeeded in getting me to lose eighty pounds by devising a secret diet so that I was unaware that I was her unsuspecting guinea pig. It not only won coveted approval from the AMA, but reprint rights were immediately purchased by the *Catholic Digest,* the *National Star* and the *London Express.* She was also offered a contract to expand it into book form under the title, "The Secret Diet Cook Book." It's no secret that she signed it.

61

CHECKLIST FOR A SALABLE ARTICLE

By Louise Boggess

When an inexperienced writer receives a rejection slip on an article, he berates the editor for not recognizing exceptional material. An analytical comparison of his article to published ones might supply the real reason for rejection: the piece needed professional techniques. The following ten techniques can mean the difference between a rejection slip and a check:

1. Reader identity idea

A salable article builds a bridge to the reader and touches him where he lives. The wider the identity, the better the article. Ask yourself who will want to read your article. If very few, find another idea.

From the *Reader's Digest* come these strong reader-identity titles:

a) "What Ails the U.S. Mails?" by Joseph Albright

b) "Will the Social Security Bubble Burst?" by Robert T. Gray

c) "A Better Way to Bank Blood," by Walter S. Ross

d) "Too Much Government by Decree!" by John Barron

e) "If You Spoil the Marriage, Spare the Child," by Paul Friggens

f) "Listen to the Sound of America," by Jean Bell Mosley

Any of these titles touches the life of most people in the United States.

2. Capsule sentence

In any published article, you can find one short sentence that will summarize the entire piece. Generally, this sentence appears within the first three paragraphs of the article. To check this technique, take any issue of *Reader's Digest* and underline this summary sentence in each article.

The *capsule sentence* summarizes your specific approach to the general subject. To find the best one for your article, write several, compare them, and select the one that expresses your point of view. Consider these capsule sentences from the article titles listed above.

340

a) For better or for worse, the industrial revolution is finally catching up with the U.S. mails.

b) There is increasing awareness that the [Social Security] system is headed for a financial crisis that can be resolved only through major tax increases—beyond the hefty ones now scheduled—or by restraint on future increases in benefits, or a combination of both.

c) Yet much of our blood-banking system is chaotically inefficient.

d) Today, Americans increasingly find their lives regulated by decrees emanating from bureaucrats who are, in effect, accountable to no one.

e) We are now raising a generation of children from broken homes—and creating a social time bomb.

f) Does she [America] have a sound? One that we cannot choose, but nevertheless is ours, made up of notes past and present and tangled into a single tone?

Make the capsule sentence specific enough to state your personal reaction to the subject, but general enough to contain the points you plan to develop in the body of the article.

3. Threads of the capsule sentence

The capsule sentence contains related threads of thought that form the body of the article. Express these thoughts in simple statements which you will incorporate exactly as written into the article. To check this technique, analyze published articles for these structural statements. Study this development from "If You Spoil the Marriage, Spare the Child."

Let your child know that you are parents forever.
Consider your child's trauma.
As you cope, so will your children.
Level with the kids, but hold your spite.
Don't use the child as a weapon.
Make visits a joyful, loving experience.

Most articles are built around approximately five statements that summarize the development of the piece. Some may use four, while others choose six, but your material will determine the number. Keep the capsule sentence in mind while you list all possible development statements. See if you can combine two or discard others to reduce the number. Remember that five strong points make a better development than eight weak ones. When you have chosen your sentences, write each on a 3 x 5 file card.

Take these cards and arrange them in the best order for discussion in the body of the article. You may want to arrange the points chronologically. Many articles work best with a logical organization. An article using much fictionalizing may require a dramatic or emotional development. Some develop from the least to the most important point. Let your material dictate the arrangement.

Now that you know the capsule sentence and the way you will expand it into an article, you must choose the correct viewpoint.

4. Viewpoint

Viewpoint means the angle from which you project the facts of the article. The type of article or your relation to the reader will suggest the best viewpoint. Consider these general rules:

If you write from your own personal experience, and this provides the "authority" of the article, choose the first-person, major-character viewpoint. This example comes from "Listen to the Sound of America."

Walking in old fence rows, I hear meadowlarks lacing the fields with song, speaking of secret things.

Writing about others, you often need to give some outside authority for the viewpoint of the article. Therefore, you use the minor-character viewpoint, as in this example from "Unforgettable Pablo Casals," by Isaac Stern (*Reader's Digest*, June 1975):

I first met Casals in the small French village of Prades, just across the Pyrenees from his native Spain, where he had exiled himself in 1939 following Franco's victory.

Implied viewpoint means you do not identify the author with an expressed personal pronoun, but you furnish the emotion of the article. With such a viewpoint, you want the reader to concentrate carefully on selected facts and share your opinion. This example comes from "A Better Way to Bank Blood."

Under the old, anarchic system of blood banking, waste had amounted to thousands of units of blood—which were lost simply because there was no way of knowing what spot had how many units of which types. The Blood Center has changed all that.

Any time the article involves interaction between the reader and the author, the dual pronoun (I-you) works best. Take this example from "If You Spoil the Marriage, Spare the Child":

Can you really pick up the pieces and carry on? Embittered couples are highly skeptical, but consider the case of Lucy Dunbar, married seven years and mother of three children when her husband deserted her for another woman.

Along with the correct viewpoint, accurate research makes articles authoritative.

5. Research

Most articles require some research, even those written from your own experience. No one can remember exactly. Nothing can so turn off an editor or a reader as an article that has doubtful facts. Most writers begin their research by reading a general account of the subject in an encyclopedia. Check several; some give more information than others. Follow through on any names or related subjects listed.

Now that you have an idea of the scope of the subject, you want to check the *Readers' Guide to Periodical Literature* for the past five years to see what articles have been published on the subject. Read these articles for the basic ideas covered, the slant, and notice points not discussed.

Search for new research on the subject. You might find this by writing to the public relations department of a corporation involved with the subject or product, and by checking newspaper coverage or government publications. Try to interview people directly associated with the subject. Museums, professional associations and organizations prove a rich source of research. Learn to knock on any related door and follow any lead no matter how small.

When the information you have collected and a certain approach to developing the article keep coming to mind, you can begin to organize your research material.

6. Hook

The hook refers to the bait in the first one to three paragraphs of the article that catches the reader's attention and makes him want to read on. Usually the hook varies in length from one sentence to several paragraphs. You have a choice of a dozen different ways to write a hook, not to mention numerous combinations of these. Pick up a magazine and read only the opening paragraphs up to the capsule sentence. Note how the hook provides the showcase for the material in the article and leads to the capsule sentence. This contrast hook comes from "If You Spoil the Marriage, Spare the Child":

Like inflation, the U.S. divorce rate is soaring. Divorce has increased as much between 1970 and 1974 as in the entire previous decade, the Census Bureau reports, with upward of one million couples now filing. About one million children are involved.

This statistical-problem hook opens the article on "A Better Way to Bank Blood":

Every day in this country, more than 18,000 units of blood (a unit is approximately one pint) are transfused—making blood the most successful and widely used of all tissue transplants. The demand for blood increases about ten percent each year as new blood products, such as gamma globulin, are developed....

The author used an action hook to open "What Ails the U.S. Mails?"

You are seated in front of a green plastic keyboard. Sixty times a minute, a rotating metal arm reaches into a tray of letters and deposits one into the chain conveyor 16 inches in front of your eyes. You have six tenths of a second to read the zip code before you hear the click. Then, within the next four tenths of a second, you must press the right three keys, like staccato notes on a piano....

Try to choose the hook that will best showcase your article and that catches the attention of the reader immediately.

7. Show business

In writing an article, you *state* the fact in your development sentence and then you *show* it with an example. The reader reaction you want determines the choice of devices. Many writers fall into the trap of narrating or preaching to the reader. To make the reader think, choose such devices as statistics, comparison, reasoning, quotations from authorities, or historical references. Most writers know these devices.

When you want the reader to react emotionally and share the experiences in the article, select devices adapted from fiction for the factual article. These include rapid-running narration, active description, series of incidents, dramatic action, or a scene.

Rapid-running narration from "What Ails the U.S. Mails?":

As for the unpredictable service: if you think what distributing 246 million pieces of different-sized mail every day entails, it seems a wonder the system works as reliably as it does. Under current practice, after first-class letters have been manually rough-sorted, they head for a Mark II facer/canceller machine.

Active description kept "Listen to the Sound of America" moving right along:

Sometimes I think I hear it, faint and far off, a high murmurous wind passing over, a wind that has known the Rockies, played hide-and-seek in the Grand Canyon, whispered in prairie grass, bent willows along some bayou, sifted snow in Montana and transferred Oklahoma dust to Kansas—a tumbleweed wind, stirring, roaring, sighing.

A series of incidents can cover a block of time, as in this device from "Will the Social Security Bubble Burst?":

Children born during the baby boom of 1946-1959 began entering the work force in the 1960s, and the influx will continue into the 1980s. Over the next 35 years, then, there will be a large work force providing benefits for a relatively small retired population. During the early 1970s, however, the birth rate dropped suddenly, to the zero-population-growth level. Therefore, when those in the baby-boom generation reach retirement age, starting about 2010, a relatively small work force will be providing high benefits for a large number of retirees.

Dramatic action takes the reader onstage with a you-are-there emotional effect. This example comes from "A Better Way to Bank Blood":

By 8:45, when a team of Center nurses began arriving, Drake and Beltran had set up nine cots in U-shaped groups of three. A large coffee machine was bubbling away, and paper cups of jellybeans, to replenish donors' blood sugar, were set out. Nurses and aides unpacked plastic bags, which have replaced the glass bottles in which blood used to be collected. Self-sticking numbers are attached to each bag and registration slip so that every donation can be traced to its source.

Dramatic action shows, while narration tells what happened. But a scene shows a conflict situation at one time and one place between two or more characters. You summarize the problem, introduce the characters, set the time and place. Show conflict in dialogue and action. Give the result. This example comes from "Too Much Government by Decree!":

In Newport Beach, Calif., an OSHA inspector visited Blackie's Boatyard, where owner Arsene "Blackie" Gadarian and six workers repair small craft. Pointing to a man without a life jacket who was working in a boat tied to the pier, the inspector asked, "What would happen if he fell in the water?"
"He would stand up," Gadarian replied. "The water's only three feet deep all along the pier." Still, the inspector thought there should be a ladder at the pier's end. Gadarian said he would nail up a ladder.

Varying the devices used gives your article a strong note of professionalism, but, more important, it makes the copy more lively and readable.

8. Exit fast

To end an article, you may simply summarize the major points, or, using a bit of dialogue, show a character in action in an amusing incident.

The last sentence of the conclusion I call the *twist*. You should restate the capsule sentence in such a way that the reader will remember it long after he has forgotten the article as a whole. Look at the general emotional tone of your article and write a last sentence that will either contrast or strengthen the dominant feeling. Basically, you can make the reader think, chuckle, act, or get choked up emotionally. An excellent illustration of conclusion and twist comes from "If You Spoil the Marriage, Spare the Child":

Following these useful guidelines, couples find that much of the anguish and stress in divorce can be reduced. But more important, they give their children a chance to know and love both parents.

9. Market

Today most editors prefer a query on an idea. This enables you to benefit from editorial comment. You may query in two ways: by brief letter or by outline.

The letter works best with editors you have sold to previously. Keep the letter to one page, single-spaced. In the first paragraph, use the hook you will incorporate in your article and add the capsule sentence to show the slant. Paragraph two asks the editor if he will be interested in an article that would include certain facts. State the length of the article and when you could deliver it. In the last paragraph, give any qualifications or writing credits.

The query outline works better for editors to whom you have not yet sold anything. In a short covering letter, state that you enclose a query outline of a prospective article. List any of your qualifications or writing credits.

On a separate sheet, leaving a two-inch margin for editorial comments, write the hook and the capsule sentence. List in numerical order the development points you will discuss. Include the conclusion and twist. Hold the outline to a single page. Select an outstanding development point and write it in full, so the editor may see your style.

To find where to send your queries, study market lists for articles in writers' magazines and in *The Writer's Handbook*. Do try to read at least six issues of the magazine you are aiming for, as well as the market listing, so you know its specific requirements. You will find many of the magazines at your library, or you can write to the editor for a copy, enclosing payment. Some second-hand stores have magazines for sale. Thorough market research gets your idea to the right editor.

10. Cool it

When you complete the first draft of an article, you often lose your objectivity. Put the article away for at least a week and let it cool. During that time, transfer your enthusiasm to a new idea and repeat this same procedure for it. Of course, you can also apply these suggestions to any rejected article, as well as using them to develop a new article idea.

62

PLOTTING THE BIOGRAPHY

By Catherine Drinker Bowen

A NOVELIST informed me, with magisterial assurance, that compared to fiction writers, biographers have an easy time. Their plot is ready to hand before they even begin to write. When I asked, what plot, exactly?—the novelist said it was self-evident: "Birth, education, marriage, career, death."

Surely the novelist was mistaken, and his five neat sequential nouns indicated a chronology rather than a plot? Consider Monday, for instance, which has its beginning and ending; the sun rises and sets. One breakfasts, works, lunches, takes a walk, goes out to dinner perhaps, comes home, goes to bed. Yet if a writer wishes to engage a reader's attention concerning Monday, his hero must that day meet with trouble, face an obstacle, a danger, a grief, and conquer it. Or if the writer prefers tragedy, then Monday's obstacle can be conqueror, and draw a reader's tears.

The book trade calls it conflict, suspense. By whatever name, it is a quality vital to biography as to fiction. The difference is that the novelist invents his plot, whereas the biographer finds it in history, in actual fact as indicated by the given material, by events as they unfold, and more particularly by the character of the biographical subject, the hero. Maurois has something to say about this. The biographer, he believes, "has greater difficulty than the novelist in composition. But he has one compensation: to be compelled to take over the form of a work ready-made is almost always a source of power to the artist. It is painful, it makes his task more difficult; but at the same time it is from this struggle between the mind and the matter that resists it that a masterpiece is born."

From *Biography: The Craft and the Calling* (Atlantic-Little, Brown). Copyright © 1968 by Catherine Drinker Bowen.

Graduate students of history, having labored for years on a thesis, often feel ambitious to see their work in print. Approaching some available professional writer they inquire how their production can be fixed up for trade publication. "Popular presentation," they have learned to call it.

The professional writer is wary of such assignments. A biography must be planned *before* it is written, not afterward. Yet as an example, the graduate student's problem can be worth careful inspection because it is actually the same problem the seasoned biographer confronts in the early stages of his books. The material is gathered, now what is to be done with it? These pages—this thesis—dry, correct, with serried footnotes, can be extremely useful as reference on a library shelf. And it covers the ground, certainly. But it moves on mechanized wooden legs, without head or guts, humor or humanity. Yet humor and humanity cannot be stuffed into a book at later convenience but must grow from the narrative as it progresses, springing hot and hearty from the writer's own bias and involvement as he sits and thinks about his subject.

Ask such a graduate student what his thesis, his book, is about. Not merely the name and life schedule of the hero, but what the book is *about*, what is its plot, what carries it along? For answer you will be given a chronology, a train of events. Let us say the biographical subject is an agent for Indian affairs on the American frontier, *circa* 1775. Captain B—— has fought the French, he knows Indians; he is prospering and minding his business, when along comes the Revolution—and he chooses the Tory side!

Divided loyalty! Here is a theme, here is plot enough to carry to the end. For what is biography but the story of a man or woman in conflict with himself? Moreover the subject is fresh; the Tory in our Revolution has not been explored in depth, as the professors say. Yet—take the manuscript in hand and what is presented on the page? Battles, boundary lines, Indian raids, with actual tallies of the scalped and the dead. Footnotes, chapter notes, bibliography. Everything neat, verified—and bloodless even though the scene itself is soaked in blood.

But the man who wrote the thesis is not dry. When he talks about his hero-captain he is entertaining, he is funny; what he says concerning his characters is quick and sharp. One knows of course that such qualities, transferred to the page, are of no help toward graduate honors. Yet this young man has not come to discuss academic degrees. Ask him then, if his hero suffered, if the captain doubted his position and his choice, felt sadness at the loss of old friends among the Americans.

For answer the young man begins to explain what it meant to be a loyalist in the Revolution, and what his captain's soul will lose or gain thereby. Suddenly his very word is gold. Write it down! the professional says. Write it on the back of an envelope, quick before it vanishes. . . .

There is, one assumes, proof of the captain's struggle, quotations available in letters, diaries, if not from the captain's hand then from someone in a like position. Did the captain have a family and did they share his views and loyalties? More legwork, as the reporters call it, was desirable, but legwork with a different end in view. Canadian libraries might yield a harvest. It would be worthwhile to visit repositories in Ottawa, Detroit. . . . The thesis is filled moreover with names of Indian tribes, Indian chiefs with whom the hero had close dealings. Is there some indirect way of repeating what they said? We must not have fictional conversation around the council fire. But treaties were made with the French, the English. The language is available, it is written down.

The young man had been excellently trained in evaluating evidence. He could spot a bad source, a dubious statement across a library room. In short, he had completed one phase of a biographer's training. But if he aimed beyond the classroom, if he wished the world to read about his hero, his Tory captain, he would find the next phase of training equally rigorous. He must move into the realm of feeling, of men and women and their emotions. Through historical evidence, fortified and animated by his own experience of living, he must pick these people up bodily from his dry pages, turn them over in his hand, stare at them long and searchingly.

And there is a further task, a pleasant one to my way of thinking. It concerns scene. What about terrain, one asks the writer—the rivers, the hills? This is an outdoor story. We must see the hero's country; a Tory captain does not float in air. In the thesis as it stands there is no field or forest or blockhouse or cellar that one can remember or describe after reading—let alone a face, a voice the figure of a man. The words on the page should be evocative, call up colors, sounds, sights, smells.

This of course is reckless counsel. Not everybody can write a scene or describe a man's face. Not everyone has eyes to see a field, a tree in life, let alone set it down in writing. There is no sense pretending that technique will take the place of talent. Yet here again, practice counts, in perception as in writing. Moreover, at certain stages heroic measures are called for, strong medicine to clear the writer's vision, turn him about to face another direction. He must free himself from his strict specific training, which for its purpose was excellent. Like the student who has mastered the fundamentals of grammar he is prepared, he is ready. Of what he has learned nothing will be forgotten, neglected or distorted. But the time has come to make the material his own, transform it into words that live, that pulse, communicate.

Once the beginner has his plot in mind—his central animating theme—he will do well to think over the chronology of the hero's life, the big things that happened. These he can note down in scenes, as for a stage play but with the dates, keeping always in mind the direction his work is heading, the climax which by now must surely have declared itself. This exercise might fill three or four pages of 8½″ x 11″ paper. Then he can begin to write his book, working from scene to scene, as the composer of a symphony heads for the next theme, whether a secondary subject or a development.

So simplified a program will not of course make a book. But it is a step taken, a map, a way out of the wilderness of research into a final choice of incident. It leads from the library into life, narration, drama, plot. An outline need not, however, be a rigid plan that must be followed letter for letter. Indeed, I have seen biographical outlines so complete, so detailed and heavy they bade fair to crush the story, deceiving the author into thinking he had written his book. What one advocates is a loose chronology which reads vividly simply because the incidents, the characters or occasional quotations from hero or heroine are themselves vivid. For example, Queen Elizabeth, as a young woman, "told the French Ambassador de Foix that whenever she thought about marriage, she felt as if someone were tearing the heart out of her bosom." Again, to her ladies, on hearing that Mary Stuart had borne a child: "The Queen of Scots is lighter of a fair son, and I am but a barren stock."

When Elizabeth Jenkins [author of *Elizabeth the Great*] came across those words in the records, surely her mind leaped forward, imagining the time and place where she could set them in her book.

It is easier to tell someone how than to do it oneself. E. M. Forster is a master of his material, a master of narrative. Yet even he confesses that "people will not realize how one flounders about."

Floundering about is endemic to writers, a phase we all go through at the outset of a work. Psychiatrists say this initial block is intrinsic to the creative process, a forcing of the writer deeper into himself. The procedure can be called by other names: thinking, brooding, dreaming. I have heard it said that most authors sit down at their typewriters too soon. Before words go on paper the biographer must put his notes away, out of sight, while he sits and thinks, or walks about and thinks—a painful exercise which may consume days or weeks while the paper remains blank in the typewriter.

This thinking may well turn upon the business of what the biography is about: its theme, the axis upon which its wheels may turn. Does the plot concern a happy man, a life fulfilled? It has been said that happiness has no story—which in itself is a challenge and a half. The biographer must write very well indeed to make his happy hero come alive; he has an extra dimension to reach, an eighth hurdle to surmount. Happiness has many definitions. Grief is part of living: *Sturm und Drang* does not necessarily mean unhappiness or unfulfillment.

But how variously lives are arranged! The biographer may choose a hero who began in poverty and climbed, or one born into luxury and place, thence falling or maintaining his position as circumstance and his spirit dictate. And how much objective history will these projected chapters include? It is a vital question. Every biography is of course a "life and times." Yet there are degrees and proportions. The life of a statesman is three-quarters "times"; the life of a painter or composer of music may show a very different mixture and balance. A biographer of Justice Holmes told me solemnly that his ambition was to "show Holmes's influence on the stream of American intellectual consciousness." But how could one aim at such an effort or be sure this intellectual stream existed? Will such a plot carry, is it feasible? A biographer can be too high-toned for his own good.

In the biographies I most admire, the story moves forward implacably, inevitably. The reader *believes* in Mary Tudor, Elizabeth the Great, Lord Melbourne, George Sand (*Lélia*), Balzac (*Prometheus*). The reader cannot but believe. There are no awkward hurdles, no holes to fall through. Nothing is stretched too far or condensed to the point of collapse. The narrative—the plot—contains us, we know where we are going.

63

THE EASIEST ARTICLE TO SELL

By Mort Weisinger

IF YOUR ambition is to crack the big slicks with nonfiction material, you may have to spend years perfecting your style of writing, learning how to open with a dramatic hook, disciplining yourself in the judicious use of anecdotes. The tricks of the trade call also for dispensing vital information palatably instead of ponderously, the expert use of smooth transitions from one set of facts to another, and the mastery of other techniques. Sad to report, you may have an excellent idea but never get it into print because of faulty treatment that dulls its brightness.

There is one type of article, however, which preempts the demand for skillful writing and focuses the spotlight on the *idea* itself. I'll bet my IBM typewriter against a dollar ballpoint pen that you can sell these features to a leading magazine without an agent, even if you don't have a single by-line to your credit.

This is the eternally popular symposium in print, known in our business as the "round-up" article. It is probably the most sure-fire sesame for entry into the major magazines, but *only* when it "name drops" national figures who populate the lofty echelons of our society. In essence, it is an adaptation of the "star system" that is almost guaranteed box-office insurance for a Hollywood film.

Ever since the late Mike Todd peppered his epic, *Around the World in 80 Days,* with "cameo" roles played by top stars, this device has put many a producer in clover. Baseball's annual All-Star Game is an inevitable sellout because fans can't resist this "round-up" of the best of the big-leaguers. Even sweet charity hitches onto the shirttails of the stars, raising millions every year corralling endless numbers of celebrities who appeal to the viewers' wallets before the telethon cameras.

It is this catering to the public's palate for stellar names that can melt the resistance of the most hard-boiled editor and will give him instant amnesia about his "overstocked inventory." Having name cards to deal from your deck is a negotiable asset! (How do *you* contact famous folk? That's known as suspense, friend, and to find out you'll have to read to the end of this article.)

I'll illustrate with some actual case histories. Like most professional writers, I always keep an eye on the calendar. A few years ago, knowing that National Library Week would be coming up in a few months, I wrote to *Better Homes and Gardens* and proposed a theme for a round-up that I felt would be appropriate for the occasion. The feature would be entitled "My Most Memorable Childhood Book," and it would list the choices of prominent figures of our time and tell, in their own words, how a book they read when they were young influenced their future lives.

I received an immediate green light for this project and was able to garner quotes from twenty-three distinguished Americans. The roster included Billy Graham, Gene Tunney, Norman Vincent Peale and other luminaries. *Better Homes and Gardens* gave the feature a seven-page spread, and paid top dollar. Happy footnote: a subsequent survey revealed the feature had polled the highest readership in the issue.

The point to remember is that, with the exception of a brief introduction, *I did not write the article;* it was my stable of stars who provided the copy. I simply quoted their own words.

Family Circle Magazine has been particularly receptive to the round-up feature. One such successful article I wrote for them was "The Day I Cried," in which I cited occasions when famous women cried, as told to me first-hand. (Here, we ruled out death of a dear one as the cause of grief, because everyone cries from this experience.) My published article reported how Senator Margaret Chase Smith had waged a bitter election campaign against an opponent who had smeared her viciously. I then told how she had cried when she was vindicated at the polls by an enormous majority. Plus similar touching sob stories.

Other round-ups I have done for *Family Circle* include "How to Enrich Your Husband's Life," a vehicle for practical suggestions by Margaret Mead, Mrs. Dale Carnegie, Sylvia Porter, and seven other notables. In the past, I've turned out such round-up pieces as "The Day I Won the Nobel Prize"; "Ten College Presidents Reveal the One Mistake Parents Make in Preparing Their Children for College"; "The One Secret I Learned about Losing Weight Permanently."

While the basic format of the round-up article consists of a stimulating title and a provocative theme that offers a showcase for direct quotes from the world's big wheels (thereby providing those coveted cover names so dear to the heart of the circulation director), the structure can be quite flexible. One variation of the round-up pattern is to weave the fabric around nationally known institutions instead of persons, as I did, for example, in an article I wrote for *Parade,* "Debunking Our Greatest Animal Myths." As my research for the piece, I polled the directors of the country's three major zoos: The Bronx Zoo, which is the most famous; the San Diego Zoo, which is the largest, and the Philadelphia Zoo, the oldest.

The directors supplied me with such information as the fact that vampire bats do not suck blood; porcupines do not fire quills; and bears do not hibernate in the winter. Of course, the directors explained why each of these beliefs is a myth. With twenty such quotes from unimpeachable authorities in the article, how could any writer miss?

Another round-up for which I depended on institutions to supply me with all the research I needed appeared in *Travel & Leisure.* This article, a catch-basin of unusual emergencies that may confront the average tourist, was titled: "What to Do When Travel Trouble Erupts." For example, what do you do if you take a cruise and discover that somehow they neglected to put your trunk on board? What do you do if you fly to Honolulu for a vacation, want to rent a car, and suddenly find that you forgot to take your driver's license with you? What do you do if you arrive in a strange city on a Sunday and discover that you've lost your glasses or had your hearing aid or pacemaker conk out? To obtain the answers to these and other travelers' dilemmas, I canvassed the public-relations directors of various airlines, steamship companies, rent-a-car companies, and the Travelers Aid Society. I felt like a thief transcribing their solutions to these problems and getting paid for it.

Similarly, for a round-up article in which I demolish popular misconceptions people have about safety, my homework was cheerfully done for me by the safety experts of such organizations as the American Red Cross, the Boy Scouts of America, the National Safety Council, the Battalion Chief of the Philadelphia Fire Department and the Safety Director of the Consolidated Edison Company of New York. The fallacies they funneled me included such eyebrow-raisers as the fact that wearing rubber gloves does not protect a person from contact with a high-tension wire; that a wet handkerchief is not a substitute for a gas mask to protect you from toxic fumes in a fire; that you should never plunge into the water yourself to rescue a drowning person; that pork is not free of trichinosis parasites even if the meat has been stamped: "Inspected and passed by U.S. Government."

I combined those experts' statements, along with their explanations and those of other safety experts as to why many survival "rules" were virtually old wives' tales, and titled the symposium, "Do You Know How to Stay Alive?" (It appeared in *Family Health* as "Caution: Play It Safe.")

Timely round-up articles are eagerly sought by editors. When the lottery craze swept thirteen of our states, I wondered how winning a million dollars affected the lives of the lucky ticket-holders. I phoned the various commissioners of the thirteen states where lotteries were legal, and they gave me the names and addresses of the top winners. I interviewed them all by phone. The resulting reactions, brimming over with emotional drama, were published in *Parade* under the title, "The Lottery Millionaires."

When *The Sting* was such a movie smash that people stood in long lines to buy tickets, I joined the queue. I noted that the audience enjoyed the clever swindling rip-offs used by the heroes, Robert Redford and Paul Newman. I quickly contacted consumer fraud agencies, insurance investigators, bank officers and Better Business Bureaus, requesting that they update me on the latest "stings" being foisted on the public by professional gyp artists. I stitched together the flow of information with which they swamped me. The finished round-up made the cover of *Parade* under the title, "New Tricks in the Con Game."

Recently, I sold *Popular Photography* an article literally assembled for me by the PR people of Polaroid and Eastman Kodak—"Twenty Ways Kids Can Make Money With a Camera." Typical tip: on Halloween, take flash shots of children who wear costumes for their "trick or treat" forays. Rare is the parent who can resist buying a print of his costume-clad offspring. Actually, most of the tips in that article were "overspill" from a round-up article I had written many years ago for the *Reader's Digest*—"Look What They're Doing With Cameras."

O.K., you say now, you've got the message, and you're convinced that the round-up treatment of a universally appealing topic can catapult you into the big time. So how do you reach famous actors, statesmen, stars, literary giants, etc.? Why should they pause in their busy day to pound out a thoughtful message for you, an unknown writer with few, if any, credits?

The answer is—human vanity, compassion for the little guy, and the constant desire of important personages to maintain their public image. Jacqueline Onassis, Gerald Ford, Jeane Dixon, and Ann Landers are but a few of the national figures who maintain staffs to handle personal mail and accommodate citizens who desire legitimate information. A courteous, intelligent letter, accompanied by a stamped, self-addressed envelope, will almost always evoke a response.

In the case of Hollywood stars, your query should be addressed to the public relations staff of the studio with which the star is associated or which is currently producing one of the actor's pictures. Similarly, if you want to get in touch with a stage celebrity in a current Broadway show, you can reach him or her through the press agent who handles that theater. If your star is off the scene, a polite query with a stamped, self-addressed envelope sent to the editor of *Variety* (154 W. 46th Street, New York, NY 10036) will give you a clue to the star's whereabouts. If your famous person is an author, like James Michener, Norman Mailer, or Betty Friedan, address your letter to them care of their publishers, who will forward them to the authors.

Who's Who is a bonanza of information, with vital statistics on numerous celebrities and also their home addresses (or office locations). You might also keep in mind a New York information center, "Celebrity Service" (171 West 57th Street, New York, NY 10019). Membership is not cheap ($40.00 a month), but it entitles you to phone them and request the current address or phone number of any of 500,000 celebrities in art, business, communications, fashion, literature, music, politics, radio, television, screen, religion, science, society, sports and stage. So fabulous are their resources that they can tell you how to reach a VIP even if he is in a remote village of the Congo. Monthly subscription allows you to make five inquiries per day, five days a week. For non-members, Celebrity Service will furnish addresses, etc., at $10 per query.

This firm also publishes a volume of brief biographies entitled *Celebrity Register,* which lists the addresses of 1800 world celebrities. The current edition is available at $35 plus tax, but it is also in most large libraries.

To get quotes from generals, admirals, even astronauts, the wisest procedure is to go through military channels. Write to the Public Relations Officer, care of the branch you are interested in—Army, Navy, Air Force, Marines, etc.—and send your communiques to the Pentagon Building, in Washington, D.C. You may be snarled in red tape, and your letter may be rerouted to another office, but eventually the wheels will turn and you will get your answer.

I think it is only fair to warn you that soliciting celebrities via the mails can be hazardous. Sometimes a secretary will reply with a firm, polite refusal; quite often your letter will lie in limbo and never be acknowledged. During the past several years, however, I have worked out a technique which works nine times out of ten. After I have an expression of interest from a magazine on an idea, I ensconce myself in a public telephone booth and fortify myself with a stack of quarters and dimes. Then I phone the celebrity at his office, person-to-person, during the lunch hour, taking into account the time zone difference. (I have found that most VIPs are so busy they rarely eat out; they brown-bag it.) If he, or his secretary, asks who's calling, I say "This is Mort Weisinger of ------- Magazine." When I reach him or her, the operator invariably says: "I have your party. Please deposit $2.75." Then I go into my ritual of inserting eleven quarters. Can you imagine the reaction of the subject at the other end? When I identify myself as a free-lance writer, he knows I have invested $2.75 of my hard-earned money and becomes sympathetic, helpful and cooperative. He regards me as an underdog and becomes quite loquacious.

If you are shy about submitting your proposal for a round-up theme to a major magazine, don't sell yourself short. If you have a viable idea for a symposium article along the lines I've mentioned, submit it to a good market, and mention that if they think it has possibilities, you will be glad to develop it on speculation. You can also list the celebrities you intend to include, and ask the editors if they have any other VIPs to suggest. Quite often they will tell you their preferences. And many times you may not even have to write an introduction to the quoted material; the magazine will simply print your quotes (some of which you may have to edit slightly or condense) under your title, say, "What I Think of Astrology," and credit you with a by-line that reads: "Compiled by John Doe." Should they reject it, you can lower your sights and try the Sunday section of your local newspaper or regional magazines. And instead of national celebrities, you can quote local politicians, school athletes and umpires, doctors, educators, barbers, etc.

Remember, this is the easiest type of article to sell—because you don't even have to write it!

64

TRAVEL WRITING

By F. A. Rockwell

"One of the good things about travel," says Alistair Cooke, "is the way it rouses some senses that tend to lie dormant, in a permanent snooze, in the country you live in." There are many other advantages for a writer. The stimulation of these places and faces inevitably provides new ideas for writers, and all expenses are deductible if you sell anything about your trip: fiction, travel, or nonfiction. After you're an established travel writer, you'll probably have expense accounts, pre-trip assignments, and a travel column! And perhaps a book series like Sydney Clark's *All the Best in South America ... Scandinavia ... France ...* etc.; Arthur Frommer's "$5 a Day" Series (later up-dated to $10 a Day); Kate Simon's *New York Places and Pleasures* and *Mexico: Places and Pleasures,* and the Fodor, Michelin, and Fielding travel guides.

Today, there is a universal need for people of different countries to know, understand, and respect each other. You can contribute to world harmony by traveling—and writing about it—in a friendly spirit that the Greeks call *philoxenia,* "love of the foreigner." This can be as much of an asset as cash or the knowledge of foreign languages, and it will enable you to write travel articles that are both salable and worthwhile, and to gather background material for your other writing.

The do's of travel writing

Work your way up to being a successful travel writer by applying these suggestions to your writing:

1. Start collecting and studying travel brochures to give you ideas for trips and places to write about. You can get excellent material from the U.S. Government Printing Office, various Chambers of Commerce, travel agents, and consulates, as well as airlines and auto clubs. Remember that writing and selling features about local places and events can finance more distant trips. A. B. Zu Tavern wrote:

By starting with trips to nearby places and radiating outward, like ripples on a pond when a stone is thrown in, travel can be made a lifelong experience with a profit.

2. Study the colorful style of travel brochures and published travel articles, and make your writing even more vivid. John Clellon Holmes, for example, described Florence, Italy, this way:

Down there, across the milky-green Arno at low water, Florence lay spread out in the shallow bowl of hills—its pale yellow piazzas, and walls of earthy pink, and tiled roofs in terraces of faded ocher as graphic as a high-definition photograph in the startling clarity of the Tuscan morning. ("Thanksgiving in Florence," *Playboy*)

3. Choose a little-known spot for your trip (and your travel article), or plan a fresh, new approach to a famous place. Perhaps you can highlight a colorful celebration, rodeo, or fiesta, or interesting side trips, local folklore, natural history, or history.

A *Westways* feature, "Walls of Carcassonne" (by Stuart Weiner), opens with a dramatic incident from the 9th century. While Charlemagne and his army laid siege to the city of Carcassonne to starve the people into submission, they saw Dame Carcas on the wall feed grain to a pig and then toss it over the wall. Thinking the city had endless reserves of food, the attackers withdrew, not knowing that the grain and the pig were the very last food and that the city was on the point of capitulation.

4. Read everything that has been written about the place you plan to visit, checking the *Readers' Guide to Periodical Literature* and the *National Geographic Index* for recently published articles. Be sure to read back issues of the magazine you want to write for to understand its slant and requirements.

5. Before going away, do enough research to query the editor of the magazine you want to submit your article to, presenting different ideas for his or her approval. Although you can write an article without a specific assignment, an editorial go-ahead can be an Open Sesame in a foreign country or a strange city, paving the way to important local people and fascinating experiences.

6. While writing your material, try to anticipate and answer questions the average reader might ask about a place. For example, a *Sunset* Magazine article on Mexico City sums up the usual questions

in its caption: "What is it really like to be a visitor? What can you eat, see, do, shop for? Where should you stay? When should you go? What about the weather? And what will it all cost?"

7. Write with enthusiasm, and not just about yourself and what you did, but about the recreational, human-interest, sports, and scenic attractions that will make a reader want to go there, too. Give honest and up-to-date information about current prices, hotels, rent-a-car-or-boat facilities, side-trip costs, and for foreign countries, rates of exchange.

8. Spruce up your writing style with contrasts and comparisons. Olympic skiing champion Sten Eriksen writes of New Zealand's Tasman glacier:

> You can visualize such formations in ice cream, but to see such tremendous walls around you! Ice-cream puffs as high as 70-story buildings!

Then he describes vividly steam from a living volcano in the same frozen area, and adds, "Although the icy, snowy-whiteness looks like fine powder, it has a curious consistency. It's a little like skiing in cement."

The following, from a *Sports Illustrated* article on Tokyo, is another good example:

> Hard by an ancient Buddhist temple two miles from the middle of downtown Tokyo, the Japanese observe their newest religion: golf. As a result, the grounds of the Shiba Driving Range ... look as if every cherry blossom in Japan had fallen at once.

Don'ts

1. Don't write a "destination piece," that is, a blow-by-blow account of your trip. That's O.K. for a mimeographed letter to enclose in Christmas cards to your friends, but the reader must be made to feel that he or she is the hero of the travel adventure, not you.

2. Don't write off the top of your head without structuring your article for a specific magazine or audience.

3. Don't write too much. Pack information into your article and give it a sharp focus. Some magazines use features as short as 300 words!

4. Take unusual photos, and submit photographs in the form the

magazine wants (black-and-white glossies, 35mm color transparencies, etc.). Don't fail to get signed releases from the people who appear in your photos and from those whom you quote.

5. Don't misrepresent the country or city to make it sound better than it is. Warn of inconveniences, but in a constructive way. Tell readers frankly to take raincoats and insect repellent instead of making negative comments about the constant rain and bugs. Prepare the reader and point out ways to help him make the best of things; avoid unfavorable comparisons. The late Richard Halliburton said, "The bee, though it finds every rose has a thorn, comes back loaded with honey from his rambles. Why should not other tourists do the same?"

6. Don't write dull, abstract descriptions or use hackneyed words like "breathtaking," "gorgeous," "never-to-be-forgotten." Use words that will paint pictures.

7. Don't write all narrative. Enliven your writing with dialogue and quotes. For instance:

"If you want to see the most beautiful country in the world," Renoir once wrote of the Côte d'Azur, "here it is." ("Côte d'Azur: the Artists' Workshop" by Ivan Fuldauer)

"Shrimp among whales," a proverb calls Korea, long a battleground for Asian power struggle. ("Rare Look at North Korea" by H. Edward Kim)

Angles and anecdotes

Be sure to focus on a sharp angle that represents your unique impression or viewpoint, and then relate everything in the article to that angle.

My article, "Should You Drive in Europe?" (*B.C. Motorist*) was written from the point of view that driving is the only way to be *of* Europe as well as *in* it, if you want to experience different national characteristics, and if you crave adventure and challenge. I wrote:

European roads are like sprawling psychiatrists' couches that reveal the individual hangups and character traits of different nationalities. French author Frossard says: "For a Canadian or American, a car is a means of transport. For an Italian, it is a means of self-expression. For a German, it is a way of aggression. For a Frenchman, it is a secondary residence."

Then I included many illustrations of driving adventures in various countries, and cited different laws, penalties, and booby traps a visitor might encounter in each nation. For example:

Italy is a nerve-jangling place to drive, with frenetic Fiats and Ferraris buzzing around like skittering bugs. You really have to watch your step, for there are rip-offs designed with you in mind.

Anecdotes are important, so choose those that enliven your writing and dramatize your angle. Ben Masselink's "A Day in Kona" (*Carte Blanche*) is studded with anecdotal gems from both the past and the present:

In the old days King Kamehameha parceled out land in a sensible way. A warrior could have as much land as he could run before he dropped.

and:

There is a story on Maui of a pet barracuda. Early in the morning fishermen go out of Lahina for opelu. In the barracuda's territory one raps on the side of the canoe with a paddle. The barracuda appears. They set their net and the barracuda rounds up the opelu, Western style, and drives them into the net.

The angle of Honor Tracy's article, "With Pride as Their Armour" (Pan Am's *Clipper* Magazine) is the stubborn pride of the Spanish character. Here is an anecdote that reinforces her theme:

There was a fisherman of Almeria who fell sick and despaired of his life. He promised the Virgin that if she made him well, he would spend the next 20 years at sea in his little boat. She did; and he did. For 20 years he bobbed up and down outside the harbor and never set foot on dry land. Once a month he rowed to the quay and a barber shaved him and cut his hair; other fishermen supplied him with water and food. When the time was up, he came ashore.

Use graphic language to create word snapshots and make the place in your article come to life. Coyote country in Arizona is the land of "tall saguaro cactus and pink desert sunsets. Sunny days and ten-gallon hats. A mesquite fire at night and a coyote yip-yipping to a skyful of a million diamond stars." Macao is "the Portuguese eyelash hanging on the mainland of China"; New Mexico is "where that which is ancient, atomic, arid and astonishing all blend together into an unbelievable mosaic as colorful as any ever designed by a Navajo blanket craftsman."

Stan Delaplane writes of Cartagena:

Coming down from Bogota's 8,700 feet to Cartagena on the emerald coast is something like stepping into a steam room. This is a tropical port whose cannon fired on the sails of Sir Henry Morgan and Admiral Vernon—at the fleet of Francis Drake and Hawkins. It took 200 years of slave labor to build the massive forts. The picture postcards you buy in the old walled city mention "El Pirate Draque."

Use your imagination and word wizardry to give a place an intriguing label or nickname. This trick dates back to 985 A.D., when explorer Erik the Red named a country that was under 10,000 feet of ice *"Greenland"* to lure chilly Scandinavians into going there!

Vivid writing brings alive the sights and sounds of a place:

[Quebec's] air is singing with the ringing of church bells, the lonesome plaint of steamboat whistles and the beeping of horn-happy motorists. Everywhere the sky is pierced by towers, cross-topped spires, statuary, and steep copper roofs designed to shed snow.

Not just sights and sounds, but smells, too!

Most Aegean isles smell of thyme, sage, oregano and of jasmine when the night is still and warm. But Samos blends with these the scent of pine woods. (Melville Bell Grosvenor in *National Geographic*)

Sprinkle your descriptions with flavorful words and phrases that are typical of the country, such as *"Velkomman til Danmark,"* *"Bienvenidos a Mexico"* or "Sure 'n' begorrah, Irish eyes smile at you all over the Emerald Isle." If you write about Greece, for example, you might shudder in the breath of the *meltimi* (winds); drink *ouzo* or *retsina* or *barbounia* wines; feast on *souvlaki* (shishkebab); play *tavali* (backgammon), or shy away from dark caves where there may be *kalikantzoroi* (gremlins).

Think up glittering titles that peg the *essence* of the place, and study published examples like these: "Belize, the Awakening Land," "Silvery Taxco: Mexico's Sterling City," "Hydra—Isle of Joy for All Escapists," "Cripple Creek: A Ghost Town with Spirit," "Amiable Amsterdam," "Caloric Copenhagen," "Paris, the Pickpocket," and "Alaska—America's Jolly White Giant."

Even a composite article, like Lowell Thomas's "Nature's Seven Greatest Wonders," uses descriptive titles for each "Wonder": "Grand Canyon: Greatest Cleft on Earth," "Victoria Falls: The Smoke That Thunders," and so forth.

Whatever title you decide upon, be sure that you continue its mood and angle throughout your feature.

Since the travel article is a where-to-go piece, it should sparkle with excitement and make the reader want to go there. Be enthusiastic about the place and its special features, whether you're reliving the past amid ancient ruins in Egypt, Turkey, Greece, or Yucatan; painting word pictures of the Taj Mahal in Agra or the Vamana Temple of the dwarf incarnation of Vishnu in Khajuraho in India; eating fresh lobster at a sidewalk cafe in Mykonos; boating through the royal blue waters of Capri's Blue Grotto or Israel's Rosh Hanikra or describing the makings of a brand new Expo or World's Fair.

Be emotionally enthusiastic about the *mood*. Contrast this:

Cuernavaca, Mexico, is the only place in the world where citizens suffer from year-round spring fever. Even the jumping beans don't jump.

with this:

Vehemence, gustiness and a tendency to rough-house have always been characteristic of Venezuela. A visitor today encounters a somewhat rowdy, even trigger-happy atmosphere.

You must take your reader to your travel destination and make him or her totally involved in the adventure. There are several ways to do this. The bargain-paradise approach implies that the reader can't afford *not* to visit the spot. The snob pitch points out how "in" this place is to Important People; therefore it's not to be missed.

Relating the exotic to the familiar is an effective technique for involving the reader:

Few foreign influences have so great an impact on the American cultural scene as the art of Japanese gardening.
Thousands of Americans come to Kyoto each year primarily to see the great gardens there. Some come simply to enjoy them. Others come to glean some bits of artistry that might be incorporated in a garden back home. (Louise Dibble)

Using the second pronoun in your article puts the reader in the scene (although it can be monotonous if overdone):

Did you ever think you'd like to own an island? A small, peaceful place in a warm climate surrounded by fish-filled waters, with a comfortable Somerset

Maugham sort of house in which you could play king of the mountain?...
Marina Cay is a 6-acre polka dot in the Virgin Islands...(Judith M. Farris)

You can do most anything—even skiing—on a tight budget. I stumbled onto
ways to schuss down some of Europe's most glamorous slopes for a song.
(Dori Lundy)

Your travel writing will be more salable if you do a lot of research
before your trip. Bone up in advance on everything you can find
about the region you will visit, all the way from ancient legends and
history to the newest roads, revolutions, politics and personalities.
Read enough to get different opinions so that you can write from your
own original angle. Give your reader accurate facts and statistics.
Don't overlook the wide market possibilities for travel articles
—squeeze as many different manuscripts as you can out of each trip,
for different publications and varying groups of readers.

For monthly magazines submit seasonal material at least six months
in advance. Send your Christmas or New Year's-slanted material in
June; a Mardi Gras in Rio or New Orleans piece in July; a feature on
Hawaii's October "Aloha Day" in April; autumn-oriented material
like Danish Days in Solvang, California, or Oktoberfest celebrations
in February or March, and so forth. Of course, the many daily and
weekly publications that use travel material work closer to the deadline, so if your article doesn't sell to a monthly market, you can try
these later on.

Don't stay home. Go away and write about it, and don't forget to
take along your *philoxenia*—your love of the foreigner. You'll
probably enjoy traveling more if you can write about it profitably.

An Israeli guide gives ten traveling commandments, the first and
last of which are:

Thou shalt not expect to find things as thou hast left them at home, for
thou hast left thy home to find things different.

and:

Remember thou art a guest in every land, and one that treateth one's host
with respect shall be treated as an honored guest. (Rena Dictor Leblanc)

65

WRITE A QUERY—GET AN ASSIGNMENT!

BY SALLY WENDKOS OLDS

MORE and more editors of major magazines are urging writers to query them first, instead of submitting completed manuscripts. It's good advice. A good query can often get an unknown writer a go-ahead to write for a top magazine. It's the route I took to get my first article assignment, for *Parents' Magazine,* in 1967. It's the route I still take to get assignments.

For the new writer, this form is often shrouded in mystery. You cannot go to the newsstand and see what kinds of queries the editors like best. There is no compilation of "The 50 Best Query Letters of 19--." The only people who see queries—also called "outlines" or "proposals"—are the writers who write them and the editors who receive them. So let's bring the query out of the closet.

The query letter is a sales tool. You use it to sell your idea and to sell yourself as the one person who's best equipped to write this particular article for this particular magazine.

A query can save you time and effort by sounding out a magazine on your idea before you invest your blood, sweat, toil, and tears in the complete article. You might write the best article in the world about a revolutionary medical discovery—and then find that the magazine you wrote it for already had an article in inventory on the exact same subject. It can't publish two articles on the same topic; so no matter how good yours is, it will be rejected. A query letter, which might have taken a couple of days of preliminary research, could have saved you the weeks or months of research you invested in your article.

At those magazines that still do read manuscripts that come in "over the transom," a query letter will get a reading from a highly placed editor instead of the reader who first goes through the articles in the "slush pile." Finally, when a query letter is successful in getting you the assignment, you and your editor can exchange views about the direction your article will take. The final result is likely to be stronger.

Now that you are convinced that you should write the query, how should you write it? You should write it well. The query letter is a sample of the way you think and the way you write. If your proposal is ungrammatical, dull, poorly organized, long-winded, or full of cliches, the editor will assume that your article will be the same. Your query should showcase the best writing you can do.

Form

An article proposal can be set up as a letter or as an "outline" sent with a covering note. The letter is more personal. The editor who receives it will get the feeling that you have designed your proposal specifically for his or her publication.

The outline is not the kind of number-and-letter affair we all learned to write in school, but a proposal on a separate sheet of paper that will indicate where you plan to go with your article. It is more practical than a letter, since you will not need to retype it if it is rejected by the first editor you send it to, unless it comes back wrinkled and dirty. Signs of rejection—the indentation of the paper clip, the curled edges, the coffee spots, the erased notations—are all obvious clues that your proposal has taken a previous trip. And no one—including editors—likes to catch a spurned offering on the rebound. So examine your outline before sending it out again as carefully as you would check your appearance before setting off for a job interview.

Either style of proposal should lock professional—typed single-space on white bond paper or business stationery. Be sure to give your name, address and telephone number; you want to make it easy for the editor to find you. It is courteous—and often conducive to a quick reply—to enclose a stamped, self-addressed envelope.

Address your letter to a specific person, *by name*: the articles editor, features editor, managing editor, or executive editor of the magazine. Find the name of the individual by looking at the masthead in a current copy. Do not get the name from an old, tattered copy. For magazines not readily available, check the listings in Part IV of *The Writer's Handbook,* or current issues of writers' magazines, or

Literary Market Place in the reference room of your library.

Be sure you're accurate. What would *you* think of the research skills of a writer who misspelled your name or got the name of the magazine wrong or addressed a query to a person who left the staff five years ago?

Length

Editors are usually bright, but they are not clairvoyant. So don't be too brief, giving only the lead paragraph and assuming the editor knows where you're going from there. Nor should you be too wordy, going on for three or four pages. The ideal query runs one to two single-spaced pages—long enough to develop your idea, short enough to be run through quickly.

Title

A catchy heading—which an editor may see as a cover line that can help to sell the magazine—may sell your idea. It pays to put some time in to think of a lively title, which you can suggest either at the top of your outline or in the body of your letter.

Lead

Start out your query letter with a strong opening paragraph, just as you would begin your article. Don't write your query until you have thought of your lead. You can change your mind later and use a different opening for the article, but the fact that you have a strong lead in your proposal attracts the editor's interest by showing that you can attract the reader's. Keep this lead to one or two paragraphs.

My husband and I used the following lead to begin a proposal for an article that we titled "The Weekend That Changes Marriages":

The weekend began badly. By the time F. Whitman Haggerson, 29, and his 28-year-old wife, Ingrid, had arrived at Cor Maria Retreat House in Sag Harbor, Long Island, they had fought vociferously throughout dinner and in the car about the packing of suitcases, about Whit's having come home late from work, and about the best route to take to the retreat home.

But by Sunday night, Ingrid and Whit, who had been married for six and a half years and were the parents of five-year-old Fritz and two-year-old William, felt like newlyweds again. "I can't remember now exactly what we said and did on that weekend," says Ingrid today. "We were in a big daze by the time we got home. I just know we held hands for the whole ride back. And, of course, I know now that these were the most important couple of days in either of our lives."

(The article was published in *LI, Newsday's* Sunday Magazine, and was reprinted by *Catholic Digest.*)

State your idea in a nutshell, proposing a specific aspect of your topic. You would not, for example, say that you want to write an article about marriage. This is too general. You need to find a narrower focus.

You also need to make clear the angle that you will take. "The Weekend That Changes Marriages," about Marriage Encounter, could be handled in several different ways. A writer could appear in the first person, drawing on his or her personal experiences and attitudes. A factual report about the overall growth of the movement could be written. Since we had already seen articles about Marriage Encounter that followed these two patterns, we proposed a profile of the Haggersons as typical "team couples" and leaders in the movement. This is how we suggested this:

That weekend in March of 1971 was the Haggersons' introduction to Marriage Encounter, a movement founded in Spain in the 1950s by a priest and a devout Catholic couple, and brought to this country in the summer of 1967 by Father Charles Gallagher, a Long Island-based Jesuit priest concerned about the ever-weakening state of American marriage. The movement's growth has been dizzying. About a thousand new couples a month are now swelling the ranks of the 25,000 American couples who, in the past five years, have gone on Marriage Encounter weekends to learn a special technique for drawing closer together.

Ingrid and Whit Haggerson have gone on to use this technique, known as Dialoguing, on virtually a daily basis ever since they "made" their first encounter. Now, as one of about 700 specially trained volunteer "team couples" around the country, they go out regularly on weekends to teach other couples how to Dialogue.

The success of the Marriage Encounter movement is in large part attributable to the enthusiasm and dedication of its team couples. They attend encounter weekends about every 6-8 weeks, leaving their children with relatives or with other "encountered couples." They attend numerous meetings that last till the early hours of the morning, write their own presentations that draw heavily on experiences from their own marriages, and do a considerable amount of administrative work. During the encounter weekends, they share intimate details about themselves and about their own marriages. They also participate fully in each weekend, making a new encounter each time.

And you need to make clear your point of view. Are you positively enthusiastic about your topic, indignantly opposed to it, amused by it, or are you setting out to write an objectively balanced report of it? We indicated our viewpoint later in the query:

Not every couple who makes an encounter will find their entire lives—or even their marriages—completely changed, as the Haggersons' have been. But we, the authors of this article, made our own encounter last July, and we agree with Ingrid Haggerson when she says, "I can't imagine any couple not being able to get something from Marriage Encounter....Every couple can grow in their marriage."

Details

Give some clues to what your article will contain. Weave in an anecdote or a case history if you did not use one in your opening. Toss out a handful of intriguing facts. Include relevant statistics.

In the query for the Marrige Encounter piece, quoted above, we did some of this in the third paragraph.

Somewhere in your proposal, you need to provide a sketchy plan of the way you will organize your article. Here's one way:

Through an in-depth profile of Ingrid and Whit, we could explain why a happily married couple would want to make an encounter in the first place. We could briefly tell the story of the movement. We could then go on to explore the reasons for the Haggersons' deep involvement, the effects of their participation on their children, and their feelings about making new encounters every couple of months (don't they run out of things to say?).

Timeliness

Why should the editor publish this article *now*? Why would readers want to read it *now*? If you can, give some reason why your article is timely—a new scientific discovery, a linkage with current news events, recently released statistics that indicate the popularity of a phenomenon.

As you can see, you need to do some preliminary research before you can even begin to write a query. You have to convey the impression that you know your subject and that you know where to go for more material.

Who are you?

By this time the editor should be so impressed by the professional way you have put your proposal together that she or he will want to know something about you. Introduce yourself. If you have professional writing experience, indicate what it has been. If not, say nothing. (Don't say, "I'm only a beginner, but....")

If you have relevant personal experience, give that, too. The editor will want to know that the author of an article about part-time jobs is the manager of an employment agency, or that someone proposing an article about "tennis elbow" is an orthopedist *and* a tennis player. But keep it relevant. The editor doesn't care that, say, your analyst feels it would be therapeutic for you to write about your relationship with your mother.

If you have special skills—say, you are a photographer who can illustrate your own story—say so. If you have special access to a unique resource—say, a prominent person who does not ordinarily grant interviews but has agreed to speak to you—mention it.

By this time, you've said it all, and it's time to end your query simply, with the brief, pointed question, "Are you interested?"

This note, addressed to Silvia Koner, Articles Editor of *Redbook,* is typical of the cover letters I usually send along with article proposals:

Dear Ms. Koner:

 I am enclosing a proposal for an article that I feel would be right for the readers of *Redbook.*

 In connection with my research for my books, *A Child's World* (McGraw-Hill, 1975), a college-level textbook on child development, and *Helping Your Child Learn Right from Wrong* (Simon & Schuster, 1976), I have heard many parents of young children express their concern about their children's moral development. My proposal offers practical advice for such parents from two of the nation's leading spokesmen in the field of moral education.

 I hope you're interested.

Sincerely,

Article proposal

HELPING CHILDREN LEARN
RIGHT FROM WRONG

One day while I was cleaning my eight-year-old daughter's room, I found a half-empty, very large bag of candy underneath a pile of Jane's school papers. I was surprised to find the candy, both because this was something my husband and I never bought and discouraged our children from buying, and also because Jane had recently complained that she didn't have enough money to get something else she wanted.

When I questioned Jane about the candy, she first looked at me blankly, then stammered a couple of weak replies, and finally admitted she had stolen it from the 5 & 10. I tried not to overreact, even though my fantasies of my daughter's turning into a shoplifter and eventually a hardened criminal terrified me. I wondered how my husband and I had failed as parents. Why didn't our child know right from wrong?

How *can* parents help their children to make moral judgments? When does learning about values begin? We all come into this world as amoral creatures, not knowing anything about the concepts of right and wrong, and not caring. But beginning in infancy, moral issues begin to fill our lives. The nursing baby bites her mother's nipple and causes pain; how should the mother react? When toddlers get together, they squabble over toys and throw sand in each other's faces; how can parents help them learn to share and keep from injuring each other? Very young schoolchildren are in situations that test their loyalty to friends, that tempt them to cheat on tests, that make lying seem the easy way out; what can parents and teachers do or say?

In this instance with Jane, my husband and I sat down with her that evening. "Why did you take that candy?" I asked her.

"I don't know," she shrugged.

"Did you want it so very badly?" my husband asked.

"I didn't even eat most of it. I gave it to some friends in school," she said. Somehow, in Jane's mind, this fact seemed to absolve her from guilt.

"What do you think we should do now?" I asked.

Another shrug, accompanied by an unintelligible grunt.

The conversation was less than satisfactory.

We adults finally decided that Jane would withdraw $1.09 from her bank account to pay for the candy. I accompanied her to the 5 & 10—and felt like an ogress as my very small, very chastened, and very embarrassed daughter held out the dollar bill and the few coins to Mr. Burns at the register. When he asked her what it was for, there was no way she could bring herself to say a word in explanation. I mumbled something about this being money that Jane owed the store, a flicker in his eyes let me know that he understood instantly, and Jane and I walked out, both sighing with relief that the ordeal was over.

At the time, my husband and I did what we thought best. Today, we might handle the situation differently. If we had spoken to Dr. Lawrence Kohlberg, for example, we might have approached the incident in this way: (Here I would construct an imaginary scenario, based on what Kohlberg would tell me in an interview.) Kohlberg, professor of education and social psychology at Harvard University, is the most prominent contemporary theorist about children's moral development. After following pre-adolescent and adolescent boys for 12 years and tracing their thinking about morality, he concluded that children's moral thinking proceeds in a definite sequence from doing the right thing because they are afraid of being punished, to doing it to gain the approval of others, to doing it because of their own internal standards of right and wrong.

If I had spoken to Dr. Sidney B. Simon, we might have handled Jane's candy-stealing along these lines: (Here would be another imaginary scenario, based on Simon's Values Clarification philosophy.) Within the past few years, Simon, professor at the Center for Humanistic Education at the University of Massachusetts, has carried his message about Values Clarification to thousands of parents, teachers, and other adults who work with children. Under this approach, adults use an assortment of specific techniques, including game-like exercises, to help children think about values and determine which ones they want to live by. It gives practical application to the theories of Kohlberg and others.

My article about children and morality would use lively anecdotes to show the ways Dr. Kohlberg's theories apply to young children and what this means in terms of parents' day-to-day dealings with them. It would also illustrate with actual examples the ways Values Clarification techniques can be applied to deal with such issues as honesty, willingness to help other people, "white lies," and other values issues.

The article that resulted from this query appeared under a slightly altered title, "Teaching Your Child Right from Wrong." It had a different opening, because before going ahead with it I checked with my daughter, who told me she would not like me to write about her. That's why her name is changed here. (Since I have three daughters, her identity can remain a mystery.) I found a similar incident to lead off the article itself.

Editors usually answer queries sooner than they make a decision on finished articles. Some Articles Editors will respond to a query within a week; more typically, you can expect an answer to a query within four weeks. If you have not heard by then, drop the editor a note or telephone asking whether she or he has come to a decision about your proposal. Indicate that if the idea is still under consideration you will be happy to allow more time. We all have our favorite horror stories with the mails, so follow-up calls after a reasonable period of time are perfectly acceptable.

If the editor's answer is "no," don't try to talk him or her out of it and don't ask why. You can make better use of your time and energy by sending other ideas to this editor and by sending this idea somewhere else.

A professional free-lance writer has to be profligate with ideas. The only way you can protect yourself from being paupered by the loss of one is to keep coming up with so many more that your stockpile won't be depleted. And remember, an idea is just an idea unless you do something with it—think about it, develop it, write it up, send it out—and then, upon getting the assignment, transform it from a proposal into a full-fledged article.

66

EVERYONE WANTS TO BE PUBLISHED, BUT...

By John Ciardi

At a recent writers' conference I sat in on a last-day session billed as "Getting Published." Getting published was, clearly, everyone's enthusiasm. The hope of getting published will certainly do as one reason for writing. It need not be the only, nor even the best, reason for writing. Yet that hope is always there.

Emily Dickinson found reasons for writing that were at least remote from publication. Yet even she had it in mind. She seems to have known that what she wrote was ahead of its time, but she also seemed to know that its time would come. If Thomas H. Johnson's biography of her is a sound guide, and I believe it is, she spent her last ten years writing her "letters to the future." The letters, to be sure, were addressed to specific friends; yet they were equally addressed *through* her friends to her future readers. As Hindemith spent ten years composing his quartets and then ten more creating the terms by which they were to be assessed critically, so Emily spent ten years writing her poems (1776 of them, if I recall the right number), and then ten more years stating the terms for their reception.

Even she, then, had an audience (which is to say, publication) in mind. Nor do I imply that the desire to publish is an ignoble motive. Every writer wants to see himself in print. No writer, to my knowledge, has ever been offended when his published offerings were well received. The desire to publish becomes ignoble only when it moves a writer to hack and hurry the work in order to get it into print.

Poetry, of course, is relatively free of commercial motive. Every generation has its Edgar Guest. Ours, I suppose, is Rod McKuen. These are writers whose remouthing of sentiments catches some tawdry emotional impulse in commercial quantities. Yet such writers—or so I have long suspected—must come to believe seriously in the inanities they write. I doubt that they have sold out to the dollar sign: more tragically, they have sold out to themselves.

Such writers aside, it is hard to imagine that anyone would think to bribe a poet to write a bad poem. It would follow then (all temptation to cheat being out of the equation) that the only reason for writing a poem is to write it as well as one possibly can. Having so written it, one would naturally like to see it published.

I was, accordingly, in sympathy with the conference members—but I was also torn. For I had just spent days reading a stack of the manuscripts these people had submitted, and I had found nothing that seemed worthy of publication. I sat by, thinking that session on getting published was an exercise in swimming in a mirage. I even suspected a few of those present of drowning in their mirages.

Then one of the hard-case pros on the conference staff delivered a statistic. "You want to get published?" he said. "Fine. Look at the magazines. What are they publishing? The answer is, roughly, 98 percent nonfiction and not quite half of one percent poetry. Yet of the manuscripts submitted at this conference, seventy-six are poetry and only two are nonfiction." He paused. "Now you tell me," he said, "where are you going to get published?"

The hard case, as it happened, was a successful nonfiction writer for the large-circulation magazines; he had dismissed from consideration the literary quarterlies that do publish poetry, sometimes without payment, but sometimes with an "honorarium." To the quarterlies, I would certainly add our two excellent poetry tabloids, *The American Poetry Review* and *Poetry Now*.

For poetry does get published, though not on terms that would be attractive to the big-circulation pros. Poets *qua* poets do not run into serious income tax problems. So be it. If a little is all one asks, then a little is enough. I have never known of anyone who turned to poetry in the expectation of becoming rich by it. Were I to impersonate the hard-case pro at that conference, I could argue that a writer writes as an alcoholic drinks—which is to say, compulsively, and for its own sake. An alcoholic expects no special recognition for being helpless in his compulsion: Why should a poet expect money and recognition for his compulsion?

The fact is that the good poets do generally find their rewards and recognitions. Ego being what it is (and the poet's ego more so), any given poet may think his true merit has been slighted. For myself, whatever I have managed to make of my writing (and it has been a love affair, not a sales campaign), I have always felt that my own satisfaction (or at least the flickering hope of it) was a total payment. Whatever else came has always struck me as a marvelous bonus. And there have been bonuses—grants, prizes, even a small, slow rain of checks. How could I fail to rejoice in that overflow of good? I wish it to every writer, and wish him my sense of joy in it.

But there is more to it. The hard case's manuscript count stayed with me. Can seventy-six poets and two nonfiction writers be called a writers' conference? He hadn't mentioned fiction, and I never learned how many fiction manuscripts had been turned in. But why, I asked myself, would seventy-six turn to poetry and only two to nonfiction? All writing is writing; all of it is part of one motion. I have enjoyed trying different sorts of writing. This present piece, for example, is nonfiction. It is part of the same exploration that poems take me on.

I asked myself the question, but I know I already had the answer —at least part of it—from the poems I had read and criticized. The poems had been bad, and I had fumbled, as one must, at trying to say why I thought they were bad. I wished on that last day that the conference were just starting and that I had ahead of me another chance to identify the badness of the poems. But perish that thought: I was emotionally exhausted.

Yet on that last day the reason so few of the conference members had turned to nonfiction seemed clear to me. Even to attempt nonfiction a writer must take the trouble of acquiring some body of information. The poems I had read lacked anything that could be called a body of information. The writers seemed to have assumed that their own excited ignorance was a sufficient qualification for the writing of poetry.

I wanted to go back and say to my conferees, "Your poems care nothing about the fact!" Isn't that another way of saying they were conceived in ignorance? Not one of the poets I read had even tried to connect fact A to fact B in a way to make an emotional experience of the connection. The writing lacked *thingness* and a lover's knowledge of thing.

Consider these lines by Stanley Kunitz (the italics are mine):

> Winter that *coils* in the thickets now,
> Will *glide* from the fields, the *swinging* rain
> Be *knotted* with flowers. On every bough
> A bird will *meditate* again.

The diction, the rhyming, the rhythmic flow and sustainment are effortless, but how knowledgeably things fall into place! Winter *coils* in the thickets because that snow that lies in shade is the last to melt, thinning down to scrolls of white by the last thaw. Winter will then *glide* from the fields—and what better (continuous, smooth) motion for the run-off of the last melt? The *swinging* rain (what word could better evoke our sense of April showers?) will then be *knotted* (as if) with flowers while birds (as if) *meditate* on every bough. The rain, of course, will not literally be knotted with flowers, nor will birds, literally, meditate. Yet what seems to be a scientific inaccuracy is of the central power of metaphor. Metaphor may, in fact, be conceived as an exactly felt error.

Metaphor is supposed to state the unknown in terms of the known. It is supposed to say X equals Y. Yet when we say "John is a lion," we do not think of John with a mane, with four clawed paws, nor with a pompon tipped tail. We extract from "lion" the emotional equivalent we need and let the rest go. The real metaphoric formula is X does-and-does-not-equal Y. Kunitz understands this formula. His knowledge of it is part of his qualification as a master poet.

There is more. More than can be parsed here. But note how the italicized words *hearken* to one another, each later term being summoned (by some knowledge and precision in the poet) by what went before. The italicized words form what I will dare to call a chord sequence by a composer who has mastered musical theory.

The passage, that is to say, is empowered by a body of knowledge of which I could find no trace in the poets I had been reading at the conference. My poets had been on some sort of trip. Their one message was "I feel! I feel!" Starting with that self-assertive impulse (and *thing* be damned), they then let every free association into the poem. They were too ignorant even to attempt a principle of selection.

I do not imply that I know what any given poem's principle of selection ought to be. To find the principle that serves best and to apply it in a way to enchant the reader is the art and knowledge of the poet. Everything in a good poem must be *chosen* into it. Even the accidents. How else could it be when one stroke of the pen will slash a thing out forever? All that has not been slashed out, it follows, is chosen in.

Ignorance, as nearly as I could say it (too late), was what had really stifled the poems I had read. The writers had not cared enough to learn their own art and use their eyes.

They will, I suppose, get published. Some of them somewhere. But have they earned the right to publication? I ask the question not to answer it. It is every writer's question to ask for himself.

67

THE INSTANT OF KNOWING

By Josephine Jacobsen

I AM neither so impertinent nor so naive as to work toward a definition of poetry, but I want to...tell a story, a true story which implies as much of a definition as I have come by....

The center of everything is the poem. Nothing is important in comparison to that. Anything which in some valid way is not directly connected with that current of energy which is the poem is dispensable....

The naming of things, which is the poet's function, is not, like a science, progressive. It is circular, and each passage of the circle is unique....

Often the poet brings back very little from the instant of knowing. Sometimes—rarely—he brings back something which combines two worlds: something germane to what Yeats called "the artifice of eternity"—the made and the eternal. Such poetry may wear any mode: the august, the raucous, the witty, the tragic. Nothing could matter less. Poetry is energy, and it is poetic energy which is the source of that instant of knowing that the poet tries to name. The test for the true poetic energy...is, it seems to me, the only universal test which can be applied to poetry.

In the process of naming things, the poet is caught at once in the problem of naming his own time, the problem of what was called "relevancy" until that word's exhaustion gave everyone empathetic fatigue. In naming his own time, the poet may be one of those rare writers who reach community in a working solitude, though seldom in a personal one. Ionesco writes: "For solitude is not *separation* but *meditation,* and we know that social groups...are most often a collection of solitary human beings...."

The phrase, "the instant of knowing," is from a poem by Richard Eberhart.

For the solitary writers, the group experience in the pursuit of their own work is a negative experience. They work alone; the poem's inception and execution is as secret as a film's development in a dark-room. They learn, ravenously, from their fellows, their betters, the great dead, their own guts; from talk, from print, by osmosis; but they are not, and can never be, group members. Most poets on the other hand, as John Ciardi pointed out, at some phase of their working life as poet, have been part of a group, and these have the stimulation and reinforcement that fly like sparks from the contact with congenial minds with the same general approach, objectives, and dislikes. But groups can also generate group-think—that curious amalgam which bounces back and forth, carrying always some measure of other-directed debris....

The brief story I want to tell is completely concerned with that energy and how it travels and the mysterious fact that certain words, in a certain arrangement and with a certain cadence, start up a chain reaction explained by nothing in the words themselves or in their content....

[Shortly after a speech I gave], a hot controversy arose as to what degree of analysis of a poem is possible without destroying the life of the poem. A number of teachers in the audience felt that poems could be, and were, dismembered to the point of death on the operating table. Others held out, very stoutly indeed, for the belief that the more you studied the poem, the more it meant to you. I understand very well the first point of view, having some years ago had a class for teachers of poetry who had been so disheartened by the poetry analysis to which they themselves had been subjected as students, that they cordially disliked poetry and were now trying to learn to reapproach it, for the sake of their students and of themselves. On the other hand, it is obviously impossible to denigrate the joy and comprehension which come from a close textual reading. It seems to me that the solution of the basic problem—as Robert Frost has pointed out—lies in acknowledging as the most important element that point of mystery which is the core of the poem, that untranslatable quasar which can never fully be put into the prose of exposition. Certain words, in a certain cadence.

"Ah sun-flower! weary of time, who countest the steps of the Sun." It would be impossible to find simpler or more daily words. Or,

"I have been one acquainted with the night." It is something which is not music and is not talk and is both; but what it does, every single time, is touch the nerve which knows. It is, literally, an instant of knowing—of something simultaneously strange and familiar; something already known but now discovered....

Almost thirty years ago, on a rather cold autumn afternoon, my husband and I were exploring some of the small side roads in the northern mountains of New Hampshire. One such road went over the crest of a hill and past a small and thoroughly overgrown cemetery, which obviously hadn't been used in the past decade. We stopped the car, and got out, and started wandering around in the tall grass, reading some of the tombstones. Some of them were tilted at angles, and some had lost letters to the weather. They said all the usual things —"Beloved wife of..." "He giveth his beloved rest...." A few said "Infant Son" or "Infant Daughter," and there were quite a lot of children. It was cold in the wind, and we started back to our car. Just before we got to the gate, which was rusted and rather lopsided, I saw a carving of a pair of clasped hands, on a leaning stone, and stooped down to look at the inscription. There was the woman's name but no relationship, and under the name and the date were carved two lines of poetry. They said:

> It is a fearful thing to love
> What Death can touch.

Eleven words, ten of them monosyllables. Immediately I thought, I know those lines; but I didn't, in the sense of placing them, and neither did my husband, though he had had exactly the same sense of recognition. They hung in my mind as though every hour they were going to place themselves. I quoted them a few times to people I thought might recognize them; always there was the same reaction: "Yes, I know that...." But no one did.

A few months later I wrote a longish and unsatisfactory poem about a wartime cemetery, and in it I quoted the epitaph from the tombstone. The poem was published in the *Junior League Magazine*— a periodical over which I doubt poets tended to hang. Later, I forgot about the poem, and I never included it in a book. But I didn't forget the two lines I did not write; they were there.

About four or five years later, after an illness, I came home from the hospital and found some piled-up issues of *Commonweal*. Leafing through them, I noticed a review of a play which had just opened in New York, by a poet whose work had interested me when I saw his Pulitzer Prize-winning play, *Hogan's Goat*. The poet was William Alfred and the verse-play under review was his *Agamemnon*. The review, a very favorable one, after praising the poetry and the stature of the play, went on to say that the play reached its climax in Cassandra's cry, "It is a fearful thing to love what death can touch."

I don't think I have ever had such an eerie sensation. I kept reading the words over, waiting for them to change in some particular. Then I sat down, in a sort of superstitious panic, and wrote a letter to William Alfred, and asked him where he had gotten those two lines, as I had a special reason for wanting to know. He wrote back at once to say that evidently the copy of the published play which he had sent me hadn't arrived. It came in the next day, and there was a note in the front which said that Cassandra's cry, "It is a fearful thing to love what death can touch," was from a poem by Josephine Jacobsen and had been quoted to him by C. Page Smith, the historian.

When I was preparing this piece, I did what I have waited all these years to do—I wrote to William Alfred and asked him what, exactly, he remembered. This is what he wrote me, as new to me then as it is to you now.

It was Columbus Day, 1950. C. Page Smith had arranged a trip under the aegis of Samuel Eliot Morison, to Plymouth, to look at where the Mayflower had first landed. Professor Morison had recently lost his wife. Part of the tour, on that gray cold day, was the graveyard...of the pilgrims, on a small hill above the harbor. As we looked out over the sea from the rise, Page told Professor Morison of that poem of yours and of the New Hampshire tombstone...it haunted me as it haunts me still.

Those eleven words, put together by an unknown human being, carved by someone's hand on a grassed-over tombstone, in a deserted New Hampshire graveyard, had struck—in a chain of energy, unbelievable but natural—into my mind, then into my poem; had extricated themselves from that inferior substance, and struck through the mind of another writer so forcefully that he had been compelled to speak them, to a poet-dramatist, who put them at the core of the poem which was his play; and the reviewer found them rising from that play to arrest him and put them, as the play's climax, onto the page of a magazine, later held by the person who had received their impact from the stone in the grass in the graveyard.

I think that the whole meaning of the instant of knowing lies in that circuit. A knowledge of what we already knew became for an instant so devastatingly fresh that it could be contained no more than a flash of lightning. The arrangement of the oldest human fact into certain special sounds, in a certain sequence. It is the thing which cannot be argued with. And I have always felt almost superstitious about the story, because it is such a complete one; it is, to me, of the essence of poetry. Whenever I hear someone trying to define poetry or hear myself working toward a definition, I think of that carved stone sending out its terrible energy to that nerve of knowledge in the hearer, the reader, which transmits it.

This is the live energy which keeps the mass from corruption: the venal poet who writes, the editor who publishes, the critic who analyzes, the reader who reads. What that energy speaks to is our knowledge, but a dormant, denied-by-habit knowledge which is kindled to response in the rare instant.

That energy is the common quality which brings poets together.

68

WRITING POETRY FOR CHILDREN

By Myra Cohn Livingston

I NEVER intended to write poetry for children. It was a complete accident, and even today I marvel that it happened at all. I was eighteen, in college, and writing what I considered far more important—poetry about love! My instructor at Sarah Lawrence College, Katherine Liddell, had given us an assignment; we were to use alliteration and onomatopoeia. I turned in some verses. "These," she said to me in her converted closet-conference room, reeking with the odor of Sano cigarettes, "would be wonderful for children. Send them to *Story Parade*" (a magazine for boys and girls published by Simon & Schuster). I grudgingly followed her instructions—the accompanying letter, the self-addressed stamped envelope. Several weeks later the envelope came back. I threw it onto a pile of papers and three weeks later became so angry with Miss Liddell's folly, that I ripped it open to confront her with her error. I caught my breath. The editor had carefully clipped three of the poems, and there was a letter accepting these for publication.

It took me eleven years for my first book, *Whispers and Other Poems,* written when I was a freshman, to be accepted for publication by the same editor, Margaret K. McElderry, who had seen the manuscript when I was in college and encouraged me to continue writing. I know now that during the war years few new books were published, and certainly poetry for children was far down on the list of desired manuscripts. In those days, I read *The Writer* religiously, hoping to find someone who would want my work, and collected a sheaf of rejection slips.

But I did not write and never have consciously written *for* children. I cannot understand why the world appeared to me from the start as through the eyes of a child—of my own childhood—or why, even today, most of the poetry I write comes out that way. The only clue I

387

have is that, even as an anthologist, I am drawn to (or write) those poems that speak to the subjects, emotions, and thoughts of children in a diction they understand.

My own poems have often been called "deceptively simple"; the first review of *Whispers* scathingly accused me of writing about "simple, everyday things," as though this were some sort of evil. Perhaps this is because many adults forget that to the child, these very things are what pique his curiosity, engage his attention. As the poet-in-residence for our school district, in my visits to schools and libraries throughout this country, and in teaching courses for teachers at U.C.L.A. Extension, I note that today's child is very different, in many respects, from the child I was, or that my children are, but that many things remain eternal. Children may know more facts, be more worldly wise, but the curiosity, wonder and fresh way of looking, the joys and pains and doubts, seem just as they always were.

I would like to suggest that anyone who wishes to write poetry that children might enjoy face up to a few basics about this vocation. The climate today is far more receptive to poetry than it was a number of years ago when the English—Walter de la Mare, Robert Louis Stevenson, and A. A. Milne—dominated the field. America has given us Elizabeth Madox Roberts, David McCord and Harry Behn, to mention but a few—and there are many exciting middle-aged and young poets publishing today whose work is excellent. We no longer have to take second place to the English, but we do have to recognize that poetry is still somewhat of a stepchild in juvenile literature. Children, themselves, are more apt to read a story in a picture book than to read poetry, for most adults and teachers feel uncomfortable about presenting it. Even Mother Goose is not as well known as once she was. And poetry demands an involvement of the emotions, whether it be laughter or wonder or a more serious way of viewing the world.

The crisis we seem to face now is the mistaken notion that *anyone* can write a poem. The Poets-in-the-Schools program, in many areas, has too often, in my opinion, fostered undisciplined writing, that which John Ciardi has called "a spillage of raw emotion." Any word or series of words written down are called "poems." This, as I see it, is a great disservice to the children who are falsely praised, but it also applies to older aspiring poets. Many of the high school and college students have had no real discipline. Metrical feet, scansion, forms are unknown. Of course, we do not want didactic, sing-song verse, the moralizing of a Henley's "Invictus" or the elusive fairies of Rose Fyleman. What we do need is true poetry that takes into account the interests and yearnings of the young and leads them toward a process of humanization.

In offering suggestions to the person who wishes to write such poetry, I would ask that he ask himself if anything of the child remains in him—a way of looking, tasting, smelling, touching, thinking; if he is in touch with the contemporary child and his way of viewing the world, if he is truly comfortable with children. I would also suggest that he make the commitment to learn the basics of writing in disciplined forms and meters. One cannot, for example, attempt a limerick without knowing how to use the iambus and anapest correctly, nor even free verse without knowing why it *is* free verse.

Another, and perhaps more elusive point, is that the writer understand and believe that poetry for children is not second-best; there is a tendency on the part of many to feel that a so-called children's poet is one who has failed in writing adult poetry, or that it is "easy" to do. The poet who writes for children exclusively is a sort of second-class citizen.

Although I have spent almost twenty years sharing with young people poetry ranging from Mother Goose to T.S. Eliot, it is difficult to give any definite answer as to what sort of poetry children like best. We know through experience that levity is always high on the list, and humor is important, for it counters the view of poems as soul-building messages in high-flown diction. But many a child prefers the more serious. The more a young person is exposed to poetry, the more refined is his taste in this, as in all arts. I would hope that any writer aspiring to publish poetry would not write for what he thinks is the juvenile market, but rather concentrate on his own strengths. The word-play of David McCord is something that comes naturally to his art; curiosity and a love for nature are intrinsic to Harry Behn's work; and Elizabeth Madox Roberts wrote about experiences of her own as a child.

My own poetry has gone through a series of changes. Trained in the traditional rhyme/meter school, I have at times broken away to free verse, knowing that the force of what I wished to say had to dictate the form. Yet I do not feel I could have made this break without a sure knowledge of the disciplines, taught to me by Robert Fitzgerald and Horace Gregory. I know that there are many who would take issue with me, who feel that anything one wishes to put down, if arranged in a certain order, is a poem.

This change may best be shown by contrasting my first published poem, "Whispers," to later work:

> Whispers
> tickle through your ear
> telling things you like to hear.
>
> Whispers
> are as soft as skin
> letting little words curl in.
>
> Whispers
> come so they can blow
> secrets others never know.

Most of my verse in *Whispers, Wide Awake, Old Mrs. Twindlytart* and *The Moon and a Star* was written in traditional forms. But in *A Crazy Flight* (published in 1969), what I wanted to say suddenly refused to be confined by rhyme. The need to use repetition and a freer form of expression asserted itself in a poem that also picked up some current speech patterns of the children I was then teaching:

> THE SUN IS STUCK
>
> The sun is stuck.
> I mean, it won't move.
> I mean, it's hot, man, and we need a red-hot
>   poker to pry it loose,
> Give it a good shove and roll it across the sky
> And make it go down
> So we can be cool,
> Man.

Yet, *The Malibu,* my poem inspired by the moon landing and America's concerns with litter, combined both the rhyming couplet and some elements of free verse:

ONLY A LITTLE LITTER

Hey moonface,
man-in-the-moonface,

do you like the way
we left your place?

can you stand the view
of footprints on you?

is it fun to stare
at the flags up there?

did you notice ours
with the stripes and stars?

does it warm you to know
we love you so?

moonface,
man-in-the-moonface,

thanks a heap for the rocks.

In *The Way Things Are,* the meter follows a child's pattern with a different rhyme pattern, in "Growing: For Louis."

It's tough being short.

Of course your father tells you not to worry,
But everyone else is giant, and you're just the
    way you were.
And this stupid guy says, "Hey shorty, where'd
    you get the long pants?"
Or some smart beanpole asks how it feels to
    be so close to the ants?
And the school nurse says to tell her again how
    tall you are when you've already told her.
Oh, my mother says there's really no hurry
And I'll grow soon enough.

But it's tough being short.

(I wonder if Napoleon got the same old stuff?)

But the rhymed couplet creeps up again and again in *4-Way Stop* (published in 1976):

OCEAN AT NIGHT

Mother Wave sings soft to sleep
the fish and seaweed of the deep

black ocean, and with quiet hands
pats to peace her tired sands,

her kelp and driftwood; fills her shoals
with gleaming tides, and gently pulls

across her bed the pale moonlight.
And this is night. And this is night.

Throughout these later books are outcroppings of free verse with which I am still experimenting, but there is an inherent pull that constantly draws me back to the containment of fixed forms. I have finally begun to tackle the haiku and cinquain, most demanding in their use of words:

Even in summer
bees have to work in their orange
and black striped sweaters.

Like any other poet, I feel that the most important factor in my poetry writing is not that I set out to write in any given form, but that I must find the right form for the subject matter. For this is when —and only when—the poem "comes right" for me.

What is right for me is not so for everybody. There are no surefire methods, although I do believe that one must know the basics and rules before breaking them. Even children need these rules, for without them, they flounder and grow dissatisfied with what they are doing. What we all have in common is that we are still learning, and, I hope, growing and changing.

69

HOW TO WRITE GOOD POETRY
AND GET IT PUBLISHED

By L. E. Sissman

CAN you write good poetry? I don't know; not everybody can. But there are ways to test the verse you've written to find out if it's good or not. First, there's the freshness test. Read over a poem you've written. Is there any phrase or image in it that is completely fresh and apt—that doesn't resemble anything else you've read before? Be objective; if you can still answer yes, you may have something as a poet. Second, there's the compression test. Write one of your poems out as a single prose paragraph. Does it read like prose? If it does, it's not a poem in the first place. But if, on the other hand, it's too terse and compact and energetic for prose, perhaps you're really a poet. Third, there's the influence test. Write down the names of the ten poets whose work means the most to you—not just important names, but people whose work holds deep meaning for you and influences what you write and how you think about poetry. O. K. Now get hold of a copy of Mark Strand's recent book, *The Contemporary American Poets,* and see how many of your favorites are included. If it's fewer than four or five, your influences are not contemporary—and your verse is probably not close enough to the mainstream of what's being written now to be good, at least by contemporary standards. There may be a few poets who are exceptions to this rule; there aren't many.

But suppose you've passed these tests. Suppose you feel very deeply that you do have a talent for poetry, and that you want to pursue it. Then, obviously, your object should be to produce a body of poems—and to get them published. I'll deal with these two points in turn, using my own (admittedly very subjective) experience as a rough guide to what you might expect.

Some years ago, I found myself with a suspected poetic talent and, at the age of thirty-five, not much to show for it. I had won a poetry prize in college; I'd published a few poems in little magazines; I had a thin sheaf of verse written ten to fifteen years before. I decided it was then or never; that if I did have talent, I would have to prove it in my thirties or forget it. So I sat down with the very cold-blooded, hard-headed objective of writing as well as I could and as much as I could, beginning right then and there. It wasn't very easy, as you might expect. But I had three invaluable assets to help me get started again. First, time. I could spare two evenings a week to concentrate on writing; every Tuesday and Thursday from eight to ten, I wrote. Second, a helpful wife. She understood what I was doing and made a time and place for me to do it in. Third, a friend. One who had a good knowledge of poetry and was willing to spend a lot of time and effort to read what I had written, to criticize and encourage me.

These three assets got me over the first hurdle: I found myself actually writing poems and slowly building up a file of them. I learned that it was absolutely necessary for me to begin with a firm idea of what the poem was about and what I wanted it to say; in addition, I learned never to set the first line down on paper until I had worked it out to my complete satisfaction in my mind. Having avoided a false start, I found it easier to go on to the next lines with confidence. And as I worked on these lines, I often found a kind of exhilaration coming over me—a feeling of excitement that the poem was beginning to shape itself, to dictate its own form, so to speak, and to carry me along with it until the end, when my own judgment would reassert itself to provide an apt ending.

At first, because the material seemed simpler to work with, I concentrated on nature poems—short quatrains about things I'd observed in the small town where I live. These soon grew into sonnets, then into sequences of sonnets. Then I began writing longer poems in four-line rhyming stanzas—and my subject matter began to expand. I found myself writing poems about my own experiences in school and college and afterward. I found myself developing that very important (and elusive) thing, a tone and style. In my case, this tone was dry, amused, analytical, a little above, in a mocking way, the experiences it described. The style made use of impacted bits of diction—sharp and smooth edges of language thrown together in such a way as to create a fresh impression of sound unlike, I hoped, anything the reader had heard before. To this I added dialogue, mimicry of sounds, parody of and allusion to other poets of every period. And the whole mix began to develop an individuality, a personality, of its own.

At this point I badly needed the outside encouragement of publishing something—somewhere, anywhere. Fortunately, it materialized. An old friend called and asked if a poem I had written years before could be printed in an English magazine of which he was an American editor. I said yes, of course; and this tiny encouragement was enough to keep me going for a while. But eventually, I knew, I would have to publish one or more of my new poems in order to establish the validity of what I was trying to do. This wasn't easy. I had to decide on my markets and besiege them with poems, in the hope that one would eventually yield and publish something. Rather than scatter my poems broadcast over dozens of literary magazines, I determined to aim high and to send them only to a few publications I particularly respected—*The New Yorker, The Atlantic, Harper's, The Kenyon Review, The Hudson Review,* and a couple of others. It was my plan to send each poem to each magazine on this list until the editors would at least become familiar with my name and style. This I did. For six months or more, I sent each new poem off to these magazines—and garnered a desk full of the usual printed rejection slips. But then a subtle change began to happen: one of the editors sent me a scrawled note of rejection instead of a printed slip; another sent me a typewritten letter of regret, with a request to see more poems. Apparently I was beginning to make some sort of impression. Four more months went by. Then, suddenly, *The New Yorker,* a magazine known for its careful reading of manuscripts submitted by unpublished writers, wrote to say that they were taking a short group of three poems; soon after, *The Atlantic* accepted a sequence of four sonnets. Next, an idea for a light, topical poem occurred to me; I wrote it in one afternoon and rushed it off to *The New Yorker.* They took it, too.

All this was more than enough to make me really serious about my writing. I began to turn out verse in quantity; in the year following my first acceptances, I must have written over 2,500 lines of poetry, much of which was, in turn, accepted by the magazines I had set my sights on. At this point, I became increasingly indebted to the poetry editors of these magazines, not only for accepting my work in the first place, but also for their skilled and excellent criticism and editorial comment, which often rescued a poem from failure. In the years since, I have come to value their judgment and to welcome their suggestions on everything I write.

Today, I still write verse (along with articles and book reviews) at a pretty consistent rate. I try to make every poem strong enough and different enough to warrant publication; then I try to get it published in one of the magazines where most of my work appears. So far, I've been most fortunate; about 75% of the poems I've written since 1964 have seen publication, and I still have hopes for some of the others. I have published three books of verse.

That, in a few hundred words, is my story. Now, let's get back to yours. At the beginning of this article, I suggested a few objective tests to determine whether you're capable of writing poetry that can be published in this day and age. Assuming that you're still reading this article because you have passed these tests, I have some more advice for you.

Though no two people, and certainly no two poets, are alike, the experience I've just outlined suggests that I've run across some basic rules that any aspiring poet can profitably follow. Let me list these and comment briefly on them.

1. *Make writing a habit.* Fortunately for all of us, good habits are as easy to get into as bad ones, and just as hard to break. If you make it an ironclad rule to spend a certain number of hours writing on one or two specific days a week—if you treat it as a hard-and-fast schedule—you'll soon find yourself with a good habit on your hands. Even if you don't have a specific writing project in mind each time you sit down, you'll discover that the leisure to think and concentrate will generate new ideas for you—ideas that will soon turn into words on the page. I don't have a lot of advice about time of day; you should just pick a time that will let you work, free of outside distractions, for a minimum of two hours at a sitting. If that's early morning or late at night, so be it. As far as writing materials are concerned, I'd recommend against a typewriter, on the grounds that typewritten copy seems so final and

unchangeable; it's better, I think, to use an ordinary #2 pencil with a good eraser.

2. *Write about what you know.* This is an ancient rule for writers of all kinds. It's still a good one. The material of poetry is not far-flung, exotic, romantic. It's your own life, what's under your nose.

3. *Think it through before you write it down.* Even with a nice, erasable #2 pencil, words have a way of crystallizing on the page once you've put them down. So don't put them down in the first place until you're reasonably sure of the form they're going to take —and the effect they're going to make. Oh, sure, detail changes and revisions are fine. But make sure that the basic structure is sound before you commit it to paper. This will save you many a false start and a dead end, especially as it applies to the beginning of a poem —and the ending. But even in the middle, when everything is (or seems to be) plain sailing, think before you write.

4. *Concentrate on those beginnings and endings.* As I've said before, those are really the parts of the poem where you're on your own; the middle tends to write itself. So labor hard and long to make every opening a model of power, grace, and impact, and to make every close a model of finality and rightness—the only possible ending for that particular poem.

5. *Use form to help you get started.* You may be absolutely dedicated to the idea of yourself as a stunning free-verse poet, but you'll find it a lot easier to start your career if you begin by working in traditional forms—the pentameter line, the couplet, the rhymed quatrain, the sonnet. Why? Because, paradoxically, following these forms makes less work for you, leaves less for you to think about, frees you to concentrate on the content rather than the form. Most free-verse poems are fiendishly difficult to write, precisely because you have to make up both form and content as you go along; conversely, a formal poem does part of the job for you by presenting you with a ready-made jig, so to speak, to assemble the words in. Also, there's this to consider: you wouldn't attempt to be a great abstract artist without first studying the rudiments of perspective, composition, and anatomy; by the same token, you shouldn't attempt to become a free-verse poet without first studying the traditional forms in which nearly all of the great

English poets have written. It's part of your basic training, no matter what kind of poet you may eventually become.

6. *Get expert criticism.* Unless you're far more objective than most of us, you can't hope to evaluate your progress all by yourself. You need some guidance from an expert. If you're lucky, as I was, you'll have a friend who can supply the needed—and continuing —criticism of your developing verse. If not, seek out such a person: perhaps the instructor in a poetry course at a local evening college or school of adult education. Secure his interest; show him your work over a period of time; take his advice and act on it.

7. *Pick your markets and bombard them.* I'll repeat for emphasis: select the places you'd like to be published; send each of them in turn every new poem you write, once you think you've reached a publishable level. Keep bombarding these chosen markets with your work; sooner or later, if you have an individual voice to offer, somebody will start to listen—and start to encourage you. Read *The Writer* to keep up on poetry markets; go to the library and familiarize yourself with the actual magazines, so you'll know whom you're submitting to and what they expect of their contributors.

8. *Keep at it.* Few poets burst into prominence overnight. Nearly all labor in obscurity for years before they find a market and an audience. You will have to do this, too. And it's not easy. But the right combination of hope, self-confidence, doggedness, and humility can keep you going until the day you get your first acceptance. And that time isn't wasted: in those long weeks and months when your work is unknown except to yourself and perhaps one mentor, you're actually dedicating yourself to the task of perfecting your outlook, your viewpoint, your style and technique, the individual voice you're striving for. In the time of obscurity, the real poet is made. It is, as the adage says, always darkest just before the dawn.

70

LIGHT VERSE: QUESTIONS
AND ANSWERS

By Richard Armour

LIGHT verse is a minor art or craft, but there is a good deal of art and craft to it. In fact there is often more technique involved in light verse than in serious poetry. Phyllis McGinley once said that light verse is (or should be) less emotional and more rational than poetry, though I think she won the Pulitzer Prize not so much for light verse as for what I would call light poetry. At any rate I agree with her that light verse is not to be taken too lightly by the writer. Quite aside from talent, and a special way with words and ideas, one must know the fundamentals, and more than the fundamentals, of versification: meter, rhyme, and all the rest.

The best modern light verse writers, such as Phyllis McGinley, Ogden Nash, David McCord, Morris Bishop, Arthur Guiterman, Samuel Hoffenstein, Dorothy Parker, Margaret Fishback, and Ethel Jacobson, have also been poets or mock poets. Having read and absorbed the writings of poets and light verse writers who went before them (and light verse is as old as Chaucer), they sharpened their skills and eventually developed styles of their own.

Some of these poets are still with us and still writing, but not quite so much and not quite so lightly. It is about time for a whole new generation. Magazine markets are fewer and book publishers more wary, but there is still a substantial readership for light verse if it is original and skillful and has something to say. I thought it might be helpful to give some basic pointers and to put them in question and answer form. These, at any rate, are the questions I am most often asked and the answers I most often give:

Q. *What is the difference between light verse and poetry?*

A. Light verse is a kind of poetry. It is poetry written in the spirit of play. Since it may not have the high thoughts or the imagery of poetry, it makes up for lack of these by emphasis on technique. The first requirement of a light verse writer is sure command of meter and rhyme. But along with technique, as in any writing, there must be something new to say, or a new way of saying something old.

Q. *What are the best subjects for light verse?*

A. Since you are writing for people, you should write about what people are most interested in. And people are most interested in people. In other words, the best subjects are those that have to do with the foibles of the human race, such as the relations of man to wife and of parents to children; the effort to get along with one's neighbors and one's colleagues and one's boss (unless one *is* the boss); the struggle with waistline and hairline; bank accounts, charge accounts, and no accounts; hosts and guests; passing fads in food and clothing and cars and sports; buying a house or building a house or running a house or being run by a house; vacations and travel and luggage and tips; pets; youth and age and the in-between adolescent; illness and doctors and remedies and recuperation and exercise; automation and the computerized society in relation to the bewildered individual; people who are meddlesome or pompous or stupid or inconsistent—in short, all aspects of the human comedy. Here is an example of a piece of light verse on a subject of universal interest:

> MONEY
> Workers earn it,
> Spendthrifts burn it,
> Bankers lend it,
> Women spend it,
> Forgers fake it,
> Taxes take it,
> Dying leave it,
> Heirs receive it,
> Thrifty save it,
> Misers crave it,
> Robbers seize it,
> Rich increase it,
> Gamblers lose it . . .
> I could use it.

Q. *Where does one look for ideas?*

A. You not only look but listen. You keep your ears open as well as your eyes. Sometimes a chance phrase or a cliché will trigger a piece of verse. In addition to looking at and listening to people, you read, read, read. You read books and magazines and newspapers. Now and then, if you are on the alert, an idea will pop up. Newspapers, especially, are mirrors reflecting the absurdities of mankind—and womankind. Light verse should concern subjects that concern people. It should strike common chords, be human, be universal.

Q. *What is the best length for a piece of light verse?*

A. Brevity is a requisite of all forms of humor. Recently a critic writing in *Esquire* made the wise observation: "Humor is like guerrilla warfare. Success depends on traveling light . . . striking unexpectedly . . . and getting away fast." This applies especially to light verse, which is a condensed, almost telegraphic, form of humor —verse being more compressed than prose anyhow. Light verse is briefer today than it was in the more leisurely nineteenth century, and less intricate than in those days of the ballade and the villanelle. Usually it runs from two lines to eight or ten or twelve. Only rarely to sixteen or more. That is, if you want to sell it. By the way, this is the shortest piece I ever sold (to the *Saturday Review*):

> MAID'S DAY OUT
> Thurs.
> Hers.

Q. *What are the best verse forms to use?*

A. Simple iambic and anapestic meter, rather short lines (trimeter or tetrameter), couplets and quatrains. If you don't know what these are, go to your local library and get Clement Wood's *Poets' Handbook* or look at the back part of Clement Wood's *The Complete Rhyming Dictionary*. You can't expect to enter a highly competitive field, in which technique plays such a large part, without knowing the fundamentals of versification.

Light verse should be technically correct in rhymes and meters, and, if possible, not only correct but fresh and original. I have mentioned short lines. You may also use the longer pentameter (five stress) line, which has been the most popular form in English poetry ever since Chaucer, but it usually leads to somewhat more serious treatment, and the rhymes (much more important in light verse than in serious poetry) are a bit far apart.

Q. *Are there any other suggestions for writing salable light verse?*

A. It should, usually, have an element of surprise or some sort of clincher at the end. (See "Money" quoted above.) But it should not rely too much on the last line, in that case spoken of slightingly as "terminal humor." Good light verse should be amusing all the way through, with maybe something a little special at the close. And it should be given the additional help of a good title—one that is original and appropriate.

Q. *How do you find markets for light verse?*

A. You can look at the market lists that appear from time to time in issues of *The Writer* (or write in for the back issue containing light verse markets). But you should also examine the magazines themselves, to see whether they are using light verse and, if so, what type. I take a good many magazines, but in addition I spend many hours on my haunches at newsstands, checking the magazines I don't take. (Forgive me, managers of drug stores and supermarkets. I still buy enough from you.)

As for knowing markets—submitting light verse to the right place at the right time—this is as important today as ever. It is perhaps more important now than it was thirty years ago, because the markets are fewer and the competition is keener. But, again, when I started out I knew my markets, *The Saturday Evening Post* and *The New Yorker,* as a long-time reader of both.

Markets change and you have to keep up with them. *The Saturday Evening Post* still uses light verse on the "Post Scripts" page, but there are few poems scattered through the back pages of the magazine. And *The New Yorker* uses less verse, and such verse as it uses is less light than in what I think of as the Good Old Days, when Harold Ross was editor.

Today, in addition to the "Post Scripts" page, there is "Light Housekeeping" in *Good Housekeeping,* and "Parting Shots" in *The American Legion Magazine.* In addition to these well-edited pages, where you have to fight off a multitude of free-lancers, there are other more specialized magazines like *Gourmet* and *Golf* that occasionally use light verse. You will find more of these in market lists or discover them for yourself by reading the magazines.

Q. *How do you submit light verse?*

A. Type it, double-spaced, one poem to a page, with your name and return address in the upper corner (it makes no difference whether left or right) of the page. Submit one to three poems at a time. You may be able to get in four, along with a stamped self-addressed envelope, for the same postage, if the paper is not heavier than sixteen-pound weight, a good weight for all manuscripts. No letter is necessary or desirable. What could you say? Editors have enough to read anyhow. Another thing—there is no need to say anything about protecting your manuscript. Editors are honest and the U.S. mails are safe. If something is bought, what is usually bought is first North American serial rights, which means the first run in a North American newspaper or magazine.

Q. *Do you need an agent?*

A. An agent might be helpful, but most agents won't bother with light verse. And most don't know the markets as well as you will know them if you study the magazines as I have suggested. It's a do-it-yourself field.

Q. *When do you do your writing?*

A. Whenever I get a chance, which isn't often enough. I long ago gave up "waiting for an inspiration"—else I would still be waiting. I also gave up trying to set aside regular hours for writing, though I would do this if I could. Since I have several other time-consuming activities, I write when I can. But my conscience or compulsion or whatever it is weighs so heavily on me that I feel frustrated and remorseful if I do not write a little something—prose or verse—each day, seven days a week. (I am writing this on a Sunday morning—

after having gone to church.) Some days I write for ten minutes; some days I write for ten hours. One advantage of light verse is that it can be written during short periods. With a schedule such as mine, I am glad I am not a novelist.

Q. *Do you still get things back?*

A. Yes, indeed. I use returned verses as scratch paper on which to write new verses. My method with editors is erosion. After a while, I wear them down. But it takes patience and postage. The difference between the professional and the amateur, in this business, is that the professional becomes discouraged less easily.

Q. *Do you get printed rejection slips or letters?*

A. Both. And sometimes I get neither—just the poem back, in the return envelope, which is really very sensible. I think rejection slips are a waste of paper. If I get a poem back, I know, without any printed explanation, that it has been rejected. Of course I am grateful for a letter, or even a brief note. One editor with whom I dealt for many years used to grade my poems, as if I were a student in Freshman Composition. Though he might buy a poem that he graded "B minus" or even "C plus," only once did he ever give me an "A." It was for this piece, which is included in my collection, *Nights With Armour:*

THE LOVE LIFE (AND DEATH) OF A MOOSE

Up in Newfoundland some 20 moose, mistaking Diesel train horns for mating calls, have been lured to death on the tracks.—*News item.*

> Imagine this beast of the frozen Northeast
> With its annual amorous craze on,
> Seduced by the toot of a choo-choo en route
> Into making a fatal liaison.
>
> Conceive of its sighs as it straddles the ties,
> Unaware of the killer it's dating.
> The honk of the train has gone straight to its brain,
> And its mind is completely on mating.
>
> Appalling? Of course, but just think how much worse
> It would be, and no words shall we weasel,

Should an engine tear loose from its tracks when a moose
Makes what sounds like the call of a Diesel.

This, by the way, is a pretty good example of playfulness, zany point of view, exaggeration, out-of-the-ordinary rhyming, and fancy footwork (with metrical feet)—some of the ingredients of light verse.

Q. *Of the light verse you have written, what is your own personal favorite?*

A. This is almost impossible to answer. Sometimes, in a depressed mood (that is, daily), I like nothing I have ever written. Other times I run onto something I wrote years ago, and had forgotten, and wonder that I had ever written anything so good. This, instead of making me happy, depresses me further, because it convinces me that I am on the downgrade and shall never do so well again. But usually I like best whatever I have written most recently. This goes not only for my light verse but for my books. Perhaps I can dodge the question by quoting a piece of light verse that seems to be a favorite of others and is fairly typical.

MY MATTRESS AND I
Night after night, for years on end,
My mattress has been my closest friend.

My mattress and I are cozy and pally;
There are hills on the sides—I sleep in the valley.

It clearly reveals the shape I'm in:
Where I'm thin it's thick, where it's thick I'm thin.

Its contours reflect the first and the last of me.
It's very nearly a plaster cast of me.

I miss my mattress when I am gone;
It's one thing I've made an impression on.

This is about all there is to it. Everything depends on your sense of humor, your original way of looking at things (including yourself), your handling of rhyme and meter and words, and your ability to be critical of what you write and to compare it honestly with what is being published.

Now I have to get back to work, because light verse, no matter how easy it looks (and it should be made to look easy) is work, hard work. And when a piece of light verse comes off right—when it is original in concept, and funny, and nicely turned—the light verse writer gets, in his way, as much of a feeling of accomplishment, even creativeness, as a serious poet.

71

THE EXPERIENCE OF THE POEM

By Ann Stanford

One may think of the ingredients of a good poem as an experience and a fresh perception of that experience. The experience need not be original or new, but the perception should be. Think of Gerard Manley Hopkins' delight in spring, a feeling old as humanity, couched in the freshest of images:

> Nothing is so beautiful as spring—
> When weeds, in wheels, shoot long and lovely and lush;
> Thrush's eggs look little low heavens, and thrush
> Through the echoing timber does so rinse and wring
> The ear, it strikes like lightnings to hear him sing;
> The glassy peartree leaves and blooms, they brush
> The descending blue; that blue is all in a rush
> With richness; the racing lambs too have fair their fling.

Hopkins' language is vital because his feeling about spring is intense and his own. He has taken the familiar ingredients of a poem about spring and made them into a new vision.

A contemporary example of a poem drawn from everyday experience is May Swenson's "Water Picture,"* which describes the reflection of objects in a pond; it begins:

> In the pond in the park
> all things are doubled:
> Long buildings hang and
> wriggle gently. Chimneys
> are bent legs bouncing
> on clouds below. A flag
> wags like a fishhook
> down there in the sky.

---

* From *To Mix with Time*. Charles Scribner's Sons. Copyright © 1963, by May Swenson.

The arched stone bridge
is an eye, with underlid
in the water. In its lens
dip crinkled heads with hats
that don't fall off. Dogs go by,
barking on their backs.
A baby, taken to feed the
ducks, dangles upside-down
a pink balloon for a buoy.

Seen in detail from a new angle, an ordinary experience becomes extraordinary and the substance of poetry. The fresh perception makes the old experience unique.

And the perception is conveyed through language. The words and combinations we choose must be carefully screened to see that they are not the old stereotypes through which we blind ourselves to the world. In his poems, e. e. cummings tore words apart and put the parts back into new combinations so that his language might reveal a new view of the world. Most of us will not follow his way, but we need to be sure we see what we see as it is, not as we think it is. There is a tree before you. What kind of leaves does it have? Are they alternating on the stem? Do they resemble plumes? Are they flat on the air like lily-pads in the water? Hopkins' journal frequently takes account of such phenomena:

Elm leaves:—they shine much in the sun—bright green when near from underneath but higher up they look olive: their shapelessness in the flat is from their being made . . . to be dimpled and dog's eared: their leaf-growth is in this point more rudimentary than that of oak, ash, beech, etc that the leaves lie in long rows and do not subdivide or have central knots but tooth or cog their woody twigs.

Such careful looking, such precision in visual perception, is a first step in writing poetry. If you cannot see what a tree looks like, it will be hard to tell anyone what a feeling feels like. Because in poetry we are dependent on the concrete manifestations of the world to use as symbols of our feelings and our experiences. This is especially true in lyric poetry. But apt suggestive details give credibility to narrative poems and character sketches as well. A good exercise in poetry is to record exactly what you see before you with no large statements about what is there. Simply describe it as if you are seeing it for the first time. An artist practices by carrying a sketch pad and drawing wherever he may be. In the same way, the result of the poet's sketch may not be a poem, but the practice will help develop a technique for handling a more complex subject when it does appear. Here is an example, a description of a shell done as an exercise:

> Being which is the size of my palm
> almost and fits the upcurled fingers
> flat-cupped the thirty-four fingers
> end in points set close together
> like the prongs of a comb
> sea-combing straining the waters
> they are printed on your back
> brown waves cutting light sand
> waves—merging inward
> lighter and lighter and closer
> whirling
> into the self-turned center
> of yourself.

Just as there are two kinds of perception—what is seen and what is experienced—there are two kinds of possibilities for exact or innovative language. And there are chances also for trite or easy observation on both levels.

A poem will not always die of a single cliché; indeed, a common observation can even be used for a deliberate artistic purpose. Only someone who has really mastered his craft, however, should dare to use a phrase which borders on the trite. Dylan Thomas sometimes uses old phrases but remakes them by small changes, so that they emerge as live word combinations like "once below a time." But I can think of no poetic situation in which a "rippling stream" or "glassy pond" can add anything but tedium. Worse than the cliché at the literal or visual level, is the cliché at the experiential level, the large abstract concept such as:

> Life, like time, moves onward.

The large concept gives the reader a stereotyped experience. Perhaps this is why some very bad poetry appeals to a number of undiscriminating readers: it repeats the stereotype of experience they have in their own minds and gives them nothing new to test it by. A good poem should jolt the reader into a new awareness of his feeling or his sensual apprehension of the world. One of the great mistakes is to make a poem too large and simple.

Poetry is an art which proceeds in a roundabout fashion. Its language is not chosen for directness of communication, for the passing on of facts, like "the plane arrives at five," or "today it is raining," although either of these facts could be a part of a poem. The truth that poetry attempts to communicate is reached by more devious means. Many of the devices thought of as being in the special province of poetry are devices of indirection: the metaphor or symbol, which involves saying one thing and meaning another; paradox, the welding of opposites into a single concept; connotations beyond the direct meaning of a word or phrase, and so on. When we think of the way things are in the world, we find that poetry is not the only area in which the immediate fact is disguised, distorted, or concealed. Poetry does this in order to reach a more complex truth. Other situations involve indirection for other reasons. Purpose determines the directness of statement. Take the guest telling his hostess he enjoyed the party. Did he really? But in saying this he is expressing some other feeling beyond the immediate situation. He may be expressing sympathy or long affection or any number of emotions rather than measuring the quality of his enjoyment of the moment. Take advertising, which often tries to pass along not so much a fact as a feeling about something. Take the art of the magician—the better the more deceiving. For the poet to speak too glibly may be to oversimplify his experience. The poet must constantly ask himself: "Is this the way it really felt? Is this the whole experience? Am I overlooking or suppressing part of it?"

As I write this, a living example has appeared before my eyes. I am looking at the tree just outside the window. If I should give you my visual experience at this moment, I should have to include a lizard that has climbed twenty feet up the trunk and is now looking at me. In my stereotyped picture of trees, birds sometimes come to rest, but not lizards. In my stereotype of the loss of a friend through death, there is sorrow, not anger. But I have felt anger at the death of a friend, and there is a lizard in this tree. The real includes these disparate elements. The poet must think of what he has really experienced. He gives certain real details, certain suggestions. The reader combines these into the experience intended by the poet, the real message of the poem, and so participates in its creation.

The poet uses three types of ingredients in his poem: at the first level is what can be immediately caught by the senses—by sight, by hearing, tasting, feeling, smelling. I call this the literal level: the poet describes what is literally there. This poem of my own is written almost entirely at this level:

THE BLACKBERRY THICKET *

I stand here in the ditch, my feet on a rock in the water,
Head-deep in a coppice of thorns,
Picking wild blackberries,
Watching the juice-dark rivulet run
Over my fingers, marking the lines and the whorls,
Remembering stains—
The blue of mulberry on the tongue
Brown fingers after walnut husking,
And the green smudge of grass—
The earnest part
Of heat and orchards and sweet springing places.
Here I am printed with the earth
Always and always the earth ground into the fingers,
And the arm scratched in thickets of spiders.
Over the marshy water the cicada rustles,
A runner snaps sharp into place.
The dry leaves are a presence,
A companion that follows up under the trees of the orchard
Repeating my footsteps. I stop to listen.
Surely not alone
I stand in this quiet in the shadow
Under a roof of bees.

The sights and sounds caught by immediate sensation are described; the memories are of the same immediate quality. Even the ending of the poem is a literal description, although the reader may find there, if he likes, connotations that go beyond the literal.

Much of modern American poetry is written at this level. If not total poems as here, at least sections of poems. Most readers of modern poetry, many editors, look for this literal quality. Here, as I said earlier, the poet must look carefully and sensitively and report exactly. Notice, next time you read a poem, how much of it contains this literal looking and what details the poet has chosen to give the appearance of reality. Even an imagined experience should have some of this literal quality.

---

* From *The Weathercock*, by Ann Stanford. Copyright © 1955, by Ann Stanford. Reprinted by permission of The Viking Press, Inc.

The next level of poetry is the metaphoric, in which one thing is compared with another. The conventional poetic devices of simile, metaphor, symbol are part of this level. Comparison often mingles with the literal. In Elizabeth Bishop's well-known poem "The Fish," * exact description is aided by comparison:

> I looked into his eyes
> which were far larger than mine
> but shallower, and yellowed,
> the irises backed and packed
> with tarnished tinfoil
> seen through the lenses
> of old scratched isinglass.

The juxtaposing of two things that are not wholly alike but that are alike in some way is one of the ways that poetry creates a new view of the world. Comparisons or analogies can be used thus as part of description, or they can make a total poem. They can be either one-way or two-way comparisons. For example, the fish's eye can be said to resemble isinglass, but isinglass does not remind one of a fish's eye. It is not always necessary or desirable that the comparisons work both ways. Another example, Shakespeare's comparison of true love to a "star to every wandering bark," is effective even though within the poem he is not also comparing a star that guides to love. He is defining love in terms of a star, but not a star in terms of love.

However, often the poet uses a two-way analogy. The doubleness of the analogy is especially effective where the whole poem is in the form of comparison. Here is a poem of mine which satirizes the work of committees.

THE COMMITTEE †
by Ann Stanford

Black and serious, they are dropping down one by one to the top of the walnut
    tree.
It is spring and the bare branches are right for a conversation.
The sap has not risen yet, but those branches will always be bare
Up there, crooked with ebbed life lost now, like a legal argument.
They shift a bit as they settle into place.

---

* From *Poems: North and South*. Houghton Mifflin Company. Copyright © 1955, by Elizabeth Bishop.
† © 1967 The New Yorker Magazine, Inc.

Once in a while one says something, but the answer is always the same;
The question is, too—it is all *caw* and *caw*.
Do they think they are hidden by the green leaves partway up the branches?
Do they like it up there cocking their heads in the fresh morning?
One by one, they fly off as if to other appointments.
Whatever they did, it must be done all over again.

Here, what is said about the crows can be applied to a committee, but it is also true of crows, at least the ones I have observed in my neighborhood. This, then, is a two-way analogy.

There is another level at which poets sometimes work: the level of statement. Much of Wordsworth's poetry is statement, as:

> This spiritual Love acts not nor can exist
> Without Imagination, which, in truth,
> Is but another name for absolute power
> And clearest insight, amplitude of mind,
> And Reason in her most exalted mood.

This is a hard and dangerous level for most poets. Much poetry, especially amateur poetry, constantly attempts statement without backing it up with the literal or analogic or comparative level. The poem which merely states, except in the hands of a master, falls flat because it does not prove anything to the reader. He is not drawn into the background of the statement. He is merely told. If his own experience backs up the statement, he may like the poem, but he likes it only because of his experience, not because of what the poem has done for him.

Masters of poetry, on the other hand, sometimes make o. large statement and spend the rest of the poem illustrating or proving it. Hopkins does this with the statement "Nothing is so beautiful as spring—"; May Swenson does it in a more specific way in "Water Picture." William Carlos Williams in "To Waken an Old Lady" defines old age by describing a flock of birds in winter. His only reference to age at all is the first line, "Old age is." Without the first line to suggest the definition, the poem could be simply a nature description. Emily Dickinson often makes an abstract idea come to life by defining it in visual terms:

> Presentiment is that long shadow on the lawn
> Indicative that suns go down;

> The notice to the startled grass
> That darkness is about to pass.

It would be a rare poem which could exist on one of these levels—that of literal description, that of metaphor, or that of statement—alone. Poems usually combine these in varying proportions. There are dangers to the poetry, besides triteness, at all levels. Flatness, dullness, and poor selection of details menace literal description. Metaphor is endangered by irrelevance; a metaphor which does not contribute in tone or feeling may turn the reader away from the poem as a whole. Statement is most dangerous, for it must be proved.

A poem which succeeds may also have a fourth level—the transcendental level, where the connotations of the poem extend on beyond the limits of the poem. But the transcendental may hardly be striven for. We only recognize it when it shimmers in the exceptional poem.

Meanwhile the poet works at what he can. He looks for the whole significance of the experience. He renders it—even more, he understands it—through language built around his own view. His new seeing is what will make the experience of the poem worth telling once more.

72

POETIC DEVICES

By William Packard

THERE is a good story about Walter Johnson, who had one of the most natural fast balls in the history of baseball. No one knows how "The Big Train" developed such speed on the mound, but there it was. From his first year of pitching in the majors, 1907, for Washington, Walter Johnson hurtled the ball like a flash of lightning across the plate. And as often as not, the opposing batter would be left watching empty air, as the catcher gloved the ball.

Well, the story goes that after a few seasons, almost all the opposing batters knew exactly what to expect from Walter Johnson—his famous fast ball. And even though the pitch was just as difficult to hit as ever, still, it can be a very dangerous thing for any pitcher to become that predictable. And besides, there were also some fears on the Washington bench that if he kept on hurtling only that famous fast ball over the plate, in a few more seasons Walter Johnson might burn his arm out entirely.

So, Walter Johnson set out to learn how to throw a curve ball. Now, one can just imagine the difficulty of doing this: here is a great pitcher in his mid-career in the major leagues, and he is trying to learn an entirely new pitch. One can imagine all the painful self-consciousness of the beginner, as Johnson tried to train his arm into some totally new reflexes—a new way of fingering the ball, a new arc of the elbow as he went into the wind-up, a new release of the wrist, and a completely new follow-through for the body.

But after awhile, the story goes, the curve ball became as natural for Walter Johnson as the famous fast-ball pitch, and as a consequence, Johnson became even more difficult to hit.

When Walter Johnson retired in 1927, he held the record for total strike-outs in a lifetime career (3409), and he held the record for total pitching of shut-out games in a lifetime career (110)—records which

415

have never been equaled in baseball. And Walter Johnson is second only to the mighty Cy Young for total games won in a lifetime career.

Any artist can identify with this story about Walter Johnson. The determination to persist in one's art or craft is a characteristic of a great artist and a great athlete. But one also realizes that this practice of one's craft is almost always painstakingly difficult, and usually entails periods of extreme self-consciousness, as one trains oneself into a pattern of totally new reflexes. It is what Robert Frost called "the pleasure of taking pains."

The odd thing is that this practice and mastery of a craft is sometimes seen as an infringement on one's own natural gifts. Poets will sometimes comment that they do not want to be bothered with all that stuff about metrics and assonance and craft, because it doesn't come "naturally." Of course it doesn't come naturally, if one hasn't worked to make it natural. But once one's craft becomes second nature, it is not an infringement on one's natural gifts—if anything, it is an enlargement of them, and an enhancement and a reinforcement of one's own intuitive talents.

In almost all the other arts, an artist has to learn the techniques of his craft as a matter of course.

The painter takes delight in exploring the possibilities of his palette, and perhaps he may even move through periods which are dominated by different color tones, such as viridian or Prussian blue or ochre. He will also be concerned, as a matter of course, with various textural considerations such as brushing and pigmentation and the surface virtue of his work.

The composer who wants to write orchestra music has to begin by learning how to score in the musical notation system—and he will play with the meaning of whole notes, half notes, quarter notes, eighth notes, and the significance of such tempo designations as *lento, andante, adagio,* and *prestissimo.* He will also want to explore the different possibilities of the instruments of the orchestra, to discover the totality of tone he wants to achieve in his own work.

Even so—I have heard student poets complain that they don't want to be held back by a lot of technical considerations in the craft of poetry.

That raises a very interesting question: Why do poets seem to resist learning the practice and mastery of their own craft? Why do they protest that technique *per se* is an infringement on their own intuitive gifts, and a destructive self-consciousness that inhibits their natural and magical genius?

I think a part of the answer to these questions may lie in our own modern Romantic era of poetry, where poets as diverse as Walt Whitman and Dylan Thomas and Allen Ginsberg seem to achieve their best effects with little or no technical effort. Like Athena, the poem seems to spring full blown out of the forehead of Zeus, and that is a large part of its charm for us. Whitman pretends he is just "talking" to us, in the "Song of Myself." So does Dylan Thomas in "Fern Hill" and "Poem in October." So does Allen Ginsberg in "Howl" and "Kaddish."

But of course when we think about it, we realize it is no such thing. And we realize also, in admiration, that any poet who is so skillful in concealing his art from us may be achieving one of the highest technical feats of all.

What are the technical skills of poetry, that all poets have worked at who wanted to achieve the practice and mastery of their craft?

We could begin by saying that poetry itself is language which is used in a specific way to convey a specific effect. And the specific ways that language can be used are expressed through all of the various poetic devices. In "The ABC of Reading," Ezra Pound summarized these devices and divided them into three categories—phonopoeia (sight), melopoeia (sound), and logopoeia (voice).

SIGHT

The image is the heart and soul of poetry. In our own psychic lives, we dream in images, although there may be words superimposed onto these images. In our social communication, we indicate complete understanding of something when we say, "I get the picture"— indicating that imagistic understanding is the most basic and primal of all communications. In some languages, like Chinese and Japanese, words began as pictures, or ideograms, which embodied the image representation of what the word was indicating.

It is not accidental that our earliest record of human civilization is in the form of pure pictures—images of bison in the paleolithic caves at Altamira in Northern Spain, from the Magdalenian culture, some 16,000 years B.C. And there are other records of stone statues as pure images of horses and deer and mammoths, in Czechoslovakia, from as far back as 30,000 years B.C.

Aristotle wrote in the "Poetics" that metaphor—the conjunction of one image with another image—is the soul of poetry, and is the surest sign of genius. He also said it was the one thing that could not be taught, since the genius for metaphor was unaccountable, being the ability to see similarities in dissimilar things.

Following are the principal poetic devices which use image, or the picture aspect of poetry:

image—a simple picture, a mental representation. "That which presents an intellectual and emotional complex in an instant of time." (Pound)

metaphor—a direct comparison. "A mighty fortress is our God." An equation, or an equivalence: A = B. "It is the east and Juliet is the sun."

simile—an indirect comparison, using "like" or "as." "Why, man, he doth bestride the narrow world/Like a Colossus..." "My love's like a red, red rose."

figure—an image and an idea. "Ship of state." "A sea of troubles." "This bud of love."

conceit—an extended figure, as in some metaphysical poetry of John Donne, or in the following lines of Shakespeare's Juliet:

<blockquote>
Sweet, good-night!
This bud of love, by summer's ripening breath,
May prove a beauteous flower when next we meet...
</blockquote>

SOUND

Rhythm has its source and origin in our own bloodstream pulse. At a normal pace, the heart beats at a casual iambic beat. But when it is excited, it may trip and skip rhythm through extended anapests or hard dactyls or firm trochees. It may even pound with a relentless spondee beat.

In dance, rhythm is accented by a drumbeat, in parades, by the cadence of marching feet, and in the night air, by churchbell tolling.

These simple rhythms may be taken as figures of the other rhythms of the universe—the tidal ebb and flow, the rising and setting of the sun, the female menstrual cycles, the four seasons of the year.

Rhythm is notated as metrics, but may also be seen in such poetic devices as rhyme and assonance and alliteration. Following are the poetic devices for sound:

assonance—rhyme of vowel sounds. "O that this too too solid flesh would melt..."

alliteration—repetition of consonants. "We might have met them dareful, beard to beard, And beat them backward home."

rhyme—the sense of resonance that comes when a word echoes the sound of another word—in end rhyme, internal rhyme, perfect rhyme, slant or imperfect rhyme, masculine rhyme, or feminine rhyme.

metrics—the simplest notation system for scansion of rhythm. The most commonly used metrics in English are:

> iamb $(\smile\,')$
> trochee $('\,\smile)$
> anapest $(\smile\smile\,')$
> dactyl $('\,\smile\smile)$
> spondee $('\,')$

VOICE

Voice is the sum total of cognitive content of the words in a poem. Voice can also be seen as the signature of the poet on his poem—his own unmistakable way of saying something. "Only Yeats could have said it that way," one feels, in reading a line like:

> That is no country for old men...

Similarly, Frost was able to endow his poems with a "voice" in lines like:

> Something there is that doesn't love a wall...

Following are the poetic devices for voice:

denotation—literal, dictionary meaning of a word.

connotation—indirect or associative meaning of a word. "Mother" means one thing denotatively, but may have a host of other connotative associations.

personification—humanizing an object.

diction—word choice, the peculiar combination of words used in any given poem.

syntax—the peculiar arrangement of words in their sentence structures.

rhetoric—"Any adornment or inflation of speech which is not done for a particular effect but for a general impressiveness..." (Eliot)

persona—a mask, an assumed voice, a speaker pretending to be someone other than who he really is.

So far these are only words on a page, like diagrams in a baseball book showing you how to throw a curve ball. The only way there can be any real learning of any of these devices is to do endless exercises in notebooks, trying to master the craft of assonance, of diction shifts, of persona effects, of successful conceits, of metrical variations.

Any practice of these craft devices may lead one into a period of extreme self-consciousness, as one explores totally new reflexes of language. But one can trust that with enough practice they can become "second nature," and an enhancement and reinforcement of one's own intuitive talents as a poet.

73

IN SEARCH OF A STORY:
THE SETTING AS SOURCE

By Katherine Paterson

LAST YEAR'S obituaries for Agatha Christie seemed apologetic for the fact that Dame Agatha's powers lay in her ability to construct ingenious plots. The implication was that great writers are strong on theme and character, and even setting, but plot is somewhat beneath them. Yet the truth of the matter is that the reason Agatha Christie is known and loved and bought by millions is that the answer to the question: "Who cares who killed Roger Ackroyd?" is: We all do, or nearly all of us do. We care desperately.

I am one of the plebeian mass who really care. I love stories. I am devoted to stories. I feel sure that at three I did not ask "Why?" but rather, "*Then* what happened?" The reason I began to write fiction was not that I believed myself to be one of those enviable artists, the "born storyteller," but that I loved stories so much, I wanted to be on the inside.

Unfortunately, loving stories is not necessarily being able to write them. This was the first hard lesson I had to learn, which explains why there is still a file drawer in my study full of unpublished manuscripts. It may also explain why I turned to historical fiction, for I discovered that an historical setting provides a rich warp for a writer's woof.

I had thus completed two novels for young people set in 12th-century Japan and was casting about for an idea for a third novel, when I made the mistake of asking my children what kind of book they would like. "You ought to write a mystery story," they said. I was horrified. They obviously didn't realize how hard plotting had always been for me. Don't you know, I said, what kind of brain it takes to plan and execute a mystery story? I reminded them that Lin, our oldest, had been beating me consistently at chess since she was six. How could a mind which couldn't plot chess moves, plot a mystery?

A few mornings later, a face glared out at me from the entertainment section of the *Washington Post.* It was that of a Japanese warrior puppet. *Bunraku,* the classical Japanese puppet theater, was coming to the Kennedy Center.

It had been fifteen years since the first time I had seen *Bunraku* in a small, dark theater in Osaka. The audience that day was made up almost entirely of little old ladies in black kimonos, and the homely smell of rice and fish and soy sauce rose from their wooden lunch boxes to permeate the theater. But when I looked at the stage, I was swept into another world. There the large, gorgeously arrayed puppets played out one of the countless stories about the forty-seven faithful retainers who spent their lives avenging the disgrace and death of their lord. The puppets, flawlessly manipulated by three operators, seemed almost to come alive. It was the "almost" which sent a little thrill of fear through me as I remembered *Bunraku.* There was something sinister about the puppets, so close to life, but not quite alive, shadowed by the hooded forms of the manipulators—the perfect setting for a mystery story, if one could write a mystery story.

Since I was convinced that I could not, the whole idea would have been folded up and put out with the papers, except that my memory of the theater, once aroused, refused to be disposed of. A week or so later, I came half awake in the middle of the night with a scene playing in my head. I was looking into the upper floor of an old Japanese storehouse. By the light of the one tiny window I could see a boy, scrabbling about in the semi-darkness. From the panicked way he was searching, I guessed both that he had no business being there in the storehouse and that the thing he was looking for was not where he had expected it to be. As I watched the frantic boy, wondering who he was and what he was looking for, I heard a thump, thump, thump on the stairs. Both the boy and I turned at the sound. In the gloom at the head of the stair, there appeared the white face of a warrior puppet, at its hand, the flash of a sword blade. Behind the puppet, almost eclipsed in shadow, was the hooded form of a single puppeteer. End of scene.

By this time, needless to say, I was fully awake, beating my brain. Who was the boy? What was he looking for in the forbidden storehouse? And who was the hooded manipulator menacing him through a puppet? But, alas, the subconscious which had served up a puzzle gratis was not about to hand me a plot free of charge. I was going to have to write the book myself and find out. So I went to the place I'd been to before: I went to a setting in search of a story.

People like to ask historical novelists about their research. For me the kind of research they are talking about comes later; first I have to search the setting for the warp of my story. Setting for me is not a background against which a story is played out, but the very stuff with which the story will be woven. The characters will not determine the setting, but the setting to a great extent will determine both what they will be like and how they will act.

For this book, then, there are two rich areas to be explored. The first was that of the puppet theater itself, a highly, and often in the past, harshly disciplined world where the individual must be willing to sacrifice everything to the demands of his art. The other was the late 18th century in a Japan ravaged by plague and famine and torn by civil disorder. Already the setting had given me a dramatic contrast— the absolute order of a puppet theater and the chaos outside its gates.

It was the characters who had to bring the two together. The conflict had to take place within them. So the boy I had glimpsed in the storehouse became the hungry son of a puppet maker who apprenticed himself to the place in Osaka where he thought he might get plenty of food. This immediately posed another puzzle. Why would there be plenty of food in the puppet theater?

History gave me an obvious answer. The rice merchants and money lenders of the city were making huge profits while the masses starved. These greedy men were still going to the theater and paying to get in —an obvious answer, but hardly one which contributed to the excitement of my story. For you see, I had gotten reckless and promised my children to write, not a true mystery, but at least an adventure story with plenty of suspense. Just how much adventure could I wring from box office receipts? No, there had to be another answer. Perhaps a person who resented the exploitation of the poor as much as I did—someone who might want to take justice into his own hands.

Saburo the bandit is not based on a historical figure, although, as devotees of samurai films well know, Japanese tradition abounds with tales of clever rogues who outwit the powerful to give succor to the weak. But the Saburo I was beginning to know was not the character so often played by Toshiro Mifune, a rude and engaging renegade whose deviling of the authorities the audience greets with guffaws and cheers. My bandit would have something of the bravado of a Robin Hood and the shrewdness of a Scarlet Pimpernel, but there was in him an element which set him apart from these hero rogues. Coming as he did, out of puppetry, Saburo would be a manipulator—a puppeteer of human lives—the sort of man, however marvelous, of whom it is well to be wary.

The setting also began to shape Jiro, the name which means simply second son that I had given my young apprentice. In searching out his history, I discovered that to have been thirteen at the climax of the Temmei famine, Jiro would have been born in a year of plague which claimed 200,000 lives.

It's hard to remember from this vantage point in what order the pieces began to tumble into position, as each answer led to another question. If he was the second son, what had happened to the first? He must, of course, have died of plague. How, then, had Jiro's parents reacted to his birth at so terrible a time? How had the long battle against starvation affected them? A scrawny, bitter woman began to emerge. Her one surviving child would not be able to understand her, even the scrap of humor she had managed to salvage from adversity would be lost on him. But I am an imperfect mother myself and I longed for someone full of life and humor to rescue her from herself and teach her guilt-ridden son to care for her. Someone who was, nonetheless, helpless to understand his own stern father, whose inscrutable behavior was tied somehow to the central question of the book—the identity of Saburo the bandit.

There are magical moments in writing historical fiction when the woof of one's invention moving through the warp of history suddenly seems to make sense. The pattern begins to emerge, filling the writer with surprise and joy. One such moment of ecstasy makes all the plodding hours fall away.

I kept waiting for my moments. Chapter after chapter I posed and answered questions, I jammed pieces into place, only to reread what I had written with leaden despair—from the richest material I'd ever worked with, I was painstakingly producing an absolute contradiction in terms—a dull adventure story.

Only pride kept me going. My publishers had doubled the advance on my second novel to allow me to go to Osaka to research this one.

My husband had managed the household and cared for the three children I had left behind for the three weeks our older daughter and I had spent in Japan. The *Bunraku* people in Osaka had given me hours of their time patiently explaining their knowledge and art. If the book for which so many people had given so much never came into being, how could I ever face them? And then, too, I had promised the children.

But I was sick. As it turned out, literally. My husband prodded and nagged me into finishing the hated draft before I went into the hospital, at which time I put it aside and turned my attention to the questions my illness posed.

Three months later our family was vacationing as usual in the barn which we rent in the Adirondacks. I wasn't feeling up to tennis, but I did feel brave enough at last to take another look at my dead story to see if there was any hope of its ever coming to life. I began to revise, little by little. It was obvious that no single correction would cure it, but time had given me distance. It didn't seem the overwhelming failure it had before. I began to believe that my physical condition had not only affected my earlier work, but also my opinion of it. Now that I was feeling better, so was the manuscript.

One night an electrical storm knocked out our lights. In a cabin in the woods, it is very dark when the lights go out. The children were restless and apprehensive, so we lighted candles, and I began to read the story out loud. As I did, I heard bumps in the rhythm that needed smoothing, and when I had failed to make some exotic detail clear, the audience stopped me and made me explain. I dared feel a faint hope.

The next day I found John, who was ten, going through the desk, looking for the manuscript. He couldn't wait until night to find out what happened next. The hope burst into flame. I knew, at last, that I had a story.

It was more than a year before the book was actually published. After the family editors passed on it, there was still my editor, who pointed out, among other things, that the scene in the storehouse, though "clever and terrifying," didn't work. I should have been warned that the scene one clings to most is very likely the one that needs lopping off, but I chose to retain it and rewrite in an attempt to make it grow more organically from what came before it. Artistically,

I've never been absolutely sure it works even yet, but it's the one scene that my young readers have relished, so I'm glad it's there. Two Japanese experts read the manuscript and suggested corrections, gently chiding me for committing the cardinal sin of Japanese puppetry. In *Bunraku,* the puppeteers must be the "shadows of the dolls"; my puppeteers were obviously overshadowing their puppets.

At last it was done, the adventure story that I had promised the children, but when I looked at it closely, I realized that the setting had given me more than a simple adventure story. It had given me a plea for justice and compassion. There it was woven through the whole pattern. I hope the children see it.

74

WHAT DO THEY WANT? WHAT DO THEY NEED?

By Winifred Madison

Every now and then I am invited to speak with children at a local intermediate school, and I love to do this because it is such a delight to look at the sometimes shining faces of the children and listen to their sometimes shining words. How pleasant it is to be with children without having to discipline them as a teacher, parent, or any other kind of adult!

We meet in the library. They sit on the floor or on small chairs clustered around me, a far cozier situation than a classroom. After a few minutes of introduction to let them know I'm not a grim and terrifying adult about to bombard them with a lecture, we become conversational and ask each other questions.

Their questions usually include these: *Where do you get your ideas? Did you write as a child? Where can I get my novel published? How much money do you make?* (How persistent they are about this, which, of course, is never really answered.) *What do you think of So-and-So?* a challenging question about a writer I've never heard of.

In turn I ask them: *Do you like to read? Is reading better than television? Do you ever like a book so much that you read it under the covers with a flashlight long after you're supposed to be asleep?* It is reassuring to find that this still goes on.

What I really want to know is what kind of books they like most and why. The answers hardly vary from class to class.

Mysteries! Science fiction! Funny books! Sports!

"Motorcycle stories! Racing cars! Wheels! Bicycles!" some boys call out.

When the hubbub dies down, there is always at least one timid person who raises his or her hand. "I like biography best. Something that's real." Encouraged by this brave revelation, a few scattered indi-

427

viduals confess to preferring books about science or other nonfiction. Then it's time for me to ask questions again.

"Do you like love stories? Do you think that children who may be ten or twelve ever fall in love? Would you like to read about it?"

The boys make gestures of disgust, but more than a few girls nod their heads quietly. Some even confess that they ask their older friends to sneak out for them a few of the more sexually advanced books from the junior high school library. I go on:

"Do you like to read about people like yourselves and your families or would you be more interested in people who are different, say very rich people or very poor people? What about children from foreign countries? Or people who live in crowded cities or else in isolated communities, such as a ranch in North Dakota?" (I ask this question in a suburban school in a university town.)

The answer is a doubtful silence and some shaking of heads. One pupil states his preference: "I like to read about people like us, not too rich, not too poor." "But with horses," a girl whispers. And then someone adds, "I like, I mean I *love*, stories about pioneers."

Do they prefer happy endings? Does it matter if someone dies in the story? Do they like a good cry? (Yes, but they would rather laugh.) What about realism? Fantasy? Now they begin to confuse books they have read with with television dramas they have seen.

It would seem as though a sugar-coated unreal realism is what most of them prefer: For the girls, the beautiful golden-haired heroine who owns a horse and solves mysteries that baffle the police from coast to coast, and for the boys, the masculine hero who wins either in outer space or here on earth. Everything must come out all right in the end. The good are rewarded and the bad are punished. Everything appears in black and white without the mitigating shade of gray.

If I'd asked them what foods they prefer, the answers would most likely be pizza, hot dogs, hamburgers, peanut butter and jelly on white bread, ice cream and Coke. Immediate gratification within accepted conventions. They believe they are supposed to prefer these foods. Yet if they were hungry and were offered a bowl of well made vegetable soup or a dish of stew, they might find that they love it. Take them to a good Chinese restaurant and see their eyes light up with interest. What they need most, perhaps, is to know that something else is there and that one can make choices.

So now I ask other questions. What would you say about a Chinese boy and his father who come to San Francisco and invent an airplane? What about a family who drink from a Fountain of Youth and live forever? What about a girl who lives in a city slum and can't think of anything excepting how much she wants a horse? They seem to be interested. And so I recommend Laurence Yep's remarkable *Dragon-wings,* Natalie Babbitt's *Tuck Everlasting,* and my own *Becky's Horse.* They sign up for these books; they are willing, perhaps eager, to try something new after all. How easy it is to pique their curiosity!

The question I dare not ask because it may be too difficult if not impossible to answer is this: What do you need that a book can give you? It is clear that children need dreams of glory and victory in which they find themselves heroes and heroines. Amuse me, they demand. Let me escape from this boring life, they seem to say. What they need most may be too deep-seated to be captured in words. Like readers of any age at all, a child may want most of all to know what experience someone else has, how he meets a challenge, and how he solves a problem that is so remarkably lifelike that the reader gains courage and understanding he did not have before.

The children could very well ask this question—and I'm somewhat relieved that they don't because it would not be easy to answer: "You are a writer. What can *you* give us?" This is a good question. Every writer must find his or her own answer, and that may take a lifetime of work to discover.

You can give only what you have. Your good sense may tell you that a novel about a golden-haired girl and her horse will pay very well, but if you do not have somewhere within you that winning heroine, and if you've never sat on a horse, it's best to forget the whole thing; readers who are true horse lovers (and there are many) will find out immediately. You may have to think about horses in an entirely new way. What you come up with may not be what is conventionally accepted, but it may be wonderful.

Knowing what children want is never enough. You can't write about sports if you never really liked baseball, fishing, motorcycles or whatever. The aficionado will know immediately that you are faking. Truth emerges from between the lines. No matter what the subject may be, every book is a self-portrait of the author.

Some writers, even good writers, copy the style of successful authors, but this has its dangers. An exaggerated example of this occurred in a first novel by a charming young writer, twelve years old and new to the craft. Influenced by Judy Blume's *Are You There God? It's Me, Margaret,* our writer, a California, set her novel in "rich" suburban New Jersey where she had never been. Here is a sample from her manuscript:

"My god!" shrieked the mother, "If you say that again, I'll go jump off the Golden Gate Bridge!"

"That's a convincing bit of dialogue," I told the writer, "but do you think that the mother would travel three thousand miles from New Jersey to San Francisco, just to jump off the Golden Gate Bridge?"

We talked for a while about the advantages of knowing what you were doing, and she shifted the locale of her highly promising story to a suburb of San Francisco, which she knows well.

Again and again one comes back to the ancient advice for writers: Write what you know! It is very good to talk with readers to find out how they feel about books and what they want from them and to ponder about what children may possibly need. But essentially all that you as a writer can do is give young readers a glimpse into the reality of your world—the world which provides *you,* as a writer, with stories. Whatever your experience may be, if it runs deep enough to touch the springs of life, then the most you can do is to put it into your stories and novels. Chances are some readers will find that this is what they have wanted all along.

75

CLUES TO THE JUVENILE MYSTERY

By Joan Lowery Nixon

When I see the words 'mystery,' 'secret,' or 'ghost' in the title of a book for children," a librarian once told me, "I automatically order five copies, because I know the books will be read so eagerly they will soon be in shreds."

And when I announced to my family that I thought I'd switch from writing for adults to writing for children, one of my young daughters immediately said, "If you're going to write for children, you have to write a book, and it has to be a mystery!"

What are the magic ingredients of a mystery novel for the eight-to-twelve age group that draw young readers to it? What does a writer need to include in his story so that his readers won't be able to put the book down until they have come to the last page?

In a mystery story the idea is often the starting point. Sometimes this idea can come from a magazine article or news item. I once read an article about artifacts being smuggled out of Mexico that led to research on the subject and eventually to a juvenile mystery novel.

Sometimes the idea can come from experience. When we moved to Corpus Christi, Texas, we found ourselves in the middle of a hurricane. The eye of the storm missed our city, but the force of the rain, wind, and waves caused tremendous damage. The area had been evacuated, but I wondered what someone would have done who couldn't leave—who, for some reason, had been left behind in the confusion. The beach houses could not withstand the force of the storm, or stay intact, but what if high on the hill there stood a stone "castle," strong enough to survive the storm and to shelter its occupants? And what if this castle were known to have as its only occupant a ghost? Out of these questons came my book *The Mystery of Hurricane Castle*.

A study of the New Orleans French Quarter, with its legends of pirate treasure and its modern day fortune-tellers, grew into a mystery novel; and the idea of someone trapped on a cruise ship, or unwilling to leave when the "all ashore" is sounded for guests, because he thinks he has just overheard the plans for a murder, developed into *The Mystery of the Secret Stowaway.*

A mystery novel should give the reader an interesting background that will expand the child's horizons. Phyllis A. Whitney, in her excellent mystery novels for children, has taken her readers to many exciting and unusual foreign settings. But even the author who cannot travel can make a small town on the coast of Maine, or a truck stop in the middle of the Arizona desert, colorful and interesting to the child for whom this too is a new experience.

Deciding upon the main character is the next step in developing the mystery novel. It is his story. He (or she) will have to solve the mystery, and he will go about it in his own individual way.

It is important to make the main characters well-rounded, interesting and actively alive. The children who read the novel will want to identify closely with them and eagerly follow their adventures to the last page. They should have a minor fault or two—something with which children feel familiar. Maybe the boy's in trouble because he can't seem to remember to keep his room tidy, or perhaps the girl's impatient and plunges into things without thinking.

The main character preferably should be twelve or thirteen years old—at the top of this age group. Eight-year-olds will read about older children, but older children do not want to identify with younger children. Plots featuring boys and stories with girls as main characters are equally popular.

Once an editor told me, "Most of the mysteries I get take place during the summer vacation. I'd like to see one in which the main character was going to school." So in *The Mysterious Red Tape Gang,* I placed my main character right in the middle of the school year. His problem with turning in homework on time gave him a character flaw and added some humor to the story.

A little light humor can be a good ingredient in a mystery novel. I learned this lesson when I was writing my first mystery. I read chapters to my children, and my fifth-grade daughter would sometimes say, "It's scary for too long. Put in something funny." What she was telling me, in essence, was to break the mood of suspense occasionally. The author can't, and shouldn't, sustain tension in the story from beginning to end. It should have peaks of suspense and valleys—breathing space, one might say, and natural humor is a good ingredient to use for this purpose.

In order to make the main character more of a "real person," I think it's good to give him a personal problem to handle along with the mystery to solve. For example, in one story I let my character's fear of a neighborhood bully turn to compassion and a tentative attempt at friendship as he began to realize what made this boy behave like a bully. In another, I matched two girls as friends—one who thinks her younger brothers and sisters are a burden, and the other an only child who lives in an adult world. Each girl learns from the other, and each learns to appreciate her own family life.

The story must be told from the main character's viewpoint only, although if there are two characters traveling this mysterious road together—friends, brothers, or sisters—the viewpoint can include them both. You are telling the story through your main character's eyes, and it's important not to have anything happen of which he or she isn't aware. She may see an obvious clue and overlook it, thinking it's not important; or he may sidetrack his efforts, and thereby come closer to danger, thinking something is important that is not; but in either case, it is that main character's story alone and the author of the juvenile mystery must keep this in mind.

As to clues, children love the puzzle in a mystery. They love to find obvious clues which the main character seems to miss. They love to search for clues which the main character has discovered, but the readers haven't figured out. Both types of clues are needed in a mystery, but the hidden clues shouldn't be too well hidden. After the solution of the mystery is reached, at the end of the story, the reader should think, "Of course! I remember that! I should have known it all along!"

Sub-mysteries, which are complications, unexpected scary situations, or new questions raised, should be used throughout the story. They all tie into the main mystery, although some of them can be solved along the way. Each chapter, through action and suspense, moves the mystery closer to its solution, and each chapter should end with something tense or a little frightening—a cliff-hanger ending—so that the reader cannot stop at the end of the chapter, but must read on to see what happens. An example is this chapter ending for *The Mysterious Red Tape Gang:*

> Linda Jean grabbed my arm and squeezed so tightly that the pressure of her fingers was painful. "Mike," she whispered, "those men might hurt my father!"
> The same thought had occurred to me. I wanted to answer her; but my mouth was dry, and I tried to swallow.
> Mr. Hartwell's face looked awful. He was like a trapped animal.
> "Mike!" Linda Jean whispered. "You've got to do something!"

Children read for pleasure, not for all the reasons for which adults read—because the book is a best seller, or because one received it as a Christmas present. If a child doesn't like a book, after the first page or two, he puts it down and looks for something else to read.

Therefore, the story should immediately introduce the main character, lead into the mystery as soon as possible, and grab the reader. In the opening paragraphs of *The Mysterious Red Tape Gang,* I set the scene, established the mood of the story, introduced my main character, told something about the other characters who would be important, and gave the first hint of mystery to come:

> My father gets excited when he reads the newspaper at the breakfast table. Sometimes a story makes him mad, and he reads it out loud to my mother. And all the time he reads, he keeps pounding his fist on the table.
> Once, when his fist was thumping up and down, my little brother, Terry, carefully slid the butter dish over next to my father just to see what would happen. Terry had to clean up the mess, but he said it was worth it.
> Sometimes my father reads a story to me, because he says a twelve-year-old boy ought to be aware of what could happen if he fell in with bad companions.
> At first I tried to tell him that Jimmy and Tommy Scardino and Leroy Parker weren't bad companions, but I found out it was just better to keep quiet and listen.
> "Michael," he said one morning, "listen to this! The crime rate in Los Angeles is rising again! People are being mugged, cars being stolen. A lot of it is being done by kids! Watch out, Michael!"
> I nodded. What I had planned to do after school was work on the clubhouse we were building behind our garage, along with Tommy and Jimmy and Leroy. None of us wanted to steal cars. In the first place, it's a crime, and in the second place, we can't drive.

The mystery novel should have plenty of action. The old-fashioned mental detection type of story, with lots of conversation and little action, is out of date even with adult readers. With children it's doubly important to include a great deal of action and excitement in mystery stories.

However, dialogue is important, too. Dialogue not only breaks up a page and makes the story look more inviting in print, but it draws the reader into the story in a way narrative description cannot do. A careful mix of dialogue with lots of action usually results in a fast-paced, suspenseful story.

The ending of a mystery novel is important to the writer, because it's one of the first things he must think about in planning his book. After he has mentally worked out the idea of the mystery, who his main character will be, and how the story will begin, he should decide how it will end. Once this is established, the middle will fit into place, with the clues planted and the direction of the action set. I find it helpful to make an outline, chapter by chapter, so vital clues and important bits of planted information won't be omitted.

A good mystery should always be logical, and the ending should be satisfying. It should never depend on coincidence. The main character must solve the mystery. If it's necessary to bring in adults to help out—such as the police or someone who could give advice—it must be the decision of the main character to do so.

The ending of a mystery novel should satisfy the reader, because it should present an exciting climax. The solution of the mystery should contain all the answers, so a drawn-out explanation of who-did-what-and-why isn't needed. Throughout the story the reader must be given reference points he can remember—well-planted clues. Just a page or two should be used to end the story and tie up all the loose ends concerning the main character's relationship with others in the book.

Stories for the reader of eight to twelve shouldn't be gory or horrifying: characters can be captured or threatened, but description should be kept within the bounds of good sense. The occult can be used in stories for this age, and can be left unexplained, if the author wishes, as the witchcraft in Scott Corbett's *Here Lies the Body*. At the author's whim, ghosts can be explained, or left forever to haunt future generations.

As for the title: Writers should remember the key words for which librarians look and make their titles mysterious or frightening. Some child who wants the pleasure of following a character through a scary adventure will reach for that book.

Mysteries for the readers of grades one to three, who are learning to read, have become increasingly popular with editors. These are "light" mystery novels—not as involved, and not as frightening as mystery novels for older brothers and sisters. The mystery tends to be more of a puzzle to solve than a threatening situation to investigate.

These stories are designed for 42 or 43 pages in a 48-page book. On each page, there are from one to eight lines, with six to eight words to a line. The vocabulary is not controlled, but is kept within the boundaries of common sense as to words a very young reader could read and understand.

As in the mystery for the eight-to-twelve-year-olds, the story opens with action and interest, and immediately introduces the main character. Within the limited number of words, the characters and the stories cannot be written with as much depth; but along with the mystery, the main character's relationship with others can still be shown. The plot should include a surprise kept from the reader, which sustains the suspense.

In *The Secret Box Mystery,* no one can guess what Michael John has brought to school in a box for his science project, even when it gets loose in the room. In *The Mysterious Prowler,* someone leaves a nose print on Jonathan's window, bicycle tracks across his muddy yard, and calls on the phone but won't speak; and Jonathan sets out to discover who the prowler is.

As in the eight-to-twelve novel, the solution of the mystery in books for beginning readers is in the hands of the main character, although he or she is allowed to have a little more help from friends.

WRITING FOR THE TEEN-AGE MARKET

By Gloria D. Miklowitz

RECENTLY, at a dinner party, a man sitting next to me said, when he learned I was writing a teen-age novel about a rape victim, "How are you qualified to write on that subject? And why are you doing it, for the money?"

When I got over my first reaction of surprise, I answered him. (A lot of people would like to ask me that question, but are embarrassed to.)

First, as to qualifications. You don't have to be a rape victim to understand how he or she might feel, I said. I've written about a black male on drugs, about a teen-age runaway, and about an unwed mother. I'm neither black nor male, never ran away, and my children are my husband's. But, certain emotions are universal, and these are the emotions I draw from. What does it feel like to be tempted by something very badly, and to fight the temptation? If you ever felt that, then you know how my black teen-ager felt when tempted by drugs again, a temptation he wants to yield to, but doesn't.

What is it like to feel anger? I've been angry. Everyone has. You just remember that feeling when you write a scene in which the character feels anger.

Haven't you ever been afraid? I asked the man at the table. When I write about my rape victim, I'm writing about her fear, after being raped, of walking down a street, of being in a crowd where she might see her attacker again.

Have you never felt insecure? I asked the man. I have. When I wrote my book about a young paramedic student who lacks confidence, I understood that feeling, because I have lacked confidence.

Now, as to the second question, do I do it for money? To that I answered No, and Yes. First, No. I write about teen problems because they concern me. I want to say something to troubled teen-agers that

437

may help them deal with their problems. I want to say something that may stop another teen-ager on the brink of making a terrible mistake, from taking that wrong step. I have a message, in other words, not a moral to be yelled out in print, but a message, nevertheless.

In my novel *Turning Off,* for example, I say in effect: If you find work that interests you and makes you respect yourself, you won't get into trouble.

In *A Time to Hurt, A Time to Heal,* a story about a 15-year-old whose problems result from her parents' divorce, I say, You must be responsible for your own behavior.

In *Runaway,* a novel about a 15-year-old girl placed in a home for delinquents because she has run away once too often, I say: You can't run away from yourself; the solution to your problems is only within you.

And in *Unwed Mother,* a story of another 15-year-old girl who has a baby out of wedlock and keeps it for a time, I say many things, such as: If you are going to be sexually active, take precautions. But mostly, I say: Love is thinking of the loved one's needs, as well as your own.

My rape book has another message: Life has its dangers; be aware of them.

Now, on the question of money. Does this come into my thinking before I write a book? Yes, of course. I don't think I'd tackle a book I didn't think had a chance of selling. I'm in the business of writing to sell. Still, when I believe in a book and think it has a good story problem and a good theme, the chances are high that it *will* sell.

What are the elements of a teen-age novel today? Well, to begin with, you are writing for the 12-to-15-year old, in seventh to ninth grade. These books are generally about 40,000 words long, or about 150-175 manuscript pages. We're talking about fifteen to twenty chapters of about 2,000 words each. We're talking about three scenes per chapter, or forty-five to sixty scenes in a book. Those are the statistics.

Since writing is a business, let's talk money. If your book sells to a hardcover house, you'll probably get from $1,500 up as an advance, depending on your subject and name. If the book goes to paperback, also, there'll be more. Three of my books were original paperbacks with Tempo Books, an imprint of Grosset and Dunlap. They are now put out by Grosset and Dunlap in hardcover editions for libraries. I get a full 10% royalty on the retail price on hardcover sales because the same publisher brings out both editions. If Tempo had sold the hardcover rights to another publisher, I'd receive only half the royalties.

Now, to the "how to's." Let's start with the idea. I'll use, as an example, how I went about researching and writing my *Runaway* book.

The idea to do a book on a home for delinquent girls was suggested by a friend. She was a volunteer at such a home in Pasadena. "Why don't you write about these girls' problems?" she asked.

My first step was to call the director and ask if I might interview him about the home and the problems the girls had. "What's a typical girl like here? What's her background? Her problems? How do you deal with these problems?" are the kind of questions I asked, while my trusty tape recorder whirred away. The director responded, but in abstract terms—nothing really specific. When I asked permission to interview some of the girls and some of the counselors, he absolutely refused. Invasion of privacy. . . . I went home, transcribed my notes, and figured that was that.

A couple of months later, the *Los Angeles Times* did a series on the terrible conditions at Juvenile Hall, a detention facility for delinquent teens, held there until their court hearings. The *Times* also did a series on runaways. My interest revived. One day, I phoned the Hollywood police station (where many runaways are brought) and arranged to interview a police officer who deals with these young people. The interview helped me understand police procedure and gave me a profile of the kids themselves.

Next step was to bone up on the subject. I went to the library and read every magazine article on runaways written during the previous two years. I learned where they ran to, the facilities for helping these children, why they ran, and so on. The more I read, the more interested and concerned I became. Finally, I called Juvenile Hall and was given a guided tour by the PR people. I saw the schoolrooms, the buildings and cells, the holding room, and learned about their daily schedules. I returned another day to attend hearings where children and parents faced the judge, and where the judge decided what was to be done with the child.

I came home from these visits eager to get to the typewriter, and quickly wrote the first two chapters of my book. The book opens in Juvenile Hall. I could describe the room Vicki was in, because I had seen it. I knew what classes she might have attended, and took her down the halls to the courtroom, where, by the end of chapter two the judge decrees that she will be placed in Lavender Lane Cottage, and warns she had better shape up or next stop for her will be Sybil Brand, a hardcore prison.

Now, I was stuck. What goes on in Lavender Lane Cottage, I had to know. I started phoning around to all the homes in the Los Angeles area where delinquent teen-agers were placed. To four calls, the answer was No; it would invade the girls' privacy. But on the fifth call, I hit a possible. Vista del Mar's director said he'd at least "talk" to me, and "see." I went down to Vista and showed the director several of my books and told him what I hoped to achieve. Finally he said, "O.K. You can have dinner with the girls in Cottage B. But you are not to ask them any direct questions about themselves."

A foot in the door. I was delighted. I went to the cottage the next evening as uptight as a spy in the enemy camp. The housemother introduced me, and I told the girls why I had come, what I hoped to learn from them. The girls were polite, but unrevealing. During dinner they talked freely—about washing their hair, the latest movie they had seen, but of nothing that showed me how they felt or thought.

After dinner, two of the girls asked if I'd be willing to read their poetry. I went into their room, read the poetry, and commented on it. Then I said, "Will you do me a favor now? Will you listen to these two chapters of my book and tell me what *you* think?"

I read them the chapters, and from that moment on, I was their friend. They identified with my character completely, saying, "That's just how it was for me in Juvie! That's just how I felt!" And they opened up to me then, telling me all the things I needed to know.

Again and again, I returned to visit, taking along new chapters as they were written, and asking more questions. I interviewed their housemother, their social workers, and their counselors. I went to a local high school and spoke with the school counselor about the special problems the teachers had with these girls. As an example, quite in passing, the high school counselor remarked that often a runaway, because she has attended school so irregularly, among other reasons, has a very poor self-image. When she returns to school, she's likely to link up with the problem kids at school, the drug users and troublemakers. I used this truth in my book.

When my main character, Vicki, first comes to the home, all she wants is to run away again. At school, she becomes involved with a boy who can only hurt her further. By the end of the book, through a nursing course she takes at school which gives her a sense of worth, she gains enough self-esteem to consider a relationship with a much nicer young man.

This, then, explains how a middle-aged woman like me, whose children have already moved on to college, can remain in touch with the teen-ager with problems.

In working on my present book, I've used much the same method of gathering information. I read all I could find about rape, its victims and their problems. Last year, I joined a rape hot line so I could understand the problems of the rape victim better, and perhaps gain firsthand contact with some. Through the hot line, and through police vice squad contacts, I've interviewed in-depth three victims, and would like to speak with even more so I can incorporate in my one character the universal problems and emotions.

Before I begin work on a book, I have two things firmly in mind. One, the story problem. This can always be put into the form of a question. In *Runaway,* it was: Will Vicki finally find a better way to deal with her life than running away? In my present book, the question is: Will Andrea be able to absorb the trauma she has experienced and face life with confidence again?

The second thing I need to know is the theme, the message I'm sending the reader. I've already mentioned the themes of several of my books. Sometimes, to be sure I don't stray from my story question and theme, I type them up and scotch tape them to the top of my typewriter.

Unlike some writers who can plan ahead, chapter by chapter, what they will do, I have only the vaguest notion of what will happen next. I do know the beginning, and I have a fair idea of how I'll develop the end, but what happens in between doesn't come to me until I'm at the typewriter and the characters take me where they're going. It's agony when the characters seem to be asleep, and you want them to wake up and *do* something, *say* something, *think* something. But, when they do wake up and take over your subconscious, it's magic, because the words just flow out through your fingers to the typewriter, and when you read them back, you can't imagine where they came from.

Finally, each chapter, like a single brick in a wall, builds a little more of the story, until the book is done and the wall is neatly in place, each brick complementing the one beside it, creating an effect of unity, grace, and—one hopes—beauty.

Now, how will you sell it? Some time before the book is done, when I'm sure I can pull all the strands together, I query. My query tells the editor the book's title, length, and audience, the story question and theme, and gives an enticing summary of its contents. I enclose a self-addressed stamped post card on which I type the name of the publisher to whom I sent the query, and list two choices: "I'd love to see your book," or "Thanks, but no. Maybe next time." One publisher crossed out the word "love" and made it "like." He wrote, "Maybe I'll change it to love after reading it." If you do not receive a response to your query within three weeks, query another publisher. My experience has been that the "yes" answers come within about two weeks. Editors not interested in a manuscript of mine often take up to two months to respond.

When you get a yes on a query, ship off the book manuscript addressed to the editor who requested it, marking your envelope, *Manuscript Requested,* so it by-passes all the sub-editors and goes direct to the editor who asked to see it. Then, get busy on another book. If it doesn't sell to the first publisher, try the next and the next. Don't be discouraged, and don't let a rejection, even a nasty one, destroy you. Maybe the editor had a fight with her husband that day, or maybe she had missed her analyst that week, or maybe her job was shaky and she was taking it out on you.

Finally, I encourage all of you who really care about young people and who have something to say to them to write for that market. It's a big market and growing, especially for paperback originals. And there's room in it for all of us.

77

WRITING FOR YOUNG CHILDREN

By Charlotte Zolotow

CHILDREN's book writing includes fiction for children from picture books on up to the young adults, non-fiction—biography, autobiography and factual books—and of course poetry. In short, it includes every category of adult writing that exists, and everything that is true of distinctive writing for adults is also true of fine literature for children.

But there is in writing for children an additional skill required. It is easier to address our peers than those who are different from ourselves. And children are different from adults because they live on a more intense level. Whatever is true of adults is true of children, only more so. They laugh, they cry, they love, they hate, they give, they take as adults do—only more so. And this is what makes writing for children different from writing for adults.

One must first of all, over and above everything, take children seriously and take writing children's books seriously. Over and over I have met people who feel that writing for children is a first step to doing "something really good." A fairly successful, but undistinguished author of many children's books said to me one night, "Some day I'm going to do something really good. I'm going to write a novel or a play."

What this gentleman's abilities as an adult writer will be, I don't know. His children's books, however, lack something. There is nothing in them that would make a child put one down and say, "What else has this person written?" (A question children have asked many times after first reading a book by Ruth Krauss, Maurice Sendak, Else H. Minarik, Laura Ingalls Wilder, Margaret Wise Brown, E. B. White, Marie Hall Ets, E. Nesbit, P. L. Travers, Beatrix Potter— the great writers of children's literature.)

This remark of his made me understand why. *He doesn't respect what he is doing.* If he ever gets to his serious play or novel, it won't be that he came via children's books, but that he finally did take seriously what he was doing. I don't think writers of this sort should be writing for children at all. Children's books are an art in themselves and must be taken seriously. Anyone who regards them simply as a step along the way to "real" writing is in the wrong field.

I should make clear here that when I use the word *seriously* I don't mean *pompously*. I don't mean that every word is holy or that it should be heavy-handed. Some of the most delightful humor in books today is in the books for children. Some of the wildest kind of nonsense is there, too. But the writers are saying something seriously in their humor and in their nonsense—something that is real to them and meaningful to them—and they are saying it the best way they can without writing down to an audience whose keenness and perception they must completely respect.

There is a popular misconception about children's books that exists even among literate people. And it exists most particularly in the area of the picture book. A television writer once told me, "I never read my children what's in a picture book. I make up my own story to go with the pictures." He was quite pleased with himself—had no idea of the absurdity his smug assumption "that anyone can write a children's book" contained. He didn't realize that though his stories might amuse his own kids, delighted with the sound of his voice, the expression of his face, and the feeling of well-being his spending time with them gave them, a *published* story must be a finished, well-rounded work of art. In cold print, a story has to be good. The wandering, sketchy bedtime stories we tell our children have to be formed and shaped and sharpened before they can be printed, illustrated, bound in a book to be read over and over again to thousands of children who are strangers to the author's face and voice.

Some of my own books have indeed come out of stories I originally told my children, but years later, and after much thought, much reforming, reshaping, pruning, and in a voice or style that was a writer's, not a mother's. There is an immense difference.

In some picture books there are just a few words on a page. Certain immortal lyrics are four lines long. A sonnet has only fourteen lines. But the brevity doesn't mean they are "easy" to write. There is a special gift to making something good with a few words. The ability to conjure up a great deal just from the sound of a word and its relation to the other words in the sentence, the gift of evocation and denotation, is not only special to the poet but to children themselves. To say that he has had a good time at school that morning, a child may simply tell you, "The teacher wore a purple skirt." The recipient of this confidence would have to be close enough to the particular child to know that purple is her favorite color; that summing up a whole morning's events by that color is equivalent to having an adult say, "excellent wine"; that, in fact, in this child's vocabulary "purple" is a value judgment and the sign of a happy morning. And since children themselves so often use this oblique, connotative language, the writer who is fortunate enough to have retained his own childlike vision can speak to them in this special poetic shorthand that evokes worlds in a word.

A picture book writer must have this gift of using words carefully, of identifying with, understanding, projecting himself into the child's world. He must know and feel what they know and feel with some of the freshness of their senses, not his experienced adult ones. He must know what children care about a given situation. This is usually quite different from what an adult in a similar situation is thinking, wanting, seeing, tasting, feeling; and sympathy and empathy (and memory) are necessary, not condescension, not smugness, not superiority, not serious observation from an adult point of view.

And while the brevity of a picture book makes the author's use of words particularly selective, the rest of what I've said applies not only to picture books but to books going up in age group to the young adults. It is a question of experiencing at that particular level how the small or "middle-aged" child feels.

The best children's book writers are those who look at the world around them with a childlike vision—not childish, which is an adult acting like a child—but with that innocent, open vision of the world that belongs to the various stages of growing up, a clearer, more immediate, more specific, more honest, less judging vision than the adult one.

Children come fresher, with less cant, less hypocrisy, less guilt, to the world around them than even the most honest adults are apt to. Children smell good and bad things without inhibition. They taste, they hear, they see, they feel with all their senses and not so much interfering intellect as the adult, who will label things by applied standards, preconceived standards of good or bad—a good smell or a bad smell, a good taste or a bad taste. Children are realists of the first order. They have fewer preconceived ideas than adults. To them, flowers may smell bad. Manure may smell good. They have no fixed judgments yet. Most things are still happening to them for the first time. The first time water comes from a faucet, heat from a radiator, snow falls, the *real* itself is *magic*.

Because of this, children are open to belief in fantasy—fairies can exist if snow can fall, magic can happen if there are cold and heat, moon and stars and sun. Nothing is routine yet. They live more immediate lives than adults, not so much of yesterday or tomorrow. They are open to the moment completely. They respond to every detail around them completely. (That is why they are so often tiring to be with.)

I remember once the poet, Edwin Honig, came to visit us. He had never met our daughter Ellen, who was then four. They liked each other immediately. And when she offered to show him the house, he left his drink on the front porch and went off into the house with her. When I came in a few minutes later, he was holding her in his arms, and she was pointing into the living room.

"That is the fireplace where we have fires in winter.

That is the rubber plant where one leaf died.

That is the radio where we had the tube fixed.

That is the best chair but our dog sits in it." She might have invited him to see if he could smell the dog in the chair if I hadn't come in.

"You know," Honig said to me, "she's living everything here for me."

A poet could understand this. And in this sense that is what everyone who writes for children must be.

Always remember that the field of children's books is exciting and specialized. It is full of pitfalls that adult writing is free from, not the least of which is that a child's point of view is so different from that of an adult—more different at three than at six, and more so at six than at nine. And even when the child and adult reaction is identical—at any age level—in being hurt, in wanting, in hating, in loving, it is more intense. Adults are like a body of water that has been dammed up, or channeled. Children haven't these constrictions yet on their emotions. They abandon themselves to emotion, and therefore everything from a cake crumb to an oak tree means more to them.

If you are to write for children, you must be absolutely honest with yourself and with them. Willa Cather once advised a young writer never to hold back on any idea or phrase when it fitted something he was writing, in the hope of using it later in something better. Never hold back on what fits the book you are writing for children either. Remember how you felt about things when you were a child; remember, remember that adults might laugh and say, "tomorrow he'll forget," but right then, at the moment, the child feels and believes in his pain or his joy with his whole being.

Ursula Nordstrom, director of children's books at Harper and Row, has, I think, discovered more wonderful children's writers than anyone. "Young people can and will accept the very best truly creative people will give them," she says. And in a recent *New Yorker* article about Maurice Sendak, one of the finest children's book artists and writers today, she said, "Too many of us . . . keep forgetting that children are new and we are not. But somehow Maurice has retained a direct line to his own childhood."

This is what anyone who wants to write for children must do.

78

NOVELS FOR TEEN-AGERS

By Hope Dahle Jordan

IF I'D hesitated over the beginning of my fiction as I have backed away from the first paragraph of this piece on the writing of that fiction, I never, never would have completed my seven novels for young adults, nor all my short stories (I've lost count there).

The problem is, I want to be honest—but to come right down to it, my working rules sound ridiculous when I put them on paper.

However, this past week I had a prompting experience that was a piece of pure luck. I walked into the public library for the armful of books I take out every week, and at one of the tables I saw a lovely young girl absolutely lost to all else in a book she held upright before her eyes. It gave me a strange feeling to see her absorbed in my *Haunted Summer* and to know that what I had conceived could be so interesting that it blotted out the world. Naturally, I circled her several times. I dawdled over the selection of what I wanted from the shelves. She seemed scarcely to breathe. Not once did she lift her eyes.

I recalled the librarian who, when I was writing short fiction for *Seventeen* and similar magazines, asked me why I didn't write books that would be warm and loving, but not lathered with sex, and that would make young readers say, "I couldn't put it down."

I must be doing something right, I thought.

I was lucky. Yet it hasn't been luck alone that's put my books on the library shelves. It's been persistence to the point of doggedness, it's been a powerful curiosity about what makes people tick, and constant study.

Study, study. I read every book I can find on what motivates people. Why do they behave the way they do? I am fascinated by biography and the revelation of character. Sometimes it's a book of philosophy which strikes a spark.

And, constantly, I am searching for writing which I wish I'd written. It's not uncommon for me to read a particularly successful chapter of a book a number of times before going on with the book. I X-ray it. What are the bones of the plot? How does the author put flesh on the bones? Why is he/she getting such complete cooperation from me, the reader?

I must have read every book written on "how to write," and they've been good guides. They've helped me to pick myself up when I've stumbled. But it took me years to learn that the art of writing is largely self-taught. There are no shortcuts, no formulas, and above all no tricks. There are no absolutes, no tangibles that one writer can communicate to another.

You've heard this often: A writer becomes a writer by writing.

It also took me a time to learn that I could write and publish only what I might like to read. Ask yourself questions. If it's fiction you're interested in, do you read to "lose yourself"? Do you feel there is a starkness about life without illusions? Or isn't there a loss of flavor for you, when romance is canceled out by constant reality?

Another thing I had to learn: All writing gets harder and harder as the writer becomes more and more practiced. No writer I know has ever discovered a way of making his life easier. However, if you work out a daily routine, that helps.

My personal, elementary rule sounds ludicrous even to me. Nevertheless, I am deadly serious when I insist it is the *only* one I conscientiously adhere to: I don't dress for the day until two pages (500 words) are written, and acceptable—to me. That is the only way I get a book finished. For as long as I stay in my blue bathrobe I stay at my typewriter.

Some writers maintain that they are at their best late at night. Not I. If I don't get started in the mornings, I won't write all day. Not even if there are open hours for it in the afternoon. Yet when I do get at it in the mornings, I often drift back to my desk between other tasks during the day, and type automatically. My writing seems to be stored in my mind; I work at the hard part of it while I'm doing other things.

Another rule: be alone in the house.

I use a card table, not my desk, and set it up before the window with the view where, isolated, I can watch the children going to school, and the milkman and the mail truck and the joggers and the cyclists. I'm alone—but there's a feeling of people. Solitude—but not the kind that drives you nearly crazy.

No electric typewriter for me. I like my old portable. I don't let anybody else use it, or it would fall apart. I have this feeling—we're such old friends it does part of my thinking.

Now that I'm writing novels for teen-age girls instead of short fiction, I have a seasonal schedule in addition to the daily one. My schedule begins the day after Labor Day, as if I were going to school.

Of course, my new novel is in my subconscious during the summer, but I don't begin making notes or getting serious about it until September. For a few weeks I become acquainted with the young woman who will become the main character and who will help me (I hope) write my story. Because the weather is too beautiful for me to tie myself to my desk yet, I live my working hours roaming, alone with her, in the car. Again, I aim for a creative solitude, surrounded by people who won't be talking to me.

I drive to one of the suburban libraries where I am a stranger, and here I do the research that may be necessary for my winter's book. I take her along. Sometimes I park under the trees alongside the pitch-and-putt golf course filled with senior citizens. Or I walk in the zoo, or attend one of the open practices of the symphony. I take her along.

I am with other people, but I am alone with my friend of the coming winter. By this time she has acquired a name which pleases me, which seems a natural for one with the basic trait (stubbornness? an intense need for appreciation? a tease? a loser?) which will put her in conflict with the others in my book. She must be likable, but nobody likes perfection in others, so she isn't perfect.

I never go anywhere with her—never—without taking along a pen and small pad for one-word or one-paragraph memory-prodders which I'll use when I get back to my typewriter. I don't keep a notebook anymore because I'd rather use the time for writing.

But I jot down key words, for by this time my character and I are having long conversations with each other, more real to me than real life. I begin to know what her background is, and in my novels this is important, because my particular readers must be able to imagine themselves there. (Never again will I set a story in a school; they have enough of that without reading about it, too.)

I have always maintained that I don't outline. That isn't correct. I don't outline on paper, but in my mind I have settled on the beginning and the end of the story before I start it, and I know many of the high points along the way. Invariably I have the title. When the opening paragraph, then the first page, are written to my satisfaction, it almost seems as if half the book is done.

The first third of the novel is a struggle. Inch by inch, I work to bring Sarah-Martha alive (or Jill, or Rilla, etc.)—not by telling what she looks like, and wears, and says (which date a book), but by showing her reactions to her life and family.

After Christmas, when there's usually too much snow to go out anyway, I don't mind sitting alone at my typewriter day after day. Because I know where I'm going in my novel, it moves along at a fast pace. I hardly have to revise the plot or story line, but I do edit conversations which sound repetitious. Also, I have found I have a tendency to put what should be the last half of a sentence first.

Along about February, I begin to have insomnia. I am positive I can't finish. The soft belly of the story seems to develop a paunch. To cure this, I overcomplicate my young friends's life. Then I cut—cut—cut.

It always surprises me when it's time to write The End. By this time, I know Sarah-Martha so well that I could live with her for weeks more. Yet this particular chapter in her life is over.

However, while I'm still in the swing of her story, I begin to revise the very next day. Therefore, I have the last clean draft ready to send to the publisher before the heat and humidity come to Wisconsin.

Having written several books, I receive many letters from readers who ask questions about my writing methods, etc. The most common question is, where do you get your ideas? I know definitely where I found the seed for Sarah-Martha's story, my last published novel (*Stranger in Their Midst*). In the center of an Illinois town I pass through whenever I drive to visit my daughter there is a large, picturesque, cumbersomely remodeled church. For years, as I've waited for the red light to turn green, I've been intrigued by it. It occurred to me you could hide in that church forever, right in the heart of town, and nobody would ever find you.

I recalled the secretary in our own church saying she was uneasy when she worked alone in the big edifice. I knew what she meant. There were unexplainable noises and strange door-bangings.

452 THE WRITER'S HANDBOOK

Suppose I put Sarah-Martha, much against her will, in that church on a summer job? Suppose out of contrariness she hides somebody. For days—for weeks—until she, too, loses the person she's been hiding. Strange things could happen in that church. Who'd be guilty—the person she's hiding?

Who in the world is she hiding? Every time I traveled to Illinois, I hid somebody else in that church. But I had no story until I happened to pass through a South Dakota city about the time it had a destructive flood. I thought, I'll move the church to a spot where there's a flood. Suddenly I had so many possible plots it was confusing.

My next problem was to find somebody who'd lived through a flood. I couldn't. So I went to four different libraries, read everything listed under FLOOD and made notes about whatever struck me emotionally. I combined details from dozens of floods into mine. When I sent the manuscript to New York my editor wrote: "My, you must have lived through a dreadful experience."

The idea of my novel *Supermarket Sleuth* came from a conversation I overheard between a supervisor for J.C. Penney's and an A & P manager about shoplifting compared to employee theft.

Haunted Summer started from a short newspaper article about a youth who had hit somebody with his car, carried the victim to a hospital and then run. What made him run? What was his life like with that episode on his mind, for he must have been a responsible person to react by going to the hospital first?

Another common question from readers: Is this *you* in your book?

I really don't know the answer. I could say "yes" or I could say "no" and be truthful. I don't consciously put myself into a novel. However, to understand with sympathy a trait which motivates the main character, I suppose I must have something of that trait in me too.

Does that mean I'm stubborn? Overly dependent? Contrary? Painfully secretive? Taken together, my characters make me sound impossible. Oh, dear, the things you learn about yourself if you write!

79

NEW TRENDS IN CHILDREN'S BOOKS

By Eve Bunting

I WENT to my dictionary for the meaning of "contemporary." It said "contemporary" meant "living, existing or occupying together in time." Then I asked one of my children what the word meant. He thought for a minute and said, "Contemporary? That's what's happening, baby!" There's the difference. The first definition is accurate. The second is contemporary!

What's happening today has always happened. There are people who hate each other and love each other. There are frightened people, confused people, happy people. But there are problems today that seem to be specifically of today. Perhaps because they are more widespread. Or perhaps because these days we are more willing to look at them, to face up to them.

We have children on drugs. Alcoholic children. Children with alcoholic parents. We probably always had those. But little Teresa used to wait outside in the snow while inside the tavern drunken old Dad drank away the grocery money. Little Teresa didn't go to Alateen and learn for herself how to cope with and live with drunken old Dad. Today we have children involved in their parents' divorces. We have child abuse, child molestation, runaways, pregnant girls. We have rape, and girls making life-and-death decisions to have or not to have abortions. We have brainwashed children joining strange and bizarre sects. Children are being used in pornography in magazines that cater to a select, sick audience. Young people are asking themselves if perhaps they are homosexual—and there is even some experimentation.

The list could go on. It almost makes one long for the good old days when all the reader had to worry about was if Laura and her family would enjoy living in the Little House on the Prairie as much as in The Little House in the Big Woods, or vice versa. But like it or not, these are things that are happening in today's world. Closing one's eyes does not make problems vanish. And there is always the rationale that it may make it easier for a child to know that another child has the same problem. It may make him say, "This is how he handled his misery. I can learn to handle mine."

I read a lot of books and I write a lot of books. I'd like to share with you my findings.

There are many new children's mysteries being written. There are lots of new sports books, though, to be sure, a good many of them deal with contemporary sports such as skateboarding, hang gliding, frisbeeing, soccer (which is new here if not in many other countries).

There are tales of high adventure—though now the adventure is as likely to take place on a U.F.O. or in another galaxy as on the Cay or on the Island of the Blue Dolphins. All of which leads one to believe that children still enjoy a plain, good old read!

There are also lots of books that involve themselves in today's problems; i.e., the recent proliferation of child abuse books: Irene Hunt's *The Lottery Rose;* Marilyn Sachs's *December Tale;* Willo Davis Roberts's *Don't Hurt Laurie;* Marion Dane Bauer's *Foster Child,* in where there is sexual molestation under the guise of religion.

Another currently "in" subject is death: *May I Cross Your Golden River?* by Paige Dixon; *Tuck Everlasting,* by Natalie Babbitt, and some nonfiction, such as Eda LeShan's *Learning to Say Goodbye.*

A couple of years ago it was homosexuality.

A year or so before that it was teen-age pregnancy. *My Darling, My Hamburger* (Paul Zindel); *Mr. and Mrs. Bo Jo Jones* (Ann Head).

There have been and are lots of orphans, foster children, disturbed children.

As authors of children's books today, we have opportunities we've never had before to write what we want to write. Nothing is taboo, or almost nothing. And the positive results we can achieve are staggering. No more is "retarded" a dirty word. In *He's My Brother* (Joe Lasker) we are given the story of a loving relationship between two children, one of whom is retarded. In *Let the Balloon Go,* Ivan Southall tells of a spastic boy who learns that before a balloon can truly be a balloon, someone has to let go of the string. He allows himself to let go of his own restraints and soar, like the balloon. There is *Ben and Annie* (Joan Tate), a book about best friends. One of them just happens to be a cripple in a wheelchair. In *Whales to See the* (Glendon Swarthout and Kathryn Swarthout), a group of autistic children inadvertently find themselves sharing the adventure with a group of "normal" children. And guess which group learns more about sharing and loving and understanding as they go to see the whales?

Yes, we are saying to children, there are other children who are different. But they are still the same. They have value. They are special and wonderful. We are all, indeed, "Free to Be You and Me."

I don't believe that authors jump on a subject for sensationalism. I think we write about these things because they are there. Or here, I should say. Because they are "what's happening."

A teacher recently said to me, "It's amazing how the subject matter in children's books comes in waves. This year we have this. Last year we had that. It must be that the thought vibrations pass through the atmosphere, and all of you pick them up."

I nodded and managed to look mysterious. But of course there is nothing mysterious or mystical about it. I know why it happens, and I'm sure you do, too. Authors have inquiring minds. We read and assimilate. I devour the *Los Angeles Times* and the *Pasadena Star News* and *Time* and the *Christian Science Monitor.* I'm not above the *National Enquirer* either. There's some pretty neat stuff in the *National Enquirer!*

Authors have trained themselves to look for ideas. Or perhaps it comes naturally. Perhaps that's why we're authors in the first place. Because everything sparks an idea. We see stars where others see only darkness. Often I'm astonished to find that all my writer friends have clipped and saved the same items from the papers at the same time!

I can spot a trend long before it comes. It's there, on the pages of the morning paper. As a matter of fact, we're bombarded with it by all phases of the media. Reporters pontificate. "Sixty Minutes" runs a special report. We find little snatches of it on radio talk shows. I don't necessarily feel qualified to handle whatever the new trend may be. Nor do I always want to. But often I do.

I would definitely say that 90% of my story seeds come from something I've read in my daily paper or in my weekly periodical. I take that seed and plant it in my conscious mind—maybe in my subconscious one too—and I let it germinate. I nurture it with lots of thinking time, often in the bathtub or before I go to sleep. After a time it begins to sprout. Now, this is the time to know not to grab. Leave it alone. Let it gather strength. If I yank at it, I'm going to pull it out, roots and all. When it's ready, I can take it and prune off all those shoots I don't need and transplant it from my head on to the paper.

And because 90% of my ideas come from reports of current news and the other 10% from what I see happening around me, I guess what I write has to be contemporary.

In the past two or three years I have written and sold many books with contemporary characters, settings, and themes:

One More Flight tells of a boy who is running away from a care center. He has run away so often that if he's caught this time he'll be sent to Juvenile Hall. Dobby is a foster child, a disturbed child, a runaway. He envies, he hates, he reaches out to belong. He is one of today's unfortunates.

Ghost of Summer is set in contemporary Northern Ireland with its political upheaval, its senseless hatreds and killings in the name of religion. In it I tried to draw a parallel between the problems there and the racial problems in the United States.

Going Against Cool Calvin tells of a gang of young boys who beat up illegal aliens as they come across the border from Mexico, on the beach by Tijuana. I read in the newspaper about an illegal alien, a Mexican teen-ager, who was on the beach on the United States side. He was arrested when he came out of hiding to rescue an American boy who was in danger of drowning. The story seed was planted in my mind. I went down to the beach and talked to border patrol officers. I saw the place where the rescue took place. Then I took pictures so I would have no trouble visualizing the locale exactly when the time came to begin writing. The book sold to the first place to which I sent it.

Not long ago, I presented an idea to a publisher who bought it in less than a week on the strength of two chapters and an outline. It was called *Finders Keepers*. I had read about two children who found money packed into an old tin can. It was a lot of money, probably more than they'd ever seen in one lump sum in their lives. They turned it over to the police. *Two* children? Did they discuss what to do? I wondered. Did one want to turn it in and one want to keep it? Did they hide it first, and look at it, and think of all the things it could buy? I knew I had the beginnings of a story, a contemporary story—contemporary because in times past the outcome would have been apparent: virtue would naturally triumph. Good children didn't keep what didn't belong to them. The temptation would be fleeting at best. Today we are more realistic. If we write about "what's happening," the child protagonist must be allowed to have weaknesses, to be human. Perhaps even to succumb to temptation—for good reason.

Cop Camp tells of a kid from the ghetto who likes to hassle the police and what happens when he goes to a camp run by cops and faces the doubts that arise from his inherent distrusts and his new-found awareness that cops are people. That there are good ones and bad ones. I read about a particular camp which was set up to let cops and problem kids become better acquainted. I went to police headquarters and talked to one of the officers who'd helped run the camp the year before. Again, I sent off an outline and a first chapter, and the book sold by return mail, literally.

All of this proves that editors are searching for contemporary stories. Write one, a good, meaty one that doesn't exploit a situation, but, rather, uses it to strengthen the story, and you will have a salable book. And I want to emphasize, too, that the educational houses are wide open for contemporary novels.

What then is the contemporary novel? I believe when we speak of it we are simply saying, "Tell a good story. Tell it as well as possible. Make sure the protagonist is believable to today's children...*is* a today's child. Make sure the language is today's, the setting, the feeling. Don't be too leisurely in the telling." If we look at books that were popular in times past, we can see that they get off to a start that is much too slow for our television-oriented generation.

Be aware.

Be honest. By this I don't mean only that we should always do careful research. I mean, be true to yourself.

If homosexuality disgusts you, don't try writing about it sympathetically. Your disgust will ooze through.

If you don't like today's children, truly like them for their guts and independence and their own special integrity, don't write about them. Write about dogs. Or locomotives. Or cobwebs. Or plutonium. Leave the kids alone.

Don't try to fool the reader that you really dig those nice, noisy dirt bikes if indeed you can't stand them. Don't pretend to admire what you despise. Don't decide that in spite of your disgust you'll go ahead anyway and write the hippest book of the season because that's what's selling. It won't work. You'll write a bad book. Editors are smart. They'll see through it and you.

When I was watching television recently, the guest on the program was Alexandra Sheedy who wrote *She Was Nice to Mice*. Alexandra is very young. I think she may be fifteen years old. She is composed and articulate and has a lot of self-confidence. The host on the show asked her who was her favorite author, and she promptly said, "Judy Blume. She remembers the way it was for her when she was young. And I say, 'Hey! That's the way I feel too.'" I'm paraphrasing Alexandra's words, because I didn't have a paper and pencil right there when I needed it—a terrible admission for an author to make! But that, in essence, was what she said.

So in the end, I guess, that's what it's all about: remembering how it was, and telling it the way it is.

80

STORYTELLING: THE OLDEST AND NEWEST ART

By Jane Yolen

SOME time ago I received one of those wonderful letters from a young reader, the kind that are always signed mysteriously "Your fiend." This one had an opening that was an eye-opener. It read:

Dear Miss Yolen:
I was going to write to Enid Blyton or Mark Twain, but I hear they are dead so I am writing to you...

Of course I answered immediately—just in case. After all, I did not want that poor child to think that all the storytellers were dead. Because that was what the three of us—Enid Blyton, Mark Twain, and Miss Yolen—had in common. Not style. Not sense. Not subject. Not "message or moral." The link was clear in the child's mind just as it was in mine. Blyton, Twain, and Yolen. We were all storytellers.

Nowadays most of the storytellers *are* dead. Instead, we are overloaded with moralists and preachers disguised as tale tellers. Our medium has become a message.

So I want to talk to you today about the art of and the heart of storytelling; about tales that begin, go somewhere, and then end in a satisfying manner. Those are the tales that contain their own inner truth that no amount of moralizing can copy. The Chinese, the *New York Times* reported in 1968, were recruiting "an army of proletarian storytellers" who were ordered to fan out into the countryside and "disseminate the thoughts of Chairman Mao." They told the kind of stories that end: "As a result, the evil wind of planting-more-watermelons-for-profit was checked." These tales waste no time in getting their message across. But they are sorry excuses for stories. As Isaac Bashevis Singer has said: "In art, truth that is boring is not true."

Storytelling may be the oldest art. The mother to her child, the hunter to his peers, the survivor to his rescuers, the priestess to her

459

followers, the seer to his petitioners. They did not just report, *they told a tale.* And the better the tale was told, the more it was believed. And the more it was believed, the truer it became. It spoke to the listener because it spoke not just to the ears but to the heart as well.

These same stories speak to us still. And without the story, would the tale's wisdom survive?

The invention of print changed the storyteller's art, gave it visual form. Since we humans are slow learners, it took a while to learn that the eye and ear are different listeners. It took a while to learn the limits and the limitlessness of two kinds of tellers—the author and the illustrator—in tandem. And it has taken us five centuries, dating from Gutenberg, to throw away the tale at last.

Children, the last audience for the storytellers who once entertained all ages, are finding it hard to read the new stories. Their literature today is full of realism without reality, diatribes without delight, information without incantation, and warning without wisdom or wit. And so the children—and the adults they grow into—are no longer reading at all. The disturbing figure I heard only last month is that 48% of the American people read no book at all in the past five years.

And so I dare. I dare to tell tales in the manner of the old storytellers. I do not simply retell the old tales. I make up my own. I converse with mermaids and monsters and men who can fly, and I teach children to do the same. It is the only kind of teaching I allow in my tales.

What of these stories? There is a form. First, a story has a beginning, an opening, an incipit. Sometimes I will use the old magical words "Once upon a time." Sometimes I vary it to please my own ear:

Once many years ago in a country far to the East....

There was once a plain but goodhearted girl....

In ancient Greece, where the spirits of beautiful women were said to dwell in trees....

Once on the far side of yesterday....

In the time before time, the Rainbow Rider lives....

Once upon a maritime, when the world was filled with wishes the way the sea is filled with fishes....

But always a story begins at the beginning. That is surely a simple thing to remember. Yet my husband begins reading any book he picks up in the middle and, if he likes it, he will continue on. He says it does not matter where he begins, with modern books—and he is right. If stories and books no longer start at the beginning, why should the reader? And if, as Joyce Cary says, "... reading is a creative art subject to the same rules, the same limitations, as the imaginative process...," then a story that begins in the middle and meanders around and ends still in the middle encourages that kind of reading.

Now I am not saying that a story has to move sequentially in time to have a beginning. One does not have to start with the birth of the hero or heroine to start the story at the beginning. Still, there must be a reason, a discernible reason, for starting a tale somewhere and not just the teller's whim. The person who invented the words "poetic license" should have his revoked.

What of the story's middle? First it should not be filled with middle-age spread. But also, it should not be so tight as to disappear. Do you remember the nursery rhyme:

> I'll tell you a story
> About Jack O'Nory,
> And now my tale's begun.
> I'll tell you another
> Of Jack and his brother,
> And now my tale is done.

Where is the middle of that story? It should be the place in the tale that elicits one question from the reader—*what then*? The middle is the place that leads the reader inevitably on to the end.

Is that not a simple task? I run a number of writers' groups and conferences, and all persuasions of writers have passed through. There are the naive novices who think that children's books must be easier to write because they are shorter and the audience less discriminating. There are the passable writers, almost-pros who have had a story or two published in religious magazines and are ready to tackle a talking animal tale or—worse—a talking prune story where inanimate objects converse on a variety of uninteresting subjects. And there are the truly professional writers whose combined publications make a reasonable backlist for any publishing company. And they all have trouble with the middles of stories.

The problem is one of caring. Too few writers today care enough about storytelling. If they should happen in the throes of "inspiration" to come upon a beginning and an ending, then they simply link the two together, a tenuous lifeline holding two climbers onto a mountain.

Of course the middle *is* the mountain. It is the most important part of the book, the tale, the story. It is where everything important occurs. Perhaps that is why so few people do it well.

What of the end? Ecclesiastes says: "Better is the end of a thing than the beginning thereof." An overstatement perhaps. But if the end is not *just* right, and is not filled with both inevitability and surprise, then it is a bad ending.

Adults are quite willing to forgive bad endings. I saw only recently a review of an adult book that said, in essence, the ending is silly, unconvincing, and weak, but the book is definitely worth reading. Children will not forgive a weak ending. They demand a rounding off, and they are very vocal in this demand. I remember reading a story of mine in manuscript to my daughter, then age seven. It was a tale about three animals—a sow, a mare, and a cow—who, tired of men and their fences, decided to live together. When I finished reading, with great feeling and taking the dialogue in special voices, I looked up at my audience of one. She looked back with her big brown eyes.

"Is that all?" she asked.

"Well, that's all in this story," I said, quickly adding "Would you like another?"

She tried again. "Is that all that happens?"

"Well, they just...I mean they...yes, that's all."

She drew in a deep breath. "That *can't* be all," she said.

"Why?" I asked, defeated.

"Because if that's all, it's not a story."

And she was right. I have not yet worked out a good ending for that story, though I am still trying. G.K. Chesterton noted this about fairy tale endings, which are sometimes bloodier than an *adult* can handle. He wrote: "Children know themselves innocent and demand justice. We fear ourselves guilty and ask for mercy."

But lots of stories can still have a beginning, a middle, and an end and not be right. If they are missing that "inner truth," they are nothing. A tale, even a small children's tale filled with delight, is still saying something. The best stories are, in Isak Dinesen's words, "a statement of our existence." Without meaning, without metaphor, without reaching out to touch the human emotion, a story is a pitiable thing; a few rags upon a stick masquerading as life.

I believe this last with all my heart. For storytelling is not only our oldest art, it is our oldest form of religion as well; our oldest way of casting out demons and summoning angels. Storytelling is our oldest form of remembering; remembering the promises we have made to one another and to our various gods, and the promises given in return; of recording our human-felt emotions and desires and taboos.

The story is, quite simply, an essential part of our humanness.

81

WRITING THE PICTURE BOOK STORY

By Mary Calhoun

You want to write for children. Picture books. You tell stories to your children or the neighbor's children, and they just love your stories. *And this is good.* If you're telling stories, you already have the first qualification for writing picture books: You are a storyteller. The person who can spin a yarn is the golden one who will fascinate the four-to-eight-year-olds.

Then why aren't the publishers snapping up your stories and publishing them in beautiful four-color editions? Just what I wanted to know when I first started writing down the stories I'd told my boys. Rejection notes from editors commented:

"Too slight."

"Not original."

"We've used this theme several times."

"Too old for the age group."

I can't tell you all the reasons editors reject picture book scripts—such as "might encourage kids to make mess in the kitchen," "might encourage kids to try this and kill themselves." You'll just have to experience some of the rejections yourself. However, these are the general heart of why picture books are rejected:

"Not enough body and plot."

"Idea not big enough."

"Not ready to be a book."

"Things happen to the hero rather than he making things happen."

"Action too passive."

"Basic situation not convincing."

And over and over, "Too slight."

Sound familiar? Use the rejection list to check your stories—my compliments. The thing is, there's a lot more to writing for children than reeling off a story.

Now about picture books.

First, definitions: A picture book is one with pictures and a story to be read to or by a child between the ages of three and eight. (Publishers usually say four-eight, but many a "mature" three-year-old can enjoy having a picture book read aloud to him.)

Of course, there are other picture books for young children. For the two- and three-year-old there are the counting books, the ABC books, the "see-the-cat" books. There are picture books with a very slim text line, books conceived by the artists mainly for the sake of the art work. (No, you don't have to supply the artist for your story; the editor will do that.) There are the "idea" books: non-fiction— exploring "what is night?", "what is time?"—and such books as *A Hole Is to Dig* and *Mud Pies and Other Recipes,* charming ramblings on an idea, but not stories.

Here let's concern ourselves with the traditional picture book, one with a story from which the artist gains his inspiration for the pictures.

What goes into a picture book story?

As I see it, the elements are four: idea, story movement, style and awareness of audience.

First of all, the *idea.* Without a good idea, the writer is dead. Most often, I'd guess, a picture book script is rejected because the idea isn't good enough. What's a good idea? Make your own definition; I suppose each writer and editor does. I'd say, though, that basically the hero is vivid, the basic situation and the things that happen in the story are fascinating to a child. And generally there is a theme, some truth you believe, such as "you can master fear." Not a moral tacked onto the story, but the essence of the story, the hero and events acting out the theme.

How do you come by good ideas? Perhaps in the long run only heaven can help you, but it seems to me that primary is rapport with children—and a strong memory of your own childhood feelings and reactions.

"Tell me a story" many times a day keeps the old idea-mill grinding. Many of my picture book and magazine stories grew directly from contact with my children.

One day I hugged Greg, saying, "You're an old sweet patootie doll." "What's a patootie doll?" asked Greg, so I launched on a spur-of-the-moment tale. The theme was (I discovered after I'd written down the story) "know who you are and be glad for it." *The Sweet Patootie Doll* was first published in *Humpty Dumpty's Magazine* and later became my first published picture book.

A magazine story, "Cat's Whiskers", came into béing because Greg was always climbing into things and getting stuck—in buckets, under the porch, even in the washing machine. I coupled this with the idea that cats use their whiskers to measure whether they can get through openings; in the story the boy sticks broomstraws on his face for whiskers, and the story goes on.

However, here was a story idea too slight for a picture book. Not enough happened, really, and there was no real theme in the sense of a universal truth.

This brings us to a point valuable to beginning writers: If your story is rejected by book editors, try it on the children's magazines. The magazines have high standards, too, of course, but they can be your training ground and means of being published while you learn. It was my lucky day when a book editor said, "Not ready to be a book. Have you thought of sending it to a magazine?" My story, "Lone Elizabeth," went through many rewritings, but finally was published in *Humpty Dumpty's Magazine*. "Bumbershoot Wind" was termed "too slight" by a book editor but appeared in *Child Life*.

Actually, all of the elements of a story are tied into the idea, but let's go on to consider them in detail.

Story movement. I choose to call it this, rather than plot, for this suggests just what a story for children must do: move. Children like a story that trots right along, with no prolonged station-stops for cute conversation or description. Keep asking yourself (as the child does), "What happened next?"

In picture books there needs to be enough change of action or scenery to afford the artist a chance to make different pictures. Some stories are very good for telling aloud, but when you look at them on paper, you see that the scene hasn't changed much.

A book editor pointed this out for me on my "Sammy and the Something Machine." In this fantasy, Sammy makes a machine out of which come in turn mice, monkeys, mudpies, pirates and hot dogs. (It grew from my Mike's chant at play, "I'm making, I'm making!") This story went down on paper perfectly well in *Humpty*

Dumpty's Magazine, where there are fewer illustrations than in a picture book. But the scene doesn't change; there's that machine, over and over, turning out different things.

When your story is moving along vigorously, the scene changes will follow naturally—*if* the idea is storybook material. If the story moves but there's not much possibility for picture change (better let the book editors decide this), it may still be a fine story for some magazine.

Style. Of course, your style will be your own, and only you can develop it through writing and trying out and thinking about it and forgetting about it as you plunge ahead in the heat of telling a story.

The story content to some extent will indicate the style, that is, choice of words, length and rhythm of sentences. The story may hop joyously, laugh along, move dreamily, or march matter-of-factly. For study, you might read aloud folk tales and attune your ears to varieties in cadence: the robust, boisterous swing of a western folk tale; the rolling, measured mysticism of an Indian folk tale; the straightforward modern "shaggy dog" story; the drawling wry humor of the southern Negro folk tale.

If you already are telling stories to children, you're on your way to developing your style. However, "telling" on paper is slightly different from telling aloud, where the *effect* is achieved by a few judiciously chosen words and the swing of sentences.

I've had some success with one approach to the written story, and I've seen examples of it in other picture books. I call it "vividry." To me it's more vivid and succinct to say that than "vivid effect," and this explains what "vividry" is: words chosen with economy for their punch. For example, in a certain book I choose to say "little mummy mice." "Mummified mice" might be more proper, but to me it sounds textbookish. "Mummy mice" rolls off the tongue and seems a more direct idea-tickler for the child.

In college journalism courses, our bible was Rudolf Flesch's *The Art of Plain Talk.* From it we learned the value, in newspaper writing, of using sentences of short or varied length; strong verbs; short, strong nouns and many personal pronouns. Flesch might have been writing a style book for children's picture books.

We all know the delight in finding "the exact word" for a spot in a story. Never is this more effective than in children's books. Magazines for children generally have word-length requirements. Try putting a full-bodied story into 800 to 1,000 words. Every word counts. Writing for the magazines can be excellent training in choosing words and cutting out the lifeless ones.

I'm not saying, however, that big words have no place in a picture book script. Writing "controlled vocabulary" books for the young is a specialized art, and those books are used mostly by teachers and parents to stimulate a child's desire to read. Several book publishers now put out series of "easy-to-read" books. If you are interested in this field, read some of the books and query the editors on requirements. In the general picture book, though, I think children like to come upon an occasional delightfully new and big word. Haven't you seen a four-year-old trotting around, happily rolling out "unconditionally" or some other mouthful he's just heard? It's the *idea* of the story that the writer suits to the age group, not every given word in the story.

And this brings us to *awareness of audience*. I've mentioned rapport with children. If you're around them you know what they're thinking and wishing, what their problems are. And you'll know if a story idea is too old for the three-to-eight-year-olds or just plain wouldn't interest them.

With a small child underfoot or in tow, you see the details of the world that fascinate him: how a spot of sunlight moves on the floor; a cat's relationship with his tail (I used this one in "Tabbycat's Telltale Tail"); or the child's own shadow. (I haven't been able to make a good story of this; maybe you can.)

A child will watch a hummingbird moth at work in a petunia bed and report wisely, "He only goes to the red ones. White petunia must not taste good."

All of this, *plus awareness of the child's emotions, plus turning your mind back to remember how it was with you as a child,* tells you what to put into a picture book.

And then there's the other way to be aware of your audience: reading, reading all the good books and stories written for that age. Then you begin to see what has pleased children. You get the feel of what is suitable for that age group. You also see what has already been done, so that your own ideas can be fresh, not trite. You read "The Three Pigs," and the books about the Melops and you say to yourself, "Very well, but a story about a pig has never been told just in *this* way," and you start off on your own particular pig story. As you read (perhaps to a child to catch his reactions, too), you may begin to draw your conclusions of what is good in children's literature, what is slightly sickening, how the stories are put together, what has worked.

It has interested me, for instance, to notice how many of the traditional stories are built on what I call a "core of three." Three brothers, three mistakes, three attempts at a solution. "The Three Pigs" makes me wonder if the composer weren't slyly trying to see just how many times he could use three. Three pigs, three encounters with men carrying building materials, three houses visited by the wolf, "chinny-chin-chin," etc. In so many of the stories, the use of three attempts to solve the problem is effective in building intensity to the climax.

So there you have it: idea, story movement, style and awareness of audience. Study them, use them in your rewrites, let them sink into your subconscious.

And then don't worry about techniques as you tell the story. For the first, last and most important thing is: you must *like* the story! You're having a ball telling it. Right at this moment, it's the most wonderful story ever told to man or child.

That, finally, is what gives the story sparkle and makes editors say, "This will make a wonderful picture book!"

82

HUMOR IS PUBLISHABLE

By Richard Armour

Two of the hardest forms of writing to publish these days are poetry and fiction. But that doesn't disturb me the slightest, because I don't write either kind. Oh, I wrote some serious, even morbid, poetry when I was in high school. However, I got that out of my system, along with whatever was causing my acne, and never again wrote poetry in the manner of Ezra Pound, T.S. Eliot, or even Edgar A. Guest.

As for fiction, I once wrote a short story. In one of my rare flashes of wisdom, I tore it up. Not at once, of course, but after it came back from sixteen magazines, each time with a printed rejection slip and no encouragement whatsoever.

I admire writers of poetry and fiction. I think they write two of the highest forms of literary art and creativity. So I am sorry if this is a difficult time for publishing their work. I hope there is a change of taste, or whatever is necessary, and that poets and writers of short stories and novels will have their editors knocking at their doors or writing them begging letters: "Please send us something—anything."

But my bent, and with the passing years I am growing more bent than ever, is humor—humor which takes the form of light verse rather than poetry and light nonfiction rather than fiction. The way my mind works, or plays, is indicated by the fact that when I typed the word "difficult" in the paragraph above, it first came out "fiddicult." The word "fiddicult" so entranced me that I found it difficult, or fiddicult, to go on.

If you study the market lists in an inclusive and reliable reference work, such as *The Writer's Handbook,* you will encounter time after time such discouraging comments as "Most articles staff written," "Currently overstocked," "No fiction," "No poetry," "No unsolicited manuscripts considered," and "Query." But you will also find, if you look hard enough, "Humor," "Humorous pieces, 1,000 to 2,000 words," "Humorous or human-interest articles," "Satire, sophisticated humor," "Light treatment, lively, enjoyable style," and so on.

Or study the magazines themselves, as I do. Often I find a magazine that uses humor occasionally, in prose or verse, yet makes no mention of it in the brief description in a market list. Many times, over the years, I have come upon a magazine that seemed to me to need humor, but perhaps its editor was not aware that it did. I have tried prose or verse humor on such a magazine and occasionally have broken in, sometimes making the market my own. Thus I had a half page in a medical journal every month for twenty-three years. My record is a magazine used largely by public speakers, *Quote: The Weekly Digest,* for which I have written a feature every week, without fail, for thirty years.

So the markets for humor exist. They take more ferreting out than they did when I started to write, forty years ago. In those days I was writing for several magazines that no longer exist, such as *Liberty* and *Look,* and others that (I think mistakenly) have given up the humor that once livened their pages.

Now we come to the heart of the matter: writing humor that will sell. I should like to be methodical about this, perhaps even a little pedagogical, and so shall list the points I have in mind. Or rather, the points I *had* in mind, because now they are out of my mind, as I myself am often thought to be. (In fact, the most wide-ranging of my books of prose humor, selected from my writings in sixteen magazines, is entitled precisely that: *Out of My Mind.*)

1. It is as hard to make readers laugh as it is to make them cry. In other words, humor of marketable caliber is no easy literary form. Humor in verse (i.e. light verse), for instance, is more than a matter of writing something that rhymes. At its best, it is more rational, if not more intellectual, than much of today's serious poetry, and it is far more concerned with both the correctness and the tricks of technique. Rarely has successful, publishable light verse been written as free verse—without rhyme or meter. Don Marquis is one of the few who managed it. And rarely has it been published when it featured purposely bad meter and outrageous rhymes. Ogden Nash was a genius at parodying poetry and contriving original, unexpected rhymes —rhymes a serious poet would never use. But it would be risky to try to follow in Nash's nimble footsteps.

There is a reason for emphasis on technique in light verse. The serious poet has lofty thoughts and evocative imagery (metaphors, similes, personification, etc.). Lacking these, the light verse writer substitutes the various techniques of meter and rhyme, often trying to surprise.

2. If you wish to write publishable humor in the form of light verse, you must do a little homework, and domework. I have written the best how-to book on the subject. I can say this categorically because it is the *only* such book. (First published in 1947 and later updated, it was subsequently expanded and brought out as *Writing Light Verse and Prose Humor* by The Writer, Inc.) The light verse part goes into subject matter, rhymes, meters, length, openings and endings, titles, markets, and everything you had always wanted to know but were afraid to ask, or didn't know whom to ask, about this minor but exacting form of humor.

3. Or, still on the subject of marketable light verse, read, study, and analyze the works of the best published writers, past and present, of humorous writing. Go back to the work of such as Samuel Hoffenstein, Arthur Guiterman, F.P.A. (Franklin Pierce Adams), Dorothy Parker, Morris Bishop, David McCord, Ogden Nash, Margaret Fishback, and Phyllis McGinley. Phyllis McGinley, by the way, was the only light verse writer to win the Pulitzer Prize, in 1961, though by that time she had become what I would call a writer of light poetry.

4. Prose humor can take the form of either fiction or nonfiction. A short story can be light, even funny. It may even be wild, zany. But it may be merely playful, or have touches that give comic relief to what would otherwise be a serious piece. Humorous or light prose can go beyond the feature or magazine short story to the novel or even to the stage—or screen. There is always the wonderful possibility that a humorous piece can be the basis of a Broadway hit or a film with a major comic star like Woody Allen. You can dream, can't you? I hope you can, because that is one of the things that keeps a writer writing.

5. One further advantage of writing humor in prose is that it can be almost any length, whereas light verse must be kept short (usually four to twelve lines). A good marketable length for prose humor is around 1,200 words, but certain publications use humor pieces that run to about 3,000 words. Thus, a piece of prose humor can be more than a

filler. It can be a feature article that will be listed in the table of contents. This gives the writer more of a showcase than a humorous poem and may lead to bigger, if not better, things.

6. But let me come back to earth, or to the more immediately possible, in the marketing of humor. Since, as I have indicated, I am not a writer of fiction, I make use of humor in nonfiction. I do this in two ways: (1) I put a light touch into what might have been a serious article on some such subject as education, the family (and divorce), politics, inflation, aging, travel—just about anything. Or (2) I toy with some personal yet universal bit of trivia, such as plastic plants, paperclips, losing my glasses case, wire coat hangers, or my neighbor's leaves that suddenly became mine.

I have placed more-or-less humorous articles in the first category in *The Christian Science Monitor, The New York Times, Parents', Woman's Day,* the in-flight magazines of several airlines, and so on. I have found even more takers of the second type of short humorous articles, including "The Phoenix Nest" (formerly in the *Saturday Review* but now syndicated by the Associated Press), *Los Angeles* and other regional magazines, and *The Saturday Evening Post.*

7. For me, humor in book form has proved one of the most marketable types of writing. This includes humor in books for children. Let me say that I think the sense of humor, like the imagination, is livelier in children than in most adults. My books of humor, on many subjects, now number fifty-five. Forty of them were published by McGraw-Hill and twenty-two are also in paperback editions. Twelve are books for children. A book of humor, if original, timely, and highly polished (though the signs of effort should not show), is almost as publishable as a how-to book. And there is always the possibility of doing a humorous how-to book, which would bring you double rewards.

Despite what many say, humor is not dead. Maybe sick humor is, after getting more and more sickening, and that's all right with me. I try to write healthy humor, perhaps because I have a healthy respect for humor, and when I have written it I try to find a market for it. Usually, but not always, I do. I have to hunt harder than I once did, but I am a determined hunter. Perhaps I need a bird dog, or a word dog.

The world needs humor today and, fortunately, some editors are aware of this. All you have to do to get your humor published is to write publishable humor, and then find the right place for it. It is as simple as that. As a matter of fact, I once wrote, and published, an article on the so-called funny bone. What is funny about the funny bone is that there is nothing funny about it.

83

THE SPECIAL PROBLEMS OF SCIENCE FICTION

By Gene Wolfe

LIKE all fiction, science fiction rests on the four sturdy legs of theme, character, style, and plot. For practical purposes, it includes all stories and novels in which "the strange" is the dominant characteristic. Sf's particular problems result from the author's need to make this element —"the strange"—acceptable to the reader.

In the broadest sense, theme is the story's central concern. In a science fiction story, for example, the theme might be the effects of a system of embalming so improved that the dead could be distinguished from the living only with difficulty. (This was the theme of my story, "The Packerhaus Method," in which the chief character's father was proven dead only by the fact that he could not get his cigar to draw.) Notice that the theme has nothing to do with what *happens* to the characters. Theme is what the story is *about*.

In science fiction, it is imperative that the theme of each story be fresh or treated from a new angle: If the theme is not original or given a fresh treatment, it cannot be "strange." The most common—and the most disastrous—error beginning sf writers make is to assume that editors want more stories on the same themes as the ones they have already published. The writer reads the collected works of Isaac Asimov and Jack Williamson, for example, and tries to write a robot story like theirs. His story cannot be "like theirs" because their stories were fresh and original when they appeared; an imitation cannot be either.

On the other hand, it is still possible to write original robot stories. In "It's Very Clean," I wrote about a girl who posed as a robot because she could not find work as a human being. I like to think that was original. In "Eyebem," I wrote about a robot forest ranger, and in "Going to the Beach," I described an encounter with a robot streetwalker down on her luck.

The trick (and I think it one of the most difficult in writing) is to see things from a new angle. I have found three questions useful in stimulating sf story ideas.

The first is: *What if something new came along?* Think of something some people (not necessarily everyone) would like to have, and imagine that it has been invented. During the Vietnam War, for example, it occurred to me that the Pentagon would probably like to be able to grow soldiers in laboratory flasks. I added an almost inevitable near-future development, the unmanned, computer-controlled battle tank, and came up with a story called, "The HORARS of War." (This story originally appeared in the Delacorte collection *Nova 1,* edited by Harry Harrison, and as a Dell paperback; it has since been reprinted by Doubleday in *A Pocketful of Stars,* edited by Damon Knight, and was selected for reprinting again in Doubleday's *Combat-SF,* edited by Gordon Dickson. Many sf stories are reprinted—and paid for—repeatedly.)

The second idea-generator is: *What if it gets better?* Take some existing art, skill, or what-you-like, and imagine that some brilliant technician is to spend his life improving it. What will it be like when he is finished? What will the social consequences of his improvements be? *What if it gets better?*—was the source of my "The Packerhaus Method." A less macabre example is "The Toy Theater," in which I had life-sized marionettes equipped with remote controls.

The third question: *What if those two got together?* Combine two existing customs, practices, sciences, or institutions. In "Beech Hill," I merged the writers' conference (where people who write fiction assemble) with the class of the poseur, the person whose life is his fiction. What I got was an annual meeting of those who pretend to be what they are not—a "secret agent," an "international adventuress," a "wild animal trainer," "the richest man in the world," and so on. My "secret agent" was really a short-order cook, and he wrote the rest of the story.

Science fiction's fictional people are hard to make believable because they are likely to be remote from the writer's experience. Who has known a Martian? A starship captain? A woman who has published scientific articles intended to prove that she is not a human being? If the writer cannot empathize with people who do not yet exist —and may never exist—he must stay out of science fiction.

In addition to empathy, there must be plausibility. A man sent to explore a new world, for example, is not likely to be a complete fool or a hopeless neurotic, though someone who finds himself in that position by accident may be either. As with other kinds of writing, character is manifested in speech and action, or by admitting the reader to the character's mind. In both these techniques, the broad scope of sf comes to the writer's aid. In "Alien Stones," for example, I provided my laconic starship commander, Captain Daw, with a young assistant named Wad. Wad was actually a computer simulation of Daw's own personality of twenty years before. This juxtaposition generated insights that could not have come from the use of a conventional younger officer acting as a foil.

But science fiction holds a number of traps for the writer trying to invent a fictional cast. People in the twenty-second century must not use current slang, for example. Yet if they belong to different social levels, or have been nurtured in different worlds, or possess radically differing personalities, their speech must reveal these differences. Sometimes the writer can coin his own new words. (A smattering of these have entered the language; Karel Capek's *robot* is an example—it did not seem exotic when I used it a few paragraphs earlier, did it? Some others are entering it now, like Robert A. Heinlein's *grok*.) In most cases, however, this is a dangerous expedient, with limited usefulness. Style of speech and habitual cast of thought are surer tools. I tried to use them in " 'A Story' by John V. Marsch":

"We had no names before men came out of the sky," the Old Wise One said dreamily. "We were mostly long, and lived in holes between the roots of trees."

Sandwalker said, "I thought we were the ones."

"I am confused," the Old Wise One admitted. "There are so many of you now and so few of us."

"You hear our songs?"

"I am made of your songs. Once there was a people using their hands —when they had hands—only to take food; there came among them another who crossed from star to star. Then it was found that the first heard the songs of the second and sent them out again—greater, greater, greater than before. Then the second felt their songs more strongly in all their bones—but touched, perhaps, by the first. Once I was sure I knew who the first were, and the second, now I am no longer sure."

"And I am no longer sure of what it is you're saying," Sandwalker told him.

"Like a spark from the echoless vault of emptiness," the Old Wise One continued, "the shining ships slipped streaming into the sea..." But Sandwalker was no longer listening. He had gone to lie between Sweetmouth and Seven Girls Waiting, reaching out a hand to each.

Science fiction has its own stylistic rules, to be broken only in exceptional cases. For example, characters must not lecture each other about things both would know. Your own small talk does not consist of explaining to your neighbor that cars must drive on the right, and that red means *stop* and green *go*. In the same way, a citizen of the year 3000 cannot expound the commonplace mechanics of his culture unless he is talking to someone who could reasonably be expected to be ignorant of them.

Frequently, writers who are aware of this prohibition try to circumvent it by having the hero discover a book (tape, vision cube) that just happens to provide the necessary data. This ploy is out of bounds, too. Of course, if the character has made a search for the "Pnakotic manuscript" and finding it is a vital part of the plot, that's different.

Many science fiction stories require coining new names. They should not be unpronounceable. (After all, one of the characters may have to pronounce them: "Come on, Xcv'tbq, it's time we met Bwbblnmx.") Furthermore, new means *new*, not taken from the work of some other writer (as in, "Pnakotic manuscript"). Writers unfamiliar with sf often discover a novel or story they believe to be completely unknown and forgotten, and only much later find that it is a "classic" work, still revered by a fanatic few and known to almost everyone in the field.

Gadgets should have logical names (in most cases) and they should be used logically. If your character has invented a "hyperspace phasor interrupter," he will probably call it a "phasor" in casual conversation; and he—and whoever controls him—will utilize it to achieve whatever goals are logically theirs.

There are only two plot rules, as far as I know. The first is that it is better to have a plot (though the story can probably do without it in a pinch, if theme, characterization, and style are good enough), and the second is to avoid the old hack plot, unless you give it a brilliant new twist. *Plot* concerns the adventures of the characters—what happens to them. Do not let the editor discover at the end of your story that the man and woman are Adam and Eve—he makes that discovery twice a week. Do not have your characters die and go to some strange new place, not unless your name is Roger Zelazny. Do not have a neighborhood tinker invent a time machine in his basement—H.G. Wells could get away with it, but no one can today.

Above all, do not convert some other type of story to science fiction by making changes in background and detail. A cowpoke buckled into a pair of ray guns (now more likely to be laser pistols) is a cowpoke still. This admonition does not mean that the theme of the lone individual fighting for life in a half-tamed wilderness is excluded from sf. But the hero's opponents should not be crooked gamblers, or livestock thieves, or claim-jumpers. The theme should be fitted with an sf plot.

Similarly, Joseph Conrad's great stories of the sea will not be improved by being shifted out to space. The officers and crew of spaceships will have their own problems—solar storms may pour out deadly radiation, but they will not toss the passengers about; mutinies may break out, but they will not be fought with belaying pins or be sparked by floggings.

Up till now I have been pointing out the difficulties of writing science fiction. It would not be fair to close without making some mention of the wonderful ease of it. The science fiction writer has escaped from the mundane world and entered the infinite universe. At various times I have wanted a girl who was really a cat, a living man without a head, a lady's maid who looked like a chest of drawers, and a world that was in fact a vast human body; and I have had them. Every writer, in sf, can have whatever he wants, if he can imagine it and make it his own.

84

WRITING FOR THE INSPIRATIONAL AND RELIGIOUS MARKET

By Dina Donohue

Not long ago, a manuscript submitted to me at *Guideposts* was accompanied by a letter reading, "Dear Editor: This article was turned down by the *Reader's Digest,* so I thought I'd send it to you." Too many writers regard the religious or inspirational magazine as an easy mark, and if a piece can't sell elsewhere, they think a church publication will want it. Perhaps this was once true, but the religious and inspirational market is different these days.

Although religious publications still offer a good open market for articles, fiction, and poetry, a great change has taken place in this market possibly because there has been a change—or more accurately, a revival—taking place in the church, combining some of the enthusiasm and devotion of the past with today's needs and tomorrow's hopes.

"Inspirational" does not necessarily serve as a synonym for "religious," although very often the two are combined in one article or story. It does not mean a sermon or theological treatise.

What then is the inspirational article? I might start with a very obvious definition—the inspirational piece is meant to inspire the reader. It can do this by depicting goodness, unselfishness, love in action, with the ultimate aim of challenging the reader to try to apply the same good qualities of strength, hope and charity to his own life and problems.

Now, as before, religious and inspirational magazines are concerned with the problems facing the world today, and the scope of the subjects discussed in their magazines bear this out. Magazines for young people are especially aware of the problems youth face and try to present articles to help solve these problems. Here are some titles recently published in the religious press:

St. Anthony Messenger (Catholic)—"Should a Mother Work?"
A.D. (United Presbyterian edition)—"Miracles Do Happen"
Reform Judaism (Jewish)—"Mixed (Up) Marriage"
Christian Century (Protestant)—"Will There Be Another Holocaust?"
Christian Life (Protestant)—"Does Your Child Listen to Garbage?"
The Church Herald (Protestant)—"The Sex Education We Often Forget"
Campus Life (Protestant)—"City Summer—Anything Good in the Ghetto?"

A word of warning: don't be frightened off by the word "religious." Sometimes a manuscript will have no mention of organized religion or any spiritual emphasis, and yet it will be well received by a religious magazine. Whether true experience or fiction, however, it should have an inherent moral point.

But you can write for more than one religious denomination or faith. My material has appeared in *Jewish Digest, Catholic Digest,* Baptist *Secret Place, Christian Herald,* and Unity publications, as well as interfaith *Guideposts.*

The *story* or narrative approach is the important ingredient. Even when writing a factual piece or an organizational article, if you use an anecdote in your lead, you have immediately aroused your readers' interest. Devotional articles also are enlivened by anecdotes. One of the major reasons an article may be rejected (aside from sloppy presentation or triteness) is that it contains a sermon-essay on the author's spiritual beliefs. Editors and readers want anecdotes to tell the story. In the religious magazine field, as in writing for the secular press, you have to use good but brief descriptions of your setting, reality in your characterizations, dialogue that moves the story along, and struggle and conflict in resolving your plot.

Some magazines which list their editorial needs as religiously oriented actually use the inspirational piece, merely giving it a different "label." *Sunshine* Magazine, on the other hand, says they do not use the religious, but only the inspirational. Hence, studying the market is particularly important if you wish to write for this relatively open field.

At *Guideposts,* we do look for a spiritual emphasis in our articles, but the inspirational quality is inherent in the line which appears each month above the name on the cover: A PRACTICAL GUIDE TO SUCCESSFUL LIVING.

We honestly believe that to be inspirational, an article or feature needs to do more than set forth an interesting idea. There should be a definite challenge or help for the reader. Take the cover feature in a recent issue. Sgt. Lysle Newberry, a state park police officer, told how he almost lost his life trying to rescue a group of people swept to the edge of Niagara Falls. They were saved by the combined concern of many. Some were involved in heroic rescue efforts, others prayed. Inspirational? Yes, because it showed us how, in time of danger, we can avert disaster by perseverance, prayer and calmness. Of course, all articles do not need to be as dramatic. Other so-called secular publications also print what can be termed the inspirational or religious piece. "Garden's Up!" by Marjorie Holmes, which appeared in *Reader's Digest*, was an inspirational piece on a different level. This was also a first-person account, a re-living of a childhood memory and the part gardens played in the author's life. The inspirational quality comes from the nostalgia that helps us relive our own early years and from the author's wish that her children could also know the joys of growing things. This perhaps will spark a similar interest in readers of the article.

Before getting involved with the specifics of style, type of article, or marketing, the first question usually asked by the writer is, "Where do I find such article ideas?"

For the dramatic rescue piece, the lost child account, or the individual achiever, your local paper can be a gold mine. (Whenever I travel, I always buy local newspapers.) The newspaper items may not always be spectacular, but the writer must read with an open eye for the story behind the article. Try to find out the motivation for an act of heroism, the scope of a difficult project, the outcome of an act of kindness. Consider the slant: One article could be told by a number of different people. The Sgt. Newberry piece was told in *Guideposts* by him. It appeared elsewhere as a third-person reporter's account. It could have been written by one of those rescued.

Another source for article material is in what you hear and see. I'm writing this on a Saturday afternoon, a day in which nothing much has happened. During the day—eating breakfast with my husband in a diner we frequent weekly, visiting the beauty salon, talking with neighbors—I have met interesting people who can serve as characters in feature articles. I have heard about situations which could provide dramatic anecdotes or leads. In one short day (it is now four P.M.), a neighbor and I discussed the importance of raising children so that they will be independent enough to leave home at an early age. We spoke of young people we knew who had made a success of this—and some who had not. I met a man who has had a real problem with alcohol and now faces a turning-point in his life and another who was disregarding doctor's orders in order to live a fuller, if shorter life. There is a good possibility here for an article.

I also spoke today to a newly-married teacher who has taken a gravely-ill friend into her home (with her husband's permission) to make sure the sick woman receives the care and treatment not available in her own town. And there were still other article possibilities in the day's conversations and meetings. Of course the writer does not use any material with real names, etc., without permission.

One of the best tools for the writer—after learning the rudiments of style and craftsmanship—is CURIOSITY. Be alert to people you know or meet. Perhaps someone in your family, neighborhood or church has a special hobby of helping people in a creative way. If the idea is different enough, something that others would wish to emulate, then you have the makings of an inspirational piece. Its success depends on how you handle your material and the market for which you intend to write it.

Listen to conversations in restaurants, elevators, subways, at conferences and conventions. In this way, you get not only anecdotes and ideas for stories but an understanding of human nature, good characterization, and, if you listen with a truly open ear, patterns of dialogue. I keep a notebook in which I record the more interesting items or ideas which may come to me—not to use verbatim but as background material for some future manuscript. After a time, I reread the notebook items, which are really in rough form, and discard those that are not worthwhile. The others I type on 3 x 5 cards and file for later use.

The important thing for the beginner as well as the established writer is to write about interesting people doing interesting things. Stress their spiritual motivation and be sure you give *facts*.

In writing the true inspirational piece, you have to have the same regard for facts as you would for a regular article. The difference is that for the inspirational you have to delve a bit deeper to make certain you leave the reader with the challenge to try to put the good actions or thoughts into his own life or, at the least, to arouse the reader from complacency to an appreciation of the finer attributes of his fellow beings.

The unselfishness of the teacher mentioned above aroused my interest, and I did try to find out from the young lady why the special attention, the sacrifice of time and effort. The answer might well be an article some day . . . or a character or situation in a fiction piece. Because we can also take true stories and characters and change them somewhat to fit the needs of a fiction piece. There would still be an inspirational quality in the young wife's desire to help her friend. For a fiction piece, I'd simply have the husband against the idea and thus develop conflict, etc.

Another source of article material can be your own life. This is where Marjorie Holmes found her idea for "Garden's Up!" Go back in memory some time and ask yourself some questions. The answers might provide an inspirational piece. For example:

What was the most memorable experience in my life?
What was the saddest day? The happiest? Funniest?
I remembered how frightened I was when . . .
I remember how much I wanted . . .
My most meaningful Christmas . . . Easter . . . Hannukah.
The day I discovered death . . . joy . . . love . . .

These are just samples to spark creative thoughts. I've used this technique in my writing classes at conferences and it's interesting to see the totally different articles which evolve.

One of the easiest ways to begin writing for the religious magazines is to do a personal-experience story. All of us, no matter how limited we might think our lives, have had scores of personal experiences which may be of interest to others. And, very often, of inspiration and help to others.

All too often we look for the truly dramatic story when the quiet one may be just waiting to be written.

All of us can benefit from a little dreaming and remembering. Try it sometime—in fact, make a habit of daily daydreaming. You might be surprised at the story material that comes to mind. You may recall interesting personalities, an incident that illustrates how to handle difficult situations, a time when your faith helped you meet a special problem. Or you may even come up with a recipe.

For church-oriented inspirational or religious stories and articles, it is necessary to give the reader something more than just an interesting piece of writing, story value, amusement or knowledge. At *Guideposts* we try to give our readers three extra ingredients which are applicable to other religious magazines as well:

Reader Identification: Make readers *feel* for the author's problem or story, even if it is not one they have been involved with themselves.

A true adventure story about an old man lost in the mountains might not appear to be within the experience of many readers. True, being lost might not; but the focal point is that an elderly man faces a seemingly insurmountable problem and has to solve it by himself. Readers can identify with his initial fear and distress and the realization that he is in danger.

Takeaway: Regardless of the problem—hating a neighbor, loss of a job, an alcoholic husband, fear of the dark, gossip—we look for a practical "how to meet and overcome the problem." The man lost in the mountains might have found it by calling to mind the Bible promise: *Fear not, I am with you always,* and, in the resultant quiet and peace of mind, his panic subsides. He is then able to think and act clearly and prudently and to save himself.

Special Emphasis: At *Guideposts* we are especially concerned with giving our readers some spiritual truth or message that they can carry away with them. Bible quotes are an easy way out, and there are other solutions. One reason for rejections is that the author will write five pages about the problem and then only one page of solution: Very often a Bible verse is remembered by the protagonist, and all is well. This doesn't mean that an appropriate quotation that really helped is not acceptable—it just mustn't be obviously brought in to provide the "religious" angle. The author has a responsibility to his readers. Showing how the main character in a story or article overcame a difficulty, not in a preachy way but with specific anecdotes and examples, can often provide readers with help.

The desperately ill person who has found a faith in God and is able to bear her pain and who shares this fortitude can help many readers who might be unhappy and disturbed in their own illness.

There might be a daughter-in-law who resented her mother-in-law's interfering. When the younger woman recognized the older one's feeling of frustration and asked her to help with cooking and caring for the children, there was a healed relationship. Practical? Yes, because it worked. Religious or spiritual? Yes, because first the daughter-in-law had to love the older lady and had to forgive what she called interference and worse. The daughter-in-law had to recognize her own fault of impatience. And in most stories there comes a time of almost complete despair when there seems no way out—usually, prayer becomes the last source of help.

Here the writer needs to be specific regarding prayer—there are so many kinds of praying. It usually isn't enough to say "I prayed for help and immediately felt better." Give details—how, why, when, where. Skimming the surface is unfair; it leaves a hole in the reader's understanding. Tell how prayer worked, or, if it didn't, tell how the characters became reconciled.

Most articles in the religious and inspirational magazines do have happy endings—readers want it and editors do look for it. But be careful you are not too much the Pollyanna, overcheerful author.

On the other hand, I have what I call my "tear duct test." If any manuscript makes me feel weepy, I give it a second reading, perhaps a third. Not that we are looking for the very sad story, but there is nothing wrong with emotion. By the same token, a little humor is also appreciated. That is why light verse can often be placed.

There is a good market for the inspirational and religious article. More and more writers are recognizing this. I am aware of it from the growing pile of manuscripts which comes across my desk each week.

To sum up, there are many varied types of magazines which use what is roughly termed inspirational material.

First, there are the denominational magazines published by the church presses. Some of them are very modern in concept and unlike what we have come to consider a "church paper." The serious writer should become familiar with these publications. Some are religiously-oriented with special denominational taboos or slants which the writer must honor. Others are quite liberal. The youth magazines vary—some are particularly creative in both art and copy.

Inspirational pieces and short items appear in many of what we term secular magazines. A good project would be to check through *Reader's Digest, McCall's, Woman's Day* and other popular magazines to see how many items could be termed "inspirational." You might find one telling how a worker or founder of a group reaches out to help others. Or an account of a terminally ill man—how he faced death with courage—might be another. Usually the presentation is the deciding factor. Take the account of a mother's thoughts on a child's first day at school. If written with tongue in cheek or irony, it might fit into a slick magazine. But if the mother has insight into what this means in the child's life, and her own, despite worries, it fits the inspirational pattern.

The writer of the inspirational piece needs a few things to help him: one, a special desire to write this type of material, perhaps a spiritual motivation; two, a grasp of good writing techniques and style; three, a knowledge of the market; and four, persistence, so that rejections are not unduly discouraging. The wealth of material coming to magazines each month means that many of the pieces are rejected not because they lack merit but because they are similar to others on hand. So "try elsewhere" can be good advice.

85

WRITING SELECTED SHORTS

BY SELMA GLASSER

IN THE days of double features, movie theatres would invariably show "selected shorts," often comedies or cartoons, between the pictures. Occasionally, they offered serious shorts on history, geography, or science, believing that not all of the audience wanted humor.

Similarly, in writing fillers, it is important to keep in mind that while there are hundreds of markets for the humorous filler, there are also many magazines that publish serious or practical short items related to the main editorial emphasis of the particular publication. Some writers tend to be more adept at writing this kind of serious filler than the funny or pun-filled piece.

Innumerable opportunities in countless categories of serious or practical filler-writing await the interested writer. In searching and researching the field, I've discovered that variety is indeed the spice of the filler writer's life. A filler writer can pick and choose the kind of writing that appeals to his or her particular aptitude or interest.

Short accounts of true incidents that illustrate the instinctive goodness of human nature are in demand by many publications, as are true cases in which unselfish acts of kindness, or unusually gracious or tactful remarks were rewarded. By studying magazines, I have found markets for short, true anecdotes that point to a moral or make an observation on human behavior.

Religious, non-sensational or juvenile publications are often a market for this type of short item. In spite of today's publicity pointing out the hazards of twentieth-century living, misguided youth, new morality, and social upheaval, there are considerate people around who perform thoughtful acts and kind deeds. It should be sheer joy for a writer to go to town on topics that portray the better side of life.

A filler may run to a few sentences or several pages. Study

published anecdotes in current and back issues of the magazines that purchase this type of material to discover length requirements, slant, and other details. In general, a good imagination, keen observation, and experience with real-life situations can help immensely.

You don't have to be female to think up, originate, or notice step-savers around the house or garden that make life easier and breezier. Take special note of shortcuts you may have been using for years. Think of party ideas, projects for youngsters, ways to save time and energy on housework (so that you'll have more time for filler-writing), tips for new mothers, shopping hints, etc. Many magazines and daily newspapers are paying anywhere from $5 to $50 each for briefs of this nature. Such tips are usually very short, no more than a sentence or two. Strive not only for brevity, but for clarity as well.

Culinary inventiveness pays extremely well and continues to be an excellent source of extra income for those dabbling in creative cooking —male or female, of course. You don't have to be an outstanding chef, cook, or homemaker. Many recipe competitions offer trips as prizes, in addition to cash and merchandise awards. Short recipe contests pay as much as $25,000 in some cases, but countless daily, weekly and monthly recipe competitions pay anywhere from $10 up on a regular basis. Old family recipes and cookbook ideas can be altered, improved, or enlivened with some new, unusual ingredient or formula. With imagination, inventiveness, and resourcefulness in concocting recipes, you can cash in on this field. In creating your recipes, combine your culinary secrets with your writing techniques. Your words add the visual interest (on paper) to your gastronomic feats (on the plate) to assure success.

Decorating, home, or women's fashion magazines frequently have contests for short pieces that may or may not require photographs or illustrations. Short items on home furnishing and decorating have an excellent opportunity to earn money for you, because professionals in the field are usually disqualified from these contests. Since originality counts, make certain you submit something that is really new, different, or unique.

Several national and regional magazines frequently use short advice or opinion items. Subjects may differ, but the general format is usually the same. Writers are requested to give advice and/or opinions on a specific problem. Subjects tend to be serious, timely, or based on personal experience. Your ideas and suggestions must be convincing, and your opinions and judgments should show genuine empathy and understanding.

Pet peeves offer the filler writer a chance to blow off steam and make money, too. Some publications accept long letters. If there is a word limit, however, condense your message, but long or short, in whatever form, turn your point into an effective filler.

New ideas to save money, time, and maybe your community or marriage are often welcome in local papers or national magazines. Here again, timely ideas can often mean a sale. You must time your writing well in advance of a special occasion or event; a Christmas item must be submitted in August or September or earlier. If you are involved in a community project, by all means write it up for publication. Not only will you receive a byline plus cash, but your community will be proud of you.

Various magazines and newspapers offer substantial amounts of money for factual question-and-answer features or a series of them on a particular subject. Reference books serve as best sources of information for gathering and verifying data. A dictionary, an encyclopedia, and an atlas are ideal for insuring accuracy and as a source of idea-starters. In anticipation of a holiday, you might write a series of questions (and answers, of course) about its origin, history, ways it is celebrated, etc. Inquiring-photographer (opinion) features are also a good source of income for the filler writer. Many daily newspapers pay at least $10 apiece for these. Topical questions of current interest are always recommended.

If you are an avid reader (and all writers should be), you have probably come across unusual facts and strange stories. Men's magazines in particular are looking for writers who can write or research strange facts and present them authentically. If this area of writing intrigues you, start searching for this kind of unusual information everywhere. Whenever you discover an odd fact or incident, write it up briefly and factually.

Do you have a special hobby? Are you thoroughly familiar with the ins and outs of the subject? Whether your hobby is hiking, sewing, or building model airplanes, others will be interested in what you write on the subject you know so well. Hobby fillers must be clear, accurate, and show that you are knowledgeable—anything fresh, novel, unusual or different. In addition to the payment you receive, won't you feel wonderful if your hobby write-up gets readers involved in pursuing it, too?

The filler writer must keep abreast of the changing features in magazines and watch the many opportunities, from month to month, or day to day in newspapers. (See market list in Part IV, "Fillers and Short Humor.")

86

PLAYWRITING: HINTS FROM A FIRST READER

By June Calender

For years I was skeptical when I heard magazine editors, book publishers and theatrical directors say, "If we could only find a good— (short story, book, play, whatever), we'd snap it up in a minute." What's wrong with them? I wondered. They must get thousands of excellent short stories, books and plays, and they probably reject them for silly, arbitrary reasons. Certainly my rejection slips were unwarranted—of course. In a sense, the shoe is now on the other foot: I am a first reader for a regional, professional theatre where we sincerely and actively search for a good new playscript to produce each year. Just one script that might be good enough to go from our theatre to Broadway.

In three years, I have read well over two hundred new scripts; we have produced two new plays, only one of which was Broadway material, and it didn't make it because of financial problems. I know now that sometimes those typical, impersonal sentences on rejection slips—"Does not fit our present requirements"—are entirely true. Most of the time the scripts simply aren't good enough. But, in any case, first impressions make a big difference.

I'd like to pass on some practical suggestions to help the free-lance playwright prepare a script that makes a good first impression and then offer several suggestions of more substance about the difficult art of playwriting.

Make it look professional. Anyone can. The standard format for a playscript is somewhat different from any other kind. Get a good handbook on playwriting, such as Sam Smiley's *Playwriting: The Structure of Action,* which gives you the usual format, along with much useful information. You don't put many words on a page, and it takes a lot of paper, but the ease with which the script can be read makes first readers, second readers, and directors happy. Many of the scripts we receive have been Xeroxed or mimeographed. This is fine; these scripts are often easier to read than an original typescript. However, carbon copies are taboo. They are hard on the eyes, they smudge the reader's fingers, they ought to stay at home in your desk drawer. Unlike the generally accepted practice in other fields, submitting the same script to half a dozen theatres or drama producers is standard practice for playwrights.

Playscripts, unlike book manuscripts, should be bound. Several styles of binder are available; anything neat is fine. You might want to choose something lightweight to make mailing less expensive. For easy handling and reading, leave a wide margin on the bound side. Neat corrections in pen are acceptable; extensive revisions should be retyped—at least the pages that are revised. Covering letters should include your background, and if you have Xerox copies of reviews of your work and they're complimentary, they can be impressive. Of course you'll always send a stamped, self-addressed envelope.

The above are purely mechanical matters. Now some suggestions that have to do with the nature of theatre. While I know that Eugene O'Neill wrote lengthy descriptions of the set and his characters, when I pick up a new script and find the first two pages a listing of characters describing each one down to the shoe size and the color of the eye shadow, followed by another two pages describing the set in elaborate detail—every piece of furniture, the pictures on the wall and the color of the lampshades—I know that I am going to feel in reading the manuscript that the writer should be a novelist. Theatre is a cooperative, group art. The set designer, the costume designer, and the director who casts the play will each bring a visual concept to your play. Never, never, never can a director find actors who look exactly like your description (you probably are visualizing your family or acquaintances anyway). If you want this kind of control over the visual presentation, write a novel and use your powers of description to your heart's content. Drama is action, not a series of tableaux.

A practical consideration: By and large, professional theatres are looking for scripts with a limited number of characters and a set that will not be too expensive. If your plays can take place in a single room, excellent. If they must take place in many locales, then some type of flexible set will be necessary. A play with six scenes, each in a different elaborate setting is almost impossible. If your imagination refuses to be confined to a single room or two, watch as many present-day productions of Shakespeare as you can and see the flexibility with which his many settings are handled in good productions. I do not believe good new scripts are rejected because they require a complex set or because they have many characters; but if there is a choice of two good plays, the one less expensive to produce may well be chosen. (I wish we had that problem more often.)

After you've written your first draft and before you begin rewriting, take time to look at your play from other people's point of view. Imagine you are a director, and ask yourself about each scene, "What is happening here?" In a sentence, state what action takes place during this scene. If you can't come up with an answer, you'd better start over again. If you want to write a script for radio, you can skip visible action; but on stage things have to happen. People have to move around; the audience must watch people doing things. Go through your play, scene by scene, asking yourself the same question again and again. If you can get yourself involved with any kind of theatrical company, no matter how amateur, get to know the director and try to understand his or her particular problems. Maybe you can take a directing course at the nearest school of drama. After the playwright, the director is the most creative person involved with a play. The more the playwright understands the director's job, the better his script will be.

Look at your script and see how many stage directions you've written. Good directors and actors generally ignore most stage directions. If you've written the speech well, you don't need to add "sarcastically," "sadly" or any other adverb; the actor will find the feeling inside himself. Most of the time you also don't need such directions as, "He paces back and forth," or "She slams the door." This, too, will arise from what the characters say and the interpretation of actors and director. The most difficult lesson for a fledgling playwright to learn is that others will add layers of flesh (action) to his skeleton of words.

Go through the script once more and imagine you are the actor in each role, one at a time. Read only that character's part and think, as an actor must, "Why am I saying or doing this at this time? What has been going on inside me since the last time I spoke? What am I revealing of my personality in this speech?" Very often a playwright is enamored of the hero, and the other characters become mere props, sticks or stereotypes.

Finally, ask yourself, "Am I telling a story or writing about characters, or have I managed to tell a story that comes out of the depths of the characters?" The latter is the ideal; it is very seldom attained.

After reading all those scripts, of which only ten or twelve gave me real pleasure, I believe that playwriting is the most difficult form of expression. After seeing plays for years and years, being moved to tears, convulsed with laughter, touched to the core by onstage drama, I believe the theatre is one of the richest forms of communication. In the beginning is the play—the concept of characters and action written down by the playwright; after that come the efforts of many other people who, the good playwright hopes, are as well trained and as professional and as serious as he is. Then wonderful things happen.

87

OPPORTUNITIES IN THE TRADE JOURNAL MARKET

By Norm Bolotin

For every general-interest publication on the market, there are dozens of trade and specialized magazines. Some are neither slick nor attractive, but many are surprisingly professional—and pay well. Few of these ever reach even the best-stocked newsstand, but they are easy to find and are one of the best markets available to free-lance writers.

Many writers don't have a clear understanding of the trade market, otherwise they would be exploiting it far more than they do. Trades are simply those magazines published for a specific industry or trade: construction, engineering, architecture, nursing, *writing;* you name the industry, and there is a magazine—or several—serving it. You probably read one regularly. Most trade magazines would be boring to someone outside the trade, but those involved read them from cover to cover.

For a writer's purposes, you can include non-trade but very specialized magazines in this same category. These cover publications serving hobbies rather than industries: skydiving, skindiving, skateboarding and so on. Each magazine exists to serve a group of readers with one common interest. Circulation may range from just a few thousand for many up to hundreds of thousands for a few of the hobby-type publications; few, very few, actual trades circulate anywhere near this many. All of these serve readers on just one subject, and for a writer, it is much easier to sell to a market where everyone is interested in the same thing as opposed to a big national publication, where at best only a fraction of the readership is interested in what you are writing about.

The basics for selling to trades are similar to those for other markets; start by acquainting yourself with the subject and the magazine. Don't write an article and then try to find a buyer. Find a subject, then write the piece to a specific market. Your success rate will be several times higher than if you do the writing first and then try to find a buyer. Trade journals are even tougher in this respect since their staffs are usually smaller than those of consumer publications. They don't have time to read unsolicited manuscripts, and their needs are so specialized that few free-lance submissions would fill the bill anyway.

Finding the proper market might seem to be the most difficult task for writers unfamiliar with trade journals. But it is amazing how many magazines writers ignore as markets even after reading them. Virtually every waiting room and office have magazines in them. More often than not, however, the writer picks up the *Newsweek, Better Homes* or *Sports Illustrated* to read. What about the trades that are sitting there? Pick those up, scan them and think of them as markets for your writing. If you are serious about selling, be thinking about it often.

The doctor's office has several health care publications as well as magazines catering to the doctor's hobbies — boating, camping, antiques, etc. Your lawyer, your neighbor the electrician, your brother-in-law the helicopter salesman, your friend the oil company executive.... They all probably receive one, two or up to a half-dozen trade magazines. You've seen them in their living rooms or their offices. And every one of these is a potential market for your articles—articles you may have already sent to the wrong markets and had rejected. There's nothing wrong with aiming at the top with your manuscripts, but the competition there is far greater.

Once you see what you think will make a good trade article, stop to think about it for a while. Don't just think of it for your favorite magazine. Examine the subject from several angles; look at it inside out and from several points of view. Remember, too, that what is new to you might be old to those in the particular trade. This is the time to study several trade magazines thoroughly. Try to find a sample copy or send for one. Virtually every article you could write involves someone doing something, or requires an interview to obtain more information. So ask the person you interview or write about what trade magazines he or she receives; ask if they have ever seen the subject or a similar one featured in any magazine.

Finding the right subject and the right market doesn't guarantee you a sale. Your query letter has to sell the article for you, even more than the article itself. Don't send a long, cumbersome letter or a too-short outline. Send what amounts to a lead, a strong paragraph or two showing the editor what you have to offer. You're not a mystery writer, so don't hold back. Hit them with the best aspect of your article and make them interested enough to want to publish it for their readers.

The key to successful freelancing to trades is the reuse of your material. The first article pays the bills; the rest provide the profit for you. And always, query first.

A few specifics illustrate just how easy it all can be. For example, you might have discovered a unique building or buildings under construction, walked through old cemeteries full of history, stopped at a local zoo, or visited a little town in the midst of a big event.

There may well be general-interest articles on each topic, perhaps for the Sunday supplement to the local newspaper. There likely wouldn't be any piece for a national consumer magazine, however. But there are several markets for the articles in trade and specialized magazines. Each of these magazines wants interesting articles as much as you want to sell them. When you consider that each of these hundreds of trade magazines buys anywhere from five to fifty manuscripts per year, the potential market is very great.

Start with the building. Don't just read a pamphlet about it or the inscription on the dedication plaque if you are aiming at a trade magazine. Call the architect, the engineer, the contractor, the owner, etc. Look on their coffee tables when you go to see them. You will find magazines such as the journal of the American Institute of Architects, trade publications for construction equipment and supplies, a civil engineering monthly, the magazine of the Associated General Contractors of America, a regional construction magazine and more. Read them all...query them...THEN write articles to the specifications of each. You will take the same basic information, rewriting and slanting it toward the needs of each.

I wrote three separate articles for three separate publications about a unique building. I needed only one interview and only one session with my camera while the building was being completed. Each of the articles contained the same basic facts and figures: building dimensions, construction techniques, individuals and companies involved. I published the first article in *Pacific Builder & Engineer Magazine,* a regional construction magazine serving the area in which the building is located. I placed the second piece about the building in *Alaska Construction & Oil,* which covers a different geographic area. The key here was that this second area was the headquarters for one of the contractors, and all I changed in writing the second article was the lead, in which I emphasized the fact that a certain contractor (the one living in the second area) was building the building, not just that it was being built. It was that simple.

Since the "unique building" was made predominantly of concrete, for the third article I selected a magazine specializing in concrete construction—*Concrete,* published in London. Because I had written articles on other concrete projects recently, I used the same facts and figures again, but for this third piece on the building I made my lead the way in which concrete was used—a factor that had been buried in the first two articles. I wrote articles for these magazines about similar projects, as well as for the *Port of Seattle Reporter* and an annual publication of a local Chamber of Commerce.

Here is a query letter I sent for one of my three articles about a unique building project. I always address a query to the editor by name if I know it. I try to find out the editor's name by looking in a market listing or in an issue of the magazine I want to sell to. This first letter followed a meeting and subsequent lunch with the editor. (I address an editor by first name if I've been lucky enough to meet and get acquainted first.)

Dear------

It was good talking to you last week, and as I said, I am very interested in doing freelance work for you.

Even though my staff work keeps me busy, I'm trying to do more and more on my own. I've published quite a few things this year already, and I'm sure several of the projects I come across through my work could be developed for your use.

The first job that comes to mind would be something on the construction at Trident. I can write to your specifications and have been to the site twice recently; the latest trip resulted in an article scheduled to run in *Pacific Builder & Engineer* magazine in June. Just let me know what you would like for an approach, length and photos.

Also, I've enclosed an article I did on a rather interesting new building in case it might be of interest. If you would like to run the photos, just let me know and I will get you copies.

Call me at the office anytime at your convenience.

Best,

(This led to a $150 sale to the *Port of Seattle Reporter,* and all they purchased was text, no photos. I spent a couple of hours one evening reworking the text from my previous two articles.)

The same approach held true in the case of the cemeteries. I was on assignment for the magazine I edit, writing an article on mining in Alaska. I found two old cemeteries where mining had been important seventy-five years ago. I also found a few odds and ends, miscellaneous relics of that period. The first article I wrote was on the history of mining, featuring photos of the old headstones and historical information I found about the people buried there. For the next sale of the "same" story I changed the emphasis. I dropped the mining history and talked only about the relics to be found—and sold it to *Western & Eastern Treasures,* a treasure-hunting magazine. I used the same facts and the same photos—all of which I had obtained at the same time. The articles were totally rewritten, but there was no new material, just a different emphasis. Later, I found a corporation that wanted the cemetery photos for an annual report. Supplying these required no other effort than the making of a duplicate 8 × 10 black-and-white print. My original research also provided the basis for historical articles that were published in *Alaskafest* (Alaska Airlines inflight magazine) and *Exxon USA.*

I turned a simple visit to a local zoo into an article on an aging seal and his keeper, for a science journal, *Pacific Search,* and another for a regional magazine, *Puget Sound Review.*

The same pattern will work with a small town holding a big event. For one writer I know the "big event" was a boat show, and he did his first article about it for *Sea Magazine,* a yachting publication highlighting the style, cost, dimension, and building of yachts on display there. He went on to tell briefly about the scenic setting of the town and a little about its history.

In writing about the same event for *Outdoors,* a general recreation magazine, he changed the emphasis and turned the historical/scenic material into the lead, telling what a great place the town was to visit because of the scenery, the old mansions, and the excellent sport fishing and boating in the area. He now has several other articles in progress for similar publications. Again, with one set of facts and photos, the result is likely to be as many as five articles—and five checks.

Here is another sample query I used successfully in selling several articles on the same subject:

Dear--

I travel extensively to Alaska on photo and writing assignments for *Alaska Construction & Oil Magazine,* as well as for other publications. Enclosed is an article on the history of mining which I thought would be of interest to you and to your readers.

"The Klondike Was Only the Beginning" should give you an idea of both my writing ability and my knowledge of the subject. Could I rework the subject for your magazine, slanting the historical material to your specifications? I also have an extensive supply of other photos: the gold rush cemetery, relics from the mining era in and around Nome and Skagway, etc.

I will look forward to hearing from you and hope that you find the subject matter of interest.

Sincerely,

(The same basic letter went out to two treasure-hunting magazines, a travel magazine and *Exxon USA.* One travel magazine never responded, one treasure hunting magazine sent me a form rejection, one asked for the article—which they bought—and *Exxon USA* asked for an article on the first oil town in the same area—which they bought.)

Once you get past the go-ahead, even if it is only on speculation and not assignment, the hardest part is over. If you were honest in your query letter, you shouldn't have much trouble with the actual article. If you miss the mark a little, an editor usually will make the changes he or she feels necessary or ask you to do it. Just remember who your audience is and what the specs are for the magazine. Some trade magazines are quite technical, but the vast majority are not. Study the magazines and their particular jargon and style; don't use a single word you don't understand. Writing for a trade is like writing for any publication: write to the style they use.

When dealing with trade journals be especially aware of similar magazines, not so much as potential markets for another article, but to avoid offending an editor. Simultaneous submissions or queries don't go over well at all. It is often difficult for the writer to tell which trades compete against one another, and if your piece were to end up in competing magazines both editors would never again consider one of your manuscripts. On the other hand, some magazines may appear to be competitors and are actually owned by the same publisher. They may want your article for both publications, but unless you are sure—take them one at a time.

Since most trade journals have relatively tight budgets and small staffs, each article won't yield a big check—usually from fifty to several hundred dollars. But when you multiply this times several publications, you have equalled a sale to a big national. The degree to which you modify your articles on the same subject will vary greatly. The case of just changing a couple of lead sentences is unusual and obviously ideal. Most often, you will change about half the text. Your length may vary from a 3,000-word piece with lots of colorful prose down to a very dry, factual article of no more than a few hundred words.

A good way to increase your sales potential is to use a camera. Some articles do not require photographs, but more than half do. Pay ranges from only a few dollars per black-and-white photo up to several hundred per color picture. You may find that some trade magazines want only the photos you offered and not the text. Remember, the big nationals have photographers to come illustrate your articles; the trades usually do not.

Your manuscript need not be perfect, but it should be clean and an original. A few corrections are fine, as long as everything is readable. Accuracy is paramount, especially with the trades, where the audience is small and well-versed in the subject matter. If something could be misunderstood or doubted, include a note to the editor about it. If the magazine uses footnotes, then follow the appropriate style.

If all this sounds very fundamental and easy, that is because it is...or it can be. The only reason more people don't sell to trades is that they just don't know about them or fail to recognize their possibilities.

There are plenty of sources for trades beyond the coffee tables and reception areas mentioned earlier. *Ulrich's International Periodical Directory* or the *Standard Periodical Directory* list many of your potential markets. Most libraries have them. Since indexing is done by title rather than subject, you may have to spend a little time searching, but it's worth the effort. Try the periodicals in the section of the library covering the particular industry, also. And don't forget universities; virtually every department has its own library or trade magazine reading room. (*The Writer* provides a trade journal list of many receptive markets.) Editors and other writers are also an excellent source of information.

As a free lancer, I've learned to turn the situation around from the one I experience as an editor. I have taken subjects I covered for one of our magazines and sold articles to other trades. And I have taken subjects that weren't right for our magazines and written articles for other publications. I have also learned what irritates me as an editor (sloppy manuscripts, annoying phone calls, photocopied submissions) and avoided them when free lancing.

It is all as easy as it sounds. I can't think of a single industry that doesn't have several trades serving it. Recognizing the market is the first step in selling for any serious free lancer.

88

Rx FOR COMEDY

By Neil Simon

THE idea of a prescription for comedy is obviously ridiculous. What works for one playwright rarely works for another, and even the fact that a certain approach succeeded for a writer before does not mean that it will surely produce an amusing play for that same scribe a second time. The knowledge of this grisly reality gives me a healthy insecurity, which I consider a great asset. Insecurity encourages a writer to be open to criticism by competent professionals; it allows him to face up to the need to revise or rewrite. Of course, *everybody* cheerily tells a playwright how to repair his script and it takes cool courage and wondrous manners to endure the amateurs' well-meant advice. In Boston during the tryout of *The Odd Couple,* I had been up till four o'clock in the morning rewriting the third act—for the fifth time. Exhausted, I finally fell asleep on my typewriter. At seven A.M. a dentist from Salem, Mass., phoned to tell me how *he* would fix the third act. I thanked him and promised myself I would call him at five the next morning to tell him how I would fix his bridgework.

I happen to like rewriting, a good deal of which is often necessary after one sees how a scene actually "plays" on stage in rehearsal or tryout. Each chance to fix, polish and tighten is a glorious reprieve— something I never had in the urgent world of weekly television. I suppose the greatest problem the writer in the theater has is to face "those ferocious critics." My problem is even greater. I write my own critics' reviews as I'm writing my play. I place Walter Kerr just behind my right shoulder holding in his hand a big stick—with rusty nails. If I get verbose or careless or stretch for jokes, Mr. Kerr lets me have it right across the knuckles.

This article originally appeared in *Playbill* Magazine, January 1966. Reprinted courtesy of Playbill, Inc.

The jokes are a special hazard. In the first of 112 versions of *Come Blow Your Horn*, the opening five minutes of the play were crammed with good jokes—in fact, some of the best I had ever written—and the scene was terrible. The audience, knowing nothing of the characters or the situation, could not have cared less. Now I know enough to start with the characters. Where do they come from? In the case of *The Odd Couple*, from a party I attended in California. All the men there were divorced, all their dates were their new girl friends. Most of these men were sharing apartments with other divorced men because alimony payments forced them to save money. In *Barefoot* and *Come Blow Your Horn*, at least one or two characters in each play resembled, perhaps in speech patterns, mannerisms or personal outlook, someone I've actually known.

Looking back at what and how I write, I seem to begin a play with two people of completely opposite nature and temperament, put them in an intolerable situation, and let the sparks fly. The extra ingredient, and very important, is that they must both emphatically believe that their way of life is the right one. Then it's the playwright's job to support *both* those beliefs. As for form, I prefer my comedies in three acts. When I start, I write extensive notes for the first act, a sketchy outline for the second and nothing for the third. I'm rather curious myself as to what will happen in the third act. Sometimes I don't find out for certain until a week before we open on Broadway.

If there is anything remotely resembling a key to comedy in theater, I'd guess that it is for the writer, director and actors to apply one simple rule. Never treat it as a comedy. The actors and characters must treat their predicament as though their lives depended on it. Not an easy achievement, I admit. Play it too seriously and the laughs are gone. Play just the comedy and ditto. In casting, my preference is not to go with the "established comic" but with a good actor who understands comedy. Walter Matthau, Robert Redford and Mildred Natwick are among the best.

One question I'm asked quite often is if I consider myself funny. I suppose I apply my own personal humor to life in the same manner as I would in a play. I need a situation. Put me around a table with real funny men like Buddy Hackett or Jonathan Winters or Mel

Brooks and I fade like a shrinking violet. No fast repartee for me. I shine trapped in an elevator with six people and a German Shepherd licking my ear.

To me, the first ten minutes of a comedy are critical. The writer must (1) set up the rules and the situation, (2) catch the audience almost immediately. Once the rules are announced, farce, satire, straight comedy or whatever game you're playing, the audience will believe you so long as you stick to those rules and that game. I believe in starting the conflict in the opening minutes (e.g., the poker game in *Odd Couple*) and to be as theatrically arresting as possible. The idea of opening on an empty stage in *Barefoot* intrigued me. Then I begin with some new event in the life of our hero, something that has never happened to him before.

My writing routines are actually rather prosaic. No midnight oil burns in my lamp. I type in an office or at home, and put in a ten to five day with a short lunch break. I may do a complete draft of a play, use it as an outline and then set to work on a more finished version. I like to get into the writing quickly to "hear how the characters speak," for once I hear the speech patterns it is easier going. I ought to point out that my insecurity is such that even as I'm writing one play, I'm beginning to think ahead to the next. So if this one doesn't quite pan out, well. . . .

Once a play goes into rehearsal, my "normal" routine ceases and the midnight oil begins to burn. There seems to be less time for social obligations, children and—horror of horrors—the Giants' football games.

Do I need quiet when I'm working? It depends. If there are no problems in the script, they could be digging the new subway under my typewriter. But one day recently my two little girls were on the other side of the house playing jacks. And as the ball bounced softly on the thick rug, I ran from the study screaming at my wife, "Can't you keep those kids quiet?"

She looked at me with knowing affection and pity.

"I'm sorry the scene's not going well, Doc," she answered with ancient female wisdom.

If there's anything I can't stand, it's a smart aleck wife—who happens to be right.

89

BOOK REVIEWING

By L. E. Sissman

AFTER years of stumping and (I hoped) dazzling other people with anything I cared to try in verse, at the hoary age of forty I became a book reviewer. Now it was my sworn and bounden duty to penetrate and unravel the obscurities of other writers' methods and messages, to dissipate the wet and inky smokescreen in which the wily squid conceals himself, and to set the delicate skeleton of the author's true design in so many words before my readers. Besides being hard, grueling detective work, this was both scary and risky; armed only with a shaky analytic gift and my spotty, idiosyncratic store of reading, I was laying my sacred honor on the line each time I tried to pick another literary lock in public.

For the first couple of years, I drove myself to write reviews like an aristocrat driving himself to the gallows, with superficial sangfroid as thin as onionskin and a real clutch of fear each time I sat down at the typewriter.

Then, mercifully, I began to learn the ropes and look a little more objectively around me. I discovered that reviewing was not simply something that a *soi-disant* literary man did to fill time, amplify his tiny reputation, and (of course) earn a little money. *Au contraire.* Reviewing, it was slowly and astoundingly revealed to me, was a vocation, a craft, a difficult discipline, with its own rules and customs, with a set of commandments and a rigid protocol. Mostly by making painful mistakes and leaping brashly into pitfalls, I began to amass some notion of the shape of a reviewer's obligations to himself, to the author he reviews, to his editor, to his readers.

In short, I became aware of the moral imperatives of book re-

Copyright © 1974, *The Atlantic.*

viewing. Funny as that may sound in a literary world raddled by cliques and claques and politics, by back-scratching and back-stabbing, by overpraise and undernotice, I now believe that the would-be conscientious reviewer must be guided by a long list of stern prohibitions if he is to keep faith with himself and his various consumers. In the interests of controversy (and, I hope, of air-clearing), I set these down herewith.

1. Never review the work of a friend. All sorts of disasters are implicit here; a man and his work should be separate in the reviewer's mind, and the work should be his only subject. If you know the man at all well, you become confused and diffident; your praise becomes fulsome, and you fail to convey the real merits and demerits of the book to the poor reader. The hardest review I ever wrote was of the (quite good) novel of a friend four years ago. Never again.

2. Never review the work of an enemy. Unless you fancy yourself as a public assassin, a sort of licensed literary hit man, you will instinctively avoid this poisonous practice like the plague it is. Corollary: never consent to be a hatchet man. If Editor X knows you are an old enemy of Novelist Y, he may (and shame on him, but it happens all the time) call on you to review Y's latest book. Beware, on pain of losing your credibility.

3. Never review a book in a field you don't know or care about. Once or twice I've been touted onto titles far from my beaten track. The resulting reviews were teeth-grindingly difficult to write and rotten in the bargain. Unless you're a regular polymath, stick to your own last.

4. Never climb on bandwagons. You are not being paid to subscribe to a consensus, nor will your reader thank you for it. If a book has been generally praised (or damned), you add nothing to anybody's understanding by praising (or damning) it in the same terms. Only if you have read the book with care and found something fresh to comment on should you attempt a review. Otherwise, find something else (how about the work of an unknown?) to write about. Or skip it; you'll earn that money you need for a new 500mm mirror lens somewhere else.

5. Never read other reviews before you write your own. This is a tough rule to follow, because all reviewers are naturally curious

about the reception of Z's latest book. Nonetheless, you can't help being subtly influenced by what *The New York Times* reviewer (or whoever) has to say. Eschew!

6. Never read the jacket copy or the publisher's handout before reading and reviewing a book. Jacket copy (I know; I used to write it) is almost invariably misleading and inaccurate. The poor (literally: these downtrodden souls are, along with retail copywriters, the most underpaid people in advertising) writer is probably working from a summary compiled by the sales department, not from a firsthand reading of the book. The handouts are more of the same, only flackier.

7. Never review a book you haven't read at least once. Believe it or not, some reviewers merely skim a book (or even depend on, horrors, the jacket copy) before reviewing it. Not only is this a flagrant abdication of responsibility; there is always the lurking danger of missing a vital clue in the text and making a public spectacle of yourself. It should happen frequently to all such lazy reviewers.

8. Never review a book you haven't understood. If *you* haven't figured out what the author is up to, there's simply no way you can convey it to your reader. Reread the book; if necessary, read some of the author's other books; if you still don't know, forget it. The cardinal sin here is to go right ahead and condemn a half-understood book on the covert grounds that you haven't found its combination.

9. Never review your own ideas instead of the author's. Unless you're the ranking pundit in the field and you have a scholarly bone to pick with the author, you have no right to use the book under inspection as a springboard for a trumpet voluntary of your own.

10. Never fail to give the reader a judgment and a recommendation on the book. And tell why. A reviewer is really a humble consumer adviser; his main job is to tell the public what to read and what to skip. It's an important job because nobody can possibly keep up with all the books being published today.

11. Never neglect new writers. First novelists, in particular, get passed over too frequently for several reasons. The obvious reason is that Norman Mailer's new novel is better copy than Hannah Furlong's maiden effort. The less obvious reason is that it's much

harder for a reviewer to get an intelligent fix on an unknown. In short, it's harder work to review a debutant.

12. Never assume that a writer is predictable. This is, in a way, the converse of the previous proposition. Part of the pleasure of picking up a new book by a writer you've read before is *knowing* what you're about to read—the themes, the style, the old, familiar tricks. But what if the novelist has *grown;* what if he does something daring and unexpected? That's when a lot of reviewers, myself included, are tempted to put him down for not rewriting himself. The only answer is to approach the book with great caution and read it on its own merits, forgetting what has gone before.

13. Never forget to summarize the story or the argument. What's more maddening than a review that rhapsodizes (or bitches) for two thousand words about the author's style, his technique, his place in letters without ever giving us a clue to the nature of the story, beyond the mention of an incident or two?

14. Never, on the other hand, write a review that is merely a plot summary and nothing more. This happens surprisingly often, especially in newspaper reviews. The reader of the review deserves a judgment, a rating, not simply a recapitulation.

15. Never impale a serious writer on his minor errors. Nobody's perfect, as the old gag line says, and, given the susceptibility of even the most powerful piece of work to ridicule, it is frighteningly easy for the reviewer to have his fun at the author's expense and end up distorting the value and import of the book. (Example: I recently read a good novel in which the author consistently misused the word "fulsome" and mixed up "she" and "her." It would have been an act of willful irresponsibility to take the author to task for these small miscues, which were also his editor's fault.)

16. Never write critical jargon. The day of the New Criticism, for all its good, is mercifully past, and so, I'd hope, is the compulsion of some reviewers to pose and posture as anointed gospelers of the true and beautiful. The reviewer who writes for a general-circulation newspaper or magazine should have his typewriter unplugged if he persists in pedagogeries.

17. Never fail to take chances in judgment. Because it forces you

to enter the mind of another on his own terms, reviewing is literally mind-expanding. Often the reviewer is astonished at his new conclusions and afraid to put them down on paper. This is a mistake; one of the highest critical acts is to arrive at a new understanding and communicate it to the reader.

18. Never pick a barn-door target to jeer at. Not long ago, one of the daily reviewers in *The New York Times* wasted an entire column on the new novel by one of the Irving Wallaces. Irving Stone? Jacqueline Susann? Or whoever. Anyway, it was painfully easy—shooting fish in a barrel—and painfully unworthy of the reviewer's taste and talent. He might far better have reviewed a good first novel.

19. Never play the shark among little fishes. Being a reviewer does not entitle you to savage the beginner, the fumbler, the less-than-accomplished writer. A sincere and decent effort demands a sincere and decent response. If you've ever struggled to write a book yourself, you know the vast amounts of pain and love it takes. To put down an honest attempt in gloating arrogance is to deal a crippling blow to a nascent career of possible promise.

20. Never compete with your subject. A reviewer is not, at least during his hours as a reviewer, a rival of the person he's reviewing. If he sees flaws in the work under inspection, he should report them, but he should not give vent to a long harangue on how *he* would have written the book. (If his hubris is that keen, perhaps he should take time off and write a book himself.)

In a word, then, the sins and temptations of reviewers are legion. As an incumbent sinner, I have more often than I like to think about been brought up short by the realization of my own weaknesses. Thus the list above. While I know I don't have the constancy and fortitude to follow it to the letter, I try to bear it in mind, like a catechism, when I sit down to write about another person's work. It is the least I can do for another poor sufferer who has taken the supreme risk of letting his dreams and talents go forth between covers, and for all those poor sufferers who simply like to read, and who rely, for better or worse, on the dim and uncertain skills of reviewers for a guide through the maze of new titles in their bright, unrevealing jackets on the shelves.

90

REALITIES OF THE GREETING CARD MARKET

By Carl Goeller

WHAT is the outlook for the greeting card free-lance writer in the seventies? On the negative side, there have been some discouraging developments for free-lancers during the past year. The economic slump has not spared the greeting card industry, and there has been a good deal of belt-tightening on the part of editors of major companies as well as smaller ones. There are fewer purchases of borderline material—material that has merit but will take working over before it is publishable. This naturally hurts greeting card writers who specialize in ideas rather than in finished, craftsmanlike writing.

But, on the positive side, this is the most exciting period in greeting card history. Editors are competing for new ideas, new gimmicks, new products, and they're paying more than ever for what they buy. And they are buying ideas as well as words. To succeed in the greeting card field during the seventies, you have to be an idea man as well as a writer.

Who is going to make it in the next decade—and who isn't—and why? Here is my appraisal of what's in store for various kinds of greeting card writers in the seventies:

The conventional writer, who writes only conventional 4- and 8-line verse for serious occasions, is in trouble. In the sixties there were as many as ten rather good markets for straight verse; today there are fewer than five, and some of these are buying only a fraction of what they once did. One reason for this is that conventional verse is a reusable commodity—a popular verse can be modified and used with a dozen or more different designs throughout a card line, and these can last for years. Greeting card editors, therefore, don't need much new conventional verse, no matter how well written it may be. The writer who is convinced that conven-

tional verse is the only type he can do will have to content himself
with a limited income from his free-lancing.

Small greeting card publishers, as well as the large ones, are insisting on fresh, new approaches which will help get their wares into
stores handling more than one line. They are stressing originality,
especially in their studio card lines.

The ostrich sits behind the typewriter day and night, writing
card ideas by the dozens—conventional, humorous, juvenile and
studio ideas. He's been at it quite a few years and has been pretty
successful because he knows what the editors want. Or so he thinks!

But he hasn't been out into the greeting card departments recently; he hasn't been reading the trade magazines to see just what's
been happening in the industry. He's neglected the research end of
his job to the point that he doesn't even realize that there have been
more changes in the greeting card business in the last three years
alone than there were in the preceding twenty. As a result, he's
showing editors only a fraction of the kinds of material they really
want to see. Unless he removes his head from the sand—quickly—
the ostrich will find his hits becoming fewer and his misses becoming commonplace.

The in-tune writer does what the ostrich fails to do—he keeps in
tune with what's happening in the industry, and he slants his efforts
accordingly. He notices, for example, that the major publishers are
coming out every year now with many new groups of "promotions"
—series of cards with some unifying theme, either design or sentiment oriented. So, instead of simply sending one batch after another
of individual card ideas, he includes some interesting promotional
idea groups. One enterprising writer last year sold six promotional
ideas to several different companies, and each brought him a handsome check. He notices, too, the trends in copy which appeal most
to the consumer. For example, American Greetings' "Soft Touch"
cards—cards using mood photography and simple, meaningful copy,
all in prose—found immediate acceptance with the youth market,
and they sold over ten million cards in less than a year. Other
companies rushed into print with their imitations of Soft Touch . . .
and a writing market was born.

The creative idea person asks himself, "Why should my creative
efforts be limited to writing? Why not sell ideas as well as words?"

and he begins approaching the card companies in a new way. He begins selling them ideas for new products and new twists to existing products. Look at what the "card" industry is making and selling these days—books, puzzles, games, party items, toys, calendars, posters, badges, candles, candy, writing instruments, gift items . . . the list is endless. The idea person is aware of these, studies them, and then comes up with fresh new ideas for them. Only recently an idea man came up with an idea for a series of books which he presented and sold to a major card company for several thousand dollars. Another sold a series of games to one of the publishers and was well paid for them. The *very* creative idea person goes one step further. He researches a product before the card companies go into it, then gets in on the ground floor. How? By reading and shopping to see what's on the market and what isn't; by talking to clerks and store managers about what is in demand that they can't supply; and by creating something to meet that demand. The method by which he sells the idea to a manufacturer may well tax his creative ability more than coming up with it—but the results can be well worth it.

The analyst takes his writing and creating seriously enough to analyze his successes and failures. Someone once defined a professional as a person who doesn't make the same mistake twice. The analyst is a professional. He periodically reviews the cards he's sold to see what slant is hitting, and, perhaps as important, he reviews his rejections to see why he missed. Further, he is willing to ask the help of others—fellow professionals or even an editor—in determining *why*. If the editor likes his work in general and feels that he has something to contribute, he will be glad to comment and suggest improvements.

Which of the five different greeting card writers we've looked at are you? If you are *the conventional writer* or *the ostrich,* the seventies are going to be rough sledding, and you had better start now to enlarge your markets by trying other types of writing. If you are *the in-tune writer, the creative idea person,* or *the analyst,* you will find the greeting card market a real challenge, and an exciting and profitable one as well.

Five years ago, the greeting card market consisted of verse for conventional, humorous, and juvenile cards, and studio card gags—

period. Today, as we have already noted, it includes new products and new twists for old categories. Let's see what new twists are in demand.

Conventional cards: There is a great interest in simplified conversational verse which avoids the clichés which have been so reliable in past years. Forget about lines like "this card has come to say," "today and all year through," and "every thought prompts wishes." Every word and every line must count. Use ideas in your verses—design, sentiment tie-ins, fresh and interesting thoughts, and unusual verse formats. Don't always use verse. If you can put your thoughts into rhythmic, readable prose, do it. Keep your verse as brief as possible but have something to say.

Humorous cards: There's more emphasis now on cleverness and less on gimmick in humorous cards. This is a matter of economics as much as anything. All the companies are finding a real cost squeeze which makes mechanical gimmicks almost prohibitive except in the highest-priced cards. Separate pieces, too, which need to be attached, are costly because of the hand labor required. This means that words and art work are practically all an editor can use at 50¢ and under. Paper is still reasonably inexpensive, so many editors are receptive to novelty folds and unusual stock ideas (paper bags, etc.). There's a definite trend away from the old cornball type of humor and toward the more youthful, sophisticated approaches. Card ideas that were considered strictly for studio cards a few years back are now used on humorous cards with pictures of bunnies, dogs, cats, etc. A word of advice—you'll sell more humorous ideas if you think design as well as words. If your gag is accompanied by some clever designing, you're saving the editor and the art director some extra work, and they will appreciate it.

Juvenile cards: There is very little demand for straight juvenile verse. Most companies are interested in "idea cards"—things to do and play with, semi-educational, and easily designed. Don't talk down to the kids with your copy—they see lots of television and their vocabularies are much broader than ours were at that age. Some greeting card companies are buying stories, both for cards and for hardback books they are now publishing.

Studio cards: As previously noted, gags that used to appear only in studio lines have now spread to the humorous lines, and studio card editors are looking for more originality and youth-oriented copy. This doesn't mean hippie-type ideas, "cool" talk, drug-culture bits, and the like; it means humor that doesn't rely on slamming the recipient (today's kids are a sentimental bunch, no matter what they say), or getting drunk, or growing old (age gags just aren't cutting it in the studio card racks these days). Love is big—and so is sex— and little digs at the Establishment—and ecology, pollution, and the like. Not every company is moving its studio line in this direction, so don't rush out and throw away your pile of straight humor. There are some editors who still want that type. But be forewarned: most major greeting card publishers are heading in this direction (upon the advice of their research people).

Books: One of the hottest items to hit the card departments in the past three years has been the little hardback book. It was pioneered by American Greetings, and now more and more companies are building sizable book lines. There are several approaches which will bring checks from editors who find they have no backlog at all of this type of material. Here are a few:

Cute stuff—Girl-to-girl or girl-to-boy messages done in a cute, almost juvenile-sounding simplicity. These are especially strong in such subjects as love, friendship, "missing you," and in birthday messages. Some are in verse; most in very simple prose.

Humorous—Often these are collections of ideas that are taken from the studio card files, but on "missing you" compliments, love, birthdays, and get-well. Items must be short and quick. Long, involved humor goes nowhere.

Studio—These have been the weakest books, and consequently bring the greatest number of rejection slips. And yet, editors need them. The material should be timely, youth-oriented humor, usually girl-to-boy stuff.

Conventional—Many of these are similar to the old *Ideals* magazine—collections of very traditional, conventional verse and poetry. This is a very small market, but it's there if you have the right idea.

This is just the start of the book business for the major greeting card publishers. The next obvious step will be larger, high-priced books, and the ideas for them could just as well come from you as from their staff writers. Here's a prediction: By 1975, at least two of the card companies will be considered major book publishers. If you get in on the ground floor now . . . who knows—you may have some published books to your credit five years from now.

Novelties: Ceramic figures are big with a dozen publishers— the little characters that say, "I wuv you," "The devil made me do it," and so on. Watch the stores to see which companies are selling figurines, then send them ideas for new approaches—not just more of the same.

Calendars are a big item with many of the major companies. They have plenty of ideas for designed calendars, but they can use you for novelty approaches.

Posters are hot. The big companies wrote them off as a fad when they were introduced about five years ago (they did that with studio cards, too), but now they realize posters are here to stay, so they're going into the business. Submit some original ideas, and they'll sell.

Puzzles and games are relatively new to most card publishers, but destined to be big items. If you have the kind of complicated mind it takes to do puzzles, etc., send them to major companies —they're interested now.

The card companies are in the business of helping people communicate with one another—and who says that cards are the only way to do this? When you're thinking of items, products, gadgets, and copy for the greeting card field, keep that in mind. If you yourself use an unusual method of communicating with your friends or relatives, you may have the makings of a new product that will be of interest to the card companies.

To return, then, to the basic question posed in this piece, does the free-lance greeting card writer stand a chance in the seventies?

Yes, but he'll have to think of himself as more than just a greeting card writer. A better title might be creative communicator.

Yes, but he'll have to remember he's living in the seventies, and writing for the future decade, not the past.

Yes, but he's going to have to stay alert to the changing times and attitudes of the people. You're in for some exciting days, months, and years ahead as you become the complete creative communicator.

91

THOUGHTS ON PLAYWRITING

By Robert Anderson

I AM AT a period in my life (52) when I would much rather be getting wisdom from someone else than trying to give it to others. I have just finished a new play, which means that I have spent over a year wrestling with what I know, what I don't know, shapes, forms, the new modes, the old modes. I have ended up with an imperfect piece of work, as we all do. Every writer knows better than he can manage to do. (I am reminded of the story of the government agriculture advisor who watched a farmer for a week and then sat him down to give him some advice. The farmer cut him short by saying, "Hell, I'm not farming as well as I know how to farm right now.") In the same way, no writer ever writes as well as he knows how to write because material just never presents itself to us that neatly. Someone said that the act of writing is the act of undoing a dream. We never end up with the near-perfect piece of work we dreamed of writing. I never read over anything I have written on a play until I have finished the whole play. If I knew day by day how far short of my "dream" I was falling, I probably wouldn't go on.

These, then, will be some rather tentative, disorganized thoughts on playwriting. They may inform and encourage the right people and inform and discourage others.

This is a really fine time for the young playwright. Never before has there been so much opportunity for him to see his work done: colleges, cafés, Off-Off-Broadway, barns, parking lots, lofts, street corners, churches. This is all to the good. But I keep worrying about these young playwrights ten years from now. Things were never worse for the "established" playwright with a family who must make his living from his work. By and large there is very little money for the young playwright in the colleges, churches, Off-Off-Broadway, etc. This is all right. He is learning, enjoying himself and entertaining others. But this can go on only so long, especially if he is a family man. I have been quoted a number of times as saying, "You can make a killing in the theatre, but not a living." (Incidentally, the killing usually goes for taxes.)

The playwright generally has to be a moonlighter in one way or another. Before *Tea and Sympathy*, I worked on my plays in the morning, wrote for radio and TV in the afternoons, and four nights a week taught from eight to eleven. My second play was an artistic success but earned me almost zero, and I started writing movies to supply me with the money for the two to three years it takes to write a play and get it produced. Very few playwrights I know make their living solely from the theatre.

Very often young playwrights say to me, "Oh, but you're established. You have it easy." This is not true. My first successful play, *Tea and Sympathy*, was turned down by almost every producer, and my agent, Audrey Wood, told me that it was still being read by one producer, but it would probably be returned and I should get on to my next play. It was not returned, and my career was started. Thirteen years later my plays, *You Know I Can't Hear You When the Water's Running*, were turned down by almost everyone, and they were on their way into my files when two young producers rescued them. The same was true of my next play, *I Never Sang for My Father*, which waited five years to be produced. In short, it never gets easier. It would be unthinkable if novelists like William Styron, Philip Roth, or John Updike couldn't get their novels published. But there are many established and successful playwrights who cannot find producers for their new plays. The cost of production is enormous now, and few people have a continuing interest in a playwright and his work. (I will pass along a terrible story. I attended a preview of Tennessee Williams' play, *The Seven Descents of Myrtle*. I was alone, as my wife was acting in one of my plays. Before the curtain went up, Tennessee appeared in one of the boxes, and some people recognized him and started to applaud. Most of the audience joined in. The lady next to me said, "Why are they applauding?" I said, "That's Tennessee Williams." She said, "Why are they applauding when they don't know whether or not they will like the play?" My blood ran cold. But I know this is the prevailing attitude. The years of great plays Williams had given us meant nothing. The lady would applaud only if *this* one pleased her.)

It is generally conceded that playwriting is the most difficult form of writing. Add to this the difficulty of getting a play produced (depending on availability of the actors, director, theatre, *and* money). Add to this the deplorable situation now prevailing in New York where a bad review from the critic on *The New York Times* can finish off your play, and one wonders why anyone wants to be a playwright.

For a playwright there is the "What?" and the "How?" *What* he feels, thinks, believes, loves, fears, hopes, and *how* to express these in terms of theatre. Very often a young playwright is first attracted by the *how's* of the theatre, the theatricality, just as a girl might be drawn to being an actress because of a striking entrance she saw some great actress make one evening. To be thus stagestruck is a good thing. Infatuation of this sort often will see a person through the inevitable doldrums to follow. But the playwright soon learns that the theatricality must convey drama, and the aspiring actress learns that there was more to the entrance than show.

Right now the theatre seems to be very much concerned with the *how,* the manner, the outward show. The Emperor's clothes. I am often inclined to think that the clothes have no Emperor, that the matter with the theatre is that the manner is the matter. But in the end this is probably healthy, fun and stimulating, to call attention to the stage as stage, the theatre as theatre. A friend of mine who teaches in a college theatre department tells me that the students come to work in the theatre full of ideas of how they want to do something on the stage—projections, soundover, turntables, lights—but they rarely have any idea of *what* they want to do, what they want to convey by all these devices.

And the *what,* of course, is what finally makes the writer. Perhaps I am old-fashioned, but I finally tire of an endless barrage of stage effects signifying little or nothing. The playwright, of course, must learn to communicate in terms of any and all techniques available to him or congenial to him, but there must be something there to communicate, a strong feeling expressed as drama or comedy. (Comedy is just as serious as drama.)

Granted that a writer knows how to write, the most important asset for him is strong feelings. I once was encouraging a young writer of short stories. I sent him to Edward Weeks, then Editor of *The Atlantic Monthly*. Mr. Weeks read his story and then said to him, "You want to be a writer, but you didn't really want to write *this* story." There is great wisdom for all writers in this sentence.

Someone has said that art gives form to feeling. There must be the feeling first. Like all writers, I am offered a number of stories or ideas by friends, acquaintances and passers-by. I hardly ever listen to such stories, first, because of a certain pride in dreaming things up for myself, but secondly because they rarely make a connection with any reservoir of feeling inside me. I think it was Tennessee Williams who said in an interview that he writes about what's bugging him at the moment. Centuries ago, Sir Philip Sidney said, "Look in thy heart and write."

One word of warning and contradiction. Often the thing that is bugging the writer most is his life as a writer. This is of little interest to anyone except another writer. I think an audience asks of a writer, "Were you there, Charlie?" This does not mean that they want a writer to write nothing but autobiography, but they want to sense the author's involvement with his story, his knowledge of the truth of whatever he is writing about. With television documentaries and movies, we are able to know so much more about the factual truth of everything that faking on this level is hardly possible any longer. But faking on the psychological level is hardly possible either. I do not want to read someone who knows no more about a situation than I know or than I could pick up from the papers and magazines and television. I want to know what it's really like. I want a letter from the front. I do not want to seem to imply by this that I just want something strange and bizarre beyond my ken. As a matter of fact, while this is sometimes fascinating, the great works usually deal with areas of life known to us all, but I want to know that the author knows that area, has suffered or laughed in that area, that he is, in short, authentic.

When I taught playwriting, I used to have a great deal to say about technique, concepts which were dramatic or not dramatic, shape and form. The more I see, the more I read, I think a great deal of the problem comes down to one word, PROGRESSION. It is the nature of an audience, any audience, to bore quickly. People in groups become restless much more quickly than they do when alone. The majority of plays I read or see which do not "work" are static. They are mood pieces, brilliant in their observation of human nature, but they start nowhere and get nowhere. Much has been said about the vanishing need for plot. It's presumably a dirty word. But whenever I start getting bored in the theatre, a voice keeps murmuring inside me, "Get on with it! Move!" And plot, no matter how slight, is what moves a play forward and holds our interest. I hate it. I fight it. It is Hell sometimes to try to wrestle with your "marvelous material" so that you can get some movement into it. I have written plays without progression and suffered the consequences. Forward-moving action is the most difficult thing to come by. But it is what holds our interest while we are absorbing the richer texture of the characters and the relationships. The developing action sometimes is relatively unimportant, but it keeps us in a frame of mind to enjoy the rest.

For example, in *Life with Father,* what we remember are the charming family scenes and the characters truly and humorously drawn, but what holds our attention though we may not know it at the time, is the simple plot of Mother trying to get Father baptized. In *Mister Roberts,* the texture is the characterizations, the humor, but the story is hung on a simple progression, Mr. Roberts' efforts to get transferred. In *The Glass Menagerie,* the story moves forward with the efforts of the family to find a gentleman caller for Laura. I have seen more beautifully written, deeply felt plays bog down after thirty minutes simply because they were going nowhere. I have often thought it would be good training for us all to write farce and melodrama, which are all forward-moving action, progression.

To give you some idea of the principle of progression . . . I was once involved in a summer theatre production of *The Emperor Jones.* You will remember that a feature of this play is the drum which starts early in the play and keeps going to the end. I remember at one rehearsal the director stopped the actors late in the play and called back to the drummer, "I can't hear you. I can't hear the drum." The drummer came forward, haggard and frazzled, and said, "I'm hitting it so hard I'm almost breaking it." The point is that we had been· listening to the drum for twenty minutes or so, and in order for us still to be conscious of it, the drummer had to beat it almost beyond the point of possibility. Progression. Lines which get laughs in the First Act will not get laughs in the Second Act. A situation which will alert an audience in the First Act will leave them nodding in the Second Act. The demand for progression is basic in human nature. Think of the sex act.

For the rest, my words of wisdom are the same as always. Work. Write, act, direct. See and read as many plays as possible. It's a long haul, depending as much on your rate of personal growth as on your acquisition of dramatic technique. And at the end of the haul, there is one man who determines whether it was worth it or in vain . . . whoever may be the critic on *The New York Times*. Madness, right? . . . I must end this now so that I can start on my next play.

PART III

THE EDITORIAL AND BUSINESS SIDE

92

THE ROLE OF THE LITERARY AGENT TODAY

By Ann Elmo

IN EXAMINING the role of the agent in today's literary marketplace, we must first look at the shifting pressures of that marketplace on all who enter it and understand the demands it makes of the writer and the editor.

In earlier days, the editor of a publishing house had the time to analyze a manuscript carefully, to sit down with it, perhaps on successive nights, for countless hours and isolate its flaws and virtues. Once, an editor could take a promising writer by the hand and, with patience, counsel, and knowledge, develop that promise.

But that was another day. That was a time when fewer than half as many books were published each year as now, when sales and marketing techniques were not what they are today. That was a time when the pressures of competition, space, distribution problems, print schedules, deadlines, and quickly changing public tastes were not a major part of the marketplace. That was a time when trends, fashions, public impact and impressions affected the book business much less than they do today.

While editors may still give patient counsel on occasion, they simply do not have the time to devote to that kind of literary analysis or author nurturing. Writers must recognize that their manuscripts must be the best they can make them when they are submitted. Because of pressures and lack of time, editors often have to turn down diamond-in-the-rough manuscripts.

Therefore, the literary agent today stands between writer and editor not only as an avenue to sales, a purveyor of talent, but in the far more subtle and necessary role the editor once had time to play. The agent today can suggest, scan, discover talent that needs nurturing, can say to the writer, "This is not salable, not professionally enough crafted," or "This is good but needs work." This can save the writer time and heartache, but it is not to suggest that the agent can be a teacher, a mentor, a step-by-step guide in a writer's literary development. The job of agenting is too time-consuming for that. But most agents can and do recognize talent that needs work and will occasionally point out in general terms the strengths and weaknesses in a manuscript.

For the editor, the agent acts as a silent partner in the promotion of talent, an extra reader. A manuscript submitted by a recognized agent says to the editor: "Here is something that will not be a waste of your valuable, crowded hours. Here is something which, whether you decide on it or not, is worth the seeing."

This silent partnership is extremely important to writers and editors in today's literary whirlpool. But the agent is more than a foot in the door for the writer, more than a guarantee to a better price for his manuscript. For the agent today fills a need of special importance to the writer in major aspects of publishing.

The writer needs an agent who knows the demands of each segment of today's literary marketplace, who sends out manuscripts selectively, not in a shotgun fashion. The writer needs an agent with know-how and with well-established channels to international publishing, motion pictures, and television. And the writer needs an agent who is honest in criticism and suggestion about a manuscript. Of course, agents have made errors in judgment on a manuscript, just as publishers have, but agents are more accessible to writers than publishers can be.

The question often asked is whether beginners need an agent. Beginning writers, completely "unsold" writers, probably do not need an agent because their work is not on the level of professionalism which major publications or publishers require. But writers who have proven their seriousness as writers and established their talents through some publication do need an agent, because the writer's purpose is to write. To devote a large portion of that time analyzing markets, getting to editors and listening to their needs, bargaining for terms, going over the fine points of the average contract—doing all of these things and more — is to divert time and attention and talents from the writer's real purpose: to write, to produce salable material for today's market.

How does a writer find an agent? There is a list of agents in that very valuable and quite complete volume known in the trade as *LMP*

—*Literary Market Place*—available at the reference desk of most public libraries, and the Society of Authors' Representatives publishes a list of its members.* Just about all active agents are listed in LMP, but it should be mentioned in passing and for whatever it's worth, that not all agents are members of the Society of Authors' Representatives.

If one finds a satisfactory agent who is willing to take on a new client, should one expect instant success? It would be nice for all parties concerned, but unfortunately it would be unrealistic. An agent is not a miracle worker. An agent is bound by the nature of the material the writer sends in, and that material is subject to the constantly shifting needs of the publishing marketplace. Quality is always important, but in today's publishing world, it is but one factor. Marketability—that element which is in tune with the needs of the current marketplace—is equally important.

Publishers are more conscious than ever before of changing trends, tastes, and moods of the public, which seems to move as an amorphous mass. When a taste for spy-adventure stories sets in, for example, it seems to affect the general buying readership. When westerns become popular, they do so across the board. Of course, every type of story has a faithful core of followers who remain constant, but the "mass market" is made up of exactly that—the mass of readers. Why one kind of story seems to spiral into popularity, to be followed by still another type, is a continuing source of speculation. Television and Hollywood have an effect. So do contemporary events, or a spectacular occurrence. Deep human needs also surge forward to create trends from time to time. The vast, instant communication of today's electronic and print media creates a national and international awareness on the part of the public, and readers are enlightened about what is going on in remote places all over the world. People everywhere are cognizant of and touched by the same things; they have a degree of awareness they never have had before, and so they move, respond, and react *en masse,* as never before.

Publishers are constantly trying to detect, to anticipate these trends, these mass inclinations toward a particular topic, new style, different

---

* A copy of this list of agents will be sent free on request, when accompanied by a stamped, self-addressed envelope, by *The Writer* (8 Arlington St., Boston, Mass. 02116).

type of book. Sometimes these trends are evident; sometimes they are dormant, waiting for the right moment to emerge. To the writer, these mass trends in taste and appeal are very significant, because they affect the marketability of a manuscript. It is not an exaggeration to say that a manuscript on a subject that publishers feel is past its peak is virtually unmarketable—regardless of the quality of the material.

This is perhaps not right, yet it is a fact of publishing life, a fact that is of the utmost importance to any author who is setting out to conquer in the arena of mass-market fiction. It is also important to the nonfiction author. If Mafia stories are on their way out, the best new one won't be bought, and if publishers feel that books on macrame are on their way out, no such offering will sell, no matter how good it is.

This marketability of a manuscript is what the agent can tell with much more accuracy than the average author. It is simply a question of being in the center of the marketplace and keeping *au courant* with the shifts and changes of that arena. Authors themselves, however, should try to pay attention to trends and directions in the publishing world by watching publishers' lists, announcements of books to be published in coming seasons, etc. Magazine writers need to be aware of topics in the news or around the world; they may be good subjects for articles or used as background and themes of short stories and novels. Often a simple query to a publisher, outlining the subject matter of a proposed manuscript, will save everyone a lot of work and time. If a writer has an agent, an inquiry to the agent describing what he has in mind will give him the benefit of the agent's knowledge of the market.

Every so often, a manuscript of special quality, craftsmanship, appeal and good timing will rise above the trends of the marketplace and become a success. This is the exception and not the rule. Unfortunately, exceptions always seem to shine brightest to new writers, but they would do better to follow the rule.

New writers, and sometimes more experienced ones, often complain that they know, are certain in their hearts, that the public would go for their literary offering, and sometimes an agent is inclined to agree. But the writer in this case may be forgetting the one salient factor that must always be kept in mind: The manuscript must be sold to the editor or publisher first. It is what the publisher wants, feels, believes, thinks, decides will sell that governs whether the manuscript is accepted and offered to the public. The publisher and editor stand between the writer and the public; publishers are the *real* literary marketplace.

And even then, the writer should understand, the mechanics of marketing, sales, distribution all go into the success of the published work. There are new, computerized methods being tried that will tell the publisher which books of his are selling in what geographic areas. Some of these new systems claim they can divide the geographic areas into local ones and pinpoint types of readers in a given store, their tastes, preferences, etc. These exercises in computer demography may help the writer in picking out subjects and genres just as they may help the publisher in ascertaining sales patterns. I say *may* because I am not at all certain that tastes, preferences, desires can be that accurately defined according to cultural, social, and economic factors. Books are read by individuals, and the strength of the publishing industry lies in its ability and desire to satisfy the tremendous variety of individual tastes and preferences. I must pause to wonder if the computerized sales information supposedly based on demographic factors will tend to encourage even greater mass-appeal publishing to the detriment of variety and individuality. This relatively new aspect of book marketing will be watched with deep interest by everyone concerned.

To the new writer, a word about submissions is in order. It is not usually necessary to submit a complete manuscript for a long work. A few chapters, and an outline of the rest of the work, or a summary of what will follow, will do. Any professional manuscript reader or editor in a publishing company, or an experienced agent, can tell from that whether the manuscript shows promise. If it does, a request to see the rest will be forthcoming. Of course there are many promising manuscripts which do not hold up when finished, and that is a problem to be taken up at that time. A busy agent looks for a certain level of writing skill, style, and quality, as well as for a marketable topic. These elements are usually present in three or so sample chapters— very often in the first chapter—or not at all. Only seldom does one find the first three chapters terrible, and the rest of the book brilliant —and the same is true the other way around.

About the future? The marketplace will continue to be a place of uncertainty, changing trends and fashions, a frantic rushing about to latch onto a hot topic. I am optimistic about the future of literature in our market. There is a distribution bottleneck that affects every publisher, and, so, every author. How to bring books to the public in the most effective way is still the major problem—a practical, mechanical, space and sales problem—but the market is there for books more than ever before. In spite of television, that absorbing and powerful medium, more and more people immerse themselves in books today, and it has been found that TV viewers are returning to reading. The printed word offers more variety, and, to allude to Marshall McLuhan, that terribly important element that a reader supplies to each book—his own subconscious mental images of the characters and what is taking place. An author can describe people and places as he sees them, but the reader forms his own very personal images.

We can immerse ourselves in reading in a way and to a degree that is not possible in any other medium. But today, every medium is helping make a more aware, more sophisticated audience. Such audiences will, I am sure, turn to books. The literary marketplace is flourishing. It will continue to do so. Whether it achieves its potential and fulfills its promise depends, in the final analysis, on the writer and his art.

93

WHAT WRITERS SHOULD KNOW ABOUT
THE NEW COPYRIGHT LAW

On October 19, 1976, the bill for the general revision of the United States copyright law was signed by President Gerald R. Ford and became Public Law 94-553 (90 Stat. 2541). The new law became effective on January 1, 1978, superseding the copyright act of 1909 (called "the old law" in this chapter).

Highlights of the New Law

Some of the highlights of the new law of special interest to writers are presented here. For detailed information about specific changes or new provisions, write to the Copyright Office (Library of Congress, Washington, DC 20559).

Single National System

The new copyright law establishes a single system of federal statutory protection for all copyrightable works, published or unpublished, and protects them from their creation. This replaces the old dual system of protecting works under the common law before publication and under Federal statute after publication.

New Definition of What Can Be Copyrighted

Under the new law, original works of authorship fixed in a tangible medium are provided with copyright protection from the time of their creation. Types of copyrightable works now include manuscripts along with books, periodicals, phonorecords, films, tapes, disks, and cards. Under the old law, unpublished manuscripts could not be copyrighted (except for certain specialized types of manuscripts such as dramatic works) and were protected by common law.

No copyright protection can be obtained for any idea, procedure, process, system, method of operation, concept, principle or discovery, regardless of the form in which it is described, explained, illustrated or embodied.

533

The new law continues the prohibition in the old law against copyright in "publications of the United States Government" but clarifies its scope by defining works covered by the prohibition as those prepared by an officer or an employee of the U.S. Government as part of that person's official duties.

Ownership of Copyright

Copyright vests in the author or authors of the work. The authors of a joint work are co-owners of copyright in the work.

Copyright in a separate contribution to a collective work (such as a periodical) vests in the author of the contribution. The owner of the copyright in the collective work acquires only the privilege of using the separate contribution as part of that collective work, unless there is a written transfer of copyright ownership signed by the owner. (A separate contribution to a collective work may bear its own copyright notice, or there may be a single copyright notice for the collective work, which satisfies the requirement for notice for all the separate contributions regardless of ownership.) A transfer of copyright by the author may be terminated 35 years from the date of the transfer, and all rights revert to the author.

In the case of a work made for hire (a work prepared by an employee in the scope of his or her employment, or a work commissioned for use as a contribution to a collective work if the parties agree in a signed document that the work shall be considered a work made for hire), the employer or person for whom the work was prepared is considered the author and owns the copyright.

Divisibility of Copyright

The new law says that any of the exclusive rights comprised in a copyright, including any subdivision of any of those rights, may be transferred and owned separately. The owner of any particular exclusive right is entitled, to the extent of that right, to all of the protection accorded to the copyright owner under this title.*

The exclusive rights of copyright owners are as follows:

---

* According to Barbara Ringer, U.S. Register of Copyrights, "There can no longer be any question about an author's rights to divide up a copyright in the most remunerative possible way, and to retain for future bargaining any rights that he or she does not wish to include in a transfer."—Ed.

(1) to reproduce the copyrighted work,

(2) to prepare derivative works based on the copyrighted work,

(3) to distribute copies of the copyrighted work by sale,

(4) to perform publicly a literary, musical, dramatic, or choreographic work, a pantomime, motion picture or other audiovisual work, and

(5) to display publicly a copyrighted literary, dramatic, musical or choreographic work, a pantomime or a pictorial, graphic or sculptural work, including the individual images of a motion picture or other audiovisual work.

Fair Use

The new law adds a provision to the statute specifically recognizing the principle of "fair use" as a limitation on the exlusive rights of copyright owners, and indicates factors to be considered in determining whether particular uses fall within this category.

These factors are as follows:

(1) The purpose and character of the use, including whether such use is of a commercial nature or is for nonprofit educational purposes;

(2) The nature of the copyrighted work;

(3) The amount and substantiality of the portion used in relation to the copyrighted work as a whole;

(4) The effect of the use upon the potential market for or value of the copyrighted work.

Photocopies by Libraries

In addition to the provision for "fair use," the new law specifies circumstances under which the making or distribution of single photocopies of works by libraries for noncommercial purposes does not constitute a copyright infringement. For detailed information, write to the Copyright Office.

Duration of Copyright for Works Created On or After January 1, 1978

For works created on or after January 1, 1978, the new law

provides a copyright term lasting for the author's life plus an additional 50 years after the author's death. In joint works, the term consists of the life of the last surviving author and 50 years after that author's death.

For works made for hire, and for anonymous and pseudonymous works (unless the author's identity is revealed in Copyright Office records), the term is 75 years from publication or 100 years from creation, whichever is shorter. The system of copyright renewal which existed under the old law does not apply to works created under the new law.

Duration of Copyright for Works in Existence But Not Copyrighted on January 1, 1978

For unpublished works that are already in existence on January 1, 1978, but that are not protected by statutory copyright, and have not yet gone into the public domain, the new law generally provides automatic federal copyright protection for the same life-plus-50-years or 75/100-year terms provided for new works.

Works already in the public domain cannot be protected under the new law. There is no procedure for restoring protection for works in which copyright has been lost for any reason.

The new law provides that all terms of copyright will run through the end of the calendar year in which they would otherwise expire. This affects not only the duration of copyrights but also the time limits for renewal.

Duration of Copyright for Works Already Copyrighted

For works already copyrighted, the new law retains the old term copyright of 28 years from first publication, renewable for a second period of protection, but it increases the length of the renewal period to 47 years. The maximum total term of copyright protection for works already copyrighted is increased from 56 years (a first term of 28 years plus a renewal term of 28 years) to 75 years (a first term of 28 years plus a renewal term of 47 years).

Copyrights in their first term on January 1, 1978, will still have to be renewed during the last (28th) year of the original copyright term. Copyrights that have already been renewed and were in their second term before January 1, 1978, do not need to be renewed again. They have been automatically extended to last for a total term of 75 years from the date they were originally secured.

As a result of the new copyright law, a copyrighted work will still be under protection in the United States if the first copyright term began on or after September 19, 1906, provided that renewal registration has been made for any work whose first copyright term began more than 28 years ago.

Termination of Transfers

Under the old law, after the first term of 28 years the renewal copyright reverts in certain situations to the author or other specified beneficiaries. The new law drops the renewal feature except for works already in their first term of statutory protection when the new law takes effect. Instead, for transfers of rights made by an author, the new law generally permits the author or certain heirs to terminate the transfer after 35 years by serving written notice on the transferee within specified time limits.

For works already under statutory copyright protection, a similar right of termination is provided with respect to transfers covering the newly added years, thus extending the maximum term of the copyright from 56 to 75 years. Within certain time limits, an author or specified heirs of the author are generally entitled to file a notice terminating the author's transfers covering any part of the period (usually 19 years) that has now been added to the end of the second term of copyright in a work already under the protection of the new law.

Notice of Copyright

The new law calls for a copyright notice on published copies of a work, but omission or errors will not immediately result in forfeiture of the copyright (as with the old law) and can be corrected. The notice may be in any position that will give reasonable notice of the claim of copyright. The form of the notice is the same as it was under the old law: the word "copyright," "copr.," or the symbol ©; the year of first publication of the work; and the name of the owner of copyright in the work. Publication is defined as the distribution of copies of a work by sale (or other transfer) to the public. Offering to distribute copies constitutes publication, but a public performance does not.

Deposit and Registration

Registration of copyright may be made at any time during the subsistence of copyright in any published or unpublished work by delivering to the Copyright Office the application, a fee of $10.00, and copies of the work, known as the deposit. The required deposit is one copy in the case of an unpublished work, such as a manuscript, and two copies of a published work.

As under the old law, registration is not a condition of copyright protection but is a prerequisite to an infringement suit. Copies or phonorecords of works published with the notice of copyright that are not registered are required to be deposited for the collections of the Library of Congress, not as a condition of copyright protection, but under provisions of the law making the copyright owner subject to certain penalties for failure to deposit after a demand by the Register of Copyrights.

Copyright Royalty Tribunal

The new law creates a Copyright Royalty Tribunal whose purpose is to determine whether copyright royalty rates in certain categories where such rates are established in the law, are reasonable and, if not, to adjust them; it will also in certain circumstances determine the distribution of those statutory royalty fees deposited with the Register of Copyrights.

Manufacturing Clause

Under the old law, certain works were required to have been manufactured in the United States to have copyright protection here. The new Act terminates this requirement completely after July 1, 1982. For the period between January 1, 1978 and July 1, 1982, it makes several modifications that narrow the coverage of the manufacturing clause, permit the importation of 2,000 copies manufactured abroad instead of the old limit of 1,500 copies, and equate manufacture in Canada with manufacture in the United States.

Further Information

Copies of the new law are available free of charge by writing to the Copyright Office, Library of Congress, Washington, DC 20559. You may also have your name added to the Copyright Office Mailing List by sending a written request to the Copyright Office.

94

EDITING THE MYSTERY AND SUSPENSE NOVEL

By Joan Kahn

BEING a mystery book editor (which is what I am primarily, though I've edited a variety of books, including an etiquette book, biographies, poetry, art books and non-mystery fiction) is like being any old kind of an editor, except that it may be a little more fun, partly because the manuscripts one gets to read are usually above the general average and usually the author seems to have rather liked writing his book.

Though I have edited non-fiction happily, I am especially interested in fiction, in the novel, and I think that the best mystery/ suspense fiction these days has many (or more) of the same qualities that make the good non-mystery novel good.

The novel, for me, is a piece of writing with a definite form, a form which has infinite variations, and gives the experimenter as much room as he needs. But a novel is a novel—it isn't a short story, or a prose poem, or an essay, or a form of biography or even a purge. In a novel the things an author saw or experienced, the emotions he felt, the information he acquired, and the ideas that came to him have been absorbed and digested and reproduced in a particular, if elastic, form—that of a novel.

A mystery novel is a novel. Once the mystery novel was fairly rigid in format, and the emphasis was primarily on detection and a puzzle. In the introduction to a 1932 book, *The Floating Admiral,* Dorothy L. Sayers (who, whether she knew it or not, widened the horizon of the detective mystery so successfully that her novels read as well today as they did when she wrote them—and Lord knows that seems to me to be no longer true of many of her contemporaries) said while talking about The Detection Club: "Its membership is confined to those who have written genuine detective stories (not adventure tales or 'thrillers')."

Genuine detective stories that are original and good are not readily available today, and Miss Sayers (who ultimately turned scornfully from all detective story writing, including her own, as her main interest became the field of religious writing), if she were still interested in the mystery novel today, might have agreed to widen the membership of The Detection Club and make it less restrictive.

The suspense novel label came into being to cover much of the widening mystery field (actually it is too generally used and often on some books not worthy of it). The suspense novel isn't limited to deductive mysteries and, in fact, some books under its free-wheeling label don't even have a detective (police or private) in them, and, though this is rare, sometimes don't include a murder.

But some of Miss Sayers' rules for Detection Club members could still be of use to today's suspense novelists: "Detectives must detect by their wits, without the help of accident or coincidence; the author must not invent impossible death rays and poison to produce solutions which no living person could expect; he must write as good English as he can, to keep the detective story up to the highest standard that its nature permits, and to free it from the bad legacy of sensationalism, claptrap and jargon."

At its best the present-day mystery novel often reaches, it seems to me, very high standards of writing, and it also is trying to explore a variety of new approaches to its story. But—and this time I quote Howard Haycraft quoting Somerset Maugham—"The reason that so many modern readers have turned to mystery fiction is that here, and here alone, they can be sure of a novel which tells a story."

The suspense novel tells a story, on many levels. We know that some of the levels appeal to Presidents of the United States, professors and provosts of colleges, lawyers and scientists. I think the average steady mystery reader is a lot brighter than the average man. The mystery is like caviar or a very good dry martini. At its best, only intelligent readers appreciate it. Today the mystery market is a vast one, reaching people who may not ordinarily be interested in book reading. Some of this vast market is the result of television and films which pluck characters out of books and return them in other mediums enticingly embodied in attractive actors and actresses.

I've been lucky, as an editor, in that I've been able to edit and publish what seem to me the best books I can find. I've never had to worry first about where or how big the market for the books will be, and I think Harper books have sold well enough to keep our authors fairly happy and to keep Harper's fairly happy, too, but how they would sell isn't what I thought about first. I feel that no writer or painter or musician should choose to enter his field primarily because he wants to make money. There are other fields in which one can make money faster and more easily and with far more certainty, though on the whole a writer has an easier time supporting himself than other creative people (there are more book buyers than there are concert goers or art collectors, and a book is easier to reproduce and to get to its audience).

To be a writer is hard work, but exciting work, even if one isn't sure one can make a living from it. To be an editor is hard work, too, and exciting work (and one does get a pay check), but publishing is a gambling game. We never *really* know what books are going to sell well—or sometimes even why a given book is selling.

I would like, as I'm sure every editor would, to find on my desk of a morning a manuscript that, when read, would have me saying, "Oh boy, is this a book!" And then I could dash around the House yelling, "Hey, you should see what *I* just found!" and the salesmen would all agree with me, and we'd turn the manuscript as fast as possible into a handsome book, and when the bookstores heard about the book, they'd take a lot of copies, and when the critics read the book they'd give it rave reviews, and when the public read the reviews, it would buy the book like mad. And then the book clubs and the reprint houses and the motion picture people would come storming in. Sometimes that does really happen. But not absolutely all the time, alas.

When it doesn't, then there is the need for an editor. An editor's job, as you probably know, is a lot of different things, Once he has decided to publish the book, he or she has to try to figure out (sort of guess) how many copies to print and what price to put on the book, and he has to consult the designer, and to worry about the jacket and the jacket copy, and the advertising and promotion, along with the various departments who watch over all these things.

But the most important thing an editor does, I think, is to help the author get his book into its best possible shape. To do this the editor has to be very gentle in part and very firm in part—and he must try to get into the author's mind and to understand what the author's intentions were as fully as he can. This is often especially hard if the editor and the author have never met (the author often lives far away) and the editor knows the author only through his manuscript and correspondence. Usually an author who has just finished a book is in a very touchy state: he's proud but defensive. The book was a part of him—for a long time his energies and his mind were devoted almost entirely to it. He must have loved it (or at least admired it) while he was working on it, or he couldn't have gone on working, and now that he's brought it into being he not only still loves it—but he's hoping it will go out and support him— and that it may also make him respected—or even famous.

An author who has just finished a book is often still infatuated with it; he hasn't the judgment he would have if he could put the book aside until time could take the rosiness out of his vision. Usually a writer can't afford to (or won't) wait for time. So he needs an editor, one who seems to understand him and to make sense to him. And the editor has to be able to respond with sensitivity, and sense, to the particular book of the particular author. To guide the author through the revision—sometimes minor, sometimes major—of the book he has written is a delicate (and often sometimes absolutely exhausting) job.

In fiction, the editor's hand must be as light and as accurate and knowledgeable as the hand of a very good surgeon as he probes the intricate network of veins and tissues, cutting away what should come out without cutting anything vital and making sure the patient will live, in a healthier condition. An author who needs the help of an editor to guide him through revisions must find the editor encouraging and reassuring as well as firm, because hard as writing often is, revision is often harder. And after the long hours at the typewriter, an author probably wants to lie down or to go dancing, or, if he's going to write, to start a completely new book.

One of the hardest things, I think, that an editor has to do (its not exactly easy on the author, either) is to turn down a book that seems to the editor so far below the author's level that publishing it won't do him any good. It's especially hard if one admires the author's work—and if the author has a reputation—because one knows that another publisher may very well take the book just to get the author and won't be concerned whether the publication of an inferior work a) will make the author sloppy and willing to do other inferior works later and b) will make the critics, bookstores and readers wonder if the author is really so hot. This is unlike the situation in other creative fields: a musician doesn't expect everything he writes to be heard, a playwright doesn't expect all his plays to be backed, a painter doesn't expect all his paintings to be hung and to be sold. Some manuscripts—even those of a good writer—*don't* work out, and, *very* hard though it is, these should be put aside. There's no easy sledding in writing or any of the arts. For artists in any field to depend upon their work to support them is a dangerous thing; it's much better to give the work a chance by doing something else for bread and butter—even if it means a double job.

I am a demanding euitor—but I'm also a painstaking editor. I care about fiction and the mystery/suspense field. And I think *care* and *caring* pay off. I still, after a long time in it, find the field very exciting. I have made the usual, or perhaps more than usual, mistakes along the way; it would be a great help to be clairvoyant but I'm not. Sometimes I fail to reach an author I admire, and the author goes away and I'm saddened.

But the author-editor relationship is, I feel, a very close one, and it has to be an honest one. An author who doesn't trust my judgment and thinks I'm foolish would be even more foolish to keep on working with me. And I cannot fight wholeheartedly for a book I don't think is any good.

I've been very lucky in getting a good many good manuscripts from good authors. And I've never felt that suspense fiction was second-class fiction or should be so treated.

More and more readers are beginning to discover the quality and pleasure of today's suspense fiction, though I'm sorry to say it is still too often reviewed in little boxes and given short shrift. Too many people say simply that they never read suspense fiction. What, I wonder, if they like fiction, are they reading instead? Not too many general novels are superior to the better suspense novels as far as writing or general reading pleasure goes.

Occasionally a novel (or a non-fiction book) in the crime field shoots up on the best seller list and is wildly heralded, and I consider how much the readers of those books would enjoy other good —and sometimes better—books in the mystery field that they haven't bothered to notice the existence of, and I think, "Oh, hell, the idiots." But the situation is getting better all the time (I'm an optimist). I do believe that books, good books, in the suspense field are not only here to stay, but here to be noticed a lot more in time to come.

95

RESEARCH AT UNCLE SAM'S BOOKSTORE

By Dee Stuart

SOMEONE once said that successful writing is 80% research and 20% rewriting. But what if you are tied to home or office and can't get away to do research? Or, if you are free to go, suppose there are no resources available?

As a beginning writer with two pre-schoolers, I hit these problems head-on while trying to research an article suggested by a friend.

"I'd love to grow gourds to make into decorative arrangements," she said. "But I've no idea how to grow them, much less preserve them."

Challenged, I, too, searched for information—with little success. Our garden book didn't cover gourds. My only other resource was the high school library. Encyclopedias were too general. The *Readers' Guide* turned up nothing. In my ignorance, I was pleased to find that nothing had been published on gourds. This would mean a plus value for my article. I soon learned there was a reason nothing had been written: No information was available.

Discouraged, I told a fellow writer I'd have to abandon the idea. Then she told me about "Uncle Sam's Bookstore."

This vast storehouse boasts more than 25,000 different titles for sale by the Superintendent of Documents, U.S. Government Printing Office, Washington, D.C. 20402. These publications range in price from 10¢ up (minimum order, $1.00, by mail). And Uncle Sam's Bookstore is as near as your mailbox.

I consulted the GPO list of publications and to my delight found two booklets on gourds. I promptly sent for them. A few weeks later I had more information about gourds than I could ever use.

Result? Two articles, two sales: "Gourds—Pretty and Practical" and "Gourds Are for the Birds."

From then on, I resolved that Uncle Sam's Bookstore would be my first resource rather than a last resort.

A pamphlet, "Consumer Guide to Federal Publications," available free from the U.S. Government Printing Office in Washington, D.C., describes the publications available by mail or at the GPO bookstores, the type and range of material and subjects covered and Subject Bibliographies that may be obtained at no cost; how material may be ordered or purchased; and other sources of federal publications in specialized subject areas. These free price lists for printed material available in specific categories and related subjects cover a wide range: *Accounting, Aging, Arts and Artists, Birds, Day Care, Dentistry, Earth Sciences, Farms and Farming, Fish and Marine Life, Grants and Awards, Astronomy and Astrophysics, Law Enforcement, Postage Stamps, Fossils, Violence, Weather* — more than 250.

One list, *Consumer Information,* includes family finances, appliances, recreation, gardening, health and safety, food, house and home, child care, and clothing and fabrics. All of these subjects are gold mines of information for writers of home, garden and women's magazine features.

Government publications are a prime source of information from many points of view. Not only will you find material on ordinary subjects, such as gourds, but you can learn all about the newest discoveries in the fields of science, space, homemaking, and other areas that you may not be able to learn about anywhere else. The data is current, valid, authoritative, and the price is low.

These publications are ideal for supplementing previous research and for double-checking factual accuracy. I know one writer working on a Civil War novel who enlarges her research by culling facts from the vast material found in the Civil War volume of the *Historical Handbooks Series.* Another friend, who writes juvenile stories about the American Indians, visited Bandelier National Monument in New Mexico, absorbed the feel of the place and developed a story. When she started writing, she found she needed more background information. Since she lives on a ranch in Montana, miles from the nearest library, additional research could have been an unsolvable problem.

She scanned the GPO Subject Bibliography under the title of *Smithsonian Institution Popular Publications* and found there "Bandelier National Monument" and ordered the booklet. From it she gleaned information on the origins and life of the Indians who lived there. She added authenticity to later Indian stories with the aid of booklets on various tribes—without ever leaving home!

Our family camping trips from coast to coast have provided raw material for many travel stories. And GPO publications have served many times to jog my memory of sites we've seen and to add "nuts-and-bolts" to the articles that followed.

Recently we camped at Sylvan Lake, South Dakota. I took detailed notes on scenery and what to see and do. Later when I began writing a roundup piece on the Black Hills, I discovered I needed a few concrete facts to give the story depth and substance. I trekked down to the Government branch bookstore in Kansas City and found all the information I needed in brochures on Wind Cave National Park and Mount Rushmore. Result? A sale to *Midwest Motorist.*

The Government Printing Office operates branch bookstores across the country. In addition to the Kansas City branch, there are similar stores in Atlanta, Birmingham, Boston, Chicago, Cleveland, Columbus, Dallas, Denver, Detroit, Houston, Jacksonville, Kansas City, Los Angeles, Milwaukee, New York City, Philadelphia, Pueblo, San Francisco, Seattle, Washington. D.C. (five stores). If you are lucky enough to live near one of Uncle Sam's Bookstores, you may find that browsing through the hundreds of publications on display or available on request from a Subject Bibliography will spark ideas for articles and stories.

Even if you do not live near one of these stores, merely perusing the titles listed in the bibliographies can turn you on. A pamphlet on John Muir, noted 19th-century naturalist and conservationist, could well be the inspiration for an article, story, or biography.

Writers in the consumer field will find of special interest the *Consumer Information Catalog,* listing over 150 free consumer information publications and about 100 sales publications that have been popular with the general public. This *Catalog* is available from the Consumer Information Center, Pueblo, Colorado 81009.

Moneymaking ideas for young people—topics such as "Catfish Farming," "Raising Rabbits," "Mushroom Growing" and "Bee-Keeping for Beginners"—could all be developed into salable articles.

If you need a few appropriate phrases for the foreign characters in your story to use, send for the *Foreign Languages* price list which includes foreign phrase books. Uncle Sam has them—from Arabic to Tagalog.

Although U.S. Government publications are primarily a source of information, you are free to quote from them without asking permission—to give your article validity. U.S. Government publications are in the public domain. Be sure, however, that the government publication is *not a reprint* of copyrighted material; if it is, the copyright remains in force, and you will have to write for permission to the copyright owner to quote from it. Subject bibliographies of special interest to writers include free price lists on publications about *Copyrights* (of special concern now with the recent changes in the copyright law), *Poetry and Literature, Reading, Stenography, Typing and Writing* (with the popular and helpful "Seven Keys to Better, Faster Typing").

One best-selling GPO publication, "Questions about the Oceans," is designed to answer questions about oceanography and marine sciences. This 120-page book also answers such questions as, "Why is the ocean salty?" "Where do waves come from?" "How deep has man gone in the ocean?" It lists colleges and universities which offer oceanographic courses and tells who hires oceanographers. An imaginative writer could transform this material into a juvenile picture book, a science article for a children's magazine or a career article for young people.

Answers to the above questions and others in over 250 subject areas are yours for the asking. The first step is to send for the leaflet, "Consumers Guide to Federal Publications," which lists the Subject Bibliographies under which all government publications for sale have been grouped. Any of these will be mailed free upon request, with price lists for the booklets available under each subject. From these lists of publications and price lists, choose those you wish, fill in the order blank on the last page of the price list, and mail with your check. Payment must be made in advance, accompanying orders (except for those who have special "deposit accounts"). Address all requests to: Superintendent of Documents, U.S. Government Printing Office, Washington, D.C. 20402.

The quickest way to order is to call or mail your request to the bookstore nearest you. If they stock what you want, they will ship it direct. If not, they will order it for you from Washington.

Thirty to forty thousand orders a day flood the Superintendent's office. Service is remarkable in the face of such a logistics nightmare. "In one section," the office reports, "all the employees do is open mail, working sixteen hours a day in two shifts." A priority desk handles bookstore orders, all of which are shipped within forty-eight hours. If possible, place your order through a branch store to take advantage of this high-speed service.

The best way to keep informed about the avalanche of new and popular government publications is to send for the free list of *Selected U.S. Government Publications,* published ten times a year, which describes 150 to 200 popular publications and includes a price list and order blank. You may receive this regularly by asking your name to be entered for this free service, and whether you think you'll need it or not, it's a good idea. You'll be surprised to find how many topics will be of interest to you—and in many cases will give you an idea for a story or article. You may also subscribe to the *Monthly Catalog of U.S. Government Publications*—12 issues with indexes—for $45.00 a year. This is a comprehensive listing of all publications issued by the departments and agencies of the federal government.

Writers today need not be discouraged or put off by lack of opportunity for doing research. If you don't drive, if you are tied down with children or otherwise housebound, if you work eight hours a day and have no time to seek out information, if you live in the boondocks and no library is near you, or if you merely want to explore untapped resources, you will find Uncle Sam's Bookstore a rich storehouse of knowledge just waiting for you to open the door.

96

LEGAL RIGHTS FOR WRITERS

By Jeanne Pollett

JOSH BILLINGS once remarked that a man's problem isn't so much the things he doesn't know, as the things he knows that aren't so.

Writers and photographers are no exception. Some of the most widely held beliefs about their legal rights and responsibilities have no foundation in law. Often the writer or the cameraman is on firmer legal ground than he thinks. He may worry about restrictions that simply don't exist. But sometimes he acts with false confidence, risking liability without realizing it.

Let's look at some of the legal principles important to those who write or take photographs for publication.

Use of the word "allegedly" or the naming of a source gives no legal protection to the writer.

There are perfectly valid reasons for a newsman to qualify a statement this way. The practice alerts the reader to the source and probable reliability of information. But it's no defense in a legal action.

"John Smith is alleged to have shot the victim" or "Police said John Smith fired the fatal shot" may literally be true, even though Smith was innocent and five hundred miles away at the time. But so far as the law of defamation is concerned, the words are the precise equivalent of the flat statement, "John Smith shot the victim." If John is innocent, he may bring a successful action for libel. (The writer's reasonable reliance on the information given him may, however, have some bearing on the question of damages.)

Inconsistently enough (and who ever said the law was consistent?), a retraction, to be legally effective, must be put forth as the writer's own statement. In the case of that shooting, it's not enough to say by way of retraction, "Police stated further investigation showed John

Smith had no connection with the shooting." The retraction must be a flat denial that Smith shot the victim.

Even reporting and denying a rumor may get the writer into a legal jam. An editorial stating, "This newspaper does not believe the report that Councilman Jones accepted any favor in return for changing his vote," may be treated as furthering a rumor that Jones did take a bribe. Courts say, perhaps somewhat unrealistically, that one may not escape liability for repeating a defamatory statement by adding that the writer does not believe it.

Recent court rulings regarding public figures have not abrogated the basic principles of libel law.

The cases of *New York Times* v. *Sullivan* and *Associated Press* v. *Walker,* and later pronouncements of the courts, do give writers considerably more leeway where public figures are concerned, but on the whole, the old concept of libel still stands:

Libel is a malicious publication, expressed either in printing, writing, typewriting, or by signs and pictures, tending either to blacken the memory of one who is dead, or the reputation of one who is alive, and expose him to public hatred, contempt, or ridicule.

Truth is a defense to an action for libel. Under the more recent decisions, it doesn't have to be an absolute, every-i-dotted-and-every-t-crossed truth. But substantial accuracy is required. One cannot imagine a twentieth-century court holding it libelous to say a man had stolen two pigs when in truth he had stolen only one (although that rule used to be the law in England).

Mere name-calling is not actionable.

A writer isn't likely to become involved in this one except perhaps indirectly, in reporting a quarrel at a meeting, for example.

William L. Prosser, former dean of the University of California School of Law, puts it this way:

"The courts have held that mere words of abuse, indicating that the defendant dislikes the plaintiff and has a low opinion of him, but without suggesting any specific charge against him, are not to be treated as defamatory. A certain amount of vulgar name-calling is tolerated, on the theory that it will necessarily be understood to amount to nothing more.''

Use of a person's name without his consent is not actionable.

Any working newsman has had the experience of watching an irate individual pound his desk, red-faced, and shout, "If you use my name again without my permission—I'll sue!"

The law doesn't give that kind of protection to even the most publicity-shy. So long as an event is newsworthy (and that's a broad definition indeed), the name of even a reluctant participant may appear in print. (A few states do prohibit publishing the identities of juvenile offenders or of victims of sex crimes.)

With very narrow exceptions, a newspaper or magazine may not be restrained from publishing—or be required to publish—anything.

A surprisingly large number of otherwise well-informed persons will speculate whether a publication "should have been allowed" to print a controversial piece.

The First (freedom of the press) Amendment is construed as allowing virtually no prior restraint on publication. After publication, writer and publisher are accountable for libel, invasion of privacy, or other actionable injury.

As to the reverse—the question whether a publication may be required to print a particular item or advertisement—the answer until recently has been a resounding "no." A publisher has been free to reject anything (even crucial legal advertising) for any reason or for no reason but pure caprice.

Today, the validity of judicial "gag orders"—orders restricting newspaper coverage of pending criminal proceedings—is still being tested in the appellate courts. And efforts are being made to require publications to accept certain advertising, notably political ads. But as far as the typical free lancer is concerned, prior restraints are non-existent.

A writer can get into trouble even if he sticks to facts which can be proved.

As we have seen, truth is ordinarily a complete defense to a civil action for libel. But a writer may risk suit on another ground—invasion of privacy—if he goes too far in exposing another's private life.

A typical example would be bringing up that Joe Blow, who has for years lived a blameless life in the community, once was prosecuted for embezzlement. If Joe is running for county treasurer, his record is very much a matter of legitimate public concern. If he's simply going his own quiet way as a private citizen, digging into and publicizing his past may well be held to be actionable. Authors of factual police and detective yarns need to be particularly aware of this problem.

The person who owns a photographic negative doesn't necessarily have the right to reproduce it.

There's a persistent belief among even professional photographers that ownership of a negative carries with it the right to reproduce the picture. The rule is neat, easily applied—and completely without legal foundation.

The test isn't who owns or holds the negative, but for whom the work was done. When a customer pays a commercial photographer to take a picture, it's the patron, not the cameraman, who owns the right to reproduce it. Conversely, an amateur or a professional photographer who takes a picture at his own expense owns the rights to it.

The same general rules govern publication of children's pictures as those of adults.

Another bit of photographic folklore has it that a minor child may not be photographed, or his picture printed, without his parents' consent.

The same rules govern the photographing of children as the portraying of adults. In general, any non-embarrassing picture taken in a public place can safely be used in the editorial pages of a magazine or newspaper. It's O.K. to photograph that schoolyard full of children without making the rounds of their parents with model release forms.

(Commercial use of a picture, of either child or adult, in an advertisement or on a product is another matter entirely.)

A writer is not free to quote from letters and diaries that have come into his possession.

Just as ownership of a photographic negative does not carry with it a right to reproduce a picture, ownership of another person's letters or diaries does not imply the right to copy their contents.

A letter, once written, mailed, and delivered, belongs to the recipient. He may save it, destroy it, sell it, frame it and hang it on the wall. He is owner of the physical object—the paper and the ink. But literary property remains with the letter writer.

An author who wants to quote from letters (even family letters) or diaries should first obtain permission. If the letter writer or the diarist has died, approval should be obtained from his heirs.

A writer may make limited use of copyrighted material.

Facts cannot be copyrighted. Otherwise research, writing, knowledge itself would come to a grinding halt. The *form of expression* of those facts is subject to copyright.

Even so, a writer may make fair use of material which has been copyrighted by others. Under the new copyright law, which went into effect on January 1, 1978, four factors enter into the determination of what is "fair use": Purpose and character of the use—for example, whether it is for commercial or for educational purposes; nature of the copyrighted work; the proportion of material used in relation to the whole; effect of the use upon the potential market for or value of the original.

The law does not specify a particular amount of copyrighted material that may be used.

Many persons in the book and music publishing industries firmly believe that up to eight bars of music (or lyrics) may be duplicated without risk.

Some countries do define fair use in mathematical terms, specifying for example that not more than eight bars may be taken from a piece of music, and not more than 1,000 words from a scientific or a literary work. As the new copyright law makes clear, there is no such specific rule in the United States.

A writer may use the title from another copyrighted work without infringement.

Titles in themselves are not subject to copyright. An author need not search to see whether the one he has in mind has been used before. But an author should not on that account dash off something under the name of *Everything You Always Wanted to Know About Sex but Were Afraid to Ask.* A title may be protected under another theory of law, unfair competition. If it's become identified with one writer's product in the public mind, the title may not be appropriated and used in such a way as to make a buyer think he's getting the first writer's work rather than another's.

There's no surefire way to avoid a lawsuit.

A writer or a photographer can be on firm legal ground, and still be sued.

Unfortunately, "Can they sue?" is an utterly meaningless question. Anybody can sue anyone, however groundlessly, if he can persuade a lawyer to take the case or if he follows the proper court procedure and files the action himself without benefit of counsel. He can sue, but he may be thrown out of court long before the action gets to the trial stage.

The sorting-out process occurs after the action has been brought. In the federal courts and in some states, the person being sued files a "motion to dismiss." Other states call the pleading a "demurrer." What it says in effect is, "Even though everything alleged in the complaint is true—and we're not admitting it except for purposes of argument—you still don't have a case."

Going back to the man who didn't want his name used without his permission: If he were to bring a lawsuit against the writer or the publisher, the defendant would demur and the court would say in effect: "Plaintiff has not suffered any wrong the law recognizes. Case dismissed."

97

LITERARY AGENTS

By James Oliver Brown

I SPEAK on occasion to writers and aspiring writers, and the assumption is that I have a special knowledge of the questions such audiences ask. A few questions have been singled out as most recurring and this piece is devoted to them.

There is a lack of understanding on the part of inexperienced writers, and some experienced, of the functions of the East Coast literary agent who, while handling all rights and forms of writing, concentrates on the selling of rights to books and magazine stories and articles. The image of these agents is of rather grasping, ill-mannered, ill-bred parasites, who resist seeing and handling the works of writers, and who make the rounds of publishing houses, manuscripts in hand, persuading publishers to publish books. If females, they probably wear large flowered hats, and if males, they probably smoke cigars. I know of no such East Coast "book" literary agents.

A writer doesn't need an agent to sell a book for him here in this country. On the other hand his book will get closer attention if it has on it the imprint of a good agent. It might even sell bearing the agent's imprint where it would not have sold without such imprint, but such a sale would be rare, because manuscripts get read, regardless of who submits them. Reactions to writing are emotional, and the endorsement of an agent who is known for his taste and success might push the emotional scales in favor of the work. If I started telling an editor why he should like and buy a book, the editor would assume I was trying to get rid of a dud. The editor knows the James Brown imprint and for what it stands. He pays attention, in relation to that standing, whatever it might be in the mind of that particular editor.

The agent for "talent" (performers) and for all phases of the performance side of our business (stage, motion pictures, television) has a job of presentation different from that of the "book" agent, and the image of this kind of agent has had greater presentation by playwrights and novelists to the general public. Partly as a result of this exposure, the public has a wrong image of the "book" agent. In the performance side of the business, the buyer more than often has to be told. He has to be made to see how to blend everything together, the writing being only a part of the whole. The added factors are things such as casting, directing, stage designing. The "book" agent, on the other hand, usually presents the finished product. Ordinarily it doesn't need to be spoken about; it speaks for itself. I don't know of any of the literary agents on the performance side who wear hats and smoke cigars.

The literary agent performs a complex and varied function, which can't be too well defined. His function depends upon the kinds of writers he represents. I can speak only for my own operation. I'm a business manager-adviser, coordinator, protector of rights, exploiter of all rights to all writings of the writers I represent, such rights including book, magazine, dramatic, motion picture, radio, television, recording, translation. My important function as an agent is bringing in money for the writer, getting the most money possible in the interests of the writer, from every possible source. When an agent starts to work on a piece of writing, a story, an article, a book, whatever, he thinks of it in terms of all rights and gets it to the people who buy the rights, here and abroad. He is an expert in knowing the markets and having the organization to get to them.

The practices of the members of our agents' professional society, the Society of Authors' Representatives, are prescribed by reasonable and rigid rules. We don't advertise, and we don't live on reader's fees and editorial fees. We get clients from recommendations of people who know us, writers, editors, and others, and we live on a percentage take of the amount we take in from a sale. Theoretically, at least, if we don't sell we don't eat. Many, and I suspect, most "book" literary agents have independent incomes or some other subsidy such as rich or working spouses. A few of us actually live on 10% of our writers' earnings. This is not enough for much more than just modest, non-caviar, non-Rolls-Royce living.

I feel that if a written contract with one of my clients is necessary, I probably shouldn't have him for a client. On the other hand, if a simple letter agreement is signed stating what the relationship is anyway, I think it is in everyone's interests. I usually send such a document (if I happen to remember to do it) to a new client and leave it up to the client. They usually sign. Except in some situations where the interests of the writer were to be protected by doing it, I advise against the signing of an agency contract which goes beyond stating what the agent-client relationship is. An agency contract, for example, may provide that the agent will continue to handle the unsold rights to a property the agent has handled, should a writer leave the agent. This is not what would happen without the contract, and a writer should know this. Except in extraordinary cases, an agent should cease being the agent when the agency relationship ends. Rarely, if ever, is it in the writer's interests to have two agents working for him on different properties. The deserted agent is a deserted agent, alas, and has left only the right to receive monies and be paid under contracts with book publishers, etc., that he negotiated before the desertion. (Who cares about a deserted parasite?)

We members of the Society of Authors' Representatives feel that a writer does well to limit his search for an agent, to fit his particular needs, to the Society's membership of almost forty agents of the eighty-seven listed in the Manhattan Telephone Directory. There are at least one or two, and perhaps more, perfectly good agents, not members of the Society. One can consult a nationally known book publisher or magazine or The Authors Guild. By correspondence the author and agent can proceed to get together. I like to meet the people I take on, but not until I have read what they write to see whether they can write.

I consider it not in the writer's interest to be handled by different agents for different rights, but this is because in the operation of my office we handle everything and every right for our clients. We are represented abroad and on the West Coast by agents who carry on our work in these areas for us. We do not take on writers who divide their representation. Some perfectly reputable agents do, I am told. This is a matter of policy, having nothing to do with ethics; rather with efficiency. Commissions are 10% on U.S.A. rights and from 15% to 20% on foreign rights.

I have been asked whether a writer should pay his agent a commission on something the writer happens to place himself. If a writer questions the payment of a commission, but the agent feels he should receive this commission, I suggest a termination of the agency relationship at once since the agent should have his commission regardless of who makes the sale. A dispute of this sort sets up bad feeling not in the interests of the writer. A writer who questions the value of his agent by wanting to withhold his commission obviously is with the wrong agent. I cannot conceive of representing someone who thought I was not earning every commission on every sale. We are underpaid for the services we perform as it is. We can exist only by taking the low and high commissions on everything. Asking about *obligation* to pay a commission indicates a bad agency relationship or a misunderstanding of the agent's function. Agents often have little to do, for example, with the conferences which result in assignments to their writers of non-fiction articles by editors. Sometimes they don't know until a check arrives that there has been a conference. The agent earns his commission even here by the over-all services he performs in the over-all writing career of the writers on his list. The agent even earns it in the case of the arrived check by being sure that the pay is what it should be and that the contract of purchase is proper.

Most experienced professional writers indoctrinated in this country have a good relationship with their agents. Occasionally one runs into a writer who feels that he must be with an agent with whom he has no social life and, in fact, has an arm's length, challenging relationship. I'm sure these are fine relationships for the parties concerned. There's nothing wrong with them, ethically. The interesting thing is that the best agents, the most successful, those with the best reputations, seem not to have this kind of relationship with their clients.

Most agents of all kinds like writers and like to see manuscripts. A writer does not have to be published to get a hearing from most of the very best agents. Some of the largest successes I have had on my list have been first novels by previously unpublished writers, and an important part of my list is made up of successful writers with whom I have worked from the beginning of their published careers. A professional writer can be unpublished. He must know how to write and have that dedication which compels him to write and to consider writing as a primary function, even if, until he gets underway, he has to have a job to eat. We agents have a special sense of who is and who is not a "pro." One lady agent (and I'm told she is not being facetious, although I hope she is) claims that she can spot a writer by observing his wrists and ankles!

I'm looking now as I write this at a list of the members of the Society of Authors' Representatives. I know most of them, some better than others. Most of us are close friends. I once was an editor with a publisher, as several of us were, and got to know most of the members then. We also meet together regularly to discuss mutual problems. You can't go wrong with any of them as far as their qualifications and ability are concerned. You can go wrong as to personality. We all are pretty much alike in our attitudes toward the business, but we differ very much as people. It would be good if every writer deciding on an agent could meet several before making a decision. It saves a lot of trouble for both parties.

Good hunting to all of you. When you find the agent who inspires the best work from you, let him or her carry the ball. They will do it better than any writer can for himself. The agent knows his area of operation. And he can take the blame for any difficulties with a buyer of the writer's product. The agent is better equipped to get the buyer (publisher, producer, whatever) to do more for his client. One of the great functions of the agent is to act as a buffer and to see that love is maintained between the principals. Most people function better when they feel they are loved and that what they are doing is being appreciated. The wise writer will let his agent be the non-loved.

When I get to the end of my talks to writers, I get the questions. Down in one of the first few rows is a young man who asks the questions, "If I can place my novel myself, why do I need an agent?"

My reply, "As long as you ask that question, you don't. It's when you don't ask it that you will need an agent."

What do I mean? When this young man, I hope not too much later in his career, discovers that his career isn't as far along as it should be and realizes what a good agent can do for him, he's ready for an agent. The writer is alone in the world without an agent. He may be the kind of person incapable of working with an agent. There are some of those, and, alas, they usually don't get as far in the commercial world as they could if they were working with the experts in the competitive market place. The young man, now older, in trouble with contracts he has signed, checks with unread endorsements he has signed, out on too many tangents and limbs, without direction and proper counseling, without anyone to fight the battle for money, respect, proper promotion, proper printings and advertising, acceptable salable titles to his work, feeling alone and unwanted, realizes why placement of his work is a minor part of the function of the agent.

98

WHAT'S IN A PEN NAME?

By Deborah N. Kassman

WHEN Queen Victoria told Charles Dodgson, author of *Alice's Adventures in Wonderland,* how much she liked his book and how eagerly she looked forward to reading something else he had written, he promptly sent her his *Syllabus of Plane Algebraical Geometry.* We do not know if the Queen was amused.

Dodgson would undoubtedly be amused, however, to learn that today, more than one hundred years after the publication of *Alice,* his pen name, Lewis Carroll, is famous throughout the English-speaking world. In fact, it is said that, with the exception of Shakespeare and the Bible, the most quoted works in the English language are *Alice* and its sequel, *Through the Looking Glass.*

Dodgson limited himself to one pen name. But most authors using pseudonyms generally find themselves in the position of William Sydney Porter, who had several pen names although he signed most of his stories O. Henry. Today, many authors erupt in a veritable rash of pen names: Don Ross, who abandoned the stage at the age of forty-nine to take up novel writing and has been described by *The New York Times* as "what must be one of the most formidable writing factories in this or any other hemisphere," uses Marilyn Ross (for Gothic novels), Rose Dana (for nurse books), Don Roberts (for Westerns), and Alice Gilmer, Ellen Randolph, and Jane Rossiter (for modern novels).

Sometimes, pen names are so well known that a reviewer could write, " 'Jeremy York' rises above his usual level and suggests one of John Creasey's better pseudonyms (perhaps 'Kyle Hunt') in *The Man I Killed."* This pen name dropper knew, of course, about Mr. Creasey's twelve other pseudonyms, which include Gordon Ashe, J. J. Marric, Anthony Morton, Richard Martin, Robert Caine Frazer, etc. (Perhaps bowing to the inevitable in the case of Mr. Creasey, his publishers noted on the cover of one of his recent books, "A Mystery Novel by John Creasey as Anthony Morton." Another well-known pen name was acknowledged by the publishers in an advertisement of a new Ellery Queen mystery, giving the names of Manfred B. Lee and Fredric Dannay as the writing team behind this pseudonym.)

Often, however, even the critics are surprised by a pen name. "Some years ago I swore off reading all detective stories except those by Michael Innes," began *New York Times* critic Orville Prescott in a review. "Only the other day did I discover that Michael Innes is the pseudonym of J. I. M. Stewart, a distinguished scholar (author of *Character in Shakespeare's Plays* and a volume of the formidable *Oxford History of English Literature*) and also the author of six non-detective novels," continued the dumbfounded Mr. Prescott.

Why all these pen names? Is a pen name a good idea for a new author? There are many valid reasons why pen names are used.

1. Prolific authors sometimes use pen names simply because publishers do not want to flood the book market with many books by the same author in one year. Mr. Creasey, who completes about a dozen books a year, has three hardcover and many paperback publishers sharing his output in the United States. John Dickson Carr uses three names for his books: One publisher brings out his books under the name of John Dickson Carr; another publisher issues his books by "Carter Dickson," a pen name, and occasionally Mr. Carr has used Carr Dickson as another pseudonym. Erle Stanley Gardner writes mysteries for his publisher both under his own name and under his pen name, A. A. Fair. (Pen names are, obviously, especially widely used in the mystery and detective field, where a bonus mystery is sometimes offered to the reader: what is the *real* name of the author?)

2. Authors who have several different specialties sometimes want to use different names for each specialty. Leo C. Rosten uses his real name for serious work, the pen name Leonard Q. Ross for humor (*The Education of H*Y*M*A*N K*A*P*L*A*N*, etc.) and Leonard Ross, without the "Q," for his "melodramas" (he wrote the original story and screenplay for *Walk East on Beacon*). Bernard De-Voto wrote novels, history, and criticism under his own name, light

fiction under the name of John August, and light essays under the name of Cady Hewes. Willard Huntington Wright, who as S. S. Van Dine created the famous detective Philo Vance, noted, when he decided to leave literary criticism and become a writer of detective stories, "I rather feared ostracism if I boldly switched from esthetics and philologic research to fictional sleuthing, and so I hid behind an old family name (Van Dyne) and the Steam-Ship initials." Historical novelist Norah Lofts occasionally uses the pseudonym of Peter Curtis for suspense fiction (*No Question of Murder, The Devil's Own*, etc.).

3. Personal confessions and revelations are sometimes published under pseudonyms. *A Grief Observed*, reflections on the death of the author's wife, was signed N. W. Clerk. This name was a pseudonym for C. S. Lewis (*The Screwtape Letters*, etc.), who felt the book was so personal he should use another name. (The real name of the author was revealed by the newspapers only after Mr. Lewis died.) *The House of Tomorrow*, the diary of an unwed mother, was published under a pen name, as was *American Woman and Alcohol* by a now happily-married member of Alcoholics Anonymous.

4. Sometimes, an assumed name has already been used for other purposes. Rebecca West (author of *The Meaning of Treason*, etc.) was born Cicily Isabel Fairfield; when she began a brief stage career, she took as a stage name Rebecca West, the name of a woman in Ibsen's play *Rosmersholm*, and then used it as a pen name when she turned to writing.

5. A doctor, lawyer, or other professional person might use a pen name for non-professional writing to keep his two spheres of activity separate. Michigan Supreme Court Justice John Donaldson Voelker, especially well known for his bestselling *Anatomy of a Murder*, writes his novels under the pseudonym of Robert Traver. Sir Anthony Hope Hawkins wrote all of his books, including the famed *Prisoner of Zenda*, using his first and middle names as a pen name, Anthony Hope. Although he later regretted the pen name, he had decided to use it when he was a successful barrister and expected to continue his career as a lawyer. When *New York Times* art critic John Caraday was teaching art at the University of Virginia some

years ago, he wrote seven mystery novels under the pseudonym of Matthew Head because he wanted to use his own name solely for his art criticism.

6. Authors of non-fiction dealing with shocking or confidential material often do not use their real names because it might be unpleasant or even dangerous for them to do so. (Books by former members of secret organizations, ex-spies, etc., come in this category.) A recently published first novel about college professors and their wives—*Tell the Time to None* by Helen Hudson (a pen name) —might also be mentioned here. Declaring that the use of a pen name in this case "was clearly motivated by prudence," *Time* Magazine explained, " 'Helen Hudson' displays such knowledge of faculty politics . . . that it is obvious she occupies, or once occupied, her own glade in the groves of academe."

7. An author who has a name similar to another author's might use a pen name simply to avoid confusion. John P. Marquand's son decided to write under the name of John Phillips, rather than as John P. Marquand, Jr. Another "Jr." using a pen name is David E. Lilienthal, Jr., son of the former Atomic Energy Commissioner, who as "David Ely" has written two well-reviewed novels: *Seconds* and *The Tour*.

8. Sometimes the sex of an author is concealed by a pseudonym. Charlotte Brontë's *Jane Eyre* first appeared under the pseudonym Currer Bell, and Emily Brontë's *Wuthering Heights* originally was printed under the name Ellis Bell. George Eliot was the famous pen name of Mary Ann Evans, and George Sand the well-known pseudonym of Amandine Aurore Lucie Dupin. These women took pen names primarily because "female authors" were unpopular. Today, many women take pen names (or use initials plus last names) because they are writing sport, western or adventure fiction—and many men will not read such books or stories if they know the authors are women. Mary Grace Chute's popular Sheriff Olsen stories were therefore published under the by-line of M. G. Chute.

9. Pen names are widely used in television today. Sometimes a television playwright will be unhappy about the changes made in his script by other writers, producers, etc., and will therefore ask that

his name be dropped from the credits. But in these days of tapes and films, if a show is repeated and there is no writing credit, the producer does not have to pay a residual fee to the writer. Therefore, for his own protection, the playwright has a pen name registered with the Writers Guild of America. When he takes his real name off the script, his pen name is substituted—and when checks arrive at the Writers Guild office, made out to his pen name, they are forwarded to him. Ernest Kinoy, a former president of the Writers Guild, used B. Chweig on scripts that had been changed; another former Guild president, David Davidson, made use of his middle names, Albert Sanders. As one television playwright put it, "I use a pseudonym to protect my scripts. My name, to me, has value. It's all I've got."

(The Writers Guild of America—East and West—represents professional writers in the fields of radio, television and motion pictures.)

10. Throughout history, pen names have been used for political reasons, and the practice continues today, of course. Baroness Blixen of Rungstedlund, better known as world-famous fiction writer Isak Dinesen, wrote what the Germans considered a harmless Gothic romance during the time that the Nazis occupied Denmark. The book, which actually made use of quite subtle symbolism in presenting a parallel between the fictional villain and the Nazis, was published under the pen name Pierre Andrézel; after the war, the real name of the author was revealed. Frank O'Connor, the Irish short story writer, was born Michael John O'Donovan, and for political reasons assumed his mother's maiden name for his writing.

11. Sometimes, a pen name will be selected because several authors are involved in a collaborative effort, and listing all the names might prove cumbersome. The recent best-seller *Hurry, Sundown,* signed K. B. Gilden, was written by the husband-wife team, Katya and Burt Gilden. Other famous writing teams include Richard Wilson Webb and H. C. Wheeler (who use the names Q. Patrick, Patrick Quentin and Jonathan Stagge for their mystery novels).

12. Some business firms and government organizations do not permit employees to use their own names for writing *not* connected with their work. David Cornwell, who wrote best-selling spy novels

(*The Spy Who Came in From the Cold, The Looking-Glass War*) under the pen name John le Carré, had to use a pseudonym because he served in the British Foreign Office and thus came under Civil Service rules and restrictions. But the air of mystery surrounding Cornwell's experiences was considerably helped by the use of the pen name; even headlines in *The New York Times* after *The Spy* reached the best-seller list announced: SPY AUTHOR SHEDS UNDER-COVER POSE . . . Cornwell (Alias le Carré) Submits to Interrogation.

13. Many writers of juvenile books use pseudonyms (some authors of books for adults want to keep their writing for children quite separate). An astonishing number of pen names in the juvenile field are controlled by The Stratemeyer Syndicate, an organization founded by Edward Stratemeyer when dime novels were being replaced by the pulp magazines. Stratemeyer, who was writing The Rover Boys series under the pen name Arthur M. Winfield, contracted with various writers to turn out books on assignment, under specified pen names, for such popular juvenile series as The Bobbsey Twins, Tom Swift, The Hardy Boys, Nancy Drew, Honey Bunch, etc. In *My Father Was Uncle Wiggily*, Roger Garis describes how his mother and father worked for Stratemeyer: The titles, the pen name, and a sketchy outline were provided by Stratemeyer, and the author did the rest, receiving a flat payment of one hundred dollars for each book. Notes Mr. Garis (who also wrote for Stratemeyer):

> There was, in fact, a practical reason for writing a series under a fictitious name. If the writer died while the series was still continuing, it might be possible to find some other writer to carry it on. But if the author's own name were used, this would be impossible.

The Stratemeyer Syndicate still operates today—impressive evidence of the soundness of this particular use of pen names.

Should a new author use a pen name? In general, it is not advisable, but if a writer has a valid reason for wishing to write under a pen name, he should indicate this to an editor. However, the new author who wants to use a pen name must have excellent reasons for doing so; there are many disadvantages connected with pen names, and these may prove especially troublesome to him.

A major disadvantage is the attitude of editors toward pen names.

Simply put, editors are suspicious of writers who use pen names, and they have good reason for their distrust. Generally, editors feel an author should be proud to have his real name connected with his writing; if he is not, then perhaps the writing should not be published. This same editorial attitude extends even to letters published in a newspaper. Most newspapers will not publish any "Letter to the Editor" unless they know the real name of the author, and, in most instances, they dislike printing letters where the name of the writer must be witheld unless there is a very good reason for this. (Sometimes, the letters as published are *anonymous*—which the new *Random House Dictionary* defines as "without any name acknowledged as that of author. . . ." and sometimes the letters are *pseudonymous,* "bearing a false or fictious name.") A new writer who decides to use a pen name must be prepared to encounter editorial suspicions—and it may prove harder for him to have manuscripts accepted if editors are not in sympathy with his reasons.

Also, the writer using a pen name faces many complications, legal and otherwise. He may run into trouble trying to cash a check made out to his pen name (usually, the procedure here is for the author to endorse the check with his pen name and then his real name, and then deposit the check at a bank where he is known). Since many bankers question whether it is legally possible for an account to be opened for two names for one person, a writer might open an account only under his pen name. However, banks report that often legal troubles arise when an author dies, leaving a bank account under a pen name, and therefore they generally require full disclosure—a written document and means of verification—to be filed with the bank when an account under a pen name is opened.

If an author will be receiving correspondence addressed to him under his pen name, he should either arrange to have his real name appear on envelopes also (pen name, *in care of* real name), or else he should make sure his local post office and his mailman know about the pen name. The Post Office generally follows the rule that name has preference over address, *e.g.* an order addressed to R. H. Macy Company at Times Square in New York City will not be left at Times Square but will be delivered to Macy's at the correct address, Herald Square, New York City. The result may be that if the postal authorities do not know about a pen name, they may not leave a letter at the street address given but may simply return it to the sender.

Pen name complications may occur if an author uses a pseudonym only for writing, and has no bank account, etc., under that name. Certainly an author using a pen name should arrange to have his editor state in writing that his real name and his pen name belong to the same person.

If an author has decided to use a pen name, and his editor has agreed to cooperate, does this mean that the author's real name will remain a secret, known only to the author and the publishing firm? Not at all!

Of course, a copyright may be taken out under a pen name since the current Copyright Act does not forbid it. (The Copyright Office recognizes the common use of pseudonyms, and the standard application form even provides space for their insertion.) A married woman may take out a copyright under her maiden name, and, if proper legal arrangements are made, the copyright may also be taken out by someone designated by the author—for instance, the publisher.

However, many people are interested in bringing to light the real name of an author using a pen name. Reporters will often unearth an author's real name if a book has news value. (For many years the real identity of Mark Epernay, pseudonymous author of *The Mac-Landress Dimension* was not revealed by the publishers, although magazines and newspapers speculated and stated that Epernay was really John Kenneth Galbraith, Harvard economist and former United States Ambassador to India. Confirmation of this was definitely made by *The New York Times*, which explained that Galbraith had made up this pen name from Mark Twain and Epernay, Napoleon III's headquarters during the Franco-Prussian war.) Librarians make an effort find out the real name of an author so that they can assemble all material written by an author in one place in their catalogues, and they will indicate cross-references for the various names. This library practice is, of course, important to any researcher who may not know all the books written by the same author if a pen name has been used. Generally, courts have not considered it a violation of privacy when the real name of an author writing under a pen name is made known.

Is there any procedure an author must take before selecting and using a pen name? Most states do not require any legal steps. However, it would be advisable for the author to make a check of the names of other authors before selecting a name, so that he does not choose a pen name that is similar to the name of another writer. (The easiest way to do this is to check through the card catalogue of a fairly large library.)

Pen names are not protected by copyright. However, the laws relating to unfair competition may often provide protection for pseudonyms.

If an author decides that he must use a pen name, the name he has selected should appear on his manuscript under the story title as a by-line. The author's real name should appear in the upper left-hand corner of the first page of the manuscript, above the address; the pen name might be put in parentheses after the author's real name.

Though the use of a pen name can often cause unpleasant or troublesome complications for an author, there are some pleasant developments that may follow, also. A famous science-fiction writer reports that recently he was given a pile of science-fiction books to review. He was most interested when he discovered that one of the titles he was asked to appraise bore a familiar by-line: his own pen name!

99

HOW BOOK PUBLISHING DECISIONS ARE MADE

By A Senior Editor

How do publishers (and their editors) find the books they eventually publish? To many writers the process may seem mysterious and even irrational, especially to those who have not been able to break into print. Yet the making of decisions at most book publishers has a logic of its own and is not likely to be capricious or inflexible. Publishers and editors are constantly looking for new voices, new ideas, new trends. Any business that in recent years has brought forth *The Whole Earth Catalog* and *Roots* and *Passages* and *Ragtime* is scarcely standing still.

As an example of how books are acquired, let me cite the experience of my own firm. Last year we published 118 books of a general nature. They came to us in various ways.

Fifty-nine of these books were written by authors whom we had previously published. The category is self-explanatory and is evidence of the firm's strength and stability: many of our authors continue to publish with us over the years.

Thirty-seven titles were submitted directly to the editors (not through literary agents) or were sought out by the editors. Editorial contacts played an important part in these acquisitions. A friend of an editor will recommend a manuscript. An editor meets a scholar at an academic convention. An editor learns that a prominent personality plans to write a book. An editor reads a magazine or newspaper article that suggests a full-length work. An editor thinks up an idea for a book and commissions the appropriate author to write it. An author may have heard about an editor through some form of publicity; frequently, in nonfiction books, the assistance of a particular editor is acknowledged.

The author is senior editor of one of America's most distinguished book publishing companies.

Eleven books were sent to our editors by literary agents on their own initiative. (Many titles in the first category were represented by agents.) There are about seventy-five literary agencies in New York City that actively submit publishable manuscripts and are sought out by publishers. They range from one-man or -woman shops to organizations with a half dozen or more agents. Editors and agents lunch and drink and play tennis and poker with each other, and in several instances, agents are married to book editors. Thus many publishing relationships begin because an agent believes a particular author is suited to a particular editor.

Eight titles were sent to us by foreign publishers, four in Britain, four in continental Europe. There is a considerable trading gap between American and foreign publishers: more American authors are published abroad than foreigners here. Nevertheless, American publishers actively search this market, because some famous writers have been first published abroad, for example, authors like Le Carré, Fowles, Gabriel Garcia Marquez, Solzhenitsyn.

One book was recommended to us by one of our bookstore sales representatives. From time to time we receive tips from our sales people, or from our college textbook travelers, who are constantly meeting scholars in the university community.

Two books were unsolicited, mailed to us unheralded and without recommendation. One is a craft book that has sold moderately well. The other is a successful work in the field of medicine.

All of these books, whether by writers familiar or unfamiliar to the publisher, went through a decision-making process. This will differ from publisher to publisher, but there is a common thread to each system.

Depending upon a publisher's size, there will be one or two or three individuals who, because of management position or seniority or specialized knowledge, can make an affirmative publishing decision without consultation of colleagues. But in fact that does not often happen. The more enthusiasts behind a book from the beginning, the better its prospects when eventually published. It is as important for an editor to create an upbeat atmosphere for a book within a publishing house as it is to do so later among reviewers and prospective readers.

Nonfiction contracts are offered on the basis of certain varying amounts of material—an idea stated verbally to an editor, a letter, a comprehensive outline, a finished manuscript. In the case of fiction, most novels submitted to a publisher are complete. An established novelist can obtain a contract for an unwritten, or partially written novel. But such a commitment to an unknown author is not likely. Publishers too often have been burned by novels that began promisingly but concluded unsuccessfully.

QUESTIONS AND ANSWERS

Q. *Can you describe in more detail the actual procedure leading up to a publishing decision?*

A. As I said, the *modus operandi* varies from house to house. Some firms hold format meetings where an editor proposes a book, and it is approved or rejected by a management who may or may not have read the manuscript. The editor's track record and presentation may be crucial in such a situation. At another firm, it may simply be a matter of discussion between an editor and the editor-in-chief. Decisions in fiction are not usually complicated; a novel should either strike an editor strongly or not: a marginal reaction is probably a sign that a book shouldn't be taken on. A nonfiction proposal may require more discussion. If it's a cookbook, what's the competition? If it's a work of history, does it break any new ground? An editor may have to read through other books on the topic to make such a judgment. If it's a biography, who else may be tackling the subject? (It's unfortunate that there's not a central registry where a publisher could check to ascertain whether a book about a particular subject is in preparation. A few years back, four biographies of Babe Ruth were published within a short period.) What are an author's qualifications in a particular field?

I should say that any author with a nonfiction proposal should thoroughly research the subject as to subject matter and competition. A very useful reference book is *Subject Guide to Books in Print,* published by Bowker and available at many public libraries. It's a reasonably accurate compendium of what books are now available.

Q. *Should a manuscript or query be submitted to the editor-in-chief of a publishing house or a lesser editor?*

A. Again, there would be different answers for different publishers.

Obviously, the best situation for an author is for an editor-in-chief to be enthusiastic about a book. On the other hand, the top editor may be overburdened with management responsibilities, and unsolicited material is likely to be referred to other editors or assistants. A middle-level editor might have more time to deal with a book. But it is the practice in most publishing houses, if an author addresses a gardening book, for example, to the wrong editor, it will be passed on to the resident authority on the subject. Editors' names are listed in *Literary Market Place*, also a Bowker publication, and available in public libraries.

Q. *How much influence has a literary agent on publishing decisions?*

A. It depends on the agent; some are better than others. (The agent who submitted the most proposals and manuscripts to us last year did not make a single contract with us.) Obtaining a good agent is actually more difficult than finding a willing publisher. Most agents are small business persons who don't have the time or capacity to deal with new, unpublished authors. And it is a misunderstanding of the agent's function to reckon that intervention will guarantee a contract with a publisher. An editor's judgment has to be the controlling factor in a decision. A proposal submitted by a trusted agent will certainly have added weight in its corner, but that fact is rarely the main determinant in a publishing decision.

Q. *Does an unsolicited manuscript really have a chance?*

A. A few publishers now return such submissions unopened. But most houses are very much accessible to new and untried talent. I suspect that fewer unrecommended manuscripts are taken on these days, because most new writers are discovered by energetic editors before their books have been completed. Editors travel around the country and abroad, searching for new writers. And it is a rare author who doesn't have a friend at or remote connection with a publishing house—perhaps through a college teacher or a journalist. If a magazine publishes a good short story or article, the author is likely to receive several letters from editors inquiring whether there are any plans for a book.

Q. *Some authors feel that publishers and agents are cliquish, since most of them operate out of New York City. Is this true?*

A. In fact, only about a third of the authors we publish live in the Boston-New York-Washington complex, even though that is still generally regarded as the intellectual and cultural hub of the nation.

I'm a great believer in regional publishing—we publish several authors whose books sell very well year after year in their home areas.

Q. *It's been written about before, but can you bring us up to date on the technical aspects of submitting a manuscript?*

A. Of course the pages should be typed double-spaced and legibly; occasionally we receive a handwritten manuscript, but it's unfair to ask an editor to read it. I don't mind a xerographic manuscript, as long as it's clear. I think that an explanatory letter, especially with a nonfiction proposal, is helpful background. Return postage (or International Reply Coupons, if abroad) is a simple matter of courtesy and protection. A strong cardboard box, the kind in which bond paper is sold, is useful. If an author doesn't hear from a publisher within six weeks (allowing two weeks for mailing both ways), he should write a follow-up letter of inquiry.

Q. *How often should a writer send out a manuscript?*

A. I think authors ought to keep trying. The history of publishing is replete with tales of editorial idiocy. *Auntie Mame* was rejected by at least fifteen publishers. Joyce Cary's *The Horse's Mouth* was turned down by seventeen, as was Irving Stone's *Lust for Life*. Beatrix Potter's *The Tale of Peter Rabbit* was returned by six houses. William L. Shirer's *The Rise and Fall of the Third Reich* was rejected by many publishers in outline form, even though Shirer was the author of two bestsellers. *The Day of the Jackal* was passed up by three or four New York publishers. I'm told that even *The Godfather* went the rounds. If an author really believes in a manuscript, he should submit it to at least ten publishers. If form rejections are the constant response, then perhaps the author should stop sending the book manuscript around until he carefully rereads it to see if improvements should be made before he resubmits it.

Q. *What kind of books are publishers looking for?*

A. Hardcover fiction is doing better than a few years ago, although $10.00 novels by unknown authors are having hard times. Books on hobbies and crafts are selling very well; this field is a good one for a new author. Many successful nonfiction titles concern social relationships. Regional books that bring out the flavor of particular sections of America are flourishing. Interest in medicine and health seems stronger than ever.

Q. *How do you feel about the future of books?*

A. There are those who prophesy the demise of the book as entertainment and a learning tool. I can't pretend to know how strongly home facsimile and video recordings will compete for the reader's time, but at the height of television's influence more people than ever are buying and reading books. And with the advent of the four-day week, there will be additional time to divide among various pursuits. Further, the book is the most compact, convenient leisure product in existence. You can take it anywhere, except underwater. No, I don't think that the book is a dinosaur, any more than I think writers are going to stop writing.

100

MANUSCRIPT PREPARATION
AND SUBMISSION

By Joyce T. Smith

A MANUSCRIPT submitted for publication competes with hundreds of others which cross the editor's desk. It follows that the manuscript which is professional in appearance, easy to read, and is free of careless mistakes is more likely to receive better attention than those which do not meet these requirements. The rules of manuscript preparation are simple, but the writer who wishes to have his manuscript considered seriously by editors should follow them carefully. For the most part, the mechanical requirements for manuscripts are the same for all publishing houses and magazines. Publications which have special style requirements will usually send such information on request.

The basic and most important rule of manuscript preparation is: *The manuscript must be typed, double-spaced, on standard 8½ × 11 white paper, on one side of the page only.* Handwritten manuscripts, however legible, are not welcome.

TYPING

Any type face which is clear and easy to read is acceptable, and the typewriter may be standard or portable, manual or electric. The size of the type is also a matter of preference; either pica type or the smaller elite type is commonly used. Some of the unusual type faces now available on typewriters, while suitable for personal use, tend to become illegible on manuscripts. The type should always be clean, and the ribbon (black) should be in good condition, producing clear, legible type. Margins of one inch to an inch and a half should be left on both sides and at the top and bottom of the page.

Manuscripts should be typed on good white bond paper (8½ × 11).

Weights of 14 lbs., 16 lbs., or even 20 lbs. for short manuscripts, are acceptable. Avoid too thin a paper (onionskin, for example) or a very heavy weight (such as parchment), which are difficult to handle and to read. Remember, too, that paper especially treated for easy erasing is also easily smudged. For making carbon copies, inexpensive "second sheet" paper is available. But whatever paper is used, a writer should always make and keep a carbon copy of every manuscript, since occasionally a manuscript is lost. Copies made by Xerox or similar duplicating processes should not be submitted to an editor, though a writer may make such copies of the original for his own use.

The name and address of the author should be typed in the upper left- or right-hand corner of the first manuscript page. About one-third down the page, the title is typed in capital letters, followed a line or two below by the author's name. Leave a three-line space and begin the text.

Pages should be numbered consecutively in the upper right- or left-hand corner, followed by the author's surname or the title of the manuscript in full or abbreviated form. This helps identify a page that may become separated from the whole manuscript. The first page does not have to be numbered.

Although not essential, the approximate number of words in the manuscript may be typed in the corner of the first page opposite the author's name and address. The figure should be *only approximate,* and may be estimated to the nearest round number by multiplying the average number of words in a line by the average number of lines on a page, and then by multiplying that answer by the number of manuscript pages.

After the manuscript has been typed, the author should read it over carefully, not only for sense and factual errors, but also for typing, spelling, and grammatical errors. If a page has only one or two errors, the corrections may be made neatly in ink by crossing out the whole word and writing it correctly in the space immediately above. Or an omitted word or short phrase may be inserted in the space above, with a slant line or caret to indicate the exact place for the insertion. If lengthy insertions are necessary, the entire page (or sometimes several pages) should be retyped.

Since editors assume factual accuracy as well as correct spelling, punctuation, capitalization, and word usage, a final check of these "mechanics" of writing is essential before you send out your manuscript. Here are a few check points:

Enclose all direct quotations in quotation marks. Quotations within quoted material are indicated by single quotes. All quoted material must appear exactly as originally printed. Whether you are quoting the Bible, Shakespeare, a few lines from a poem that you remember (song lyrics, however brief, *always* require permission for quotation), recheck these before you send your manuscript out; do not rely on your memory.

When quoting material of more than three lines, indent the passage quoted, omit quotation marks except to indicate quoted dialogue, and type it single space. (If you wish to quote copyright material of more than a few words, it is advisable to obtain permission of the copyright owner.)

Dialogue is enclosed in quotation marks, with the words of each new speaker beginning a new paragraph.

Italics to indicate emphasis should be used sparingly for maximum effect, but there are some "rules" for italicizing. Book and play titles names of magazines and newspapers, and foreign words are generally italicized. (Titles of short stories, essays, poems, and other parts of books or longer works are enclosed in quotation marks.)

The pages of short manuscripts should be fastened with a paper clip. Do not pin, tie, bind, or staple the pages together in any other way. The pages of a book manuscript should be left loose and mailed in a box.

Book manuscripts

Follow general rules for manuscript preparation, and also include a title page (not required for short manuscripts) on which the title is typed in capital letters about half-way down the page. On the line immediately below type the word "By" and your name. The entire manuscript should be numbered consecutively from the first page to the last. (Do not number the pages of the individual chapters separately.) Begin each new chapter on a new page, typing the chapter number and chapter title (if any) about three inches from the top. Leave two or three spaces and then proceed with the text.

Sometimes the question of illustrations arises, especially in writing children's books. Most publishers assign artists after the manuscript is accepted. If the author has collaborated with an artist, then, of course, the text and sample illustrations may be submitted together. Similarly, if the author is also the artist, it is not advisable to submit *complete*, original illustrations, unless the publishers request you to do so.

Short Items

Type poetry double-spaced, leaving three or four spaces between stanzas. Begin each new poem—no matter what its length—on a separate page, putting your name and address at the top right of each.

Fillers are also typed double-spaced, one to a page, with your name and address on each, and for fact fillers the source should be indicated. Because of the volume of manuscripts received, many magazines do not acknowledge or return fillers, but the author may assume that if he has not heard in three months, he may offer it for sale again.

Greeting card publishers sometimes have special specifications for the submission of verses or ideas, i.e., ideas should be submitted on 3 × 5 cards, one idea to a card, etc. Requirements for art work also vary greatly, and prospective contributors should check directly with the companies and should study manuscript market lists.

Play and television scripts

In typing dramatic material for the stage or for television, you must follow a special format. Specifications and illustrations for television scripts may be found in Chapter 93, "Television Writing Today." There are two commonly used styles in typing plays: (a) Type the names of the characters in capital letters at the left margin, followed by the dialogue in upper and lower case; (b) Type names of characters in capital letters at center of page. On next line, begin the speech at the left margin, in upper and lower case.

Footnotes

Research publications and other scholarly works may require footnotes and bibliographies, and in typing these manuscripts, writers should follow standard accepted forms as given in the widely accepted reference manual, *A Manual of Style* (University of Chicago Press).

If the manuscript requires footnotes, type these in the body of the manuscript, immediately after the line to which the note refers, using a raised number or a symbol such as an asterisk in the text and correspondingly at the beginning of the footnote. Footnotes more than one line long should be typed single-space and set off from the text by a rule above and below it.

QUERY LETTERS

Before you submit a complete nonfiction manuscript—either article or book length—it is advisable to send a brief query letter to the editor describing the proposed article or book. The letter should also include information about the author's special qualifications for dealing with the particular subject, and for a book-length manuscript, an outline of the book and a sample chapter may be included. Otherwise, no covering letter is necessary when submitting a manuscript, though the writer may include a brief note simply indicating that the manuscript is submitted for possible publication. No amount of self-praise will bring about a sale if the manuscript is unsuitable, nor will the absence of a letter discourage an editor from accepting it. If you are submitting a manuscript following a positive response to your query letter, you may indicate this fact in a brief note accompanying it. For book manuscripts, a letter is often sent separately, stating that the manuscript has been mailed under separate cover.

REPORTS ON MANUSCRIPTS

Monthly or weekly magazines, as well as large publishing houses, may take several weeks—and often longer—to read and report on manuscripts. For bi-monthlies, quarterlies, some literary magazines, and small publishing houses with limited editorial staffs, two or more months may elapse before reports are made to authors.

If you have had no report on a manuscript after a reasonable time —six to eight weeks for a large company—you may write a brief, courteous letter inquiring about the status of your manuscript.

To save time and postage—and to approach the business of marketing manuscripts in a professional way—it is essential for free-lance writers to study editorial requirements of various publications as described in market lists and by examining the publications themselves. Read several issues of any magazine to which you may wish to submit material. Familiarize yourself with the types of books published by various publishers by browsing in a library or bookshop, and by watching their advertising.

It is common practice to submit a manuscript to only one publisher at a time. Although this may seem unfair and time-consuming, it is the only way to avoid the difficulties that may arise if, for example, two editors wish to buy the same manuscript. The same practice also applies to writing query letters—send only *one at a time*.

When submitting a manuscript, address it to the editor by name, if you know it, or to the editor of the particular part of the magazine— Fiction Editor, Articles Editor, Features Editor, etc., also by name, if possible, otherwise by title. The same is true for book publishers: Address your manuscript to the editor in charge of the particular division for which your book is suited: Juvenile Editor, Religious Editor, etc.

RIGHTS

As a rule, a writer submitting a manuscript to a magazine should not stipulate on his manuscript or in an accompanying letter what rights he is offering. Although most magazines buy only "First North American Serial Rights," some publications buy *all* rights as a matter of policy. It is therefore best to discuss what rights the magazine is interested in—and what limitations the writer may wish to set— *after* a manuscript is accepted.

First North American serial rights means that a magazine is buying the exclusive right to publish the material for the first time and only once. Purchase of *second serial rights* gives the magazine the right to reprint the material once after its original publication— twice in all. Some magazines buy *all periodical rights*, that is, the exclusive right to print and reprint the material here and abroad in magazine form. Generally, magazines buy only periodical rights, and all further rights—for television, motion pictures, book use, etc., belong to the author.

Books are handled quite differently, and if your book manuscript is accepted, you will receive a contract from the publishers outlining carefully the rights they are buying and those the author retains. These contracts are fairly standard throughout the industry, and writers may have confidence in the good faith of any reputable publishing company. When a writer has established an important reputation and achieved prestige and success, he may (directly or through his agent) be justified in negotiating with the publishers for higher royalties and other more liberal terms which he may want (and will often be able to arrange with the book or magazine publishers).

MAILING

Short manuscripts should be mailed flat in Manila envelopes. If the manuscript is only 3 or 4 pages in length, it may be folded twice, and sent in an ordinary long (#10) envelope. Book manuscripts should be sent loose, in a cardboard box, such as the kind typing paper comes in.

Under present postal regulations, manuscripts for books and periodicals may be mailed at the regular first-class mail rate, or, less expensively, by the Special Fourth Class Rate for Manuscripts; ask at your Post Office for this rate. Manuscripts or boxes sent by this rate must be marked Special Fourth Class Rate—Manuscript. If you wish to include a letter with a manuscript sent via the Special Fourth Class Rate, you may do so, provided you note on the outside of the box or envelope that first-class material is enclosed, and that you place additional first-class postage on the package.

Manuscripts sent at the Special Fourth Class Rate may also be insured at the post office.

A stamped self-addressed return envelope should always be enclosed when a manuscript is submitted to a publisher, in case the manuscript is rejected. If you are using the Special Fourth Class Rate, be sure that the return envelope is marked Special Fourth Class Rate—Manuscript.

PART IV

THE WRITER'S MARKETS
Where to Sell

WHERE TO SELL

This section of THE WRITER'S HANDBOOK is devoted to manuscript market information that will help writers sell their manuscripts. All information concerning the needs and requirements of markets comes directly from the editors of the periodicals, publishing companies, and television programs listed.

Although we have taken every precaution to have the information accurate, there will undoubtedly be some changes in the requirements listed as the needs of editors change from time to time. Therefore writers are advised to study recent issues of a publication before submitting any manuscripts to it. New magazines and television programs should always be checked carefully, since frequent changes occur in these markets.

FICTION MARKETS

This list is divided into three categories: general magazines; college, literary and little magazines; religious and denominational magazines. See *The Popular Market* for lists of magazines using male-oriented and "adult" fiction, confession and romance stories, science fiction, and mysteries. Juvenile fiction markets are listed under *Juvenile, Teen-Age and Young Adult Magazines*. Publishers of book-length adult and juvenile manuscripts are listed under *Book Publishers*.

GENERAL MAGAZINES

ADAM—8060 Melrose Ave., Los Angeles, CA 90046.
Fiction, 2,000 to 3,500 words, on erotic subjects. Limited free-lance market. Pays $50 to $100.

ALFRED HITCHCOCK'S MYSTERY MAGAZINE—229 Park Ave. South, New York, NY 10003. After June 1, 1978: 122 East 42nd St., New York, NY 10017. Eleanor Sullivan, Editor.
Well-plotted, plausible mystery, suspense and crime stories, 1,000 to 10,000 words; no sensationalism or actual crimes. Pays 3¢ to 8¢ a word, on acceptance.

THE ATLANTIC ADVOCATE—Gleaner Bldg., Phoenix Sq., Fredericton, N.B. Canada.
Some fiction, 1,000 to 2,000 words, with regional slant. Pays 5¢ a word.

THE ATLANTIC MONTHLY—8 Arlington St., Boston, MA 02116. Robert Manning, Editor.
Short stories, 2,000 to 6,000 words, of highest literary quality. Occasional stories to 14,000 words. Pays on acceptance.

AUSTIN—Austin Chamber of Commerce, Box 1967, Austin, TX 78767. Hal Susskind, Editor.
Business- or community-oriented fiction, 800 to 1,000 words, with Texas or Austin angle. Pays varying rates.

BOY'S LIFE—North Brunswick, NJ 08902. Stan Pashko, Fiction Editor.
Short stories, to 3,500 words, for 10- to 17-year old boys. Short shorts, 1,200 words. Pays from $400.

CAT FANCY—P.O. Box 4030, San Clemente, CA 92672. Mike Criss, Managing Editor.
Fiction, to 4,000 words, directly or indirectly about cats. Pays 3¢ a word, on publication.

CAVALIER—316 Aragon Ave., Coral Gables, FL 33134.
Fiction, to 6,000 words, for sophisticated young men. Pays to $300, on publication.

CHATELAINE—481 University Ave., Toronto, Ont., Canada M5W 1A7. Doris Anderson, Editor; Almeda Glassey, Fiction Editor.
Fiction, to 4,000 words, for women, on serious issues in women's lives, relationships, adventure, romance. Pays from $400, on acceptance.

CHESAPEAKE BAY—130 Severn Ave., Annapolis, MD 21403. Betty Rigoli, Editor.
Short stories with some connection to the Chesapeake Bay region. Pays $35 to $60, on acceptance and sometimes on publication.

CLASSIC—551 Fifth Ave., New York, NY 10017. Andrew Crichton, Executive Editor.
Occasional short stories, 2,000 to 4,000 words, related to horses used primarily for pleasure and sport, to interest horse owners and others who attend horse shows, belong to polo clubs, etc. Pays good rates, on acceptance. Query.

CO-ED—Scholastic Magazines, Inc., 50 West 44th St., New York, NY 10036. Address Fiction Editor.
Fiction, 2,000 to 3,000 words, on problems and interests of contemporary teenagers: family, dating, social prejudice, personal identity. Humor, sports and adventure, stories with foreign settings. Pays from $150, on acceptance.

COLORADO WOMEN'S DIGEST—2480 West 26th Ave., Diamond Hill Suite 125B, Denver, CO 80211. Patricia Cox, Editorial Director.
Short stories relevant to women, ages 20 to 60. Length, 1,200 to 1,500 words. Regional publication, but seeks material of national interest. Pays 3¢ per word, on publication.

COLUMBIA—Box 1670, New Haven, CT 06507. Elmer Von Feldt, Editor.
Journal of the Knights of Columbus. Fiction, 2,000 to 3,000 words, with a Christian viewpoint. Pays $200 to $300, on acceptance.

COMMENTARY—165 East 56th St., New York, NY 10022. Norman Podhoretz, Editor.
Fiction of high literary quality, on social or Jewish issues. Pays around 7¢ a word.

THE COMPASS—Mobil Sales and Supply Corp., 150 East 42nd St., New York, NY 10017. R.G. MacKenzie, Editor.
Short stories, to 3,500 words, on the sea and sea trades. Pays to $250, on acceptance. Query.

COSMOPOLITAN—224 West 57th St., New York, NY 10019. Harris Dienstfrey, Fiction Editor.
Fiction for sophisticated young career women; short shorts, 1,500 to 3,000 words: short stories, 5,000 to 6,000 words. Pays $1,000 for short stories, $300 to $600 for short shorts, on acceptance.

THE COUNTRY GENTLEMAN—1100 Waterway Blvd., Indianapolis, IN 46202. Frederic Birmingham, Editor.
Short stories, to 3,500 words. Pays varying rates, on publication.

DELL CROSSWORD PUZZLES—245 East 47th St., New York, NY 10017. Kathleen Rafferty, Editor.
Mysteries, 500 words, with clues for solution. Pays $25, on acceptance.

DOG FANCY—P.O. Box 4030, San Clemente, CA 92672. Mike Criss, Managing Editor.
Fiction, to 4,000 words, about dogs. Pays 3¢ a word, on publication.

ELITE—606 Avenue Rd., Suite 404, Toronto, Ont., Canada H3H 2G1. David S. Wells, Editor.
Sophisticated fiction, mystery and satire, to 3,500 words. Pays $100 to $300, on publication.

THE ELKS MAGAZINE—425 West Diversey Pkwy., Chicago, IL 60614. Jeffrey Ball, Editor.
Short, humorous fiction for a family audience; suspense, mystery and detective stories. Pays to $350.

ELLERY QUEEN'S MYSTERY MAGAZINE—229 Park Ave. South, New York, NY 10003. After June 1, 1978: 122 East 42nd St., New York, NY 10017. Ellery Queen, Editor. Eleanor Sullivan, Managing Editor.
Detective, crime and mystery stories, 4,000 to 6,000 words. Pays 3¢ to 8¢ a word, on acceptance.

FAMILY CIRCLE—488 Madison Ave., New York, NY 10022. Myrna Blyth, Fiction Editor.
Short stories, 2,500 words, for women. Pays on acceptance.

FIELD & STREAM—383 Madison Ave., New York, NY 10017. Jack Samson, Editor.
Fiction on outdoor topics. Limited free-lance market. Pays from 20¢ a word, on acceptance.

FLORIDA GEORGIA BASS—2639 North Monroe St., Suite 230B, Tallahassee, FL 32304. Greg Sefton, Editorial Director.
Humorous short stories, to 2,500 words, to interest members of the Florida Georgia Bass Fisherman's Association. Pays up to $150, on publication.

GALLERY—99 Park Ave., New York, NY 10016.
Fiction, to 6,000 words, for sophisticated men. Short humor, satire. Pays $350 to $750, after acceptance. Query.

GEM—303 West 42nd St., New York, NY 10036. Will Martin, Editor.
Contemporary, erotic fiction, 500 to 1,500 words. Pays $35 to $50, after acceptance. Same address and requirements for *The Swinger*.

GENESIS—770 Lexington Ave., New York, NY 10021. J.J. Kelleher, Editor.
Adult fiction for men, 3,000 to 6,000 words. Pays on publications.

GOLF DIGEST—495 Westport Ave., Norwalk, CT 06956. Nick Seitz, Editor.
Unusual or humorous stories, to 2,000 words, about golf; golf "fables," 750 to 1,000 words. Pays from 20¢ a word.

GOOD HOUSEKEEPING—959 Eighth Ave., New York, NY 10019. Naome Lewis, Fiction Editor.
Short stories, 2,000 to 5,000 words, with strong identification for women, by published writers and "beginners with demonstrable talent." Novelettes, to 20,000 words. Pays top rates, on acceptance.

GRAY'S SPORTING JOURNAL—1330 Beacon St., Brookline, MA 02146.
Short stories, 2,000 to 4,000 words, on hunting and fishing. Pays good rates, on acceptance.

HARLEQUIN—240 Duncan Mill Rd., Suite 605, Don Mills, Ont., Canada M3B 1Z4. Beth McGregor, Editor.
Short stories, 2,500 to 5,000 words, with short shorts, 1,000 to 2,000 words: light romance, mystery, humor. Pays varying rates, on acceptance.

HARPER'S—2 Park Ave., New York, NY 10016.
Short stories, 2,000 to 4,000 words, of highest literary quality. Pays from $300, on acceptance. Send 300-word summary to Queries Editor before submitting.

HUGHES RIGWAY—Hughes Tool Co., P.O. Box 2539, Houston TX 77001. Tom Haynes, Managing Editor.
Short stories, 2,000 to 2,500 words, and historical narratives, for oil- and gas-drilling personnel. Pays 10¢ a word, on acceptance.

HUSTLER—2029 Century Park East, Los Angeles, CA 90067.
Erotic fiction, 800 to 1,500 words. Pays $150 to $1,000, on publication.

ISAAC ASIMOV'S SCIENCE FICTION MAGAZINE—Box 13116, Philadelphia, PA 19101. George Scithers, Editor.
Short, good science fiction, to 12,500 words. Pays 3¢ to 5¢ a word, on acceptance.

JEWISH LIFE—116 East 27th St., New York, NY 10016. Yaakov Jacobs, Editor.
Short stories, to 3,000 words, involving Orthodox Judaism.

LADIES' HOME JOURNAL—641 Lexington Ave., New York, NY 10022.
No longer reads unsolicited short story manuscripts; will only read manuscripts submitted through agents.

McCALL'S—230 Park Ave., New York, NY 10017. Helen DelMonte, Fiction Editor.
Short stories, to 3,000 words, and novels (to be condensed or excerpted), for literate, sophisticated women. Pays top rates, on acceptance.

MADEMOISELLE—350 Madison Ave., New York, NY 10017. Mary E. McNichols, Fiction and Poetry Editor.

Short stories 2,500 to 6,500 words, of high literary quality. Pays from $300 on acceptance.

MAN TO MAN—280 Madison Ave., New York, NY 10016. Everett Meyers, Editor.
Contemporary fiction, 1,500 to 5,000 words, on male-female relationships. Pays from $100, on publication.

MIDSTREAM—515 Park Ave., New York, NY 10022. Joel Carmichael, Editor.
Fiction on Jewish, social or political issues. Pays 7¢ a word, on publication.

MIKE SHAYNE MYSTERY MAGAZINE—P.O. Box 1084, Reseda, CA 91335.
Detective and mystery fiction; short stories, 1,500 words; novelettes, 12,000 words. Pays from 1¢ a word, on acceptance.

MODERN MATURITY—215 Long Beach Blvd., Long Beach, CA 90801. Hubert Pryor, Editor.
Short stories for readers over 55. Pays to $500, on acceptance.

MS.—370 Lexington Ave., New York, NY 10017. Address Editorial Department, Fiction.
Short stories on women's changing self-image and status. Pays on acceptance.

NATIONAL JEWISH MONTHLY—1640 Rhode Island Ave. N.W., Washington, DC 20036. Charles Fenyvesi, Editor.
Short stories with Jewish angle. Pays 5¢ to 8¢ a word.

THE NEW YORKER—25 West 43rd St., New York, NY 10036.
Short stories, 1,000 to 6,000 words; humor and satire. Pays on acceptance.

NRTA JOURNAL—215 Long Beach Blvd., Long Beach, CA 90801. Hubert C. Pryor, Editor.
Magazine of National Retired Teachers Association. Short stories, 500 to 2,500 words. Pays $50 to $500.

OUI—8560 Sunset Blvd., Los Angeles, CA 90069. Richard Cramer, Editor.
Short stories, 1,000 to 2,000 words, preferably erotic. Pays $1,000 to $1,200, on acceptance.

OUR FAMILY—Box 249, Dept. E, Battleford, Sask., Canada S0M 0E0. Reb Materi, O.M.I., Editor.
Fiction, 1,000 to 3,000 words, for Catholic family readers. Pays 3¢ a word, on acceptance.

PENTHOUSE—909 Third Ave., New York, NY 10022. Paul Bresnick, Fiction Editor.
All types of short fiction; high literary quality a must. Pays on acceptance; top rates.

PLAYBOY—919 North Michigan Ave., Chicago, IL 60611. Vicky Haider, Fiction Editor.
Top quality science fiction and mystery short stories; always welcomes serious fiction and humorous fiction. Preferred length, 1,000 to 10,000 words. Pays from $1,000 to $3,000, on acceptance. Bonus of $1,000 for best story of the year, best first appearance, and best longer work.

PLAYERS—8060 Melrose Ave., Los Angeles, CA 90046. Joe Nazel, Editor.
Fiction, 2,000 to 6,000 words, for black men. Pays from 5¢ a word, on publication.

PLAYGIRL—1801 Century Park East, Suite 2300, Los Angeles, CA 90067. Joyce Dudney Fleming, Editor.
Contemporary fiction, suspense, adventure, humor and romance, 1,500 to 5,000 words, for modern young women. Pays $250 per 1,000 words, after acceptance.

POWDER—P.O. Box 1028, Dana Point, CA 92629. Neil Stebbins, Associate Editor.

Fiction, 800 to 1,500 words, on skiing. Pays $25 to $100, on acceptance.

REDBOOK—230 Park Ave., New York, NY 10017 Eileen Schnurr, Fiction Editor.
Fresh, intelligent short stories, for young women, on relationships, young parenthood, first jobs and unusual subjects, reflecting a raised consciousness. Pays from $850 for short shorts (1,800 words), $1,000 for short stories (around 5,000 words), $7,500 for novels, on acceptance. Manuscripts without stamped, self-addressed envelopes will not be returned.

ROAD KING—P.O. Box 319, Park Forest, IL 60466. George Friend, Editor.
Short stories, 2,500 words, appealing to or about truck drivers. Pays $100, on acceptance.

THE SATURDAY EVENING POST—1100 Waterway Blvd., Indianapolis, IN 46202.
Short stories, 1,000 to 3,500 words, that lend themselves to illustration. Pays varying rates.

THE SCANDINAVIAN REVIEW—127 East 73rd St., New York, NY 10021. Howard E. Sandum, Editor.
Short stories, 2,000 to 3,000 words, about Scandinavia; translations. Pays $20 to $100, on publication.

SCHOLASTIC SCOPE—Scholastic Magazines, Inc. 50 West 44th St., New York, NY 10026. Katherine Robinson, Editor.
For 15- to 18-year olds with 4th to 6th grade reading ability. Short stories, 500 to 1,000 words, on teen-age interests, relationships, family, job and school situations. Realistic stories from viewpoint of member of minority group, not necessarily about race relations. Pays good rates, on acceptance.

SEVENTEEN—850 Third Ave., New York, NY 10022. Annette Grant, Fiction Editor.
Sophisticated fiction for (but not necessarily about) young adults. Pays good rates, on acceptance.

SHORT STORY INTERNATIONAL—6 Sheffield Rd., Great Neck, NY 11021. Sylvia Tankel, Editor.
Reprints previously published contemporary stories by living authors. Stories in non-English languages will be considered and translated. Length, 6,000 words preferred. Payment negotiated individually.

SPRINT—Scholastic Magazines, Inc., 50 West 44th St., New York, NY 10036. Vicky Chapman, Editor.
For 9- to 12-year old remedial reading students. Short stories, 300 to 500 words, with strong plot and action; science fiction, mystery, sports stories and humor. Pays from $125.

STAG—See *Swank*.

SUNSHINE MAGAZINE—Litchfield, IL 62506.
Wholesome short stories, to 1,250 words, with well-concealed moral. Pays varying rates, on acceptance.

SURFER MAGAZINE—Box 1028, Dana Point, CA 92629. Steve Pezman, Editor.
Well-plotted fiction, 1,000 to 2,500 words, on surfing. Pays from 8¢ a word, on publication.

SWANK—888 Seventh Ave., New York, NY 10019. Richard Milner, Managing Editor.
Men's magazine. Sophisticated fiction, 1,800 to 3,500 words. Pays $300 and up for articles, $200 and up for fiction, on publication. Query with outline. Same address and requirements for *Stag*.

TALK (formerly *GirlTalk*)–380 Madison Ave., New York, NY 10017. Berenice Connor
    Kennedy, Editor.
    Fiction, to 2,000 words, for women. Pays varying rates.

'TEEN–8490 Sunset Blvd., Los Angeles, CA 90069. Kathy McCoy, Feature Editor.
    Short stories, 2,000 to 4,000 words, and two-part serials, 6,000 words: mystery,
    travel, adventure, romance, humor. Pays from $100 on acceptance.

TODAY'S SECRETARY–1221 Ave. of the Americas, New York, NY 10020. Lauren
    Bahr, Editor.
    Short stories, 800 to 1,000 words, on secretaries' business lives (rarely uses romance).
    Pays $50, on acceptance.

TWIN CITIES WOMAN–512 Nicollet Mall, Minneapolis, MN 55402. Marcia Appel,
    Editor.
    Short fiction to interest upwardly mobile women in the Minneapolis-St. Paul region.
    Pays on publication at varying rates.

VOGUE–350 Madison Ave., New York, NY 10017. Address Leo Lerman, Consulting
    Features Editor.
    Fiction, around 2,000 words. Pays on acceptance.

THE WESTERN PRODUCER–Box 2500, Saskatoon, Sask., Canada S7K 2C4.
    R.H.D. Phillips, Editor.
    Short stories, to 1,500 words, on western Canadian subjects, for intelligent farm and
    rural readers. Pays varying rates, on acceptance.

WOMAN'S DAY–1515 Broadway, New York, NY 10036. Eileen Herbert Jordan,
    Fiction Editor.
    Short fiction, humorous or serious. Pays top rates, on acceptance.

WOODMEN OF THE WORLD MAGAZINE–1700 Farnam St., Omaha, NE 68102.
    Leland A. Larson, Editor.
    Family-oriented fiction. Pays 2¢ a word, on acceptance.

YANKEE–Dublin, NH 03444. Deborah Stone, Fiction Editor.
    Short stories, either located in New England or with some New England connection.
    No stories relying heavily on sex, alcoholism, or the drug scene. Manuscripts should
    not exceed 4,000 words. Pays up to $600, on acceptance.

COLLEGE, LITERARY AND LITTLE
MAGAZINES

THE AGNI REVIEW–P.O. Box 349, Cambridge, MA 02138. Askold Melnyczuk and
    Sharon Dunn, Editors.
    Short stories, to 10,000 words. Pays in copies.

THE ANTIGONISH REVIEW–St. Francis Xavier University, Antigonish, N.S. Canada.
    R.J. MacSween, Editor.
    Short stories, 1,800 to 2,500 words.

ANTIOCH REVIEW—Yellow Springs, OH 45387. Nolan Miller, Fiction Editor.
Fiction of high literary quality. Pays $8 per printed page, on publication.

APALACHEE QUARTERLY—DDB Press, P.O. Box 20106, Tallahassee, FL 32304.
Short stories. Pays in copies.

APPALACHIAN JOURNAL—134 Sanford, Appalachian State University, Boone, NC
28608. J.W. Williamson, Editor.
Short stories, 2,000 to 5,000 words, about the mountains. Pays in copies.

ARARAT—628 Second Ave., New York, NY 10016. Leo Hamalian, Editor.
Publication of the Armenian General Benevolent Union of America. Short stories,
1,000 to 5,000 words, on Armenian experience in America. Pays $30 to $50, on
publication.

ARIZONA QUARTERLY—University of Arizona, Tucson, AZ 85721. Albert F.
Gegenheimer, Editor.
Fiction, to 3,500 words. Pays in copies; annual awards.

AURA—Box 348 NBSB, University Sta., Birmingham, AL 35294.
Short fiction; especially interested in contemporary, experimental and avant-garde
writing. Manuscripts should be 20 typed pages long or shorter. Pays in copies.

BACHY—Papa Bach Bookstore, 11317 Santa Monica Blvd., West Los Angeles, CA
90025.
Serious fiction, experimental or traditional. Pays in copies; cash awards.

BACK ROADS—Box 543, Cotati, CA 94928. Stella Nathan, Editor.
Short stories. Pays in copies. Query for theme of issue.

BALL STATE UNIVERSITY FORUM—Ball State University, Muncie, IN 47306. Merrill
Rippy and Frances Mayhew Rippy, Editors.
Short stories, 500 to 4,000 words. Pays in copies.

BEYOND BAROQUE—1639 West Washington Blvd., Venice, CA 90291.
Experimental fiction, to 7,500 words.

BLACK MARIA—815 West Wrightwood Ave., Chicago, IL 60614.
Feminist short stories and experimental fiction, to 3,500 words. Pays in copies.

THE BLACK WARRIOR REVIEW—P.O. Box 2936, University, AL 35486. Sarah Teal
DeMiller, Editor.
High quality fiction, in experimental and mainstream styles. Pays in copies.

BOSTON UNIVERSITY JOURNAL—775 Commonwealth Ave., Boston, MA 02215.
Serious fiction, 2,500 to 6,000 words. Pays $10 per printed page, on publication.

BOUNDARY 2—SUNY Binghamton, Binghamton, NY 13901.
Experimental short stories, sections from longer fiction.

THE CALIFORNIA QUARTERLY—100 Sproul Hall, University of California, Davis, CA
95616. Elliot L. Gilbert, Editor.
Fiction, to 8,000 words. Graphics. Pays $2 per page, extra for graphics, on publica-
tion.

THE CANADIAN FICTION MAGAZINE—Box 46422, Station G, Vancouver, B.C.,
Canada V6R 4G7.
Fiction, to 5,000 words, preferably by Canadians: short stories, novel excerpts, ex-
perimental fiction. Pays $3 per page, on publication.

THE CANADIAN FORUM—3 Church St., Suite 401, Toronto, Ont. Canada M5E 1M2.
Dennis Smith, Editor.
Short fiction. Pays $50.

CANTO—c/o Realforms, 11 Bartlet St., Andover, MA 01810.
Fiction by new writers. Pays on publication.

THE CARLETON MISCELLANY—Carleton College, Northfield, MN 55057. Wayne Carver, Editor.
Short stories, to 7,500 words. Pays $8 per page, on publication.

CAROLINA QUARTERLY—Box 1117, Chapel Hill, NC 27514. Michael Carter, Editor; address Fiction Editor.
Innovative fiction, to 8,000 words, by new or established writers; excerpts from longer works. Pays $3 per printed page.

THE CHARITON REVIEW—Northeast Missouri State University, Division of Language and Literature, Kirksville, MO 63501. Andrew Grossbardt, Editor.
Short stories, to 5,000 words. Pays in copies.

CHELSEA—Box 5880, Grand Central Station, New York, NY 10017. Sonia Raiziss, Editor.
Short fiction. Pays in copies. Overstocked.

THE CHICAGO REVIEW—University of Chicago, Chicago, IL 60637. Richard Vine, Editor.
Serious fiction, traditional or experimental; translations. Pays in copies.

CHOMO URI—P.O. Box 1057, Amherst, MA 01002.
Feminist short stories, 12 to 15 pages. Pays in copies.

CIMARRON REVIEW—Oklahoma State University, Stillwater, OK 74074. Jeanne Adams Wray, Managing Editor.
Serious fiction on contemporary life. Pays in copies.

CITY—Dept. of English, The City College, Convent Ave. at 138th St., New York, NY 10013.
Fiction, 1 to 25 pages, typed double space. Pays in copies.

THE COLORADO QUARTERLY—Hellems 134, University of Colorado, Boulder, CO 80309. Walter Simon, Editor.
Serious fiction, 3,000 to 6,000 words. Pays $50 on acceptance.

CONFRONTATION—Dept. of English, Long Island University, Brooklyn, NY 11201. Martin Tucker, Editor.
Serious fiction, 750 to 6,000 words. Pays on publication.

CONNECTICUT FIRESIDE—Box 5293, Hamden, CT 06518. Albert Callan, Editor.
Short fiction. Pays in copies.

CUMBERLANDS (formerly *Twigs*)—Pikeville College Press, Pikeville, KY 41501.
Short fiction. Pays in copies.

CUTBANK—Dept. of English, University of Montana, Missoula, MT 59801.
Short stories. Pays in copies.

THE DEKALB LITERARY ARTS JOURNAL—c/o W.S. Newman, Editor, DeKalb College, 555 Indian Creek Dr., Clarkson, GA 30021.
Short stories; one act plays; illustrations and photos. Pays in copies.

DECEMBER—4343 North Clarendon, Apt. 615, Chicago, IL 60613.
Short stories, 2,000 to 3,000 words. Pays in copies.

DESCANT—Texas Christian University, T.C.U. Station, Fort Worth, TX 76129. Betsy Colquitt, Editor.
Fiction, to 6,000 words. Pays in copies.

EPOCH—245 Goldwyn Smith Hall, Cornell University, Ithaca, NY 14853.
Serious fiction. Pays in copies.

EVENT—Douglas College, Box 2503, New Westminster, B.C., Canada V3L 5B2. John S. Levin, Editor.
Short stories, novellas, plays; photography and graphics. Pays modest rates, after publication.

THE FALCON—Belknap Hall, Mansfield State College, Mansfield, PA 16933. T.E. Porter, Fiction Editor.
Contemporary short stories and excerpts from novels, 2,000 to 6,000 words. Pays in copies.

THE FAULT—33513 Sixth St., Union City, CA 94587. Terrence Ames, Literature Editor.
Innovative short fiction; plays; graphics and photos. Pays in copies.

FICTION—Dept. of English, CCNY, Convent Ave. and 138th St., New York, NY 10031. Mark J. Mirsky, Editor.
Serious fiction.

FICTION INTERNATIONAL—Dept. of English, St. Lawrence University, Canton, NY 13617. Joe David Bellamy, Editor and Publisher.
Short stories, any length, especially with innovative forms or rich personal styles. Pays $25 to $150.

THE FIDDLEHEAD—The Observatory, University of New Brunswick, Fredericton, N.B., Canada.
Serious fiction, 2,500 words, preferably by Canadians. Pays around $5 per printed page, on publication.

FIRESCAPES—Box 322, Hunter College, 695 Park Ave., New York, NY 10021. Laurie Pearson, Editor.
Short fiction. Pays in copies.

FORUM—University of Houston, Houston, TX 77004. William L. Pryor, Editor.
Short stories of moderate length. Overstocked until September, 1978.

FOUR QUARTERS—LaSalle College, Philadelphia, PA 19141. John Keenan, Editor.
Short stories with strong characterization. Pays to $25, on publication.

FRONT STREET TROLLEY—2125 Acklen Ave., Nashville, TN 37215. Molly McIntosh, Editor.
Short stories, to 2,000 words, preferably by southern writers. Pays in copies.

THE GEORGIA REVIEW—University of Georgia, Athens, GA 30602. John T. Irwin, Editor.
Short fiction. Pays on publication.

GONE SOFT—Dept. of English, Salem State College, Salem, MA 01970.
Short stories, 2,000 to 6,000 words. Pays in copies.

GREEN RIVER REVIEW—SVSC Box 56, University Center, MI 48710. Raymond Tyner, Editor.
Short stories, to 3,000 words. Pays in copies.

THE GREENFIELD REVIEW—Greenfield Center, NY 12833. Joseph Bruchac III, Editor.
Very short fiction, especially by third world and new writers. Pays in copies.

GREEN'S MAGAZINE—P.O. Box 313, Detroit, MI 48231.
Fiction, 1,500 to 4,000 words. Pays $3 to $25, on publication.

THE GREENSBORO REVIEW—University of North Carolina, Greensboro, NC 27412.
Fiction, to 5,000 words. Pays in copies. Reads manuscripts only in September and
October.

THE GRUB STREET WRITER—English Dept., Kean College, Union NJ 07083.
Short stories and essays, in traditional or experimental forms. Pays in copies.

HAWAII REVIEW—2465 Campus Rd., University of Hawaii, Honolulu, HI 96822.
Short stories of any length. Pays in copies, or up to $30, on publication.

HEIRS—657 Mission St., San Francisco, CA 94105. Alfred Durand Garcia, Editor.
Short fiction, to 2,500 words, for multi-cultural magazine. Pays various rates, on
publication.

HUDSON REVIEW—65 East 55th St., New York, NY 10022. Frederick Morgan and
Paula Deitz, Editors.
Fiction to 10,000 words, of high literary quality. Pays 2½¢ a word, on publication.

HUDSON RIVER ANTHOLOGY—Vassar College, Poughkeepsie, NY 12601.
Short stories, traditional or experimental. Pays in copies.

INLET—Dept. of English, Virginia Wesleyan College, Norfolk, VA 23502. Joseph H.
Harkey, Editor.
Short fiction. Submit between September and March.

INTERSTATE—P.O. Box 7068, University Station, Austin, TX 78712. Loris Essary and
Carl D. Clark, Editors.
Experimental literature in all genres. Pays in copies.

THE IOWA REVIEW—EPB 321, The University of Iowa, Iowa City, IA 52242.
Short stories, prose poems. Pays $5 per page, on publication.

JAPANOPHILE—Box 223, Okemos, MI 48864. Earl R. Snodgrass, Editor.
Fiction, to 3,500 words, with a Japanese setting, preferably showing interaction
between Japanese and foreigners. Pays to $20, on publication.

KANSAS QUARTERLY—Dept. of English, Kansas State University, Manhattan, KS
66506.
Fiction. Pays in copies, annual awards.

KARAMU—Dept. of English, Eastern Illinois University, Charleston, IL 61920. Allen
Neff, Editor.
Serious fiction, 2,000 to 7,000 words, traditional or experimental. Pays in copies.
Submit between September and June.

KINEO WRITING—Kineo Island Club, Rockwood, ME 04478. Patrick Flynn, Lisa
Schmid, Richard Warren, Editors.
Maine-based essays and fiction, to 5,000 words. Pays varying rates, on publication.

THE LITERARY REVIEW—Fairleigh Dickinson University, Madison, NJ 07940. Charles
Angoff, Editor.
Serious fiction. Pays in copies.

THE LITTLE MAGAZINE—P.O. Box 207, Cathedral Station, New York, NY 10025.
David G. Hartwell and Barbara Damroseh, Editors.
Fiction, to 5,000 words. Pays in copies.

THE MALAHAT REVIEW—University of Victoria, P.O. Box 1700, Victoria, B.C., Canada V8W 2Y2. Robin Skelton, Editor.
Serious fiction, 2,000 to 5,000 words; translations. Photos; drawings. Pays $25 per
1,000 words, on acceptance.

THE MASSACHUSETTS REVIEW—Memorial Hall, University of Massachusetts,
Amherst, MA 01002. L.R. Edwards, John H. Hicks and M.T. Heath, Editors.

Short fiction. Pays modest rates, on publication.

THE MIDATLANTIC REVIEW—P.O. Box 398, Baldwin Place, NY 10505. Innovative short stories, to 20 pages. Pays in copies.

MISSISSIPPI REVIEW—Dept. of English, University of Southern Mississippi, Southern Station, Box 37, Hattiesburg, MS 39401. Bernard Kaplan and D.C. Berry, Editors. Serious fiction, 5,000 words. Pays $3 per printed page, on publication.

MOONS AND LION TAILES—Lake Street Station, Box 8434, Minneapolis, MN 55408. H. Schjotz-Christensen and Jim Perlman, Editors. Short fiction. Pays in copies.

MOUNTAIN REVIEW—Box 660, Whitesburg, KY 41858. Betty Edwards, Editor. Short stories, to 3,000 words. Pays in copies.

MOVING OUT—4866 Third, Wayne State University, Detroit, MI 48202. Feminist short stories; plays; graphics; photos. Pays in copies.

MUNDUS ARTIUM—University of Texas at Dallas, Box 688, Richardson, TX 75080. Rainer Schulte, Editor-in-Chief. Short fiction; translations.

NEW MAGAZINE (formerly *Newletters*)—1639 West Washington Blvd., Venice, CA 90291. George Drury Smith, Editor. Fiction. Pays in copies.

NEW ORLEANS REVIEW—Loyola University, New Orleans, LA 70118. Serious fiction. Pays $50, on publication.

NEW YORK ARTS JOURNAL—560 Riverside Dr., New York, NY 10027. Richard Burgin, Editor. Short stories, to 25 pages. Pays $3 per page, on publication. Query.

NIMROD—Dept. of English, University of Tulsa, Tulsa, OK 74104. Francine Ringold, General Editor. Serious fiction, experimental and traditional. Pays in copies; cash awards.

THE NORTH AMERICAN REVIEW—University of Northern Iowa, Cedar Falls, IA 50613. Address Fiction Editor. Fiction of high literary quality. Pays from $10 per printed page.

NORTHWEST REVIEW—University of Oregon, Eugene, OR 97403. Michael Strelow, Editor. Serious fiction. Pays varying rates.

THE OHIO REVIEW—Ellis Hall, Ohio University, Athens, OH 45701. Short stories, around 5,000 words. Pays from $5 per page, plus copies, on publication.

THE ONTARIO REVIEW—6000 Riverside Rd. East, Windsor, Ont., Canada N8S 1B6. Short stories, to 5,000 words. Pays in copies.

OYEZ REVIEW—Roosevelt University, 430 South Michigan Ave., Chicago, IL 60605. Fiction, preferably experimental. Pays in copies.

PARIS REVIEW—45-39 171st Pl., Flushing, NY 11358. Address Fiction Editor. Fiction of high literary quality. Pays on publication.

PARTISAN REVIEW—Rutgers University, One Richardson St., New Brunswick, NJ 08903. Serious fiction. Manuscripts held at least 3 months. Pays 1½¢ a word, on publication.

THE PAWN REVIEW—P.O. Box 29250, Dallas, TX 75229. Michael Anderson, Editor.

Short stories, 2,000 to 5,000 words, especially from unknown writers in Texas and the Southwest. Pays in copies.

PHOEBE—4400 University Dr., Fairfax, VA 22030.
Fiction to 8,000 words. Graphics. Include cover letter. Pays in copies.

PRAIRIE SCHOONER—201 Andrews Hall, University of Nebraska, Lincoln, NE 68588. Bernice Slote, Editor.
Short stories, to 5,000 words. Pays in copies; prizes.

PRIMER—18 East 40th St., #1, Indianapolis, IN 46205. Ron Wray, Editor.
Short stories, 5 to 10 pages. Pays in copies.

PRISM INTERNATIONAL—c/o Creative Writing, University of British Columbia, Vancouver, B.C., Canada V6T 1W5.
Fiction, to 5,000 words; short plays. Pays $5 per printed page, on publication.

PSYCHOLOGICAL PERSPECTIVES—c/o Harvey Mudd College, Claremont, CA 91711. J'nan Sellery, Associate Editor.
Fiction, 5,000 to 7,000 words, on psychological themes. Pays in copies.

PUERTO DEL SOL—Writing Center, Box 3E, New Mexico State University, Las Cruces, NM 88003.
Short stories, sections of novels, fiction works in progress, by native American and Chicano writers. Pays varying rates, on publication.

QUARTET—1119 Neal Pickett Dr., College Station, TX 77840. Richard Hauer Costa, Editor.
Short stories, some experimental, to 4,000 words. Query for theme of issue.

RED CEDAR REVIEW—Dept. of English, Morrill Hall, Michigan State University, East Lansing, MI 48824. Rebecca Howard and Michael Tanamura, Editors.
Fiction, 4,000 to 8,000 words. Pays in copies. Query.

THE REMINGTON REVIEW—505 Westfield Ave., Elizabeth, NJ 07208. Joseph A. Barbato, Fiction Editor.
Fiction, 1,500 to 10,000 words. Pays in copies.

RIVERSIDE QUARTERLY—Box 14451, University Station, Gainesville, FL 32604. Address Redd Boggs, Box 1111, Berkeley, CA 94701.
Science fiction and fantasy, to 3,500 words. Pays in copies.

SALT LICK—Box 1064, Quincy, IL 62301. James Haining and Dan Castelaz, Editors.
Fiction, any length. Drawings, photos, collages. Pays in copies.

SAM HOUSTON LITERARY REVIEW—English Dept., Sam Houston State University, Huntsville, TX 77340. Paul Ruffin, Editor.
Fiction, to 25 typed pages. Pays in copies.

SCHOLIA SATYRICA—Dept. of English, University of South Florida, Tampa, FL 33620. R.D. Wyly, Editor.
Original satire, to 5,000 words, mocking the scholarly community. Pays in copies.

SEQUOYA—University Center, St. John's University, Grand Central and Utopia Pkwys., Jamaica, NY 11439.
Annual magazine. Short stories, any length. Pays in copies.

SEWANEE REVIEW—Sewanee, TN 37375. George Core, Editor.
Fiction, to 8,000 words, of high literary quality. Pays $10 to $12 per printed page, on publication.

SHANTIH—P.O. Box 125, Bay Ridge Station, Brooklyn, NY 11220. John S. Friedman and Irving Gottesman, Editors.

Fiction, preferably experimental, to 3,000 words. Pays in copies.

SHENANDOAH—Box 722, Lexington, VA 24450. James Boatwright, Editor. Short fiction. Pays varying rates, on publication.

THE SMITH—5 Beekman St., New York, NY 10038. Harry Smith, General Editor. Serious fiction, short shorts to novellas. Pays modest rates, on acceptance, plus copies.

SNOWY EGRET—Dept. of English, Otterbein College, Westerville, OH 43081. William T. Hamilton, Literary Editor. Short stories and excerpts of novels, to 10,000 words, on people and nature. Pays $2 a page, on publication.

SOUTH CAROLINA REVIEW—c/o Dept. of English, Clemson University, Clemson, SC 29631. Short stories, 3,000 to 5,000 words. Pays in copies.

SOUTH DAKOTA REVIEW—Box 111, University Exchange, Vermillion, SD 57069. John R. Milton, Editor. Fiction, any length or style, preferably with western setting. Pays in copies.

SOUTHERN EXPOSURE—Institute for Southern Studies, P.O. Box 230, Chapel Hill, NC 27514. Short stories, to 3,500 words, on southern life and social change. Pays to $50.

SOUTHERN HUMANITIES REVIEW—Auburn University, Auburn, AL 36830. Short stories, 3,500 to 5,000 words. Pays in copies.

SOUTHERN REVIEW—Drawer D, University Station, Baton Rouge, LA 70893. Donald Stanford and Lewis Simpson, Editors. Fiction, 4,000 to 8,000 words, of high literary quality. Manuscripts held for 2 to 3 months. Pays from 3¢ a word, on publication.

SOUTHWEST REVIEW—Southern Methodist University, Dallas, TX 75275. Margaret L. Hartley, Editor. Stories, 3,000 to 5,000 words, with strong characterization. Pays on publication.

SPECTRUM—University of California, P.O. Box 14800, Santa Barbara, CA 93107. Short fiction, in any genre, about 2,500 words. Pays in copies. Stamped, self-addressed envelope required.

STORY QUARTERLY—220 Myrtle St., Winnetka, IL 60093. Short stories. Pays in copies.

THE SUNSTONE REVIEW—P.O. Box 2321, Santa Fe, NM 87501. Sandra Prewitt Edelman, Manuscript Editor. Short stories, to 1,500 words. Pays in copies.

TALES—Box 24226, St. Louis, MO 63130. Jonathan Moreno and Barry Glassner, Editors. Short fiction. Pays in copies.

TEXAS QUARTERLY—Box 7517, University Station, Austin, TX 78712. Thomas M. Cranfill and Miguel Gonzales-Gerth, Editors. Short fiction. Pays in copies and offprints.

TRIQUARTERLY—1735 Benson Ave., Northwestern University, Evanston, IL 60201. Fiction for international audience. Pays varying rates, on publication.

TWIGS—See *Cumberlands*.

THE UNIVERSITY OF DENVER QUARTERLY—University of Denver, Denver, CO 80210.
Fiction, any length. Pays $5 per printed page, after publication.

THE UNIVERSITY OF PORTLAND REVIEW—University of Portland, Portland, OR 97203. Thompson M. Faller, Editor.
Contemporary fiction, 500 to 2,500 words. Pays in copies.

THE UNIVERSITY OF WINDSOR REVIEW—Dept. of English, University of Windsor, Windsor, Ont., Canada. Alistair MacLeod, Fiction Editor.
Fiction, 2,500 to 5,000 words. Pays $10, plus copies.

VAGABOND—P.O. Box 879, Ellensburg, WA 98926. John Bennett, Editor.
Short fiction. Pays in copies.

THE VILLAGER—135 Midland Ave., Bronxville, NY 10708. Amy Murphy, Editor.
Fiction, 900 to 2,000 words: mystery, adventure, humor, romance. Pays in copies.

VIRGINIA QUARTERLY REVIEW—One West Range, Charlottesville, VA 22903.
Fiction, 3,000 to 5,000 words, of high literary quality. Pays $10 per page, on publication.

WASCANA REVIEW—c/o Dept. of English, University of Regina, Regina, Sask., Canada S4S 0A2.
Short stories, 2,000 to 6,000 words. Pays $3 per page, after publication.

WASHINGTON REVIEW OF THE ARTS—404 Tenth St., S.E., Washington, DC 20003. Jean Lewton, Editor.
Original fiction, 1,500 to 2,500 words, concerning all areas of the arts, with emphasis on Washington, DC area. Pays in copies.

WAVES—Room 128, Founders College, York University, 4700 Keele St., Downsview, Ont. Canada M3T 1P3.
Short stories, 1,000 to 5,000 words. Pays in copies.

WEBSTER REVIEW—Webster College, Webster Groves, MO 63119. Nancy Schapiro and Harry J. Cargas, Editors.
Fiction; translations. Pays in copies.

WEST COAST REVIEW—Simon Fraser University, Burnaby, B.C., Canada V5A 1S6.
Fiction, 1,000 to 3,000 words, preferably experimental. Pays $5, on acceptance.

WESTERN HUMANITIES REVIEW—University of Utah, Salt Lake City, UT 84112. Jack Garlington, Editor.
Serious fiction, any length. Pays $75 to $100.

WIND LITERARY JOURNAL—RFD Route #1, Box 810, Pikeville, KY 41501. Quentin R. Howard, Editor.
Short stories, to 3,000 words (will consider longer ones). Pays in copies.

WISCONSIN REVIEW—Box 118, Dempsey Hall, University of Wisconsin, Oshkosh, WI 54901.
Fiction, to 3,000 words. Pays in copies.

WOMEN: A JOURNAL OF LIBERATION—3028 Greenmount Ave., Baltimore, MD 21218.
Fiction, to 3,000 words, about women. Pays in copies.

YALE REVIEW—1902A Yale Station, New Haven, CT 06520. J.E. Palmer, Editor; Mary Price, Managing Editor.
Short stories of high literary quality. Pays on publication.

RELIGIOUS AND DENOMINATIONAL MAGAZINES

BREAD–6401 The Paseo, Kansas City, MO 64131. Dan Ketchum, Editor.
Church of the Nazarene. Religious short stories, to 1,500 words, for teen-agers. Pays from 2¢ a word, on acceptance.

THE CANADIAN MESSENGER–833 Broadview Ave., Toronto, Ont., Canada M4K 2P9. F.J. Power, S.J., Editor. Address Ms. M. Pujolas.
Catholic. Short stories, 1,800 to 2,000 words with Catholic emphasis. Pays 2¢ a word, on acceptance.

CHRISTIAN LIFE MAGAZINE–Gunderson Dr. and Schmale Rd., Wheaton, IL 60187. Robert Walker, Editor.
Fiction, 1,500 to 2,500 words, on problems faced by Christians. Pays to $150, on publication.

THE CHURCH HERALD–1324 Lake Drive, S.E., Grand Rapids, MI 49506.
Magazine of the Reformed Church in America. Children's stories only. Pays 2¢ to 4¢ a word, on acceptance.

COLUMBIA–Box 1670, New Haven, CT 06507. Elmer Von Feldt, Editor.
Journal of Knights of Columbus. Fiction from a Christian viewpoint. Pays $100 to $300, on acceptance.

COMMENTARY–165 East 56th St., New York, NY 10022. Norman Podhoretz, Editor.
Serious fiction, relevant to Jewish affairs. Pays on publication.

THE COMPANION–15 Chestnut Park Rd., Toronto, Ont., Canada M4W 1W5. N. Weiss, O.F.M. Conv., Editor.
Fiction, 1,200 to 1,500 words. Pays 2¢ a word, on acceptance.

CONTACT–302 Lake St., P.O. Box 650, Huntington, IN 46750. Stanley Peters, Editor.
Fiction, 1,000 to 1,500 words, on Christian subjects. Pays 1¢ a word, on acceptance.

THE EVANGEL–999 College Ave., Winona Lake, IN 46590. Vera Bethel, Editor.
Free Methodist. Fiction, 1,500 to 1,800 words, on Christian solutions to problems. Pays 2¢ a word, on acceptance.

FACE-TO-FACE–201 Eighth Ave. South, Nashville, TN 37202. Sharilyn S. Adair, Editor.
United Methodist. Fiction, 2,500 to 3,000 words, for 15- to 18-year-olds. Pays 3¢ a word, on acceptance.

HOME LIFE–127 Ninth Ave. North, Nashville, TN 37234. George W. Knight, Editor.
Southern Baptist. Fiction, to 2,000 words. Pays 3¢ a word, on acceptance.

INSPIRATION MAGAZINE–Petersen Publishing Co., 8490 Sunset Blvd., Los Angeles, CA 90069.
Limited amount of sensitively-written fiction, of inspirational interest. Pays from $150, after acceptance.

LIVE–1445 Boonville Ave., Springfield, MO 65802. Gary Leggett, Adult Editor.
Sunday school paper for adults. Fiction, 1,500 to 2,000 words. Pays on acceptance.

THE LOOKOUT–8121 Hamilton Ave., Cincinnati, OH 45231. Mark A. Taylor, Editor.
Fiction expressing Christian principles. Pays 3¢ a word.

LUTHERAN STANDARD–426 South Fifth St., Minneapolis, MN 55415. George H. Muedeking, Editor.

Fiction to 1,000 words. Pays from 3¢ a word, on acceptance.

MATURE LIVING–127 Ninth Ave. North, Nashville, TN 37234. Zada Malugen, Assistant Editor.
Short stories, 875 words, for people 60 years of age and older, on Christian topics; uses one story per issue. Pays 2½¢ per word, on acceptance.

MATURE YEARS–201 Eighth Ave. South, Nashville, TN 37203. Daisy D. Warren, Editor.
United Methodist. Humorous and serious short stories, 1,200 to 1,500 words, especially on Christmas or Thanksgiving, for adults. Pays 3¢ a word, on acceptance.

MIDSTREAM–515 Park Ave., New York, NY 10022. Joel Carmichael, Editor.
Fiction, to 8,000 words, of Jewish interest. Pays 7¢ a word, on publication.

THE MIRACULOUS MEDAL–475 East Chelton Ave., Philadelphia, PA 19144. Robert P. Crawley, C.M. Editorial Director.
Fiction, to 2,000 words, with Catholic awareness, but not necessarily religious. Pays from 2¢ a word, on acceptance.

MOMENT–55 Chapel St., Newton, MA 02160.
Sophisticated fiction, 2,000 to 5,000 words, on Jewish topics. Pays $200 to $400, on publication.

NEW CATHOLIC WORLD–1865 Broadway, New York, NY 10023. Robert J. Heyer, Managing Editor.
Fiction, 2,000 words, reflecting religious concern about modern problems. Pays from $75, on publication.

OUR FAMILY–Box 249, Dept. E., Battleford, Sask., Canada S0M 0E0. Reb Materi, O.M.I., Editor.
Catholic. Fiction, 1,000 to 3,000 words, for family readers. Pays 3¢ a word, on acceptance.

PURPOSE–610 Walnut Ave., Scottdale, PA 15683. David E. Hostetler, Editor.
Fiction, to 1,200 words, on Christians confronting issues. Pays to 3¢ a word, on acceptance.

QUEEN–40 South Saxon Ave., Bay Shore, NY 11706. James McMillan, S.M.M., Editor.
Publication of the Montfort Missionaries. Fiction, 1,000 to 2,000 words, relating to the Virgin Mary. Pays on acceptance.

THE RECONSTRUCTIONIST–432 Park Ave. South, New York, NY 10016. Ira Eisenstein, Editor.
Fiction, 2,000 to 3,000 words, relating to Judaism. Pays $15 to $25, on publication.

ST. JOSEPH'S MESSENGER–P.O. Box 288, Jersey City, NJ 07303. Sister Ursula Marie Maphet, Editor.
Inspirational fiction, 1,000 to 1,500 words. Pays 1¢ a word. Query.

SCOPE–426 South Fifth St., Minneapolis, MN 55415. Lily M. Gyldenvand, Editor.
Journal of American Lutheran Women. Fiction, 1,000 to 1,500 words. Pays on acceptance.

SEEK–8121 Hamilton Ave., Cincinnati, OH 54231. J. David Lang, Editor.
Fiction, 400 to 1,200 words, on inspirational subjects. Pays about 2¢ a word, on acceptance.

THE SIGN–Monastery Place, Union City, NJ 07087. Arthur McNally, C.P., Editor.
General-interest and religious fiction, to 4,000 words. Pays to $300, on acceptance.

SUNSHINE MAGAZINE–Litchfield, IL 62056. Monta Henrichs Crane, Editor.
Short stories, 1,250 words, on living. Pays varying rates, on acceptance.

THE POPULAR MARKET

The popular market includes the magazines that used to be called the "pulps": men's magazines, detective and mystery, science fiction, confession and romance magazines. Included among the men's magazines are publications seeking so-called adult material. Most of the popular magazines use fiction, many use both stories and articles, while a few detective and adventure magazines want only factual material. Book publishers also have a continuing need for western, mystery, science fiction, romance and adventure novels; many paperback book publishers particularly are in the market for paperback originals in these areas. Writers should consult the list of *Paperback Book Publishers* for their requirements.

MEN'S AND ADULT MAGAZINES

ADAM—8060 Melrose Ave., Los Angeles, CA 90046. Carlton Hollander, Editor.
 Articles, 1,000 to 3,000 words, on social themes, sexuality, personalities, etc. Sexy humor, satire. Hard-hitting topical fiction. Pays $50 to $150, on publication.

ARMY TIMES—475 School St. S.W., Washington, DC 20024. Gene Famiglietti, Editor.
 Articles on military service, personnel policies, current developments, etc. Cartoons. Pays varying rates.

BEAVER—Reese Publishing Co., Inc., 235 Park Ave. South, New York, NY 10003. Jayson Rollands, Editor.
 Short, erotic fiction, 1,500 to 3,000 words; articles to interest male audience, 18 to 34. Pays from $300, on acceptance. Fillers, humor, jokes.

CAVALIER—316 Aragon Ave., Coral Gables, FL 33134. Nye Willden, Managing Editor.
 Articles and fiction, 3,000 to 6,000 words, for hip young men. Pays to $400 for articles, to $300 for fiction, on publication.

CHIC—1888 Century Park East, Suite 1606, Los Angeles CA 90067. Peter Brennan, Editor.
 Articles, 2,500 to 5,000 words, and fiction, from 3,000 words, for sophisticated men. Fillers and short humor, 100 to 450 words. Pays $600 to $750 for fiction, $750 to $1,200 for articles, on acceptance. Query.

DAPPER—21335 Roscoe Blvd., Canoga Park, CA 91304. Kent Roland, Editor.
 Factual articles, 2,000 to 3,000 words, on sex, sports, adventure, etc. Fiction; humor. Pays from $100, on acceptance. Same address and requirements for *Nymphet*.

ELITE—606 Avenue Rd., Suite 404, Toronto, Ont., Canada H3H 2G1. David S. Wells, Publisher.
 Articles, 1,500 to 3,500 words, on sports, politics, money, health, sex, etc. Fiction, to 3,500 words: science fiction, mystery, suspense, erotic, etc. Fillers. Pays $125 to $350 for articles, $110 to $300 for fiction, on publication.

ESQUIRE—488 Madison Ave., New York, NY 10022.
Articles, 1,500 to 5,000 words, for intelligent adult audience. Features, 1,000 words, on dramatic news pieces. Pays $350 to $1,250, on acceptance. Query.

FOR MEN ONLY—575 Madison Ave., New York, NY 10022. Ivan Prashker, Editorial Director.
Fiction, 3,000 to 5,000 words, for men: humor, adventure, rugged action, etc., with some sex. Pays to $400, on acceptance.

GALLERY—99 Park Ave., New York, NY 10016. Eric Protter, Editorial Director.
Articles and fiction, to 5,000 words, for sophisticated men. Short humor, satire. Photos. Pays $350 to $750, after acceptance. Query.

GEM—303 West 42nd St., New York, NY 10036. Will Martin, Editor.
Articles and fiction, 500 to 1,500 words, on sexy topics. Pays after assignment. Same address and requirements for *The Swinger.*

GENESIS—770 Lexington Ave., New York, NY 10021. J.J. Kelleher, Editor.
Articles, 2,500 to 6,000 words: profiles, exposés, interviews, etc. Fiction, 3,000 to 6,000 words. Photo essays, photos. Pays varying rates, on publication.

GENTLEMEN'S QUARTERLY(GQ)—488 Madison Ave., New York, NY 10022. Jack Haber, Editor.
Queries only. No fiction, poetry, or cartoons. Unsolicited manuscripts returned unread.

HIGH SOCIETY—801 Second Ave., Room 705, New York, NY 10017. Richard Barraclough, Editorial Director.
Articles and fiction, to 2,500 words, personality pieces and interviews. All material should have sexual slant. Pays to $350, on publication. Query first.

HUSTLER—2029 Century Park East, Los Angeles, CA 90067.
Articles, 1,500 to 6,000 words, and fiction, 800 to 1,500 words, on sexy topics. Pays $150 to $1,000, on publication.

KNIGHT—Publisher's Service, Inc., 8060 Melrose Ave., Los Angeles, CA 90046. Jared Rutter, Editor.
Articles on sexuality; interviews. Erotic fiction for men and women. Pays $60 to $250, on publication.

MALE—575 Madison Ave., New York, NY 10022. Carl Sifakis, Editor.
Articles, 3,500 to 4,000 words: true adventures with exotic backgrounds; exposés; profiles; World War II and contemporary cold war stories. Pays to $400, on acceptance. Query. Same address and requirements for *Men.*

MAN TO MAN—280 Madison Ave., New York, NY 10016. Everett Meyers, Editor.
Fiction, 1,500 to 5,000 words, on male-female relationships. Articles, 2,000 to 5,000 words, on sex, travel, art, entertainment, etc. Pays from $75, on or before publication. Same requirements for *Mr. Magazine* and *Sir!.*

MEN—See *Male.*

MR. MAGAZINE—See *Man to Man.*

NYMPHET—See *Dapper.*

OUI–8560 Sunset Blvd., Los Angeles, CA 90069. Address Articles Editor.
Articles and fiction, 2,500 to 5,000 words, on sexy topics. Short pieces for "Openers." Pays to $1,200, $50 to $100 for short pieces.

PENTHOUSE–909 Third Ave., New York, NY 10022.
Sophisticated, sexy fiction, 3,000 to 5,000 words, and general-interest or controversial articles, to 6,000 words. Pays to 25¢ a word, after acceptance.

PENTHOUSE FORUM–909 Third Ave., New York, NY 10022. Barbara Schrank, Executive Editor.
Articles, 1,500 to 2,500 words, on contemporary emotional, psychological, medical and sexual conflicts, problems, innovations, etc. Pays $200 to $400.

PLAYBOY–919 North Michigan Ave., Chicago, IL 60611. Address Articles Editor.
Articles, 4,000 to 8,000 words, for urban men. Humor; satire. Top quality science fiction and mystery short stories and serious fiction, 1,000 to 10,000 words. Vicky Haider, Fiction Editor. Pays to $3,000.

PLAYERS–8060 Melrose Ave., Los Angeles, CA 90046. Joe Nazel, Editor.
Articles, 1,000 to 4,000 words, with photos, for black men: travel, business, entertainment, sports; interviews. Fiction, 2,000 to 6,000 words. Humor; satire. Movie, theatre and record reviews, 100 to 500 words. Pays from 5¢ a word, on publication.

SAGA–333 Johnson Ave., Brooklyn, NY 11206. Martin M. Singer, Editor.
Articles, 4,000 to 5,000 words, for men: adventure, humor, travel, hunting, sports, war. Interviews, profiles. Photo essays on action sports, dangerous pastimes. Pays from $250.

SIR!–See *Man to Man.*

STAG–See *Swank.*

SWANK–888 Seventh Ave., New York, NY 10019. Richard Milner, Managing Editor.
Men's magazine. Articles, 2,500 to 3,500 words, on personalities, sports, politics, sex and behavior; interviews. Sophisticated fiction, 1,800 to 3,500 words. Pays $300 and up for articles, $200 and up for fiction, on publication. Query with outline. Same address and requirements for *Stag.*

THE SWINGER–See *Gem.*

DETECTIVE AND MYSTERY MAGAZINES

ALFRED HITCHCOCK'S MYSTERY MAGAZINE–229 Park Ave. South, New York, NY 10003. After June 1, 1978: 122 East 42nd St., New York, NY 10017. Eleanor Sullivan, Editor.
Well-plotted mystery, suspense and crime fiction, 1,000 to 10,000 words. No cheap thrills. Pays 3¢ to 8¢ a word, on acceptance.

ARMCHAIR DETECTIVE–3656 Midland, White Bear Lake, MN 55110. Allen J. Hubin, Editor.
Articles on mystery and detective fiction: biographical sketches, critiques, book reviews, etc. No payment.

ELLERY QUEEN'S MYSTERY MAGAZINE—229 Park Ave. South, New York, NY 10003. After June 1, 1978: 122 East 42nd St., New York, NY 10017. Ellery Queen, Editor.
Detective, crime, mystery and spy fiction, 4,000 to 6,000 words. Suspense or straight detective stories. Pays 3¢ to 8¢ a word, on acceptance.

FRONT PAGE DETECTIVE—See *Inside Detective.*

INSIDE DETECTIVE—235 Park Ave. South, New York, NY 10003.
Timely, true detective stories, 3,500 to 4,500 words, with photos, stressing suspense, detective work, characterization and emotion. Crime shorts, to 1,500 words. No fiction. Pays from $200, $25 to $50 for shorts, on acceptance. Same address and requirements for *Front Page Detective.*

MASTER DETECTIVE—235 Park Ave. South, New York, NY 10003. A. P. Govoni, Editor.
Detailed articles, 5,000 to 6,000 words, with photos, on current cases (some older, solved cases considered), emphasizing human motivation and detective work. No fiction. Pays to $200, extra for photos. Query.

MIKE SHAYNE MYSTERY MAGAZINE—P.O. Box 1084, Reseda, CA 91335.
Detective and mystery stories. 1,500 to 12,000 words. Pays from 1¢ a word, on acceptance.

OFFICIAL DETECTIVE STORIES—235 Park Ave. South, New York, NY 10003. A. P. Govoni, Editor.
True detective stories, 5,000 to 6,000 words, on current investigations, strictly from the investigator's point of view. No fiction. Pays $200, extra for photos. Query.

STARTLING DETECTIVE—Globe Communications Corp., 1440 St. Catherine St. West, Montreal, Que., Canada H3G I52. Dominick A. Merle, Editor.
Articles, 3,000 to 6,000 words, with photos, on current sensational crimes in U.S., detailing police investigation leading to arrest. No fiction. Pays $125 to $225.

TRUE DETECTIVE—235 Park Ave. South, New York, NY 10003. A. P. Govoni, Editor.
Articles, from 5,000 words, with photos, on current police cases, emphasizing detective work and human motivation. Special series on older, solved cases. No fiction. Pays $200, extra for photos. Query.

TRUE POLICE CASES—Globe Communications Corp., 1440 St. Catherine St. West, Montreal, Que., Canada H3G I52. Dominick A. Merle, Editor.
Factual articles, 3,000 to 6,000 words, with photos, on sensational crimes in U.S. No old or unsolved cases. Pays $125 to $225.

SCIENCE FICTION AND FANTASY MAGAZINES

ALGOL: THE MAGAZINE ABOUT SCIENCE FICTION—P.O. Box 4175, New York, NY 10017. Andrew Porter, Editor.
Articles, 3,000 to 10,000 words, on writing science fiction and on science-fiction writers. Interviews with authors, editors, etc. Artwork. Pays 1¢ a word, on acceptance.

ANALOG: SCIENCE FICTION & FACT—350 Madison Ave., New York, NY 10017. Ben Bova, Editor.

Science fiction, with human characters in believable future or alien setting: short stories, 3,500 to 7,500 words; novelettes, 10,000 to 20,000 words; serials, to 70,000 words. "Fact" articles, 3,500 to 5,000 words, on probable future developments of current facts. Pays to 4¢ a word, 5¢ a word for short stories, on acceptance. Query on novelettes and articles.

BEYOND REALITY—303 West 42nd St., New York, NY 10036. Harry Belil, Editor.
Well-researched articles, 2,500 words, on ESP, UFOs, psychic phenomena, new age philosophy, strange happenings and parapsychology. Pays 3¢ a word, on publication.

COSMOS—Baronet Publishing Co., 509 Madison Ave., New York, NY 10022. David Hartwell, Editor.
Science fiction short stories, to 15,000 words. Pays 2¢ to 6¢ a word, on acceptance.

FANTASY & SCIENCE FICTION—P.O. Box 56, Cornwall, CT 06753. E. Ferman, Editor.
Science fiction and well-plotted fantasy, short-shorts to serials. Light material. Pays 2¢ a word, on acceptance.

GALAXY MAGAZINE—720 White Plains Rd., Scarsdale, NY 10583.
Science fiction, on situations and environments based on current scientific knowledge or hypothesis: short stories, to 7,200 words; novelettes, to 17,000 words; novellas, to 20,000 words, usually by arrangement. No fantasy. Pays by arrangement.

HEAVY METAL—635 Madison Ave., New York, NY 10022.
Adult fantasy and science fiction, 2,000 to 3,000 words. Pays 10¢ a word, part on acceptance, the remainder on publication.

ISAAC ASIMOV'S SCIENCE FICTION MAGAZINE—Box 13116, Philadelphia, PA 19101. George Scithers, Editor.
Short, good science fiction, to 12,500 words. One-page fillers. Pays 3¢ to 6¢ a word, on acceptance. Contributors' sheets available. Send stamped, self-addressed envelope.

POLLUTION CONTROL JOURNAL—144 West 12th Ave., Denver, CO 80204.
Science fiction, 2,500 to 3,000 words, using pollution theme. Pays 3¢ a word, on publication.

RIVERSIDE QUARTERLY—Box 14451, University Sta., Gainesville, FL 32604. Leland Sapiro, Editor. Address Redd Boggs, Box 1111, Berkeley, CA 94701.
Science fiction and fantasy, to 3,500 words. Pays in copies.

UNEARTH—102 Charles St., Suite 190, Boston, MA 02114. Jonathan Ostrowsky-Lantz, Editor.
Science fiction, fantasy, and speculative stories, to 10,000 words. Also book and movie reviews. Pays $20 for short stories, varying rates for other submissions, on acceptance.

WEIRDBOOK—Box 35, Amherst Branch, Buffalo, NY 14226. W. Paul Ganley, Editor.
Horror and fantasy adventure fiction, to 20,000 words; poetry, to 15 lines. No straight science fiction. Pays from $2 per printed page, on publication.

WHISPERS—Box 904, Chapel Hill, NC 27514. Stuart David Schiff, Editor.
Fantasy and horror stories, 1,000 to 8,000 words, and articles, 1,000 to 5,000 words, on fantasy writing and writers. Pays 1¢ a word for fiction, half on acceptance, half on publication, in copies for articles.

CONFESSION AND ROMANCE MAGAZINES

BRONZE THRILLS—Good Publishing Co., 1220 Harding St., Fort Worth, TX 76102. Edna K. Turner, Editor.
Confession stories, 5,000 to 8,000 words, for black readers. Photos. Pays on acceptance. Same address and requirements for *Hep, Jive* and *Soul Confessions*.

DARING ROMANCES—See *Intimate Story.*

HEP—See *Bronze Thrills.*

HERS—IPC Magazines, Ltd., Room 1705, 205 East 42nd St., New York, NY 10017.
First-person stories with strong reader identification, 5,000 to 8,000 words, on emotional, romantic, realistic subjects. No pornography. Pays on acceptance. Same address and requirements (3,000- to 6,000-word stories) for *True.*

INTIMATE ROMANCES—See *True Secrets.*

INTIMATE SECRETS—See *True Secrets.*

INTIMATE STORY—2 Park Ave., New York, NY 10016. Janet Wandel, Editor.
First-person stories, to 7,000 words, on love, courtship, marriage and family problems, resolved in uplifting manner, and stories on sexy topics. No nonfiction. Pays to $180, after acceptance. Same address and requirements for *Daring Romances.*

JIVE—See *Bronze Thrills.*

MODERN LOVE—See *Real Confessions.*

MODERN ROMANCES—Macfadden Women's Group, 205 East 42nd St., New York, NY 10017. Jean Sharbel, Editor.
Confession stories with reader identification and emotion, 1,500 to 7,000 words; articles of interest to blue-collar, family-oriented women, 300 to 1,000 words; light, romantic poetry, to 24 lines. Pays 5¢ a word, on publication.

MY ROMANCE—See *True Secrets.*

PERSONAL ROMANCES—2 Park Ave., New York, NY 10016. Johanna Roman Smith, Editor.
Confession stories, 2,000 to 6,500 words, on emotional, sexual and family conflicts of young married women, singles and teen-agers, and their resolution. Pays on acceptance.

REAL CONFESSIONS—261 Fifth Ave., New York, NY 10016. Susan Silverman, Editor.
First-person confession stories, to 7,000 words, with female narrator, on relationships with family, husband, lovers, children, etc.: timely, original, colloquial; with much dialogue. Pays on acceptance. Same address and requirements for *Modern Love.*

REAL ROMANCES—21 West 26th St., New York, NY 10010. Ardis Sandel, Editor.
Sexy, well-plotted first-person confession stories, to 7,500 words, with convincing characterization and motivation; teen-age courtship and young-married stories. Some male viewpoint; no racial themes. Pays $100 to $150, on publication. Same address and requirements for *Real Story.*

REAL STORY—See *Real Romances.*

SECRETS—Macfadden Women's Group, 205 East 42nd St., New York, NY 10017. Jean Sharbel, Editor.
Confession stories with emotion and realism, articles on subjects of interest to family-oriented women, 300 to 850 words. Short stories, 1,500 to 7,000 words; light, romantic poetry, to 24 lines. Pays 3¢ a word, on publication.

SOUL CONFESSIONS—See *Bronze Thrills.*

TRUE—See *Hers.*

TRUE CONFESSIONS—205 East 42nd St., New York, NY 10017. Jean P. Silberg, Editor.
Confession stories, 2,500 to 12,000 words, with female narrator, on emotional conflicts in male-female relationships. Short shorts, 1,500 to 2,500 words. Pays 5¢ a word, on publication.

TRUE EXPERIENCE—205 East 42nd St., New York, NY 10017. Lydia E. Paglio, Editor.
Realistic first-person stories, 4,000 to 8,000 words (short shorts to 2,000 words), on family life, love, courtship, health, religion, etc. Pays 3¢ a word.

TRUE LOVE—205 East 42nd St., New York, NY 10017. Erma E. Benedict, Editor.
Fresh, realistic first-person stories, to 8,000 words. No conventional confession stories. Pays 3¢ a word.

TRUE ROMANCE—205 East 42nd St., New York, NY 10017. Barbara J. Brett, Editor.
Timely, emotional first-person stories, 2,000 to 7,500 words, on romance, family life and problems of contemporary women. Articles, 300 to 700 words, for young blue-collar class women. Pays 3¢ a word, on publication.

TRUE SECRETS—667 Madison Ave., New York, NY 10021. Cara Sherman, Editorial Director.
First-person stories, 1,500 to 7,000 words, on romantic or emotional problems: sex, love, teen-age romance, children, etc. Mystery-gothic confession stories. Pays to $150. Same address and requirements for *Intimate Secrets, My Confession, My Romance,* and *Secret Story.*

TRUE STORY—205 East 42nd St., New York, NY 10017. Helen Vincent, Editor.
First-person stories, 3,000 to 8,000 words, on hopes, fears, drama and humor of women's lives. Articles, 1,500 to 3,000 words, of general interest to women. Pays from 5¢ a word on publication.

ARTICLE MARKETS

The magazines in this list are in the market for free-lance articles of many types. The list is divided into the following categories: general magazines; college, literary and little magazines; religious and denominational magazines; publications devoted to sports, outdoors, travel, cars, etc.; magazines that emphasize women's interests and home and garden magazines; magazines with specialized interests: trade and business, city and regional, house and company magazines; also travel, technical, education, health and hobbies, crafts, fine arts and the like.

Only the largest trade and business publications that particularly want to see free-lance material are listed. Writers who are able to write articles in a particular technical or business field can find the names of thousands more in *Ayer Directory of Publications,* available in most libraries. Periodicals in a wide variety of specialized areas are also listed. The *Directory,* which contains an index according to classification, does not list editorial requirements, and writers should query these magazines before submitting manuscripts.

Juvenile article markets are listed under *Juvenile, Teen-Age and Young Adult Magazines.* Markets for male-oriented or adult articles, true detective stories, etc., are listed under *The Popular Market.*

GENERAL MAGAZINES

ADAM—8060 Melrose Ave., Los Angeles, CA 90046. Norman Scott, Editor.
Articles, 2,000 to 5,000 words, on social themes, sexuality, personalities, etc. Sexy humor, satire. Pays $75 to $200 for first rights, $35 to $75 for second rights, on publication. Query.

ADAM FILM WORLD—8060 Melrose Ave., Los Angeles, CA 90046.
Articles on film erotica.

AFRICA REPORT—833 U.N. Plaza, New York, NY 10017. Anthony Hughes, Editor.
Well-researched articles by specialists, 1,000 to 4,000 words, with photos, on current African affairs and life styles. Pays $40 to $150, on publication.

AFTER DARK—10 Columbus Circle, New York, NY 10019. William Como, Editor.
Features and reviews on regional theaters, people in entertainment field, etc. Photos. Pays $75 for features, $15 to $25 for reviews, extra for photos, on publication.

ALLIED PUBLICATIONS—P.O. Box 9820, Fort Worth, TX 76107. Didi Scott, Associate Editor.
Articles, with photos, on home and family, travel, beauty, decorating, hobbies, etc. Profiles; how-to pieces; articles of interest to hair-stylists. Pays 5¢ a word, $5 per photo, on acceptance.

AMERICAN ASTROLOGY—2505 North Alvernon Way, Tucson, AZ 85712.
Articles, to 3,000 words, on popular astrology. Pays from $20 per printed page, on publication.

AMERICAN BAR ASSOCIATION JOURNAL—77 South Wacker Dr., Chicago, IL 60606. Richard B. Allen, Editor.
Articles, 3,000 to 3,500 words, on law, legal history, public affairs, political science. No payment. Query.

AMERICAN HERITAGE—10 Rockefeller Plaza, New York, NY 10020. Alvin M. Josephy, Jr., Editor.
Articles, 4,000 to 6,000 words, on historic background of American life and culture today. Pays varying rates, on acceptance. Query.

AMERICAN HUMANE MAGAZINE (formerly *National Humane Review*)—5351 South Roslyn St., Englewood, CO 80110. Anne Brennan, Editor.
Articles, 500 to 2,000 words, on protection of children and animals; general interest features about people and animals. Photo essays. Pays $25 to $75, on publication. Query.

AMERICAN LEGION MAGAZINE—1608 K St. N.W., Washington, DC 20006. Raymond J. McHugh, Editor.
Articles on national and international affairs, American history and military history. Pays to $1,000, after acceptance.

THE AMERICAN SCHOLAR—1811 Q St., N.W., Washington, DC 20009. Joseph Epstein, Editor.
Nontechnical articles and essays, 3,500 to 4,000 words, on current affairs, the American cultural scene, politics, the arts, religion and science. Pays $250, on acceptance.

AMERICAN WAY—American Airlines, 633 Third Ave., New York, NY 10017. Address Articles Editor.

General-interest articles, 1,500 to 2,000 words. Pays $200 to $500, after acceptance.

AMERICAN WEST—20380 Town Center Ln., Suite 160, Cupertino, CA 96014. Ed Holm, Editor and Publisher.
Well-researched, illustrated articles, 3,000 to 5,000 words, on the West, past and present. Pays $100 to $250, on acceptance. Query.

AMERICANA—American Heritage Society, 10 Rockefeller Plaza, New York, NY 10020. Michael Durham, Editor.
Illustrated articles, 1,000 to 2,000 words, on travel to historic places, crafts, decorating old houses, gardening, cooking, etc. Pays varying rates, on acceptance. Query.

ANDY WARHOL'S INTERVIEW MAGAZINE—860 Broadway, New York, NY 10003. Interviews with well-known or unusual people. Pays $25, on publication. Query.

ANIMAL CAVALCADE—See *Today's Animal Health*.

ANIMAL KINGDOM—Zoological Park, Bronx, NY 10460.
Articles, 2,500 words with photos, on natural history, ecology and animal behavior, preferably based on original scientific research. No articles on pets. Pays $150 to $325, on acceptance.

ANIMAL LOVERS—P.O. Box 918, New Providence, NJ 07974.
Human-interest articles, 600 words, on pets. Photos. Pays 1¢ a word, $2 per photo, on acceptance.

ANIMALS—MSPCA, 350 South Huntington Ave., Boston, MA 02130. Deborah Salem, Editor.
Journal of the Massachusetts Society for the Prevention of Cruelty to Animals. Articles, to 3,000 words, on animals. Photos. Pays 2¢ a word, on publication. Query.

ARIZONA MAGAZINE—*The Phoenix Republic,* 120 East Van Buren St., Phoenix, AZ 85001.
Articles, 1,000 to 3,000 words, with unusual Arizona angle. Photos. Pays $50 to $175, before publication.

ARMY MAGAZINE—1529 18th St., N.W., Washington, DC 20036. L. James Binder, Editor-in-Chief.
Features, 4,000 words, on military subjects. Essays, humor, news reports, first-person anecdotes. Pays 7¢ to 9¢ a word, $5 to $25 for anecdotes, on publication.

THE ATLANTIC—8 Arlington St., Boston, MA 02116. Robert Manning, Editor.
In-depth articles on public issues, politics, social sciences, education, business, literature and the arts. Pays around $100 per printed page, on acceptance.

THE ATLANTIC ADVOCATE—Gleaner Bldg., Phoenix Sq., Fredericton, N.B., Canada. H. P. Wood, Editor.
Articles on the Atlantic provinces of Canada. Photos. Pays varying rates, on publication.

BC OUTDOORS—Box 900, Postal Station A, Surrey, B.C., Canada V3S 4P4. Art Downs, Editor.
Articles, 2,000 to 3,000 words, on camping, fishing, wildlife, history, travel and general-interest topics related to British Columbia and the Yukon. Pays $50 to $150, on acceptance.

BEACON MAGAZINE (formerly *Pictorial Living Magazine*)—*Boston Sunday Herald American,* 300 Harrison Ave., Boston, MA 02106.
Articles, 1,000 to 3,000 words, on local and human-interest subjects, profiles. Pays $40 to $100, on publication.

BETTER HOMES AND GARDENS—1716 Locust St., Des Moines, IA 50336. James A. Autry, Editor.
"While our material is over 75% staff-produced, free-lance contributions are used in areas of travel, health, cars, money management, family entertainment and do-it-yourself projects, which should be accompanied by 'before' and 'after' snapshots. Articles should run from 250 to 1,000 words. We prefer a query first with an outline. We pay top rates, on acceptance."

BLACK STARS—820 South Michigan Ave., Chicago, IL 60605.
Articles on black entertainers. Pays $100 to $200, on publication. Articles on assignment only. Query.

THE BLADE SUNDAY MAGAZINE—See *Toledo*.

BON APPETIT—5900 Wilshire Blvd., Los Angeles, CA 90036. Paige Rense, Editor-in-Chief.
Covers gourmet cooking, fine living. Queries welcome. Enclose samples of published work. Rates vary. Payment is on acceptance.

CALIFORNIA HIGHWAY PATROLMAN—1225 8th St., Suite 150, Sacramento, CA 95814. Richard York, Editor.
Articles, with photos, on transportation safety, driver education, travel in California and historic California. Cartoons. Pays 2½¢ a word, $2.50 per photo, $10 for cartoons, on publication.

CALIFORNIA LIVING—*The San Francisco Examiner*, 110 Fifth St., San Francisco, CA 94119. Harold I. Silverman, Editor.
Articles, to 5,000 words, and photo essays, on life styles, leisure and service related to Bay area. Pays varying rates, on publication.

CALIFORNIA TODAY—750 Ridder Park Dr., San Jose, CA 95131. Fred Dickey, Editor.
Factual, historical or humorous articles on California, particularly northern and western regions. Pays varying rates, on acceptance.

CAMPAIGN INSIGHT—Suite 516, Petroleum Bldg., Wichita, KS 67202. Linda Donlay, Editor.
Articles, 800 to 1,000 words, on successful political campaign techniques. Pays 5¢ a word, on acceptance. Query.

THE CANADIAN MAGAZINE—Simpson Tower, 401 Bay St., Suite 1100, Toronto, Ont. Canada M5H 2Y8. Don Obe, Editor.
Articles, to 4,000 words, on controversial topics with Canadian appeal. Profiles; sports, adventure; human-interest and entertainment pieces. Pays $300 to $800, on acceptance.

CAPPER'S WEEKLY—616 Jefferson St., Topeka, KS 66607. Dorothy Harvey, Editor.
Articles, 300 to 500 words: human interest, personal experience, historical. Pays varying rates, on publication.

CARTE BLANCHE—3460 Wilshire Blvd., Los Angeles, CA 90010. Margaret M. Volpe, Editor-in-Chief.
Articles, 2,000 to 2,500 words, with photos, on travel, dining and entertainment, for family audience and professional men and women. Pays around $300, on acceptance.

CAT FANCY—P.O. Box 4030, San Clemente, CA 92672. Mike Criss, Managing Editor.
Articles, from 1,500 words, on cat care, health, grooming, etc., Pays 3¢ a word, on publication.

CATS–P.O. Box 4106, Pittsburgh, PA 15202.
Articles, 1,000 to 2,000 words, with illustrations, on cats: unusual anecdotes, medical pieces, humor, articles on cats in art, literature or science. Pays 3¢ a word, extra for illustrations, on publication.

CAVALIER–316 Aragon Ave., Coral Gables, FL 33134.
Articles, 2,500 to 5,000 words, for hip young males with sophisticated tastes. Pays from $200, on publication. Query.

CHATELAINE–481 University Ave., Toronto, Ont., Canada M5W 1A7. Doris Anderson, Editor.
Articles, 3,000 words, for women, on controversial subjects, personalities, medicine, psychology, etc. Pays from $300, on acceptance.

CHICAGOSTYLE (formerly *Midwest Magazine*)–*Chicago Sun-Times,* Chicago, IL 60611. Richard Takeuchi, Editor.
Articles, to 1,500 words, on Chicago area subjects. Pays $75 to $300, on publication.

THE CHRISTIAN SCIENCE MONITOR–One Norway St., Boston, MA 02115. John Hughes, Editor.
Articles on travel, education, homemaking, science, environment, consumer affairs, etc. Humorous or human-interest articles for People page; literary essays, to 1,000 words, for Home Forum; guest columns, to 800 words, for editorial page. Pays varying rates.

THE CIVIL LIBERTIES REVIEW–American Civil Liberties Union, 22 East 40th St., Room 1020, New York, NY 10016. Albert Robbins, Staff Editor.
Articles, 1,200 to 7,000 words, on civil liberties topics: political, social, cultural, legal. Pays varying rates, on acceptance. Query.

CLASSIC–551 Fifth Ave., New York, NY 10017. Andrew Crichton, Executive Editor.
Feature articles, 2,000 to 4,000 words, and shorter column-length pieces, on horses, used for pleasure or sport. Pays from $500 for articles, $250 for columns, and a $25 finders fee for "Comment" section items, on acceptance. Query.

COLORADO–Box 4305, Denver, CO 80204.
Illustrated articles, 2,500 to 3,000 words, on the Rocky Mountain West: adventure, current or historical; how-to and service pieces. Pays 10¢ a word, on acceptance.

COLUMBIA–Box 1670, New Haven, CT 06507. Elmer Von Feldt, Editor.
Journal of Knights of Columbus. Illustrated articles, 1,000 to 3,000 words, on science, history, sports, current events, religion, education and art. Humorous pieces, to 1,000 words. Pays $100 to $300, on acceptance.

COLUMBUS DISPATCH SUNDAY MAGAZINE–Columbus, OH 43216. Daniel F. Flavin, Editor.
Articles, to 1,800 words, with local angle. Pays from 3¢ a word, $5 per photo, after publication.

COMMENTARY–165 East 56th St., New York, NY 10022. Norman Podhoretz, Editor.
Articles, 5,000 to 7,000 words, on contemporary issues, Jewish affairs, social sciences, community life, religious thought, cultural activities. Pays around 3½¢ a word, on publication.

COMMON CENTS–172 Madison Ave., New York, NY 10016.
Sunday newspaper supplement on family money management. Short pieces on the home, car care, health, food, retirement, travel, etc. Fillers. Pays varying rates on publication. Query.

COMMONWEAL–232 Madison Ave., New York, NY 10016. James O'Gara, Editor.
Catholic. Articles, to 3,000 words, on political, social, religious and literary subjects. Pays 2¢ a word, on acceptance.

THE CONTINENTAL MAGAZINE—Room 961, World Headquarters, Ford Motor Co., Dearborn, MI 48121. Robert M. Hodesh, Editor-in-Chief.
Sophisticated service articles, 1,300 to 1,500 words, on travel, entertainment, shopping, collecting, cuisine, for an affluent readership. Pays from $350, on acceptance. Query.

COSMOPOLITAN—224 West 57th St., New York, NY 10019. Helen Gurley Brown, Editor; Roberta Ashley, Articles Editor.
Articles, to 5,000 words, and features, 1,000 to 2,500 words, for young career women. Pays around $750 to $1,500 for articles, less for features, on acceptance. Query.

THE COUNTRY GENTLEMAN—1100 Waterway Blvd., Indianapolis, IN 46202. Michael New, Managing Editor.
Articles, 1,000 to 1,500 words, on rural living: recreational sports, hobbies and crafts, environment, gardening, food, camping, animals. Pays varying rates, on publication. Query.

CREDIT UNION LIFE (formerly CU Insight)—P.O. Box 1, Eau Claire, WI 54701. Stephen A. Franzmeier, Editor.
Articles, to 1,500 words, on life styles, personalities, country living, with Upper Midwest locale. Pays $200 to $250.

THE CRISIS—N.A.A.C.P., 1790 Broadway, New York, NY 10019. Warren Marr II, Editor.
Articles, 3,000 words, on the problems and achievements of blacks and other minorities. Pays in copies.

THE DES MOINES SUNDAY REGISTER PICTURE—Des Moines Register and Tribune, 715 Locust St., Des Moines, IA 50304.
Articles, to 1,000 words, with photos, on Iowa and residents. Pays on publication.

DESERT MAGAZINE—Palm Desert, CA 92260. William Knyvett, Editor.
Illustrated articles, 500 to 2,000 words, on the Southwest: history, travel, nature, ghost towns, etc. Pays 2¢ a word, to $35 per photo, on publication.

DETROIT—Detroit Free Press Sunday Magazine, 321 West Lafayette Blvd., Detroit, MI 48231. Rogers Worthington, Editor.
Articles, to 3,000 words, on issues of Detroit area: crime, politics, business, etc. Personality and service pieces; interviews. Pays $100 to $250, after publication.

DISCOVER—Sunday Bulletin, 30th and Market Sts., Philadelphia, PA 19101. Jack Wilson, Editor.
Articles, 300 to 1,500 words, with photos, of interest to Philadelphians. Pays varying rates, on publication.

DIXIE—The Times-Picayune, 3800 Howard Ave., New Orleans, LA 70140. Terence P. Smith, Editor.
Factual articles with Louisiana or Mississippi angle. Anecdotes, 750 to 1,000 words, on the Deep South. Pays from $40 for articles, $20 for anecdotes, on publication. Query.

DOG FANCY—P.O. Box 4030, San Clemente, CA 92672. Mike Criss, Managing Editor.
Articles, from 1,500 words, on dog care, health, grooming, etc. Photos. Pays 3¢ a word, on publication.

DOWN EAST—Camden, ME 04843. Duane Doolittle, Editor.
Articles, 1,500 to 2,500 words, on Maine. Photos. Pays from 3¢ a word, $5 to $25 for photos, on acceptance.

DYNAMIC YEARS (formerly Dynamic Maturity)—215 Long Beach Blvd., Long Beach, CA 90801. Hubert Pryor, Editor.
Articles, 1,000 to 2,500 words, on pre-retirement planning, career changes, sideline

businesses, personal adjustments, financial and legal problems and crafts, for 50- to 64-year-olds. Profiles; humor; photos. Pays $400, extra for photos, on acceptance.

EARLY AMERICAN LIFE—Box 1831, Harrisburg, PA 17105. Robert G. Miner, Editor.
Illustrated articles, 1,000 to 4,000 words, on early American life: arts, crafts, furnishings, architecture. Pays $50 to $300, on acceptance. Query.

EBONY—820 South Michigan Ave., Chicago, IL 60605. Herbert Nipson, Executive Editor.
Articles, with photos, on blacks: achievement, civil rights, etc. Pays from $150, on publication.

ELITE—606 Avenue Rd., Suite 404, Toronto, Ont., Canada M4V 2K9. David S. Wells, Publisher.
Articles, 1,500 to 3,500 words, on sports, politics, money, health, sexual behavior, and topical issues, for 18- to 40-year-old men. Pays $75 to $450, on publication.

THE ELKS MAGAZINE—425 West Diversey Pkwy., Chicago, IL 60614. Jeffrey Ball, Articles Editor.
Articles, 3,000 words, on business, money management, and scientific or technical advances, for rural audience with above-average income. Informative or humorous pieces, to 2,800 words. Pays $150 to $350 for short pieces, from $400 for articles, on acceptance. Query.

EMPIRE MAGAZINE—*The Denver Post,* Denver, CO 80201. Carl Skiff, Editor.
Articles, to 2,000 words, on regional personalities, history, oddities and true adventure. Photos. Pays around 5¢ a word, on acceptance. Query.

ENVIRONMENT—560 Trinity Ave., St. Louis, MO 63130. Julian McCaull, Editor.
Factual articles, 5,000 to 7,000 words, on environmental pollution, effects of technology, etc. Pays $100 to $150. Query.

ESQUIRE—488 Madison Ave., New York, NY 10022. Clay Felker, Editor-in-Chief.
Articles, 1,500 to 5,000 words, for intelligent adult audience. Features, 1,000 words, on dramatic news pieces, or major issues. Pays $350 to $1,000, on acceptance. Query.

ESSENCE—1500 Broadway, New York, NY 10036.
"The magazine for today's black woman." Pays varying rates, after publication. Query.

FAMILY CIRCLE—488 Madison Ave., New York, NY 10022. Babette Ashby, Articles Editor.
Articles on family, marriage, consumer affairs, health, jobs and finances, travel and gardening, for women. Service pieces; human-interest stories. Pays top rates, on acceptance.

FAMILY WEEKLY—641 Lexington Ave., New York, NY 10022. Scott De Garmo, Executive Editor.
Short, lively articles on prominent individuals; family advice. Pays on acceptance. Queries only; no unsolicited manuscripts accepted.

FATE—Clark Publishing Co., 500 Hyacinth Pl., Highland Park, IL 60035. Mary M. Fuller, Editor.
Documented fact articles, to 3,000 words, on strange happenings. First-person accounts, to 300 words, of true psychic or unexplained experiences, for "True Mystic Experiences" and "My Proof of Survival." Pays 3¢ a word for articles, $10 for short pieces, on publication.

FIREHOUSE—33 East 53rd St., New York, NY 10022. Dennis Smith, Editor-in-Chief.
Articles, 500 to 3,000 words, on trends in firefighting equipment and practice, profiles of firefighters, on-the-scene accounts of fires, etc. Pays to 10¢ a word, on publication. Query.

FLING—1485 Bayshore Blvd., San Francisco, CA 94124. Arv Miller, Editor.
Articles, 2,500 to 4,500 words, on crime, sports figures, travel, pornography, new sex activities, health, etc., for men. Profiles, interviews; humor, satire; exposés. Pays $125 to $500, on acceptance.

FLORIDA SPORTSMAN—2701 South Bayshore Dr., Miami, FL 33133. Bill Hallstrom, Executive Editor.
Articles and how-to pieces, 800 to 2,000 words, with photos, on fishing, boating and camping in Florida, the Bahamas and West Indies. Pays from $50, on publication.

THE FLORIDIAN—*St. Petersburg Times,* Box 1121, St. Petersburg, FL 33731. Anne L. Goldman, Editor.
Profiles, lifestyle and travel pieces, with Florida angle preferred. Photos. Pays $100 to $400. Query.

FOCUS/MIDWEST—928A North McKnight, St. Louis, MO 63132. Charles L. Klotzer, Editor.
Articles, 900 to 4,000 words, on controversial political, social and cultural issues, particularly in Chicago, St. Louis and Kansas City. Pays from $25, on publication.

FORD TIMES—Ford Motor Co., 3000 Schaefer Rd., Dearborn, MI 48121. Richard L. Routh, Managing Editor.
Articles, 1,200 to 1,500 words, on motor travel, sports, fashion, vacation ideas, cities and towns, the arts, Americana and nostalgia. Pays from $250, on acceptance. Query.

FOREIGN SERVICE JOURNAL—2101 E St. N.W., Washington, DC 20037. Shirley Newhall, Editor.
Articles on American diplomacy and foreign affairs and subjects of interest to Americans representing U.S. abroad. Pays on publication.

THE FREEMAN—Foundation for Economic Education, Irvington-on-Hudson, NY 10533. Paul L. Poirot, Editor.
Articles, to 3,000 words, on economic, political and moral implications of private property. Pays 5¢ a word, on publication.

FRIENDS—30400 Van Dyke, Warren, MI 48093.
Photo essays on travel, recreation, sports, personalities, etc. Pays $75 to $150 per page, on acceptance. Query.

FRONTIERS—Academy of Natural Sciences, 19th St. and The Parkway, Philadelphia, PA 19103. Vi Dodge, Editor.
Articles, 1,000 to 2,000 words, on natural history and ecology. Photos. Pays $25 to $50 per printed page.

GARDEN—The Garden Society, Botanical Garden, Bronx, NY 10458. Jeffrey Katz, Assistant Editor.
Articles, 500 to 1,000 words, on horticulture, forestry and ecology, etc. Also poetry and fillers. Pays to $300, extra for photos, on publication. Query.

GEM—303 West 42nd St., New York, NY 10036. Will Martin, Editor.
Articles, 500 to 1,500 words, on contemporary issues, preferably sex-oriented. Pays after assignment. Same address and requirements for *The Swinger.*

GENESIS—770 Lexington Ave., New York, NY 10021. J.J. Kelleher, Editor.
Articles, 2,500 to 6,000 words: profiles, exposés, interviews, etc. Photo essays, photos. Pays varying rates, on publication. Query.

GENTLEMEN'S QUARTERLY (GQ)—488 Madison Ave., New York, NY 10022. Roger C. Sharpe, Managing Editor.
Sophisticated features on travel, good living, fitness, grooming, etc., for men. Pays after acceptance. Query; no unsolicited manuscripts accepted.

GLAMOUR—350 Madison Ave., New York, NY 10017. Ruth Whitney, Editor-in-Chief; Phyllis Starr, Managing Editor.
Service articles of interest to young women; features, 2,000 to 3,000 words, on current topics. Pays $300 to $700, on acceptance.

GOOD HOUSEKEEPING—959 Eighth Ave., New York, NY 10019. Jean Block, Articles Editor.
Dramatic personal-experience articles on relationships, individual achievement, practical living, romance, etc. Research reports on news of interest to women, for "Better Way." Pays top rates, on acceptance. Query.

GOURMET—777 Third Ave., New York, NY 10017. Gail Zweigenthal, Managing Editor.
Articles, 2,500 to 3,000 words, on food, travel and good living, for a sophisticated audience. Recipes only in connection with articles. Pays on acceptance.

GRIT—208 West Third St., Williamsport, PA 17701.
Articles, to 2,500 words, with captioned photos, on small towns, people, patriotism, etc. Pays 5¢ a word, extra for photos, on acceptance.

HARPER'S—2 Park Ave., New York, NY 10016. Lewis H. Lapham, Editor.
Articles, 1,500 to 5,000 words, on social, political, economic and cultural affairs. Pays on acceptance. Query.

HARPER'S BAZAAR—717 Fifth Ave., New York, NY 10022. Anthony T. Mazzola, Editor-in-Chief.
Query; no unsolicited manuscripts accepted.

HOLIDAY—See *Travel/Holiday*.

HOW TO, THE HOMEOWNERS' HANDBOOK—380 Madison Ave., New York, NY 10017. Jim Liston, Editor.
Articles, 500 to 600 words, with photos, on do-it-yourself household construction and gardening projects. Pays $100 to $150 per printed page, on acceptance. Query.

HORIZON—American Heritage Publishing Co., 10 Rockefeller Plaza, New York, NY 10020. Otto Fuerbringer, Editor.
Articles reporting on contemporary urban culture, including life in metropolitan areas, intellectual and social trends, urban planning, science, history, and the arts. Length, 3,500 words. Pays on acceptance, at varying rates. Queries are a must.

HUMAN BEHAVIOR—12031 Wilshire Blvd., Los Angeles, CA 90025.
Articles, 1,500 to 4,000 words, with photos, on new developments in social sciences and human behavior research. Pays from $150 to $500, on acceptance. Query.

HUMAN NATURE—757 Third Ave., 23rd Floor, New York, NY 10017. Elizabeth Hall, Editor.
Articles in the human sciences written for the educated layman by researchers describing their work. Fields covered include genetics, health and medicine, psychology, sociology, anthropology, archaeology, economics, and paleontology. Pays from $500 to $1,000 for an article of 4,000 to 5,000 words. Queries are a must.

THE HUMANIST—923 Kensington Ave., Buffalo, NY 14215. Paul Kurtz, Editor.
Articles, 2,000 to 4,000 words, on social, ethical, moral issues. Pays on publication. Query.

HUSTLER—2029 Century Park East, Los Angeles, CA 90067.

Articles, exposés, and interviews, 4,000 words. Pays varying rates, on acceptance. Query first.

I-AM—527 Madison Ave., New York, NY 10022. Ron DePaolo, Executive Editor.
Articles, 1,500 to 3,000 words, to interest Americans of Italian heritage: arts, leisure, politics, food, books, music, nostalgia, etc. Pays varying rates, on acceptance. Query first.

INFANTRY—Box 2005, Fort Benning, GA 31905.
Articles, 2,000 to 5,000 words, on military organizations, equipment, leadership, etc., for U.S. infantry personnel. Pays on publication. Query.

INSIGHT—*Milwaukee Journal,* 333 West State St., Milwaukee, WI 53201. Mike Moore, Editor.
Articles, 1,000 to 3,000 words, on local, humorous human-interest subjects. Pays $75 to $300, on acceptance.

JURIS DOCTOR—730 Third Ave., New York, NY 10017. Zachary Sklar, Editor.
Articles, to 3,500 words, on new developments in the legal profession; profiles on outstanding young lawyers. "Muckraking" pieces, 3,500 words, on conflicts of interest, legal fees, the organized bar. Pays from $400 for investigative articles, from $250 for profiles, on acceptance. Query with outline and sample of published work. Also publishes *Medical Dimensions,* for doctors; *MBA,* for business students; *New Engineer,* for engineers.

KEYNOTER—101 East Erie St., Chicago, IL 60611. John A. Mars, Executive Editor.
Articles, 1,200 to 2,500 words, on social issues, the environment and sports, of interest to high school students. Pays on acceptance.

THE KIWANIS MAGAZINE—101 East Erie St., Chicago, IL 60611. David B. Williams, Executive Editor.
Well-researched articles, 1,500 to 2,500 words, on domestic problems in U.S. and Canada, economics, etc. Pays $200 to $500, on acceptance.

KNIGHT—8060 Melrose Ave., Los Angeles, CA 90046. Jared Rutter, Editor.
Articles, 1,200 to 4,500 words, on sexuality; humor. Pays $80 to $300, on publication. Query on long articles.

LADIES' HOME JOURNAL—641 Lexington Ave., New York, NY 10022. Lenore Hershey, Editor.
Articles on contemporary subjects of interest to women. Personal-experience pieces; articles, 1,000 words, for regional sections, "How America Lives" and "Prime Showcase." Pays top rates, on acceptance. Query.

LADY'S CIRCLE—21 West 26th St., New York, NY 10010. Shirley Howard, Editor.
Articles, 2,000 to 2,500 words, with photos, on child-raising, crafts, diet, marriage, gardening, finances and people who have overcome handicaps. Pays $125, $15 per photo, on publication.

LEATHERNECK—Box 1775, Quantico, VA 22134. Ronald D. Lyons, Editor.
Articles, 1,500 to 3,000 words, with photos, on U.S. Marines. Pays to $300, on acceptance. Query.

LEISURETIME MAGAZINE—Box 11626, Santa Ana, CA 92711. Ann Terrill, Editor.
Articles, 600 to 2,500 words, with photos, on unique travel destinations. Pays varying rates, on publication. Query.

LISTEN MAGAZINE—6830 Laurel St. N.W., Washington, DC 20012. Francis A. Soper, Editor.
Articles, 500 to 1,500 words, on development of mental and physical health for teen-agers: medical reports on drugs and alcohol; personality profiles, etc. Pays 2¢ to 5¢ a word, on acceptance.

THE LOOKOUT–Seamen's Church Institute, 15 State St., New York, NY 10004. Carlyle Windley, Editor.

Factual articles on the sea. Features, 200 to 1,500 words, on the merchant marine, sea oddities, etc. Photos. Pays $15 to $45, on publication.

MBA–See *Juris Doctor.*

McCALL'S–230 Park Ave., New York, NY 10017. Helen Markel, Articles Editor.

Timely features and articles, 2,500 to 3,500 words, of interest to suburban women. All service articles staff-written. Pays top rates, on acceptance. Querv.

MACLEAN'S NEWS MAGAZINE–481 University Ave., Toronto, Ont. Canada. M5W 1A7.

Articles, 2,000 to 3,000 words, on entertainment, sports, politics, business, etc., in Canada. Query with outline.

MADEMOISELLE–350 Madison Ave., New York, NY 10017. Mary Cantwell, Managing Editor.

Articles, 1,000 to 2,500 words, on controversial subjects of interest to literate young women. Pays on acceptance. Query.

MAGAZINE OF THE MIDLANDS–*Omaha World Herald,* World-Herald Square, Omaha, NE 68102. Hollis Limprecht, Editor.

Articles, 300 to 2,300 words, on regional-interest subjects. Humor; photos. Pays $25 to $75, on publication.

MAN TO MAN–See *Mr. Magazine.*

MANKIND–8060 Melrose Ave., Los Angeles, CA 90046.

Articles, 2,000 to 4,000 words, on historical events. Pays to $200, on publication. Query with outline.

MARRIAGE & FAMILY LIVING–St. Meinrad, IN 47577.

Articles, to 2,500 words, on husband-wife and parent-child relationships. Pays 5¢ a word, on acceptance. Query.

MEDICAL DIMENSIONS–See *Juris Doctor.*

MIDNIGHT–c/o Selig Adler, Editor, 200 Railroad Ave., Greenwich, CT 06830. Canadian Magazine.

Factual articles, 500 to 1,000 words, with photos: exposés; interviews with celebrities; consumer pieces. Pays from $150, on acceptance.

MIDSTREAM: A MONTHLY JEWISH REVIEW–515 Park Ave., New York, NY 10022. Joel Carmichael, Editor.

Articles; book reviews. Pays 7¢ a word, on acceptance.

MIDWEST MAGAZINE–See *ChicagoStyle.*

MILITARY LIFE/MALE CALL–c/o Taylor & Ives, 30 East 42nd St., New York, NY 10017. Will Lieberson, Editor.

Articles, 700 to 1,000 words, with military angle, on sports and adventure. Pays $75, on acceptance. Query.

MINNESOTA AAA MOTORIST–7 Travelers Trail, Burnsville, MN 55337. Ronald D. Johnson, Editor.

Articles, 800 to 1,000 words, on travel, motoring, car care, etc. Photos. Pays from $150, $15 to $75 for photos, on acceptance.

MODERN MATURITY–215 Long Beach Blvd., Long Beach, CA 90802. Hubert Pryor, Editor.

Service articles on living, food, health, employment and activities, for persons over 55 years. Nostalgia, inspirational articles, personality pieces, Americana, to 2,000 words. Pays $50 to $600, extra for photos, on acceptance.

MODERN PEOPLE–11058 West Addison St., Franklin Park, IL 60131.
Articles, 500 to 700 words, on people in television, movies, sports, politics, etc. Photos. Pays $40 to $125, on acceptance.

MOMENT–55 Chapel St., Newton, MA 02160. William Novak, Executive Editor.
Sophisticated articles, 2,000 to 4,000 words, on Jewish political, social and religious issues. Pays $200 to $400, on publication. Query.

MONEY–Time & Life Bldg., Rockefeller Center, New York, NY 10020.
No free-lance material.

MONTANA: THE MAGAZINE OF WESTERN HISTORY–Montana Historical Society, 225 North Roberts, Helena, MT 59601. Vivian A. Paladin, Editor.
Documented articles, 3,500 to 6,500 words, on history of the West. Photos, drawings. Pays 1½¢ a word, on acceptance. Query.

MOTHER JONES–607 Market St., San Francisco, CA 94105.
Alternative news magazine. No free-lance material.

THE MOTHER EARTH NEWS–P.O. Box 70, Hendersonville, NC 28739.
Articles of any length dealing with ecology and back-to-the-land movement; down-home cooking, alternative energy systems, homesteading, etc. Pays $20 to $500, on acceptance. Queries recommended.

MR. MAGAZINE–280 Madison Ave., New York, NY 10016. Everett Meyers, Editor.
Articles, 2,000 to 3,500 words, on travel, music, sex, art, unusual entertainment and other subjects of interest to men. Photos. Pays from $125 for articles, extra for photos, on publication. Same address and requirements for *Man to Man* and *Sir!*

MS.–370 Lexington Ave., New York, NY 10017. Address Manuscript Editor.
Reports, interviews, and personal-experience pieces, to 3,000 words, on women's changing self-image and status. Pays on acceptance. Query.

NASHVILLE GOSPEL–521 Fifth Ave., New York, NY 10017. Jesse Gifford, Managing Editor.
Articles, 2,000 words, on country music stars and topics of interest to women, for family audience. Pays 10¢ a word, on acceptance. Query.

THE NATION–333 Sixth Ave., New York, NY 10014. Blair Clark, Editor.
Articles, 2,000 to 2,500 words, on current issues. Pays 2¢ a word, on publication. Query.

NATIONAL ENQUIRER–Lantana, FL 33644.
Articles, any length, for mass audience: topical news, the occult, how-to, scientific discoveries, human drama, adventure, personalities. Photos. Pays from $300. Query; no unsolicited manuscripts accepted.

NATIONAL GEOGRAPHIC–17th and M Sts. N.W., Washington, DC 20036. Gilbert M. Grosvenor, Editor.
First-person articles, 2,000 to 4,000 (8,000 words maximum), on travel, exploration, mountaineering, seafaring, archaeological discoveries, natural history, festivals and folkways. Pays $1,500 to $4,000, extra for photos, on acceptance. Query.

THE NATIONAL GUARDSMAN–One Massachusetts Ave. N.W., Washington, DC 20001. Luther Walker, Editor.
Articles, 2,000 to 4,000 words, with photos, on Army and Air National Guard and their role in national and international defense. Short, humorous military anecdotes for "Tales from the Troops." Pays $50 per printed page, 3¢ a word for anecdotes.

THE NATIONAL HUMANE REVIEW—See *American Humane Magazine.*

NATURAL HISTORY MAGAZINE—Central Park West at 79th St., New York, NY 10024. Alan Ternes, Editor.
Articles, to 3,500 words, by experts, on anthropology and natural sciences. Photos. Pays $600, on acceptance. Query.

NEW ENGINEER—See *Juris Doctor.*

NEW ENGLAND MAGAZINE—*Boston Globe*, Boston, MA 02107. Anthony C. Spinazzola, Editor.
General-interest articles, 1,000 to 5,000 words, on New England. Photo essays. Pays $100 to $300, $150 for photo essays, on publication. Query.

NEW HAMPSHIRE PROFILES—2 Steam Mill Court, Concord, NH 03301. Sharon L. Smith, Editor.
Articles, 1,500 to 3,000 words, on current events and activities, personalities, history, antiques, nostalgia, conservation, country living, recreation, cooking and crafts, related to New Hampshire; how-to pieces. Photos. Pays varying rates, on publication.

NEW REALITIES (formerly *Psychic*)—680 Beach St., San Francisco, CA 94109. James Bolen, Editor.
Factual articles, pro and con, on psychic phenomena, parapsychology, etc. Pays to $150, on acceptance. Query.

THE NEW REPUBLIC—1220 19th St., N.W., Washington DC 20036. Martin Peretz, Editor.
Articles, to 1,500 words, on social, economic, political and cultural issues. Pays 8¢ a word.

NEW TIMES—One Park Ave., New York, NY 10016. Jonathan Z. Larsen, Editor.
Articles, 1,500 to 4,000 words, on current controversial subjects. Pays from $250, on acceptance. Query.

NEW WEST—9665 Wilshire Blvd., Beverly Hills, CA 90212.
Regional articles. Query.

NEW YORK—775 Second Ave., New York, NY 10017. John Berendt, Editor.
Feature articles on New York subjects. Query; no unsolicited manuscripts accepted.

THE NEW YORK TIMES MAGAZINE—229 West 43rd St., New York, NY 10036. Edward Klein, Editor.
Timely articles, around 4,500 words, on news items, forthcoming events, trends, anniversaries, etc. Features, 1,000 to 2,000 words. Pays $850, $500 for short pieces, on acceptance.

THE NEW YORKER—25 West 43rd St., New York, NY 10036. Address The Editors.
Factual, historical and biographical articles, for "Profiles," "Reporter at Large," "That Was New York," "Annals of Crime," "Onward and Upward with the Arts," etc. Pays good rates, on acceptance. Query.

NORTHWEST—*Sunday Oregonian*, 1320 S.W. Broadway, Portland, OR 97201. J.R. Bianco, Editor.
Articles, 800 words, on outdoor activities in Pacific Northwest. Photos. Pays $40, $15 per photo, after publication.

NOW—8060 Melrose Ave., Los Angeles, CA 90046. Dick Robb, Editor.
Human-interest articles, to 1,000 words, profiling well-known black Americans. Pays $200, on publication. Query.

OCEANS—240 Fort Mason, San Francisco, CA 94123. Keith K. Howell, Editor.
Articles, to 5,000 words, with photos, on marine life, oceanography, undersea ex-

ploration, seaports, conservation, etc. Some features on travel, fishing, diving and boating. Pays $60 per printed page, on publication. Query.

OPTIMIST MAGAZINE—4494 Lindell Blvd., St. Louis, MO 63108. Gary Adamson, Editor.
Articles on Optimist Club projects. Photos; cartoons. Pays varying rates, on publication. Query.

OUI—8560 Sunset Blvd., Los Angeles, CA 90069. Richard Cramer, Editor.
Articles, 2,500 to 3,000 words, on entertainment, politics, trends, etc., for 18- to 34-year-old-men. Pays $1,200, on acceptance. Query.

PAGEANT—1010 St. Catherine St., West, Suite 304, Montreal, Que., Canada H3G 1Z2. Blanche Hodder, Editor.
Articles on current social trends, medicine, etc. Self-help; humor; how-to. Pays from $100, before publication. Query.

PARADE—733 Third Ave., New York, NY 10017. Address Articles Editor.
Articles, to 2,500 words, on important general-interest news items. Short pieces of interest to families. Pays good rates, on acceptance. Query.

PARADE REST—Taylor & Ives, Inc., 30 East 42nd St., New York, NY 10017. Will Lieberson, Editor.
General-interest articles, 750 to 1,000 words, on leisure-time activities: outdoor recreation, hi-fi, cars, sports, movies, photography. Pays $100 to $150, on publication. Query.

PARENTS' MAGAZINE—52 Vanderbilt Ave., New York, NY 10017. Genevieve Millet Landau, Editor-in-Chief.
Articles, 2,000 words, on physical, emotional and mental development of infants, school children and adolescents, family, adults in the community, etc. Lively articles on research in medicine, science, education, etc. Prefers colloquial style with quotes from experts. Pays on acceptance.

PENTHOUSE—909 Third Ave., New York, NY 10022. Art Cooper, Executive Editor; Heidi Handman, Managing Editor.
General-interest or controversial articles, to 6,000 words; sexy nonfiction and humor, to 5,000 words. Pays from 20¢ a word, on acceptance.

PENTHOUSE FORUM—909 Third Ave., New York, NY 10022. Barbara Schrank, Executive Editor.
Articles, 1,500 to 2,500 words, on contemporary emotional, psychological, medical and sexual conflicts, problems, innovations, etc. Pays $200 to $400, on acceptance.

PEOPLE ON PARADE—Meridian Publishing Co., 1720 Washington Blvd., Ogden, UT 84404. Melissa Arlene Hamblin, Managing Editor.
Articles, 900 to 1,200 words, on people who overcame adversity; humorous features about individuals who enjoy life; shorter pieces, 200 to 500 words. Pays 10¢ a word, extra for photos, on acceptance.

PETROLEUM TODAY—2101 L St. N.W., Washington, DC 20037. Patricia Maloney Merkon, Executive Editor.
Articles, 500 or 1,000 to 2,000 words, on oil industry issues: energy crisis, Alaska pipeline, environment, deep-water ports, off-shore leasing, etc. Pays from $200, on publication. Query.

PICTORIAL LIVING MAGAZINE—See *Beacon Magazine.*

PLANNING MAGAZINE—1313 East 60th St., Chicago, IL 60637. Robert Cassidy, Editor.
Journal of the American Society of Planning Officials (city planners). News and

feature articles, 500 to 2,000 words, on urban affairs, environment, transportation, etc. Related book reviews. Pays varying rates, on acceptance. Query.

PLAYBOY—919 North Michigan Ave., Chicago, IL 60611. Laurence Gonzales, Peter Ross Range, Senior Editors.
Sophisticated articles, 4,000 to 8,000 words, of interest to urban men. Humor; satire. Pays to $3,000, on acceptance. Query.

PLAYGIRL—1801 Century Park East, Century City Suite 2300, Los Angeles, CA 90067. Joyce Dudney Fleming, Editor.
Articles of interest to contemporary women. Humor; satire. Pays $250 per 1,000 words, after acceptance. Query.

PRESENT TENSE—165 East 56th St., New York, NY 10022. Murray Polner, Editor.
Serious reportage, 3,000 to 5,000 words, with photos, on international developments concerning Jews; memoirs; profiles of Jewish life abroad. Pays $100 to $250, on acceptance. Query.

THE PROGRESSIVE—408 West Gorham St., Madison, WI 53703. Erwin Knoll, Editor.
Articles, 1,000 to 3,500 words, on political, social, economic and international problems. Light features; profiles. Pays $75 to $150, on publication.

PSYCHIC—See *New Realities.*

PSYCHOLOGY TODAY—One Park Ave., New York, NY 10016. Mary Marcus, Manuscripts Editor.
Well-researched articles on current trends in psychology and behavior. Query.

QUEST/78—1133 Ave. of the Americas, New York, NY 10036. Molly McKaughan, Managing Editor.
Articles, to 5,000 words, on "pursuit of excellence." Pays on acceptance, 50¢ a word for commissioned articles, $600 minimum for shorts under 1,200 words. Query.

READER'S DIGEST—Pleasantville, NY 10570. Edward T. Thompson, Editor-in Chief.
Outstanding personal-experience articles, 2,500 to 3,000 words, for "First Person" and "Drama in Real Life," and general interest pieces. Accounts of true psychic and supernatural experiences, to 2,500 words. Pays a minimum of $2,400, to $3,000, on acceptance. Query with outline.

REAL WEST—Charlton Bldg., Derby, CT 06418.
Articles, 1,000 to 3,000 words, on pioneering experience in the West. Photos. Pays 2¢ a word, on acceptance.

REDBOOK—230 Park Ave., New York, NY 10017. Sey Chassler, Editor-in-Chief; Sylvia Koner, Articles Editor.
Articles, 1,500 to 3,500 words, on social and political issues; subjects related to work, marriage and the family. Pays good rates, on acceptance. Query with outline.

THE RETIRED OFFICER—1625 Eye St., N.W., Washington, DC 20006. Minter L. Wilson, Jr., Editor.
Articles, 1,000 to 2,500 words, of interest to military retirees. Humor; pieces on second-career opportunities. Pays $25 to $250, on publication. Query.

RETIREMENT LIVING—150 East 58th St., New York, NY 10022. Roy Hemming, Editor.
Articles, 500 to 1,500 words, with photos, on planning or beginning retirement: health, housing, money management, travel, hobbies, personalities. Case-history and how-to pieces; no nostalgia. Pays $50 to $125, extra for photos. Query.

THE RHODE ISLANDER—*Providence Sunday Journal*, 75 Fountain St., Providence, RI 02902. Douglas Riggs, Editor.

Articles, to 1,500 words, on Rhode Island and subjects of interest to residents of southern New England. Pays $50 to $200, on publication.

ROLL CALL: THE NEWSPAPER OF CAPITOL HILL–428 Eighth St. S.E., Washington, DC 20003.
Factual, breezy articles with political or Congressional angle: history, human-interest subjects, political lore, etc. Political satire and humor. Pays modest rates, on publication.

ROLLING STONE–745 Fifth Ave., New York, NY 10022. Jann Wenner, Editor.
Query; no unsolicited manuscripts accepted.

ROSICRUCIAN DIGEST–Rosicrucian Park, San Jose, CA 95191. Robin M. Thompson, Editor.
Articles, to 2,500 words, on mysticism, the arts, personal experiences, scientific achievements. Pays 4¢ a word, on acceptance.

THE ROTARIAN–1600 Ridge Ave., Evanston, IL 60201. Willmon L. White, Editor.
Articles, 1,200 to 2,000 words, on social and economic problems, business ethics, community and family, travel, etc., of interest to business and professional men. Pays good rates, on acceptance. Query.

SAGA–333 Johnson Ave., Brooklyn, NY 11206. David J. Elrich, Editor.
Articles, 4,000 to 5,000 words, for men: adventure, humor, travel, hunting, sports, war. Interviews, profiles. Photo essays on action sports, dangerous pastimes. Pays from $250, on acceptance.

THE SATURDAY EVENING POST–1100 Waterway Blvd., Indianapolis, IN 46202. Starkey Flythe, Jr., Managing Editor.
Articles, 2,500 to 3,500 words, on education, the arts, science, politics, etc. Photo essays. Pays varying rates, on publication. Query with outline.

SATURDAY NIGHT–69 Front St. East, Toronto, Ont., Canada M5E 1R3. Robert Fulford, Editor.
Articles, to 3,000 words, on current affairs, economics, literature, etc., of interest to Canadians. Pays to $700, on publication.

SATURDAY REVIEW–1290 Ave. of the Americas, New York, NY 10019. Norman Cousins, Editor.
Articles, 1,000 to 3,000 words, on cultural affairs. Pays $500 to $750, less for short pieces, on publication. Query with outline.

SCANDINAVIAN REVIEW–127 East 73rd St., New York, NY 10021. Howard E. Sandum, Editor.
Articles, 2,000 to 3,000 words, about Scandinavia and Scandinavians in America. Photos. Pays around $100, on publication.

SCENE–*The Dallas Morning News*, Communications Center, Dallas, TX 75222. Betty Cook, Editor.
Well-researched articles, 1,000 to 3,000 words, with photos, preferably with Texas angle. Pays 5¢ to 10¢ a word, on acceptance. Query.

SEATTLE TIMES SUNDAY MAGAZINE–Box 70, Seattle, WA 98111. Larry Anderson, Editor.
Articles, 800 to 1,500 words, of interest to residents of Pacific Northwest. Pays from $40 per printed page, after publication.

SEXOLOGY–200 Park Ave. South, New York, NY 10003.
Nonfiction, to 2,000 words, on sex, interpersonal relationships. Pays from $175 to $300, on acceptance. Queries preferred.

SHOW-BOOK WEEK–*Chicago Sun Times,* 401 North Wabash Ave., Chicago, IL 60611. Jean Adelsman, Editor.
Articles, profiles and interviews, to 1,500 words, relating to fine arts or lively arts. Pays to 10¢ a word, on publication. Query.

SIGNATURE–260 Madison Ave., New York, NY 10016. Robin Nelson, Managing Editor; Josh Eppinger, Executive Editor.
Magazine of the Diners Club. Articles on travel, sports, business, entertainment, personalities and social issues, for well-traveled business executives. Pays $400 to $750, on acceptance. Query.

SIR!–See *Mr. Magazine.*

SKEPTIC–812 Presidio Ave., Santa Barbara, CA 93101. Christiane Schlumberger, Editor.
Current events, controversial points of view. Query.

SMALL WORLD–Volkswagen of America, 818 Sylvan Ave., Englewood Cliffs, NJ 07632. Burton Unger, Editor.
Articles, 600 to 1,500 words, for Volkswagen owners: personality profiles of well-known Volkswagen owners; inspirational or human-interest pieces with Volkswagen angle; travel, humor. Pays $100 per printed page, on acceptance. Query.

SMITHSONIAN MAGAZINE–Arts and Industries Bldg., 900 Jefferson Dr., Washington, DC 20560. Edward K. Thompson, Editor.
Articles on wildlife, the environment, art, science, cultural history. Pays good rates, on acceptance. Query.

THE SOUTH–P.O. Box 2350, Tampa, FL 33601. Roy B. Bain, Editor.
News features, to 1,800 words, on business, economic, and political trends and issues, explaining cause and effect, of interest to leaders in southern states. Pays to $300, on acceptance. Query.

THE SOUTHERN ISRAELITE–P.O. Box 77388, Atlanta, GA 30357. Jack Geldbart, Editor and Publisher.
Weekly newspaper; articles. Pays modest rates or in copies.

SPORT MAGAZINE–641 Lexington Ave., New York, NY 10022. Berry Stainback, Editor.
Articles, 2,500 to 3,500 words, on current controversies and personalities in major spectator sports. Features on college athletes. Pays $350 to $750. Query.

SPORTS ILLUSTRATED–Rockefeller Center, New York, NY 10020. Robert W. Creamer, Articles Editor.
Articles, 2,000 to 5,000 words, on major sports personalities, issues and events. Offbeat news features, 1,000 to 2,000 words; humor; nostalgia. Pays $250 for short features, from $750 for articles, on acceptance. Most articles are staff-written.

STAG–See *Swank.*

THE STAR–730 Third Ave., New York, NY 10017.
Topical articles, 300 to 2,000 words, on human-interest subjects, social and moral issues, life styles, the sciences, sports, etc., for family audience. Pays varying rates.

STAR MAGAZINE–*The Indianapolis Star,* 307 North Pennsylvania St., Indianapolis, IN 46206. Fred D. Cavinder, Editor.
Articles with Indiana angle. Photos. Pays from $35, on publication. Query.

SUCCESS UNLIMITED–6355 Broadway, Chicago, IL 60660. Diana Maxwell, Executive Editor.

Inspirational and self-help articles, to 2,000 words, with photos, on success. Personality pieces on well-known people who succeed through perseverance and hard work. Pays 10¢ a word, on acceptance. Query.

SUNDAY NEW YORK NEWS MAGAZINE—*Sunday News,* 220 East 42nd St., New York, NY 10017. Richard C. Lemon, Editor.
Articles, 1,000 to 3,000 words, on New York area subjects (preferably people). Pays $150 to $750, on acceptance.

SWANK—888 Seventh Ave., New York, NY 10019. Richard Milner, Managing Editor.
Articles, 2,500 to 3,500 words, on politics, social trends, personalities, sex and behavior; how-to pieces. Pays from $300, on publication. Query with outline. Same address and requirements for *Stag.*

THE SWINGER—See *Gem.*

TEXAS MONTHLY—P.O. Box 1569, Austin, TX 78767. Judy Benson, Assistant Managing Editor.
Articles, 2,000 to 8,000 words, on Texas, its residents and related subjects. Pays varying rates, on acceptance.

THE TIMES MAGAZINE—Army Times Publishing Co., 475 School St. S.W., Washington, DC 20024. Jim Scott, Managing Editor.
Articles, 1,500 words, on military life. Photos. Pays $50 to $250, on publication.

TODAY MAGAZINE—*Philadelphia Inquirer,* Broad and Callowhill Sts., Philadelphia, PA 19101. David Boldt, Editor.
Local interest features, 500 to 2,000 words, and "how to cope" articles on contemporary problems. Pays varying rates, on publication. Query.

TODAY'S ANIMAL HEALTH (formerly *Animal Cavalcade*)—8338 Rosemead Blvd., Pico Rivera, CA 90660. Richard S. Glassberg, Editor.
Articles, 1,500 words, with photos, on animal health and responsible pet ownership. Pays to $10, extra for photos, on publication.

TODAY'S SECRETARY—1221 Ave. of the Americas, New York, NY 10020. Lauren S. Bahr, Editor.
Features, 1,000 to 1,500 words, with photos, on young secretaries. Articles, 500 to 800 words, on self-improvement, career tips, office techniques and trends, etc. Pays $75 to $150, on acceptance. Query.

TOLEDO (formerly *Blade Sunday Magazine*)—Toledo *Blade,* Toledo, OH 43660. Tom Gearhart, Editor.
Articles, to 4,000 words, on Toledo area personalities, news, etc. Photos. Pays $35 to $125, on publication. Query.

TOWN & COUNTRY—717 Fifth Ave., New York, NY 10022. Frank Zachary, Editor.
Articles on medicine, finance, personalities, social customs, etc., for an affluent readership. Humor; satire. Pays from $400, on acceptance. Query with outline.

TRAVEL & LEISURE—1350 Ave. of the Americas, New York, NY 10019. Pamela Fiori, Editor-in-Chief.
Articles, 1,000 to 2,500 words, on travel and leisure-time activities. Regional pieces for regional editions. Pays $500 to $1,500. Query.

TRAVEL HOLIDAY—Travel Bldg., Floral Park, NY 11001.
Articles, 1,500 to 2,000 words, with photos, about foreign and domestic travel destinations; shorter "featurettes," 1,000 words. Pays $100 to $225.

THE TRIBUNE MAGAZINE—*Chicago Tribune,* 435 North Michigan Ave., Chicago, IL 60611. Robert Goldsborough, Editor.
Articles, 2,000 to 3,000 words, of interest to Chicago area residents. Pays from $200, on acceptance. Query.

TROPIC—*The Miami Herald*, One Herald Plaza, Miami, FL 33101. Stephan L. Petranek, Editor.
General-interest articles, 1,000 to 4,000 words, for sophisticated audience; personality profiles. Pays to $300. Query.

TV GUIDE—Radnor, PA 19088. Andrew Mills, Assistant Managing Editor.
Articles on television subjects. Pays on acceptance. Query.

TWA AMBASSADOR—1999 Shepard Rd., St. Paul, MN 55116. James Morgan, Editor.
Articles, 1,000 to 2,500 words, on travel, humor, sports, business, personalities and modern living. Photos. Pays $100 to $600, on acceptance. Query.

UNDERSTANDING—Star Route Box 588F, Tonopah, AZ 85354. Daniel W. Fry, Editor.
Articles, to 800 words, on ESP, UFOs and related phenomena. Pays 1¢ a word, on publication.

US MAGAZINE—488 Madison Ave., New York, NY 10022. Bill Davis, Editor and Publisher.
Features on human interest and self-improvement topics, on government, literature, arts, movies, sports, science, etc. Query first.

VFW MAGAZINE—Broadway at 34th, Kansas City, MO 64111.
Journal of Veterans of Foreign Wars. Articles, 1,000 words, on current issues, solutions to everyday problems, personalities, sports, etc. How-to and historical pieces. Pays 5¢ to 10¢ a word, extra for photos, on acceptance.

VILLAGE VOICE—80 University Pl., New York, NY 10003.
Articles, 500 to 3,000 words, on current or controversial topics. Pays $50 to $200, on publication.

VIVA—909 Third Ave., New York, NY 10022. Ernest Baxter, Executive Editor.
Articles, 2,500 to 5,000 words, on problems of modern women: social, sexual, economic, emotional, etc. Humor; personal-experience pieces. Pays $250 to $1,000, after acceptance. Query.

VOGUE—350 Madison Ave., New York, NY 10017. Leo Lerman, Consulting Features Editor.
Articles, to 1,500 words, on women, the arts, travel, medicine and health. Limited free-lance market. Pays good rates, on acceptance. Query.

THE WASHINGTON MONTHLY—1028 Connecticut Ave. N.W., Washington, DC 20036. Charles Peters, Editor.
In-depth articles, 1,500 to 5,000 words, on government. Pays 5¢ to 10¢ a word, on publication. Query.

THE WASHINGTONIAN—1828 L St. N.W., Washington, DC 20036. John Limpert, Editor.
Articles, 1,000 to 4,000 words, on Washington-related subjects, for sophisticated audience. Pays 7¢ to 10¢ a word, on publication. Query.

WEEKDAY—20 North Wacker Dr., Chicago, IL 60606.
Articles, to 1,000 words, on community affairs. Pays to $40, on acceptance.

WEIGHT WATCHERS MAGAZINE—149 Fifth Ave., New York, NY 10010. Bernadette Carr, Editor.
Articles, 500 to 2,750 words, on weight loss; no "how to get thin" or dieting pieces. Pays from $300, on acceptance. Query.

WESTWAYS—Box 2890, Terminal Annex, Los Angeles, CA 90051. Frances Ring, Editor.

Articles, 1,000 to 3,000 words, and photo essays, on western U.S., Canadian and Mexican activities, natural science, travel, personalities, western history, etc. Pays from 10¢ a word, extra for photos, on acceptance. Query.

WOMAN'S DAY–1515 Broadway, New York, NY 10036. Geraldine Rhoads, Editor. Address Rebecca Greer, Articles Editor.
Serious or humorous articles, 1,500 to 3,500 words, on marriage, child care, family health, money management, vacations, education, leisure activities, etc. Pays top rates, on acceptance.

WOMEN'S WORK–Suite 203, 1302 18th St. N.W., Washington, DC 20036. Frances Knight Palmeri, Editor.
Articles, 1,000 to 3,000 words, on how to find a job, choose a career, etc. Pays varying rates, on publication. Query.

WOODMEN OF THE WORLD MAGAZINE–1700 Farnam St., Omaha, NE 68102. Leland A. Larson, Editor.
Articles on history, travel, do-it-yourself projects, science etc. Pays 2¢ a word, from $10 per photo, on acceptance.

WORKING WOMAN–110 East 59th St., New York, NY 10022. Bette-Jane Raphael, Articles Editor.
Articles on business and personal sides of working women's lives. Humor; articles for regular feature, "Day in the Life of." Pays from $200, on acceptance. Query with published writing samples.

YANKEE–Dublin, NH 03444. Judson D. Hale, Editor.
Articles to 3,000 words, with New England angle. Photos. Pays $50 to $500 ($300 to $400 average), on acceptance.

YANKEE MAGAZINE'S GUIDE TO NEW ENGLAND–581 Boylston St., Boston, MA 02116. Georgia Orcutt, Editor.
Articles, 500 to 2,000 words, with photos, on family activities and recreation in New England. Features, 2 pages. Pays $50 to $200, on publication.

YOUR PLACE–230 Park Ave., New York, NY 10017. Dick Friedman, Articles Editor.
Articles of interest to young people in their twenties: careers, relationships, health, home furnishings, crafts, travel, etc. Pays varying rates, on acceptance. Query.

COLLEGE, LITERARY AND LITTLE MAGAZINES

AMERICAN QUARTERLY–Van Pelt Library, 3420 Walnut St., University of Pennsylvania, Phildelphia, PA 19174. Bruce Kuklick, Editor.
Scholarly essays, 5,000 to 10,000 words, on any aspect of U.S. culture. No payment.

THE AMERICAN SCHOLAR–1811 Q St. N.W., Washington, DC 20009. Joseph Epstein, Editor.
Articles, 3,500 to 4,000 words, on science, politics, literature, the arts, etc. Book reviews. Pays $250, $50 for reviews, on publication.

ANTIOCH REVIEW–Yellow Springs, OH 45387. Paul Bixler, Editor.

Timely articles, 2,000 to 8,000 words, on social sciences, politics, economics, literature and humanities. Pays $8 per printed page, on publication.

ARARAT—628 Second Ave., New York, NY 10016. Leo Hamalian, Editor.
Publication of Armenian General Benevolent Union of America. Articles, 1,000 to 5,000 words, on the Armenian experience in America. Pays $30 to $60, on publication.

ARIZONA QUARTERLY—University of Arizona, Tucson, AZ 85721. Albert F. Gegenheimer, Editor.
Literary essays; regional material; general-interest articles. Pays in copies; annual awards.

ASPECT—66 Rogers Ave., Somerville, MA 02144. Edward J. Hogan, Editor.
Essays, 100 to 1,600 words, on literature, politics, history, etc. Pays in copies.

BACHY—Papa Bach Bookstore, 11317 Santa Monica Blvd., West Los Angeles, CA 90025.
Essays and reviews on literary and cultural topics. Pays in copies; cash awards.

BALL STATE UNIVERSITY FORUM—Ball State University, Muncie, IN 47306. Merrill Rippy and Frances Mayhew Rippy, Editors.
General-interest articles, 500 to 4,000 words. Pays in copies.

THE BERKELEY BARB—P.O. Box 1247, Berkeley, CA 94701. Ray Riegert, Editor.
Hard-news stories, investigative reporting, news analysis and cultural feature articles, 500 to 2,000 words, for Bay area readers. Pays 3¢ a word.

THE BLACK COLLEGIAN—3217 Melpomene Ave., New Orleans, LA 71025. Kalamu ya Salaam, Editor.
Articles, to 2,000 words, on conditions or experiences of black students. Pays on publication. Query.

THE BLACK SCHOLAR—Box 908, 2656 Bridgeway, Sausalito, CA 94965. Robert L. Allen, Editor.
Essays, 2,000 to 5,000 words, on the black movement and community; book reviews. Pays in copies plus subscription. Query.

BOOK FORUM—38 East 76th St., New York, NY 10021.
Essays, 800 to 2,000 words, on books about literature, sociology and behavioral studies; book reviews. Pays in copies.

BOOKS ABROAD—See *World Literature Today*.

BOSTON UNIVERSITY JOURNAL—775 Commonwealth Ave., Boston, MA 02115.
Articles on any subject; literary criticism. Pays $10 per printed page, on publication.

BUCKNELL REVIEW—Bucknell University, Lewisburg, PA 17837. Harry R. Garvin, Editor.
Scholarly articles on sciences, arts and letters. Pays in offprints.

THE CANADIAN FORUM—3 Church St., Suite 401, Toronto, Ont., Canada M5E 1M2. Denis Smith, Editor.
Articles, 1,500 to 2,000 words, with Canadian angle, on current events, politics, art, etc. Pays $50.

THE CENTENNIAL REVIEW—110 Morrill Hall, Michigan State University, East Lansing, MI 48824. David Mead, Editor.
Articles, 2,000 to 3,000 words, on sciences and humanities. Pays by subscription.

THE CHICAGO REVIEW—University of Chicago, Chicago, IL 60637. Mary Ellis Gibson, David Shields, Editors.
Essays; interviews; book reviews. Pays in copies plus subscription.

CIMARRON REVIEW—Oklahoma State University, Stillwater, OK 74074. Jeanne Adams Wray, Managing Editor.
Articles, 1,500 to 3,500 words, on history, philosophy, political science, etc. Pays in copies.

COLORADO QUARTERLY—Hellems 134, University of Colorado, Boulder, CO 80309. Walter Simon, Editor.
Articles, 4,000 to 6,000 words, by specialists in humanities, sciences, economics, politics, etc., for a general readership. Pays $50, on acceptance.

CONFRONTATION—Dept. of English, Long Island University, Brooklyn, NY 11201. Martin Tucker, Editor.
Serious literary essays, to 2,500 words. Pays on publication. Query.

CRITICAL INQUIRY—University of Chicago, Wieboldt Hall 123, 1050 East 59th St., Chicago, IL 60637. Sheldon Sacks, Editor.

DASEIN—G.P.O. Box 2121, New York, NY 10001. Percy Johnston, Editor.
Scholarly articles on film, aesthetics, social philosophy. Query.

THE DEKALB LITERARY ARTS JOURNAL—c/o W. S. Newman, Editor, DeKalb College, 555 Indian Creek Dr., Clarkston, GA 33021.
Essays, reviews, critiques on the humanities, particularly literature. Pays in copies.

DESCANT—Texas Christian University, T.C.U. Sta., Fort Worth, TX 76129. Betsy Colquitt, Editor.
Critical articles, to 3,000 words, on modern literature and philosophy. Pays in copies.

EVENT—Douglas College, Box 2503, New Westminister, B.C., Canada. John S. Levin, Editor.
Reviews and essays, to 3,500 words. Pays modest rates, after publication.

FORUM—University of Houston, Houston, TX 77004.
Scholarly articles on arts, letters and science. Overstocked until September 1978.

FOUR QUARTERS—La Salle College, Philadelphia, PA 19141. John Keenan, Editor.
Critical articles, 1,500 to 6,000 words, on writers and literary works; "think pieces" on history, politics, the arts. Pays to $25, on publication. No submissions in July or August.

THE FREE LANCE—6005 Grand Ave., Cleveland, OH 44104. Casper L. Jordan and R. Atkins, Editors.
Short critical essays, experimental or avant-garde. Pays in copies. Query.

FRONT STREET TROLLEY—2125 Acklen Ave., Nashville, TN 37215. Molly McIntosh, Editor.
Articles on southern literature. Pays in copies.

THE GEORGIA REVIEW—University of Georgia, Athens, GA 30602.
Articles on the humanities. Pays on publication.

HUDSON REVIEW—65 East 55th St., New York, NY 10022. Frederick Morgan and Paula Deitz, Editors.
Essays on literature, the arts, cultural subjects; reviews. Pays 2½¢ a word, on publication.

INVISIBLE CITY—Red Hill Press, 6 Gabriel Dr., Fairfax, CA 94930. John McBride and Paul Vanyelisti, Editors.
Reviews, translations. No payment.

THE IOWA REVIEW—EPB 321, University of Iowa, Iowa City, IA 52242. Thomas R. Whitaker, Editor.
Critical essays. Pays $5 per page, on publication.

JOURNAL OF POPULAR CULTURE—Center for the Study of Popular Culture, Bowling Green State University, Bowling Green, OH 43402.
Articles. Photos; drawings. No payment. Query.

JOURNAL OF POPULAR FILM—Bowling Green State University, 101 University Hall, Bowling Green, OH 43403.
Articles, to 3,000 words, on popular films, directors, genres, etc. Pays in copies.

JOURNAL OF THE WEST—Box 1009, Manhattan, KS 66502. Robin Higham, Editor.
Documented articles, 2,500 to 7,500 words, on history and geography of the West. Book reviews. Pays in copies.

KANSAS QUARTERLY—Dept. of English, Kansas State University, Manhattan, KS 66506.
Articles and criticism on history, sociology, art and folklore of Midwest area. Pays in copies. Query.

KINEO WRITING—Kineo Island Club, Rockwood, ME 04476. Patrick Flynn and Richard Warren, Editors.
Maine- and rural-based essays, to 3,000 words. Pays various rates, on publication.

THE LITERARY REVIEW—Fairleigh Dickinson University, Madison, NJ 07940. Martin Green and Harry Keyishian, Co-editors.
Sketches and essays on literature. Pays in copies.

THE MALAHAT REVIEW—University of Victoria, Victoria, B.C., Canada. Robin Skelton, Editor.
Serious articles, 2,000 to 5,000 words. Translations of Latin American, European and Asian literature. Pays $25 per 1,000 words, on acceptance.

MASSACHUSETTS REVIEW—Memorial Hall, University of Massachusetts, Amherst, MA 01002.
Literary criticism; articles on public affairs, scholarly disciplines. Pays modest rates, on publication.

MIDWEST QUARTERLY—Pittsburg State University, Pittsburg, KS 66762. V. J. Emett, Jr., Editor.
Scholarly articles, 2,500 to 5,000 words, on contemporary issues. No payment.

MONTHLY REVIEW—62 West 14th St., New York, NY 10011. Paul M. Sweezy and Harry Magdoff, Editors.
Serious articles, 5,000 words, on politics and economics from independent socialist viewpoint. Pays $25 to $50, on publication.

MOSAIC—208 Tier Bldg., University of Manitoba, Winnipeg, Man., Canada R3T 2N2.
Scholarly articles, around 5,000 words, on relationship of literature to social, critical and philosophical themes.

MUNDUS ARTIUM—UTD, Box 688, Richardson, TX 75080. Rainer Schulte, Editor.
Interdisciplinary essays.

NEW BOSTON REVIEW—109 Museum St., Cambridge, MA 02138. J. M. Alonso, Jeffrey C. Hart, Editors.
Essays, 3,500 to 5,000 words, on artists, musicians, film makers, writers. No payment.

NEW DIRECTIONS FOR WOMEN—223 Old Hook Rd., Westwood, NJ 07675. Paula S. Kassell, Editor.
Articles, 500 to 1,000 words, on feminism; career, legal problems, life styles, health, books, etc. Pays in copies. Query.

NEW ENGLAND QUARTERLY—Hubbard Hall, Brunswick, ME 04011. Herbert Brown, Editor.

Historical, biographical and critical articles, around 5,000 words, on New England life and letters. No payment. Query.

NEW MAGAZINE—1639 West Washington Blvd., Venice, CA 90291. George Drury Smith, Editor.
Articles and literary criticism on West Coast literary scene. Pays in copies. Query.

NEW ORLEANS REVIEW—Loyola University, New Orleans, LA 70118.
Scholarly, scientific or general-interest articles, to 6,000 words; book reviews. Pays $50 for articles, on publication.

THE NEW YORK QUARTERLY—P.O. Box 2415, Grand Central Station, New York, NY 10017. William Packard, Editor.
Critical essays on poetry, with emphasis on technique. Pays in copies. Query.

THE NORTH AMERICAN REVIEW—University of Northern Iowa, Cedar Falls, IA 50613. Robley Wilson, Jr., Editor.
Articles on contemporary affairs, especially ecological. Pays from $20 per printed page. Query.

THE OHIO REVIEW—Ellis Hall, Ohio University, Athens, OH 45701.
Essays, to 6,000 words, on interdisciplinary subjects in humanities. Pays from $5 a page, plus copies, on publication.

THE ONTARIO REVIEW—6000 Riverside Dr. East, Windsor, Ont., Canada N8S 1B6. Raymond J. Smith, Editor.
Essays, to 4,000 words, on contemporary Canadian and American authors and artists. Pays in copies.

OYEZ REVIEW—Roosevelt University, 430 South Michigan Ave., Chicago, IL 60605.
Essays on the arts. Pays in copies.

PARABOLA—150 5th Ave., New York, NY 10011. Rick Fields, Lorraine Kisly, Editors.
Articles, 2,500 to 7,500 words, on mythology, comparative religions, anthropology, etc. Book reviews. Pays varying rates. Query.

PHOEBE—4400 University Dr., Fairfax, VA 22030. Samuel J. O'Neal, Jr., Editor.
Essays, reviews; interviews. Pays in copies.

PRAIRIE SCHOONER—201 Andrews Hall, University of Nebraska, Lincoln, NE 68588. Bernice Slote, Editor.
Criticism bearing on contemporary American scene. Pays in copies: prizes.

PRISM INTERNATIONAL—c/o Creative Writing, University of British Columbia, Vancouver, B. C., Canada V6T 1W5.
Literary essays, to 5,000 words. Pays $5 per printed page, on publication.

THE RUFUS—P.O. Box 16, Pasadena, CA 91102. Patricia Ann Bunin, Editor.
Essays on contemporary poetry, forms, movements; articles about and interviews with well-known poets, 500 to 1,000 words. Pays in copies. Query.

THE SALT LICK—Box 1064, Quincy, IL 62301. James Haining and Dan Castelaz, Editors.
Articles, essays, reviews. Drawings, photos. Pays in copies.

SCHOLIA SATYRICA—Dept. of English, University of South Florida, Tampa, FL 33620. R. D. Wyly, Editor.
Critical essays, to 5,000 words, on satiric technique, themes and individual works. Pays in copies.

SEWANEE REVIEW—Sewanee, TN 37375. George Core, Editor.
Literary articles of high quality. Pays $10 to $12 per printed page, on publication.

SMALL POND MAGAZINE–10 Overland Dr., Stratford, CT 06497. Napoleon St. Cyr, Editor.
Articles, to 2,500 words. Reviews of poetry books. Pays in copies.

SMALL PRESS REVIEW–Box 1056, Paradise, CA 95969. Len Fulton, Editor.
News pieces and reviews, to 250 words, about small presses and little magazines. Pays by arrangement or in copies.

THE SMITH–5 Beekman St., New York, NY 10038. Harry Smith, General Editor.
Nonfiction of any type. Pays modest rates, on acceptance, plus copies.

SNOWY EGRET–Dept. of English, Otterbein College, Westerville, OH 43081. William T. Hamilton, Literary Editor.
Articles, to 10,000 words, on naturalists and nature subjects, from literary, artistic or philosophical viewpoint. Pays $2 per printed page, on publication.

SOUTH DAKOTA REVIEW–Box 111, University Exchange, Vermillion, SD 57069. John R. Milton, Editor.
Articles, to 5,000 words, on history, biography and literature, preferably with regional emphasis. Pays in copies.

SOUTHERN EXPOSURE–Institute for Southern Studies, P.O. Box 230, Chapel Hill, NC 27514.
Documented articles, 2,000 to 6,000 words, on political, economic and cultural affairs related to the South. Pays $50.

SOUTHERN HUMANITIES REVIEW–Auburn University, Auburn, AL 36830.
Essays and articles, 3,500 to 5,000 words. Pays in copies.

SOUTHERN REVIEW–Drawer D, University Station, Baton Rouge, LA 70893. Donald E. Stanford and Lewis P. Simpson, Editors.
Serious essays, 4,000 to 8,000 words. Pays from 3¢ a word, on publication.

SOUTHWEST REVIEW–Southern Methodist University, Dallas, TX 75275. Margaret L. Hartley, Editor.
Articles, 1,500 to 4,000 words. Pays on publication. Query.

STUDIES IN AMERICAN FICTION–Dept. of English, Northeastern University, Boston, MA 02115. James Nagel, Editor.
Reviews, 750 words; scholarly essays, 1,200 to 6,300 words, on American fiction. No payment.

SUN & MOON–4330 Hartwick Rd., #418, College Park, MD 20740. Douglas Messerli, Literary Editor.
Traditional or experimental literary criticism and interviews. Pays in copies.

THE TEXAS QUARTERLY–Box 7517, University Station, Austin, TX 78712.
Essays on the humanities, sciences and social sciences. Pays in copies. Query with summary.

TRIQUARTERLY–1735 Benson Ave., Northwestern University, Evanston, IL 60201.
Articles on the arts, letters and opinion. Pays varying rates, on publication.

THE UNIVERSITY OF DENVER QUARTERLY–University of Denver, Denver, CO 80210.
Literary cultural essays and articles; book reviews. Pays $5 per printed page, after publication.

THE UNIVERSITY OF PORTLAND REVIEW–University of Portland, Portland, OR 97203. Thompson M. Faller, Editor.
Scholarly articles and essays, 500 to 2,500 words. Pays in copies.

THE UNIVERSITY OF WINDSOR REVIEW—Dept. of English, University of Windsor, Windsor, Ont., Canada.
Articles, 3,500 to 5,000 words, on arts, sciences, politics and social sciences. Pays $25, plus copies.

UTAH HISTORICAL QUARTERLY—Utah State Historical Society, 603 East South Temple, Salt Lake City, UT 84102.
Scholarly articles, to 7,500 words, on Utah history. Pays in copies.

VILLAGE VOICE—80 University Pl., New York, NY 10003.
Articles, 500 to 3,000 words, on current issues. Pays $50 to $200, on publication.

VIRGINIA QUARTERLY REVIEW—One West Range, Charlottesville, VA 22903.
Serious essays and articles, 3,000 to 6,000 words, on literature, science, politics, economics, etc. Pays $10 per printed page, on publication.

WASCANA REVIEW—c/o Dept. of English, University of Regina, Regina, Sask., Canada S4S 0A2.
Nonfiction, 2,000 to 6,000 words. Pays $3 per page, after publication.

WAVES—Room 128, Founders College, York University, 4700 Keele St., Downsview, Ont., Canada M3T 1P3.
Articles and essays, to 3,000 words, on literature and the arts; reviews, 500 words. Pays in copies.

WEST COAST REVIEW—Simon Fraser University, Burnaby, B. C., Canada V5A 1S6.
Essays, 1,000 to 3,000 words. Pays $5, on acceptance.

WESTERN FOLKLORE—c/o Elliott Oring, Editor, Dept. of Anthropology, California State University, Los Angeles, CA 90039.
Scholarly articles, 2,000 to 3,000 words, on folklore. No payment.

WESTERN HUMANITIES REVIEW—University of Utah, Salt Lake City, UT 84112. Jack Garlington, Editor.
Interdisciplinary articles on art, politics, world affairs, music, cinema and literature. Pays $75 to $100.

WORLD LITERATURE TODAY (formerly *Books Abroad*)—University of Oklahoma, Norman, OK 73019.
Essays on contemporary world literature and literary figures. No payment. Query.

YALE REVIEW—1902A Yale Sta., New Haven, CT 06520. J. E. Palmer, Editor; Mary Price, Managing Editor.
Serious articles, 2,000 to 4,500 words. Pays on publication.

RELIGIOUS AND DENOMINATIONAL MAGAZINES

AGLOW—P.O. Box I, Lynwood, WA 98036.
Articles, 500 to 2,000 words, by and for Christian women; personal testimonies. Pays from $10, on publication. Also book-length nonfiction; query.

AMERICA—106 West 56th St., New York, NY 10019. Joseph A. O'Hare, S.J., Editor.
Articles, 1,000 to 1,500 words, on current events, international and domestic problems, family life, literary trends. Pays $50 to $75, on acceptance.

AMERICAN BIBLE SOCIETY RECORD—1865 Broadway, New York, NY 10023. Clifford P. Macdonald, Managing Editor.
Material related to work of American Bible Society: translating, publishing, distributing. Pays on acceptance. Query.

ANNALS OF ST. ANNE DE BEAUPRÉ—Basilica of St. Anne, Quebec, Canada G0A

3C0. Jean-Claude Nadeau, C.SS.R., Managing Editor.
Articles, 1,500 to 1,600 words, on Catholic subjects and on St. Anne. Photos, illustrations. Pays 1½¢ to 2¢ a word, on acceptance.

BAPTIST HERALD—One South 210 Summit Ave., Oakbrook Terrace, Villa Park, IL 60181. R. J. Kerstan, Editor.
Articles, 800 to 1,600 words, on Baptist subjects. Photos, drawings. Pays around $10 for 900 words, after publication.

BAPTIST LEADER—Valley Forge, PA 19481. V. Alessi, Editor.
Articles, 750 to 1,600 words, on church-school work. Photos. Pays from 2¢ a word, on acceptance.

BREAD—6401 The Paseo, Kansas City, MO 64131. Dan Ketchum, Editor.
Church of the Nazarene. Devotional, Bible study and Christian guidance articles, to 1,200 words, for teen-agers. Pays from 2¢ a word for prose, on acceptance.

BRIGADE LEADER—P.O. Box 150, Wheaton, IL 60187. Rick Mould, Managing Editor.
Articles, to 1,200 words, for Christian men helping boys. Pays from 3¢ a word.

CAM—General Council of Assemblies of God, 1445 Boonville, Springfield, MO 65802.
Articles, to 1,500 words, for Pentecostal Christians at secular colleges. Pays 1¢ to 3¢ a word.

THE CANADIAN MESSENGER—833 Broadview Ave., Toronto, Ont., Canada M4K 2P9. F. J. Power, S.J., Editor. Address Ms. M. Pujolas.
Articles, 1,800 to 2,000 words, with Catholic emphasis, on daily life and problems; humor. Pays 2¢ a word, on acceptance.

CATHOLIC DIGEST— P.O. Box 3090, St. Paul, MN 55165. Address Articles Editor.
Articles, 2,000 to 2,500 words, on Catholic and general subjects. Fillers. Pays $200, $100 for reprints, $4 to $50 for fillers. Overstocked.

CATHOLIC LIFE—9800 Oakland Ave., Detroit, MI 48211. Robert C. Bayer, Editor.
Articles, 600 to 1,200 words, on Catholic missionary work in Hong Kong, India, Latin America, Africa, etc. Photos, drawings. Pays 4¢ a word, $2 per photo, on publication.

THE CHAPLAIN—Suite 301, 5100 Wisconsin Ave., N.W., Washington, DC 20016. Norman G. Folkers, Editor.
Interdenominational journal for chaplain-ministers in military service. Articles, 1,500 to 2,000 words, on chaplaincy history, biography and programs. Pays in copies.

CHICAGO STUDIES—Box 665, Mundelein, IL 60060. Address The Editors.
Scholarly articles, 5,000 to 6,000 words, on Scripture, theology, liturgy, catechetics, canon law, and philosophy. Pays varying rates, on acceptance.

CHORAL PRAISE—See *The Church Musician.*

THE CHRISTIAN ATHLETE—812 Traders National Bank Bldg., 1126 Grand Ave., Kansas City, MO 64106. Gary Warner, Editor.
Articles, to 2,500 words, on sports in relation to faith; profiles of Christian athletes and coaches. Photos. Pays $25, $10 to $15 per photo, on publication.

CHRISTIAN BOOKSELLER—Gundersen Dr. and Schmale Rd., Wheaton, IL 60187.
Trade magazine for Christian booksellers, publishers and suppliers. Articles, 800 to 1,500 words, with photos, on operating religious book and supply stores. Pays $25 to $75, on publication. Query.

THE CHRISTIAN CENTURY—407 South Dearborn St., Chicago, IL 60605. James M. Wall, Editor.
Ecumenical. Articles, 1,500 to 2,500 words, with religious angle, on political and

social issues, international affairs, culture, the arts, etc. Cartoons; photos. Pays 2¢ a word, $10 to $15 per cartoon, $10 to $30 per photo, on publication.

CHRISTIAN HERALD–Chappaqua, NY 10514. Kenneth L. Wilson, Editor.
Interdenominational. Articles and personal-experience pieces, to 2,500 words, on current social issues, religious or moral topics. Pays from $100 for full-length features, from $10 for short pieces.

CHRISTIAN LIFE MAGAZINE–Gundersen Dr. and Schmale Rd., Wheaton, IL 60187. Robert Walker, Editor.
Articles, 1,500 to 2,500 words, on evangelical subjects, Christian living, Christians in politics, sports or entertainment. Photos. Pays to $150, on publication.

CHRISTIANITY AND CRISIS–537 West 121st St., New York, NY 10027. Wayne H. Cowan, Editor.
Articles, 1,000 to 4,000 words: political, social and theological commentary from ecumenical Protestant perspective. Pays to $50, on publication.

CHRISTIANITY TODAY–465 Gundersen Dr., Carol Stream, IL 60187. Harold Lindsell, Editor.
Doctrinal, devotional, and interpretive essays, 1,500 to 2,500 words, from evangelical Protestant perspective. Pays $75 to $150, on acceptance.

CHURCH ADMINISTRATION–127 Ninth Ave. North, Nashville, TN 37234. George Clark, Editor.
Southern Baptist. Articles, 750 to 1,500 words, on administrative planning, staffing, organization, financing, etc. Pays 2½¢ a word, on acceptance.

CHURCH & STATE–8120 Fenton St., Silver Spring, MD 20910. Edd Doerr, Editor.
Articles, 600 to 2,600 words, dealing with religious liberty and church-state relations issues. Pays varying rates, on acceptance. Query.

CHURCH EDUCATOR–Education Ministries, Inc., 1406 Westwood, Lakewood, OH 44107. Robert G. Davidson, Jill Porter, Editors.
Articles, 200 to 3,000 words, with a "person-centered" approach to Christian education. Pays 3¢ to 5¢ a word, extra for photos, on publication.

THE CHURCH HERALD–1324 Lake Drive, S.E., Grand Rapids, MI 49506.
Magazine of Reformed Church in America. Articles, 500 to 1,500 words, on Christianity and culture, politics, marriage and the home, evangelism, etc. Pays 2¢ to 4¢ a word, on acceptance.

CHURCH MANAGEMENT–4119 Terrace Ln., Hopkins, MN 55343. Manfred Holck, Jr., Editor.
Articles, 500 to 1,800 words, on Protestant church administration, education, worship, law, etc. Pays from $10.

THE CHURCH MUSICIAN–127 Ninth Ave. North, Nashville, TN 37234. W. M. Anderson, Editor.
For Southern Baptist music leaders. Articles, 500 to 2,000 words, on church music. Profiles of musicians. Puzzles; cartoons. Pays around 2¢ a word, on acceptance. Same address and requirements for *Gospel Choir* and *Choral Praise* (for adults) and *Opus One* and *Opus Two* (for teenagers).

THE CHURCHMAN–1074 23rd Ave. North, St. Petersburg, FL 33704. Edna Ruth Johnson, Editor.
Articles, to 1,000 words, on current social scene, from liberal viewpoint. No payment.

COLUMBIA–Box 1670, New Haven, CT 06507. Elmer Von Feldt, Editor.
Journal of Knights of Columbus. Articles, 1,000 to 3,000 words, for Catholic family,

on current events, social problems, education, general-interest topics. Pays $100 to $300, on acceptance.

COMMENTARY—165 East 56th St., New York, NY 10022. Norman Podhoretz, Editor.
Articles, 5,000 to 7,000 words, on contemporary issues, Jewish affairs, social sciences, religious thought, culture. Book reviews. Pays on publication.

COMMONWEAL—232 Madison Ave., New York, NY 10016. James O'Gara, Editor.
Catholic. Articles, to 3,000 words, on political, religious, social and literary subjects. Pays 2¢ a word, on acceptance.

THE COMPANION—15 Chestnut Park Rd., Toronto, Ont., Canada M4W 1W5. N. Weiss, O.F.M. Conv., Editor.
Articles, 1,200 to 1,500 words, on current affairs, moral and social issues, better living. Photos. Pays 2¢ a word, on acceptance.

THE CONGREGATIONALIST—484 East Grand Blvd., Detroit, MI 48207.
Articles, 800 to 1,500 words preferred, 2,000 maximum, on the free church and moral-spiritual concepts. Pays $25 to $75, on publication.

CONGRESS MONTHLY—15 East 84th St., New York, NY 10028. Herbert Poster, Editor.
Fact or opinion articles, 1,500 to 2,500 words, for liberal Jewish readers. Book, movie and theater reviews with Jewish angle. Pays $60 to $75, on publication. Stamped, self-addressed envelope required for return of manuscript.

CONTACT—302 Lake St., P.O. Box 650, Huntington, IN 64750. Stanley Peters, Editor.
Articles, 1,000 to 1,500 words, on Christian subjects; self-help and inspirational pieces, 500 to 900 words. Pays 1¢ a word, on acceptance.

CROSS AND CROWN—1909 South Ashland Ave., Chicago, IL 60608. J. J. McDonald, O.P., Editor.
Doctrinal, biblical, liturgical, ecumenical and biographical articles, 3,000 to 4,000 words. Pays 1¢ a word, on publication.

DAILY BLESSING—P.O. Box 2187, Tulsa, OK 74171. Oral Roberts, Editor.
Simple devotionals, 300 words, with Scripture quotation and blessing for the day. Pays $5 to $15, on acceptance. Send for writer's guide.

DAILY MEDITATION—Box 2710, San Antonio, TX 78299. Ruth S. Paterson, Editor.
Inspirational nonsectarian articles, 650 to 2,000 words, on spiritual growth; pieces on new Mayan archaeological discoveries. Fillers, to 350 words. Submit seasonal material 6 months in advance. Pays ½¢ to 1¢ a word, on acceptance.

DECISION—Billy Graham Evangelistic Association, 1300 Harmon Pl., Minneapolis, MN 55403. Roger C. Palms, Editor.
Articles, 2,000 words; Christian testimonials. Narratives, 400 to 750 words, for editorial feature section. Pays varying rates, on publication.

THE DISCIPLE—Box 179, St. Louis, MO 63166. James L. Merrell, Editor.
Journal of Disciples of Christ. Articles on Christian living; devotionals, 150 words. Pays $5 to $15, on acceptance.

THE EDGE—6401 The Paseo, Kansas City, MO 64131. Melton Wienecke, Editor.
Church of the Nazarene. Short articles on Christian education. Pays $20 per 1,000 words, on acceptance.

ENGAGE/SOCIAL ACTION MAGAZINE—100 Maryland Ave. N.E., Washington, DC 20002. Allan R. Brockway, Editor.
Articles, 1,500 to 2,000 words, on social issues, for church-oriented audience. Pays $35 to $50, on publication.

THE EPISCOPALIAN—1930 Chestnut St., Philadelphia, PA 19103.
Articles, 500 to 1,200 words, for Episcopal Church members. Photos. Pays varying rates, on publication.

ETCETERA—6401 The Paseo, Kansas City, MO 64131. J. Paul Turner, Editor.
Church of the Nazarene. Devotional, Bible study and Christian-living articles, to 1,200 words, for young adults. Pays 2¢ a word, on acceptance.

ETERNITY—1716 Spruce St., Philadelphia, PA 19103. Stephen Board, Executive Editor.
Articles, to 2,000 words, with religious or evangelic angle. Pays $15 to $65, on acceptance. Query.

EUCHARIST—194 East 76th St., New York, NY 10021. William J. O'Halloran, S.S.S., Editor.
Post-conciliar Catholic. Devotional and inspirational articles, 500 to 2,000 words, related to liturgy and the Eucharist. Pays 2¢ a word, on publication.

THE EVANGEL—999 College Ave., Winona Lake, IN 46590. Vera Bethel, Editor.
Free Methodist. Articles, 1,500 to 1,800 words, on Christian solutions to problems. Human-interest pieces, 500 to 1,000 words. Pays 2¢ a word, on acceptance.

EVANGELICAL BEACON—1515 East 66th St., Minneapolis, MN 55423. George Keck, Editor.
Magazine of Evangelical Free Church. Articles, 500 to 1,750 words, on religious topics; testimonials. Pays 2¢ a word, on publication.

FACE-TO-FACE—201 Eighth Ave. South, Nashville, TN 37202. Sharilyn S. Adair, Editor.
United Methodist. Articles, 2,000 to 2,500 words, illustrated pieces, 1,200 to 1,500 words, for 15- to 18-year-olds. Pays 3¢ a word, on acceptance.

FRIAR—Butler, NJ 07405. Rudolf Harvey, O.F.M., Editor.
Catholic. Articles, to 3,000 words, on religious, humorous, patriotic and family subjects. Pays varying rates, on acceptance.

FRIENDS JOURNAL—152-A North 15th St., Philadelphia, PA 19102. Ruth Kilpack, Editor.
Articles, to 1,500 words, on religious and social issues. No payment. Query.

GOOD NEWS BROADCASTER—Box 82808, Lincoln, NE 68501.
Timely articles, to 1,500 words, biblical in principle. Pays 3¢ a word, on acceptance.

GOSPEL CARRIER—Pentecostal Church of God, P.O. Box 850, Joplin, MO 64801.
Articles, 500 to 800 words, on Christian living. Pays ½¢ per word, quarterly.

GOSPEL CHOIR—See *The Church Musician.*

GOSPEL HERALD—Scottdale, PA 15683. Daniel Hertzler, Editor.
Mennonite. Articles, to 1,500 words, on Christian experience. Pays to 3¢ a word, on acceptance.

GUIDEPOSTS—747 Third Ave., New York, NY 10017. Jack Haring, Articles Editor.
True first-person articles, 250 to 1,500 words; anecdotal fillers, to 250 words. Pays $10 to $20 for fillers, $100 to $300 for articles, on acceptance.

HIS—5206 Main St., Downers Grove, IL 60515.
Scripture-oriented articles on Christian living on the college campus, for students, faculty, etc.; biography. Pays 2¢ a word, on acceptance.

HOME LIFE—127 Ninth Ave. North, Nashville, TN 37234. George W. Knight, Editor.
Southern Baptists. Articles, preferably personal-experience, and fiction, to 2,000 words, on child development, marriage, parent-teen-ager relationships, family fi-

nances, etc. Human-interest pieces, 200 to 500 words. Pays 2½¢ a word, on acceptance. Send for writer's guide.

THE ILLUSTRATOR—Sunday School Dept., MSN #176 5 NW, 127 Ninth Ave. North, Nashville, TN 37234.
Articles, to 2,400 words, on archaeology, geography and history of biblical lands. Fillers; photos. Pays 2½¢ a word, extra for photos, on acceptance. Query.

INSIGHT—6856 Eastern Ave. N.W., Washington, DC 20012. Donald John, Editor.
Seventh-day Adventist. Personal-experience narratives and articles, to 1,800 words, for high school and college students. Parables; shorts. Photos. Pays 2¢ to 4¢ a word, extra for photos, on acceptance. Query. Send for writer's guide.

INSPIRATION MAGAZINE—Petersen Publishing Co., 8490 Sunset Blvd.,, Los Angeles, CA 90069.
Vibrant, up-beat articles about human experiences: child-rearing, morality, money management, etc.; travel-oriented features; humorous pieces. Pays from $150, $350 to $500 for major pieces, after acceptance. Query.

INTERACTION—3558 South Jefferson, St. Louis, MO 63118. Mervin A. Marquardt, Editor.
Inspirational articles, to 2,000 words, for Christian teachers. Pays $20 to $30.

JEWISH LIFE—116 East 27th St., New York, NY 10016. Yaakov Jacobs, Editor.
Articles, to 4,000 words, relating to Orthodox Judaism. Book reviews, to 1,200 words. Pays $8 per printed page for articles; $6 per page for book reviews. Query.

KEY TO CHRISTIAN EDUCATION—8121 Hamilton Ave., Cincinnati, OH 45231. Marjorie Reeves Miller, Editor.
Articles, with photos, on teaching methods, success stories, for workers in Christian education. Pays varying rates, on acceptance.

LIBERTY MAGAZINE—6840 Eastern Ave. N.W., Washington DC 20012. Roland R. Hegstad, Editor.
Timely articles, to 2,500 words, with photos, on religious freedom and church-state relations. Pays 5¢ a word, on acceptance. Query.

THE LIGUORIAN—Liguori, MO 63057.
Articles, 500 to 1,500 words, on Christian values in modern life. Photos. Pays 7¢ a word, on acceptance.

LIVE—1445 Boonville Ave., Springfield, MO 65802. Gary Leggett, Adult Editor.
Sunday School paper for adults. Articles, 1,000 to 1,500 words, on applying Bible principles to everyday living. Pays on acceptance. Send for writer's guide.

THE LIVING LIGHT—Our Sunday Visitor, Inc., 1312 Massachusetts Ave. N.W., Washington, DC 20005. Robert P. Stamschror, Editor.
Theoretical and practical articles, 1,500 to 4,000 words, on current trends and problems in religious education. Pays 2½¢ a word, on publication.

LOGOS JOURNAL—201 Church St., Plainfield, NJ 07060. Howard Earl, Senior Editor.
Interdenominational, emphasizing charismatic aspect of church. Personal-experience articles on spiritual and physical healing; opinion pieces, 1,200 words; testimonials, mission reports and humor, 2,000 words. Pays 5¢ a word, on publication.

THE LOOKOUT—8121 Hamilton Ave., Cincinnati, OH 45231. Mark A. Taylor, Editor.
Articles, 1,000 to 1,500 words, on people overcoming problems by Christian principles. Inspirational or humorous shorts, 100 to 500 words. Pays to 3¢ a word.

THE LUTHERAN—2900 Queen Ln., Philadelphia, PA 10129. Albert P. Stauderman, Editor.
Articles, to 2,000 words, on Christian ideology, personal religious experiences,

Christian family life, church and community. Pays $75 to $250. Query.

LUTHERAN STANDARD—426 South Fifth St., Minneapolis, MN 55415. George H. Muedeking, Editor.
Articles, 500 to 1,000 words, on social, economic and political aspects of church and Christian living; human-interest items; personality profiles. Pays from 3¢ a word, on acceptance.

MARRIAGE—Abbey Press Publishing Div., St. Meinrad, IN 47577. Ila Stabile, Editor.
Interviews, personal-experience pieces, humor, 1,500 to 3,000 words, dealing with marital relationships. Pays 5¢ a word, on acceptance.

MATURE LIVING—127 Ninth Ave. North, Nashville, TN 37234. Zada Malugen, Assistant Editor.
Articles, 875 to 1,400 words, for people 60 years of age or older; nostalgia, character sketches, how-to pieces. Pays 2½¢ per word, on acceptance.

MARYKNOLL--Maryknoll Fathers, Maryknoll, NY 10545.
Articles, to 1,500 words; profiles of mission people, socio-economic studies of mission countries. Pays $150 to $200 for articles with photos, on acceptance, usually. Query.

MIDSTREAM—515 Park Ave., New York, NY 10022. Joel Carmichael, Editor.
General-interest articles and book reviews, of Jewish interest. Pays 7¢ a word, on acceptance.

MOMENT—55 Chapel St., Newton, MA 02160.
Sophisticated articles, 2,000 to 5,000 words, on Jewish topics. Pays $200 to $400, on publication.

MOMENTUM—National Catholic Educational Association, Suite 350, One Dupont Circle N.W., Washington, DC 20036. Carl Balcerak, Editor.
Articles, 1,500 to 3,000 words, on outstanding programs, issues and research in education. Book reviews. Pays 2¢ a word, on publication. Query.

THE NATIONAL JEWISH MONTHLY—B'nai B'rith, 1640 Rhode Island Ave. N.W., Washington, DC 20036. Charles Fenyvesi, Editor.
Shorts, 200 to 800 words, and articles, 1,000 to 3,500 words, on contemporary Jewish topics. Pays 5¢ to 10¢ a word, on publication.

NEW CATHOLIC WORLD—1865 Broadway, New York, NY 10023. Robert J. Heyer, Managing Editor.
Articles, to 2,000 words, on politics, science, literature, etc. Pays from $75, on publication.

NEW WORLD OUTLOOK—475 Riverside Dr., New York, NY 10027. Arthur J. Moore, Jr., Editor.
Articles, 1,500 to 2,500 words, on Christian missions. Pays on publication.

THE OBLATE WORLD AND VOICE OF HOPE (formerly *OMI Missions*)—The Oblate Fathers, Box 96, San Antonio, TX 78291.
Catholic. Mission stories, 1,000 to 1,600 words, about Oblate Fathers in Texas, Mexico, Phillipines or Asia. Pays 1¢ to 2¢ a word, on acceptance.

OPUS ONE—See *The Church Musician.*

OPUS TWO—See *The Church Musician.*

OUR FAMILY—Box 249, Dept. E, Battleford, Sask., Canada S0M 0E0. Reb Materi, O.M.I., Editor.
Articles, 1,000 to 3,000 words, for Catholic family readers, on modern society, family, marriage, current affairs. Humor. Pays 3¢ a word, on acceptance.

OUR SUNDAY VISITOR—Huntington, IN 46750.

Articles, 1,000 to 1,200 words, on personalities, Catholic lay groups, philosophy, theology. Pays $75 to $100, $10 to $20 for cartoons.

PASTORAL LIFE, THE MAGAZINE FOR TODAY'S MINISTRY—Canfield, OH 44406. Victor Viberti, S.S.P., Editor.
Articles for priests and ministers, on pastoral activities and contemporary issues. Book reviews. Pays from 3¢ a word, on acceptance. Query.

THE PENTECOSTAL EVANGEL—1445 Boonville, Springfield, MO 65802. Robert C. Cunningham, Editor.
Publication of Assemblies of God. Religious personal-experience and devotional articles, 500 to 1,000 words. Pays 1¢ a word, on publication.

PLAIN TRUTH—Ambassador College, Pasadena, CA 91123. Herbert Armstrong and Garner Ted Armstrong, Editors.
Articles, 500 to 2,000 words, with biblical approach to world news; commentary. Pays 15¢ a word, on publication.

POWER FOR LIVING—Box 513, Glen Ellyn, IL 60137.
Articles on Christian themes: personality profiles, 1,200 to 1,500 words; first-person or as-told-to pieces, 1,000 to 1,500 words; commentaries on contemporary issues, 300 to 500 words; photo essays, 500 to 1,000 words. Pays to 7¢ a word, extra for photos, on acceptance.

PRESENT TENSE—165 East 56th St., New York, NY 10022. Murray Polner, Editor.
Serious reportage, 3,000 to 5,000 words, with photos, on international developments concerning Jews; memoirs. Pays $100 to $250, on acceptance. Query.

THE PRIEST—St. John's University, Grand Central and Utopia Pkwys., Jamaica, NY 11439.
Contemporary articles, to 2,500 words, on life and ministry of priest, current theological developments, etc., for priests and seminarians.

PURPOSE—610 Walnut Ave., Scottdale, PA 15683. David E. Hostetler, Editor.
Articles, 350 to 1,200 words, with photos, on Christians confronting issues. Historical, biographical and scientific material. Pays to 3¢ a word, $5 to $25 for photos, on acceptance.

QUAKER LIFE—Friends United Meeting, 101 Quaker Hill Dr., Richmond, IN 47374. Fred Wood, Editor.
Articles, 600 to 1,500 words. No payment.

QUEEN—40 South Saxon Ave., Bay Shore, NY 11706. James McMillan, S.M.M., Editor.
Publication of Montfort Missionaries. Articles and fiction, 1,000 to 2,000 words, relating to the Virgin Mary. Pays varying rates, on acceptance.

THE RECONSTRUCTIONIST—432 Park Ave. South, New York, NY 10016. Ira Eisenstein, Editor.
Articles, 2,000 to 3,000 words, relating to Judaism. Pays $15 to $25, on publication.

ST. ANTHONY MESSENGER—1615 Republic St., Cincinnati, OH 45210. Jeremy Harrington, O.F.M., Editor.
Articles, 2,500 to 3,500 words, on personalities, major movements in Church, education, hobbies. Human-interest and humor pieces; fiction. Photos, photo essays. Pays from 6¢ a word, on acceptance. Query.

ST. JOSEPH'S MESSENGER—P.O. Box 288, Jersey City, NJ 07303. Sister Ursula Marie Maphet, Editor.
Inspirational articles, 500 to 1,000 words, on Catholic topics. Pays 1¢ a word. Query.

SCIENCE OF MIND—P.O. Box 75127, Los Angeles, CA 90075.

Inspirational articles, 1,500 to 2,000 words, on metaphysical aspects of science, philosophy and religion. Pays varying rates, on publication.

SCOPE—426 South Fifth St., Minneapolis, MN 55415. Lilly M. Gyldenvand, Editor.
Journal of American Lutheran Women. Self-help and inspirational articles, 1,000 to 1,500 words, on women's roles in home, church and community. Pays moderate rates, on acceptance.

SEEK—8121 Hamilton Ave., Cincinnati, OH 45231. J. David Lang, Editor.
Articles, 400 to 1,200 words, on inspirational subjects, controversial topics and timely religious issues. Christian testimonials. Pays around 2¢ a word, on acceptance.

SH'MA—Box 567, Port Washington, NY 11050. Eugene B. Borowitz, Editor.
Articles, 750 to 2,000 words, on ethics, Zionism, Jewish living, etc. Pays in copies.

THE SIGN—Monastery Place, Union City, NJ 07087. Arthur McNally, C.P., Editor.
Articles, to 3,500 words, on Catholic topics: Sacraments, prayer, liturgy, family life. Pays to $300, on acceptance.

SIGNS OF THE TIMES—1350 Villa St., Mountain View, CA 94042. Lawrence Maxwell, Editor.
Seventh-day Adventist. Devotionals to 800 words.

SOCIAL JUSTICE REVIEW—3835 Westminster Pl., St. Louis, MO 63108. Harvey J. Johnson, Editor.
Articles, 2,000 to 4,000 words, on social problems in the light of Catholic social teaching and current scientific studies. Pays 1¢ a word, on publication.

SPIRITUAL LIFE—2131 Lincoln Rd. N.E., Washington, DC 20002. Christopher Latimer, O.C.D., Editor.
Professional religious journal. Religious essays, 3,000 to 5,000 words, on spirituality in contemporary life; no first-person accounts. Pays from $50, on acceptance.

SUNDAY DIGEST—850 North Grove Ave., Elgin, IL 60120. Darlene McRoberts, Editor.
Articles, to 1,500 words, with photos, on application of Christian faith to current problems. Anecdotes and inspirational fillers, to 300 words. Pays from 3¢ a word, on acceptance. Send for writer's guide.

SUNSHINE MAGAZINE—Litchfield, IL 62056. Monta Henrichs Crane, Editor.
Inspirational articles, to 600 words, on living. Short stories, 1,250 words, and juveniles, 600 words. Pays varying rates, on acceptance.

THE TEXAS METHODIST/UNITED METHODIST REPORTER—P.O. Box 1076, Dallas, TX 75221. Spurgeon M. Dunnam III, Editor.
United Methodist. Religious features and news stories, 500 words. Action photos. Pays 3¢ a word, on acceptance. Send for writer's guide.

THEOLOGY TODAY—Box 29, Princeton, NJ 08540. Hugh T. Kerr, Editor.
Articles, to 3,500 words, or to 1,500 words, on theology, religion and related social issues. Literary criticism. Pays $35 to $50, on publication.

THESE TIMES—Box 59, Nashville, TN 37202. K. J. Holland, Editor.
Articles, to 2,500 words, on moral issues, health, inspirational and patriotic themes, the Bible, marriage and the home, for family audience. Pays to 10¢ a word, on acceptance.

TODAY'S CHRISTIAN PARENT—8121 Hamilton Ave., Cincinnati, OH 45231. Wilma L. Shaffer, Editor.
Articles, 600 to 1,000 words, on application of Christian principles in child-rearing. Helpful, inspirational family articles; devotional ideas. Pays after acceptance.

THE UNITED CHURCH OBSERVER—85 St. Clair Ave. East, Toronto, Ont., Canada. A. C. Forrest, Editor.

Factual articles, 1,500 to 2,500 words, on religious trends, human problems, personalities. Cartoons with religious angle. Pays from $50, before publication. Query.

UNITED EVANGELICAL ACTION—Box 28, Wheaton, IL 60187. Harold Smith, Editor.
Publication of National Association of Evangelicals. Articles, 1,500 to 2,500 words, on religious, social, and political problems in evangelical context. Pays 2¢ to 5¢ a word, on publication. Query.

UNITED SYNAGOGUE REVIEW—155 Fifth Ave., New York, NY 10010. Alvin Kass, Editor.
Articles, 1,000 to 1,500 words, on synagogue programs and projects, Jewish worship services, rituals, etc.

UNITY MAGAZINE—Unity School of Christianity, Unity Village, MO 64065. Thomas E. Witherspoon, Editor.
Inspirational and metaphysical articles, 500 to 2,500 words. Pays from 2¢ a word, on acceptance.

THE UPPER ROOM—1908 Grand Ave., Nashville, TN 37203.
Meditations on Bible texts, 250 words, with illustrations, prayer and "thought for the day." Pays $7, on publication.

VISTA—Box 2000, Marion, IN 46851.
Devotional and biographical articles; photo essays. Pays 2¢ a word, on acceptance.

THE YOUTH LEADER—1445 Boonville Ave., Springfield, MO 65802. Glen Ellard, Editor.
How-to articles, 500 to 2,000 words, for Christian youth leaders. Pays 2½¢ to 3½¢ a word, on acceptance.

SPORTS, RECREATION, CONSERVATION
AND OUTDOOR MAGAZINES

ACROSPORTS—410 Broadway, Santa Monica, CA 90401. Glenn Sundby, Publisher.
U.S. Sports Acrobatic Federation publication. Articles on competitive acrobatics, balancing, trampoline, tumbling. No payment.

AERO MAGAZINE—P.O. Box 4030, San Clemente, CA 92672. Dennis Shattuck, Editor.
Factual articles on aircraft ownership: single-engine business jets, general-aviation aircraft. Pays $25 to $50 per printed page, on publication. Query.

AMA NEWS—See *American Motorcyclist*.

THE AMERICAN BLADE—13222 Saticoy St., North Hollywood, CA 91605. Ken Faust, Editor.
Articles on cutlery, for collectors, users, manufacturers. Photos. Pays 5¢ a word, $5 per photo after publication. Query.

AMERICAN BOATING ILLUSTRATED—2019 Clement Ave., Alameda, CA 94501. Michael Dobrin, Editor.
How-to pieces, 50 to 1,000 words, on repair, modification, rigging, for power- and sailboats. Pays $1.20 per column inch, extra for illustrations, on publication. Query.

THE AMERICAN FIELD—222 West Adams St., Chicago, IL 60606. William F. Brown, Editor.
Yarns about hunting trips and bird-shooting experiences. Short articles, to 1,500 words, on hunting dogs, field trials. Emphasizes conservation of game resources. Pays varying rates, on acceptance.

AMERICAN FORESTS—1319 18th St. N.W., Washington, DC 20036. Bill Rooney, Editor.

Well-documented articles, to 1,800 words, with photos, on outdoor subjects, environment. Photos. Pays on publication.

THE AMERICAN HANDGUNNER—See *Guns.*

THE AMERICAN HUNTER—1600 Rhode Island Ave. N.W., Washington, DC 20036. Ken Warner, Editor.
Articles, 1,000 words, on hunting in America. Photos. Pays top rates, on acceptance.

AMERICAN MOTORCYCLIST (formerly *AMA News*)— American Motorcyclist Association, Box 141, Westerville, OH 43081.
Articles and fiction, to 3,000 words, on motorcycling: news coverage, personalities, tours. Photos. Pays varying rates, on publication.

THE AMERICAN RIFLEMAN—1600 Rhode Island Ave. N.W., Washington, DC 20036. Ken Warner, Editor.
Factual articles on use and enjoyment of sporting firearms. Pays on acceptance.

ARCHERY—Rt. 2, Box 514, Redlands, CA 92373. Dan Gustafson, Editor.
Articles, 1,000 to 2,500 words, on bow-and-arrow hunting, fishing; interviews with field archers, how- and where-to-hunt pieces. Photos. Pays to $50 per printed page, on publication. Query.

ARCHERY WORLD—225 East Michigan, Milwaukee, WI 53202. Glenn Helgeland, Editor.
Articles, 1,000 to 3,000 words, on all aspects of archery, for hunters and competitive shooters, beginners and professionals. How-to pieces; photo tips; photos. Pays from $35, $10 per photo, near acceptance.

ARGOSY—420 Lexington Ave., New York, NY 10017. Lou Sahadi, Editor.
Articles, 3,000 to 3,500 words, with photos, on adventure, life styles, exploration, outdoors. Pays $350 to $500 for articles, on publication. Query.

ARMS GAZETTE—13222 Saticoy St., North Hollywood, CA 91605. Ken Faust, Managing Editor.
Articles, any length, on firearms, edged weapons, armor, from ancient to modern times. Photos. Pays 5¢ a word, after publication. Query.

AUTO RACING DIGEST—See *Baseball Digest.*

B. C. HORSEMAN—7614 17th Ave., Burnaby, B. C., Canada V3N 1L7. R. K. Cross, Editor.
Profiles of horse ranches, trainers, 1,500 to 2,000 words. Payment rates vary. Query.

BC OUTDOORS—Box 900, Postal Station A, Surrey, B.C., Canada V3S 4P4. Art Downs, Editor.
Articles, 2,500 to 3,000 words, on hunting, fishing, conservation, travel, boating, hiking, nature, wildlife, in British Columbia and Yukon. No poetry. Pays $75 to $100, extra for photos, on acceptance. Query.

BACKPACKER—65 Adams St., Bedford Hills, NY 10507. Andrea Scott, Editor.
Articles, 1,500 to 3,000 words, on backpacking: where to go, what to do. No beginners' how-to articles. Photos, cartoons, poetry. Pays from $75 for articles, on acceptance.

BACKPACKING JOURNAL—229 Park Ave. South, New York, NY 10003. Andrew J. Carra, Editor.
Articles on backpacking, for beginners and experts: personal experiences, trails, sites, etc. Photos; fillers. Pays $50 to $250, after acceptance. Query.

THE BACKSTRETCH—19363 James Couzens Hwy., Detroit, MI 48235. Ruth LeGrove, Editor.

United Thoroughbred Trainers of America publication. Feature articles with photos. Pays after publication.

BASEBALL DIGEST—1020 Church St., Evanston, IL 60201. John Kuenster, Editor.
Articles, 800 to 2,500 words, on baseball and players. Pays on publication. Query. Same address and requirements for *Auto Racing Digest, Basketball Digest, Football Digest,* and *Hockey Digest.*

BASKETBALL DIGEST—See *Baseball Digest.*

BAY & DELTA YACHTSMAN—2019 Clement Ave., Alameda, CA 94501. Michael Dobrin, Editor.
News, features, how-to pieces, 500 to 2,000 words, for boating readers in San Francisco Bay-Northern California area. Pays $1 per column inch, extra for photos, on publication. Query.

BICYCLING—119 Paul Dr., P.O. Box 4450, San Rafael, CA 94903.
Articles and fiction, 500 to 1,500 words, for cycling enthusiasts, on recreational riding, commuting, equipment, touring. Photos; humor. Pays $1 per column inch, extra for photos, on publication.

BIKE WORLD—P.O. Box 366, Mountain View, CA 94042. Bob Anderson, Editor.
Articles on bicycle touring, racing, training. Related fiction. Photos. Pays from $15 per published page, extra for photos, on publication. Same address and requirements for *Down River, Nordic World, Soccer World.*

BOATING—One Park Ave., New York, NY 10016. Richard L. Rath, Editor.
Illustrated articles, 1,000 to 2,000 words, on boating, fresh- and salt-water; no fishing, water-skiing, or skin-diving material. Pays good rates, on acceptance.

BOW & ARROW—Box HH, 34249 Camino Capistrano, Capistrano Beach, CA 92624. Jack Lewis, Editor.
Practical articles, 1,200 to 2,600 words, with photos, on bow hunting, target archery, do-it-yourself projects. Pays $50 to $200, on acceptance. Same address and requirements for *Gun World.*

BOWHUNTER MAGAZINE—P.O. Box 5377, Fort Wayne, IN 46805. M. R. James, Editor.
Adventure, how-to and where-to-go articles, 500 to 5,000 words (2,500 preferred), on bow-and-arrow hunting. Pays $50 to $125, on acceptance.

BOWLING—5301 South 76th St., Greendale, WI 53129. David DeLorenzo, Editor.
Articles, to 1,000 words, with photos, on league or tournament bowling. Pays $35 to $100, on acceptance. Query.

CAMPING JOURNAL—229 Park Ave. South, New York, NY 10003. Andrew J. Carra, Editor.
Travel features, profiles, interviews, to 2,500 words, with photos. Short how-to articles, with photos. Pays from $75 for how-to articles, from $150 for features, on acceptance. Query.

CAMPING MAGAZINE—Bradford Woods, Martinsville, IN 46151. Glenn T. Job, Editor.
American Camping Association publication. Articles, to 1,500 words, on children's camps. No payment.

CANADIAN GEOGRAPHICAL JOURNAL—488 Wilbrod St., Ottawa, Ont., Canada K1N 6M8. David Maclellan, Editor.
Articles, photo-features, 2,000 to 3,000 words, on Canada. Research and photos essential. Pays from $150 to $350, on publication.

CANOE—1999 Shepard Rd., St. Paul, MN 55116. Peter Sonderegger, Publisher.

Articles, to 1,800 words, on competitive, recreational and wilderness canoeing and kayaking, including conservation, safety, camping. Pays varying rates, on acceptance.

CAR AND DRIVER—One Park Ave., New York, NY 10016. David E. Davis, Editor/ Publisher.
Articles, to 2,500 words, for enthusiasts, on car manufacturers, auto sports, new developments in cars, safety on highways; profiles. Pays to $1,000, on acceptance.

CAR CRAFT—8490 Sunset Blvd., Los Angeles, CA 90069. Rick Voegelin, Editor.
Articles and photo-features on unusual street machines, drag cars, racing events; technical pieces; action photos. Pays from $100 per page, on acceptance.

CAROLINA SPORTSMAN—P.O. Box 9248, Charlotte, NC 28299. Sidney L. Wise, Editor.
Fiction and articles, 1,000 to 1,500 words, on outdoor sports (hunting, fishing, boating, camping, riding, backpacking, etc.) in North and South Carolina. Photos. Pays 1¢ to 2¢ per word, on publication.

CLASSIC—551 Fifth Ave., New York, NY 10017. Andrew Crichton, Executive Editor.
Articles and fiction, 2,000 to 4,000 words, on horses for sport and pleasure. Short items for "Comment." Pays from $500, $250 for columns, $25 for shorts, on acceptance. Query.

COUNTRY CLUB GOLFER—2171 Campus Dr., Irvine, CA 92715. Edward Pazdur, Editor.
Articles, 2,500 to 5,000 words, on country-club golf. Poetry, 8 to 16 lines. Pays varying rates for articles, $5 to $10 for poems, on publication.

CRUISING WORLD—P.O. Box 452, Newport, RI 02840. Murray Davis, Editor.
Articles, 500 to 3,500 words, on technical and recreational aspects of cruising under sail. Poetry; fillers; cartoons; photos; photo-essays. Pays $50 to $300 for features, on publication.

CURLING NEWS—7614 17th Ave., Burnaby, B. C., Canada V3N 1L7. R. K. Cross, Editor.
Articles, 1,500 to 2,000 words, and photographs, on curling activities in the US and abroad, and profiles of famous curlers. Pays varying rates, on publication. Query.

CYCLE—1 Park Ave., New York, NY 10016. Cook Neilson, Editor.
Staff-written; no free-lance material at present.

CYCLE GUIDE—P.O. Box 6040, Compton, CA 90220. Suzanne Whitfield, Managing Editor.
Articles, 2,000 to 4,000 words, technical pieces, short stories, photos, relating to motorcycles. Pays from $50 per page, on publication.

CYCLE TIMES—222 W. Adams St., Chicago, IL 60606. Denis Schmidlin, Editor.
Articles, 1,500 words, maximum, geared toward the knowledgeable midwestern motorcyclist, local race reports, technical pieces and interviews, with artwork and photos. Pays $1.00 per column inch, $2.50 for photos, on publication.

CYCLE WORLD—1499 Monrovia Ave., Newport Beach, CA 92663. Allan Girdler, Editor.
Accurate technical and feature articles, 1,500 to 2,500 words, for motorcycle enthusiasts. Humor; fiction; photos. Pays $75 to $100 per page, on publication. Query.

DEFENDERS OF WILDLIFE—1244 19th St. N.W., Washington, DC 20036.
Conservation. No freelance material.

DIRT BIKE—16200 Ventura Blvd., Encino, CA 91316.
Short articles on off-road motorcycle riding and racing. Photos. Pays varying rates, on publication. Query.

DOWN RIVER—See *Bike World*.

DRESSAGE & C.T.—P.O. Box 2460, Cleveland, OH 44112. Ivan Bezugloff, Jr., Editor.
Articles and fiction, 800 to 1,400 words, on dressage, combined training and eventing. Drawings. Pays around 2½¢ a word.

DUNE BUGGIES AND HOT VWS—P.O. Box 2260, Costa Mesa, CA 92626.
Articles, 1,500 words, on dune buggies. Pays $50 per printed page, on publication.

EASYRIDERS MAGAZINE—Box 52, Malibu, CA 90265. Lou Kimzey, Editor.
Articles, 2,000 to 3,000 words, and fiction, to 4,000 words, on motorcycling. Interviews; poetry; fillers; cartoons. Photos. Pays 5¢ to 10¢ a word, on acceptance.

ENTHUSIAST—Harley-Davidson Motor Co., Inc., P.O. Box 653, Milwaukee, WI 53201. Robert H. Klein, Editor.
Articles, to 3,000 words, cartoons, photo-essays, on motorcycle racing, tours, etc., featuring Harley-Davidson cycles. Pays 5¢ a word, extra for photos, on publication.

FIELD & STREAM—383 Madison Ave., New York, NY 10017. Jack Samson, Editor.
Articles, 1,500 to 2,500 words, with photos. Some fiction. Pays from 20¢ a word, on acceptance.

FIGHTING WOMAN NEWS—Box 5416 Grand Central Sta., New York, NY 10017. Valerie Eads, Editor.
Articles, to 2,000 words, and fiction, 1,000 to 1,500 words, on martial arts for women. Pays in copies.

FISH AND GAME SPORTSMAN—P.O. Box 737, Regina, Sask., Canada. Red Wilkinson, Editor.
Articles, to 2,500 words, on fishing, camping, snowmobiling, outdoor trips and experiences in Alberta and Saskatchewan; how-to pieces. Photos. Pays $40 to $175, on publication (on acceptance if article will not be used within three months).

FISHING WORLD—51 Atlantic Ave., Floral Park, NY 11001. Keith Gardner, Editor.
Factual articles, 1,500 to 3,000 words, with photos, on angling in fresh and salt water; how-to pieces. Pays $200 for articles, on acceptance.

FLIGHT LINE TIMES—Box 186, Brookfield, CT 06804. David A. Shugarts, Editor.
Aviation news and features, 700 to 1,500 words. Photos. Pays to $20 for features, $5 per photo, after publication. Same address and requirements for *North Atlantic Aircraft Bulletin, Great Lakes Aircraft Bulletin, Southern Aviation Times*. Correspondents needed.

THE FLORIDA HORSE—P.O. Box 699, Ocala, FL 32670. Lauren Marks, Marianne Upson, Editors.
Articles, 1,500 words, on Florida thoroughbred racing. Pays $50 to $100, on publication.

THE FLYFISHER—390 Bella Vista Way, San Francisco, CA 94127. Michael Fong, Editor.
Articles, 2,000 to 3,000 words, on fly-fishing technique, lore, history and on conservation, for sophisticated anglers. Photos. Pays $75 to $175. Query.

FLYING MAGAZINE—One Park Ave., New York, NY 10016. Richard Collins, Editor.
Articles on personal flying experiences, 1,500 words. Pays varying rates, on acceptance. Query.

FOOTBALL DIGEST—See *Baseball Digest*.

THE FOOTBALL NEWS—17820 East Warren, Detroit, MI 48224. Roger Stanton, Editor.
In-depth articles, 750 to 1,000 words, on football teams, sports personalities. Pays $30 to $50, after acceptance. Query.

FUR-FISH-GAME—2878 East Main St., Columbus, OH 43209. A. R. Harding, Editor.
Illustrated articles, 2,000 to 2,500 words, on hunting, fishing, camping, trapping, etc.
Pays 1½¢ to 3½¢ a word, on acceptance.

GEORGIA SPORTSMAN—Box 741, Marietta, GA 30061. John Spears, Editor.
Articles, 900 to 1,200 words, with photos, on fishing, hunting and outdoor recreational activities in Georgia. Pays 10¢ a word, on publication, maximum of $120.
Query.

GOLF DIGEST—495 Westport Ave., Norwalk, CT 06856. Nick Seitz, Editor.
Articles, 500 to 2,000 words, on golf personalities, events, instruction (especially
authorized by golf professional), humor. Fillers, photos, cartoons. Pays from 20¢ a
word, $50 for cartoons, on acceptance. Query.

GOLF JOURNAL—United States Golf Association, Far Hills, NJ 07931. Robert
Sommers, Editor and Publisher.
U. S. Golf Association publication. Articles on golf personalities, history, rules,
Photos. Pays on publication.

GOLF MAGAZINE—380 Madison Ave., New York, NY 10017. John M. Ross, Editor-in
Chief.
National-interest articles, 2,000 words, with photos, on golf. Light fiction; shorts, to
750 words; cartoons. Pays $500, $75 to $300 for shorts, $75 for cartoons.

GRAY'S SPORTING JOURNAL—1330 Beacon St., Brookline, MA 02146. Ed Gray,
Editor.
Articles and fiction, 2,000 to 4,000 words, on hunting and fishing. Photos. Pays good
rates, on acceptance. Query.

GREAT LAKES AIRCRAFT BULLETIN—See *Flight Line Times.*

GUN DIGEST AND HANDLOADER'S DIGEST—20604 Collins Road, Marengo, IL
60152. John T. Amber, Editor.
Well-researched articles, to 5,000 words, on guns and shooting equipment. Photos.
Pays 10¢ to 15¢ a word, on acceptance. Query.

GUN WORLD—See *Bow & Arrow.*

GUNS—8150 North Central Park Blvd., Skokie, IL 60076. J. Rakusan, Editor.
Articles, 1,500 to 2,500 words, on target shooting, hunting, history or design of guns.
Photos. Pays around 5¢ a word, on publication. Query. Same address and requirements for *The American Handgunner.*

GUNS & AMMO—8490 Sunset Blvd., Los Angeles, CA 90069. Howard French, Editor.
Technical articles, 1,500 to 2,000 words, on guns, ammunition, target shooting, etc.
General articles on guns and accessories. Photos, fillers. Pays from $125, on
publication.

GYMNAST—See *International Gymnast.*

HANDBALL—4101 Dempster St., Skokie, IL 60076. Terry Muck, Editor.
Articles, 200 to 400 words, on handball and handball players. Photos; cartoons;
fillers, 30 to 40 words. Pays $25 to $75, on acceptance.

HOCKEY DIGEST—See *Baseball Digest.*

HOCKEY ILLUSTRATED—333 Johnson Ave., Brooklyn, NY 11206. Randy O'Neill,
Editor.
Articles, 1,500 to 2,000 words, with photos, on hockey players. Fillers, puzzles,
short humor. Pays $100 for articles, extra for photos, on publication. Query.

HORSE & RIDER—P.O. Box 555, Temecula, CA 92390. Ray Rich, Editor.
Articles, 250 to 3,000 words, with photos, on Western riding: training, feeding, vet

advice, grooming, and general horse care. Cartoons. Pays varying rates, before publication.

HORSE, OF COURSE—Temple, NH 03084. R. A. Green, D.V.M., Editor.
How-to articles, 600 to 2,000 words, on horse ownership, training, riding, care; profiles of horses or people. Photos. Pays from $50, on publication.

HORSE PLAY—Box 545, Gaithersburg, MD 20760. Susanne Saver, Editor.
Articles, 2,500 words, on horse shows, three-day eventing, fox hunting, steeplechase, etc., for experts. Pays $50 to $75, on publication.

HORSEMAN—5314 Bingle Rd., Houston, TX 77018. Allen L. Bird, Editor.
Articles, 2000 to 3,000 words, with photos, on techniques of western horsemanship, horse management. Pays 4¢ to 6¢ a word, $6 to $7 per photo, on publication. Query.

HORSEMEN'S JOURNAL—Suite 317, 6000 Executive Blvd., Rockville, MD 20852. William McDonald, Editor.
Articles, 500 to 3,000 words, reflecting inside knowledge of thoroughbred (flat) racing. Pays $25 to $100, on publication.

HOT ROD—8490 Sunset Blvd., Los Angeles, CA 90069. John Dianna, Editor.
How-to pieces and articles, 500 to 5,000 words, on auto mechanics, hot rods, track and drag racing, hill climbing, other hot-rod competitions. Photo-features on custom or performance-modified cars. Pays to $125 per page, on publication.

HUNTING—8490 Sunset Blvd., Los Angeles, CA 90069.
How-to articles on practical aspects of hunting. At least 15 photos required with articles. Pays $200 to $300 for articles, extra for color photos, on publication. Send for writer's guide.

HUNTING DOG—9714 Montgomery Rd., Cincinnati, OH 45242. George R. Quigley, Managing Editor.
Articles, 1,000 to 2,000 words, on sporting dogs and outdoors. Pays from 2¢ a word, from $5 per photo, on publication.

INTERNATIONAL GYMNAST (formerly *Gymnast*)—410 Broadway, Santa Monica, CA 90401. Glenn Sundby, Publisher.
Gymnast news: competitions, instruction, personalities, with many photos. Fillers. Pays modest rates.

JEWISH SPORTS REVIEW—198 Mt. Vernon St., Dedham, MA 02026. Richard Braude, Editor.
Sports features, 500 to 1,000 words, on Jewish athletes. Photos. Pays $5 to $15, on publication.

THE LIVING WILDERNESS—The Wilderness Society, 1901 Pennsylvania Ave. N.W., Washington, DC 20006. James G. Deane, Editor.
Articles, to 5,000 words, with photos, on wilderness, wildlife, environment and nature subjects. Pays varying rates, on publication. Query.

MARIAH MAGAZINE—3401 West Division St., Chicago, IL 60651.
Articles, 2,500 to 5,000 words, on wilderness expeditions, shorter pieces on equipment and techniques. Pays about $50 per page, more for photos, on publication. Query.

MASSACHUSETTS WILDLIFE—Mass. Division of Fisheries and Game, Field Headquarters, Westboro, MA 01581. Jack Clancy, Managing Editor.
Articles, with photos, on wildlife and environmental and conservation issues. No payment.

MICHIGAN OUT-OF-DOORS—P.O. Box 30235, Lansing, MI 48909. Kenneth S. Lowe, Editor.

Features, 1,500 to 2,500 words, on hunting, fishing, camping and conservation in Michigan. Photos. Pays $50 to $100, on publication. Query.

MODERN CYCLE—7950 Deering Ave., Canoga Park, CA 91304. Rick Sieman, Editor.
Articles, 1,000 to 2,500 words, preferably with action photos, on motorcycle racing, personalities, major competitions, etc. Pays varying rates. No recent report. Query.

MOTOR TREND—8490 Sunset Blvd., Los Angeles, CA 90069. Robert E. Brown, Publisher.
Articles, 1,000 to 2,000 words, on foreign and domestic autos, racing, events; how-to pieces, profiles; photos. Pays from $350 for features, on acceptance.

MOTORBOAT—38 Commercial Wharf, Boston, MA 02110. Pete Smith, Editor.
Articles, 1,500 to 2,500 words, on powerboats: design, construction, power, equipment, use. Pays $350 to $400, on acceptance. Query.

MOTORCYCLE WEEKLY—4222 Campus Dr., Newport Beach, CA 92663. John Bethea, Editor.
Articles on motorcycles. Query on features and fiction; race coverage on assignment. Photos. Pays varying rates, $3 to $5 for photos.

MOTORCYCLIST—8490 Sunset Blvd., Los Angeles, CA 90069.
Articles, 1,000 to 3,000 words. Action photos. Pays varying rates, on acceptance. Query.

MOTORHOME LIFE—23945 Craftsman Rd., Calabasas, CA 91302. Beverly Edwards, Managing Editor.
Articles, to 2,000 words, with photos, on motorhomes, campers, self-propelled recreational vehicles; travel and how-to pieces. Pays $75 to $200, on publication.

MOUNTAIN GAZETTE—2025 York St., Denver, CO 80205. Gaylord Guenin, Editor.
Articles, 1,000 to 2,500 words, with photos, on mountaineering, skiing, outdoor recreation, environment, wilderness preservation. Fiction, 500 to 5,000 words. Pays $50 to $200, extra for photos, on acceptance. Query.

THE NATIONAL BOWLERS JOURNAL AND BILLIARD REVUE—Suite 3734, 875 North Michigan Ave., Chicago, IL 60611. Mort Luby, Jr., Editor.
Trade and consumer articles, 1,200 to 2,000 words, with photos, on bowling and billiards. Cartoons. Pays $50 to $75, $5 for cartoons, on publication.

NATIONAL FISHERMAN—Camden, ME 04843. David Getchell, Editor.
Serious news and feature stories, 50 to 3,500 words, on commercial fishing, workboat and pleasure-boat construction, maritime history. Photos. Pays around 2½¢ a word, extra for photos, within a month of acceptance.

NATIONAL PARKS AND CONSERVATION MAGAZINE—1701 18th St. N.W., Washington, DC 20009. Eugenia Horstman Connally, Editor.
Illustrated articles, 1,500 to 2,000 words, on national parks and monuments, endangered species, environmental problems and solutions, natural history, etc. Photos. Pays $75 to $100, on acceptance.

NATIONAL WILDLIFE AND INTERNATIONAL WILDLIFE—225 East Michigan, Milwaukee, WI 53202. Bob Strohm, Managing Editor.
Articles, 1,000 to 2,500 words, on wildlife, conservation, environment; outdoor how-to pieces. Photos. Pays varying rates, on acceptance. Query, with photos.

NATURAL HISTORY MAGAZINE—Central Park West at 79th St., New York, NY 10024. Alan Ternes, Editor.
Articles, 2,500 to 3,500 words, by specialists, on natural sciences, geology, astron-

omy, anthropology, environment, no travel pieces. Photos. Pays $500 for full-length articles, extra for photos, on publication.

NEW ENGLAND OUTDOORS—737 Statler Office Bldg., Boston, MA 02116. James Barry, Managing Editor.
Features, 100 to 4,000 words, on natural history and conservation in New England. Pays $75 to $150, on acceptance or publication. Query.

NORDIC WORLD—See *Bike World.*

NORTH ATLANTIC AIRCRAFT BULLETIN—See *Flight Line Times.*

NORTHEAST OUTDOORS—95 North Main St., Waterbury, CT 06702. John Florian, Editor.
Articles, from 800 words, on camping: tips, places to camp in Northeast, recreational vehicle hints, etc. Pays from $25, from $50 for articles with photos.

NORTHWEST SKIER—P.O. Box 5029, University Station, Seattle, WA 98105. Stephanie French, Editor.
Fiction, 250 to 2,500 words, and articles, 250 to 3,500 words, on skiing in Pacific Northwest. Pays from $1 per column inch, on publication.

1001 TRUCK & VAN IDEAS—12301 Wilshire Blvd., Los Angeles, CA 90025.
Brief illustrated articles on customized vans; technical how-to pieces, with photos, on do-it-yourself truck and van projects. Pays to $50 per printed page, on publication. Query.

OUTDOOR LIFE—380 Madison Ave., New York, NY 10017. John Fry, Editorial Director.
Articles on hunting, fishing and related subjects. Pays top rates, on acceptance. Query.

OUTDOORS—Outdoors Bldg., Columbia, MO 65201. Lee Cullimore, Editor.
Articles, to 1,200 words, with photos, on recreation, especially boating. Pays $35 to $125, on acceptance.

OUTDOORS IN GEORGIA—Dept. of Natural Resources, Room 714, 270 Washington St. S.W., Atlanta, GA 30334. Aaron Pass, Editor.
Articles, 1,200 to 1,800 words, with photos, on environment, historic sites, hunting and fishing in Georgia. Pays from $35, extra for photos, on acceptance. Query.

OUTSIDE—625 Third St., San Francisco, CA 94107. Will Hearst, Managing Editor.
High-quality articles on nature and the outdoors. Pays varying rates, on publication. Query, and enclose clippings of published work.

PACIFIC SKIPPER—P.O. Box 1698, Newport Beach, CA 92663. Wayne Carpenter, Editor.
Illustrated cruising and boating articles; how-to and historical pieces. Pays $50 to $250, on publication.

PADDLE WORLD—370 Seventh Ave., New York, NY 10001. Robert E. Abrams, Editor.
Articles on unusual platform-tennis tournaments, courts and players. Pays varying rates, on publication.

PARACHUTIST—U.S. Parachute Assn., 806 15th St., N.W., Suite 444, Washington, DC 20005. Michael Leeds, Director.
Articles on sport parachuting. Photos. Pays in copies.

PENNSYLVANIA ANGLER—Pennsylvania Fish Commission, P.O. Box 1673, Harris-

burg, PA 17120. J. F. Yoder, Editor.
Articles, 750 to 2,500 words, with photos, on freshwater fishing, boating and camping in Pennsylvania. Pays $35 to $175, on acceptance.

PENNSYLVANIA GAME NEWS—Game Commission, Harrisburg, PA 17120. Bob Bell, Editor.
Articles, to 2,500 words, with photos, on outdoor subjects, except fishing and boating. Pays from 3¢ a word, extra for photos, on acceptance.

PICKUP, VAN & 4WD (PV4)—1499 Monrovia Ave., Newport Beach, CA 92663. Don E. Brown, Editor.
How-to articles, 2,500 words, on off-road driving or camping with pickups, vans or four-wheel drive vehicles. Features on older models. Photos. Pays $50 per page, on publication.

POOL 'N' PATIO—3923 West Sixth St., Los Angeles, CA 90020. Fay Coupe, Editor.
Articles, 500 to 1,500 words, for owners of residential swimming pools. Pays 5¢ a word, on acceptance.

POPULAR SCIENCE MONTHLY—380 Madison Ave., New York, NY 10017. Hubert P. Luckett, Editor-in-Chief.
Factual articles, to 2,000 words, with photos, on new products for home, car, boat, workshop or outdoor activities. Pays around $150 per printed page, on acceptance. Query.

POWDER MAGAZINE—P.O. Box 1028, Dana Point, CA 92629. Dave Moe and Neil Stebbins, Editors.
Articles and fiction, 100 to 2,500 words, on skiing, racing, touring, equipment, instruction, travel, etc. Photos. Pays 7¢ to 10¢ a word, extra for photos, on publication.

POWERBOAT—P.O. Box 3842, Van Nuys, CA 91407. Bob Brown, Editor.
Articles, to 1,500 words, with photos, for powerboat owners, on outstanding achievements, water-skiing, competition; nontechnical how-to pieces. Pays around $50 per page, on publication.

PRIVATE PILOT—2377 South El Camino Real, San Clemente, CA 92672. Dennis Shattuck, Editor.
True-experience articles, technical analyses, 1,000 to 4,000 words, for aviation enthusiasts. Photos. Pays $25 to $200, on publication. Query.

PV4—See *Pickup, Van & 4WD.*

RAILROAD MAGAZINE—420 Lexington Ave., New York, NY 10017. Freeman Hubbard, Editor.
Technical, anecdotal articles, 2,000 to 3,000 words, on railroading, by experts; no hobby pieces. Photos. Pays 5¢ a word, on or before publication.

ROAD RIDER MAGAZINE—P.O. Box 678, South Laguna, CA 92677. R. L. Carpenter, Managing Editor.
Articles, to 2,500 words, on motorcycle touring. Cartoons. Pays $50 to $100, on publication.

RUDDER—See *Sea.*

RUNNER'S WORLD—P.O. Box 366, Mountain View, CA 94042. Richard Benyo, Managing Editor.
Articles, 500 to 3,000 words, on races and running meets; personal-experience pieces; personality profiles, interviews; short opinion pieces for "Runner's Forum." Pays $30

to $50 per printed page, extra for photos, on publication. Query.

SAIL—38 Commercial Wharf, Boston, MA 02110. Keith Taylor, Editor.
Articles, 1,500 to 2,000 words, with photos, on sailing, sailboats, equipment, etc.
Pays $75 to $350, on publication.

SAILORS' GAZETTE—6727 1st Ave., South, Suite 107, St. Petersburg, FL 33707.
John A. Weber, Editor.
Articles, 500 to 2,000 words, with photos, on Southeastern sailing, cruising and technical how-to's. Pays 3¢ to 6¢ a word, $5 for photos, on publication.

SALMON TROUT STEELHEADER—P.O. Box 02112, Portland, OR 97202. Frank W.
Amato, Editor.
Factual articles, 750 to 2,500 words, with photos, on salmon, trout and steelhead
fishing in western states and British Columbia. Pays $45 to $100, on publication.

SALT WATER SPORTSMAN—10 High St., Boston, MA 02110. Frank Woolner, Editor.
How-to-articles, 2,500 to 3,000 words, on saltwater sport fishing. Fishing tips, 500
to 700 words. Action photos or illustrations required. Pays from 5¢ a word, on
acceptance.

SEA (Combining *Rudder*)—1499 Monrovia Ave., Newport Beach, CA 92663. Chris
Caswell, Editor.
Western, Eastern and Southern editions. How-to articles, 2,000 words, on boat operation and cruising destinations. Humor; photos. Pays from 10¢ a word, extra for
photos, on acceptance. Query.

SHOOTING TIMES—News Plaza, Peoria, IL 61601. Alex Bartimo, Executive Editor.
Articles, 1,000 to 2,000 words, with photos, on guns, hunting, gunsmithing. Pays on
acceptance. Query.

SKATEBOARD WORLD—Daisy Publishing, 16200 Ventura Blvd., Encino, CA 91436.
Jill Sherman, Editor.
Articles, 200 to 2,000 words, for teens, on all facets of skateboarding in the U. S.,
Europe and Asia. Pays from $25 to $250, on publication. Query.

SKATING—Sears Crescent, Suite 500, City Hall Plaza, Boston, MA 02108. Gregory
Smith, Editor.
Articles, to 1,500 words, on amateur ice figure skating, clubs, skaters. Photos. Pays
2½¢ a word, $5 per photo, on publication.

SKI MAGAZINE—380 Madison Ave., New York, NY 10017. Dick Needham, Editor.
Articles, 1,300 to 2,000 words, with photos, on skiing. Pays $75 to $200, on acceptance. Query.

SKI RACING—75 Main St., Fair Haven, VT 05743. Pam Penfold, Managing Editor.
Interviews, articles and how-to pieces, to 1,500 words, relating to national and international ski competitions. Photos. Pays from $1 per column inch, on publication.

SKIER—22 High St., Brattleboro, VT 05301. Jack Soper, Editor.
Eastern Ski Assn. publication. Articles on skiing, techniques, history, etc. Human-interest pieces, profiles. Photos; cartoons. Pays $35, on publication.

SKIER'S DIRECTORY—38 Commercial Wharf, Boston, MA 02110. Tina Bentley,
Managing Editor.
Articles, 1,500 words, on any subject relating to skiing. Pays varying rates, on
publication.

SKIING MAGAZINE—One Park Ave., New York, NY 10016. Al Greenberg, Editor-in-
Chief.
Articles, 1,000 to 3,000 words, on skiing, travel, technique. Short pieces, from 800

words; profiles, humor, Pays $100 to $500, on acceptance.

SKIN DIVER MAGAZINE—8490 Sunset Blvd., Los Angeles, CA 90069. Paul Tzimoulis, Editor.
Illustrated articles, 1,000 to 2,000 words, on skin-diving activities, equipment and personalities. Pays $35 per page, on publication.

SMITHSONIAN—Arts and Industries Bldg., 900 Jefferson Dr., Washington, DC 20560. Edward K. Thompson, Editor.
Articles, 700 to 4,000 words, on wildlife, environment, science (hard and natural), art, history. Pays on acceptance. Query.

SNOTRACK—225 East Michigan Ave., Milwaukee, WI 53202. Bill Vint, Editor.
Articles, 700 to 2,000 words, with photos, on snowmobiling, races, rallies, trail rides. How-to pieces; humor; cartoons; photos. Pays to $100, on acceptance. Query.

SNOWMOBILE WEST—P.O. Box 981, Idaho Falls, ID 83401. Loel H. Schoonover, Editor.
Articles, around 1,200 words, on snowmobiling in the western states. Photos. Pays 3¢ a word, $5 per photo, on publication. Query.

SOCCER AMERICA MAGAZINE—P.O. Box 23704, Oakland, CA 94623. Clay Berling, Publisher.
Articles, to 3,000 words, on soccer; news, features, profiles, coaching tips, etc. Pays 1¢ per word, or 50¢ per column inch, within 60 days of publication.

SOCCER CORNER MAGAZINE—16200 Ventura Blvd., Encino, CA 91316. Grahame Jones, Editor.
Articles, 750 to 2,500 words, with photos, on U.S. soccer; some pieces on foreign soccer. Pays varying rates, extra for photos, on publication.

SOCCER WORLD—See *Bike World.*

SOUTHERN AVIATION TIMES—See *Flight Line Times.*

SPORT—641 Lexington Ave., New York, NY 10022. Sheryl Flatow, Managing Editor. Overstocked.

SPORTS AFIELD—250 West 55th St., New York, NY 10019. David Maxey, Editor.
Articles, 500 to 2,000 words, on hunting, fishing, conservation, travel, camping, personal experiences. Photo-essays; how-to pieces; humor, fiction; photos. Pays top rates, on acceptance.

SPORTS AFIELD FISHING ANNUAL—250 West 55th St., New York, NY 10019.
How-to and personal-experience articles, 3,000 words, with photos, on fishing. How-to fillers. Pays from $400, on acceptance. Query. Same address and requirements for *Sports Afield Hunting Annual.*

SPORTS ILLUSTRATED—Rockefeller Center, New York, NY 10020. Robert W. Creamer, Articles Editor.
Articles, 1,500 to 5,000 words, on sports personalities, issues, trends, events, off-beat news features. Pays from $1,000 to $1,750, $250 to $450 for shorter features, on acceptance.

SPORTSWOMAN—630 North Court St., Palatine, IL 60067.
Articles, 1,000 to 2,000 words; interviews with female sports stars. Photos. Pays $25 to $100, extra for photos, on publication. Query.

STOCK CAR RACING—1420 Prince St., Alexandria, VA 22314. Dick Berggren, Editor.
Articles, 1,000 to 3,000 words, on stock-car racing, personalities, etc. Photos. Pays $50 to $150, extra for photos, on publication. Query.

STREET CHOPPER—2145 West La Palma, Anaheim, CA 92801. Bob Clark, Editor.
Technical articles, 4,000 words, with photos, on motorcycles. Pays $50 per printed page, on acceptance.

SURFER MAGAZINE—Box 1028, Dana Point, CA 92629. Steve Pezman, Editor.
Articles, 500 to 5,000 words, on surfing, places, surfers, etc. Photos. Pays 5¢ to 10¢ a word, on publication.

SWIMMING WORLD—8622 Bellanca Ave., Los Angeles, CA 90045. Bob Ingram, Editor.
Articles, from 500 words, for high school, collegiate and national competitive swimmers and divers, on nutrition, training, motivation, etc.; profiles. Pays varying rates, on acceptance.

TAE KWON DO DIGEST—144 West 12th Ave., Denver, CO 80204.
Articles and fiction, 1,500 to 4,000 words, on personalities in the martial arts, tournaments, etc. Book reviews; poetry; fillers; photos. Pays 1¢ to 3¢ a word, on publication.

TENNIS—495 Westport Ave., Norwalk, CT 06856. Shepherd Campbell, Editor.
Instructional articles, features, profiles of tennis stars, 500 to 2,000 words. Fillers; humor. Photos, drawings. Pays $100 to $500, from $25 for fillers and humor, on publication. Query.

TENNIS DIRECTORY—38 Commercial Wharf, Boston, MA 02110. Tina Bentley, Managing Editor.
Articles, 1,500 words, on any subject relating to tennis. Pays varying rates, on publication.

TENNIS U.S.A.—Chilton Co., Chilton Way, Radnor, PA 19089. Robert L. Gillen, Editor.
Articles, 500 to 3,000 words, on tennis personalities, events, fashion, travel, equipment, instruction. Humorous poetry, 5 to 25 lines; cartoons, photos. Pays $50 to $350, on acceptance. Query.

TRACK AND FIELD NEWS—Box 296, Los Altos, CA 94022. Garry Hill, Editor.
Features on track and field; profiles. Photos. Pays varying rates, on publication. Query.

TRAILER BOATS—1440 West Walnut, P.O. Box 7030, Compton, CA 90224. Ralph Poole, Editor.
Factual articles, 1,500 to 2,500 words, on boat, trailer or car maintenance and operation, skiing, fishing, cruising. Fillers; humor. Pays 7¢ to 10¢ a word, on publication. Query.

TRAILER LIFE—23945 Craftsman Rd., Calabasas, CA 91302. Denis M. Rouse, Publisher.
Articles, to 2,500 words, with photos, on trailering, truck campers, motorhomes, hobbies, etc.; how-to pieces. Pays to $175, on publication. Send for writer's guide.

TROUT—4620 East Evans, Denver, CO 80222. Alvin R. Grove, Editor.
Articles, 800 to 2,500 words, with photos, on trout management, related conservation projects. Pays $25 to $80, $5 per photo, on acceptance. Query.

TURF AND SPORT DIGEST—511-13 Oakland Ave., Baltimore, MD 21212. Michael Yockel, Editor.
Articles, 1,500 to 4,000 words, on national turf personalities and approaches to handicapping. Pays $75 to $125, on publication. Query.

VAN WORLD (formerly *RV World*)—16200 Ventura Blvd., Encino, CA 91316. Chris Hosford, Editor.

Articles, to 1,500 words, with photos, on custom vans; how-to pieces on van customizing and CB radio. Pays $40 per printed page, on publication.

VIRGINIA WILDLIFE—4010 West Broad St., P.O. Box 11104, Richmond, VA 23230. Harry Gillam, Editor.
Articles, around 1,500 words, on Virginia hunting, fishing, boating, resource management. Photos. Pays 3 ¢ a word, from $5 per photo, on acceptance. Query.

WASHINGTON FISHING HOLES—114 Ave. C, Snohomish, WA 98290. Milt Keizer, Co-Editor.
Detailed articles, 800 to 1,500 words, on specific Washington State fishing areas; must follow magazine style. Pays $25 to $50, on publication.

WATER SKIER—P.O. Box 191, Winter Haven, FL 33880. Thomas C. Hardman, Editor.
Offbeat articles and photo-essays on water-skiing. Pays varying rates, on acceptance.

THE WESTERN HORSEMAN—P.O. Box 7980, Colorado Springs, CO 80933. Chan Bergen, Editor.
Articles, around 1,500 words, with photos, on care and training of horses; historical pieces. Pays varying rates, on acceptance. Query.

WESTWAYS—Box 2890, Terminal Annex, Los Angeles, CA 90051. Frances Ring, Editor.
Articles, 700 to 2,500 words, on western U.S., Canada and Mexico; natural science, travel, history, personalities, sports, etc. Poetry; photos. Pays 10¢ a word, on acceptance, $25 to $100 for photos, $25 for poetry, on publication. Query.

WOMAN GOLFER—Daisy Publishing Co., 16200 Ventura Blvd., Encino, CA 91316. Rhonda Glenn, Editor.
Instructional articles by nationally-known pros; golfing personality pieces; competition coverage; fashion layouts and tournament action. Fillers, humorous pieces, jokes, etc. No fiction. Pays $40 per page, extra for photos, on publication. Query.

WOODALL'S TRAILER & RV TRAVEL—500 Hyacinth Pl., Highland Park, IL 60035. Kirk Landers, Editor.
Articles, 300 to 3,000 words, on family camping, travel, outdoor living; how-to pieces on renovating, maintaining and utilizing recreational vehicles. Pays to 10¢ a word, on acceptance. Query, with illustrations. Incorporating *Camping and Trailering Guide.*

WOODENBOAT—P.O. Box 78, Brooklin, ME 04616. Jonathan A. Wilson, Editor/ Publisher.
Articles, 1,000 to 4,000 words, on wooden sail- and powerboats, repair and restoration, boatbuilding, designers and design; no cruising tales. Photos, drawings. Pays from $50, after acceptance. Send for writer's guide.

THE WORLD OF RODEO—Box 660, Billings, MT 59103. Dave Allen, Editor.
Articles, to 1,000 words, with photos, cartoons, and drawings, on rodeo and the people involved in it. Fillers and humor, up to 100 words, and western poetry, to 30 lines. Pays $1 an inch, minimum, extra for photos, on publication.

WORLD TENNIS—385 Madison Ave., New York, NY 10017. Ronald Bookman, Editor.
Features and instructional articles, 1,000 to 2,000 words, with photos, on tennis. Photos of tournaments. Pays varying rates, on publication. Query.

YACHTING—50 West 44th St., New York, NY 10036. William W. Robinson, Editor.
Articles on recreational boating (sail and power), history; technical pieces on yachting. Pays $250 to $350, on acceptance.

YANKEE MAGAZINE'S GUIDE TO NEW ENGLAND—581 Boylston St., Boston, MA 02116. Georgia Orcutt, Editor.

Articles, 1,000 to 2,000 words, on unusual New England activities; no history or biography. Photos. Pays $50 to $200, on acceptance. Query with outline.

YOUNG ATHLETE—Box 513, Edmonds, WA 98020. Dan Zadra, Editor.

Features, to 1,800 words, on pro athletes. Profiles of boy or girl and handicapped athletes; how-to pieces; tips from coaches for "Coaches Corner"; inspirational personal experiences; humor. Photos, photo-essays. Pays 7¢ a word, on publication. Query with outline.

WOMEN'S MAGAZINES, HOME AND GARDEN PUBLICATIONS

ALLIED PUBLICATIONS, INC.—P.O. Box 9820, Fort Worth, TX 76107. Didi Scott, Associate Editor.

Articles, with photos, on home and family, travel, beauty, decorating, hobbies, etc. Profiles; how-to pieces; articles of interest to hairstylists. Pays 5¢ a word, $5 per photo, on acceptance.

AMERICAN BABY—575 Lexington Ave., New York, NY 10022. Judith Nolte, Editor.

Articles, 400 to 1,500 words, for new or expectant parents; pieces on child care. Pays varying rates, on publication.

THE AMERICAN ROSE MAGAZINE—P.O. Box 30,000 Shreveport, LA 71130. Harold S. Goldstein, Editor.

Articles on home rose gardens: varieties, products, etc. Fillers. No payment.

THE ANTIQUES JOURNAL—P.O. Box 88129, Dunwoody, GA 30338. John Mebane, Editor.

Illustrated articles, to 2,000 words, on antiques and collectibles. Pays $50 to $75, on acceptance. Query.

BABY CARE—52 Vanderbilt Ave., New York, NY 10017. Evelyn A. Podsiadlo, Editor.

Articles, to 1,800 words, on infant care, emotional and physical development of infants, etc. Humorous or serious features, to 1,000 words. Cartoons; short poetry; fillers. Pays $10 to $125, on acceptance.

BABY TALK—66 East 34th St., New York, NY 10016. Patricia Irons, Editor.

Articles, 500 to 1,000 words, by mother or father, on babies, baby care, etc.

BETTER HOMES AND GARDENS—1716 Locust St., Des Moines, IA 50336. James A. Autry, Editor.

Articles on home and family entertainment, money management, health, travel and cars. Pays top rates, on acceptance. Query with outline.

BON APPETIT—5900 Wilshire Blvd., Los Angeles, CA 90036. Paige Rense, Editor-in-Chief.

Covers gourmet cooking, fine living. Queries welcome. Enclose samples of published work. Rates vary. Payment is on acceptance.

BRIDE'S—350 Madison Ave., New York, NY 10017. Peyton Bailey, Articles Editor.

Articles, 1,000 to 3,000 words, for brides and brides-to-be. Pays $300 to $500. Query.

CAPPER'S WEEKLY—616 Jefferson St., Topeka, KS 66607. Dorothy Harvey, Editor.

Articles, 300 to 500 words: human interest, personal experience, historical. Poetry, to 15 lines, on nature, home, family. Letters on women's interests, for "Heart of the Home." Jokes, cartoons. Pays varying rates, on publication.

CHATELAINE—481 University Ave., Toronto, Ont., Canada M5W 1A7. Doris Anderson, Editor.

Fiction, 4,000 words, on romance, family and social themes. Articles, 3,000 words, on controversial subjects and personalities of interest to Canadian women. Personal-experience pieces. Pays $300 for personal-experience pieces, from $600 for articles, from $400 for fiction, $25 to $200 for fillers, on acceptance.

CHOMO-URI—P.O. Box 1057, Amherst, MA 01003.
Articles, fiction and poetry on women in a changing society. Pays in copies.

THE CHRISTIAN HOME—201 Eighth Ave. South, Nashville, TN 37202. David Bradley, Editor.
Educational or humorous articles, 1,000 to 2,000 words, for parents. Poetry. Pays 2½¢ a word, 50¢ a line for poetry, on acceptance.

THE CHRISTIAN SCIENCE MONITOR—One Norway St., Boston, MA 02115. John Hughes, Editor. Nan Trent, Women's Editor. Phyllis Hanes, Food Editor.
Articles on homemaking, food, fashion, family, consumer affairs, women of achievement, etc. Pays varying rates.

COACHING: WOMEN'S ATHLETICS (formerly *Woman Coach*)—P.O. Box 867, Wallingford, CT 06492. Cindy Whitman, Editor.
Articles, 1,000 to 2,500 words, on coaching techniques and strategies in women's sports. Features, 800 to 1,000 words, on coaching sidelights. Pays 2½¢ a word, on publication. Query.

COSMOPOLITAN—224 West 57th St., New York, NY 10019. Helen Gurley Brown, Editor; James Watters, Managing Editor; Harris Dienstfrey, Fiction Editor.
Articles, to 4,000 words, and features, 2,000 to 3,000 words, on issues affecting young career women. Fiction on male-female relationships: short shorts, 1,500 to 3,000 words; short stories, 5,000 to 6,000 words; mystery and other novels; condensed books, 30,000 words. Pays $1,000 to $1,500 for full-length articles, $1,000 for short stories, $300 to $600 for short shorts.

DECORATING AND CRAFT IDEAS—1303 Foch St., Fort Worth, TX 76107. Frederica Daugherty, Editor.
Articles, about 500 words, on unique craft projects, with original patterns and instructions. Pays $100 to $150, on acceptance.

EARLY AMERICAN LIFE—Box 1831, Harrisburg, PA 17105. Robert G. Miner, Editor.
Illustrated articles, 1,000 to 4,000 words, on early American life: arts, crafts, furnishings and architecture. Pays from $25 to $200, on acceptance. Query.

ESSENCE—1500 Broadway, New York, NY 10036.
"The magazine for today's black woman." Pays varying rates, after publication. Query.

EXPECTING—52 Vanderbilt Ave., New York, NY 10017. Evelyn A. Podsiadlo, Editor.
Articles, 700 to 1,800 words, for expectant mothers. Medical pieces by professionals. Pays $50 to $125, on acceptance.

FAMILY CIRCLE—488 Madison Ave., New York, NY 10022. Arthur Hettich, Editor.
Articles on family, consumer affairs, health, jobs and finances, food, travel and gardening. Pays top rates.

THE FAMILY FOOD GARDEN—Route 1, Box 877, McCourtney Rd., Grass Valley, CA 95945. George S. Wells, Editor.
Practical articles, with photos, on home gardening and livestock. Pays modest rates, on publication.

THE FAMILY HANDYMAN—1999 Shepard Rd., St. Paul, MN 55116.
Non-technical articles, to 1,000 words, with photos, on do-it-yourself home improvement. How-to pieces on gardening. Fillers, 100 to 300 words. Pays $40 to $100 for articles, $5 to $15 for fillers, on publication.

FAMILY HEALTH—149 Fifth Ave., New York, NY 10010.
Articles, to 3,000 words, and photo essays, on health, beauty, child care, nutrition, medical subjects and personal experiences. Pays from $500 for features, on acceptance. Query with outline.

FAMILY WEEKLY—641 Lexington Ave., New York, NY 10022; Scott DeGarmo, Executive Editor; Tim Mulligan, Managing Editor.
Short, lively articles on prominent individuals and family advice. Pays $300 to $500, on acceptance. Queries only.

FLOWER & GARDEN MAGAZINE—4251 Pennsylvania, Kansas City, MO 64111. Rachel Snyder, Editor-in-Chief.
How-to articles, to 1,500 words, with photos, on indoor and outdoor gardening. Pays from 4¢ a word, on acceptance.

GLAMOUR—350 Madison Ave., New York, NY 10017. Ruth Whitney, Editor-in-Chief.
Articles on subjects of interest to young women: medicine, mental health, unusual careers, and social, economic or emotional problems. (Fashion and beauty material staff-written.) Personal-experience or opinion pieces, 1,500 to 3,000 words. Pays from $300.

GOOD HOUSEKEEPING—959 Eighth Eve., New York, NY 10019. Jean Block, Articles Editor.
Dramatic personal-experience articles on relationships, individual achievement, practical living, romance, etc. Fiction, 2,000 to 5,000 words, by published writers and "beginners with demonstrable talent." Pays top rates, on acceptance.

GOURMET—777 Third Ave., New York, NY 10017. Gail Zweigenthal, Managing Editor.
Articles, 2,500 to 3,000 words, on food, travel and good living, for a sophisticated audience. Recipes only in connection with articles. Pays on acceptance.

GREENLEAVES—420 Lexington Ave., Rm. 2540, New York, NY 10017. Mary Byrnes, Editor.
Articles, to 3,000 words, on indoor gardening, with a sophisticated approach on a broad range of subjects: houseplant how-to information, herbs, terrace gardening, decorating, etc. Pays varying rates.

HANDY ANDY—Parents' Magazine Enterprises, 52 Vanderbilt Ave., New York, NY 10017.
Short pieces, 250 to 750 words, on do-it-yourself home improvements. Pays on acceptance. Query.

HARLEQUIN—Harlequin Enterprises, Ltd., 240 Duncan Mill Rd., Suite 605, Don Mills, Ont., Canada M3B 1Z4. Beth McGregor, Editor.
Upbeat romantic fiction, 1,000 to 5,00 words. Inspirational articles, 1,000 to 2,000 words; travel pieces; general-interest features. Pays varying rates, on acceptance. Query with outline and sample paragraph.

HORTICULTURE—300 Massachusetts Ave., Boston, MA 02115. Paul Trachtman, Editor.
Authoritative articles, 500 to 3,000 words, on gardening, horticulture and ecology. Pays varying rates.

HOUSE BEAUTIFUL—717 Fifth Ave., New York, NY 10022. Wallace Guenther, Editor.
Query with detailed outline. Pays on acceptance.

HOUSE & GARDEN—350 Madison Ave., New York, NY 10017. Denise Otis, Associate Editor.
Articles on decorating, entertaining and crafts. Rarely buys unsolicited articles.

HOUSE PLANTS AND PORCH GARDENS—1 Aldwyn Center, Villanova, PA 19085.

Articles, 1,500 to 5,000 words, on horticulture: types of plants, techniques, new developments, etc. Photos. Pays 10¢ a word, on publication. Query with outline.

HOUSTON HOME & GARDEN—2472 Bolsover, Houston, TX 77006. Karleen Koen, Editor.
Articles on decorating, regional gardening, home management, household repairs, etc. Pays $2.50 per column inch, on publication. Query.

HOW TO, THE HOMEOWNER'S HANDBOOK—380 Madison Ave., New York, NY 10017. Jim Liston, Editor.
Articles, 500 to 600 words, with photos, on do-it-yourself household construction and gardening projects. Pays $100 to $150 per printed page, on acceptance. Query.

LADIES' HOME JOURNAL—641 Lexington Ave., New York, NY 10022.
Limited market: most articles staff-written or assigned through agents.

LADYCOM—1800 M St., N.W., Suite 650 So., Washington, DC 20036.
Articles, to 2,000 words, for military wives in the U.S. and overseas. Pays $50 to $150, after acceptance. Query.

LADY'S CIRCLE—21 West 26th St., New York, NY 10010. Shirley Howard, Editor.
Articles, 2,000 to 3,000 words, with photos, on crafts, hobbies, baby care, home management and gardening. Pays $125, extra for photos, on publication. Query with outline.

LADY'S CIRCLE HOME CRAFTS—21 West 26th St., New York, NY 10010. Frank W. Coggins, Editor.
Articles, with photos, on handicrafts: weaving, engraving, woodworking, embroidering, etc. Pays varying rates, on publication.

LILITH—Box 16C, 500 East 63rd St., New York, NY 10021. Susan W. Schneider, Editor.
Articles and fiction, 1,500 to 3,000 words, on relating the women's movement to Jewish issues. Pays in copies. Query.

LUTHERAN WOMEN—2900 Queen Ln., Philadelphia, PA 19129.
Articles, with photos, on subjects of interest to Christian women. Pays $50, on publication.

McCALL'S—230 Park Ave., New York, NY 10017. Robert Stein, Editor.
Articles, 3,000 words, on current issues; reportorial pieces, 300 to 800 words, for "Right Now." Fiction. Pays top rates, on acceptance.

McCALL'S NEEDLEWORK & CRAFTS MAGAZINE—230 Park Ave., New York, NY 10017. Margaret Gilman, Managing Editor.
Directions for making original handicraft items; articles on unusual handcrafts. Pays varying rates, on acceptance.

MADEMOISELLE—350 Madison Ave., New York, NY 10017. Mary Cantwell, Managing Editor; Beth McNichols, Fiction Editor.
Articles and fiction, 1,200 to 6,500 words, for young women. Pays varying rates for articles, from $300 for fiction, on acceptance.

MOBILE LIVING—P.O. Box 1418, Sarasota, FL 33578. Frances Neel, Editor.
Articles, 500 to 1,000 words, for travel-trailer and camper owners, on travel clubs, vacation trips, etc. Pays 1¢ a word, on publication. Query.

MODERN BRIDE—One Park Ave., New York, NY 10016.
Articles, from 1,500 words, for bride and groom, on etiquette, the home, honeymoon travel, etc. Pays on acceptance.

MODERN MATURITY—215 Long Beach Blvd., Long Beach, CA 90801. Hubert Pryor, Editor.

Service articles on housing, food, health, employment and hobbies, for persons over 55. Nostalgia, inspirational articles, personality pieces, Americana, personal accounts. Short stories. Pays $50 to $500, extra for photos, on acceptance.

THE MOTHER EARTH NEWS—P.O. Box 70, Hendersonville, NC 28739. John Shuttleworth, Editor.
Articles on ecology, back-to-the-land movement, down-home cooking, first-hand accounts of homesteading or adventurous journeys. Pays $20 to $500, on acceptance.

MOTHER'S MANUAL—176 Cleveland Dr., Croton-on-Hudson, NY 10520. Beth Waterfall, Editor.
Well-researched articles on early childhood learning and behavior, family life styles, etc. Personal-experience articles about mothers. Pays on publication.

MOVING OUT—4866 Third Ave., Wayne State University, Detroit, MI 48202. Margaret Kaminski, Editor.
Feminist short stories, essays and short poetry; interviews with prominent women. Pays in copies.

MS.—370 Lexington Ave., New York, NY 10017. Address Manuscript Editor.
Articles and fiction on topics relevant to women. Pays varying rates, on acceptance.

NEW WOMAN—P.O. Box 9820, Fort Worth, TX 76107.
Articles for women combining career and marriage. Regular features on finance, legal rights, divorce, food, personalities, travel, beauty, etc. Pays varying rates.

1001 CHRISTMAS IDEAS—Lopez Publications, 21 West 26th St., New York, NY 10010. Barbara Jacksier, Editor.
Craft and needlework projects, photos, and instructions. Pays $25 to $75, on publication. Query.

ORGANIC GARDENING AND FARMING—33 East Minor St., Emmaus, PA 18049. M. C. Goldman, Managing Editor.
Articles, to 2,500 words, on organic agriculture: biological pest control, natural fertilizers, etc. Photos; fillers. Pays $50 to $250, $25 to $50 for fillers, on publication.

OVER THE GARDEN FENCE—3960 Cobblestone, Dallas, TX 75229. Jay Altes, Editor.
Articles, to 2,000 words, on natural living in Texas: nutrition, organic gardening, environmental protection, how-tos, etc. Pays in copies, after publication.

PARENTS' MAGAZINE—52 Vanderbilt Ave., New York, NY 10017. Genevieve Millet Landau, Editor-in-Chief.
Articles, 2,000 words. on physical, emotional and mental development of infants, school children and adolescents, family, adults in the community, etc. Lively articles on research in medicine, science, education, etc. Prefers colloquial style with quotes from experts. Pays on acceptance.

PARTY, THE MAGAZINE OF HOME ENTERTAINING—Box P, Manhattan Beach, CA 90266. Sandra A. Shaw, Editor.
Features, 1,500 to 2,500 words, on how to plan successful parties, aimed at women. Pays to $200, on publication. Query.

PERFECT HOME—427 Sixth Ave. S.E., Cedar Rapids, IA 53400. Donna Nichols Hahn, Editor.
Photo essays on moderate-cost homes, remodeling projects, unusual decorating, etc. Query.

PLANTS ALIVE—5509 First Ave. South, Seattle, WA 98108.
Articles, to 1,000 words, on houseplants, greenhouses and outdoor container gardening. Pays 3¢ a word, $10 per photo, on publication.

PLAYGIRL—1801 Century Park East, Century City, Suite 2300, Los Angeles, CA

90067. Joyce Dudney Fleming, Editor.
In-depth articles of interest to contemporary women. Fiction, 1,000 to 7,500 words. Humor; satire. Pays $300 to $1,000, after acceptance. Query.

QUILT WORLD—Box 338, Chester, MA 01011. Barbara Hall Pederson, Editor.
Articles, 1,000 words, with photos, or illustrations: innovative quilt-making techniques; original quilt designs; history, nostalgia, and short humor related to quilt-making. Pays 2¢ to 5¢ a word, extra for photos, on publication.

REDBOOK—230 Park Ave., New York, NY 10017.

Articles and fiction of special interest to young women. Pays from $1,000 for short stories, $850 for short shorts (1,400 to 1,600 words), from $3,000 for novellas (12,000 to 25,000 words), $7,500 for full-length novels, on acceptance. Manuscripts without stamped, self-addressed envelopes will not be returned. Query for articles.

THE SECRETARY—2440 Pershing Rd., G-10, Kansas City, MO 64108. Shirley S. Englund, Editor.
Articles, 800 to 2,000 words, on office procedures, secretarial skills, administrative responsibilities, unusual secretarial careers, etc. Pays on publication.

SPHERE—420 Lexington Ave., New York, NY 10017.
Imaginative how-to articles for women. Queries only.

SPORTSWOMAN—630 North Court St., Palatine, IL 60067.
Articles, 1,000 to 2,000 words, on unusual sports; interviews with women sports stars. Cartoons; photos. Pays $25 to $100 for articles, $25 for cartoons, $25 per photo, on publication. Query.

SUNSET MAGAZINE—Menlo Park, CA 94025. Proctor Mellquist, Editor.
No free-lance material at present.

TALK—380 Madison Ave., New York, NY 10017. Berenice C. Kennedy, Editor.
Articles and fiction, to 2,000 words, of interest to women. Short, humorous poems; fillers. Pays varying rates, on publication.

TODAY'S CHRISTIAN PARENT—8121 Hamilton Ave., Cincinnati, OH 45231. Wilma L. Shaffer, Editor.
Articles, 600 to 1,200 words, on application of Christian principles in child-rearing. Ideas for children's activities. Pays varying rates.

TODAY'S SECRETARY—1221 Ave. of Americas, New York, NY 10020. Lauren Bahr, Editor.
Articles, 1,000 to 1,500 words, with photos, on young secretaries, new office techniques and trends, self-improvement, etc. Fiction, 500 to 1,000 words, on secretaries' business lives (rarely uses romance). Pays $60 to $150 for articles, $50 for fiction. Query.

US MAGAZINE—Taylor & Ives Publishing Co., 30 East 42nd St., New York, NY 10017.
Articles, 1,000 to 1,200 words, of interest to military wives and families overseas. Pays varying rates. Query.

VIVA—909 Third Ave., New York, NY 10022. Ernie Baxter, Executive Editor.
Articles, 2,500 to 5,000 words, on problems of modern women: social, sexual, economic, emotional, etc. Humor. Pays $250 to $1,000. Query.

VOGUE—350 Madison Ave., New York, NY 10017. Leo Lerman, Consulting Features Editor.
Articles, to 1,500 words, on women, the arts, travel, medicine and health. Sometimes buys unsolicited manuscripts. Pays good rates, on acceptance.

WEIGHT WATCHERS MAGAZINE—149 Fifth Ave., New York, NY 10010. Bernadette Carr, Editor.
Articles on weight loss; how-to pieces. Pays on acceptance.

THE WOMAN—235 Park Ave. South, New York, NY 10003. Diana Lurvey, Editor.
First-person articles from viewpoint of married or once-married woman. Pays $50, on acceptance.

WOMAN COACH—See *Coaching: Women's Athletics.*

WOMAN GOLFER—16200 Ventura Blvd., Encino, CA 91316. Rhonda Glenn, Editor.
Instructional articles, golfing personality pieces, competition coverage, fashion layouts and tournament action. Fillers, humorous pieces, jokes, etc. Pays $40 per page, extra for photos, on publication. Query; articles on assignment only.

WOMAN'S DAY—1515 Broadway, New York, NY 10036. Rebecca Greer, Articles Editor. Eileen Herbert Jordan, Fiction Editor.
Serious, human-interest or humorous articles, to 3,500 words, on marriage, child-rearing, health, relationships, money management, leisure activities, etc. Short stories. Pays top rates, on acceptance. Query for articles.

WOMEN: A JOURNAL OF LIBERATION—3028 Greenmount Ave., Baltimore, MD 21218.
Articles and fiction, to 3,000 words, about women. Poetry; artwork; photos. No payment.

WOMEN'S CIRCLE HOME COOKING—Box 338, Chester, MA 01011. Barbara Hall Pedersen, Editor.
Food-related articles, to 1,200 words; hints, anecdotes, fillers, short verse to 8 lines, for cooks. Pays to 5¢ a word, on publication.

WOMENSWEEK—250 West 57th St., New York, NY 10019. Paulett Smith, Editor.
Articles and fiction, 1,000 words, on areas of interest to women. No payment. Query.

THE WORKBASKET—4251 Pennsylvania, Kansas City, MO 64111. Mary Ida Sullivan, Editor.
Articles, 500 to 700 words, on home improvement. Short how-to pieces on home-crafts. Fillers, to 200 words, on crafts to make and sell, for "Women Who Make Cents." Pays $5.

THE WORKBENCH—4251 Pennsylvania, Kansas City, MO 64111.
Illustrated how-to articles on do-it-yourself projects. Pays $75 to $150 per printed page, on acceptance.

WORKING WOMAN—600 Madison Ave., New York, NY 10022. Bette-Jane Raphael, Articles Editor.
Articles on business and personal sides of working women's lives. Humor; articles for regular feature, "Day in the Life of." Pays from $200, on acceptance. Query with published writing samples.

SPECIALIZED MAGAZINES

HEALTH

ACCENT ON LIVING—P.O. Box 700, Bloomington, IL 61701. Raymond C. Cheever, Editor.
Articles on rehabilitation of the handicapped, success stories, self-help, etc. Pays to $100, on publication.

AMERICAN BABY—575 Lexington Ave., New York, NY 10022. Judith Nolte, Editor.
Articles, 400 to 1,500 words, for new or expectant parents, on infant care. Pays varying rates, on publication.

AMERICAN FAMILY PHYSICIAN—1740 West 92nd St., Kansas City, MO 64114. Walter H. Kemp, Managing Publisher.
Illustrated articles, 1,600 to 3,200 words, on clinical medicine. Pays from $100, on publication. Query.

AMERICAN JOURNAL OF NURSING—10 Columbus Circle, New York, NY 10019. Thelma M. Schorr, Editor.
Articles, 1,500 to 2,000 words, with photos, on nursing. Pays $20 per printed page, on publication. Query.

BEHAVIORAL MEDICINE (formerly *Practical Psychology for Physicians*)—475 Fifth Ave., New York, NY 10017. Robert McCrie, Editor.
Articles on clinical medicine, physician-patient communication, sexology, behavior, etc., for physicians. Pays 10¢ to 25¢ a word, extra for photos, after acceptance.

BESTWAYS—466 Foothill Blvd., La Canada, CA 91011. Barbara Farr, Editor.
Articles, 1,500 to 3,000 words, on health: food, life styles, exercise, etc. Pays $75 to $125, on publication.

CANADIAN DOCTOR—310 Victoria Ave., Westmount, Que., Canada H3Z 2M9. Peter Williamson, Managing Editor.
Articles, to 2,000 words, on medical economics (no clinical material). Pays 5¢ to 10¢ a word, on publication. Query.

DENTAL ECONOMICS—P.O. Box 1260, Tulsa, OK 74101. Richard Henn, Editor.
Articles, 1,200 to 1,500 words, with photos, on money management and business side of dental practice. Pays around $100, on acceptance.

EMERGENCY PRODUCT NEWS—P.O. Box 159, Carlsbad, CA 92008. Linda Olander, Managing Editor.
Features on emergency medical treatment. Pays $75 to $200, on publication. Query.

THE EXCEPTIONAL PARENT—708 Statler Office Bldg., Boston, MA 02116. Stanley D. Klein, Editor.
Articles, 600 to 3,000 words, on practical advice for parents of disabled children. Pays to 5¢ a word, on publication.

EXPECTING—52 Vanderbilt Ave., New York, NY 10017. Evelyn A. Podsiadlo, Editor.
Articles, 700 to 1,800 words, for expectant mothers. Medical pieces by professionals (R.N.s and M.D.s). Pays $50 to $125, on acceptance.

THE GREEN PAGES—641 West Fairbanks, Winter Park, FL 32789. Peggy Furman, Coordinator.
Articles on success stories, rehabilitation activities, etc., for the handicapped. Profiles; humor. Pays $75 per printed page, extra for photos, on publication. Query.

HEALTH—212 East Ohio St., Chicago, IL 60611. Barbara E. Peterson, Executive Editor.
Articles, 1,000 to 1,500 words, with photos, on health and medicine, for the lay reader. Cartoons. Pays 4¢ a word, $5 per photo, $7.50 per cartoon, on acceptance.

HOSPITAL PROGRESS–1438 South Grand Blvd., St. Louis, MO 63104. Robert J. Stephens, Editor.
Journal of the Catholic Hospital Association. Features, 1,500 to 3,000 words, on hospital management and administration. Pays $1 per column inch., on publication, or by arrangement. Query.

LIFE AND HEALTH–6856 Eastern Ave. N.W., Washington, DC 20012. Don Hawley, Editor.
Well-researched human-interest articles, to 2,000 words, on health with emphasis on prevention, for the lay reader. Pays $50 to $150, on acceptance.

MD–30 East 60th St., New York, NY 10022. Betty Hamilton, Administrative Editor.
Not in the market at present.

MEDICAL DIMENSIONS–730 Third Ave., New York, NY 10017. Decia Fates, Editor.
Articles, 1,000 to 4,000 words, for young physicians: medical how-to pieces; investigative reporting on the profession, institutions, events, etc. Pays 10¢ a word, on publication.

MEDICAL SELF-CARE MAGAZINE–P.O. Box 718, Inverness, CA 94937. Tom Ferguson, Editor.
Articles, to 1,500 words, on health-related topics; reports on happenings in health consumer/patient education movement. Pays in copies. Query.

NURSING 78–414 Benjamin Fox Pavilion, Jenkintown, PA 19046. Daniel L. Cheney, Editor.
Most articles by experts on assignment. Pays $25 to $350, on publication. Query.

THE PHYSICIAN AND SPORTSMEDICINE MAGAZINE–4530 West 77th St., Minneapolis, MN 55435. Jack Martin, Managing Editor.
Articles, 500 to 1,000 words, for physicians who treat athletic injuries. Pays $50 to $200, on acceptance.

PHYSICIAN'S MANAGEMENT–757 Third Ave., New York, NY 10017. Patrick Flanagan, Editor.
Articles on finance and office management, for physicians. Pays $100 to $300, on acceptance. Query.

PRACTICAL PSYCHOLOGY FOR PHYSICIANS–See *Behavioral Medicine.*

RN MAGAZINE–Oradell, NJ 07649.
Articles. to 2,000 words, preferably by R.N.s, on nursing, clinical care, etc. Pays to 10¢ a word, on acceptance. Query.

STRENGTH AND HEALTH–P.O. Box 1707, York, PA 17405. Bob Karpinski, Editor.
Articles, from 1,500 words, on weightlifting, physical fitness, sports, etc. Pays from $50, on publication.

TIC–P.O. Box 407, North Chatham, NY 12132. Joseph Strack, Editor.
Articles, 800 to 3,000 words, for dentists: starting a practice, office procedures, etc. Photos. Pays on acceptance.

WELL-BEING–833 West Fir, San Diego, CA 92101. Allan Jaklich, Editor.
Articles, to 5,000 words, on do-it-yourself healing: herbs, diet, etc. Pays about $5 per published page, on publication.

EDUCATION

AMERICAN EDUCATION–400 Maryland Ave. S.W., Washington, DC 20202. William A. Horn, Editor.

Articles, 1,000 to 3,000 words, on innovative education programs or activities supported by federal funds: preschool through college, adult, vocational, etc. Photos. Pays varying rates, on acceptance. Query with outline and lead paragraph.

AMERICAN SCHOOL & UNIVERSITY—401 North Broad St., Philadelphia, PA 19108. Rita Robison, Editor.
Articles and case studies, 1,200 to 1,500 words, on design, construction, operation and maintenance of school and college plants. Pays $25 per printed page, on publication. Query.

AMERICAN SCHOOL BOARD JOURNAL—National School Boards Association, 1055 Thomas Jefferson St. N.W., Washington, DC 20007.
Articles on problems of school administration and local control of education. Pays on acceptance. Query.

CHANGE—NBW Tower, New Rochelle, NY 10801. George W. Bonham, Editor.
Reports, 1,500 to 2,000 words, on programs, people and institutions of higher education. Intellectual essays, 3,000 to 5,000 words, on higher education today. Pays $150 for reports, $350 for essays, on acceptance.

CHILDREN'S HOUSE—P.O. Box 111, Caldwell, NY 07006. Kenneth Edelson, Editor.
Articles, 800 to 2,500 words, on children's education; features on Montessori programs, learning disabilities, special education, etc. Pays $15 to $25, on publication.

CROFT TEACHER'S SERVICE—24 Rope Ferry Rd., Waterford, CT 06386. Amby Burfoot, Editor.
Lesson plans, 1,800 words, in science, social studies, mathematics and English, for kindergarten through high school. Pays from $60, on publication.

DAY CARE AND EARLY EDUCATION—72 Fifth Ave., New York, NY 10011. Vittorio Maestro, Managing Editor.
Articles, 1,000 to 3,000 words, on preschool education and development: teaching methods and trends, innovative programs, activities, etc. Pays $35 to $150, on publication.

ELEMENTARY SCHOOL JOURNAL—5835 Kimbark Ave., Chicago, IL 60637. Philip W. Jackson, Editor.
Articles, 2,000 to 5,000 words, on classroom procedure, supervision and school administration. No payment.

FORECAST FOR HOME ECONOMICS—50 West 44th St., New York, NY 10036. Gloria S. Spitz, Editor.
Articles, to 1,500 words, for home economics teachers, by specialists. Pays varying rates, on publication.

FOUNDATION NEWS—888 Seventh Ave., New York, NY 10019.
Articles, to 2,000 words, on grant-making foundations. Pays $300, on acceptance. Query.

THE HORN BOOK MAGAZINE—Park Sq. Bldg., 31 St. James Ave., Boston, MA 02116. Ethel L. Heins, Editor.
Articles, 600 to 3,000 words, on children's books and related subjects, for librarians, teachers, parents, etc. Pays $20 per printed page, on publication. Query.

INDUSTRIAL EDUCATION—One Fawcett Pl., Greenwich, CT 06830. Paul Cuneo, Editor.
Instructional material, projects and how-to pieces, 1,000 to 2,000 words, with photos, for industrial arts, vocational and technical education classes. Pays $30 per printed page, on publication.

INSTRUCTOR—7 Bank St., Dansville, NY 14437. Leanna Landsmann, Editor.
Articles on elementary school teaching, by teachers. Pays varying rates, on acceptance.

KEY TO CHRISTIAN EDUCATION—8121 Hamilton Ave., Cincinnati, OH 45231. Marjorie Miller, Editor.
Articles, 600 to 2,000 words, on Christian education; tips for teachers. Pays varying rates, on publication.

LEARNING—530 University Ave., Palo Alto, CA 94301. Morton Malkofsky, Editor.
Articles for elementary school teachers, on techniques, research, philosophy, etc. Pays $50 to $300, on acceptance.

LEARNING TODAY—P.O. Box 956, Norman, OK 73069. Howard Clayton, Editor.
Articles, 1,500 words, with photos, on library-centered methods of learning. Pays 10¢ a word.

THE NATIONAL ELEMENTARY SCHOOL PRINCIPAL—1801 North Moore St., Arlington, VA 22209.
Articles, 3,000 to 3,500 words, on school administration, instruction, educational issues, etc.

PARKS & RECREATION—National Recreation and Park Association, 1601 North Kent St., Arlington, VA 22209. Margaret Smith, Editor.
Articles, 2,000 words and 400 to 500 words, on recreation, park programs, crafts, camping, etc. Photos. No payment.

PHI DELTA KAPPAN—Eighth St., and Union Ave., Box 789, Bloomington, IN 47401. Stanley Elam, Editor.
Articles, 1,000 to 4,000 words, on education. Pays $25 to $250, on publication. Query.

SCHOOL ARTS MAGAZINE—72 Printers Bldg., Worcester, MA 01608. George F. Horn, Editor.
Articles, 800 to 1,000 words, on art education: classroom techniques, multi-media material, art history instruction, etc. Photos. Pays varying rates, on publication.

SCIENCE ACTIVITIES—4000 Albemarle St. N.W., Suite 510, Washington, DC 20016.
Articles, 2,500 to 5,000 words, on classroom activities for science teachers. Photos. Pays $10 per printed page, on publication.

SCIENCE AND CHILDREN—National Science Teachers Association, 1742 Connecticut Ave. N.W., Washington, DC 20009. Phyllis R. Marcuccio, Editor.
Informative articles, 800 to 1,200 words, for elementary school science teachers. No payment.

TEACHER—One Fawcett Pl., Greenwich, CT 06830. Joan Sullivan Baranski, Editor.
Articles, on curriculum, new teaching methods, etc., for teachers of kindergarten through junior high. Pays on publication.

TEACHING ENGLISH IN THE TWO-YEAR COLLEGE—Dept. of English, East Carolina University, Greenville, NC 27834.
Articles on teaching English in two-year colleges.

TODAY'S CATHOLIC TEACHER—2451 East River Rd., Suite 200, Dayton, OH 45439. Ruth A. Matheny, Editor.
Articles, 600 to 800 words and 1,200 to 1,500 words, on Catholic education, parent-teacher relationships, innovative teaching, etc. Pays $15 to $75, on publication.

TODAY'S EDUCATION—1201 16th St. N.W., Washington, DC 20036. Walter A. Graves, Editor.
Articles, 800 to 2,400 words, on education. Pays varying rates, on acceptance.

WILSON LIBRARY BULLETIN–950 University Ave., Bronx, NY 10452.
Articles, 1,000 to 3,000 words, on library-related material, education, etc. News reports on libraries; opinion pieces, 900 words, for "Overdue." Pays from $35, extra for photos, on publication.

AGRICULTURE

AMERICAN FRUIT GROWER–Willoughby, OH 44094.
Articles, to 750 words, with photos, on solutions to marketing or production problems of commercial fruit growers. Pays around 2¢ a word, from $3 per photo, on acceptance or publication. Query. Same address and requirements for *American Vegetable Grower.*

AMERICAN VEGETABLE GROWER–See *American Fruit Grower.*

BEEF–1999 Shepard Rd., St. Paul, MN 55116. Paul D. Andre, Editor.
Articles on beef cattle feeding in confined facilities. Pays to $200, on acceptance. Query.

BIG FARMER–131 Lincoln Hwy., Frankfort, IL 60423. Rich Fee, Managing Editor.
Articles, 1,500 words, with photos, for and about high-income commercial farmers. Short items on cost-cutting or money-making ideas. Pays varying rates, on acceptance.

BROILER BUSINESS–P.O. Drawer 947, Cullman, AL 35055. Mike Butler, Editor.
Articles, 1,000 to 2,500 words, with photos, on broiler production, processing, marketing, etc. Pays $60 to $250, on acceptance.

DAIRY GOAT JOURNAL–Box 1908, Scottsdale, AZ 85252. Kent Leach, Editor.
How-to articles, 250 to 750 words, relating to dairy goats. Photos. Pays 5¢ a word, on publication. Query.

FARM FUTURES–225 East Michigan, Milwaukee, WI 53202. Royal Fraedrich, Editor.
Articles, to 1,500 words, on successful marketing of agricultural commodities, and the use of commodity futures for agricultural producers. Pays 30 to 60 days after acceptance. Query with outline.

FARM JOURNAL–Washington Square, Philadelphia, PA 19105. Lane Palmer, Editor.
Articles, 500 to 1,500 words, with photos, on new ideas in farming to increase profit, save time or improve living. Humor. Pays 10¢ to 15¢ a word, on acceptance. Query.

FARM SUPPLIER–Mt. Morris, IL 61054. Ray Bates, Editor.
Articles, 600 to 1,200 words, with photos, on feed, fertilizer, agricultural chemicals, and supplies product news, to and through retail farm trade outlets. Pays around 7¢ a word, on acceptance.

THE FURROW–Deere & Company, John Deere Rd., Moline, IL 61265. George Sollenberger, Editor.
Specialized illustrated articles on farming. Limited free-lance market. Pays to $400, on acceptance.

THE KENTUCKY FARMER–2311 Nashville Rd., P.O. Box 645, Bowling Green, KY 42101.
How-to articles on farming in Kentucky. Photos. Pays varying rates, on publication.

MICHIGAN FARMER–3303 West Saginaw, Lansing, MI 48901.

Articles on Michigan farming, rural situations and problems. Pays $5 to $10 per printed column, on acceptance.

THE NATIONAL FUTURE FARMER—Box 15130, Alexandria, VA 22309. Wilson Carnes, Editor.
Articles, to 1,000 words, on vocational, educational, social and recreational interests of Future Farmers members. Profiles of members; agricultural information. Pays to 4¢ a word, on acceptance.

NORDEN NEWS—Norden Laboratories, 601 West Cornhusker Hwy., Lincoln, NE 68521. Patricia Pike, Editor.
Articles, 1,200 to 1,500 words, on veterinary medicine. Jokes; photos. Pays $100, $7.50 per photo, on publication.

ORGANIC GARDENING AND FARMING—Emmaus, PA 18049. M. C. Goldman, Managing Editor.
Articles, 1,000 to 2,500 words, with photos, on gardening, farming, livestock, houseplants, conservation, etc., with emphasis on natural gardening techniques: use of organic and ground mineral fertilizers, mulching, composting, etc. Pays $25 to $200, extra for photos, on publication.

THE PEANUT FARMER—559 Jones Franklin Rd., Suite 150, Raleigh, NC 27606. Stephen Denny, Editor.
Articles, 1,500 words, on peanut production. Photos. Pays $125. Query first.

PENNSYLVANIA FARMER—P.O. Box 3665, Harrisburg, PA 17105. Robert H. Williams, Editor.
Articles on farmers, their farm operations, families, life styles, etc. Pays $15 for first 15 inches, 50¢ an inch thereafter, on publication.

POULTRY TRIBUNE—Mt. Morris, IL 61054. Milton R. Dunk, Editor.
Articles, 200 to 1,000 words, on egg production, processing and marketing. Pays to 8¢ a word, on acceptance.

SUCCESSFUL FARMING—1716 Locust St., Des Moines, IA 50336. Dick Hanson, Editor.
Articles on farm management, operations, etc. Helpful hints for farm shops. Pays varying rates, on acceptance.

WALLACES FARMER—Des Moines, IA 50305. Monte Sesker, Editor.
Features, 600 to 700 words, on farming in Iowa, methods and equipment; interviews with farmers. Pays 4¢ to 5¢ a word, on acceptance. Query.

THE WESTERN PRODUCER—Box 2500, Saskatoon, Sask., Canada S7K 2C4. R. H. D. Phillips, Editor.
Articles and fiction, to 2,500 words, with photos, on western Canadian subjects, for intelligent farm and rural readers. Pays to $75 per printed page, $5 to $35 for photos, on acceptance.

WISCONSIN AGRICULTURIST—2976 Triverton Pike, Madison, WI 53711. Ralph Yohe, Editor.
Articles on farming in Wisconsin; how-to pieces. Pays $50 to $175, on acceptance. Query.

THE WYOMING STOCKMAN FARMER—110 East 17th St., Cheyenne, WY 82001. Kirk Knox, Editor.
Features, to 500 words, with photos, on agriculture in Wyoming, Nebraska and Rocky Mountain area. Pays varying rates, on publication.

PERFORMING ARTS, MUSIC, FINE ARTS, BROADCAST/FILM,
PHOTOGRAPHY, HOBBIES, CRAFTS, COLLECTING

ACQUIRE—See *Collector Editions Quarterly.*

AFTER DARK—10 Columbus Circle, New York, NY 10019. William Como, Editor.
Features and reviews on regional theaters, people in entertainment, etc. Photos. Pays $15 to $75, extra for photos, on publication.

THE AMERICAN ART JOURNAL—40 West 57th St., 5th Floor, New York, NY 10019. Jane Van N. Turano, Editor.
Scholarly articles, 2,000 to 6,000 words, on American art of the 18th, 19th and 20th centuries. Photos. Pays $200 to $300, on acceptance.

AMERICAN COLLECTOR—Box A, Reno, NV 89506. John F. Maloney, Editor.
Articles, 1,000 to 2,000 words, with mass appeal, on antique collecting, collectibles, specific collections. Photos. Pays $1.20 per column inch, extra for photos.

AMERICAN FILM—The American Film Institute, John F. Kennedy Center for the Performing Arts, Washington, DC 20566. Hollis Alpert, Editor.
Articles, 3,000 words, on subjects related to film or television; 1,500-word columns; book reviews, 750 to 1,000 words. Payment varies. Query first.

THE ANTIQUES DEALER—1115 Clifton Ave., Clifton, NJ 07013. Stella Hall, Editor.
Articles, 1,200 to 2,000 words, on trends, pricing, retailing hints, hard news stories, in antiques trade. Pays 4¢ a word for articles, $30 per page for longer features, on publication. Query.

THE ANTIQUES JOURNAL—P.O. Box 88129, Dunwoody, GA 30338. John Mebane, Editor.
Well-researched articles, to 2,000 words, with photos, on antiques. Submit seasonal material 7 months in advance. Pays $25 to $65, on acceptance. Query.

ASTROLOGY '78—127 Madison Ave., New York, NY 10016. Henry Weingarten, Editor.
Serious articles on astrology. Pays $2 per page.

AUDIO—401 North Broad St., Philadelphia, PA 19108. Eugene Pitts III, Editor.
Semi-technical articles for hi-fi enthusiasts, music lovers and audio professionals. Pays $35 per page, on publication.

BEYOND REALITY—303 West 42nd St., New York, NY 10036.
Documented articles, to 2,000 words, on parapsychological phenomena. Personal accounts, 300 to 500 words, on mystical experiences. Pays around 3¢ a word, on publication.

BLUEGRASS UNLIMITED—Box 111, Broad Run, VA 22015. Peter V. Kuykendall, Editor.
Articles, to 2,000 words, on bluegrass music. Pays 1¢ to 2¢ a word, extra for photos. Query.

BRIGHT LIGHTS—P.O. Box 26081, Los Angeles, CA 90026. Gary Morris, Editor.
Articles, 2,000 to 12,000 words, analyzing the work of American film directors. Book reviews, 500 words. Pays in copies.

BROADCASTER—77 River St., Toronto, Ont., Canada M5A 3P2. Michael L. Pollock, Editor.
Articles, 500 to 2,000 words, on communications business in Canada, controversies, innovations of broadcast engineers. Profiles; industry news. Pays from $25, on acceptance. Query.

CAMERA 35—420 Lexington Ave., New York, NY 10017.
Illustrated instructional articles, 800 to 3,900 words, on practice and techniques of serious photography. Pays varying rates, on publication.

CANADIAN THEATRE REVIEW—York University, Downsview, Ont., Canada M3J 1P3.
Critical articles on professional theater, particularly in Canada. Pays $35 to $100, on publication. Query.

THE CB TIMES—1005 Murfreesboro Rd., Nashville, TN 37217. Guy L. Smith, Editor.
Articles on unique and unusual uses of CB radio; human-interest stories on its use; CB-personality pieces, fillers, jokes and short humor. Pays on acceptance. Query first.

COLLECTOR EDITIONS QUARTERLY (formerly *Acquire*)—170 Fifth Ave., New York, NY 10010. Robert Rowe, Editor.
Articles, 750 to 3,000 words, on collectibles: porcelain, *objets d'art,* modern Americana, etc. Pays $75 to $250, on publication. Query.

CONTEMPORARY KEYBOARD MAGAZINE—Box 907, Saratoga, CA 95070. Tom Darter, Editor.
Articles, 1,500 to 3,000 words, on keyboard instruments and players. Photos. Pays $50 to $90, on acceptance. Query.

COUNTRY RAMBLER—7400 Waukegan Rd., Niles, IL 60648.
Articles, 6 to 8 triple-spaced typewritten pages, on progressive country music. Photos, cartoons. Pays $200, on acceptance for articles. Query first.

COUNTRYSTYLE—11058 West Addison St., Franklin Park, IL 60131. James Neff, Associate Editor.
Articles, 800 to 1,200 words, on country music and country living; profiles, interviews. Pays 5¢ a word, on acceptance.

CRAFT MARKET NEWS—521 Fifth Ave., Suite 1700, New York, NY 10017. Marvin David, Publisher.
Articles for owners of craft shops and makers of hand-crafted items: marketing, unique promotions and advertising; reports of new shops and galleries and their crafts needs, 150 words. Pays 10¢ a word, on publication.

CREATIVE CRAFTS MAGAZINE—P.O. Box 700, Newton, NJ 07860. Sybil C. Harp, Editor.
How-to articles, 200 to 1,500 words, with photos, on adult handicrafts. Pays $50 per printed page, on publication.

DANCE MAGAZINE—10 Columbus Circle, New York, NY 10019. William Como, Editor.
Features on dance, personalities and trends. Photos. Pays $50, $10 to $15 for photos, on publication.

DANCE SCOPE—1619 Broadway, Room 603, New York, NY 10019. Richard Lorber, Editor.
Articles, 2,000 to 2,500 words, on history, aesthetics of dance; interviews with dance artists. Pays $20 per article. Query.

DESIGN—1100 Waterway Blvd., Indianapolis, IN 46202. Cindy Worl, Editor.
Articles, 1,000 to 1,500 words, on unusual art projects, useful crafts, innovative teaching methods, etc., for art teachers, students, artists and craftspersons. Pieces, 200 words, on arts and crafts activities. Photos. Pays $15 to $70, on publication.

DISCOWORLD MAGAZINE—352 Park Ave. South, New York, NY 10010. Richard Altschuler, Editor.
Articles, 1,000 to 3,000 words, on disco, jazz, rock and roll personalities, trends, etc. Pays varying rates, on publication.

THE DRAMA REVIEW—School of the Arts, New York University, 51 West Fourth St., New York, NY 10012. Michael Kirby, Editor.
Articles, with photos, on contemporary, avant-garde theater, theatrical theory and history. Pays 2¢ a word, on publication.

DRAMATICS—3368 Central Pkwy., Cincinnati, OH 45225. S. Ezra Goldstein, Editor.
Articles, 2,000 to 2,500 words, on the performing arts: theater, puppetry, dance, mime, children's theater, etc. Pays $15 to $100, on acceptance.

EAST WEST JOURNAL—233 Harvard St., Brookline, MA 02146. Sherman Goldman, Editor.
Articles, 1,000 to 5,000 words, on natural life styles, organic gardening, etc. Pays 1¢ to 3¢ a word, on publication.

EXHIBIT—P.O. Box 9820, Fort Worth, TX 76107. Didi Scott, Editor.
Articles, to 900 words, with photos, on fine arts, new movements, etc.; profiles of artists. Pays 5¢ a word, $5 per photo, on acceptance.

FILM QUARTERLY—University of California Press, Berkeley, CA 94720.
Film reviews, historical and critical articles, production projects, to 5,000 words. Pays 1½¢ a word, on publication. Query.

GEMS AND MINERALS—P.O. Box 687, Mentone, CA 92359. Jack R. Cox, Editor.
Articles, with photos, on collecting, cutting and identifying gems and materials. How-to pieces on making jewelry. Pays 50¢ per column inch or $15 per page, on publication. Query.

GUITAR PLAYER MAGAZINE—Box 615, Saratoga, CA 95070.
Articles, 1,500 to 2,500 words, on guitarists and guitars. Pays $50 to $85, on acceptance.

HAM RADIO—Greenville, NH 03048. James R. Fisk, Editor.
Articles, to 2,500 words, on amateur radio, construction, etc. Pays to 5¢ a word, on acceptance. Query.

HIGH FIDELITY—Great Barrington, MA 01230. Leonard Marcus, Editor.
Articles, 2,500 to 3,000 words, on music, records and sound reproduction. Pays on acceptance. Query.

INDUSTRIAL PHOTOGRAPHY—750 Third Ave., New York, NY 10017.
Articles on techniques and trends in professional photography, audiovisuals, motion pictures and videotape, for industrial photographers and communications executives. Pays on publication. Query.

JOURNAL OF POPULAR FILM—Bowling Green State University, 101 University Hall, Bowling Green, OH 43403.
Articles, to 3,000 words, on popular films, directors, genres, etc. Pays in copies.

LOST TREASURE (formerly *True Treasure*)—P.O. Drawer L, Conroe, TX 77301. John H. Latham, Editor.
Factual articles, 100 to 3,500 words, on buried and sunken treasure or lost mines. Photos. Pays 2¢ a word, $5 for photos, on acceptance.

McCALL'S NEEDLEWORK & CRAFTS MAGAZINE—230 Park Ave., New York, NY 10017. Margaret Gilman, Managing Editor.
Directions for making original handicraft items. Pays varying rates, on acceptance.

MAINE ANTIQUE DIGEST—Box 358, Waldoboro, ME 04572. Samuel Pennington, Editor.
Authoritative, entertaining articles, anecdotes and interviews on antiques market in New England. Photos. Pays $35 to $50, on acceptance. Query.

MAKE IT WITH LEATHER—Box 1386, Fort Worth, TX 76101. Earl F. Warren, Editor.
How-to articles, to 2,000 words, with photos and diagrams, on leathercraft. Pays from $50 per printed page, extra for illustrations, on publication.

MILLIMETER—12 East 46th St., New York, NY 10017.
Articles, 400 to 1,500 words, on film personalities, developments in the industry, TV and videotape. Pays $50 to $75, on publication.

THE MINIATURE MAGAZINE—P.O. Box 700, Newton, NJ 07860. Sybil C. Harp, Editor.
How-to articles on scale dollhouse miniatures as a hobby; pieces on antique miniatures and collectors' miniatures. Pays $50 per printed page, on publication.

MODEL AIRPLANE NEWS—White Plains Plaza, One North Broadway, White Plains, NY 10601. Arthur F. Schroeder, Editor.
Scientific or technical articles, with photos, on model aviation. Construction projects with drawings, photos, directions. Pays on publication.

MODEL RAILROADER—1027 North Seventh St., Milwaukee, WI 53233. Linn H. Westcott, Editor.
Articles, with photos of layout and equipment, on model railroads. Pays $36 per printed page, on acceptance. Query.

MODERN DRUMMER—47 Harrison St., Dept. 4, Nutley, NJ 07110. Ronald L. Spagnardi, Editor.
Articles, 500 to 2,000 words, on drumming: how-tos, interviews, etc. Pays 4¢ a word, on publication.

MUSICAL AMERICA—130 East 59th St., New York, NY 10022.
Authoritative articles, 1,000 to 1,500 words, on musical subjects. Pays around 10¢ a word.

MUSICAL NEWSLETTER—654 Madison Ave., Suite 1703, New York, NY 10021. Patrick J. Smith, Editor.
Articles, to 4,000 words, on classical music and occasionally jazz, rock and folk. Pays 10¢ a word, on acceptance. Query.

NATIONAL STAMP NEWS—Drawer Y, Sullivan's Island, SC 29482. Marcia Byars-Warnock, Editor.
Articles, to 2,000 words, on stamp collecting. Payment negotiable, on publication.

OLD BOTTLE MAGAZINE—Box 243, Bend, OR 97701. Shirley Asher, Editor.
Articles, to 2,000 words, on bottle collecting. Pays $20 per printed page, extra for photos, on acceptance.

OPERA NEWS—The Metropolitan Opera Guild, 1865 Broadway, New York, NY 10023. Robert Jacobson, Editor.
Articles, 600 to 3,500 words, on all aspects of opera; humorous anecdotes. Pays from 8¢ a word, on publication.

PERFORMING ARTS REVIEW—Law-Arts Publication, 453 Greenwich St., New York, NY 10013. Dr. Joseph Taubman, Editor.
Professional or scholarly articles, to 2,000 words, on fine arts management. No payment.

PETERSEN'S PHOTOGRAPHIC—8490 Sunset Blvd., Los Angeles, CA 90069.
Articles and how-to pieces, with photos, on all aspects of still and motion-picture photography, for amateurs and advance beginners. Pays $60 per printed page, on publication.

PHOTO LIFE—P.O. Box 3646, Vancouver, B. C. Canada V6B 3Y8.
Articles, 500 to 2,500 words, with photos, on different aspects of photography. Pays 5¢ a word, extra for photos, on publication.

PHOTOMETHODS—One Park Ave., New York, NY 10016. Fred Schmidt, Editor.
Articles, 1,500 to 3,000 words, on innovative techniques in imaging (still, film, video), working situations, etc., for the functional photographer. Pays from $75, on publication.

PICKIN'—401 North Broad St., Philadelphia, PA 19108. Don Kissil, Editor.
Articles, to 3,000 words, on bluegrass and old-time country music; interviews. Pays $5 to $50, on publication.

PLAYBILL—151 East 50th St., New York, NY 10022. Joan Rubin, Editor.
Sophisticated articles, 800 to 2,000 words, with photos, on theater and subjects of interest to theater-goers. Pays $100 to $300, on publication.

POPULAR ARCHAEOLOGY—Box 4211, Arlington, VA 22204.
Nontechnical articles, to 2,000 words, on archaeological subjects. No payment. Query.

POPULAR PHOTOGRAPHY MAGAZINE—One Park Ave., New York, NY 10016.
How-to articles, 500 to 2,000 words, for amateur photographers. Pays from $100 per printed page, and $25 for illustrated photo tips. Query with outline and photos.

RAILROAD MODEL CRAFTSMAN—P.O. Box 700, Newton, NJ 07860. J. Anthony Koester, Managing Editor.
How-to articles on scale model railroading: cars, operation, scenery, etc. Pays on publication.

R/C MODELER MAGAZINE—P.O. Box 487, Sierra Madre, CA 91024. Don Dewey, Editor.
Technical and semi-technical how-to articles on radio-controlled model aircraft. Pays $25 to $400, 30 days after publication. Query.

RELICS—P.O. Box 3338, Austin, TX 78764. Pat Wagner, Editor.
Articles, 500 to 2,000 words, on American frontier relics, historical Americana and collectibles. Photos. Pays from 2¢ a word, on acceptance. Query.

RIO GRANDE HISTORY—University Library, Box 3475, New Mexico State University, Las Cruces, NM 88003.
Well-researched articles, 1,000 to 4,000 words, for history enthusiasts. Pays in copies.

ROCK AND GEM—16001 Ventura Blvd., Encino, CA 91436.
How-to articles, to 2,000 words, with photos, on rock collecting, field trips, etc. Pays $40 per printed page, on publication.

ROCKHOUND—P.O. Drawer L, Conroe, TX 77301. John H. Latham, Editor.
Articles, 100 to 3,500 words, with photos, on mineral collecting sites: location, conditions, etc. Pays 2¢ a word, $5 per photo, on acceptance. Query.

SHOW-BOOK WEEK—*Chicago Sun Times,* 401 North Wabash Ave., Chicago, IL 60611. Jean Adelsman, Editor.
Articles, interviews and profiles, to 1,000 words, on the lively and fine arts. Pays to 10¢ a word, on acceptance.

STEREO QUARTERLY—State Rd., Great Barrington, MA 02130.
Factual articles, to 4,000 words, on stereo music systems and related equipment. Pays to 10¢ a word, on acceptance. Query.

SUPER-8 FILMAKER—3161 Fillmore St., San Francisco, CA 94123. Bruce Anderson, Editor.
Features, 2,500 words, on Super-8, organizations, productions, etc.; how-to pieces. Articles, 500 to 2,000 words, on film technique; related book reviews. Pays $70 to $100 for features, $25 to $75 for short pieces, on publication. Query.

TAKE ONE—Box 1778, Station B, Montreal, Que., Canada H3B 3L3. Phyllis Platt, Managing Editor.
Articles, interviews and reviews related to film. Pays modest rates.

TRUE TREASURE—See *Lost Treasure.*

VIDEOGRAPHY—750 Third Ave., New York, NY 10017. Peter Caranicas, Managing Editor.
Articles, 1,000 to 3,000 words, on video in education, business and industry, pay and cable television, video art, etc. Pays $50, on publication.

WESTART—Box 1396, Auburn, CA 95603.
Features, 350 to 700 words, on fine arts and crafts. Photos. Pays 30¢ per column inch, on publication.

WESTERN & EASTERN TREASURES—1440 West Walnut St., Compton, CA 90220. Ray Krupa, Managing Editor.
Articles on searches for buried and sunken treasures using metal detectors, etc. Historical articles on early American inhabitants, places to look for treasure, treasure discoveries. Pays 2¢ a word, $5 for photos, $100 maximum, on publication.

THE WORKBASKET—4251 Pennsylvania Ave., Kansas City, MO 64111.
How-to articles, 300 to 500 words, with photos, on women's homecrafts. Pays 5¢ a word, $5 per photo, on acceptance.

THE WORKBENCH—4251 Pennsylvania Ave., Kansas City, MO 64111. Jay W. Hedden, Editor.
How-to articles, with photos, on do-it-yourself home improvement, maintenance, construction, etc. Pays from $150 per printed page, on acceptance.

TECHNICAL AND SCIENTIFIC

THE AOPA PILOT—7315 Wisconsin Ave., Bethesda, MD 20014.
Magazine of the Aircraft Owners and Pilots Association. First-person how-to articles, with photos, on general aviation, for beginning and experienced pilots. Pays to $300, extra for photos.

ASTRONOMY—411 East Mason St., 6th Floor, Milwaukee, WI 53202.
Articles on astronomy, astrophysics, space travel, extraterrestrial life, research, etc. Hobby pieces on equipment, etc.; short news items. Pays varying rates, on publication.

BYTE MAGAZINE—70 Main St., Peterborough, NH 03458. Carl T. Helmers, Jr., Editor.
Articles on personal microcomputers. Photos. Pays $20 to $30 per printed page.

CB LIFE—Petersen Publishing Co., 8490 Sunset Blvd., Los Angeles, CA 90069. Ormel Duke, Editor.
Articles, to 2,500 words, with photos, of interest to CB enthusiasts: technical, how-to's, personality pieces, etc. Pays varying rates, on publication.

COMPUTER DECISIONS—50 Essex St., Rochelle Park, NJ 07662. Hesh Wiener, Editor.
Articles, 800 to 4,000 words, on generic uses of computer systems and on effective ways to use data processing systems. Pays $30 to $50 per printed page, on publication.

CREATIVE COMPUTING—P.O. Box 789-M, Morristown, NJ 07960. Stephen Gray, Editor.
Articles, 500 to 3,000 words, on educational and recreational applications of computers, the effects of computers on society and building computers at home. Pays 1¢ to 3¢ a word, on acceptance.

ENVIRONMENT—560 Trinity Ave., St. Louis, MO 63130. Julian McCaull, Editor.
Factual articles, 3,000 to 4,000 words, on environmental pollution. Pays $100 to $150. Query.

THE LIVING WILDERNESS—1901 Pennsylvania Ave. N. W., Washington, DC 20006.
Articles, to 5,000 words, on wilderness experiences, studies, wildlife, environmental concerns, conservation. Nature photos. Pays varying rates. Query.

MECHANIX ILLUSTRATED—1515 Broadway, New York, NY 10036. Robert G. Beason, Editor.
Features, 1,500 words; short pieces and photo essays; how-to articles; useful tips.

Pays from $400 for features, $75 to $500 for shorter articles, $15 for tips.

NATURAL HISTORY—Central Park West and 79th St., New York, NY 10024. Alan Ternes, Editor.
Well-researched articles, 2,500 to 3,500 words, on biological sciences, archaeology, ecology, earth sciences, astronomy and anthropology. Pays $350 to $600 for articles, extra for photos, on acceptance.

NEW ENGINEER—730 Third Ave., New York, NY 10017. Steven S. Ross, Editor.
Articles, 1,500 to 5,000 words, on engineering profession, technical projects, etc. Pays $50 to $100 per printed page, on publication. Query.

POPULAR ELECTRONICS—One Park Ave., New York, NY 10016. Arthur P. Salsberg, Editor.
Articles on consumer electronics technology: hi-fi, CB, radio, TV servicing, computers, etc. Pays to $350 for features, to $500 for construction articles, on acceptance.

POPULAR MECHANICS—224 West 57th St., New York, NY 10019. John Linkletter, Editor.
Features on scientific, mechanical and industrial subjects, with elements of action or adventure; articles on sports, automotives and housing. How-to pieces on crafts projects and shop work. Photo essays, to 250 words; photos. Pays $300 to $500 for features, from $12 for shorts, on acceptance.

POPULAR SCIENCE MONTHLY—380 Madison Ave., New York, NY 10017. Hubert P. Luckett, Editor.
Articles, to 2,000 words, with photos, on new developments in applied science and technology. Short illustrated articles on new inventions and products; photo essays, to 5 pages. Pays from $150 per printed page, on acceptance.

PSYCHOLOGY TODAY—One Park Ave., New York, NY 10016. Mary Marcus, Manuscript Editor.
Well-researched articles on current trends in psychology and behavior. Query first.

RADIO-ELECTRONICS—200 Park Ave. South, New York, NY 10003. Larry Steckler, Editor.
Technical articles, 2,000 to 3,000 words, with photos, on electronics: new technology, hi-fi, construction projects, servicing, etc. Pays on acceptance.

SCIENCE AND MECHANICS—229 Park Ave. South, New York, NY 10003. Joseph Daffron, Editor.
Articles, 1,000 to 1,500 words, with photos, on unusual developments in physical sciences; how-it-works pieces. Pays on acceptance. Query.

SCIENCE DIGEST—224 West 57th St., New York, NY 10019. Daniel E. Button, Editor.
Timely articles, 1,500 to 2,000 words, on the sciences for the lay reader. Pays $50 to $500, after acceptance. Query.

SCIENCE NEWS—1719 N St. N.W., Washington, DC 20036. Kendrick Frazier, Editor.
Articles, 1,500 to 1,800 words, on scientific developments. Limited free-lance market.

SEA FRONTIERS—International Oceanographic Foundation, 3979 Rickenbacker Causeway, Virginia Key, Miami, FL 33149. F. G. Smith, Editor.
Illustrated articles, 2,000 words, on scientific advances and discoveries related to the sea, interesting physical, chemical or geological phenomena, etc. Pays from 6¢ a word, on acceptance. Query.

UFO REPORT—333 Johnson Ave., Brooklyn, NY 12206. Martin M. Singer, Editorial Director.

Articles, from 4,000 words, on sightings of or first-hand experiences with unidentified flying objects and on ancient advanced civilizations. Photos. Pays from $250, on acceptance. Query.

TRADE AND BUSINESS MAGAZINES

AERO–P.O. Box 4030, San Clemente, CA 92672.
Factual articles, any length, with photos, on skills and technical know-how for pilots and aircraft owners. Pays $35 to $50 per printed page, after publication. Query.

AMERICAN BICYCLIST AND MOTORCYCLIST–461 Eighth Ave., New York, NY 10001. Stan Gottlieb, Editor.
Articles, 1,500 to 2,800 words, on sales and repair practices of successful bicycle and moped dealers. Pays from 4¢ a word, $5 a photo, on publication. Query.

AMERICAN COIN-OP–500 North Dearborn, Chicago, IL 60610. Phil Sneiderman, Managing Editor.
Articles, to 1,000 words, with photos, on successful coin-operated laundries and dry-cleaners: promotion, equipment, maintenance, security, etc. Pays 3¢ to 5¢ a word, $5 per photo, on publication. Query.

AMERICAN DRYCLEANER–500 North Dearborn, Chicago, IL 60610. Paul T. Glaman, Editor.
Well-documented articles on development in drycleaning industry of important programs in merchandising, production, etc. Photos. Pays 3¢ a word and up, on publication.

AMERICAN LAUNDRY DIGEST–500 North Dearborn, Chicago, IL 60610. Ben Russell, Editor.
Articles, 300 to 2,500 words, on operation of hospital and hotel laundries, linen supply plants and self-service laundries: production, management, marketing. Pays from 3¢ per word, $5 per photo, two weeks before publication; $5 per cartoon, on acceptance. Query.

AMERICAN PAINT AND WALL COVERINGS DEALER–2911 Washington, St. Louis, MO 63103. Clark Rowley, Editor.
Articles, 1,000 to 2,000 words, about successful paint and wall coverings stores, merchandising campaigns, etc. Photos. Pays $100, extra for photos, on publication. Queries preferred.

AMERICAN PAINTING CONTRACTOR–2911 Washington Ave., St. Louis, MO 63103. John Cleveland, Editor.
Technical articles, to 2,500 words, with photos, on residential and commercial decorating, industrial maintenance painting and management of painting business, for painting contractors, architects, plant maintenance engineers. Pays 5¢ a word and up, extra for photos, on publication.

AMERICAN ROOFER AND BUILDING IMPROVEMENT CONTRACTOR–915 Burlington, Downers Grove, IL 60515. J. C. Gudas, Editor.
Articles, 600 words, on problem solving, sales, manufacturing and estimating in roofing and siding field. Pays 3¢ a word and up, on publication.

AMUSEMENT BUSINESS–1717 West End Ave., Nashville, TN 37203. Tom Powell, Editor.
Articles, any length, for owners, managers, booking agents of amusement enterprises: fun parks, fairs, stadiums, circuses, tourist attractions, shopping centers, arenas, race tracks. Pays varying rates, monthly. Query.

THE ANTIQUES DEALER–1115 Clifton Ave., Clifton, NJ 07013. Miss Stella Hall, Editor.
Articles, 500 to 2,000 words, on national and international news and trends in

antiques business. Occasional features by authorities in specific fields. Pays 4¢ per word, $5 per photo, on publication.

THE APOTHECARY—401 Commonwealth Ave., Boston, MA 02115.
Articles with a non-technical orientation on pharmacy and/or relation to health care, 1,000 to 5,000 words. Photos. Pays modest rates, on acceptance.

AQUARIUM INDUSTRY—Toadtown, Magalia, CA 95954. Bob Behme, Editor.
Articles 300 to 1,000 words on business, sales and news in aquarium industry. Pays 10¢ a word, on acceptance.

ARCHERY RETAILER—225 East Michigan, Milwaukee, WI 53202. Glenn Helgeland, Editor.
Case histories of successful archery retail shops. how-to pieces on selling archery equipment. Photos. Pays $50 to $75, after acceptance.

ARCHITECTURAL RECORD—1221 Ave. of the Americas, New York, NY 10020. Walter Wagner, Editor.
Business articles on building management, costs, and activity. Limited free-lance market. Pays varying rates. Query.

AREA DEVELOPMENT MAGAZINE—432 Park Ave. South, New York, NY 10016. Albert H. Jaeggin, Editor.
Instructive articles, for top executives of manufacturing companies, on industrial and office facility planning: site selection, plant relocation and expansion, design, financing, etc. Pays $40 per printed page. Query.

AUDECIBEL—20361 Middlebelt Rd., Livonia, MI 48152.
Articles, 200 to 2,000 words, on hearing aids, sound and related topics, for hearing specialists. Send for writer's "Fact Sheet."

AUDIO TIMES—325 East 75th St., New York, NY 10021. Michael Dillon Thomas, Editor.
Articles, 300 to 1,500 words, for audio components retailers. Dealer profiles, how to improve profits, etc. Pays 10¢ a word, on publication. Query.

AUTO AND FLAT GLASS JOURNAL—1929 Royce Ave., Beloit, WI 53511. David Benjamin, Editor.
Interviews, 500 to 1,000 words, with photos, of successful auto glass replacement shop managers. Pays 5¢ a word, on publication.

AUTO TRIM NEWS—129 Broadway, Lynbrook, NY 11563. Nat W. Danas, Editor.
Articles to 1,000 words, with photos, on management and merchandising in auto trim shops, seat-cover specialty stores, etc. How-to pieces, 300 to 400 words, on marine or aircraft upholstery and recreational vans. Pays $30 per printed page, on publication. Query.

BARRISTER—American Bar Association, 1155 East 60th St., Chicago, IL 60637. Elizabeth Cameron, Managing Editor.
Articles to 3,000 words, on matters affecting young lawyers. Pays $150 to $400, on acceptance. Fillers. Query first.

BARRON'S—22 Cortlandt St., New York, NY 10007. Robert M. Bleiberg, Editor.
Articles of national interest, 1,200 to 2,500 words, on business and finance. Pays from $500, on publication. Query.

BATH PRODUCTS & DOMESTICS BUYER—76 S.E. Fifth Ave., Delray Beach, FL 33444. Bill Dogan, Editor.
Articles, 1,000 to 1,500 words, with photos, on merchandising and display techniques for buyers of bathroom accessories. Pays varying rates. Query.

BICYCLE DEALER SHOWCASE–P.O. Box 19531, Irvine, CA 92713. Steve Ready, Editor.
Well-researched, technical articles, 1,000 to 1,500 words, for bicycle dealers, on business, sales, service and repair, with emphasis on merchandising. Photos. Pays $50 to $75, on publication.

BIG FARMER–Big Farmer, Inc., 131 Lincoln Hwy., Frankfort, IL 60423. Richard Fee, Editor.
Articles, 1,500 words, with photos, for and about high-income farmers. Short pieces on cost-cutting and money-making ideas. Pays $75 to $300, on publication.

BLACK ENTERPRISE–Earl G. Graves Publishing Co., 295 Madison Ave., New York, NY 10017. Phil W. Petrie, Managing Editor.
Articles, 2,000 words, with photos, on black businesses, businessmen, etc. Pays from $300, on acceptance. Query.

BOATING INDUSTRY–205 East 42nd St., New York, NY 10017. Dave Kendall, Senior Editor.
Business articles, 1,000 to 1,500 words, on boat dealers. Pays 4¢ to 5¢ a word, $5 to $10 for photos, on publication. Query.

BODY FASHIONS/INTIMATE APPAREL–757 Third Ave., New York, NY 10017. Mimi Finkel, Editor.
Merchandising features on retail intimate apparel; interviews with merchandisers and buyers. Pays 10¢ a word, $5 per photo. Query preferred. Incorporating *Hosiery & Underwear.*

BROADCAST ENGINEERING–9221 Quivira Rd., Overland Park, KS 66212. Ron Merrell, Editor.
Practical articles on engineering and production, 1,000 to 2,800 words, on cable TV, commercial AM and FM, educational radio and TV, recording studios. Engineer's Exchange column on short cuts and equipment modification. Photos. Pays $75 to $200 per article, $10 to $25 for column, on acceptance. Query.

BOYS OUTFITTER–See *Teens and Boys.*

BURROUGHS CLEARING HOUSE–Box 418, Detroit, MI 48232. Norman E. Douglas, Managing Editor.
Articles, 1,800 to 2,000 words, for finance officers in banks, corporations and insurance companies, on lending, investment management, controllership, personnel, etc. Pays 10¢ a word, on acceptance. Query.

BUSINESS AND COMMERCIAL AVIATION–Ziff-Davis Publishing Co., Hangar C-1, Westchester Airport, White Plains, NY 10604. Archie Trammell, Editor.
Articles, 2,500 words, with photos, for pilots, on use of private aircrafts for business transportation. Pays $100 to $500, on acceptance. Query.

BUSINESS AND SOCIETY REVIEW–870 Seventh Ave., New York, NY 10019. Theodore Cross, Editor.
Articles, 1,500 to 6,000 words, on social responsibilities of business. Pays in copies. Query.

BUSINESS WEEK–1221 Ave. of the Americas, New York, NY 10020. Lewis H. Young, Editor.
Staff-written.

BUSINESS WORLD–P.O. Box 1234, Rahway, NJ 07065. Gretchen Mirrielees, Editor.
Career-related articles, 300 to 2,500 words, for graduating college seniors. Two issues a year for women entering business.

THE CALIFORNIA HIGHWAY PATROLMAN—2030 V St., Sacramento, CA 95818. Richard York, Editor.
Articles, 800 to 3,500 words, on traffic safety, recreational vehicle use, driver education, travel, historic California. Photos; cartoons. Pays 2½¢ per word, $2.50 for photos, $10 for cartoons, on publication.

CAMPAIGN INSIGHT—516 Petroleum Bldg., Wichita, KS 67202.
How-to articles, 500 to 1,000 words, on political campaigning techniques; case histories. Pays 5¢ a word, on acceptance. Query.

CAMPGROUND MANAGEMENT—500 Hyacinth Pl., Highland Park, IL 60035. James D. Saul, Editor.
Detailed articles, 300 to 1,200 words, with photos, on park owners' business operations. Pays to $50, on publication. Query.

CAMPGROUND MERCHANDISING—327 Wagaraw Rd., Hawthorne, NJ 07506. Debby Roth, Editor.
Articles, 1,500 words, on equipment and merchandise sold by campground managers to recreational-vehicle owners. Pays 4¢ per word, $10 per photo, on publication.

CANDY AND SNACK INDUSTRY—777 Third Ave., New York, NY 10017. Mike Lench, Editor.
Illustrated features, 1,000 to 1,250 words, on production and promotion of national candy snack firms and local retailers. Short news pieces. Pays 5¢ a word, $5 for photos, on publication. Query on features.

CARS & TRUCKS—8400 Westpark Dr., McLean, VA 22101. Ronald D. Nelson, Publisher.
Publication of National Automobile Dealers Association. Articles, 750 to 2,000 words, with photos, on management of car dealerships. Pays on acceptance. Query.

THE CATTLEMAN—410 East Weatherford, Ft. Worth, TX 76102. Paul W. Horn, Editor.
Factual, well-documented articles, 1,500 to 2,000 words, on beef cattle raising, range management and related subjects in the Southwest. Pays varying rates, on acceptance. Sample copies available. Queries suggested.

CERAMIC SCOPE—Box 48643, Los Angeles, CA 90048. Mel Fiske, Editor.
Articles, 1,000 to 1,500 words, on business operations of hobby ceramic studios: merchandising, promotion, display, inventory systems, management on retail or wholesale levels. Photos. Pays 3¢ a word, $5 a photo, on acceptance. Query.

CGA MAGAZINE—535 Thurlow St., Suite 700, Vancouver, B.C. Canada V6E 3L2.
Articles, 1,500 to 3,000 words, on business and financial issues of interest to Canadian accountants, financial reporters and politicians. Fillers. Pays $100 to $200 for articles, from $1 for fillers, on acceptance. Query.

CHAIN SAW AGE—3435 N.E. Broadway, Portland, OR 98232. Norman Raies, Publisher.
Merchandising features, to 500 words, on dealers, distributors and users of chain saws. Pays 2½¢ a word, extra for photos, on publication. Query.

CHEMICAL WEEK—1221 Ave. of the Americas, New York, NY 10020. Patrick McCurdy, Editor-in-Chief.
News pieces, to 200 words, on chemical business. Pays $3.50 per column inch. Query.

CHINA, GLASS & TABLEWARES—P.O. Box 2147, Clifton, NJ 07015. Sue Grisham, Editor.
Interviews or studies of china and glass departments in department stores, with photos, 1,500 to 2,500 words. Pays $40 a page, on publication. Query.

CHRISTIAN BOOKSELLER—Gundersen Dr. and Schmale Rd., Wheaton, IL 60178. Jan Lokay, Editor.

Articles, 1,200 to 1,500 words, with photos, on sales promotions, successful businesses, merchandising in bookstores; features on retail outlets of religious books. Pays $60 to $75, on publication.

CLEANING MANAGEMENT—17915-B Sky Park Blvd., Irvine, CA 92714. R. Daniel Harris, Jr.,
Instructive articles, 1,000 words, for cleaning and maintenance personnel, on increasing efficiency and upgrading performance. No case histories. Pays 8¢ a word, $6 for photos, on publication.

COINAMATIC AGE—60 East 42nd St., New York, NY 10017.
Articles, 1,000 to 1,500 words, with photos, on ingenuity of store owner in coin laundry and drycleaning. Include list of trade-named equipment. Pays 3¢ a word and up, extra for photos, on publication. Query.

COMMERCIAL CAR JOURNAL—Chilton Way, Radnor, PA 19089. James D. Winsor, Editor.
Factual articles, any length, on truck and bus fleet operation and maintenance. Pays from $50, on acceptance. Query.

COMMODITIES—219 Parkade, Cedar Falls, IA 50613. Darrell Jobman, Editor.
Articles, 1,000 to 3,000 words, on trading commodity futures and stock options. Cartoons. Pays 6¢ to 10¢ a word, on publication. Query.

COMMUNICATION NEWS—402 West Liberty Dr., Wheaton, IL 60187. Bruce Howat, Editor.
Technical articles, 500 to 1,500 words, on developments in voice, signal and data communications; news, case histories, how-to pieces. Pays 3¢ per word, $7.50 per photo, on publication.

COMMUNICATIONS RETAILING—CES Publishing Corp., 325 East 75th St., New York, NY 10021. Mitchell Ratliff, Editor.
Articles to 2,000 words, for retailers who sell, install and service Citizens Band radios, monitor scanners, marine radios, telephone accessories, etc. Photos; fillers. Pays 10¢ a word, on acceptance.

COMPUTER DECISIONS MAGAZINE—50 Essex St., Rochelle Park, NJ 07662. Hesh Weiner, Editor.
Articles, 800 to 4,000 words, on generic uses of computer systems, and on social, economic and political aspects of computing. Pays $30 to $50 printed page. Query.

CONCRETE CONSTRUCTION—329 Interstate Rd., Addison, IL 60101. William C. Panarese, Editor.
Technical articles, 1,500 to 2,000 words, with illustrations, on on-site construction with concrete. Pays varying rates, on acceptance. Query.

CONCRETE PRODUCTS—300 West Adams St., Chicago, IL 60606. William J. Blaha, Editor.
Articles, 1,400 words, on production methods and marketing of precast and prestressed concrete. Pays 3¢ a word, extra for photos, on acceptance. Query.

CONSUMER ELECTRONICS PRODUCT NEWS—St. Regis Publications, 6 East 43rd St., New York, NY 10017. Kathleen Lander, Managing Editor.
Articles, 500 to 2,000 words, on sales training and merchandising techniques in consumer electronics (hi-fi, TV, calculators, CB, telephone accessories, etc.). Pays varying rates, on acceptance. Query, with writing sample.

CONTACTS—Box 407, North Chatham, NY 12132. Joseph Strack, Editor.
Articles, 300 to 1,000 words, on management of dental laboratories, lab techniques, equipment, etc. Cartoons. Pays 3¢ to 5¢ a word, on acceptance.

CRAFT HORIZONS—44 West 53rd St., New York, NY 10019. Rose Slivka, Editor.

Articles, with photos, on professional handcrafts and craftspersons: weaving, ceramics, metalworking, woodworking, etc. Pays to $100, after publication. Query.

CREDIT & COLLECTION MANAGEMENT BULLETIN—24 Rope Ferry Rd., Waterford, CT 06386. Claire Sherman, Editor.
Interview-based articles, 800 to 1,250 words, from industrial credit managers, on handling delinquent accounts and solving problems. Pays 10¢ a word, on acceptance, after editing. Query.

CREDIT AND FINANCIAL MANAGEMENT—475 Park Ave. South, New York, NY 10016. James J. Andover, Editorial Director.
Articles, 2,000 words, on business credit, financial and business conditions and management. Pays in copies. Query.

CURTAIN, DRAPERY & BEDSPREAD MAGAZINE—Columbia Communications, 370 Lexington Ave., New York, NY 10017. Ruth L. Lyons, Editor.
Articles, to 1,500 words, with photos, on merchandising or promotional techniques. Pays 5¢ a word, $5 per photo, on publication. Query.

CYCLE AGE—Babcox Publications, Babcox Bldg., 11 South Forge St., Akron, OH 44304.
Articles, 1,250 words, for cycle dealers, on business, marketing and maintenance; personality profiles. Photos. Pays varying rates, on publication. Query.

DAIRY HERD MANAGEMENT—P.O. Box 67, Minneapolis, MN 55440. George Ashfield, Editor.
Articles, 500 to 2,000 words, with photos, on large dairy operations and techniques and equipment used by major U.S. dairies. Fillers. Pays $10 to $150, on acceptance. Query.

D/E JOURNAL—See *Domestic Engineering.*

DECOR—408 Olive, St. Louis, MO 63102. William M. Humberg, Editor. Address William G. Cotner.
Retailer profiles on art galleries, picture framers, and interior accessories retailers. Pays from $25 per printed page. Queries preferred.

DEFENSE TRANSPORTATION JOURNAL—1612 K St. N.W., Washington, DC 20006. G. W. Collins, Publisher.
Articles, 1,500 to 3,000 words, on concepts and developments in domestic and international transportation industry. Pays to $150, on publication.

DENTAL MANAGEMENT—757 Third Ave., New York, NY 10017. M. J. Goldberg, Editor.
Articles to 2,000 words, on taxes, insurance, offices, etc., of interest to dentists. No technical or clinical material. Pays 10¢ to 15¢ a word, on acceptance. Query.

THE DISCOUNT MERCHANDISER—641 Lexington Ave., New York, NY 10022. Nathaniel Schwartz, Editor.
Articles on mass-merchandising techniques and ideas for discount stores. Pays to $150 for articles, $7.50 for photos, on acceptance. Query.

DOMESTIC ENGINEERING (formerly *D/E Journal*)—110 North York Rd., Elmhurst, IL 60126. Stephen J. Shafer, Editor.
Articles, to 3,000 words, on plumbing, heating, air conditioning, process piping, etc. Photos. Pays $20 to $35 per printed page, on publication.

DRUG TOPICS—680 Kinderkamack Rd., Oradell, NJ 07649. Barbara P. Johnson, Editor.
News pieces, 500 words, with photos, on retailers and associations in retail drug field. Merchandising features, 1,000 to 1,500 words; query. Pays $25 to $50 for pieces, $50 to $200 for features, on acceptance.

EARNSHAW'S INFANTS' & CHILDREN'S REVIEW–393 Seventh Ave., New York, NY 10001. Thomas W. Hudson, Editor.
Articles on fashion manufacturers, retail promotions and statistics and figures for the children's wear industry. Pays $50 to $150, on publication. Query.

EASTERN AUTOMOTIVE JOURNAL–P.O. Box 373, Cedarhurst, NY 11516. Stan Hubsher, Publisher.
Articles, 1,000 to 1,500 words, with photos, on wholesale automotive replacement parts trade from Maine to Virginia. Pays varying rates, on publication. Query.

EDITOR & PUBLISHER–575 Lexington Ave., New York, NY 10022. Robert U. Brown, Editor.
Articles, to 1,200 words, with photos, on newspapers and newspaper persons. Pays varying rates, after publication. Query.

ELECTRICAL CONTRACTOR–7315 Wisconsin Ave., Washington, DC 20014. Larry C. Osius, Editor.
Articles, 1,000 to 1,500 words, with photos, on construction or management techniques for electrical contractors. Pays $60 per printed page, before publication. Query.

ELECTRONIC TECHNICAL DEALER–One East First St., Duluth, MN 55802. J. W. Phipps, Editor.
Articles, 1,500 to 2,500 words, for radio and communications service technicians and dealers, on successful dealers, CCTV, sound systems, MATV, two-way radio, etc. Cartoons. Pays $25 per printed page, $7.50 per cartoon, on acceptance.

ENERGY NEWS–P.O. Box 1589, Dallas, TX 75221. Gregory Martin, Managing Editor.
Brief news items on the natural gas industry. Pays 10¢ per word, within a month of publication.

EXECUTIVE REVIEW–224 South Michigan Ave., Chicago, IL 60604.
How-to articles, profiles on successful companies and individuals, human-interest pieces, hunting and fishing articles. Reprints from business publications preferred. Pays varying rates, on publication.

EXPORT–386 Park Ave. South, New York, NY 10016. Martha Downing, Editor.
Articles, to 1,500 words, on new products and trends in air conditioning and refrigeration, hardware, consumer electronics, etc. Pays 10¢ a word, on acceptance. Query.

FARM AND POWER EQUIPMENT MAGAZINE–10877 Watson Rd., St. Louis, MO 63127. Glenn S. Hensley, Editor.
Articles, to 1,500 words, with photos, on retailers selling light industrial power equipment and farm implements. Pays to $300, on acceptance. Query.

FASHION ACCESSORIES MAGAZINE–22 South Smith St., Norwalk, CT 06855. Renee Brown, Editor.
Articles, with photos, for handbag and accessory buyers, on store displays, retail promotions; profiles of designers and manufacturers. Pays $50 for short articles, from $100 for features, on publication. Query.

FAST SERVICE–757 Third Ave., New York, NY 10017. Tom Farr, Editor.
Articles, with photos, on fast-food restaurants: how-to pieces; executive profiles; features on advertising and management. Fillers; photos. Pays 7¢ to 10¢ a word, $5 to $10 per photo. Query.

FEED INDUSTRY REVIEW–3055 North Brookfield Rd., Brookfield, WI 53005. Bruce W. Smith, Publisher.
Feature articles, 1,200 to 2,500 words, with photos, on full-scale manufacturing of brand-name feeds. Query.

FENCE INDUSTRY—6285 Barfield Rd., Atlanta, GA 30328. Bill Coker, Editor.
Articles on fence industry: history, gross volume, sales, promotion, management; interviews with dealer-erectors; on-the-job pieces. Pays 5¢ per word, $10 for photos, on publication. Query.

FINANCIAL EXECUTIVE—633 Third Ave., New York, NY 10017. Carl Cerminaro, Editor.
Articles, 3,000 to 4,000 words, on business and finance. No payment. Query.

FIREHOUSE—33 East 53rd St., New York, NY 10022. Dennis Smith, Editor-in-Chief.
Articles, 500 to 3,000 words, on major fires, firefighting equipment, firefighters, etc. How-to articles, fire kitchen recipes, fillers. Pays to 10¢ a word, on publication. Queries only.

FIRE TIMES—1100 N.E. 125th St., North Miami, FL 33161. Thomas Moore, Editor.
Articles, 500 to 1,200 words, on fire equipment, departments and personnel. Photos. Pays 2¢ a word, $5 per photo, on publication.

THE FISH BOAT—P.O. Box 217, 1700 North Causeway St., Mandeville, LA 70448. William A. Sarratt, Editor.
Articles on commercial fishing, promotion and merchandising of seafood products. Short items on commercial fishers and boats. Pays varying rates, on acceptance. Query.

FISHING GAZETTE—461 Eighth Ave., New York, NY 10001. Frank P. Margiotta, Editor.
Articles, to 2,000 words, with photos, on commercial fisheries, boat construction, fish processing and freezing plants. No game fishery material. Pays varying rates. Query.

FLOORING MAGAZINE—757 Third Ave., New York, NY 10017. Michael Korsonsky, Editor.
Articles, 1,500 to 2,000 words, for floor-covering industry, on merchandising, display, advertising, promotion, distribution. Photos. Pays 5¢ to 7¢ per word, on acceptance. Query.

FLORIST—29200 Northwestern Hwy., P.O. Box 2227, Southfield, MI 48037. William P. Golden, Editor.
Articles, to 1,000 words, with photos, on retail florist business improvement. Pays 5¢ a word, $7.50 per photo.

THE FOOD BROKER SALES AND MARKETING—P.O. Box 28, Barrington, RI 02806.
Articles on activities, trends, merchandising techniques and views of food brokers and their clients. Pays 3¢ per word, $5 per photo, on publication.

THE FOREMAN'S LETTER—Bureau of Business Practice, 24 Rope Ferry Rd., Waterford, CT 06386. Frank Berkowitz, Editor.
Interviews, with photos, of successful industrial supervisors and foremen. Pays 8¢ to 10¢ per word, extra for photos, on acceptance. Query.

FURNITURE AND FURNISHINGS—1450 Don Mills Rd., Don Mills, Ont., Canada M3B 2X7. Ronald H. Shuker, Editor.
Merchandising and management articles, with photos, for retailers, buyers, decorators, distributors and manufacturers' representatives, on distribution, sales displays, promotion of furniture, floor coverings, draperies, lamps and accessories in Canada. Pays varying rates, on publication. Query.

GASOLINE NEWS—100 North Grant St., Columbus, OH 43215. Paul Hendershot, Editor.
Trade paper for service stations. Clippings on service stations, automotive after market, car wash and snowmobile industries. Pays 50¢ per clipping, on publication. Query.

GIFT AND TABLEWARE REPORTER–1515 Broadway, New York, NY 10036. Jack McDermott, Editor.
Illustrated articles and news items, 300 to 500 words, on merchandising, for giftware and tableware retail buyer. Pays varying rates, on acceptance. Query.

GIFTS AND DECORATIVE ACCESSORIES–51 Madison Ave., New York. NY 10010. Phyllis Sweed, Editor.
Articles, 1,500 to 3,000 words, with photos, on promotions, display techniques, design features, business activities of quality retail shops for gifts, stationery and greeting cards. Pays to $50, extra for photos, on publication.

GLASS DIGEST–15 East 40th St., New York, NY 10016. Oscar S. Glasberg, Editor.
Articles, 1,200 to 1,500 words, on building projects and glass/metal dealers, distributors, storefront and glazing contractors. Pays 5¢ to 7¢ per word, $7 to $8 for photos, on publication.

GOLF INDUSTRY–915 N.E. 125th St., Suite 2-C, North Miami, Fl 33161. Michael Keighley, Editor.
Articles, 1,200 words, on marketing golf equipment. Photos. Pays 5¢ a word, on publication. Query.

GOLF SHOP OPERATIONS–495 Westport Ave., Norwalk, CT 06856. James McAfee, Editor.
Articles, 200 to 800 words, on successful golf shop operations; new ideas for merchandising, display, bookkeeping, etc. Short pieces on golf professionals. Pays $50 to $100, on publication.

GRAPHIC ARTS MONTHLY–222 South Riverside Plaza, Chicago, IL 60606. Bertram D. Chapman, Editor.
Technical articles, 2,000 to 3,000 words, on printing industry. Pays 6¢ per word, on acceptance. Query.

GROCERY COMMUNICATIONS–P.O. Box 925, Woodland Hills, CA 91365.
Articles, any length, with photos, for grocery retailers and food industry executives, on merchandising techniques. Pays 3¢ per word, $5 per photo, on publication.

HARDWARE AGE–Chilton Way, Radnor, PA 19089. M. Jay Holtzman, Editor.
Articles on merchandising methods in hardline outlets. Photos. Pays on acceptance.

HARDWARE MERCHANDISER–7300 North Cicero Ave., Chicago, IL 60646. W. P. Farrell, Editor.
Articles, to 1,000 words, with photos, on hardware marketing: merchandising of lines in hardware stores, discount stores, mass merchandisers, home centers. Query.

HEALTH FOODS BUSINESS–225 West 34th St., New York, NY 10001. Michael Spielman, Editor.
Articles, 1,500 words, with photos, on managing health-food stores: security, health cosmetics advertising, etc. Pays $25 per printed page, on publication. Query.

HEATING/PIPING/AIR CONDITIONING–2 Illinois Cntr., Chicago, IL 60601. Robert T. Korte, Editor.
Articles, to 5,000 words, on heating, piping and air conditioning systems in industrial plants and large buildings; engineering information. Pays $30 per printed page, on publication. Query.

HOME AND AUTO–757 Third Ave., New York, NY 10017.
Articles on merchandising methods of auto supply stores, home and auto stores, etc. Photos. Pays varying rates, on publication. Query. Unsolicited manuscripts not returned.

HOMESEWING TRADE NEWS–129 Broadway, Lynbrook, NY 11583. Senta Mead, Editor.
Articles, 750 to 1,000 words, with photos, for fabric shop owners and department store buyers in homesewing field. Pays $35 to $50 on publication. Query.

HOSIERY & UNDERWEAR–see *Body Fashions/Intimate Apparel.*

HOSPITAL SUPERVISOR'S BULLETIN–24 Rope Ferry Rd., Waterford, CT 06386. Barbara Kelsey, Editor.
Interview based articles, for nonmedical hospital supervisors, on solving problems of absenteeism, low morale, turnovers, etc. Pays on acceptance. Query, enclosing stamped, self-addressed envelope. Editorial guide available.

HOTEL & MOTEL MANAGEMENT–845 Chicago Ave., Evanston, IL 60202. Bob Freeman, Editor.
Articles, 1,000 to 2,000 words, on hotel and motel managements. Pays 6¢ a word, on acceptance. Query.

HOUSEWARES–757 Third Ave., New York, NY 10017. Jack BenAry, Editor.
Articles on merchandising by retail housewares outlets. Pays 10¢ per word, on acceptance. Query a must!

HOUSTON BUSINESS JOURNAL–5314 Bingle Rd., Houston, TX 77092. Mike Weingart, Editor.
Articles, to 3,000 words, on business news in Houston area. Cartoons; photos. Pays $2.50 per column inch, $7.50 for photos and cartoons, on publication.

THE JEWELERS' CIRCULAR-KEYSTONE–Chilton Way, Radnor, PA 19089. George Holmes, Editor.
Articles, 200 to 1,500 words, with photos, on retail jewelry store merchandising or operation. Shorts, 200 to 300 words, on activity that built sales or cut costs.

JOBBER & WAREHOUSE EXECUTIVE–53 West Jackson Blvd., Chicago, IL 60604. James Halloran, Editor.
Articles, 800 to 1,200 words with photos, for management personnel in automotive wholesaling firms. Pays varying rates, on acceptance.

JURIS DOCTOR–730 Third Ave., New York, NY 10017. Zachary Sklar, Editor.
Articles, 1,000 to 5,000 words, on legal profession. Profiles; short essays on leisure-time activities for "Off Hours." Pays 10¢ a word, on publication. Query. Also publishes *MBA, Medical Dimensions,* and *New Engineer.*

KIRKLEY PRESS, INC.–Box 200, Lutherville, MD 21093. Walter Kirkley, Editor.
Articles, 400 or 2,200 to 2,400 words, on good employee relations and efficiency. Pays $40 for folders, $200 to $300 for booklets, on acceptance. Query with sample of piece.

KITCHEN BUSINESS–1515 Broadway, New York, NY 10036. Patrick Galvin, Editor and Publisher.
Articles, 500 to 2,000 words, with photos and drawings, on management or merchandising methods of successful kitchen/bath dealers, designers, distributors. Must have how-to angle. Query first; uses little free-lance material. Pays $50 to $100.

KNITTING INDUSTRY–630 Third Ave., New York, NY 10017. Perry Antoshak, Editor.
Articles, 1,500 to 2,000 words, with photos, on manufacturing processes in knitting industry; outerwear, underwear, hosiery, packaging. Pays $1 per inch, $5 per photo, after publication. Query.

LAWN & GARDEN MARKETING–9221 Quivira Rd., Overland Park, KS 66212. Wendall J. Burns, Editor.

Brief articles on management, for retailers of landscaping and gardening supplies. Pays $65 per printed page, on acceptance. Query.

LP-GAS MAGAZINE—One East First St., Duluth, MN 55802. Zane Chastain, Editor.
Articles, 750 to 2,000 words with photos, on LP-Gas dealer operations: marketing, management, etc. Pays to 7¢ a word, $5 to $10 per photo, on acceptance. Query.

MADISON AVENUE MAGAZINE—750 Third Ave., New York, NY 10017. Jenny Greenberg, Editor.
Feature articles on advertising and marketing. No payment.

MAINE ANTIQUE DIGEST, INC.—Box 358, Waldoboro, ME 04572.
Lively, authoritative articles on antiques market in New England. Photos. Pays to $50, on acceptance. Query.

MANAGE—2210 Arbor Blvd., Dayton, OH 45439. Doug Shaw, Editor.
Articles, 1,500 to 2,200 words, with photos, on management and supervision, for first line and middle managers. Pays 5¢ a word, $10 for cartoons, on acceptance.

MARKING INDUSTRY—666 North Lake Shore Dr., Chicago, IL 60611. A. W. Hachmeister, Editor.
Technical or sales material on manufacture and distribution of steel stamps, checks, badges, seals, etc. in U.S. or Latin America. Pays on acceptance.

MBA—See *Juris Doctor.*

MEDICAL DIMENSIONS—See *Juris Doctor.*

MEETINGS & CONVENTIONS—One Park Ave., New York, NY 10016. Mel Hosansky, Editor.
Articles, 500 to 1,500 words, with photos, on ways to make corporate and association meetings more effective: ice-breaking techniques, seminar techniques, menus, etc. Pays from $150, on acceptance. Overstocked until June 1978.

MERCHANDISING 2-WAY RADIO—See *Personal Communications.*

MILITARY REVIEW—U.S. Army Command and General Staff College, Fort Leavenworth, KS 66027. Col. Edward M. Bradford, Editor-in-Chief.
Articles, 2,500 to 6,000 words, on military tactics, history, forces, strategy, etc. Pays about $50, on publication. Query.

MILK HAULER AND FOOD TRANSPORTER—P.O. Box 625, Washington, IN 47501.
Success stories, with photos, on transporters who haul cheese and other dairy products, liquid sugar, molasses, citrus juice, etc. Pays about $35 per article, $5 for photos, on acceptance. Query.

MODERN HEALTHCARE—740 North Rush St., Chicago, IL 60611. Donald E. L. Johnson, Editor.
No longer seeks free-lance manuscripts.

MODERN JEWELER—15 West 10th St., Kansas City, MO 64105. Dorothy Boicourt, Managing Editor.
Feature stories, with photos, about specific jewelers, on solving problems, building sales, etc., 6 to 7 typewritten pages. Pays from $60 to $90, on acceptance.

MODERN PACKAGING—1221 Ave. of the Americas, New York, NY 10017. Paul E. Mullins, Editor.
Articles, to 1,000 words, with tables, charts, graphs or photos, for packers of con-

sumer, industrial or military products. Pays $30 per printed page, on publication. Query.

MODERN TIRE DEALER–P.O. Box 5417, 77 North Miller Rd., Akron, OH 44313. Stephen LaFerre, Editor.
Merchandising, management and service articles, 1,000 to 1,500 words, with photos, on independent tire dealers and retreaders. Pays 7¢ a word and up, on publication.

MOTEL/MOTOR INN JOURNAL–306 East Adams Ave., Temple, TX 76502. Walter T. Proctor, Editor.
Articles, with photos, on motel and motor inn management, operation, maintenance and promotion. Pays $10 per manuscript page, extra for photos, on acceptance. Query.

MOTOR–1790 Broadway, New York, NY 10019. Joe Oldham, Editor.
Articles, 750 to 1,500 words, with photos, on new trends, ideas and products in automotive service business, and on merchandising and management techniques. Pays $75 to $240, on acceptance. Query.

MOTOR IN CANADA–1077 St. James St., Box 6900, Winnipeg, Man., Canada. Ralf Neuendorff, Editor.
Merchandising and service articles, 250 to 1,000 words, for automotive trade in western Canada. Pays $1.50 per column inch, extra for pictures, on publication. Query.

NATIONAL BOWLERS JOURNAL AND BILLIARD REVUE–Suite 3734, 875 North Michigan Ave., Chicago IL 66011. Mort Luby, Jr., Editor, Jim Dressel, Managing Editor.
Articles, 1,200 to 1,500 words, with photos, on promotions for bowling and billiard proprietors. Pays $60 to $75, on publication.

NATIONAL BUSINESS WOMAN–2012 Massachusetts Ave. N.W., Washington, D.C. 20036. Louise G. Wheeler, Editor.
Articles, to 1,200 words, for business and professional women, on career development, opportunities, responsibilities, etc. Pays 3¢ a word, on acceptance.

NATIONAL LIVESTOCK PRODUCER–733 North Van Buren, Milwaukee, WI 53202. Frank Lessiter, Editor.
Articles, any length, for livestock producers on marketing. Pays about $100 per article, on acceptance. Query.

THE NATIONAL PUBLIC ACCOUNTANT–1717 Pennsylvania Ave. N.W., Washington, DC 20006. Stanley H. Stearman, Editor.
Articles, 1,800 to 5,000 words, on accounting, tax, bookkeeping, data processing, administration, etc. No payment.

NEW CAREER WAYS NEWSLETTER–358 Main St., Suite 20, Haverhill, MA 01830. William J. Bond, Editor.
How-to articles, 1,500 to 2,000 words, on new ways to succeed in business career. Pays varying rates, on publication. Query with outline.

NEW ENGINEER–See *Juris Doctor*.

NORTHERN HARDWARE TRADE–5901 Brooklyn Blvd., Suite 112, Minneapolis, MN 55429. Betty Braden, Managing Editor.
Articles, 800 to 1,000 words, on unusual hardware stores and promotions in Northwest and Midwest. Pays 4¢ a word, $5 per photo, on publication. Query.

OCCUPATIONAL HAZARDS–614 Superior Ave. West, Cleveland, OH 44113. Peter J. Sheridan, Editor.

Articles, 500 to 2,000 words, on industrial safety, health, fire prevention and security. Photos. Pays from 3¢ a word, on publication, $5 for cartoons, on acceptance.

OFFICE PRODUCTS—Hitchcock Bldg., Wheaton, IL 60187. Thomas J. Trafals, Editorial Director.
Illustrated merchandising articles, any length, for office-supply, machine and furniture dealers. Pays from $25 per printed page, on acceptance.

OFFICE SUPERVISOR'S BULLETIN—24 Rope Ferry Rd., Waterford, CT 06386. Ruth Norcia, Editor.
Interview-based articles, 900 to 1,350 words, for first- and second-line supervisors, on solving management problems. Pays 10¢ a word, on acceptance, after editing. Query.

THE OSHA COMPLIANCE LETTER—24 Rope Ferry Rd., Waterford, CT 06386. Ruth Norcia, Editor.
Interview-based articles, 800 to 1,250 words, for safety professionals, on solving OSHA-related safety problems. Pays 10¢ a word, on acceptance, after editing. Query.

PACKING AND SHIPPING—735 Woodland Ave., Plainfield, NJ 07062. C. M. Bonnell, Jr., Editor.
Illustrated articles, 1,000 words, on distribution, industrial packing, handling, shipping-room practice. Short items. Pays varying rates, on publication.

PAPER, FILM AND FOIL CONVERTER—200 South Prospect, Park Ridge, IL 60068. Peter Rigney, Editor.
Articles, 2,500 to 5,000 words, or photo-essays, on converter processes, production, product development. No payment.

PAPERBOARD PACKAGING—777 Third Ave., New York, NY 10017. Joel J. Shulman, Editor.
Articles, any length, on paperboard mills, corrugated containers, folding cartons, set-up boxes, etc. Pays $50 per 1,000 words, on publication. Query with outline.

PERSONAL COMMUNICATIONS (formerly *Merchandising 2-Way Radio*)—14 Vandeventer Ave., Port Washington, NY 11050. Eric Ian Mathieson, Editor.
How-to articles, 2,000 words, with photos, on merchandising CB radio. Pays from $150 to $250, on publication. Query.

PET DEALER—225 West 34th St., New York, NY 10001. William G. Reddan, Editor.
Merchandising articles, 900 to 1,500 words, on specialty pet shops or departments. Photos. Pays $25 per printed page, on publication. Query.

PETROLEUM TODAY—2101 L St. N.W., Washington, DC 20037. Don Sweeney, Director, Editorial Dept.
Articles, 500 or 1,200 to 2,000 words, on oil industry issues: energy crisis, Alaska pipeline, environment, deep-water ports, personalities, etc. Pays from $200, on publication. Query.

PETS/SUPPLIES/MARKETING—One East First St., Duluth, MN 55802. Paul A. Setzer, Editor.
Articles, 1,500 to 2,000 words, with photos, for pet and pet product retailers, wholesalers and manufacturers, on successes of pet shops. Short pieces, with photos, on merchandising or display ideas. Pays 5¢ per word, $6 to $15 for photos. Query.

PHOTO MARKETING—603 Lansing Ave., Jackson, MI 49202. Michael F. Buda, Managing Editor.
Articles, 500 words, on camera store and finishing plant successes in promotion, advertising, personnel management, etc. Pays 5¢ to 7¢ per word, $5 to $7.50 per photo, on publication.

PHYSICIAN'S MANAGEMENT—757 Third Ave., New York, NY 10017. Patrick Flanagan, Editor.

Articles, 400 to 2,000 words, for doctors, on office management, socio-economic subjects; interviews. Pays 5¢ to 20¢ a word, on acceptance. Query.

POLICE TIMES—1100 NE 125th St., Miami, FL 33101. Donald Anderson, Editor.
Articles, 200 to 2,000 words, on law enforcement officers, departments, (including prisons, jails), forest rangers, game wardens, private security, courts, etc. Photos. Fillers and humor, 100 to 200 words. Pays 2¢ a word, $1 to $5 per photo, on publication.

POOL NEWS—Leisure Publications, 3932 West Sixth St., Los Angeles, CA 90020. Fay Coupe, Editor.
News pieces on swimming pool industry. Pays 5¢ a word, $5 per photo, on publication. Query.

POULTRY TRIBUNE—Mt. Morris, IL 61054. Milton R. Dunk, Editor.
Articles, 200 to 1,000 words, on egg production, processing and marketing. Pays 6¢ to 8¢ a word, on acceptance. Query.

POWER ENGINEERING—1301 South Grove Ave., Barrington, IL 60010. John Papamarcos, Editor.
Specialized articles, 1,000 to 2,400 words, on design, construction, operation and maintenance of large power facilities for industry and utilities. Pays $40 per printed page, on acceptance.

PRODUCTION MAGAZINE—Bramson Publishing Co., P.O. Box 101, Bloomfield Hills, MI 48013. Robert F. Huber, Editor.
Articles, 300 to 3,000 words, with photos, on improved metalworking operations. Pays varying rates, on acceptance.

PROFITABLE CRAFT MERCHANDISING—News Plaza, Peoria, IL 61601. Ellen M. Dahlquist, Editor.
Articles, 1,000 to 1,500 words, with photos, for small independent craft retailers, on store management: sales displays, accounting systems, etc.; profiles of successful retailers; how-to pieces on craft projects and techniques. Pays $45 to $250, on acceptance. Query.

PROGRESSIVE GROCER—708 Third Ave., New York, NY 10017. Edgar B. Walzer, Editor.
Factual articles, to 2,500 words, on supermarket management, merchandising and promotion. Shorts, 100 to 200 words, on sales promotion ideas. Photos. Pays varying rates, on acceptance.

PROOFS—P.O. Box 1260, Tulsa, OK 74101. Jon Finch, Editor.
Articles, 800 to 1,200 words, with photos, on dental product sales and dealerships. Pays up to $100, on acceptance.

THE PUBLIC RELATIONS QUARTERLY—44 West Market St., Rhinebeck, NY 12572. Howard Penn Hudson, Editor.
Articles on public relations techniques and personalities. Pays in copies. Query.

PUBLICIST—Public Relations Aids, Inc., 221 Park Ave. South, New York, NY 10003. Lee Levitt, Editor.
Case histories, 400 to 800 words, of successful national public-relations campaigns. Humor, cartoons, fillers, photos. Pays $50 to $100, on acceptance.

PURCHASING—221 Columbus Ave., Boston, MA 02116. Robert Haavind, Editor.
Articles, 1,200 to 1,500 words, on buying techniques in industrial purchasing departments, industry personalities. Pays about $50 per printed page, on publication.

PURCHASING EXECUTIVE'S BULLETIN—24 Rope Ferry Rd., Waterford, CT 06386. Claire Sherman, Editor.
Interview-based articles, 800 to 1,250 words, from industrial purchasing agents or

managers, on coping with problems in the field. Pays 10¢ a word, on acceptance, after editing. Query.

THE PURCHASING PROFESSIONAL—1070 Sibley Tower, Rochester, NY 14604. Peter O. Allen, Editor.
Articles, 2,000 to 3,000 words, on industrial purchasing. Pays varying rates, on publication.

RADIO AND TELEVISION WEEKLY—254 West 31st St., New York, NY 10001. Cy Kneller, Editor.
News on radio, television wholesale and retail delears. Pays $2 per inch, after publication. Query.

RADIO-ELECTRONICS—200 Park Ave. South, New York, NY 10003. Larry Steckler, Editorial Director.
Technical articles, 1,500 to 3,000 words, on electronic equipment. Pays $50 to $500, on acceptance.

RECREATIONAL VEHICLE RETAILER—23945 Craftsman Rd., Calabasas, CA 91302. Alice Robison, Editorial Director.
Articles 2,000 to 3,500 words, with photos, on selling and servicing recreational vehicles, increasing profits in dealer business, opening new markets. Pays to $150, on publication.

REFRIGERATED TRANSPORTER—1602 Harold St., Houston, TX 77006.
News articles, with illustrations, on transportation under refrigeration, by for-hire and private motor carriers. Pays from $50 per printed page.

RENT ALL—Harcourt Brace Jovanovich, One East First St., Duluth, MN 55802. Roy Johnson, Editor.
Business articles, 1,000 to 1,500 words, with photos, on rental field. Pays 8¢ per word, $7.50 per photo, on acceptance. Query.

RESORT MANAGEMENT—1509 Madison Ave., P.O. Box 4169, Memphis, TN 38104. Allen J. Fagans, Editor.
Articles, 1,000 to 1,500 words, on successful resort operation and management: attracting and entertaining guests, saving money, servicing bar, kitchen, housekeeping, etc. Pays to $75 for articles, $5 for photos, on publication. Query with outline.

ROCK PRODUCTS—300 West Adams St., Chicago, IL 60606. Roy A. Grancher, Editor.
Articles, from 1,000 words, on production methods in construction minerals field: cement, lime, gypsum, sand and gravel, crushed stone, slag and lightweight aggregates. Pays $35 per printed page, after publication.

SALESMAN'S OPPORTUNITY—John Hancock Center, Suite 1460, 875 North Michigan Ave., Chicago, IL 60611. Jack Weissman, Managing Editor.
Articles, 900 words, on sales psychology, techniques, self-improvement. Cartoons. Pays $25, $5 per cartoon, on publication.

SECURITY MANAGEMENT: PLANT AND PROPERTY PROTECTION—24 Rope Ferry Rd., Waterford, CT 06386. Carol McGarry, Editor.
Interview-based articles, 800 to 1,250 words, from security professionals, on solving security problems. Pays 10¢ a word, on acceptance, after editing. Query.

SELLING SPORTING GOODS—717 North Michigan Ave., Chicago, IL 60611. Thomas B. Doyle, Managing Editor.
Articles, 1,000 to 1,200 words, with black-and-white photos, on retail sporting goods stores with outstanding promotions, advertising, merchandising, training programs, etc. Pays $75 to $125, on acceptance. Query.

SHOPPING CENTER WORLD—6285 Barfield Rd., Atlanta, GA 30328. Eric Petersen, Editor.

Articles, to 4,000 words, on new developments in shopping center design, construction and operation. Pays to $400, on acceptance. Query.

SIMMENTAL SCENE—Suite 120, Petroleum Bldg., 310 Ninth Ave. S.W., Calgary, Canada T2P 1K5. Keith J. Wilson, Editorial Production.
Articles, up to 2,000 words, on subjects of interest to North American purebred cattle producers: farming and ranching methods, scientific and technological advances in breeding techniques, profiles. Also articles of interest to rural women, offbeat rural stories. Pays 2¢ to 5¢ a word, on publication, extra for photos. Queries preferred.

SKIING TRADE NEWS—One Park Ave., New York, NY 10016. Carol Feder, Editor.
How-to articles, 1,500 words, with photos, on making profits in retail ski shops. Pays 10¢ a word, on publication.

SNACK FOOD MAGAZINE—Harcourt Bldg., Duluth, MN 55802. Jerry Hess, Editor.
Articles, 1,200 to 1,600 words, on trade news, personalities, promotions, production in snack food manufacturing industry. Short pieces; photos. Pays 5¢ to 7¢ per word, $5 to $7 per photo, on acceptance. Query.

THE SOUTH MAGAZINE—Trend Publications, Inc., P.O. Box 2350, Tampa, FL 33601. Roy B. Bain, Editor.
Articles, 150 to 1,500 words, on southern business: companies, people, successes and failures, urban problems and solutions. Pays $50 to $300, on acceptance. Query.

SOUTHERN HARDWARE—1760 Peachtree Rd., Atlanta, GA 30309. Ralph E. Kirby, Editor.
Articles, 800 to 1,000 words, on merchandising and operational methods of specific southern hardware retailers. Pays $50 per printed page and up, on acceptance. Query.

SOUVENIRS AND NOVELTIES—327 Wagaraw Rd., Hawthorne, NJ 07506.
Articles, 1,500 words, quoting souvenir shop managers on items that sell, display ideas, problems in selling and industry trends. Pays from $1 per column inch, $10 for photos.

SPECIALTY SALESMAN—307 North Michigan Ave., Chicago, IL 60601. Susan Loeb, Editor.
Articles, 300 to 1,200 words, for independent salespersons selling to homes, stores, industries and business. Pays 3¢ a word, on acceptance.

THE SPORTING GOODS DEALER—1212 North Lindbergh, St. Louis, MO 63166. Steve Blackhurst, Managing Editor.
Articles, 500 words, on news of sporting goods stores. Pays from 2¢ a word for articles, on publication.

SUFFOLK SENTINEL—See *Trooper Magazine.*

SUPERMARKET MANAGEMENT—209 Dunn Ave., Stamford, CT 06905. Kenneth Jones, Editor.
Articles, with photos, on assignment only. Pays $50 per printed page. Query.

SUPERVISION—424 North Third, Burlington, IA 52601. B. Pollard, Editor.
Self-help articles, 1,000 to 1,500 words, for management executives, supervisors, foremen and production managers. Pays 2¢ a word, on publication. Query.

TEENS & BOYS (formerly *Boys Outfitter*)—71 West 35th St., New York, NY 10001. Ellye Bloom, Editor.
Articles on the retailing and merchandising of male-youth fashions, 1,000 to 2,000 words. Pays from $30 to $150. Query.

TENNIS INDUSTRY—915 N.E. 125th St., Suite 2C, North Miami, FL 33161. Michael Keighley, Editor.
Articles, 1,000 to 2,000 words, on tennis industry: tennis products, new court sur-

faces, recreation center planning, costs of operating tennis complexes at schools, etc. Pays 5¢ a word, on publication. Query.

TEXTILE WORLD—1175 Peachtree St. N.E., Atlanta, GA 30361. L. A. Christiansen, Editor.
Articles, 500 to 2,000 words, with photos, on manufacturing and finishing textiles, increasing efficiency, management techniques, marketing, etc. Pays varying rates, on acceptance.

TRAILER/BODY BUILDERS—1602 Harold St., Houston, TX 77006. Paul Schenck, Editor.
Articles on engineering, sales and management ideas for truck body and truck trailer manufacturers. Pays from $50 per printed page, on acceptance.

TRAINING—731 Hennepin Ave., Minneapolis, MN 55403. Philip G. Jones, Managing Editor.
Articles, 1,500 to 2,000 words, on how organizations train employees. Pays 5¢ to 10¢ a word, on acceptance. Query.

TRAVEL AGE EAST—888 Seventh Ave., Suite 600, New York, NY 10019.
Articles, 400 to 600 words, with photos, on travel agency operations; new travel packages; destinations, hotels, sightseeing, transportation. Pays about $35 per article, on publication. Query.

THE TRAVEL AGENT—2 West 46th St., New York, NY 10036.
Articles, 1,500 words, with photos, on travel trade, for travel agents. Pays $50 to $75, on acceptance.

TROOPER MAGAZINE—(formerly *Suffolk Sentinel*)—1616 Soldiers Field Rd., Boston, MA 02135. Sue Himmelrich, Editor.
Articles, 2,000 to 3,500 words, on police operations, society, medicine, adventure, etc. Photos. Pays 5¢ per word, on publication. Query. Same address for "brother" publications for Massachusetts, Illinois, Indiana, Iowa, Arizona, Virginia, Nebraska, Alabama, Colorado.

VENDING TIMES—211 East 43rd St., New York, NY 10017. Arthur E. Yohalem, Editor.
Feature and news articles, with photos, on vending machines. Pays varying rates, on acceptance. Query.

VIDEO SYSTEMS—P.O. Box 12901, Overland Park, KS 66212.
How-to articles, with photos, on new uses for closed-circuit video systems. Pays $100, extra for photos. Query.

WALLS & CEILINGS—14006 Ventura Blvd., Suite 204, Sherman Oaks, CA 91423. Robert F. Welch, Editor.
Articles for plaster and drywall contractors on building techniques, management skills, reducing overhead. Photos; fillers. Pays 3¢ a word, on publication.

THE WELDING DISTRIBUTOR—614 Superior Ave. West, Cleveland, OH 44113. Charles Berka, Executive Editor.
Articles, 1,000 to 3,500 words, on selling welding and safety equipment, running a small business, keeping records and management. Cartoons; photos. Pays 2½¢ per word, on publication. Query.

WESTERN OUTFITTER—5314 Bingle Rd., Houston, TX 77092. Mary J. House, Editor.
Articles, to 1,500 words, with photos, on merchandising western wear and equipment. Pays 5¢ per word, $6 per photo, on publication. Query.

WESTERN PAINT REVIEW—2354 West 3rd St., Los Angeles, CA 90057. E. C. Ansley, Editor.
Articles, 1,000 to 2,000 words, with photos, on paint and painting industries in

western states. Pays 4¢ per word, $3 per photo, on publication. Query.

WINES & VINES—703 Market St., San Francisco, CA 94103. Philip Hiaring, Editor.
Articles, 1,000 words, with photos, for wine industry, emphasizing marketing and production. Pays 3¢ a word, on acceptance.

WOODWORKING & FURNITURE DIGEST—Hitchcock Bldg., Wheaton, IL 60187. R. D. Rea, Editor.
Articles, 1,200 to 1,600 words, with photos, on management, production and engineering in industries using wood as primary material. No sawmill, logging, paper industry or forestry pieces. Pays $35 to $50 per printed page. Query.

WORLD OIL—Gulf Publishing Co., P.O. Box 2608, Houston, TX 77001. R. W. Scott, Editor.
Engineering and operations articles, 3,000 to 4,000 words, on petroleum industry exploration, drilling or producing. Photos or drawings. Pays from $25 per printed page, on acceptance. Query.

TRAVEL

AIRFAIR INTERLINE MAGAZINE—9800 South Sepulveda Blvd., Suite 520, Los Angeles, CA 90045. Crista C. Gillette, Editor.
Travel articles, 1,000 to 1,500 words, with photos, for airline employees, on shopping, sightseeing, dining, etc., including prices and addresses. Pays to $75, after publication.

ALOFT—2701 South Bayshore Dr., Miami, FL 33133. Karl Y. Wickstrom, Editor.
National Airlines' in-flight magazine. Articles, 1,300 words, on cities along National route: offbeat approaches to sightseeing, shopping, dining, etc. Pays $150 to $200. Query.

ARIZONA HIGHWAYS—2039 West Lewis St., Phoenix, AZ 85009. Tom Cooper, Editor.
Queries only.

AWAY—ALA Auto and Travel Club, 888 Worcester St., Wellesley, MA 02181. Gerard J. Gagnon, Editor.
Travel articles, 1,000 to 1,200 words, on tourist attractions, auto trips and outdoor activities in New England. Light articles, 600 to 800 words. Photos, photo essays. Pays 10¢ a word, on acceptance, $5 to $10 per photo, on publication. Query.

BON APPETIT—5900 Wilshire Blvd., Los Angeles, CA 90036. Paige Rense, Editor-in-Chief.
Travel articles, 1,200 to 1,500 words, on fine food, wine, restaurants, new products and culinary equipment, mentioning specific restaurants, hotels, foods, wines and recipes. Pays 20¢ a word, $10 to $25 per photo.

BRANIFF'S FLYING COLORS—15383 N.W. Seventh Ave., Miami, FL 33169. Seymour Gerber, Editor and Publisher.
Braniff airlines' in-flight magazine. Travel articles, 750 to 2,000 words, with photos, on cities along Braniff route; personality profiles. Pays $125 to $250. Query.

BUYWAYS—1000 Sunset Ridge Rd., Northbrook, IL 60062. Charles E. McKillip, Editor.
Publication of the National Association of Consumers and Travelers. Travel articles, 500 to 2,500 words, emphasizing budget. Submit seasonal material 4 months in advance. Pays 10¢ to 20¢ a word, on acceptance. Query.

CALIFORNIA MAGAZINE (formerly *PSA, The California Magazine*)—East/West Net-

work, Inc., 5900 Wilshire Blvd., Suite 300, Los Angeles, CA 90036. Thomas Shess, Editor.
Pacific Southwest Airlines' in-flight magazine. Articles, 1,500 words, of interest to business travelers. Travel features staff-written. Pays $100, 60 days after acceptance. Most articles written on assignment. Query first. Same address for Allegheny *Flightime*, Continental *Flightime*, Ozark *Flightime*, *Holiday Inn Companion*, *Mainliner*, *Ramada Reflections*, *ReView*, *Sky*, *Sundancer*. Query first.

CHEVRON USA—P.O. Box 6227, San Jose, CA 95150. Marian May, Editor.
Articles, 800 to 1,500 words, on travel in western, southern and eastern states. Humorous anecdotes, 100 to 250 words; cartoons. Pays from 15¢ a word, $35 to $200 per photo, on acceptance.

CHICAGO TRIBUNE—Travel Section, Tribune Square, Chicago, IL 60611. Alfred S. Borcover, Associate Travel Editor.
Travel articles, 800 to 1,200 words, with photos, from second- or third-person point of view. Pays $40 to $100, extra for photos, on acceptance.

CLIPPER MAGAZINE—East/West Network, Inc., 5900 Wilshire Blvd., Los Angeles, CA 90036. Address queries to Robert L. Sammons, Travel Editor, *Clipper*, 488 Madison Ave., New York, NY 10022.
Articles, 1,000 to 1,500 words, on international travel along Pan Am route. Pays $200 to $400, after acceptance.

THE CONTINENTAL MAGAZINE—Room 956, Central Office Bldg., Ford Motor Co., Dearborn, MI 48121. Robert M. Hodesh, Editor-in-Chief.
Sophisticated service articles, 1,300 to 1,700 words, on travel, entertainment, shopping, sports, etc., for an affluent readership. Pays on acceptance. Query.

COSMOPOLITAN—224 West 57th St., New York, NY 10019. Roberta Ashley, Articles Editor.
Travel articles, 2,500 to 3,000 words, of interest to young career women. Pays $400 to $500. Query.

DESERT MAGAZINE—Palm Desert, CA 92260. Bill Knyvett, Editor.
Articles, 500 to 2,500 words, with photos, on travel in the West. Pays 2¢ a word, from $5 per photo, on publication.

DISCOVERY—Allstate Motor Club, Northbrook, IL 60062. Alan Rosenthal, Editor.
Articles, 1,000 to 2,500 words, with photos: first-person accounts of vacation trips, humor pieces related to motoring. Pays $100 to $400, on acceptance.

EASY LIVING—1999 Shepard Rd., St. Paul, MN 55116. Jean Marie Hamilton, Editor.
Articles, 1,500 to 2,000 words, for travelers over 50, on travel in Europe, Mexico, Far East, etc. Photos. Pays $100 to $250, on acceptance. Query.

ENTHUSIAST—Harley-Davidson Motor Co., P.O. Box 654, Milwaukee, WI 53201. Robert H. Klein, Editor.
Articles and fiction, to 2,500 words, and photo essays, on motorcycling. Travel pieces on places not readily accessible by car. Pays 5¢ a word, $7.50 to $15 per photo, on publication.

FLAIR—6500 Midnight Pass Rd., P.O. Box 2527, Sarasota, FL 33581. Laurie Storey, Editor.
Personal-experience travel articles, 250 to 400 words, with photos, on destinations in Florida and the Bahamas. Pays $25, on publication.

FLIGHTIME (Allegheny)—See *California Magazine*.

FLIGHTIME (Continental)—See *California Magazine*.

FLIGHTIME (Ozark)—See *California Magazine*.

FORD TIMES—Ford Motor Co., The American Rd., Dearborn, MI 48121. Richard L. Routh, Managing Editor.
Articles, to 1,500 words, for young adults, on travel and recreation related to car ownership. Humor. Pays from $250, on acceptance. Query.

GOING PLACES—211 East 43rd St., New York, NY 10017. Maurice L. Fisher, Editor.
Travel destination articles, 2,000 to 2,500 words, of interest to upper-income customers. Pays $250 to $300, on acceptance.

HOLIDAY—See *Travel Holiday*.

INCENTIVE TRAVEL MANAGER—Bentwood Publishing Corp., 825 South Barrington Ave., Los Angeles, CA 90049. Martin Waldman and Hal Spector, Editors.
Articles, 3,000 to 5,000 words, to help corporation sales and marketing executives plan incentive travel programs: destination selection, promotional procedures, etc. Pays $125 to $150, on acceptance. Query first.

LATITUDE 20—1649 Kapiolani Blvd., Suite 28, Honolulu, HI 96814. Rita Witherwax, Editor.
Articles, to 1,500 words, on travel in Hawaii: costs, activities, sights, etc. Pays $50, on publication.

THE LUFKIN LINE—P.O. Box 849, Lufkin, TX 75901. Virginia R. Allen, Editor.
Articles, 1,000 to 1,200 words, with photos, on travel in U.S. and Canada. Pays $50, extra for photos, on acceptance.

MAINLINER—See *California Magazine*.

THE MIDWEST MOTORIST—201 Progress Pkwy., Maryland Heights, MO 63043.
Articles, 1,000 to 1,500 words, with photos, on travel, transportation and consumerism in Midwest. Pays $50 to $200, on acceptance.

MINNESOTA AAA MOTORIST—7 Traveler's Trail, Burnsville, MN 55337. Ron D. Johnson, Editor.
Articles, 800 to 1,000 words, on domestic and foreign travel, motoring, safety, recreation, etc. Cartoons; photos. Pays from $150, from $15 per photo, $15 for cartoons, on acceptance.

MOTOR NEWS—Auto Club Dr., Dearborn, MI 48126.
Articles, 800 to 2,000 words, on travel in U.S.: costs, planning, sights, etc. Pieces on travel in Michigan. Photos. Pays from $100, on acceptance.

NATIONAL GEOGRAPHIC—17th and M Sts. N.W., Washington, DC 20036. Gilbert M. Grosvenor, Editor.
First-person articles, 2,000 to 8,000 words (shorter lengths preferred), on geography: travel, exploration, natural history, archaeology, etc. Photos. Pays $1,500 to $3,500, on acceptance. Query.

NATIONAL MOTORIST—One Market Plaza, Suite 300, San Francisco, CA 94105. Jim Donaldson, Editor.
Illustrated articles, 300 or 1,100 words, for California motorists, on motoring in the West, car care, roads, personalities, places, etc. Pays from 10¢ a word, $15 to $25 per photo, on acceptance.

THE NEW EAST—See *Tar Heel.*

THE NEW YORK TIMES—229 West 43rd St., New York, NY 10036. Robert W. Stock, Travel Editor.
Travel articles, 1,000 to 2,500 words. Query first, indicating approach, time and purpose of visit (no articles based on sponsored trips) and author's credentials. Pays 10¢ a word, $50 per photo.

NORTHLINER—7101 York Ave. South, Minneapolis, MN 55435.
North Central Airlines' in-flight magazine. Travel articles, 1,000 to 2,000 words, with photos, on cities along North Central route: business, personalities, humor, etc. Cartoons. Pays $50 to $400, on acceptance. Query.

NORTHWEST—*Sunday Oregonian,* 1320 S. W. Broadway, Portland, OR 97201. J. R. Bianco, Editor.
Articles, to 1,500 words, with photos, on travel in Pacific Northwest. Pays $40 per printed page, $15 per photo.

OFF DUTY—250 East 63rd St., New York, NY 10021. Jim Shaw, Editor.
Travel articles, 800 to 2,500 words, with anecdotes, dialogue, description, etc.; useful information on transportation arrangements and prices. Pays 7¢ to 10¢ a word, extra for photos, on acceptance and publication.

PSA, THE CALIFORNIA MAGAZINE—See *California Magazine.*

REVIEW—See *California Magazine.*

SIGNATURE—260 Madison Avenue, New York, NY 10016. Josh Eppinger, Executive Editor.
Sophisticated articles, to 2,500 words, on foreign and domestic travel; no "destination" pieces. Articles on sports, business and social issues, for an affluent readership. Pays $650. Query.

SKY—See *California Magazine.*

SUNDANCER—See *California Magazine.*

TAR HEEL (formerly *The New East*)—223 West 10th St., Greenville, NC 27834. James Wise, Editor.
Well-researched articles, 1,200 to 3,000 words, on North Carolina. Some fiction; poetry. Pays from 2¢ a word, on publication.

TRAVEL AGE WEST—582 Market St., San Francisco, CA 94104. Don Langley, Managing Editor.
Articles, 800 to 1,000 words, with photos, on any aspect of travel useful to travel agents, including addresses, etc. Pays $1.50 per inch, after publication. Query.

TRAVEL & LEISURE—1350 Ave. of the Americas, New York, NY 10019. Pamela Fiori, Editor-in-Chief.
Articles, 1,500 to 2,500 words, on accessible destinations and leisure-time activities. Regional pieces. Pays $500 to $1,500. Articles on assignment. Query.

TRAVELDAY/VISA—532 D St., San Rafael, CA 94902.
Articles, 250 to 1,000 words, with photos, on consumer-oriented travel, U.S. and world-wide travel. Pays $25 to $100, extra for photos, on publication.

TRAVEL HOLIDAY—Travel Bldg., Floral Park, NY 11001.
Articles, 1,500 to 2,000 words, with photos, about foreign and domestic travel destinations; shorter "featurettes" 1,000 words. Pays $100 to $225.

TWA AMBASSADOR—1999 Shepard Rd., St. Paul, MN 55116. James Morgan, Editor.
TWA's in-flight magazine. Travel articles, 1,000 to 2,000 words, with photos, with

strong, well-developed angle. Pieces on sports, business, personalities, modern living, etc. Pays to $600, on acceptance. Query.

WESTERN'S WORLD–141 El Camino Dr., Suite 110, Beverly Hills, CA 90212. Frank M. Hiteshew, Editor.
Western Airlines' in-flight magazine. Travel and special-interest articles, 1,500 to 2,000 words, on the West: artists, food, sports, etc, Pays 10¢ a word, on publication. Query.

WOODALL'S TRAILER & RV TRAVEL–500 Hyacinth Place, Highland Park, IL 60035. Kirk Landers, Editor.
Articles, 1,200 to 2,500 words, with photos, on recreational-vehicle travel: routes, costs, recreation, campgrounds, scenery, etc. Pays from 10¢ a word, on acceptance. Query.

CITY AND REGIONAL MAGAZINES

The following list gives a representative sample of the many city and regional magazines published across the country. These publications offer writers an excellent market for all types of material: general-interest and business articles, travel pieces, profiles, photo-features, fillers, and, occasionally, short stories. Most editors require that articles and features focus specifically on the region or city, its history, people, and events. Many of the city magazines are published by chambers of commerce and seek to build local pride by emphasizing local business, politics, cultural and urban affairs.

It is essential that writers query editors of these publications before sending completed manuscripts, and enclose a list of photos available or even a few sample prints. Always study past issues of the publications carefully to learn what has been used recently, and to determine a magazine's style and slant.

See the list of *General Magazines* for names of newspaper magazine supplements, many of which buy regional-interest articles.

ADIRONDACK LIFE–Keene, NY 12942. Lionel A. Atwill, Editor.
Articles, 750 to 2,000 words, with photos, on Adirondack personalities, history, geography, wildlife, etc. Pays $75 to $175, $10 to $30 for photos, on publication. Query.

ALABAMA REVIEW–Dept. of History, University of Alabama, University, AL 35486. Sarah W. Wiggins, Editor.
Historical, scholarly articles on Alabama and the South.

ALASKA GEOGRAPHIC–Alaska Geographic Society, Box 4-EEE, Anchorage, AK 99509.
Informative articles, with photos, on geography of Alaska and northern Canada, Siberia and Japan: exploration, geology, biology, resources, etc. Pays to $500, on publication. Query.

ALASKA JOURNAL–Box 4-EEE, Anchorage, AK 99509. William S. Hanable, Editor.
Well-researched articles, 500 to 5,000 words, with photos, on Alaska and Yukon history and on Alaska artists. Pays around 2¢ a word, on publication. Query.

ALASKA, THE MAGAZINE OF LIFE ON THE LAST FRONTIER–Box 4-EEE, Anchorage, AK 99509. Bob Henning, Editor and Publisher.
Factual articles, to 3,000 words, on life in Far North, preferably by residents. Photos. Pays $10 to $200, on publication.

THE AMERICAN WEST–20380 Town Center Ln., #160, Cupertino, CA 95014. Ed Holm, Editor and Publisher.

Articles, 2,500 to 4,000 words, on western history, natural history, conservation, etc. Pays to $200, after acceptance. Query.

ARIZONA—The Arizona *Republic,* Box 1950, Phoenix, AZ 85001.
Articles, 500 to 2,500 words, on Arizona. Fillers, cartoons. Photos, drawings. Pays $25 to $175, before publication.

ARIZONA AND THE WEST—University of Arizona, Library C327, Tucson, AZ 85721. Harwood P. Hinton, Editor.
Scholarly articles, 4,000 to 6,000 words, on history of the West. Photos, maps. No payment.

ARIZONA HIGHWAYS—2039 West Lewis Ave., Phoenix, AZ 85009. Tom Cooper, Editor.
Articles on Arizona. Overstocked; no free-lance material.

THE ATLANTIC ADVOCATE—Gleaner Bldg., Phoenix Sq., Fredericton, N.B., Canada E3B 5A2. Harold P. Wood, Editor.
Well-researched articles on eastern Canada and general-interest articles. Fiction, to 2,000 words. Pays 5¢ a word, on publication.

AUSTIN—Austin Chamber of Commerce, Box 1967, Austin, TX 78767. Hal Susskind, Editor.
Articles, 800 to 1,500 words, on Austin. Photos; cartoons. Pays varying rates. Query.

BALTIMORE MAGAZINE—Baltimore Chamber of Commerce, 22 Light St., Baltimore, MD 21202.
Articles, to 3,500 words, on metropolitan area problems, institutions, personalities. Photos. Pays on publication. Query.

THE BEAVER—Hudson's Bay House, Winnipeg, Manitoba, Canada R3C 2R1. Helen Burgess, Editor.
Factual articles, 3,000 words, and fillers, 700 to 1,500 words, on historical or modern aspects of northwest Canada and Arctic regions. Photos. Pays around 5¢ a word, on acceptance.

BERKELEY BARB—Box 1247, Berkeley, CA 94701. Ray Riegert, Editor.
Fast-paced, accurate articles, 1,000 words, on social issues, of interest to Bay Area readers. Pays 75¢ per column inch, on publication.

BLADE SUNDAY MAGAZINE—See *Toledo Magazine*.

BOSTON MAGAZINE—1050 Park Sq. Bldg., Boston, MA 02116.
Compelling, entertaining features, 1,000 to 5,000 words, on Boston area personalities, institutions and phenomena. Pays $100 to $500, on acceptance. Query.

BROWARD LIFE MAGAZINE—3801 East Commercial Blvd., Ft. Lauderdale, FL 33308. Joanne Myers, Editor.
Articles, 2,000 words and up, on life styles, problems and pleasures of South Florida. Poems up to 50 lines. Pays various rates, on publication. Query first.

BUCKS COUNTY PANORAMA—57 West Court St., Doylestown, PA 18901. Mrs. Gerry Wallerstein, Editor.

Articles, 1,500 to 2,500 words, on Delaware Valley area. Fiction, 1,000 to 2,500 words. Poetry, to 16 lines. Photos. Pays $15 to $25, $5 for poetry, on publication or acceptance.

BUFFALO SPREE MAGAZINE—P.O. Box 38, Buffalo, NY 14226. Richard G. Shotell, Editor.
Articles, 2,000 to 4,000 words, on social, artistic and environmental issues. Fiction to 4,000 words. Poetry, 2 to 52 lines. Pays to $75, after publication.

CALIFORNIA JOURNAL—1617 10th St., Sacramento, CA 95814. Ed Salzman, Editor.
Analytical articles on California state politics. Query.

CALIFORNIA TODAY—750 Ridder Park Dr., San Jose, CA 95131. Fred Dickey, Editor.
Articles and photo essays on sports, outdoors, leisure, home, etc. in California. Pays varying rates, on acceptance.

CHARLOTTE MAGAZINE—P.O. Box 15843, Charlotte, NC 28210. James L. Townsend, Editor.
Articles, 500 to 3,000 words, with photos, on business, personalities and unusual life styles in North Carolina, and on distinguished former residents. Pays $30 to $150, on publication.

CHEVRON USA—P.O. Box 6227, San Jose, CA 95150. Helen Bignell, Editor.
Articles, 250 to 1,500 words, on travel in western, southern and eastern states, emphasis on family activities. Travel anecdotes, 100 to 250 words. Cartoons; photos. Pays 15¢ a word, extra for photos, on acceptance.

CHICAGO—500 North Michigan Ave., Chicago, IL 60611. John Fink, Editor.
Articles and fiction, 1,000 to 5,000 words, related to Chicago. Pays varying rates, on publication. Query.

CHICAGO HISTORY—Clark St. at North Ave., Chicago, IL 60614. Fannia Weingartner, Editor.
Articles, to 4,500 words, on regional, social and cultural history. Pays to $250, on acceptance. Query.

CHICAGO LIFE—120 West Madison St., Chicago, IL 60602. Carol Felsenthal, Editor.
Articles on Chicago subjects, profiles of Chicago personalities, poetry and cartoons. Query.

CHICAGOSTYLE (formerly *Midwest Magazine*)—Chicago *Sun-Times,* Chicago, IL 60611. James Toland, Editor.
Articles on architecture, interiors, fashions, food and products in Chicago area. Pays $100 per page, on publication.

CINCINNATI—120 West Fifth St., Greater Cincinnati Chamber of Commerce, Cincinnati, OH 45202.
Articles, 800 to 1,800 words, on people and issues of Cincinnati area. Pays 6¢ a word, on publication.

CLEVELAND—1632 Keith Bldg., Cleveland, OH 44115. Michael Roberts, Editor.
Articles, 750 to 5,000 words, on people and issues of Cleveland area. Pays 10¢ a word, on publication.

COLORADO MAGAZINE—1139 Delaware Plaza, P.O. Box 4305, Denver, CO 80204. Jacqueline Lovelace Choitz, Editor.
Adventure stories, 1,500 to 3,000 words, with photos, on people and events in Rocky Mountain area. Pays 10¢ a word, on publication.

COLUMBUS DISPATCH SUNDAY MAGAZINE—Columbus, OH 43216.

Articles, to 1,800 words, related to Ohio. Pays from 3¢ a word, $5 for photos, after publication.

COMMONWEALTH—Virginia State Chamber of Commerce, 611 East Franklin, Richmond, VA 23219. James S. Wamsley, Editor.
Sophisticated articles, 1,500 to 3,000 words, on Virginia. No stock history or travel pieces. Pays around 5¢ a word. Query.

CONTEMPORARY—*The Denver Post,* Denver, CO 80201. Joan White, Editor.
News features, 500 to 1,500 words, with photos, on Rocky Mountain subjects. Pays $20 to $75, on publication. Query.

D MAGAZINE—2902 Carlisle, Dallas, TX 75204. Charles Matthews, Managing Editor.
Articles, 2,000 to 4,000 words, on business, life styles, politics, fashion, etc. in Dallas-Fort Worth area. Pays varying rates. Query.

DALLAS—1507 Pacific Ave., Dallas, TX 75201.
Articles, 4,000 words, on business trends and business community in Dallas, by local writers only. Pays from $150, on acceptance. Query.

THE DALLAS SUN—P.O. Box 8366, Dallas, TX 75205. Ken Badt, Editor.
Articles on local personalities and events, 500 words; material for regular departments on houseplants, films, and the arts. Pays $1.35 per column inch, on publication. Query.

DAYTON, U.S.A.—111 West First St., Dayton, OH 45402. Kathleen Turner, Editor.
Articles, 2,000 to 3,000 words, with photos, for community leaders. No payment. Query.

DELTA SCENE—Delta State University, Box B-3, Cleveland, MS 38733. Curt Lamar, Editor.
Features about history, customs, current activities of lower Mississippi River valley. Short-short stories, poetry with regional flavor. Pays various rates, on publication. Query.

DENVER—8000 East Girard, Suite 210, Denver, CO 80231. Jan Golab, Editor.
Articles, 1,000 to 4,000 words, on regional issues, life styles, etc. Photos. Pays to $100, extra for photos, on publication. Query.

THE DES MOINES SUNDAY REGISTER PICTURE—*Des Moines Register and Tribune,* 715 Locust St., Des Moines, IA 50304.
Articles, to 1,000 words, with photos, on Iowa. Pays on publication.

DETROIT—*Detroit Free Press* Sunday Magazine, 321 West Lafayette Blvd., Detroit, MI 48321. Rogers Worthington, Editor.
Articles, to 3,000 words, on issues of Detroit area: crime, politics, business, etc. Personality and service pieces; interviews. Pays $100 to $250.

DISCOVER—Sunday *Bulletin,* 30th and Market Sts., Philadelphia, PA 19101. Jack Wilson, Editor.
Articles, 300 to 1,500 words, with photos, of interest to Philadelphians. Pays varying rates.

DOWN EAST—Camden, ME 04843. Davis Thomas, Editor.
Articles, 1,500 to 2,500 words, on Maine. Photos. Pays from 3¢ a word, $5 to $25 for photos, on acceptance.

THE DULUTHIAN—Chamber of Commerce and Convention and Visitors Bureau, 325 Harbor Drive, Duluth, MN 55802.
Articles, 750 to 1,500 words, on Duluth area: people, business developments, civic problems or activities and sports. No payment.

EMPIRE MAGAZINE—*The Denver Post,* P.O. Box 1709, Denver, CO 80201. Carl Skiff, Editor.
Articles, 500 to 2,500 words, on people, events, history, issues, etc., in Denver area. Photos. Pays around 5¢ a word, on acceptance. Query.

EXCLUSIVELY YOURS—161 West Wisconsin Ave., Milwaukee, WI 53202. Wallace F. Patten, Editor.
Articles, 750 to 2,000 words, with constructive, humorous or inspirational approach. Pays 5¢ a word, on publication.

FLORIDA FIESTA—140 North Federal Hwy., P. O. Box 820, Boca Raton, FL 33432. Paul T. Hutchens, Editor.
Articles, 1,000 to 2,000 words, on people, places and events in south Florida. Poetry, to 20 lines. Pays $10 per printed page, in copies for poetry.

FLORIDAGRICULTURE—P. O. Box 730, Gainesville, FL 32602. Andy Williams, Editor.
Published by the Florida Farm Bureau Federation. Articles, 500 to 1,500 words, on all aspects of Florida agriculture. Pays from $50 to $250 per article, on acceptance.

FLORIDA TREND—P.O. Box 2350, 1901 13th St., Tampa, FL 33601.
Articles, to 1,800 words, on Florida business and businesspersons. Photos. Pays around 10¢ a word. Query.

THE FLORIDIAN—St. Petersburg *Times,* Box 1121, St. Petersburg, FL 33731.
In-depth articles on Florida: personality profiles, features on controversial subjects in medicine, law, education, politics. Short, factual pieces, 800 to 1,500 words, on nature, wildlife, science, crime, history. Photos. Pays $50 to $150, on acceptance. Query.

FOCUS-MIDWEST—928a North McKnight, St. Louis, MO 63132. Charles L. Klotzer, Editor.
Articles, 900 to 4,000 words, on controversial issues in Chicago, St. Louis and Kansas City. Pays on publication.

GREAT LAKES GAZETTE—Box 47, Grand Marais, MI 49839. Rose Mary Marshall, Editor.
Articles on Great Lakes subjects; fiction, poetry, cartoons, humor, fillers. Pays in copies.

GULFSHORE LIFE—1039 Fifth Ave. North, Naples, FL 33940. Lanny Sherwin, Editor.
Articles, 500 to 1,000 words, on community activities, personalities, etc. in southwestern Florida. Pays $25 to $50, on publication.

HAMPTON LIFE—20 Hampton Rd., Southampton, NY 11968. Bonnie P. Barton, Editor.
Articles, to 3,000 words, on life in the Hamptons. Pays from $50 to $175. Query.

HOUSTON BUSINESS JOURNAL—5314 Bingle Rd., Houston, TX 77092. Mike Weingart, Editor.
Articles, 3,000 words, on business in Houston area. Cartoons. Pays $2 per column inch, $7.50 for cartoons, on publication.

HOUSTON HOME & GARDEN—2472 Bolsover, Houston, TX 77005. Karleen Koen, Editor.
Articles on home management, decorating, furnishings, gardening, etc. in Houston area. Photos. Pays $2.50 per column inch, extra for photos, on publication. Query.

ILLINOIS ISSUES—226 Capital Campus, Sangamon State Univ., Springfield, IL 62708. Caroline S. Gherardini, Managing Editor.
Articles, 750 to 2,250 words, focusing on issues in Illinois. Pays 5¢ to 10¢ a word, on publication. Query.

INCREDIBLE IDAHO—Room 108, Capital Bldg., Boise, ID 83720. Dorine Goertzen, Editor.
Articles, 1,000 to 2,500 words, with photos, on Idaho. Poetry. Pays in copies. Query.

INDIANAPOLIS MAGAZINE—320 North Meridian St., Indianapolis, IN 46204. Craig G. Beardsley, Editor.
Feature articles with photos, 500 to 5,000 words, on regional topics. No fiction. Pays from $75 to $100, on publication. Query first.

JACKSONVILLE MAGAZINE—P.O. Box 329, Jacksonville, FL 32201.
Articles, 1,500 to 3,000 words, on Jacksonville area. Photos. Pays on publication. Query.

LONG ISLAND FORUM—P.O. Box 215, West Islip, NY 11795. Carl A. Starace, Editor.
Articles, to 2,400 words, on Long Island history and folklore. Photos. No payment. Query.

LOS ANGELES MAGAZINE—1888 Century Park East, Los Angeles, CA 90067. Geoff Miller, Editor.
Articles, to 3,000 words, of interest to affluent southern Californians. Photo essays; humor. Pays 5¢ to 10¢ a word, on publication. Query.

LOUISVILLE—300 West Liberty St., Louisville, KY 40202. Betty Lou Amster, Editor.
Articles, 1,000 to 2,000 words, on community problems and local business success stories, for business leaders of Louisville area. Photos. Pays from $35, on acceptance. Query.

LURE OF THE LITCHFIELD HILLS—Cornwall Press, Box 907, West Cornwall, CT 06970.
Articles, 2,000 words, on Connecticut history and folklore. Pays $25, on publication. Query.

MAINE ANTIQUE DIGEST—Box 358, Waldoboro, ME 04572. Samuel Pennington, Editor.
Authoritative, entertaining articles on antiques market in New England. Anecdotes; interviews. Photos. Pays $35, on acceptance. Query.

MIAMI MAGAZINE—3361 S. W. Third Ave., Miami, FL 33145. James Kukar, Executive Editor.
Sophisticated articles, to 1,500 words, on South Florida life styles. Pays varying rates, on publication.

MIDWEST MAGAZINE—See ChicagoStyle.

MISSOURI LIFE—1209 Elmerine Ave., Jefferson City, MO 65101. W. R. Nunn, Editor.
Articles, 1,500 to 3,000 words, with photos, on Missouri: history, commerce, culture, people. Photo essays; original art. Pays $75 for articles with color illustrations, $50 for articles with black-and-white photos. Query.

MONTANA MAGAZINE OF THE NORTHERN ROCKIES—Box 5630, Helena, MT 59601. Rick Graetz, Editor.
Articles, with photos, on Montana. Pays varying rates. Query.

MONTANA: THE MAGAZINE OF WESTERN HISTORY—Montana Historical Society, 225 North Roberts, Helena, MT 59601. Vivian A. Paladin, Editor.

Documented articles, 3,500 to 6,500 words, on history of the West, preferably lesser-known facets. Photos, drawings. Pays 1½¢ a word, on acceptance. Query.

MPLS.–512 Nicollet Mall Bldg., Suite 615, Minneapolis, MN 55402. Kate Richardson, Editor.
Minneapolis-region personality pieces, investigative articles, etc., 500 to 2,000 words. Short stories, 1,500 to 3,000 words; short humor, puzzles; regional photo-essays. Pays $75 to $300.

NASHVILLE!–One Vantage Way, Nashville House, Nashville, TN 37228. C. Turney Stevens, Jr., Editor.
Articles on Nashville current events and subjects of interest to residents. Payment by arrangement. Query.

NEBRASKALAND–Nebraska Game and Parks Commission, 2200 North 33rd St., Lincoln, NE 68503. Lowell Johnson, Managing Editor.
Articles on Nebraska: people, environment, travel, outdoors and history. Photos. No payment.

NEVADA MAGAZINE–State Dept. of Economic Development, Carson City, NV 89710.
Articles, 1,000 to 2,500 words, with photos, on Nevada recreation, history, scenery, etc. Pays 5¢ to 8¢ a word, $15 to $50 for photos, on publication.

THE NEW ENGLANDER–Dublin, NH 03444.
Articles, 1,500 to 2,500 words, with photos, on New England business and public affairs: real estate, manufacturing, education, insurance, agriculture, travel, politics, etc. Pays from $50 per printed page. Query.

NEW ENGLAND GALAXY–Old Sturbridge Village, Sturbridge, MA 01566. Catherine Fennelly, Editor.
Articles, to 3,000 words, on New England history. Poetry, to 32 lines. Photos. Pays $75 to $150, on publication. Query.

NEW HAMPSHIRE PROFILES–2 Steam Mill Ct., Concord, NH 03301. Sharon L. Smith, Editor.
Articles, to 2,000 words, on country living, history, nostalgia, etc., related to New Hampshire. Photo essays, photos. Pays varying rates, on publication.

NEW MEXICO MAGAZINE–Bataan Memorial Bldg., Santa Fe., NM 87503; Sheila Tryk, Editor.
Articles, 250 to 2,000 words, on specific New Mexico subjects. Photos. Pays $25 to $300, $50 to $300 for photo assignments. Query.

NEW NORFOLK–475 St. Paul's Blvd., P. O. Box 327, Norfolk, VA 23501. Marilyn Goldman, Managing Editor.
Articles on business, civic or city topics in southeastern Virginia. Query.

NEW ORLEANS–6666 Morrison Rd., New Orleans, LA 70126. George H. Curtner, Editor.
Articles about New Orleans and Louisiana people, five typed pages, with photos. Poems, 5 to 10 stanzas long. Pays $150 to $400, to $25 for poems, on acceptance. Query.

NEW WEST–NYM Corporation, 9665 Wilshire Blvd., Beverly Hills, CA 90212. Frank Lalli, Executive Editor.
Published by *New York* Magazine. For California and the people of the West. Feature articles, 1,000 to 2,500 words, on life styles, trends, personalities, etc. Filler-length regional news for "Intelligencer" column. Pays from $200 to $2,000, on publication. Query.

NEW WORLDS—P.O. Box I, 550 Newport Center Dr., Newport Beach, CA 92663. Frank C. McGee, Editor.
Articles, 2,000 words, on the Newport Beach/Irvine area, its people, places, events. Pays $150, after acceptance. Query first; all articles on assignment.

NEW YORK—755 Second Ave., New York, NY 10017. John Berendt, Editor.
Articles on New York City subjects. Query.

NORTH COUNTRY ANVIL—Box 37, Millville, MN 55957. Jack Miller, Editor.
Articles and fiction, 1,500 to 3,000 words, on alternative ways of living and thinking, preferably by writers from Midwest. Verse. Pays in copies.

NORTHWEST—1320 S.W. Broadway, Portland, OR 97201.
Sunday magazine of the *Sunday Oregonian.* Articles, to 1,500 words, on individuals and issues in Pacific Northwest. Pays $50 per printed page, $15 per photo. Same address and requirements for *Outdoors.*

OKLAHOMA TODAY—Will Rogers Memorial Bldg., State Capitol, Oklahoma City, OK 73105. Bill Burchardt, Editor.
Articles, to 1,500 words, on Oklahoma. Pays 5¢ a word, on publication.

ORBIT—*The Daily Oklahoman,* P. O. Box 25125, Oklahoma City, OK 73125. Dave Funderburk, Managing Editor.
Articles, with photos, on subjects related to Oklahoma. Pays $75 to $100 per printed page, extra for photos, on publication. Query.

OREGON HISTORICAL QUARTERLY—Oregon Historical Society, 1230 S.W. Park Ave., Portland, OR 97205. Thomas Vaughan, Editor.
Articles, 1,000 to 20,000 words, on North Pacific history: diaries, recollections, etc. Photos. Pays in copies.

OUTDOORS—See *Northwest.*

PACIFIC MAGAZINE—109 West Whittier Blvd., Montebello, CA 90640. Dana Howard Jones, Editor.
Articles, 1,000 to 2,000 words, for Southern Californians, 18 to 30, relating to that age group and the area. Pays about $200, on publication. Also photos, drawings.

PENNSYLVANIA ILLUSTRATED—P.O. Box 657, Camp Hill, PA 17011. Albert E. Holliday, Editor.
Short and long articles and photos on Pennsylvania's people, places, travel, history, events, etc. Pays various rates, on acceptance. Query.

PHILADELPHIA—1500 Walnut St., Philadelphia, PA 19102. Art Spikol, Executive Editor.
Articles, 1,000 to 5,000 words, relating specifically to Philadelphia area. Pays $50 to $500, on acceptance. Query.

PHILADELPHIA INQUIRER TODAY MAGAZINE—400 North Broad St., Philadelphia, PA 19101. Scott De Garmo, Editor.
Articles, 500 to 3,500 words, on local subjects. Photos. Pays varying rates, on publication. Query.

PHOENIX MAGAZINE—4707 North 12th St., Phoenix, AZ 85014. Anita J. Welch, Editor.
Articles, 1,000 to 2,500 words, with photos, on Phoenix area. Pays from $50, on publication. Query.

PITTSBURGH—4802 Fifth Ave., Pittsburgh, PA 15213. Herb Stein, Editor.
Articles, 3,000 words, and shorter pieces, 850 words, of interest to western Pennsylvania readers. Pays $50 to $200 for features, $40 to $75 for shorter pieces, on publication.

THE PITTSBURGHER MAGAZINE—The Express House, Station Sq., Pittsburgh, PA 15219. Gail Balph, Editorial Assistant.
Articles, 5,000 to 9,000 words, on Metropolitan Pittsburgh; shorter pieces, to 1,500 words. Pays 10¢ a word, on acceptance.

THE PORTLAND OREGON JOURNAL—Portland, OR 97201. Donald J. Sterling, Jr., Editor.
Articles, 1,200 words, on regional subjects. Pays $25 to $50, after publication.

THE RHODE ISLANDER—Providence Sunday *Journal,* Providence, RI 02902. Douglas R. Riggs, Editor.
Anecdotal articles, 1,000 to 1,500 words, on southern New England subjects. Pays $50 to $200, on publication.

THE ST. LOUISAN—7110 Oakland Ave., St. Louis, MO 63117.
Articles on food and restaurants, people, arts, medicine, environment, education, etc., in St. Louis area. Photo essays, photos. Pays varying rates, after publication. Query.

SAN ANTONIO MAGAZINE—Chamber of Commerce, P.O. Box 1628, San Antonio, TX 78296. Sammye Johnson, Editor.
Articles on San Antonio area. Pays on publication. Query.

SANDLAPPER: THE MAGAZINE OF SOUTH CAROLINA—P.O. Box 1668, Columbia, SC 29202. Bob W. Rowland, Editor.
Articles, to 2,500 words, with photos, on people, places and events in South Carolina. Short fiction and poetry. Pays $20 to $125, from $125 for fiction, $10 for poetry, after publication. Query for articles.

SEATTLE BUSINESS—Seattle Chamber of Commerce, 215 Columbia St., Seattle, WA 98104.
Articles on business in western Washington. Human-interest features. Pays on publication.

SEATTLE TIMES SUNDAY MAGAZINE—Box 70, Seattle, WA 98111. Larry Anderson, Editor.
Articles, 800 to 1,500 words, on Pacific Northwest. Pays $40 per printed page, on publication. Query.

SEAWAY REVIEW—Harbor Island, Maple City Postal Sta., MI 49664. Jacques LesStrang, Editor.
Articles, 500 to 3,000 words, with photos, on Great Lakes water transportation, and on St. Lawrence Seaway. Pays $50 to $150, on publication.

SOUTH CAROLINA MAGAZINE—Box 89, Columbia, SC 29202. Sidney Wise, Editor.
Articles, 1,000 to 2,000 words, on South Carolina and residents. Pays modest rates, on publication.

SOUTHERN EXPOSURE—Institute for Southern Studies, Box 230, Chapel Hill, NC 27514.
Documented, investigative articles, book reviews, historical analyses and opinion pieces, 2,000 to 6,000 words, on political, economic and cultural affairs related to the South. Fiction, 1,500 to 5,000 words. Pays $50, on publication.

THE SOUTH MAGAZINE—Trend Publications, Inc., P.O. Box 2350, Tampa, FL 33601. Roy B. Bain, Editor.

Articles, 1,000 to 3,500 words on companies, successes and failures related to business in the South, for business leaders. Pays $70 to $300, on publication. Query.

THE STATE: DOWN HOME IN NORTH CAROLINA—Box 2169, Raleigh, NC 27602. Bill Wright, Editor.
Features, 500 to 1,500 words, on North Carolina subjects. Pays $10 to $35, on acceptance.

SUNDAY NEW YORK NEWS MAGAZINE—Sunday *News,* 220 East 42nd St., New York, NY 10017. Richard C. Lemon, Editor.
Articles, 500 to 2,500 words, with photos, on New York and residents. Pays $150 to $750, on acceptance.

SUNSET MAGAZINE—Menlo Park, CA 94025. Proctor Mellquist, Editor.
Western regional. Queries considered but not encouraged.

TEXAS MONTHLY—P.O. Box 1569, Austin, TX 78767. Judy Benson, Assistant Managing Editor.
Articles, 2,000 to 8,000 words, on Texas, its residents and related subjects. Pays varying rates, on acceptance.

TEXAS PARADE—2446 Cee Gee, Suite 204, San Antonio, TX 78217. Kenneth Lively, Editor.
Articles, 1,500 to 2,000 words, on business in Texas. Photos. Pays from $40 per printed page, on publication. Query.

TOLEDO MAGAZINE (formerly *Blade Sunday Magazine*)—Toledo, OH 43660. Tom Gearhart, Editor.
Articles, to 4,000 words, on Toledo area personalities, news, etc. Photos. Pays $35 to $125, on publication. Query.

TORONTO LIFE—59 Front St. East, Toronto, Ont., Canada M5E 1B3. Alexander Ross, Editor.
Articles, 1,000 to 4,500 words, on Toronto. Pays $150 to $600. Query.

TRENTON—Mercer County Chamber of Commerce, P.O. Box 4533, Trenton, NJ 08608.
Articles, 500 to 1,500 words, about interesting people in Mercer County area. Pays $25 to $50. Query.

TROPIC—*The Miami Herald,* One Herald Plaza, Miami, FL 33101. John Parkyn, Editor.
General-interest articles, 1,500 to 3,000 words, for South Florida readers. Personality profiles. Pays to $300, on acceptance. Query.

TULSA—Metropolitan Tulsa Chamber of Commerce, P.O. Box 1620, Tulsa, OK 74101. Larry P. Silvey, Editor.
Factual, human-interest articles, 800 to 1,600 words, on Tulsa area, primarily for business community. Pays $25 to $75, on publication. Query.

UPCOUNTRY—Eagle Publishing Co., 33 Eagle St., Pittsfield, MA 01201. William H. Tague, Managing Editor.
Articles, 500 to 2,500 words, with photos, on New England. Humorous stories, 1,500 words. Pays varying rates, on acceptance.

UTAH—65 West Fayette Ave., Salt Lake City, UT 84101. Duane S. Crowther, Editor.
Articles, 800 to 1,000 words, on history, culture and wildlife in Utah. Poetry; some fiction. Photos. Pays 5¢ a word, $5 to $35 for photos, on publication. Query.

UTAH HISTORICAL QUARTERLY—Utah State Historical Society, 603 East South Temple, Salt Lake City, UT 84102. Stanford J. Layton, Managing Editor.
Documented, scholarly articles, to 7,500 words, on history of Utah. Photos. Pays in copies.

VERMONT LIFE—61 Elm St., Montpelier, VT 05602. Brian Vachon, Editor.
Articles, 1,500 to 3,000 words, on any subject related to Vermont. Photos. Pays $200 to $400, on acceptance. Query.

THE WASHINGTONIAN—1828 L St., N.W., Suite 200, Washington, DC 20036. Laughlin Philips, Editor.
Sophisticated articles, 1,000 to 4,000 words, on any subject related to Washington. Pays 7¢ to 10¢ a word, on publication. Query.

WEEKEND MAGAZINE—390 Bay St., Suite 504, Toronto, Ont., Canada M5H 2Y2. John Macfarlane, Editor.
Articles and essays, 1,500 to 2,500 words, of interest to Canadians. Pays $400 to $750, on acceptance.

WESTCHESTER ILLUSTRATED—16 School St., Yonkers, NY 10701. Peter Porco, Editor.
Feature articles, 1,500 to 4,000 words, on Westchester lifestyles, arts, media, ecology, etc. Shorter features, 750 to 1,500 words. Fillers, cartoons, photos. Pays $50 to $100 for features; $5 to $50 for fillers and shorter features, after publication. Query.

THE WESTERN PRODUCER—Box 2500, Saskatoon, Sask., Canada S7K 2C4. R. H. MacDonald, Executive Editor.
Articles and fiction, to 2,500 words, with photos, on western Canadian subjects, for intelligent farm and rural readers. Pays to $75 per printed page, $5 to $35 for photos, on acceptance.

WESTERN RESERVE MAGAZINE—Box 243, Garrettsville, OH 44231. Mary Folger, Editor.
Historical and contemporary articles, 600 to 2,400 words, on Ohio's Western Reserve only. Fillers on little-known Western Reserve history. Pays $30 to $50, on publication.

WESTWAYS—Box 2890, Terminal Annex, Los Angeles, CA 90051. N. J. Kockler, Managing Editor.
Articles, 1,000 to 2,500 words, on western U.S., Canada and Mexico: natural science, travel, history, personalities, towns, etc. Verse, to 45 lines. Photos. Pays from 10¢ a word, from $25 for photos, on acceptance. Query.

WESTWORLD—P.O. Box 6680, Vancouver, B.C., Canada V6B 4L4. Bill Mayrs, Editor.
Articles, 1,500 to 2,500 words, with photos, dealing with events, places, people, travel, history of the four western Canadian provinces. No U.S. travel. Pays 5¢ a word, $15 per cartoon, on publication.

WICHITA—Chamber of Commerce, 350 West Douglas, Wichita, KS 67202. Marge Setter, Editor.
Articles, 300 to 600 words, on Wichita. Pays $50 to $100, half on acceptance, half on publication. Query.

WISCONSIN TRAILS—P.O. Box 5650, Madison, WI 53705. Jill Dean, Editor.
Articles, 1,500 to 3,000 words, on Wisconsin: history, industry, personalities, recreation, etc. Photos. Pays $50 to $200, extra for photos, on publication. Query.

WONDERFUL WEST VIRGINIA—Information and Education Division, Dept. of Natural Resources, Charleston, WV 25305. Edward R. Johnson, Editor.
Articles, 1,200 words, on West Virginia. Fillers; photos. No payment. Query.

YANKEE—Dublin, NH 03444. Judson D. Hale, Editor.
Articles and fiction, to 2,500 words, on New England and residents. Photos. Pays $200 to $400 for features, $300 to $500 for fiction, on acceptance.

YANKEE MAGAZINE'S GUIDE TO NEW ENGLAND–581 Boylston St., Boston, MA
02116. Georgia Orcutt, Editor.
Articles, 500 to 2,000 words, with photos, on interesting and unusual places to visit
in New England. Short features. Pays from $50 to $250, on acceptance. Same address
and requirements for *Yankee Magazine's Guide to the State of New York*. Query.

HOUSE MAGAZINES AND COMPANY
PUBLICATIONS

House magazines (also called company publications) are published by a company or
corporation (and sometimes trade associations) to promote good will, familiarize readers
with the company's services and products, and interest customers in these products. A
large percentage of the material published in house organs is frankly promotional–but
editors also look for general-interest articles, travel or regional features, humor, and even
some short stories. These magazines are also an excellent market for photographs.
The house magazines in the following list represent only a sampling of the many
publications in the field. For a complete list of house magazines–both those that buy
free-lance material and those that do not–see the *Gebbie House Magazine Directory*,
published by National Research Bureau, Inc. (424 North Third St., Burlington, IA
52601), available in most libraries.

AIR LINE PILOT–Air Line Pilots Association International, 1625 Massachusetts Ave.
N.W., Washington, DC 20036. C. V. Glines, Editor.
Articles, to 3,000 words, on aviation, stressing pilot's point of view; articles on safety
and air transport history; profiles on ALPA members. Pays varying rates, on
publication.

CHANNELS OF BUSINESS COMMUNICATION–Northwestern Bell Telephone Co.,
Room 930, 100 South 19th St., Omaha, NE 68102. Gerald T. Metcalf, Editor.
Case-history articles, 500 to 1,200 words, and articles on communications, for business leaders in Iowa, Minnesota, Nebraska, North and South Dakota. Pays from $150,
from $20 for cartoons, on acceptance.

THE COMPASS–Mobile Sales and Supply Corp., 150 East 42nd St., New York, NY
10017. R. G. MacKenzie, Editor.
Short stories and articles, to 3,500 words, on the sea and deep sea trade. Photos. Pays
to $250, on acceptance. Query.

THE CONTINENTAL MAGAZINE–Room 332, Ford Motor Co., 3000 Schaefer Rd.,
Dearborn, MI 48121. Robert M. Hodesh, Editor-in-Chief.
Sophisticated service articles, 1,300 to 1,500 words, on travel, entertainment, cuisine,
shopping, sports. Pays from $300, on acceptance. Query.

ENTHUSIAST–Harley-Davidson Motor Co., P.O. Box 653, Milwaukee, WI 53201.
Robert H. Klein, Editor.
Fiction, photo essays and articles, to 2,500 words, on motorcycling subjects featuring
Harley-Davidson products. Pays 5¢ a word, $7.50 to $15 per photo, on publication.

FLAGSHIP NEWS–American Airlines, Inc., 633 Third Ave., New York, NY 10017. Bill
Hunter, Editor.
Articles for American Airlines employees. Limited free-lance market. Pays within 30
days of publication. Query.

THE FURROW–Deere & Company, John Deere Rd., Moline, IL 61265. George R.
Sollenberger, Editor, North America.

Articles and humor, to 1,500 words; researched agricultural-technical features; rural social- and economic-trend features. Pays to $400, on acceptance.

GAYLORD TRIANGLE—Gaylord Bros., Inc., P.O. Box 4901, Syracuse, NY 13221. E. R. Vrooman, Director of Advertising.
Brief articles about new company products; photos and write-ups on products in use.

GO GREYHOUND—Greyhound Tower, Phoenix, AZ 85077. Kathleen L. Meell, Publications Assistant.
Human-interest travel articles, 600 to 800 words, with photos. Pays $300, on publication. Query.

GOING PLACES—211 East 43rd St., New York, NY 10017.
Company-related articles, on assignment only. Pays varying rates, on acceptance. Query.

GOLF JOURNAL—Golf House, Far Hills, NJ 07931.
Articles, 500 to 4,000 words, on subjects of interest to serious amateur golfers. Pays on publication.

HUGHES RIGWAY MAGAZINE—Hughes Tool Co., P.O. Box 2539, Houston, TX 77001. Address Ken Whanger.
Fact features and topical articles, 2,000 to 2,500 words, for oilfield-drilling personnel. Pays 10¢ a word, on acceptance.

ILLINOIS CENTRAL GULF NEWS—Illinois Central Gulf Railroad, 233 North Michigan Ave., Chicago, IL 60601. R. A. Einbinder, Editor.
Articles, to 1,500 words, with pictures and captions, on Illinois Central Gulf Railroad only.

IMPERIAL OIL FLEET NEWS—111 St. Clair Ave. West, Toronto Ont., Canada M5W 1K3. Betty Schill, Editor.
Articles, 1,000 words, of interest to tankermen, preferably with Canadian angle. Photos to illustrate articles. Query.

INLAND—Inland Steel Co., 30 West Monroe St., Chicago, IL 60603. Sheldon A. Mix, Managing Editor.
Imaginative articles, essays, commentaries, any length, of special interest in Mid-West: humor, history, folklore, sports, etc. Pays about $300, on acceptance. Sample issues available on request.

THE IRON WORKER—Lynchburg Foundry, A. Mead Co., Lynchburg, VA 24505. P. M. Early, Editor.
In-depth, well-documented, factual, historical articles, Virginia-related Americana, 3,500 to 5,000 words. Payment varies, on acceptance. Query.

THE LOOKOUT—Seamen's Church Institute of New York, 15 State St., New York, NY 10004. Carlyle Windley, Editor.
Articles, 1,000 to 1,500 words, relating to merchant marine: oddities, adventure, etc. Graphics, occasional short verse. Pays to $40 for articles with art, $20 for black-and-white cover photos, on publication.

THE LUFKIN LINE—P.O. Box 849, Lufkin, TX 75901. Virginia R. Allen, Editor. Quarterly.
Uses one travel article per issue, 1,000 words, with minimum of ten color transparencies, 2¼ x 2¼ or professional quality 35mm photos. Pays $50, on acceptance.

MARATHON WORLD—Marathon Oil Co., 539 South Main St., Findlay, OH 45840. Robert Ostermann, Editor.
Petroleum- and business-oriented narrative approach preferred; current issues and events. Pays $250 to $750 for feature-length articles, on acceptance. Request sample copy. Query a must.

MIRACLE MAID WHISTLER—West Bend Co., 400 Washington, West Bend, WI 53095.
Kitt Egan, Editor.
Articles on "party plan" selling techniques, 2 to 3 typed pages. Pays 10¢ per word,
on acceptance.

THE MODERN WOODMEN—Modern Woodmen of America, Mississippi River at 17th
St., Rock Island, IL 61201. Robert E. Frank, Editor.
Juvenile and general-interest fiction and nonfiction, 1,500 to 2,000 words, strongly
plotted. Pays $35 and up, on acceptance; more with photos. Publication is not copy-
righted.

OUR SUN—1608 Walnut St., Philadelphia, PA 19103.
Petroleum industry-related articles, 500 to 1,500 words. Most material internally
generated. Pays various rates, on acceptance. Query first.

OUTDOORS—Outdoors Bldg., Columbia, MO 65201.
Informative articles, to 1,200 words, accompanied by 8 x 10 black-and-white and
color transparencies, on recreational subjects, with emphasis on boating. Pays $35 to
$125, on acceptance.

PEOPLE ON PARADE—Meridian Publishing Co., 1720 Washington Blvd., Ogden, UT
84404. Melissa Arlene Hamblin, Managing Editor.
Success stories, inspirational accounts of overcoming adversity, and humorous
features, 900 to 1,200 words, with photos; short pieces, 200 to 500 words. Pays 10¢
a word, extra for photos, on acceptance. Query.

SEVENTY SIX MAGAZINE—Union Oil Co. of California, Box 7600, Los Angeles, CA
90051. Karen Saunders, Editor.
Articles, 750 to 1,750 words, about the petroleum industry and company employees;
anecdotes, quotes. No dealer stories. Pays 10¢ to 30¢ a word, extra for photos, on
acceptance. Query.

SPERRY NEW HOLLAND—Division of Sperry Rand Corp., New Holland, PA 17557.
Michael A. Balas, Editor.
Articles, 1,000 to 1,500 words, with photos, about farming, mentioning Sperry New
Holland equipment only as used in farm operation. Pays on publication.

THINK—International Business Machines Corp., Armonk, NY 10504. C. B. Hansen,
Editor.
In-company magazine. Business/management-related articles, 2,000 to 3,000 words.
Pays competitive rates, on acceptance. Query first.

TILE AND TILL—Eli Lilly and Company, Indianapolis, IN 46206.
Management and scientific articles about pharmacy, by qualified writers. Query.

TRAINING DIGEST—International Correspondence Schools, Scranton, PA 18515.
Articles, for management officials, 1,000 to 3,000 words, on new methods,
emphasizing industrial training and development. Photos encouraged. Pays $6 to $10
per page, on acceptance.

THE WATER SKIER—American Water Skier Association, P.O. Box 191, Winter Haven,
FL 33880. Thomas C. Hardman, Editor.
Occasional off-beat articles to 2,500 words and/or photo features involving water
skiing. Payment varies, on acceptance. Query.

POETRY MARKETS

The following list is divided into four categories: general magazines, college, literary, and
little magazines, and those using only poetry; religious and denominational magazines;
and greeting card markets. Each tends to use a certain type of poetry, but many poems

may meet the requirements of markets in more than one of the categories. Markets for both serious and light verse are included in each group.

In addition to the markets listed here, many daily and weekly newspapers use verse occasionally. Though they may not specifically seek poetry from free-lancers, the papers often print verse submitted to them, especially on holidays and other special occasions.

The markets for juvenile poetry are listed under *Juvenile, Teen-Age and Young Adult Magazines;* markets for book-length poems or poetry collections are listed under *Book Publishers.*

GENERAL MAGAZINES

THE AMERICAN LEGION MAGAZINE–1608 K St. N.W., Washington, DC 20006. Address Parting Shots Editor.
Humorous verse, to 16 lines. Pays $10 and up, on acceptance.

THE AMERICAN SCHOLAR–1811 Q St. N.W., Washington, DC 20009. Joseph Epstein, Editor.
Poetry, 10 to 32 lines, that develops an image or thought without cliches. Pays $35 to $75, on acceptance.

THE ATLANTIC–8 Arlington St., Boston, MA 02116. Peter Davison, Poetry Editor.
Poetry of highest quality. Limited market: only 3 or 4 poems an issue. Interest in young poets. Occasionally uses light verse. Pays varying rates, on acceptance.

THE ATLANTIC ADVOCATE–Gleaner Bldg., Phoenix Sq., Fredericton, N.B., Canada.
Poetry related to Canada's Atlantic provinces. Pays $2 per column inch, on publication.

BABY CARE–52 Vanderbilt Ave., New York, NY 10017. Evelyn A. Podsiadlo, Editor.
Poetry, to 24 lines. Pays varying rates, on acceptance.

BREEZY–See *Humorama, Inc.*

CAT FANCY–P.O. Box 4030, San Clemente, CA 92672. Address Poetry Editor.
Poetry about cats. Pays $10, on publication.

CATS MAGAZINE–P.O. Box 4106, Pittsburgh, PA 15202. Jean Laux, Editor.
Poems to 30 lines, preferably light, about cats. Pays 30¢ a line, on publication.

CHATELAINE–481 University Ave., Toronto, Ont., Canada. Doris Anderson, Editor.
Verse to 25 lines. Pays to $30, on acceptance.

CHILD LIFE–1100 Waterway Blvd., P.O. Box 567B, Indianapolis, IN 46206. Peg Rogers, Editor.
Poetry for children to 14 years old. Pays about 3¢ a word, $5 minimum.

CHILDREN'S PLAYMATE–1100 Waterway Blvd., P.O. Box 567B, Indianapolis, IN 46206. Beth Wood Thomas, Editor.
Humorous poetry for children 3 to 8 years old. Buys all rights. Pays about 3¢ a word, $5 minimum, on publication.

THE CHRISTIAN SCIENCE MONITOR–One Norway St., Boston, MA 02115. Henrietta Buckmaster, Editor, The Home Forum.
Fresh, vigorous poems of high quality, on various subjects. No downbeat material. Pays varying rates, on acceptance.

COMEDY MAGAZINE–See *Humorama, Inc.*

COSMOPOLITAN—224 West 57th St., New York, NY 10019. Jo Hynes, Poetry Editor. Poetry (typed originals only) about personal relationships, for young, active career women. Enclosed stamped, self-addressed envelope. Pays from $25, on acceptance.

ESSENCE—1500 Broadway, New York, NY 10036.
Poetry, to 40 lines. Pays $25 and up, after publication.

FAMILY CIRCLE—488 Madison Ave., New York, NY 10022. Eleanore Lewis, Poetry Editor.
Poetry, to 20 lines. Pays from $10, on acceptance.

FUN HOUSE—See *Humorama, Inc.*

GAZE—See *Humorama, Inc.*

GEE WHIZ—see *Humorama, Inc.*

GIRLTALK—See *Talk.*

GOLF DIGEST MAGAZINE—495 Westport Ave., Norwalk, CT 06856. Lois Hains, Poetry Editor.
Humorous verse, 4 to 8 lines, on golf. Pays $10 to $20, on acceptance.

GOLF MAGAZINE—380 Madison Ave., New York, NY 10017. John M. Ross, Editor.
Light or humorous verse, to 25 lines, on golf. Pays $25 and up, on acceptance.

GOOD HOUSEKEEPING—959 Eighth Ave., New York, NY 10019. Address Poetry Editor.
Good, serious poetry of interest to women. Send short, light verse to Gay Norton, Associate Editor. for Light Housekeeping page. Pays $5 a line, on acceptance.

GOURMET MAGAZINE—777 Third Ave., New York, NY 10017.
Sophisticated light verse with food angle. Avoid mention of dieting, calories, etc. Pays $25 to $50, on acceptance.

GREAT LAKES GAZETTE—Box 47, Grand Marais, MI 49839. Rose Mary Marshall, Editor.
Short poetry. Pays in copies.

HARPER'S MAGAZINE—2 Park Ave., New York, NY 10016.
No unsolicited poetry accepted. Overstocked.

THE HARTFORD COURANT—285 Broad St., Hartford, CT 06115. Malcolm L. Johnson, Poetry Column Editor.
Verse, to 50 lines. Pays in copies.

HUMORAMA, INC.—100 North Village Ave., Rockville Centre, NY 11570. Ernest N. Devver, Editor.
Breezy, humorous erotic verse, 4 to 48 lines. Pays 60¢ a line, before publication. Same address and requirements for *Jest, Laugh Riot, Laugh Digest, Comedy, Stare, Zip, Fun House, Romp, Joker, Gaze, Gee Whiz, Breezy, Quips, Popular Jokes, Popular Cartoons.*

JEST—See *Humorama, Inc.*

JOKER—See *Humorama, Inc.*

LADIES' HOME JOURNAL—641 Lexington Ave., New York, NY 10022. Address Poetry Editor.
Uses a limited amount of poetry. Enclose stamped, self-addressed envelope. Pays $5 a line, on acceptance.

LAUGH DIGEST–See *Humorama, Inc.*

LAUGH RIOT–See *Humorama, Inc.*

LEATHERNECK–Box 1775, Quantico, VA 22134. Ronald D. Lyons, Editor.
Publication of U. S. Marine Corps. Marine-oriented poetry. Pays from $10, on acceptance.

McCALL'S MAGAZINE–230 Park Ave., New York, NY 10017. Address Poetry Editor.
Poetry and light verse, 4 to 20 lines. Pays top rates, on acceptance.

MADEMOISELLE–350 Madison Ave., New York, NY 10017. Mary Elizabeth McNichols, Poetry Editor.
Outstanding poetry of high quality, to 65 lines. Pays from $25, on acceptance.

MAINE LIFE–RFD 1, Liberty, ME 04949. David E. Olson, Editor.
Poetry on Maine. No payment.

MODERN BRIDE–One Park Ave., New York, NY 10016. Cele G. Lalli, Executive Editor.
Short verse appealing to bride and groom. Pays on acceptance.

MS.–370 Lexington Ave., New York, NY 10017.
Poetry of high quality, not necessarily on feminist subjects. Pays $75, on acceptance.

THE NATION–333 Sixth Ave., New York, NY 10014. Grace Schulman, Poetry Editor.
Poetry of high quality. Pays after publication.

NEW-ENGLAND GALAXY–Old Sturbridge Village, Sturbridge, MA 01566. Catherine Fennelly, Editor.
Poetry, to 30 lines, on New England subjects. Pays $50, on publication.

THE NEW YORKER–25 West 43rd St., New York, NY 10036. Address The Editors.
Light verse (topical, satirical or humorous) and serious poetry. Pays top rates, on acceptance.

NRTA JOURNAL–215 Long Beach Blvd., Long Beach, CA 90801. Hubert C. Pryor, Editor.
Publication of the National Retired Teachers Association. Short verse. Pays from $10, on acceptance.

THE OHIO MOTORIST–P.O. Box 6150, Cleveland, OH 44101. A. K. Murway, Editor.
Humorous poems, 4 to 6 lines, on motoring and vacation topics (foreign and domestic). Pays $7 to $10, on acceptance.

OREGONIAN VERSE–*Northwest Magazine, The Oregonian,* Portland, OR 97201. Penny Avila, Editor.
Poetry to 24 lines. Rarely uses religious or humorous poetry. Pays $5 per poem, after publication.

PLAYBOY–919 North Michigan Ave., Chicago, IL 60611. Address Party Jokes Editor.
Limericks only; no other verse. Pays $50.

POPULAR CARTOONS–See *Humorama, Inc.*

POPULAR JOKES–See *Humorama, Inc.*

QUAKER LIFE–Friends United Meeting, 101 Quaker Hill Dr., Richmond, IN 47374.
Verse, 10 to 30 lines. Pays in copies.

QUIPS–See *Humorama, Inc.*

QUOTE MAGAZINE–P.O. Box 4073, Anderson, SC 29621.
Light verse, to 4 lines, of value to ministers, toastmasters, club leaders and other public speakers.

ROLL CALL: THE NEWSPAPER OF CAPITOL HILL–428 Eighth St. S. E., Washington, DC 20003.
Light, humorous satire on Congress or politics. Pays on acceptance.

ROMP–See *Humorama, Inc.*

THE ROTARIAN–1600 Ridge Ave., Evanston, IL 60201. Willmon L. White, Editor.
Humorous or philosophical verse. Pays varying rates, on acceptance.

ROUNDUP–The Denver *Post,* P.O. Box 1709, Denver, CO 80201. Walter Hall, Editor, Poetry Forum.
Poetry, to 20 lines, by Rocky Mountain area poets. Pays $2, on acceptance.

RURAL ELECTRIC MISSOURIAN–2722 East McCarty St., Jefferson City, MO 65101. Don Yoest, Editor.
Poetry, 4 to 12 lines, with rural flavor. Pays from $7, on acceptance.

THE SATURDAY EVENING POST–1100 Waterway Blvd., Indianapolis, IN 46202. Astrid Henkels, Poetry Editor.
Short poetry, in any form. Light verse for Post Scripts pages. Pays varying rates, on publication.

SATURDAY REVIEW–488 Madison Ave., New York, NY 10022.
No unsolicited poetry accepted.

SCANDINAVIAN REVIEW–127 East 73rd St., New York, NY 10021. Howard E. Sandum, Editor.
Short poems translated from Scandinavian languages. Pays varying rates, on publication.

SEVENTEEN–850 Third Ave., New York, NY 10022.
Poetry, to 20 lines, by teens. Pays to $25. No manuscripts returned. Allow 8 weeks reading time.

STARE–See *Humorama, Inc.*

UNDERSTANDING–Star Route Box 588F, Tonopah, AZ 85354.
Poetry, to 36 lines, expressing good will among all peoples of the world. Pays 10¢ a line, on publication.

WESTWAYS–P.O. Box 2890, Los Angeles, CA 90051. Frances Ring, Editor.
Serious verse, to 24 lines, preferably on western theme: travel, history, conservation, etc. Pays from $25, on acceptance. Overstocked.

YANKEE–Dublin, NH 03444. Jean Burden, Poetry Editor.
Serious poetry of high quality, to 30 lines. Pays $25 per poem, on publication. Annual awards.

ZIP–See *Humorama, Inc.*

COLLEGE, LITERARY AND POETRY MAGAZINES

ALEPH—7319 Willow Ave., Takoma Park, MD 20012. Mel Raff and L. R. Fox, Editors.
Poetry, any length. Pays in copies.

THE AMERICAN POETRY REVIEW—1616 Walnut St., Rm. 405, Philadelphia, PA
19103.
High-quality modern poetry. Pays in copies.

ANTAEUS—1 West 30th St., New York, NY 10001. Susan Dwyer, Editor.
Poetry. Pays on publication. Query. Overstocked.

THE ANTIGONISH REVIEW—St. Francis Xavier University, Antigonish, N.S., Canada.
R. J. MacSween, Editor.
Poetry on any subject. Pays in copies.

APALACHEE QUARTERLY—DDB Press, P.O. Box 20106, Tallahassee, FL 32304.
Poetry. Pays in copies.

APPALACHIAN JOURNAL—134 Sanford, Appalachian State Univ., Boone, NC 28608.
J. W. Williamson, Editor.
Poetry with a regional flavor. Pays in copies.

ARIZONA QUARTERLY—University of Arizona, Tucson, AZ 85721. Albert F. Gegenheimer, Editor.
Poetry. Pays in copies and subscription; annual award.

ASPEN ANTHOLOGY—Box 3185, Aspen, CO 81611. Kurt Brown, Editor.
Poetry, graphics, photos. Pays in copies; awards.

BACHY—Papa Bach Bookstore, 11317 Santa Monica Blvd., West Los Angeles, CA
90025.
Serious poetry. Pays in copies. Occasional cash awards.

BACK ROADS—Box 543, Cotati, CA 94928. Stella Nathan, Editor.
Poetry, to 2 pages. Pays in copies.

BALL STATE UNIVERSITY FORUM—Ball State University, Muncie, IN 47306. Merrill
Rippy and Frances Mayhew Rippy, Editors.
Poetry, 4 to 200 lines. Pays in copies.

BARBEQUE PLANET—4414 Illinois Ave., Nashville, TN 37209. Bob Millard, Editor.
Imaginative poetry, serious or humorous, 5 to 55 lines. Pays in copies.

BARDIC ECHOES—1036 Emerald Ave. N.E., Grand Rapids, MI 49503. Clarence L.
Weaver, Editor.
Poetry, to 40 lines, in good taste. Pays in copies; awards.

BELOIT POETRY JOURNAL—Box 2, Beloit, WI 53511.
Poetry to any length, experimental or traditional. Occasional chapbooks. Pays in
copies.

BERKELEY BARB—Box 1247, Berkeley, CA 94701. Ray Riegert, Editor.
Poetry, 2 to 20 lines. Pays $10, on publication.

BEST FRIENDS—c/o Carolyn Maisel, 329 Montclaire N.E., Albuquerque, NM 87108.
Poetry, any length, by women only. Pays in copies.

BEYOND BAROQUE—P.O. Box 806, Venice, CA 90291.
Avant-garde poetry. Pays in copies.

THE BITTER OLEANDER—310 Bradford Pkwy., Syracuse, NY 13224. Paul B. Roth,
Editor.
Poetry, up to 30 lines. Pays $5 per poem.

BITTERROOT—Box 51, Blythebourne Sta., Brooklyn, NY 11219. Menke Katz, Editor.
Poetry. Pays in copies; annual awards.

BOX 749—Box 749, Old Chelsea Station, New York, NY 10011. David Ferguson,
Editor.
Poetry, any length. Pays in copies.

CANADIAN FORUM—3 Church St., Suite 401, Toronto, Ont., Canada. MSE 1M2. Denis
Smith, Editor.
Poetry, any length. Pays $8, plus copies.

THE CAPE ROCK—Southeast Missouri State University, Cape Girardeau, MO 63701.
R. A. Burns, Editor.
Poetry, to 70 lines, of any kind. No obscenity or sentimentality. Pays in copies.

CAROLINA QUARTERLY—Box 1117, Chapel Hill, NC 27514. Jeff Richards, Editor.
Poems of any length, form and subject by well-known and new poets. Pays $5, on
publication; annual awards.

CHELSEA—Box 5880, Grand Central Sta., New York, NY 10017. Sonia Raiziss, Editor.
Poetry, translations. Pays in copies.

CHICAGO REVIEW—The University of Chicago, Faculty Exchange Box C, Chicago, IL
60637. Richard Vine, Editor.
Poetry, translations. Pays in copies.

CHOMO-URI—P.O. Box 1057, Amherst, MA 01002.
Poetry by women which offers perspectives on a changing society. Submit no more
than 5 poems. Pays in copies.

CHOOMIA—Yarrow Press, P.O. Box 4204, Tucson, AZ 85719. Ann Guido and Jay
Barwell, Editors.
Modern poetry. Pays in copies.

CIMARRON REVIEW—Oklahoma State University, Stillwater, OK 74074. Jeanne
Adams Wray, Managing Editor.
Verse, any length, particularly on contemporary society. Pays on copies.

CONFRONTATION—Dept. of English, Long Island Univ., Brooklyn, NY 11201. Martin
Tucker, Editor.
Poetry. Pays on publication.

CONNECTIONS—Bell Hollow Rd., Putnam Valley, NY 10579. Toni Ortner Zimmerman,
Editor.
Modern poetry, one page, especially by women. Pays in copies.

THE COOPERATOR—8570 Wilshire Blvd., Beverly Hills, CA 90211.
Poetry and translations, to 30 lines. Poetry reviews and criticism. Pays in copies.

CREATIVE MOMENT—BOX 391, Sumter, SC 29150. Syed Amanuddin, Editor.
Poetry and translations, to 30 lines. Poetry reviews and criticism. Pays in copies.

CUMBERLANDS (formerly *Twigs*)—Pikeville College Press, Pikeville, KY 41501.
Poetry on Appalachian subjects. Pays in copies, awards.

THE DEKALB LITERARY ARTS JOURNAL—DeKalb College, 555 Indian Creek Dr.,
Clarkston, GA 30021. William S. Newman, Editor.
Original poetry. Pays in copies. No carbons, Xeroxes.

DESCANT—Texas Christian University, T. C. U. Sta., Fort Worth, TX 76129. Betsy
Colquitt, Editor.
Poetry, any length; short poetry preferred. Pays in copies.

THE DICKINSON REVIEW—Dept. of English, Dickinson State College, Dickinson, ND
58601.
Short poetry. Pays in copies.

DRAGONFLY: A QUARTERLY OF HAIKU—4102 N.E. 130th Pl., Portland, OR

97230. Larraine Ellis Harr, Manuscripts Editor.
Classical haiku preferred (not necessarily 5-7-5). Cash and book awards each issue.

EN PASSANT POETRY QUARTERLY–1906 Brant Rd., Wilmington, DE 19810. James
A. Costello, Editor.
Poetry, including translations. Pays in copies.

EPOCH–245 Goldwin Smith Hall, Cornell University, Ithaca, NY 14850. Tom Merwin,
Editor.
Serious verse, to 4 pages; contemporary but not necessarily experimental. Pays in
copies.

EVENT–Douglas College, P.O. Box 2503, New Westminster, B.C., Canada V3L 5B2.
John Levin, Editor.
Poetry of highest quality. Small honorarium and copies.

THE FAULT–33513 Sixth St., Union City, CA 94587. Rustie Cook, Editor.
Poetry. Pays in copies.

THE FIDDLEHEAD–The Observatory, University of New Brunswick, Fredericton, N.B.,
Canada. Roger Ploude, Editor.
Serious poetry, preferably short and Canadian. Pays about $5 per page, on pub-
lication.

FIELD–Rice Hall, Oberlin College, Oberlin, OH 44074.
Serious poetry, any length, by established and unknown poets. Pays $15 per page, on
publication.

FORUM–University of Houston, Houston, TX 77004. William Lee Pryor, Editor.
Poetry, to 50 lines. Pays in copies. Overstocked until September 1978.

FOUR QUARTERS–La Salle College, Philadelphia, PA 19141. John Keenan, Editor.
Poetry, to 30 lines. Pays $5, on publication. No manuscripts read June through
August.

FREE LANCE–6005 Grand Ave., Cleveland, OH 44104. Casper L. Jordan, and Russell
Atkins, Editors.
Experimental, avant-garde poetry, any length. Pays in copies.

FRONT STREET TROLLEY–2125 Acklen Ave., Nashville, TX 37212. Molly McIntosh,
Editor.
Serious and satirical poetry, any length, preferably by southern writers. Pays in
copies.

GEORGIA REVIEW–University of Georgia, Athens, GA 30602. John T. Irwin, Editor.
Poetry, any length. Pays 50¢ per line, on publication.

GRAVIDA–P.O. Box 76, Hartsdale, NY 10530.
Poetry. Pays in copies.

THE GREENFIELD REVIEW–Greenfield Centre, NY 12833. Joseph Bruchac III,
Editor.
Contemporary poetry, any length, by established and new poets, third world writers.
Translations. Pays in copies.

GREEN'S MAGAZINE–P.O. Box 313, Detroit, MI 48321. David Green, Editor.
Poetry, to 36 lines. Pays $2 to $3, on publication.

GROVE: CONTEMPORARY POETRY AND TRANSLATION–Pitzer College, Claremont, CA 91711. Barry Sanders, Editor.
Original poetry and translation of foreign-language poems. Pays in copies.

THE HAMPDEN-SYDNEY POETRY REVIEW–P.O. Box 126, Hampden-Sydney, VA

23943. Tom O'Grady and Michael Egan, Editors.
Highest quality poetry, any length. Pays in copies.

HIRAM POETRY REVIEW–P.O. Box 162, Hiram, OH 44234. David Fratus, Editor.
Poetry, any length. Pays in copies and subscription.

HUDSON REVIEW–65 East 55th St., New York, NY 10022. Frederick Morgan and
Paula Dietz, Editors.
Poetry. Pays on publication.

IMAGES–Wright State University, Dayton, OH 45431. Gary Pacernick, Editor.
Poetry, to 250 lines. Pays in copies.

IN A NUTSHELL–Hibiscus Press. P.O. Box 22248, Sacramento, CA 95822. Margaret
Wensrich, Managing Editor.
Poetry, no length or subject limit. Pays from $3, plus copies, on publication.

INLET–Dept. of English, Virginia Wesleyan College, Norfolk, VA 23502. Joseph
Harkey, Editor.
Published annually. Poetry, to 50 lines, accepted from September to March. Pays in
copies.

THE IOWA REVIEW–EPB 321, University of Iowa, Iowa City, IA 52242.
Poetry and prose poems. Pays 50¢ a line, on publication.

KAMADHENU MAGAZINE–Dept. of English, Washington State University, Pullman,
WA 99164. G. S. Sharat Chandra, Editor.
Serious contemporary poetry, to 100 lines. Reviews and translations. Encourages
minority groups. Pays varying rates, on publication.

KANSAS QUARTERLY–Dept. of English, Kansas State University, Manhattan, KS
66506.
Poetry. Pays in copies. Annual poetry awards.

KARAMU–Dept. of English, Eastern Illinois University, Charleston, IL 61920. Carol
Elder, Poetry Editor.
Poetry, 4 to 60 lines, with clear, strong imagery. Pays in copies.

THE LITERARY REVIEW–Fairleigh Dickinson University, Madison, NJ 07940. Martin
Green and Harry Keyishian, Co-Editors.
Serious poetry, any length. Pays in copies.

THE LITTLE MAGAZINE–P.O. Box 207, Cathedral Sta., New York, NY 10025. David
G. Hartwell, Editor.
Poetry, any length. Pays in copies.

LONG ISLAND REVIEW–360 West 21st St., New York, NY 10011. Stephen Sossa-
man and Edward Faranda, Editor.
Poetry, any length. Pays in copies.

LOON–P.O. Box 11633, Santa Rosa, CA 95406. D. L. Emblen, Richard Welin and
Richard Speakes, Editors.
Poetry and short essays on poetics. Pays $5 a poem and copies.

THE LYRIC–307 Dunton Dr. S.W., Blacksburg, VA 24060. Leslie Mellichamp, Editor.
Serious traditional poetry, preferably upbeat. No payment; cash prizes and annual
college contest.

MACABRE–26 Fowler St., New Haven, CT 06515. Joseph Payne Brennan, Editor.
Verse to 30 lines, on eerie, macabre, supernatural subject matter. No science fiction
or light verse. Pays in copies.

MASSACHUSETTS REVIEW—Memorial Hall, University of Massachusetts, Amherst, MA 01003.
Poetry. Pays modest rates, on publication.

THE MIDWEST QUARTERLY—Pittsburg State University, Pittsburg, KS 66762. V. J. Emmett, Jr., Editor.
Serious poetry, to 50 lines. Pays in copies.

MISSISSIPPI REVIEW—Dept. of English, Southern Sta., Box 37, University of Southern Mississippi, Hattiesburg, MS 39401. Bernard Kaplan, Editor.
Serious poetry, any length. Pays $5 per poem. Do not submit during summer months.

THE MODULARIST REVIEW—Wooden Needle Press, 65-45 Yellowstone Blvd., Forest Hills, NY 11375. R. C. Morse, Editor.
Contemporary poetry, to 5 pages. Pays in copies and subscription.

MOONS AND LIONS TAILES—Lake Street Sta., Box 8434, Minneapolis, MN 55408.
Lyrical poetry, essays, translations and reviews. Pays in copies for poetry, $10 per page for translations and prose, on publication. Query for essays.

MOVING OUT: FEMINIST LITERARY & ARTS JOURNAL—Wayne State University, 4866 Third, Rm. 207, Detroit, MI 48202.
Poetry. Pays in copies.

MR. COGITO—Box 627, Pacific University, Forest Grove, OR 97116.
Poetry, translations. Pays in copies.

MUNDUS ARTIUM—UTD, Box 688, Richardson, TX 75080. Rainer Schulte, Editor.
Journal of international literature and arts. Bilingual poetry, conceptual, not descriptive.

THE NANTUCKET REVIEW—P.O. Box 1444, Nantucket, MA 02554. Richard Cumbie and Richard Burns, Editors.
Poetry of any length, translations. Pays in copies.

NEBULA—970 Copeland, North Bay, Ont., Canada P1B 3E4. K. Stange, Editor.
Literate poetry. Pays in copies.

NEW COLLAGE MAGAZINE—5700 North Tamiami Trail, Sarasota, FL 33580. A. McA. Miller, Editor.
Expressive, unsentimental poetry. Do not submit during summer. Pays in copies.

NEW LAUREL REVIEW—Box 1083, Chalmette, LA 70044. Alice Moser Claudel, Editor. Calvin Andre Claudel, Asst. Editor, Translations.
Contemporary poetry, to 35 lines, and translations. Pays in copies.

NEW ORLEANS REVIEW—Loyola University, New Orleans, LA 70118.
Innovative poetry, and skillfully done traditional forms. Pays $10, on publication.

NEW YORK QUARTERLY—P.O. Box 2415, Grand Central Sta., New York, NY 10017.
Poetry of all genres. Critical essays on poetry (query). Pays in copies.

NIMROD—University of Tulsa, Tulsa, OK 74104.
Serious poetry and translations. Pays varying rates.

NORTH AMERICAN REVIEW—University of Northern Iowa, Cedar Falls, IA 50613. Peter Cooley, Poetry Editor.
Poetry of high quality. Pays 50¢ a line, on publication.

NORTH CAROLINA REVIEW—3329 Granville Dr., Raleigh, NC 27609. Carol Lynn Wilkinson, Editor.
Poetry of literary merit, to 100 lines. Pays 50¢ a line, on acceptance.

NORTHERN LIGHT—University of Manitoba Press, 605 Fletcher Argue Bldg., Winnipeg, Man., Canada R3T 2N2.
Poetry, preferably by young Canadians. Reviews of recent Canadian poetry. Good photography. Pays in copies.

NORTHWEST REVIEW—University of Oregon, Eugene, OR 97403. Michael Strelow, Editor.
Poetry. Pays in copies; occasional cash payments.

OHIO REVIEW—Ellis Hall, Ohio University, Athens, OH 45701. S. W. Lindberg, Editor.
Poetry. Pays on publication.

PAINTBRUSH—Ishtar Press, Inc., Comparative Literature, State University of New York, Binghamton, NY 13901. B. M. Bennani, Editor.
Semi-annual. Serious poetry and translations. Pays varying rates.

PANACHE—Box 77, Sunderland, MA 01375. David Lenson, Editor.
Poetry, any length. Payment varies.

PARIS REVIEW—541 East 72nd St., New York, NY 10021. Michael Benedikt, Poetry Editor.
Poetry of high quality. Pays $10 to $50, on publication.

PARTISAN REVIEW—Rutgers University, One Richardson St., New Brunswick, NJ 08903. William Phillips, Editor.
No unsolicited poetry.

THE PENNY DREADFUL—c/o Dept. of English, Bowling Green University, Bowling Green, OH 43403.
Serious poetry. Pays in copies.

PLOUGHSHARES—Dept. W, Box 529, Cambridge, MA 02139.
Poetry of highest quality. Pays $10. Overstocked.

POEM—Box 1247, West Station, Huntsville, AL 35807. Robert L. Welker, Editor.
Serious poetry, any length. Pays in copies.

POET LORE—4000 Albemarle St., N.W., Suite 302, Washington, DC 20016.
Traditional and experimental poetry, original and translation. Verse plays. Pays in copies; annual awards.

POETRY—1228 North Dearborn Pkwy., Chicago, IL 60610. Daryl Hine, Editor.
Poetry of highest quality. Pays $1 a line, on publication. Enclose stamped, self-addressed envelope.

POETRY NEWSLETTER—Dept. of English, Temple University, Philadelphia, PA 19122. Richard O'Connell, Editor.
Poetry and translations. Pays in copies.

POETRY NORTHWEST—University of Washington, Seattle, WA 98195. David W. Wagoner, Editor.
Poetry. Pays in copies and subscription.

POETRY VIEW—1125 Valley Rd., Menasha, WI 54952. Dorothy Dalton, Editor.
Serious poetry, to 24 lines; free verse preferred. Light verse, 4 to 8 lines. No religious or sentimental poetry. Submit seasonal material 2 to 3 months in advance. Pays $3 per poem, after publication.

PRAIRIE SCHOONER—Andrews Hall 201, University of Nebraska, Lincoln, NE 68588. Bernice Slote, Editor.
Good verse of any style. Payment plus copies, reprints and prizes.

PRISM INTERNATIONAL—c/o Creative Writing, University of British Columbia, Vancouver, B. C., Canada.
Serious poetry, any length. Pays $5 per printed page, on publication.

PSYCHOLOGICAL PERSPECTIVES—10349 West Pico Blvd., Los Angeles, CA 90064.
Serious poetry. Pays in copies. Send to J'nan M. Sellery, Poetry Editor, c/o Department of Humanities, Harvey Mudd College, Claremont, CA 91711.

QUARTERLY REVIEW OF LITERATURE—26 Haslet Ave., Princeton, NJ 08540. T. Weiss, Editor.
Poetry.

RED CEDAR REVIEW—Dept. of English, Morrill Hall, Michigan State University, East Lansing, MI 48824.
Poetry. Pays in copies.

THE REMINGTON REVIEW—505 Westfield Ave., Elizabeth, NJ 07208. Dean Maskevich, Editor.
Serious poetry, to 100 lines. Interested in new writers. No carbons or Xeroxes. Pays in copies.

REVIEW LE BOOCHE—110 South 9th St., Columbia, MO 65201.
Poetry. Pays in copies.

ROANOKE REVIEW—Dept. of English, Roanoke College, Salem, VA 24153. R. R. Walter, Editor.
Serious poetry. Pays in copies.

ST. ANDREWS REVIEW—St. Andrews Presbyterian College, Laurinburg, NC 28352.
Poetry. Pays in copies, awards.

SEQUOYA—c/o University Center, St. John's University, Grand Central & Utopia Pkwys., Jamaica, NY 11439. Patty Gordon, Associate Editor.
Poetry, any length. Pays in copies.

SEVEN—115 South Hudson, Oklahoma City, OK 73102. James Neill Northe, Editor.
Serious, original poems, any form; free verse only if genuine. Pays $4 per poem, on acceptance. Query.

SEWANEE REVIEW—Sewanee, TN 37375. George Core, Editor.
Serious poetry, to 60 lines, of highest quality. Pays about 60¢ per line, on publication.

SHANTIH—P.O. Box 125, Bay Ridge Sta., Brooklyn, NY 11220. John S. Friedman and Irving Gottesman, Editors.
Poetry and translations. Pays in copies.

SHENANDOAH—Box 722, Lexington, VA 24450. Eleanor Taylor, Poetry Editor.
Poetry. Pays varying rates, on publication. No manuscripts considered June through August.

THE SMALL FARM—P.O. Box 563, Jefferson City, TN 37760. Jeff Daniel Marion, Editor.
Poetry of highest quality, especially by poets from Tennessee. Pays in copies.

THE SMALL POND MAGAZINE—10 Overland Dr., Stratford, CT 06497. Napoleon St. Cyr, Editor.
Poetry, to 100 lines, of any style. Pays in copies.

THE SMITH—5 Beekman St., New York, NY 10038. Harry Smith, Editor.
Poetry, any length. Interested in young and unknown poets. Pays modest rates, on acceptance, plus copies.

SNOWY EGRET–c/o Dept. of English, Otterbein College, Westerville, OH 43081. William T. Hamilton, Literary Editor.
Serious poetry, any length, related to natural history. Pays from $2 per printed page, on publication.

THE SOUTH CAROLINA REVIEW–c/o Dept. of English, Clemson University, Clemson, SC 29631.
Poetry, any length. Pays in copies.

SOUTH DAKOTA REVIEW–Box 111, University Exchange, Vermillion, SD 57069. John R. Milton, Editor.
Serious poetry, from 10 lines. Pays in copies. Overstocked.

SOUTHERN HUMANITIES REVIEW–Auburn University, Auburn, AL 36803.
Poetry, to 2 pages. Pays in copies.

SOUTHERN POETRY REVIEW–Dept. of English, UNCC, UNCC Sta., Charlotte, NC 28223.
Serious poems, preferably short. No light verse, inspirational or nature poetry. Pays in copies.

SOUTHERN REVIEW–Drawer D, University Sta., Baton Rouge, LA 70893. Donald E. Stanford and Lewis P. Simpson, Editors.
Serious poetry of highest quality. Pays $20 per printed page, on publication. Manuscripts submitted without stamped, self-addressed envelopes will not be returned. Allow 1 to 2 months for editorial decision.

SOUTHWEST REVIEW–Southern Methodist University, Dallas, TX 75275. Margaret L. Hartley, Editor.
Short verse and some longer poetry. Pays $5, on publication.

SPECTRUM–U.C.S.B., Box 14800, Santa Barbara, CA 93107.
Poetry, primarily by college students. Pays in copies; awards.

SPIRIT–Seton Hall University, South Orange, NJ 07079. David Rogers, Editor.
Poetry, any length. Pays in copies.

THE SUNSTONE REVIEW–P.O. 2321, Santa Fe, NJ 87501. William Farrington, Editor.
Serious poetry, any length. Pays in copies. Manuscripts without stamped, self-addressed envelopes not returned.

SYRACUSE GUIDE–500 South Warren St., Syracuse, NY 13202. James Svejda, Poetry Editor.
Serious poetry, to 30 lines. Pays $5, plus copies, on publication.

TEXAS QUARTERLY–Box 7517, University Station, Austin, TX 78712.
Poetry. Pays in copies.

TWIGS–See *Cumberlands.*

UNIVERSITY OF DENVER QUARTERLY–University of Denver, Denver, CO 80210. Burton Raffel, Editor.
Serious or light verse, any length. Pays $10 per page, on publication.

UNIVERSITY OF WINDSOR REVIEW–Dept. of English, University of Windsor, Windsor, Ont., Canada. John Ditsky, Editor.
Poetry. Pays $10 and two copies.

VAGABOND–P.O. Box 79, Ellensburg, WA 98926. John Bennett, Editor.

Hard-hitting, concise poetry, any length. Pays in copies.

THE VILLAGER—135 Midland Ave., Bronxville, NY 10708. Amy Murphy, Editor.
Short verse. Pays in copies.

VIRGINIA QUARTERLY REVIEW—One West Range, Charlottesville, VA 22903. Staige
Blackford, Editor.
Poetry of high quality, by established poets and promising newcomers. Pays 50¢ a
line, on publication.

WASCANA REVIEW—c/o Dept. of English, University of Regina, Regina, Sask., Canada
S4S 0A2.
Poetry, 4 to 100 lines. Pays $10, after publication.

WEST COAST POETRY REVIEW—1335 Dartmouth Dr., Reno, NV 89509. William L.
Fox, Editor.
Experimental poetry. Pays in copies.

WEST COAST REVIEW—Simon Fraser University, Burnaby, B. C., Canada.
Verse, any length. Pays from $5, on acceptance.

WESTERN HUMANITIES REVIEW—University of Utah, Salt Lake City, UT 84112.
Jack Garlington, Editor.
Serious poetry, any length. Single poems or groups. Pays to $35 per poem, on ac-
ceptance.

WESTERN POETRY—3253 Q San Amadeo, Laguna Hills, CA 92653. Joseph Rosenzweig,
Editor.
Highest quality poetry and light verse, to 24 lines, not limited to western themes.
Pays in copies; awards. Enclose stamped, self-addressed envelope.

WIND—RFD Route 1, Box 810, Pikeville, KY 41501. Quentin R. Howard, Editor.
Poetry to 30 lines. Pays in copies.

THE WINDLESS ORCHARD—Dept. of English, Indiana-Purdue University, Ft. Wayne,
IN 46805. Robert Novak, Editor.
Favors contemporary poetry. Pays in copies. Enclose stamped, self-addressed en-
velope.

WISCONSIN REVIEW—Box 118, Dempsey Hall, University of Wisconsin, Oshkosh, WI
54901.
Poetry. Pays in copies.

THE WORMWOOD REVIEW—P.O. Box 8840, Stockton, CA 95024. Marvin Malone,
Editor.
Modern poetry and prose poems, to 400 lines. Pays in copies. Enclose stamped
self-addressed envelope.

XANADU—Long Island Poetry Collective, 1704 Auburn Rd., Wantagh, NY 11793. C.
Fishman, G. W. Fisher and B. Lawn, Editors.
Serious contemporary poetry, to 60 lines. Pays in copies.

YALE REVIEW—1902A Yale Station, New Haven, CT 06520. J. E. Palmer, Editor.
Serious poetry, to 200 lines. Pays on publication.

ZEUGMA—6 Mt. Vernon Terr., Newtonville, MA 02160. Marrill Kaitz, Editor.
Poems, any length, and drawings. Pays in copies.

RELIGIOUS AND DENOMINATIONAL MAGAZINES

BREAD (formerly *Conquest*)—6401 The Paseo, Kansas City, MO 64131. Dan Ketchum, Editor.
Church of the Nazarene. Inspirational poetry, to 20 lines. Pays 15¢ per line, on acceptance.

THE CHRISTIAN ATHLETE—812 Traders National Bank Bldg., 1125 Grand Ave., Kansas City, MO 64106. Gary Warner, Editor.
Free verse, of any length, to interest Christian athletes and coaches. Pays on publication.

THE CHRISTIAN CENTURY—407 South Dearborn St., Chicago, IL 60605. James M. Wall, Editor.
Ecumenical. Verse, to 20 lines. No payment.

CHRISTIAN HERALD—Chappaqua, NY 10514. Kenneth L. Wilson, Editor.
Interdenominational. Short verse.

CHURCH MANAGEMENT—4119 Terrace Ln., Hopkins, MN 55343. Manfred Holck, Jr., Editor.
Protestant. Verse. No payment.

CONTACT—302 Lake St., P.O. Box 650, Huntington, IN 46750. Dennis Miller, Assistant Editor.
Poetry on Christian subjects. Pays 7¢ a line, on acceptance.

DAILY MEDITATION—Box 2710, San Antonio, TX 78299. Ruth S. Paterson, Editor.
Nonsectarian. Verse. Pays 14¢ a line, on acceptance.

DECISION—Billy Graham Evangelistic Association, 1300 Harmon Pl., Minneapolis, MN 55403. Roger C. Palms, Editor.
Poems, 12 to 30 lines, preferably free verse; devotional thoughts and verse, 5 to 8 lines. Pays on publication.

THE DISCIPLE—Box 179, St. Louis, MO 63166. James L. Merrell, Editor.
Journal of Disciples of Christ. Poetry. Pays $2.50 to $5, on acceptance.

THE EVANGEL—999 College Ave., Winona Lake, IN 46590. Vera Bethel, Editor.
Free Methodist. Serious poetry, 8 to 12 lines. Pays 25¢ a line, on acceptance.

EVANGELICAL BEACON—1515 East 66th St., Minneapolis, MN 55423. George Keck, Editor.
Magazine of Evangelical Free Church. Poetry. Pays on publication.

GOSPEL HERALD—Scottdale, PA 15683. Daniel Hertzler, Editor.
Mennonite. Poetry, to 10 lines. Pays $5, on acceptance.

HOME LIFE—127 Ninth Ave. North, Nashville, TN 37234. George W. Knight, Editor.
Southern Baptist. Short lyrical verse, some humorous. Pays on acceptance.

MARRIAGE—Abbey Press Publishing Div., St. Meinrad, IN 47577. Ila M. Stabile, Editor.
Some verse. Pays on acceptance.

MATURE YEARS—201 Eighth Ave. South, Nashville, TN 37203. Daisy D. Warren, Editor.

United Methodist. Poetry, to 12 lines. Pays 50¢ a line, on acceptance.

THE MIRACULOUS MEDAL—475 East Chelten Ave., Philadelphia, PA 19144. Robert
    P. Crawley, C.M., Editor.
    Catholic. Religious verse, to 20 lines. Pays 50¢ a line, on acceptance.

NEW CATHOLIC WORLD—1865 Broadway, New York, NY 10023. Robert J. Heyer,
    Managing Editor.
    Verse, 3 to 22 lines. Pays on publication.

NEW WORLD OUTLOOK—475 Riverside Dr., New York, NY 10027. Arthur J. Moore,
    Jr., Editor.
    Poetry, to 16 lines. Pays on publication.

OUR FAMILY—Box 249, Dept. E., Battleford, Sask., Canada S0M 0E0. Reb Materi,
    O.M.I., Editor.
    Catholic. Verse. Pays on acceptance.

PENTECOSTAL EVANGEL—1445 Boonville, Springfield, MO 65802. Robert C.
    Cunningham, Editor.
    Publication of Assemblies of God. Verse, 12 to 50 lines. Pays on publication.

PURPOSE—610 Walnut Ave., Scottdale, PA 15683. David E. Hostetler, Editor.
    Poetry, 3 to 24 lines. Pays $5 to $15, on acceptance.

THE RECONSTRUCTIONIST—432 Park Ave. South, New York, NY 10016. Ira Eisen-
    stein, Editor.
    Poetry, related to Judaism. Pays on publication.

ST. JOSEPH'S MESSENGER—P.O. Box 288, Jersey City, NJ 07303. Sister Ursula Marie
    Maphet, Editor.
    Verse, 4 to 40 lines.

SCOPE—426 South Fifth St., Minneapolis, MN 55414. Lily M. Gyldenvand, Editor.
    Journal of American Lutheran Women. Poetry. Pays on acceptance.

THE TEXAS METHODIST/UNITED METHODIST REPORTER—P.O. Box 1076,
    Dallas, TX 75221. Spurgeon M. Dunnam III, Editor.
    United Methodist. Religious verse, 4 to 12 lines. Pays on acceptance.

UNITY MAGAZINE—Unity School of Christianity, Lee's Summit, MO 64063. James A.
    Decker, Editor.
    Religious poetry to 20 lines. Pays from 50¢ a line, on acceptance.

VISTA—Box 2000, Marion, IN 46952.
    Poetry. Pays 25¢ a line, on acceptance.

THE GREETING CARD MARKET

AMBERLEY GREETING CARD COMPANY—P.O. Box 37902, Cincinnati, OH 45222.
    J. Jupiter, Editor.
    Humorous studio greeting card ideas, for birthday (general and relative), illness,
    friendship, wedding, birth, and other congratulations; miss you, thank you, retire-
    ment, apology, goodbye, promotion, new home, expectant parents. Risqué humor.
    No conventional verse or seasonal cards. Motto ideas and bumper stickers. Pays from
    $15.

AMERICAN GREETINGS CORPORATION—10500 American Rd., Cleveland, OH
    44144. S. H. McGuire, Editorial Director.
    Ideas for humorous or juvenile cards, promotions and books. No conventional verse.

Short messages, not poetic or humorous or risqué in tone, on love and friendship themes. Address Myra Zirkle. Pays top rates, on acceptance.

BARKER GREETING CARD COMPANY—Rust Craft Park, Dedham, MA 02026.
Ideas for studio and novelty greeting cards, everyday and seasonal. Special interest in dimensional products. Pays from $25.

D. FORER & COMPANY, INC.—511 East 72nd St., New York, NY 10021.
Ideas and designs for whimsical everyday and Christmas lines. Pays from $15 per idea on acceptance.

FRAN MAR GREETING CARDS, LTD. Box 1057, Mt. Vernon, NY 10550.
Whimsical greeting card copy, to 4 lines, with appeal to teen and college market. Birthday, get well, friendship and special titles. Pays $15 per idea, within 30 days of acceptance.

FRAVESSI-LAMONT, INC.—11 Edison Pl., Springfield, NJ 07081. Address Editor.
Short verse, mostly humorous or sentimental; studio cards with witty prose. No Christmas material. Pays varying rates, on acceptance.

GALLANT GREETINGS CORPORATION—2725 West Fullerton, Chicago, IL 60647.
Ideas for humorous and serious greeting cards. Pays $12.50 to $20 per idea, in 60 days.

GIBSON GREETING CARDS, INC.—2100 Section Rd., Cincinnati, OH 45237. Address Editorial Dept.
Studio, humorous, and general material. Pays $25 for humor (must be short and punchy); $50 for studio; $3 per line for rhymed verse; $20 for "cutes" or prose. Especially interested in good "page 2" material appropriate for a season, occasion, or relationship, tied in with direct message for "page 3." Birthday (including all family birthdays), illness, cheer, wedding anniversary, sympathy for everyday line; general and family captions for all seasons. Pays $100 for small books (no poetry collections). Pays following acceptance.

HALLMARK CARDS, INC.—25th and McGee, Kansas City, MO 64141.
Contemporary and Humorous Illustrated departments consider all funny, sendable greeting card ideas. Pays $50 per idea, on acceptance. Address humorous ideas to Freelance Editor, ask for guide sheet. Hallmark General Verse and Prose: previously published writers should acquaint Hallmark with their experience before submitting poetic verse and prose. Not presently in the market for books, photos or artwork.

ALFRED MAINZER, INC.—27-08 40th Ave., Long Island City, NY 11101. Arwed H. Baenisch, Art Director.
Everyday, Christmas, Mother's Day, Father's Day verses. Pays varying rates.

MISTER B GREETING CARD CO.—4370 N.W. 128th St., Opa-Locka, FL 33054. Marguerite Barker, Editor.
Humorous, risqué or novelty ideas and serious, conventional or sentimental material, no more than 4 lines: anniversary, birthday, Mother's Day, St. Patrick's Day, Christmas, get well, etc. No Easter or religious material. Illustrations optional. Pays varying rates.

NORCROSS, INC.—950 Airport Rd., West Chester, PA 19380.

Everyday and seasonal verse. Pays $1.50 to $3 a line. Studio and humorous ideas. Pays $20 to $50. Sensitivity ideas without romantic overtones.

THE PARAMOUNT LINE, INC.—Box 678, Pawtucket, RI 02862. Dorothy Nelson, Editor.
Humorous ideas and ideas for sensitivity or prose cards; 4 to 8 line verses, everyday and seasonal. Prefers material that is conversational and casual rather than sentimental. Pays varying rates, on acceptance.

RED FARM STUDIO—334 Pleasant St., Pawtucket, RI 02860.
Informal cards for birthdays, weddings, anniversaries, Valentine's Day, etc. Prose copy must be short, cute, whimsical; some four-line verse. Pays varying rates.

REED STARLINE CARD CO.—3331 Sunset Blvd., Los Angeles, CA 90026. Reed Stevens, Editor.
Short, humorous studio card copy, conversational in tone, for sophisticated adults; no verse or jingles. Everyday copy, with emphasis on birthday, friendship, get well, anniversary, thank you, travel, congratulations. Submit material for fall holidays in January; for Valentine's Day and St. Patrick's Day in April; and for Easter, Mother's Day, Father's Day and graduation in August. Pays $40 per idea, on acceptance.

RUST CRAFT GREETING CARDS, INC.—Rust Craft Park, Dedham, MA 02026. Address Editorial Director.
Greeting cards for birthday, illness, friendship, etc., both humorous and general. Pays from $15 for informal and cute cards with strong illustration possibilities, from $10 for imaginative, sentimental prose; from $25 for juvenile and humorous ideas; from $60 for book ideas, all on acceptance.

UNITED CARD CO.—107 North Hickory, Arlington Heights, IL 60004.
Humorous contemporary studio greeting cards, seasonal or general. Submit in any form, but no finished artwork. Pays from $25 to $50 per idea, on acceptance.

VAGABOND CREATIONS—2560 Lance Dr., Dayton, OH 45409. George F. Stanley, Jr., Editor.
Birthday, everyday, Valentine, Christmas and graduation studio card copy in good taste with punch line. Humor slanted to younger age group. Mildly risqué humor with *double entendre* acceptable. Ideas for buttons and motto postcards. Pays $10, on acceptance.

WARNER PRESS PUBLISHERS—Anderson, IN 46011. Mrs. Dorothy Smith, Verse Editor.
Religious greeting card verse, from 4 to 6 lines, with suggested Scripture text for each verse. Sensitivity or prose cards, if religious. Begins reading everyday sentiments September 1, Christmas sentiments, November 1. Pays $1 a line, on acceptance.

FILLERS AND HUMOR

Included in the following list are magazines which are noted for their excellent filler departments, plus a cross-section of representative publications that use fillers and short humor pieces. However, almost all magazines use some type of filler material, and writers can find dozens of markets by studying copies of magazines at a library or newsstand.

Many magazines do not acknowledge or return filler material. In such cases, writers may assume that after ninety days have passed from the time of submission, a filler may be submitted to another market.

ALASKA, MAGAZINE OF LIFE ON THE LAST FRONTIER–Box 4-EEE, Anchorage, AK 99509.
Short features, with photos, on Alaska by residents. Pays $10 to $50, on publication.

ALIVE! FOR YOUNG TEENS–Christian Board of Publication, P.O. Box 179, St. Louis, MO 63166.
Cartoons, puzzles, brainteasers, word games, short poetry. Pays $6 for cartoons, to $8 for puzzles and fillers, 25¢ a line for poetry.

THE AMERICAN FIELD–222 West Adams St., Chicago, IL 60606.
Short fact items and anecdotes on outdoor sports and field trials for bird dogs. Pays varying rates, on acceptance.

AMERICAN FRUIT GROWER–37841 Euclid Ave., Willoughby, OH 44094.
Personal-experience pieces, 200 to 500 words, on commercial production and selling of fruit. Pays varying rates.

AMERICAN LEGION MAGAZINE–1608 K St. N.W., Washington, DC 20006. Address Parting Shots Editor.
Anecdotes, to 300 words; humorous light verse, to 16 lines; epigrams. Pays $20 for anecdotes, $2.50 a line for verse, $10 for epigrams.

THE AMERICAN ROSE MAGAZINE–P.O. Box 30,000, Shreveport, LA 71130.
Fillers on home rose gardening. No payment.

THE AMERICAN WEST–20380 Town Center Ln., #160, Cupertino, CA 95014. Ed Holm, Editor.
Illustrated articles, 1,000 words, on unusual people, places or events of Old West, for "Collector's Choice." Pays $75.

ARIZONA–120 East Van Buren St., Phoenix, AZ 85004.
Sunday magazine of *The Arizona Republic*. Short fillers, humor, cartoons, related to Arizona. Pays before publication.

ARIZONA'S HOST–7302 East Sixth Ave., Scottsdale, AZ 85251.
Fillers, short humor, 150 to 200 words, on Arizona and the Southwest. Pays various rates.

THE ATLANTIC–8 Arlington St., Boston, MA 02116.
Sophisticated humorous or satirical pieces, 1,000 to 3,000 words. Some light poetry. Pays varying rates, on acceptance.

BABY CARE–52 Vanderbilt Ave., New York, NY 10017. E. Podsiadlo, Editor.
Short items for "Focus on You" (500 words), "Family Corner" (100 words). Short poetry, cartoons. Pays $10 to $25.

BABY TALK–66 East 34th St., New York, NY 10016.
Short features on child care.

THE BEAVER–Hudson's Bay House, Winnipeg, Manit., Canada R3C 2R1. Helen Burgess, Editor.

Fillers, 700 to 1,000 words, on historical or modern aspects of northwest Canada and Arctic regions. Pays on acceptance.

BICYCLING!—119 Paul Dr., P.O. Box 4450, San Rafael, CA 94903.
For cycling enthusiasts. Humor, photos. Pays $1 per column inch, extra for photos, on publication.

BITS AND PIECES—Box 746, Newcastle, WY 82701. Mabel E. Brown, Editor.
Fillers, 500 to 1,000 words, on history of Wyoming and surrounding states. Source must be given. Pays in copies.

BOYS' LIFE—North Brunswick, NJ 08902.
How-to features, to 750 words, with photos, on hobbies, crafts, science, outdoor skills, etc. Pays from $150.

BREEZY—See *Humorama, Inc.*

BUCKS COUNTY PANORAMA—57 West Court St., Doylestown, PA 18901.
Humor and cartoons on Delaware Valley area. Pays various rates.

CAPPER'S WEEKLY—616 Jefferson St., Topeka, KS 66607.
Short 500- to 700-word human interest and personal experience articles; letters on women's interests, for "Heart of the Home," jokes, cartoons. Pays on publication.

CARTOON FUN & COMEDY—See *Humorama, Inc.*

CATHOLIC DIGEST—P.O. Box 3090, St. Paul, MN 55165.
Features, to 300 words, on instances of kindness rewarded, for "Hearts Are Trumps." Stories about conversions, for "Open Door." Reports of tactful remarks or actions, for "The Perfect Assist." Accounts of good deeds, for "People Are Like That." Humorous pieces on parish life, for "In Our Parish." Picturesque figures of speech, for "Flights of Fancy." Amusing signs, for "Signs of the Times." Jokes; fillers. Source must be given. Pays $4 to $50, on publication.

THE CB TIMES—1005 Murfreesboro Rd., Nashville, TN 37217.
Fillers, jokes, short humor about citizens' band radio. Pays on acceptance.

CHANGING TIMES: THE KIPLINGER MAGAZINE—1729 H St. N.W., Washington, DC 20006.
Epigrams, topical quips, for "Notes on These Changing Times." Pays $10 per item.

CHARLOTTE MAGAZINE—P.O. Box 15843, Charlotte, NC 28210.
Fillers to 750 words, relevant to North Carolina. Pays on publication.

CHATELAINE—481 University Ave., Toronto, Ont., Canada M5N 1V5.
Light verse. Pays $10 to $25, on acceptance.

CHILD LIFE—1100 Waterway Blvd., Box 567B, Indianapolis, IN 46206.
Mystery and science-fiction magazine for intermediate readers up to 14. Uses quizzes, puzzles, games, and simple craft projects. Pays varying rates, on publication.

CHILDREN'S PLAYMATE—1100 Waterway Blvd., P.O. Box 567B, Indianapolis, IN 46206.
Verse, puzzles, games, mazes, tricks, for 3- to 8-year-olds. Pays around 3¢ a word, on publication.

CHORAL PRAISE—See *The Church Musician.*

THE CHRISTIAN ADVENTURER—Messenger Publishing House, P.O. Box 850, Joplin, MO 64801.

Inspirational fillers, to 300 words, and Bible puzzles, for teen-agers. Pays ½¢ a word, on publication.

CHRISTIAN HERALD—40 Overlook Dr., Chappaqua, NY 10514.
Personal-experience pieces, 500 words; unusual anecdotes; poetry, 4 to 24 lines; photos with an inspirational message. Pays $5 to $15.

THE CHRISTIAN HOME—201 Eighth Ave. South, Nashville, TN 37202. United Methodist. David Bradley, Editor.
Articles, 800 to 1,000 words, relating to family living. Seasonal, inspirational or humorous verse, to 16 lines. Pays $10 to $15, 50¢ a line for poetry, on acceptance.

CHRISTIAN LIFE—Gundersen Dr. and Schmale Rd., Wheaton, IL 60187.
News items, 100 to 200 words, on trends, ideas, personalities and events of interest to Christians. Photos. Pays on publication.

THE CHURCH MUSICIAN—127 Ninth Ave. North, Nashville, TN 37234. W. M. Anderson, Editor.
For Southern Baptist music leaders. Fillers. Pays around 2¢ a word, on acceptance. Same address and requirements for *Gospel Choir* and *Choral Praise* (for adults), and *Opus One* and *Opus Two* (for teen-agers).

CLASSIC—551 Fifth Ave., New York, NY 10017.
Magazine about horses for sport and pleasure. Short items for "Comment" column. Pays $25, on acceptance.

COLUMBIA—Box 1670, New Haven, CT 06507.
Journal of the Knights of Columbus. Humor and satire, to 1,000 words; captionless cartoons. Pays to $100, $25 for cartoons, on acceptance.

COLUMBIA JOURNALISM REVIEW—700 Journalism Bldg., Columbia University, New York, NY 10027.
Amusing mistakes in news stories, headlines, etc. (original clipping required), for "Lower Case." Fillers, 250 words, on non-New York media happenings. Pays $10 to $25, on acceptance.

THE COUNTRY GENTLEMAN—1100 Waterway Blvd., Indianapolis, IN 46202.
Appropriate fillers relating to rural living, crafts, environment, gardening, etc. Pays on publication.

COUNTRY WORLD (formerly *Oklahoma Ranch and Farm World*)—Box 1770, Tulsa, OK 74102. Sunday supplement of the *Sunday World.* Herb Karner, Editor.
Farm, suburban, homemaking pieces, to 800 words, with photos. Pays from $10 per column, on publication. Query.

CREEM—P.O. Box P-1064, Birmingham, MI 48012. Susan L. Whitall, Features Editor.
Off-beat news items, to 500 words; cartoons. Pays varying rates.

CRUISING WORLD—Box 452, Newport, RI 02840.
Fillers, poetry, cartoons, photos and photo-essays related to technical and recreational aspects of cruising under sail. Pays on publication.

CRUSADER—1548 Poplar Ave., Memphis, TN 38104.
Southern Baptist. For boys 6 to 11. Hobbies, games, nature pieces. Pays 2½¢ a word, on acceptance.

CYCLE WORLD—1499 Monrovia Ave., P.O. Box 1757, Newport Beach, CA 92663.
Humor, 1,500 to 2,000 words, of interest to motorcycle enthusiasts. Racing reports, 400 to 600 words, with photos. Cartoons; news items on motorcycle industry, legislation, trends. Pays $75 to $100 per printed page, on publication.

DENTAL MANAGEMENT—757 Third Ave., New York, NY 10017.
Time- and money-saving tips for dental assistants for "Time-saving Tips." Pays $5.

DIXIE-ROTO—*The Times-Picayune,* New Orleans, LA 70140.
Humorous shorts involving children from Louisiana or Mississippi, for "Bright Talk."
Documented historical anecdotes related to the South. Pays $20 for anecdotes, $2 to
$3 for shorts.

DOWN EAST—Camden, ME 04843.
Anecdotes and stories about Maine, to 300 words, for "It Happened Down East" and
"I Remember." Features, 1,000 words, for "Room with a View." Amusing or in-
formative observations about contemporary Maine, for "North by East." Photos.
Pays $10 to $35, on acceptance.

EBONY—820 South Michigan Ave., Chicago, IL 60605.
Features, to 200 words, on blacks in traditionally non-black jobs. Pays $35.

ELITE—606 Avenue Rd., Suite 404, Toronto, Ont., Canada H3H 2G1.
Men's magazine. Fillers. Pays on publication.

THE ELKS MAGAZINE—425 West Diversey Pkwy., Chicago, IL 60614. Jeffrey Ball,
Editor.
General-interest humor, 1,500 to 2,500 words, for a family audience. Non-political
satire. Pays from 10¢ a word.

THE EMPIRE MAGAZINE—*Denver Post,* Denver, CO 80201.
Fillers with photos, of interest to Rocky Mountain readers. Pays 4¢ to 5¢ a word, $10
per photo.

EXPECTING—52 Vanderbilt Ave., New York, NY 10017. E. Podsiadlo, Editor.
Anecdotes about pregnancy, for "Happenings." Sophisticated light verse. Pays $10,
$5 to $10 for verse.

FAMILY CIRCLE—488 Madison Ave., New York, NY 10022. Patricia Curtis, Copy
Director.
Humor, how-to and inspirational pieces, to 1,500 words. Fillers, 50 to 75 words, on
ideas for better everyday living. Pays to $500, $10 for fillers.

FAMILY DIGEST PARISH MONTHLY—See *Parish Monthly.*

THE FAMILY FOOD GARDEN—Route 1, Box 877, McCourtney Rd., Grass Valley, CA
95945. George S. Wells, Editor.
Fillers and cartoons on home food gardening; some recipes. Pays modest rates, on
acceptance.

THE FAMILY HANDYMAN—1999 Shepard Rd., St. Paul, MN 55116.
Tips and shortcuts, 100 to 300 words, on do-it-yourself projects. Pays $5 to $15, on
publication.

FARM JOURNAL—Washington Sq., Philadelphia, PA 19105.
Verse, 4 to 8 lines, and humor, on the farm or farm family. Pays on acceptance.

FATE—Clark Publishing Co., 500 Hyacinth Pl., Highland Park, IL 60035.
Factual fillers, to 200 words, on strange or psychic happenings. True stories, to 300
words, on psychic or mystic personal experiences. Pays $1 to $10.

FIELD AND STREAM—383 Madison Ave., New York, NY 10017.
Features, to 2,500 words, on hunting, camping and fishing. How-to pieces, to 1,000
words. Pays from $500 for features, $250 for how-to pieces.

FIREHOUSE—33 East 53rd St., New York, NY 10022. Dennis Smith, Editor-in-Chief.
For firefighters and their families. Recipes from a firefighter's kitchen, appropriate
fillers and poems. Pays on acceptance.

FLING—1485 Bayshore Blvd., Suite 400, San Francisco, CA 94124.
Men's magazine. Humor and satire, 1,500 to 3,000 words. Pays from $100.

FUN HOUSE—See *Humorama, Inc.*

GALLERY—99 Park Ave., New York, NY 10016.
Men's magazine. Short humor, satire. Pays from $350, after acceptance. Query.

GARDEN—The Garden Society, Botanical Garden, Bronx, NY 10458. Jeffrey Katz, Assistant Editor.
Fillers on botanical subjects. Pays on publication.

GASOLINE NEWS—100 North Grant St., Columbus, OH 43215.
Clippings on service stations, car wash and snowmobile industries. Pays 50¢ per clipping, on publication. Query.

GAZE—See *Humorama, Inc.*

GIRLTALK—See *Talk.*

GOLF DIGEST—495 Westport Ave., Norwalk, CT 06856.
Short fact items, anecdotes, quips, jokes, light verse related to golf. True humorous or odd incidents, to 200 words. Pays from $15, on acceptance.

GOLF MAGAZINE—380 Madison Ave., New York, NY 10017.
Fillers, to 750 words, and short humor, on golf. Cartoons. Pays from $25, on acceptance.

GOOD HOUSEKEEPING—959 Eighth Ave., New York, NY 10019. Robert M. Liles, Features Editor.
Light verse and very short humorous prose. Pays from $10 to $100, from $5 a line for verse.

GOSPEL CARRIER—Messenger Publishing House, P.O. Box 850, Joplin, MO 64801.
Inspirational fillers, to 300 words. Pays ½¢ a word, on publication.

GOSPEL CHOIR—See *The Church Musician.*

GOURMET MAGAZINE—777 Third Ave., New York, NY 10017.
Sophisticated light verse with a food or drink angle. Pays on acceptance.

GUIDEPOSTS—747 Third Ave., New York, NY 10017. Dina Donohue, Senior Editor.
Inspirational anecdotes, to 250 words. Pays $10 to $25.

HANDBALL—4101 Dempster St., Skokie, IL 60076.
Fillers, 30 to 40 words, on handball and handball players. Cartoons, photos. Pays on acceptance.

HAPPY TIMES—3558 South Jefferson Ave., St. Louis, MO 63118.
Short poems, action games, suggestions for home activities, puzzles, etc. Pays varying rates, on acceptance.

HOCKEY ILLUSTRATED—333 Johnson Ave., Brooklyn, NY 11206. Randy O'Neill, Editor.
Fillers, puzzles, short humor. Pays on publication.

HOME LIFE—127 Ninth Ave., North, Nashville, TN 37234. George Knight, Editor.
Southern Baptist. Personal-experience pieces, 100 to 500 words, on family relationships. Pays 2½¢ a word, on acceptance.

HOSPITAL PHYSICIAN—405 Lexington Ave., New York, NY 10017.
Short items by physicians, for "Here's How I Do It," "What's Wrong with This Patient?," "Your Next Step?," and "Pediatricks." Pays $10 to $15.

HOW TO, THE HOMEOWNER'S HANDBOOK—380 Madison Ave., New York, NY 10017. Jim Liston, Editor.
Captioned photos, illustrating worksaving, or problem-solving device, for "Problem Solvers." Pays $25.

HUMORAMA, INC.—100 North Village Ave., Rockville Centre, NY 11570.
Topical satire, epigrams, humorous fillers, to 600 words. Light verse, to 24 lines. Pays $1.50 for one-line fillers, 60¢ a line for verse, 5¢ a word for prose, before publication. Same address and requirements for *Joker, Pop Cartoons, Pop Jokes, Laugh Riot, Quips, Stare, Gaze, Fun House, Zip, Cartoon Fun & Comedy, Wink,* and *Breezy.*

HUNTING—Petersen Publishing Co., 8490 Sunset Blvd., Los Angeles, CA 90069.
How-to fillers on hunting. Pays $50.

THE ILLUSTRATOR—Sunday School Dept., MSN #176, 5 NW, 127 Ninth Ave. North, Nashville, TN 37234.
Fillers, photos, on archaeology, geography and history of biblical lands. Pays 2½¢ a word, on acceptance.

JACK AND JILL—1100 Waterway Blvd., P.O. Box 567B, Indianapolis, IN 46206. William Wagner, Editor.
Poems, short plays, puzzles, games, science and craft projects, for 5- to 12-year-olds. Instructions for activities should be clearly written, accompanied by diagrams and a list of materials needed. Pays varying rates, on publication.

JOKER—See *Humorama, Inc.*

LADY'S CIRCLE—21 West 26th St., New York, NY 10010.
Fillers, 600 words, with black-and-white photos, on antiques, bringing up children, gardening, nostalgia, etc. "Sound Off" department pays $10. "Readers' Exchange Cookbook" pays $5 for recipes.

LAUGH RIOT—See *Humorama, Inc.*

THE LOOKOUT—8121 Hamilton Ave., Cincinnati, OH 45231. Mark A. Taylor, Editor.
Inspirational or humorous shorts, 100 to 500 words. Pays 3¢ a word.

LOST TREASURE (formerly *True Treasure*)—Box 328, Conroe, TX 77301. John H. Latham, Editor.
Fillers, 100 to 250 words, on lost mines and buried or sunken treasure, for "Treasure Nuggets." Pays $12.50, on acceptance.

McCALL'S—230 Park Ave., New York, NY 10017.
Fillers on ideas for better living, for "Survival in the Suburbs." Pays $50. Manuscripts are not acknowledged or returned. Phone number must be included with submissions.

MAGAZINE OF THE MIDLANDS—*Omaha World Herald,* World-Herald Sq., Omaha, NE 68102.
Regional-interest humor, from 300 words. Pays on publication.

MAKE IT WITH LEATHER—Box 1386, Fort Worth, TX 76101.
How-to fillers on leathercraft, for "Tips and Hints." Pays $10.

MATURE YEARS—Methodist Publishing House, 201 Eighth Ave. South, Nashville, TN 37202.
Poems, cartoons, puzzles, jokes, anecdotes, to 300 words, for older adults. Pays 3¢ per word, on acceptance.

MECHANIX ILLUSTRATED—1515 Broadway, New York, NY 10036.
Single photos with captions and tips for shortcuts in shop, garage or home, for "It's New" and "Home & Shop Shorts." Cartoons for "Freddie Fumbles." Ideas for

inventions, for "Inventions Wanted." Fillers, to 500 words. Pays $5 to $75.

MODERN BRIDE—One Park Ave., New York, NY 10017.
Humorous pieces, 500 to 1,500 words, and poetry, for brides. Pays on acceptance.

MODERN MATURITY—215 Long Beach Blvd., Long Beach, CA 90802. Hubert C. Pryor, Editor.
Money-saving ideas and how-to and crafts tips, for "Tips Worth Considering." Quizzes, cryptograms, riddles, brainteasers, etc., for "Fun Fare." Quotes from people over 54. Seasonal material (submit 6 months in advance). Pays $5 to $20.

MODERN PHOTOGRAPHY—130 East 59th St., New York, NY 10022.
How-to pieces, 200 to 300 words, with photos, on photography. Pays $25 to $50, on acceptance.

MPLS.—512 Nicollet Mall Bldg., Suite 615, Minneapolis, MN 55402. Kate Richardson, Editor.
Short humor, puzzles, photo-essays on Minneapolis region. Pays various rates.

NATIONAL ENQUIRER—Lantana, FL 33462. Address Fillers Editor.
Short humorous fillers, quotations (give source), witticisms, anecdotes, tart comments. Pays $15.

NATIONAL GUARDSMAN—One Massachusetts Ave. N.W., Washington, DC 20001.
True Army and Air Force anecdotes, for "Tales from the Troops." Pays $10, on publication.

NATIONAL LAMPOON—635 Madison Ave., New York, NY 10022.
Short humor; satire.

NATIONAL REVIEW—150 East 35th St., New York, NY 10016.
Satire, to 900 words. Pays $35 to $75, on publication.

NEBRASKALAND—2200 North 33rd St., Lincoln, NE 68503. Lowell Johnson, Editor.
Verse of interest to Nebraska residents. Cartoons on outdoor subjects. Pays $5 for cartoons. No payment for verse.

THE NEW YORKER—25 West 43rd St., New York, NY 10036.
Amusing mistakes in newspapers, books, magazines, etc. Entertaining anecdotes. Pays from $5, extra for headings and tag lines, on acceptance.

NORDEN NEWS—Norden Laboratories, 601 West Cornhusker Hwy., Lincoln, NE 68521. Patricia Pike, Editor.
Jokes, photos related to veterinary medicine. Pays on publication.

NRTA JOURNAL—215 Long Beach Blvd., Long Beach, CA 90801. Hubert C. Pryor, Editor.
Short verse, humor, "Find-the-Word" puzzles, tips, crafts, cartoons, for older readers. Pays $5 to $50.

THE OHIO MOTORIST—P.O. Box 6150, Cleveland, OH 44101.
Humorous poems, 4 to 6 lines, on motoring and vacation topics. Pays $7 to $10.

OKLAHOMA RANCH AND FARM WORLD—See *Country World.*

ON THE LINE—616 Walnut Ave., Scottdale, PA 15683.
Light verse, 8 to 24 lines, cartoons, puzzles, quizzes, human-interest photos with captions, for 10- to 14-year-olds. Pays $4 to $8 for verse, from $4 for puzzles and quizzes, $7.50 to $15 for photos.

OPUS ONE and OPUS TWO—See *The Church Musician.*

ORBEN'S CURRENT COMEDY—801 Wilmington Trust Bldg., Wilmington, DE 19801.

Send manuscripts to Robert Orben, Apt. 1122, 1200 North Nash St., Arlington, VA 22209.
Original, funny, performable one-liners and brief jokes on news, fads, topical subjects, etc. Pays $3. Stamped, self-addressed envelope required for return of manuscripts.

ORGANIC GARDENING AND FARMING—33 East Minor St., Emmaus, PA 18049.
Fillers, 100 to 500 words, on gardening experiences: how-to's, solution of problems, etc. Material for various departments; news items. Pays $25 to $50, before publication.

OUTDOOR LIFE—380 Madison Ave., New York, NY 10017.
Short instructive or informative items on hunting, fishing, camping gear, boats, outdoor equipment. Photos. Pays on acceptance.

OUI—8560 Sunset Blvd., Los Angeles, CA 90069.
Men's magazine. Short pieces for "Openers." Pays various rates.

PARENTS' MAGAZINE—52 Vanderbilt Ave., New York, NY 10017.
Humorous children's sayings, for "Out of the Mouths of Babes." Short items on solutions of child care-related problems (allowances, nap-taking, etc.), for "Family Clinic." Pays $5 to $10, on publication.

PARISH MONTHLY (formerly *Family Digest Parish Monthly*)—Noll Plaza, Huntington, IN 46750. Robert A. Willims, Editor.
Humorous anecdotes. Pays $5, on acceptance.

PENTHOUSE—909 Third Ave., New York, NY 10022.
Adult magazine. Sexy humor, to 5,000 words. Pays from 20¢ a word, on acceptance.

PLAYBOY—919 North Michigan Ave., Chicago, IL 60611. Address Party Jokes Editor or After Hours Editor.
Jokes; short humorous items on topical subjects, for "After Hours." Pays $50 for jokes, $50 to $350 for "After Hours" items.

PLAYERS—8060 Melrose Ave., Los Angeles, CA 90046. Art Aveilhe, Editor.
For black men. Humor, satire. Movie, theater and record reviews, 100 to 500 words. Pays on publication.

PLAYGIRL—1801 Century Park East, Suite 2300, Century City, Los Angeles, CA 90067.
Fillers, 500 to 800 words, humor, satire and cartoons, for contemporary women.

POP CARTOONS—See *Humorama, Inc.*

POP JOKES—See *Humorama, Inc.*

POPULAR PHOTOGRAPHY—One Park Ave., New York, NY 10016.
Illustrated how-to pieces, for "Photo Tips." Pays $25, on publication.

POPULAR SCIENCE MONTHLY—380 Madison Ave., New York, NY 10017.
Short fact items and hints, with photos or sketches, for "Taking Care of Your Car" and "Short Cuts and Tips." Pays $25, on acceptance.

POWER FOR LIVING—Box 513, Glen Ellyn, IL 60137.
Comments on contemporary issues, 300 to 500 words, for "Viewpoint" column, personal-experience articles reflecting a Christian interpretation of life. Pays from $50. Query.

PROCEEDINGS—U.S. Naval Institute, Annapolis, MD 21402. Clayton R. Barrow, Jr., Editor.
Short humorous anecdotes for members of Navy. Pays $25, on acceptance.

PUBLICIST—Public Relations Aids, Inc., 221 Park Ave. South, New York, NY 10003.
Lee Levitt, Editor.
Short case histories of successful national public-relation campaigns and projects, 400
to 800 words; cartoons; fillers; photos; humor relating to professional public
relations. Pays after publication. Queries preferred.

QUILT WORLD—Box 338, Chester, MA 01011. Barbara Hall Pedersen, Editor.
Fillers, jokes and humor; light verse, 12 lines. Pays 2¢ to 5¢ a word, on publication.
Query.

QUIPS—See *Humorama, Inc.*

QUOTE MAGAZINE—P.O. Box 4073, Station B., Anderson, SC 29621.
Light verse, to 4 lines, of value to ministers, toastmasters, club leaders and other
public speakers.

RAINBOW—American Baptist Board of Education and Publication, Valley Forge, PA
19481.
For 8- to 11-year-olds. Poetry, puzzles, prayers, cartoons, art. Pays to 3¢ a word, on
acceptance.

READER'S DIGEST—Pleasantville, NY 10570.
Anecdotes, for "Life in These United States," "Humor in Uniform," "Campus
Comedy" and "All in a Day's Work." Pays $300, on publication. Short items, for
"Toward More Picturesque Speech." Pays $35. Anecdotes, for "Laughter, the Best
Medicine," "Personal Glimpses," etc. Pays $15 per two-column line ($35 for re-
prints). No fillers acknowledged or returned.

REFLECTION—Box 788, Wheaton, IL 60187.
Publication of Pioneer Girls. Cartoons, quizzes, games, photos, with Christian
emphasis. Pays various rates, on acceptance.

ROAD KING—P.O. Box 319, Park Forest, IL 60466.
Jokes and cartoons, for "Loads of Laughs"; recipes, for "Wives are Winners." Pays $5
for jokes, $25 for cartoons, $10 for recipes.

ROLL CALL—428 Eighth St. S.E., Washington, DC 20003.
Humorous items on Congress; anecdotes, puzzles, quips on political subjects. Pays on
acceptance.

ROTARIAN—1600 Ridge Ave., Evanston, IL 60201. Willmon L. White, Editor.
Humorous articles, 1,200 words, for business and professional men. Pays top rates.
Query.

RUNNER'S WORLD—P.O. Box 366, Mountain View, CA 94042. Richard Benyo, Managing Editor.
For middle- and long-distance competition or fitness runners. Short opinion pieces
for "Runner's Forum." Pays on publication. Query.

THE SATURDAY EVENING POST—1100 Waterway Blvd., Indianapolis, IN 46202.
Starkey Flythe, Jr., Managing Editor.
Humor and satire, 1,500 to 2,000 words; cartoons, light verse for "Post Scripts,"
short quizzes (boxed and illustrated), two-paragraph anecdotes. Pays varying rates.

SATURDAY REVIEW—1290 Ave. of the Americas, New York, NY 10019.
News items, newspaper clippings, etc. for "Front Runners" column. Pays $25.

SCIENCE DIGEST—224 West 57th St., New York, NY 10019. Daniel E. Button, Editor.
Humorous and factual fillers and short poems in the area of science and technology.
Pays varying rates, on acceptance.

SCOPE—Augsburg Publishing House, 426 South 5th St., Minneapolis, MN 55415.
Journal of the American Lutheran Church Women. Religious, humorous, or inspirational fillers. Pays on acceptance.

SEA—1499 Monrovia Ave., Newport Beach, CA 92663.
Humor on boat operation and cruising destinations in western states. Pays 10¢ a word, on acceptance. Query.

SEVENTEEN—850 Third Ave., New York, NY 10022.
Fillers, to 500 words, for "Mini-Mag." Articles, 800 words, by teens, for "In My Opinion." Fact and fiction, 20 to 200 words, by teens, for "Free For All." Photos, cartoons, poetry, by teens. Pays varying rates, on acceptance.

SKEPTIC—812 Presidio Ave., Santa Barbara, CA 93101. Christiane Schlumberger, Editor.
Short pieces, to 1,000 words, provoking controversy and debate, for "Short Stuff." Pays varying rates.

SKIING MAGAZINE—One Park Ave., New York, NY 10016.
Articles, 500 to 1,000 words, on skiing of the past; personal anecdotes, humorous vignettes. One-paragraph fillers on skiing oddities. Articles, 1,200 to 1,500 words, on skiing experiences in distant places, for "Letters From." Pays from 10¢ a word, on acceptance.

SMALL WORLD—Volkswagen of America, 818 Sylvan Ave., Englewood Cliffs, NJ 07632.
Anecdotes, to 100 words, about Volkswagen owners' experiences; cartoons, humorous photos of Volkswagens. Pays from $15, on acceptance.

SNOTRACK—225 East Michigan Ave., Milwaukee, WI 53202. Bill Vint, Editor.
Magazine of United States Snowmobile Association. Short humor and cartoons. Pays $15 to $25 for cartoons, varying rates for humor.

SOAP OPERA DIGEST—420 Lexington Ave., New York, NY 10017. Ruth J. Gordon, Executive Editor.
Crossword puzzles ("Soapuzzles") and recipes with a soap-opera tie-in. Pays various rates. Query.

SPORTS AFIELD—250 West 55th St., New York, NY 10019.
Unusual, useful tips, 100 to 700 words, with photos, on hunting, fishing, camping, boating, etc. Pays $50 to $400, on acceptance.

THE STAR (formerly *The National Star*)—730 Third Ave., New York, NY 10017.
Unusual news stories, with photos, for broad family readership. Pays varying rates.

STARE—See *Humorama, Inc.*

SUNDAY DIGEST—850 North Grove Ave., Elgin, IL 60120. Darlene McRoberts, Editor.
Humorous or inspirational Christian anecdotes, to 500 words. Timely vignettes (submit seasonal material 12 months in advance) and quotations, to 300 words. Short poems, jokes and epigrams, on Christian virtues or frailties. Pays $2 to $25, on acceptance. Stamped, self-addressed envelope required for return of manuscript.

TENNIS—495 Westport Ave., Norwalk, CT 06856.
Fillers, humor. Pays from $25, on publication. Query.

TENNIS USA—Chilton Co., Chilton Way, Radnor, PA 19089. Robert L. Gillen, Editor.
Cartoons on tennis. Pays to $25, on acceptance.

TODAY'S CHRISTIAN PARENT—8121 Hamilton Ave., Cincinnati, OH 45231. Wilma
L. Shaffer, Editor.
Creative children's activities; short items on Christian living, for "Happenings at Our
House." Quips, short poems. Pays varying rates, on acceptance.

TRAILER BOATS—1440 West Walnut, Compton, CA 90220. Ralph Poole, Editor and
Publisher.
Fillers, humor and jokes, on boats. Pays 7¢ to 10¢ a word, on publication.

THE TRAVEL ADVISOR—141 Parkway Rd., Suite 18, Bronxville, NY 10708. Patricia
Morrisroe, Associate Editor.
Original travel tips, 50 to 150 words. Pays $20, on publication.

TRUE CONFESSIONS—205 East 42nd St., New York, NY 10017.
Fillers, 300 to 800 words, of interest to young wives, for "Feminine Side of Things."
Pays from $50, on acceptance.

TRUE ROMANCE—205 East 42nd St., New York, NY 10017.
Articles, 300 to 700 words, of interest to young blue-collar women. Pays flat rate.

TRUE STORY—205 East 42nd St., New York, NY 10017.
Short humorous or inspirational personal-experience pieces, for "Women Are Wonderful." Features on home and children; light verse. Pays 5¢ a word.

TRUE TREASURE—See *Lost Treasure.*

TV GUIDE—Radnor, PA 19088.
Short humor, one magazine page in length, on television, for "TV Jibe." Pays varying rates.

UNITY MAGAZINE—Unity School of Christianity, Unity Village, MO 64065.
Fillers, to 500 words. Pays on acceptance.

WESTART—Box 1396, Auburn, CA 95603.
Features and current news items, 350 to 500 words, on crafts and fine arts. No
hobbies. Pays 30¢ per column inch, on publication.

WESTERN RESERVE MAGAZINE—Box 243, Garrettsville, OH 44231. Mary Folger,
Editor.
Fillers on little-known Western Reserve history. Pays on publication.

WINK—See *Humorama, Inc.*

WOMAN'S DAY—1515 Broadway, New York, NY 10036.
Short items on instructive family experiences, for "Neighbors"; practical suggestions
for homemakers. Photos. Pays $25.

WOMEN'S CIRCLE HOME COOKING—Box 338, Chester, MA 01011. Barbara Hall
Pedersen, Editor.
Magazine for cooks. Humorous fiction, to 400 words; hints; anecdotes; fillers; verse
to 8 lines. For "Cooks' Photo Album," recipe with snapshot of cook. Pays on
publication.

THE WORKBASKET—4521 Pennsylvania, Kansas City, MO 64111.

Illustrated how-to articles, 200 to 400 words, on crafts. Brief instructions for crafts women can make and sell (include selling price), for "Women Who Make Cents." Pays 4¢ a word for how-to pieces, $5 for instructions, on acceptance.

WOW—American Board of Educational Ministries, Valley Forge, PA 19481.
For 6- to 7-year-olds. Poetry, puzzles, cartoons, Bible verses. Pays on acceptance.

YACHTING MAGAZINE—50 West 44th St., New York, NY 10036. William W. Robinson, Editor.
Short fillers and anecdotes. Pays modest rates, on publication.

YANKEE MAGAZINE—Dublin, NH 03444.
Features, to 400 words, on small New England businesses and hobbies. Unusual or humorous stories, 500 to 2,500 words, with photos, related to New England. Pays $15 for short features, $25 to $400 for articles, $15 to $25 per photo.

YOUNG ATHLETE—Box 513, Edmonds, WA 98020. Dan Zadra, Editor.
Dedicated to boys' and girls' amateur sports. Jokes for "Sports Humor." Brief profiles of boys and girls who have achieved sports success. Pays on publication.

YOUNG JUDEAN—817 Broadway, New York, NY 10003. Barbara Gingold, Editor.
For 8- to 12-year-olds. Fillers, humor, reviews relating to Jewish-American life, Jewish History, Israel, etc. Pays various rates.

YOUNG MISS—52 Vanderbilt Ave., New York, NY 10017.
How-to pieces, to 100 words, particularly on things to make with odds and ends, for teen-age girls. Pays $5, on acceptance.

ZIP—See *Humorama, Inc.*

JUVENILE, TEEN-AGE AND YOUNG ADULT MAGAZINES

Publications for both children and teen-agers are listed here. Markets for book-length fiction for young people of all ages are listed under *Book Publishers.*

JUVENILE MAGAZINES

THE BEEHIVE—201 Eighth Ave. South, Nashville, TN 37203.
Stories, to 700 words, for 4th to 6th graders. Some poetry. Pays 2¢ to 3¢ a word, 50¢ a line for poetry, on acceptance.

CHILD LIFE—1100 Waterway Blvd., P.O. Box 567B, Indianapolis, IN 46206. Peg Rogers, Editor.
Mystery and science-fiction stories, to 1,800 words, for children up to 14; may include sports, nature, ethnic themes. Articles, to 900 words, with photos, and mystery or science-fiction theme. Quizzes, puzzles, games and simple craft projects. Pays about 3¢ a word for stories, $2.50 per photo, on publication. Stamped, self-addressed envelope required for return of manuscript.

CHILDREN'S CHURCH: THE LEADER'S GUIDE—1445 Boonville Ave., Springfield, MO 65802. James E. Erdmann, Editor.
Articles and fiction for 6- to 8-year-olds for use in Bible learning situations. Pays on acceptance. Send stamped, self-addressed envelope for guidelines.

CHILDREN'S EXPRESS—257 Park Ave. South, New York, NY 10019. Dorriet Kavanaugh, Editor.
News and features written by children to age 13. Pays $10 to $25, on publication.

CHILDREN'S PLAYMATE—1100 Waterway Blvd., P.O. Box 567B, Indianapolis, IN 46206. Beth Wood Thomas, Editor.

Stories, to 600 words, for 3- to 8-year-olds. Crafts pieces with clear, brief instructions. Simple science articles. "All About . . ." features, 300 to 500 words, on people, animals, events, etc. Pays around 3¢ a word, on publication. Submit seasonal material 8 months in advance. Stamped, self-addressed envelope required for return of manuscript.

THE CHRISTIAN SCIENCE MONITOR—One Norway St., Boston, MA 02115. Address Editor for Children.
Puzzles, quizzes, news features and some stories, 500 to 600 words, for children to 12 years old. Pays $10 to $50, on acceptance.

CRICKET—Open Court Publishing Co., Box 100, La Salle, IL 61301.
Articles and fiction, 200 to 2,000 words, for 6- to 12-year-olds. Poetry, to 100 lines. Pays to 25¢ a word, to $3 a line for poetry, on publication.

CRUSADER—1548 Poplar Ave., Memphis, TN 38104. Phil Burgess, Editor.
Southern Baptist. Articles and fiction, to 900 words, with photos, for 6- to 11-year-old boys. Hobbies, games; nature pieces. Pays 2½¢ a word, from $5 per photo, on acceptance.

DASH—Christian Service Brigade, Box 150, Wheaton, IL 60187. Address Managing Editor.
Articles, to 800 words, for 8- to 11-year-old boys, on Christian life styles, current issues, etc. Photos and photo essays; cartoons. Pays $30 to $60, $7.50 per cartoon, $15 to $25 for photos, on publication.

DISCOVERIES—6401 The Paseo, Kansas City, MO 64131. Ruth Henck McCreery, Editor.
Stories, to 1,200 words, for 3rd to 6th graders, with Christian emphasis. Features, 500 to 800 words, on nature, travel, history, crafts, science, etc. Cartoons. Poetry, 4 to 20 lines. Pays 2¢ a word, 25¢ a line for poetry, on acceptance.

DISCOVERY—Light and Life Press, 999 College Ave., Winona Lake, IN 46590. Vera Bethel, Editor.
Stories, 1,800 to 2,000 words, for 8- to 11-year-olds. How-to features, 500 to 1,000

THE FRIEND—50 East North Temple, Salt Lake City, UT 84150. Lucile C. Reading, Managing Editor.
Stories, to 1,000 words, with character-building theme: suspense, adventure, holiday, humor. "Tiny tot" stories, 300 to 500 words. Pays from 3¢ a word, 25¢ to 50¢ a line for poetry, on acceptance.

THE GOOD DEEDER—Berrien Springs, MI 49103. Colleen S. Garber, Editor.
Realistic stories, 750 to 1,600 words, for 10- to 14-year-olds, with character-building theme. Pays 1¢ a word, after acceptance.

HIGHLIGHTS FOR CHILDREN—803 Church St., Honesdale, PA 18431. Caroline C. Myers, Managing Editor.
Stories, to 1,000 words, for 3- to 12-year-olds. Easy-to-read stories, 400 to 600 words, with strong plot and urban setting or ethnic American characters. Overstocked on verse. Pays from 6¢ a word, on acceptance.

HUMPTY DUMPTY'S MAGAZINE—52 Vanderbilt Ave., New York, NY 10017. Karen Craig, Editor.
Read-Aloud Stories, to 900 words, for 3- to 8-year-olds, with 3rd or 4th grade vocabulary. Tell-Me Stories, to 1,000 words, for parents to read to children. Verse, 4 to 12 lines. Pays $50, $10 for verse, on acceptance.

INSTRUCTOR—Instructor Park, Dansville, NY 14437. Leanna Landsmann, Editor-in-Chief.

Short stories, 400 to 600 words, for primary grade children; 500 to 1,000 words for middle-grade children (for teachers to read aloud). Plays for classroom production; short poems. Pays varying rates, on acceptance.

JACK AND JILL—1100 Waterway Blvd., Box 567B, Indianapolis, IN 46206. William Wagner, Editor.

Short, factual articles, for 5- to 12-year-olds, on nature, science, etc. Longer features: "My Father/My Mother Is a . . .," first-person stories of life in foreign countries, historical or biographical pieces. Stories, 500 to 1,200 words; two-part serials, 1,200 words per installment: realistic stories, fantasy, adventure, etc. Short plays, puzzles, jokes, poems, games, songs, science projects, etc. Photos. Pays 3¢ a word, $2.50 per photo, on publication. Stamped, self-addressed envelope required for return of manuscript.

JET CADET—8121 Hamilton Ave., Cincinnati, OH 45231. Dana Eynon, Editor.

Christian stories, 900 to 1,200 words, for 11- to 12-year-olds, on young teen-agers in situations involving mystery, sports, adventure, school or relationships with parents and friends. Two-part serials, to 2,000 words. Articles, 400 to 500 words, on hobbies, nature, life in other lands or seasonal subjects, with religious emphasis. Poems, to 12 lines. Pays to 1½¢ a word, 25¢ to 35¢ a line for poetry, on acceptance.

THE KINDERGARTNER—Graded Press, 201 Eighth Ave. South, Nashville, TN 37202. Arba O. Herr, Editor.

United Methodist. Stories, to 300 words, for kindergarten children. Poems. Pays varying rates, on acceptance.

NATIONAL GEOGRAPHIC WORLD—National Geographic Society, 17th and M Sts. N.W., Washington, DC 20036.

Photo essays, for 8- to 13-year-olds, on animals, people, locales, etc. Puzzles, games; adventure. Pays $150 per page for photos, on publication. Query.

NURSERY DAYS—Graded Press, 201 Eighth Ave. South, Nashville, TN 37202. Doris Willis, Editor.

United Methodist. Stories, 250 words, for 2- to 4-year-olds, on church, family, friends, Bible, etc. Poems, 4 to 8 lines. Pays on acceptance.

ON THE LINE—616 Walnut Ave., Scottdale, PA 15683. Helen Alderfer, Editor.

Religious articles and fiction, 750 to 1,000 words, for 10- to 14-year-olds. Poetry, quizzes, puzzles, cartoons. Pays to 3¢ a word.

OUR LITTLE FRIEND—Pacific Press Publishing Assn., 1350 Villa St., Mountain View, CA 94042. Louis Schutter, Editor.

Seventh-day Adventist. Stories, 500 to 1,000 words, for 2- to 6-year-olds. Verse, 8 to 12 lines. Puzzles; photos. Pays 1¢ a word, 10¢ a line for verse.

PIZZAZZ—575 Madison Ave., New York, NY 10022. Bobby Miller, Editor.

Articles, 500 words, and features on sports, media and national events, for 10- to 13-year-olds. Puzzles, games, and short stories. Pays varying rates, on acceptance. Query.

PLAYS, THE DRAMA MAGAZINE FOR YOUNG PEOPLE—8 Arlington St., Boston, MA 02116. Carol Kountz, Managing Editor.

One-act plays, programs, skits and creative dramatics material, suitable for production by 7- to 17-year-olds: comedies, satires, farces, melodramas, dramatized classics, folktales and fairy tales, puppet plays. Plays with one set preferred. Manuscript specification sheet on request. Pays good rates, on acceptance.

PRIMARY TREASURE—Pacific Press Publishing Assn., 1350 Villa St., Mountain View, CA 94042. Louis Schutter, Editor.

Seventh-day Adventist. Stories, 500 to 1,500 words, for 7- to 9-year-olds. Serials. Verse, 8 to 12 lines. Puzzles; photos. Query on serials. Pays 1¢ a word, 10¢ a line for verse, on acceptance.

RAINBOW—American Baptist Board of Education and Publication, Valley Forge, PA 19481. Gracie McCay, Editor.
Articles and fiction, 800 to 1,000 words, for 8- to 11-year-olds. Poetry, puzzles, prayers, cartoons, art. Pays to 3¢ a word, on acceptance.

RANGER RICK'S NATURE MAGAZINE—National Wildlife Federation, 1412 16th St. N.W., Washington, DC 20036. Trudy Dye Farrand, Editor.
Articles, to 900 words, for young people, on nature, natural science, conservation, etc. Pays $5 to $250, before publication.

SPRINT—Scholastic Magazines, Inc., 50 West 44th St., New York, NY 10036. Vicky Chapman, Editor.
For 9- to 11-year-olds with 4th to 6th grade reading ability. High-interest, easy-to-read stories, 300 to 500 words, and one-act plays, 450 to 550 words: sports, humor, mystery, science fiction, adventure. Pays from $75.

STONE SOUP, THE MAGAZINE BY CHILDREN—Box 83, Santa Cruz, CA 95063. Gerry Mandel and William Rubel, Editors.
Stories, poems, plays, book reviews and illustrations by children under 13. Manuscripts should be in original form. Pays in copies.

STORY FRIENDS—Mennonite Publishing House, Scottdale, PA 15683. Alice Hershberger, Editor.
Stories 350 to 900 words, for 4- to 9-year-olds, on Christian faith in everyday experiences. Quizzes, riddles. Poetry. Pays to 3¢ a word, to $5 per poem, on acceptance.

TRAILS—Box 788, Wheaton, IL 60187. Sara Robertson, Editor.
Publication of Pioneer Girls. Christian articles and fiction, to 2,000 words, for 8- to 12-year-old girls. Cartoons, quizzes, games. Photos. Pays varying rates, on acceptance.

THE VINE—201 Eighth Ave. South, Nashville, TN 37202. Betty M. Buerki, Editor.
Short stories, about 800 words, for 3rd and 4th graders. Poetry; puzzles, quizzes. Pays 3¢ a word, 50¢ to $1 a line for poetry.

WEE WISDOM—Unity Village, MO 64065. Jim Leftwich, Editor.
Character-building adventure stories, 750 words, for boys and girls. Science and nature stories, projects, crafts ideas.

WONDER TIME—6401 The Paseo, Kansas City, MO 64131. Elizabeth B. Jones, Editor.
Stories, 200 to 750 words, for 6- to 8-year-olds, with Christian emphasis. Features 200 to 500 words, on nature, travel, crafts, Bible, etc. Poetry, 4 to 16 lines. Pays 2¢ a word, from 25¢ a line for verse, on acceptance.

WOODMEN OF THE WORLD MAGAZINE—1700 Farnam St., Omaha, NE 68102. Leland A. Larson, Editor.
Stories, 400 to 1,200 words, for 8- to 16-year-olds. Pays 2¢ a word, on acceptance.

WOW—American Baptist Board of Educational Ministries, Valley Forge, PA 19481. Gracie McCay, Editor.
Stories, 300 to 400 words, for 6- to 7-year-olds. Articles, short poetry; puzzles, cartoons, Bible verses. Pays to 3¢ a word, on acceptance.

YOUNG CRUSADER—1730 Chicago Ave., Evanston, IL 60201. Michael Vitucci, Editor.
Character-building stories, 600 to 850 words, for 6- to 12-year-olds. Pays ½¢ a word, on publication.

YOUNG WORLD—1100 Waterway Blvd., P.O. Box 567B, Indianapolis, IN 46206. Julie Plopper, Editor.
Articles, to 1,200 words, and fiction, to 1,800 words, for 10- to 14-year-olds, on young people in community action, sports, entertainment, etc. Verse; puzzles.

Photos. Pays 3¢ a word, varying rates for poetry and puzzles, $2.50 to $5 for photos, on publication. Stamped, self-addressed envelope required for return of manuscript.

TEEN-AGE, YOUNG ADULT MAGAZINES

ALIVE!—Christian Board of Publication, Beaumont and Pine Blvd., St. Louis, MO 63166. Darrell Faires, Editor.
Fiction, 1,200 to 1,600 words, for junior high young people. First-person articles, to 1,500 words, with photos, on outstanding youths, projects and activities. Poetry, to 16 lines. Cartoons, puzzles, brain-teasers. Pays 2¢ a word, extra for photos, 25¢ a line for poetry, $6 for cartoons, on publication. Query for articles.

AMERICAN GIRL—830 Third Ave., New York, NY 19022. Cleo Paturis, Editor.
Publication of Girl Scouts. Articles, 500 to 1,000 words, for 12- to 16-year-old girls. Fiction, 1,000 to 2,000 words: mystery, school and family life, sports, career, romance, etc. Pays varying rates, on acceptance. Query for articles.

AMERICAN NEWSPAPER BOY—915 Carolina Ave. N.W., Winston-Salem, NC 27101. Charles Moester, Editor.
Light fiction, 1,800 to 2,000 words, for 14- to 17-year-old newspaper carriers: mystery, adventure, etc. Inspirational articles, editorials. Pays $10 to $25, on acceptance.

BOYS' LIFE—North Brunswick, NJ 08902. Robert E. Hood, Editor.
Publication of Boy Scouts. Articles, 300 to 1,500 words, and fiction, 1,000 or 2,500 to 3,200 words, for 8- to 18-year-old boys. Photos. Pays from $150 for articles, from $350 for fiction. Query for articles.

BREAD—6401 The Paseo, Kansas City, MO 64131. Dan Ketchum, Editor.
Religious and nonreligious articles, 500 to 1,200 words, and fiction, to 1,500 words, for teen-agers. Poetry, to 20 lines. Pays from 2¢ a word, on acceptance.

CAMPUS LIFE—Box 419, Wheaton, IL 60187. Philip Yancey, Editor.
Articles and fiction, 1,500 words, for 16- to 19-year-old Christian young people. Photo essays; cartoons. Pays from 3¢ a word.

THE CHRISTIAN ADVENTURER—P.O. Box 850, Joplin, MO 64801. Marthel S. Wilson, Editor.
Articles, 100 to 700 words, and fiction, to 1,500 words, for 13- to 18-year-olds, on Christian living. Fillers. Pays ½¢ a word, quarterly.

CHRISTIAN LIVING—See *Looking Ahead*.

CO-ED—Scholastic Magazines, Inc., 50 West 44th St., New York, NY 10036. Address Features Editor.
Fiction, to 3,000 words, for 13- to 18-year-olds, on problems of contemporary teen-agers: personal identity, relationships with family and friends, boy-girl situations, etc. Adventure and humor. Pays to $300, on acceptance.

CRAWDADDY—72 Fifth Ave., New York, NY 10011.
Rock interviews and celebrity pieces, 1,000 to 2,000 words, for 18- to 30-year-olds. "Hip" humor and fiction. Pays varying rates, on publication. No recent report. Query.

ENCOUNTER—See *In Touch*.

ETCETERA—6401 The Paseo, Kansas City, MO 64131. Ernie McNaught, Editor.
Religious and nonreligious articles, 500 to 1,200 words, for 18- to 24-year-olds. Poetry, to 20 lines. Pays from 2¢ a word, on acceptance.

EXPLORING—Boy Scouts of America, North Brunswick, NJ 08902. Dick Pryce, Editor.

Articles, 500 to 2,500 words, for 15- to 21-year-olds, on careers, education, travel, history, music, relationships, etc.; interviews and profiles. Pays $150 to $500, on acceptance. Query.

FREE WAY—Scripture Press Publications, 1825 College Ave., Wheaton, IL 60187. Anne Harrington, Editor.
Articles, to 2,000 words, for 15- to 19-year-olds, on Christian faith. Fiction; photos. Pays $70, extra for photos, on acceptance. Query.

GLAD (formerly *Straight*)—8121 Hamilton Ave., Cincinnati, OH 45231. Judy Trotter, Editor.
Short, humorous fiction, 700 to 1,000 words, for 16- to 19-year-olds, on dating, college life, getting a job, etc.; serious, thought-provoking fiction, 1,000 to 1,200 words. Articles on current issues: TM, drugs, politics, etc. Religious emphasis. Pays 2¢ a word; extra for photos.

GRIT—Williamsport, PA 17701. Kenneth D. Loss, Feature Editor.
Articles, 300 to 800 words, with photos, on personalities and small towns, emphasis on human interest. Pays 5¢ a word, on acceptance, extra for photos. Stamped, self-addressed envelope required for return of manuscript.

GROUP MAGAZINE—P.O. Box 481, Loveland, CO 80537.
Articles, to 3,000 words, on activities, service projects and worship ideas for high-school-age church youth groups. Short plays. Photos. Pays from 1¢ a word, on publication.

HICALL—1445 Boonville Ave., Springfield, MO 65802. Kenneth D. Barney, Youth Editor.
Articles, 500 to 1,000 words, and fiction, 1,200 to 2,000 words, for 12- to 19-year-olds, with evangelical emphasis. Pays on acceptance.

IN TOUCH (formerly *Encounter*)—The Wesleyan Church, Box 2000, Marion, IN 46952.
Fiction, 1,000 to 1,500 words, for 15- to 18-year-olds, with Christian emphasis. Articles, 500 to 1,000 words: personal witness, devotional, etc. Poetry, 4 to 16 lines. Pays 2¢ a word, 25¢ a line for poetry, on acceptance.

LISTEN MAGAZINE—6830 Laurel St., N.W., Washington, DC 20012. Francis A. Soper, Editor.
Articles, 500 to 1,500 words, on development of mental and physical health for teen-agers: medical reports on drugs and alcohol; personality profiles, etc. Pays 2¢ to 5¢ a word, on acceptance. Query.

LOOKING AHEAD—David C. Cook Publishing Co., 850 North Grove Ave., Elgin, IL 60120.
Feature articles and fiction, 1,200 to 1,500 words, for junior high Sunday school students. Pays 3¢ to 5¢ a word, on acceptance. Same address and requirements for *Christian Living* (for senior high).

THE NATIONAL FUTURE FARMER—Box 15130, Alexandria, VA 22309. Wilson Carnes, Editor.
Articles, to 1,000 words, for high school agriculture students, on activities of Future Farmers of America, new developments in agriculture, etc. Cartoons. Pays to 4¢ a word, $7.50 for cartoons, on acceptance.

NEW ERA—50 East North Temple, Salt Lake City, UT 84150. Brian Kelly, Editor.
Articles, 500 to 3,000 words, and fiction, 700 to 3,000 words, on young Mormons. Poetry; photos. Pays 3¢ to 5¢ a word, 25¢ a line for poetry, on acceptance.

NOW (formerly *Straight*)—8121 Hamilton Ave., Cincinnati, OH 45231. Sherry Morris, Editor.

Fiction and non-fiction, 1,000 to 1,500 words, for 12- to 15-year-olds, on teenage problems, parents, school, etc. Religious emphasis. Pays 2¢ a word, extra for photos.

PROBE—1548 Poplar Ave., Memphis, TN 38104. Mike David, Editor.
Brotherhood Commission of Southern Baptist Convention. Articles, to 1,500 words, for 12- to 17-year-old boys, on teen problems, current events, etc. Photo essays on sports personalities. Pays 2½¢ a word, $5 to $10 for photos, on acceptance.

PUZZLE SCENE—Children's Television Workshop, One Lincoln Place, New York, NY 10023. Jack L. Roberts, Editor.
Crossword puzzles and "word hunts," focusing on celebrities in music, TV, sports. Pays $10 to $15, on publication. Query.

REFLECTION—Box 788, Wheaton, IL 60187. Sara Robertson, Editor.
Publication of Pioneer Girls. Articles and fiction, to 2,000 words, for 13- to 18-year-old girls, with Christian emphasis. Cartoons, quizzes, games; photos. Pays varying rates, on acceptance.

ROLLING STONE—745 Fifth Ave., New York, NY 10022. Jann Wenner, Editor.
Not in the market at present.

SCHOLASTIC SCOPE—Scholastic Magazines, Inc., 50 West 44th St., New York, NY 10036. Katherine Robinson, Editor.
For 15- to 18-year-olds with 4th to 6th grade reading ability. Fiction, 400 to 1,200 words, and plays, to 3,000 words, on problems of high school students, relationships, etc. Action stories and realistic stories from viewpoint of member of a minority group (not necessarily about race relations). Articles, 400 to 800 words, on interesting teen-agers. Photos. Pays $100 for 500- to 600-word articles and short stories; from $150 for longer pieces, on acceptance.

SEVENTEEN—850 Third Ave., New York, NY 10022. Phyllis Schneider, Fiction Editor.
Sophisticated fiction, for (but not necessarily about) young adults. Pays good rates, on acceptance.

STRAIGHT—See *Glad* and *Now*.

'TEEN MAGAZINE—8831 Sunset Blvd., Los Angeles, CA 90069. Kathy McCoy, Feature Editor.
Fiction, 2,500 to 4,000 words, depicting today's teen-age girl. Pays from $100, on acceptance.

TEEN POWER—Box 513, Glen Ellyn, IL 60137.
First-person articles, with photos, on solution of teen-age problem through Christian teachings. Short stories and 2- or 3-part serials, with urban settings, dealing with teen-age problems. Pays up to $60 for fiction, up to $75 for nonfiction, on acceptance. Query.

TEENS TODAY—6401 The Paseo, Kansas City, MO 64131. Roy F. Lynn, Editor.
Realistic fiction, to 2,500 words, and articles, to 1,500 words, for high school students, on Christian faith. Profiles; poetry. Pays 2¢ a word, to 25¢ a line for poetry, on acceptance.

TIGER BEAT—Laufer Company, Suite 800, 7060 Hollywood Blvd., Hollywood, CA 90028. Sharon Lee, Editor.
Articles, to 4 pages, on young people in show business. Pays varying rates, on acceptance. Query.

VENTURE—Christian Service Brigade, Box 150, Wheaton, IL 60187. Address Managing Editor.
Articles, 1,500 words, for 12- to 18-year-old boys, on Christian living, relationships, etc. Photos, photo essays; cartoons. Pays $30 to $75, $15 to $25 for photos, $7.50 for cartoons, on publication.

WIND—Box 2000, Marion, IN 46952. Robert Black, Editor.
Publication of The Wesleyan Church. Religious or educational articles, to 1,000 words, for teens. Pays 2¢ a word, more for photos and cartoons, on publication.

WORLD OVER—426 West 58th St., New York, NY 10019. Stephen Schaffzir, Editor.
Fiction, 600 to 1,200 words, for 9- to 14-year-olds, on Jewish subjects (holidays, history, etc.). Pays 4¢ to 5¢ a word, on acceptance. Query.

YOUNG AMBASSADOR—Box 82808, Lincoln, NE 68501. Robert H. Sink, Managing Editor.
Articles and fiction, 2,000 words, for young teens, with religious emphasis. Pays from 3¢ a word, on acceptance.

YOUNG ATHLETE—Box 513, Edmonds, WA 98020. Dan Zadra, Editor.
Profiles of boys and girls who have achieved sports success; 1,800-word features on today's professional athletes; how-to pieces; articles by coaches; jokes; dramatic action photos. Pays 7¢ to 10¢ a word, on publication.

YOUNG JUDEAN—817 Broadway, New York, NY 10003. Barbara Gingold, Editor.
Articles, 500 to 1,500 words, with photos, for 8- to 12-year-olds, on Jewish-American life, Jewish history, Israel, etc. Fiction, 800 to 1,500 words. Poetry, from 8 lines. Fillers, humor; reviews. Pays to $5 per printed page.

YOUNG MISS—52 Vanderbilt Ave., New York, NY 10017. Rubie Saunders, Editor.
Realistic stories, 2,000 to 2,300 words, for 10- to 14-year-old girls, on contemporary teen-age problems. Articles, 1,000 to 2,000 words, on sports, careers, crafts, etc. Pays from $50 for articles, $50 to $150 for fiction, on acceptance. Query for articles.

YOUTH ALIVE!—1445 Boonville Ave., Springfield, MO 65802.
Interviews and biographical sketches, 300 to 1,200 words, for junior and senior high school students, of outstanding Christian young people. Photos, photo essays; how-to features. Some poetry, fiction. Pays 1½¢ a word, on acceptance.

YOUTH IN ACTION—Winona Lake, IN 46590.
Publication of Free Methodist Youth Ministries. Articles, 500 to 1,500 words, on activities of youth in churches and on Christian living. Poetry; photos. Pays 1½¢ a word, on publication.

REPRINT MAGAZINES

If an author has sold an article or story to a magazine and retains the reprint rights, he or she may submit the piece to a publication that uses reprints. The following list gives a few digest magazines that regularly use reprints.

Many of the smaller and more specialized magazines listed elsewhere as markets for unpublished material occasionally buy reprint rights, and sometimes even the larger magazines will reprint material of general interest that appeared first in a specialized publication. Writers can submit copies of published articles or stories, together with information about when and where the material was originally published, if they are certain that they have the permission of the original publisher to do so.

CATHOLIC DIGEST—P.O. Box 3090, St. Paul, MN 55165.

CHILDREN'S DIGEST—52 Vanderbilt Ave., New York, NY 10017.

EASTERN REVIEW—East/West Network, Inc., 5900 Wilshire Blvd., Suite 300, Los Angeles, CA 90036.

READER'S DIGEST—Pleasantville, NY 10570.

SHORT STORY INTERNATIONAL—6 Sheffield Rd., Great Neck, NY 11021.

TELEVISION AND PLAYS

This section includes markets for dramatic material: television, publishers of plays for the amateur stage, community and college theatres, and literary magazines that occasionally print plays.

The television world is constantly changing. New shows are tried out, and may continue as a series or be dropped after a season; old shows go off the air or become inactive script markets. Therefore, the following list of programs should not be considered complete or permanent.

Before submitting material to any television program, you should always query the show's script editor or producer, outlining your writing background. If the address of a particular program is not available, write to the script editor in care of the national network televising the program. If the producers express an interest in seeing a script, they will probably require that you send a signed release form when the script is submitted. The form may be obtained by sending a self-addressed stamped envelope to the program for which you are writing. However, most television programs require that scripts be submitted through recognized agents. Although it is often difficult for new television playwrights to find a reputable literary agent who is willing to represent them, some agents will read scripts, provided the author queries first. (A list of agents appears at the end of this book.)

There are relatively few markets for free-lance material in radio at the present time. For full information, write to the major networks listed below.

Publishers of plays for school, community and church groups offer a hospitable market for free-lance writers. This field has rewards and pleasures of its own, and playwrights who are interested in writing for television and the professional theatre will find the amateur stage a good training ground.

A number of regional and community theaters, college dramatic groups, and little theaters are actively looking for new plays by free-lance writers for stage production. Payment is seldom great, but usually college and community theaters buy only the right to produce a play, and all further rights revert to the author.

As a rule, Broadway producers will not read plays sent in by an unknown playwright. Writers with plays they wish to have considered for Broadway production should query one of the recognized literary agents listed at the end of this book.

Some literary, university and little magazines are interested in publishing plays, particularly innovative or experimental drama, or plays with little chance of appearing in more popular media. They are not an active play market, however, because of space limitations, and dramatic material can appear only infrequently, if at all.

MAJOR TELEVISION AND RADIO NETWORKS

THE AMERICAN BROADCASTING COMPANIES, INC.—1330 Ave. of the Americas, New York, NY 10019.

COLUMBIA BROADCASTING SYSTEM, INC.—51 West 52nd St., New York, NY 10019.

NATIONAL BROADCASTING COMPANY—30 Rockefeller Plaza, New York, NY 10019.

PUBLIC BROADCASTING SERVICE—985 L'Enfant Plaza West S.W., Washington, DC 20024.

TELEVISION PROGRAMS

ALICE—*Network:* CBS-TV. *Length:* 30 minutes.
 Script: Comedy, based on movie, *Alice Doesn't Live Here Anymore,* about a recent

widow working as a waitress, trying to make a good life for herself and her precocious 12-year-old son. Scripts through accredited agents, or with signed release only. *Contact:* Bruce Johnson, Producer, Warner Bros. Television, 4000 Warner Blvd., Burbank, CA 91505.

ALL IN THE FAMILY—*Network:* CBS-TV. *Length:* 30 minutes.
Script: Situation comedy about opinionated middle-class man and his family. Scripts through recognized agents only, or through release form. *Contact:* Mort Lachman, Executive Producer, Tandem Productions, 5752 Sunset Blvd., Los Angeles, CA 90028.

BARNABY JONES—*Network:* CBS-TV. *Length:* 1 hour.
Script: Suspense drama about veteran private investigator working in Los Angeles and Southern California. Scripts on assignment through recognized agents only. *Contact:* Robert Sherman, Associate Producer, QM Productions, Goldwyn Studios, 1041 North Formosa, Los Angeles, CA 90046.

BARNEY MILLER—*Network:* ABC-TV. *Length:* 30 minutes.
Script: Comedy about the captain of detectives in a Manhattan police precinct. Scripts through recognized agents only. *Contact:* Danny Arnold, Executive Producer, Tony Sheehan, Producer, 4D Productions, c/o ABC-TV, 1313 North Vine St., Los Angeles, CA 90028.

THE BIONIC WOMAN—*Network:* NBC-TV. *Length:* 1 hour.
Script: Suspense drama about a woman who leads a double life as a result of an operation that gives her bionic limbs and organs. Scripts through recognized agents only. *Contact:* Jim Parriott, Universal Television, 100 Universal City Plaza, Universal City, CA 91608.

CBS-TV PROGRAM PLANNING AND DEVELOPMENT—New program ideas.
Scripts or queries through recognized agents only. *Contact:* Mike Marden, Director of Program Development, Alan Wagner, Vice President, Nighttime Programs, CBS-TV, 51 West 52nd St., New York, NY 10019.

CBS PLAYHOUSE 90—*Network:* CBS-TV. *Length:* 90 minutes.
Script: Occasional plays by well-known and new writers. Scripts through recognized agents only. *Contact:* Mike Marden, CBS-TV, 51 West 52nd St., New York, NY 10019.

CANADIAN BROADCASTING CORPORATION—Copyright and Script Services Dept., P.O. Box 500, Postal Terminal A, Toronto, Ont., Canada.
TV and radio drama, 30 and 60 minutes in length.

CHARLIE'S ANGELS—*Network:* ABC-TV. *Length:* 1 hour.
Script: Detective adventure about three glamorous women who work for a successful but never-seen detective, Charlie. Scripts on assignment through recognized agents only. *Contact:* Aaron Spelling, Leonard Goldberg, Executive Producers, Spelling/Goldberg Productions, 20th Century-Fox, 10201 West Pico, Los Angeles, CA 90035.

CHICO AND THE MAN—*Network:* NBC-TV. *Length:* 30 minutes.
Script: Situation comedy about embittered elderly garage owner and an energetic Chicano youth who works at garage. Scripts through recognized agents only. *Contact:* Jerry Ross, Chuck Stewart, Producers, Komack Company with Wolper Productions, c/o NBC Television City, 3000 West Alameda Ave., Burbank, CA 91503.

CPO SHARKEY—*Network:* NBC-TV. *Length:* 30 minutes.
Script: Situation comedy about Chief Petty Officer Sharkey, in command of a training unit at the San Diego Training Center. Scripts through recognized agents only. *Contact:* Aaron Ruben, Executive Producer, R. and R. Productions, NBC Studios, 3000 West Alameda Ave., Burbank, CA 91503.

FAMILY—*Network:* ABC-TV. *Length:* 1 hour.
Script: Drama about the Lawrences, a family. Scripts through recognized agents only. *Contact:* Aaron Spelling, Leonard Goldberg, Executive Producers, Spelling/Goldberg Productions, 20th Century-Fox, 10201 West Pico, Los Angeles, CA 90035.

GOOD TIMES—*Network:* CBS-TV. *Length:* 30 minutes.
Script: Situation comedy about a black family in Chicago high-rise ghetto. Scripts staff-written. Inquiries through recognized agents only. *Contact:* Austin and Irma Kalish, Executive Producers, c/o Tandem Productions, KTTV, 5746 Sunset Blvd., Los Angeles, CA 90028.

HAPPY DAYS—*Network:* ABC-TV. *Length:* 30 minutes.
Script: Family situation comedy about life in the 50s and 60s. Scripts through recognized agents only. *Contact:* Bob Brunner, Producer, Marty Nadler, Executive Story Editor, Paramount Television, 5451 Marathon, Los Angeles, CA 90028.

HAWAII FIVE-O—*Network:* CBS-TV. *Length:* 1 hour.
Script: Police adventure set in Hawaii. Scripts on assignment only; market closed for season. *Contact:* Curtis Kenyon, Story Editor, CBS Studio Center, 4030 Radford, Studio City, CA 91604.

THE JEFFERSONS—*Network:* CBS-TV. *Length:* 30 minutes.
Script: Comedy about a *nouveau-riche* black couple living in a New York high-rise. Scripts through recognized agents only. *Contact:* Roger Shulman, John Baskin, Executive Story Editors, TAT Communications, 5752 Sunset Blvd., Hollywood, CA 90028.

KOJAK—*Network:* CBS-TV. *Length:* 1 hour.
Script: Police drama about Lieutenant Kojak and captain of detectives McNeil. Scripts through recognized agents only. *Contact:* Matt Rapf, Executive Producer, Jim McAdams, Executive Producer, Universal Television, 100 Universal City Plaza, Universal City, CA 91608.

LAVERNE AND SHIRLEY—*Network:* ABC-TV. *Length:* 30 minutes.
Script: Situation comedy about two women, one a realist, the other a dreamer, working in a Milwaukee brewery in the early 1960s, who would like to marry and settle down. Scripts through recognized agents only. *Contact:* Arthur Silver, Producer, Paramount Television, 5451 Marathon, Los Angeles, CA 90038.

THE LIFE AND TIMES OF GRIZZLY ADAMS—*Network:* NBC-TV. *Length:* 1 hour.
Script: Wildlife adventures of a 19th century fugitive, a mountain man who is pursued for a crime he did not commit. Scripts through recognized agents only. *Contact:* Charles E. Sellier, Jr., Executive Producer, Sunn Classic Productions, 1554 South Sepulveda Blvd., Los Angeles, CA 90025.

LITTLE HOUSE ON THE PRAIRIE—*Network:* NBC-TV. *Length:* 1 hour.
Script: Family pioneer drama set in southwestern Minnesota 100 years ago. Scripts through recognized agents only; market closed for season. *Contact:* John Hawkins, Producer, Paramount Television, 5451 Marathon, Hollywood, CA 90038.

LOU GRANT—*Network:* CBS-TV. *Length:* 1 hour.
Script: Newspaper drama with comic overtones, about city editor of the Los Angeles Tribune. Scripts through recognized agents only. *Contact:* Leon Tokatyan, Story Editor, MTM Enterprises, Inc., CBS Studio, 4030 Radford, Studio City, CA 91604.

M*A*S*H—*Network:* CBS-TV. *Length:* 30 minutes.
Script: Situation comedy about the high jinks of the madcap Mobile Army Surgical Hospital unit. Scripts on assignment through recognized agents only. *Contact:* Jay Folb, Story Consultant, 20th Century-Fox TV, 10201 West Pico, Los Angeles, CA 90064.

THE NANCY DREW/HARDY BOYS MYSTERIES—*Network:* ABC-TV. *Length:* 1 hour.
Script: Mystery dramas alternating weekly, based on the classic stories. Scripts through recognized agents only. *Contact:* Glen Larson, Executive Producer, Universal Television, 100 Universal City Plaza, Universal City, CA 91608.

POLICE STORY—*Network:* NBC-TV. *Length:* 2 hours.
Script: Special anthology dramas based on true stories from the files of the nation's police departments. Scripts through recognized agents only. *Contact:* David Gerber, Executive Producer, Columbia Pictures Television, Colgems Sq., Burbank, CA 91505.

POLICE WOMAN—*Network:* NBC-TV. *Length:* 1 hour.
Script: Police drama about women officers in law enforcement. Scripts from recognized agents only; market is closed. *Contact:* Edward DeBlasio, Story Editor, David Gerber Productions/Columbia Pictures Television, Colgems Square, Burbank, CA 91505.

RHODA—*Network:* CBS-TV. *Length:* 30 minutes.
Script: Comedy about Rhoda and her friends. Scripts through recognized agents

only. *Contact:* MTM Enterprises, CBS Studio Center, 4024 Radford Ave., Studio City, CA 91604.

THE ROCKFORD FILES—*Network:* NBC-TV. *Length:* 1 hour.
Script: Suspense drama about a private investigator. Scripts mainly staff-written; market is closed. *Contact:* Meta Rosenberg, Executive Producer, Universal City Studios, 100 Universal City Plaza, Universal City, CA 91608.

SHICK SUNN CLASSIC PRODUCTIONS—556 East 200 South, Salt Lake City, UT 84102. Dave Balsiger, Director of Research Development.
Television series ideas. Wholesome, entertaining material with family appeal sought. Also ideas for episodes of "Grizzly Adams," TV series. Before submitting, request a copy of "Film Concept Submission Procedures." Only two- to four-page treatments wanted.

THE SIX MILLION DOLLAR MAN—*Network:* ABC-TV. *Length:* 1 hour.
Script: Suspense drama about Steve Austin, who uses his bionic powers in carrying out government assignments. Scripts through recognized agents only; market closed for season: *Contact:* Silverton Productions/Universal Television, 100 Universal City Plaza, Universal City, CA 91608.

STARSKY AND HUTCH—*Network:* ABC-TV. *Length:* 1 hour.
Script: Police drama about two plainclothes detectives: Starsky, cool and street-wise, and Hutch, clean-cut and conservative. Scripts through recognized agents only; market is closed. *Contact:* Joseph Naar, Producer, Michael Fisher, Executive Story Editor, Spelling Goldberg Productions at 20th Century-Fox, 10201 West Pico, Los Angeles, CA 90064.

THE TONY RANDALL SHOW—*Network:* CBS-TV. *Length:* 30 minutes.
Script: Comedy about a Philadelphia judge, competent in court but less than competent off the bench. Scripts through recognized agents only. *Contact:* Hugh Wilson, Gary Goldberg, Producers, MTM Enterprises, Inc., CBS Studio Center, 4024 Radford, Studio City, CA 91604.

THE WALTONS—*Network:* CBS-TV. *Length:* 1 hour.
Script: Family drama about a family living in the Blue Ridge Mountains of Virginia in 1939–40. Scripts on assignment through recognized agents only; market is closed. *Contact:* Lorimar Productions, Burbank Studios, 4000 Warner Blvd., Burbank, CA 91505.

WELCOME BACK, KOTTER—*Network:* ABC-TV. *Length:* 30 minutes.
Script: Comedy about a young teacher assigned to the same tough Brooklyn high school he graduated from ten years earlier. Scripts on assignment through recognized agents only. *Contact:* Jewel and Jerry Rannow, Executive Script Consultants, Komack Company/Wolper Productions, c/o ABC Television Center, 4151 Prospect Ave., Los Angeles, CA 90027.

THE WONDERFUL WORLD OF DISNEY—*Network:* NBC-TV. *Length:* 1 hour.
Script: Suspense, adventure, nature stories, comedy to appeal to all age groups. Scripts through recognized agents only. *Contact:* Frank Paris, Executive Story Editor, Walt Disney Productions, 500 South Buena Vista St., Burbank, CA 91521.

PLAY PUBLISHERS

ALL-MEDIA DRAMATIC WORKSHOP—612 North Michigan, Suite 316, Chicago, IL 60611. Michelle M. Faith, Associate Producer.
Original radio scripts. Pays $25 per minute, up to $1,500 per script.

ART CRAFT PLAY COMPANY—Box 1058, Cedar Rapids, IA 52406.
Three-act comedies and one-act comedies or dramas, with one set, for production by junior and senior high schools. Pays on royalty basis or by outright purchase.

WALTER H. BAKER COMPANY (*Baker's Plays*)—100 Chauncy St., Boston, MA 02111.
Scripts for amateur production: one-act plays for competition, children's plays, religious drama, monologues, readings and recitations.

CHILD LIFE—1100 Waterway Blvd., P.O. Box 567B, Indianapolis, IN 46206. Peg Rogers, Editor.
Mystery and science-fiction plays, 700 to 900 words, for classroom or living-room production by children up to 14. Pays around 3¢ a word, on publication.

CHILDREN'S PLAYMATE MAGAZINE—1100 Waterway Blvd., P.O. Box 567B, Indianapolis, IN 46206. Beth Wood Thomas, Editor.
Plays, 200 to 500 words, for children 3 to 8. Pays around 3¢ a word, on publication.

CONTEMPORARY DRAMA SERVICE—Box 457, Downers Grove, IL 60515. Arthur L. Zapel, Editor.
Easy-to-stage comedies, skits and one-act plays for schools and churches. Documentaries, adaptations of classics and improvisational material for classroom use. Storyteller collections for one or two narrators, reader's theater scripts, chancel drama for Christmas and Easter church use, role-playing materials or games, to 4,000 words. Include synopsis. Pays by fee arrangement or on royalty basis.

THE DRAMATIC PUBLISHING COMPANY—4150 North Milwaukee Ave., Chicago, IL 60641.
Full-length and one-act plays, musical comedies for amateur and stock groups. Pays on royalty basis.

DRAMATICS—3368 Central Parkway, Cincinnati, OH 45225. S. Ezra Goldstein, Editor.
One-act plays, to 30 minutes, for high school production. Pays on acceptance.

ELDRIDGE PUBLISHING COMPANY—Franklin, OH 45005. Kay Myerly, Editorial Dept.
Three-act and one-act plays for schools, churches, community groups, etc. Christmas comedies, sacred plays and pageants. Best to submit in summer. Pays varying rates, on acceptance.

SAMUEL FRENCH, INC.—25 West 45th St., New York, NY 10036.
One- and three-act plays for Broadway and off-Broadway production, stock community theater, colleges, schools, children's theater, churches, organizations. Pays on royalty basis.

HEUER PUBLISHING COMPANY—Drawer 248, Cedar Rapids, IA 52406. J. Vincent Heuer, Editor.

One-act comedies and dramas for contest work; three-act comedies with one interior setting, for high school production. Pays on acceptance.

INSTRUCTOR—Dansville, NY 14437.
Plays, around 2,000 words, for very young children and for third to sixth graders. Holiday and seasonal plays. Pays $25 to $50, on acceptance.

PERFORMANCE PUBLISHING—978 North McLean Blvd., Elgin, IL 60120. Virginia Butler, Editor.
One- and three-act plays. Pays on royalty basis.

PIONEER DRAMA SERVICE—P.O. Box 22555, Denver, CO 80222. Shubert Fendrich, Editor and Publisher.
Full-length plays and musicals for the educational market, children's theatre plays to be produced by adults for children, and old-fashioned melodrama. Outstanding one-act plays. "No unproduced plays, one-acts with more than one set, or plays which have a largely male cast." Pays on a royalty basis or by outright purchase. Buys all rights. Free catalogue available.

PLAYS, THE DRAMA MAGAZINE FOR YOUNG PEOPLE—8 Arlington St., Boston, MA 02116. Carol Kountz, Managing Editor.
One-act plays, with simple settings, for production by young people 7 to 17: holiday plays, comedies, dramas, skits, dramatized classics, farces, puppet plays, melodramas, dramatized folktales, and creative dramatics. Maximum lengths: lower grades, 10 double-spaced pages; middle grades, 15 pages; junior and senior high, 25 pages. Casts may be mixed, all-male or all-female; plays with one set preferred. Manuscript specification sheet available on request. Pays good rates, on acceptance.

SCHOLASTIC SCOPE—Scholastic Magazines, Inc., 50 West 44th St., New York, NY 10036. Katherine Robinson, Editor.
For ages 15 to 18 with 4th to 6th grade reading ability. Plays, to 3,000 words, on problems of contemporary teen-agers, relationships between people in family, job and school situations. Some mysteries and science fiction; plays about minorities. Pays good rates, on acceptance.

TEACHER—One Fawcett Pl., Greenwich, CT 06830. Joan Sullivan Baranski, Editor.
Tested school entertainment material: assembly programs, seasonal celebrations, plays with audience participation, improvisations. Ten or more characters preferred. Pays from $25, on acceptance.

REGIONAL AND UNIVERSITY THEATERS

The following list includes theaters that seek new plays throughout the year; query before submitting material to be sure they are still looking for new scripts.

ACADEMY THEATRE—3213 Roswell Rd., N.E., Atlanta, GA 30305. Address New Scripts.
Full-length and one-act experimental drama, comedy, etc. Writer-in-residence program.

AMERICAN CONSERVATORY THEATER—450 Geary St., San Francisco, CA 94102. William Ball, General Director.
Full-length and one-act plays: experimental, drama, comedy. Pays $300 and up.

AMERICAN PLACE THEATER—111 West 46th St., New York, NY 10036. Wynn Handman, Director.
Experimental plays, comedies and dramas. Pays $1,500 for full production, $100 up for workshop production.

ARENA STAGE–6th and Maine Ave., S. W., Washington, DC 20024. Zelda Fichandler, Producing Director.
Full-length and one-act experimental plays, adaptations, musicals, comedies, and dramas. Submissions in spring preferred. Payment is negotiable.

CHELSEA THEATRE CENTER–Brooklyn Academy of Music, 30 Lafayette St., Brooklyn, NY 11217.
Full-length "new" plays. Payment based on standard Dramatists Guild contract for off-Broadway productions.

CIRCLE REPERTORY COMPANY–186 West 4th St., New York, NY 10012. Marshall W. Mason, Artistic Director.
Traditional drama, comedy, musicals. Allow 6 months for report.

THE CLEVELAND PLAY HOUSE–2040 East 86th St., Cleveland, OH 44106. Robert Snook, New Script Department.
Plays. Manuscripts should be bound. Pays on royalty basis.

DES MOINES COMMUNITY PLAYHOUSE THEATER FOR YOUNG PEOPLE–831-42nd St., Des Moines, IA 50312.
Scripts, 60 to 75 minutes. Pays on royalty basis. Query.

EARPLAY–Vilas Communication Hall, 821 University Ave., Madison, WI 53706. Howard Gelman, Script Editor.
Radio plays of literary quality. Plays purchased for 3 years of unlimited use on 200 public radio stations in U.S. Pays $2,000 for 60-minute scripts, on acceptance. Stamped, self-addressed envelope required for return of manuscript. Send for writers' fact sheet.

THE GUTHRIE THEATER–Vineland Place, Minneapolis, MN 55403. Michael Langham, Artistic Director.
Full-length plays, experimental scripts, with simple production requirements. No musicals or children's plays. Query.

HARTFORD STAGE COMPANY–65 Kinsley St., Hartford, CT 06103. Paul R. Weidner, Producing Director.
Full-length comedies, dramas and experimental plays. Query with description of cast and sets. Pays on royalty basis.

HONOLULU THEATRE FOR YOUTH–Box 3257, Honolulu, HI 96801.
Children's plays, one hour, for performance by adult casts; plays for family audience. Pays on royalty basis.

HOPE COLLEGE–Dept. of Theater, Holland, MI 49423.
Traditional and experimental productions on small scale, for proscenium, thrust and arena-studio stages. Pays on royalty basis.

THE INVISIBLE THEATRE–P.O. Box 12, Tucson, AZ 85702. Rebecca Peters, Production Manager.
Full-length and one-act comedies, dramas, musicals and adaptations, for simple production. Experimental and children's plays. Pays on royalty basis or by outright purchase.

LONG WHARF THEATRE–222 Sargent Dr., New Haven, CT 06511. John Tillinger, Literary Manager.
Full-length and one-act dramas, comedies and adaptations. Also reading productions. Payment rates are negotiable.

MANHATTAN THEATRE CLUB–321 East 73rd St., New York, NY 10021. Stephen Pascal, Literary Manager.
Produces 10 to 15 new plays a year. Query.

MARLBORO GUILD THEATER—Marlboro, VT 05344. Geoffry Brown, Producing Director.
Plays for production on thrust stage. Pays on royalty basis for summer repertory season. Query. Same address and requirements for *Marlboro College-Theater Workshop.*

NEW YORK SHAKESPEARE FESTIVAL—425 Lafayette St., New York, NY 10003. Lynn Holst, Coordinator, Department of Play Development.
Full-length plays and musicals; no one-acts or children's plays. Interested in "works on any subject, in any style, but we tend toward works of a more subjective nature and away from commercial theater." Pays on royalty basis.

EUGENE O'NEILL MEMORIAL THEATER CENTER—Suite 1012, 1860 Broadway, New York, NY 10023, and 305 Great Neck Rd., Waterford, CT 06385.
Plays for production during summer Conference in Waterford, Connecticut. Previously unproduced plays (one play per playwright) may be submitted between September 15 and December 31 only, to New York Office. Two copies of the script are required with stamped envelope for return of scripts. Pays stipend, room and board at Conference.

THE PLAYWRIGHT'S LAB—3800 Park Ave. South, Minneapolis, MN 55407. Tom Dunn, Managing Director.
One-act or full-length plays, traditional or experimental, particularly by midwestern playwrights. Pays varying rates.

SEATTLE REPERTORY THEATER—Seattle Center, P.O. Box B, Seattle, WA 98109. W. Duncan Ross, Artistic Director.
Full-length dramas and experimental plays. Also workshop and reading productions.

THE SHADE COMPANY—c/o Valk, 19 Seaman Ave., New York, NY 10034. Toni Dorfman, Producing Director.
Plays. Pays on royalty basis.

STUDIO ARENA THEATER—681 Main St., Buffalo, NY 14203. Neal Du Brock, Executive Producer.
Full-length dramas, comedies, adaptations and musicals, with 12 characters maximum. Payment rates are negotiable.

MARK TAPER FORUM—135 North Grand Ave., Los Angeles, CA 90012.
Plays, any length, on any subject, for production in thrust theater, or flexible theater. Pays on royalty basis or by outright purchase.

THEATRE AMERICANA—Box 245, Altadena, CA 91001. Address Playreading Chairperson.
Full-length comedies, tragedies, farces, musicals (include piano arrangements), for production in community theater. One-set plays preferred. Award of $300 for best play of season.

THEATRE AT ST. CLEMENT'S —423 West 46th St., New York, NY 10036. Stephen Roylance, Production Dept.
Original American plays.

THEATRE FOR THE NEW CITY—113 Jane St., New York, NY 10014. Crystal Field, George Bartenieff, Artistic Directors.
Experimental plays.

URBAN ARTS CORP.—26 West 20th St., New York, NY 10011. Vinnette Carroll, Artistic Director.
Plays by black playwrights; classics.

VIRGINIA MUSEUM THEATRE—Boulevard and Grove, Richmond, VA 23221. Loraine Slade, General Manager.
Full-length dramas. Payment rates are negotiable.

YALE REPERTORY THEATER—222 York St., New Haven, CT 06520. Robert Brustein, Director.
Full-length dramas, comedies, adaptations, and experimental plays. "No standard, Broadway-style entertainments. Realistic, domestic dramas and comedies are not for us. We look for out-of-the-ordinary, formally experimental plays with a dramaturgically poetical dimension." Pays on royalty basis.

LITERARY MAGAZINES

CANADIAN THEATRE REVIEW—Theater Dept., York University, Downsview, Ont., Canada.
Plays by Canadians. Pays varying rates, on publication. Query.

THE DEKALB LITERARY ARTS JOURNAL—DeKalb College, 555 Indian Creek Dr., Clarkston, GA 30021. W. S. Newman, Editor.
One-act plays. Pays in copies.

EVENT—Dept. of English, Douglas College, Box 2503, New Westminster, B.C., Canada V3L 5B2. John S. Levin, Editor.
Short drama. Pays in copies.

THE FAULT—33513 Sixth St., Union City, CA 94587. Terrence Ames, Literature Editor.
Short, innovative plays. Pays in copies.

THE LITERARY REVIEW—Fairleigh Dickinson University, Madison, NJ 07940.
Liberary plays, radio and television plays. Pays in copies.

PRISM INTERNATIONAL—Creative Writing, University of British Columbia, Vancouver, B. C., Canada V6T 1W5. Michael Bullock, Editor-in-Chief.
Short plays. Pays $5 per printed page, plus copies, on publication.

SUN AND MOON—4330 Hartwick Rd., College Park, MD 20740. Douglas Messerli, Literary Editor.
Drama; publishes literature of all kinds but prefers experimental work. Pays in copies.

WIND LITERARY JOURNAL—RFD Rte. #1, Box 810, Pikeville, KY 41501. Quentin R. Howard, Editor.
Publishes one one-act drama per year. Pays in copies.

BOOK PUBLISHERS

Three lists are included here: hardcover book publishers (although many of these have paperback subsidiaries as well), publishers of paperback originals; and university presses, which publish a limited number of scholarly and specialized books.

Royalty rates for hardcover books usually start at 10% of the retail price of the book, and increase after a certain number of copies have been sold. Paperbacks generally have a somewhat lower rate, about 5% to 8%. It is customary for the publishing company to pay the author a cash advance against royalties when the book contract is signed or when the finished manuscript is received.

Book manuscripts may be sent by first-class mail, but the most inexpensive and commonly used method at present is by "Special Fourth Class Rate—Manuscript." For a summary of postal regulations for the "Special Fourth Class Rate—Manuscript," see Chapter 100, *Manuscript Preparation and Submission*, and for rates, details of insurance, etc., inquire at your local post office.

HARDCOVER BOOK PUBLISHERS

ABBEY PRESS—St. Meinrad, IN 47577. John J. Bettin, Editor.
Religious books; nonfiction on family relationships. Pays on royalty basis. Query with table of contents and writing sample.

ABELARD-SCHUMAN, LTD. (Division of *Thomas Y. Crowell Co.*)—666 Fifth Ave., New York, NY 10019. Morrill Gipson, Editor.
Juvenile books. Not accepting manuscripts at present.

ABINGDON PRESS—201 Eighth Ave. South, Nashville, TN 37202.
Religious books, juveniles, college texts. General nonfiction: biography, Americana, marriage and family, social issues and recreation. Query with outline and sample chapters.

HARRY N. ABRAMS, INC. (Subsidiary of *Times Mirror Co.*)—110 East 59th St., New York, NY 10022.
Art, photography, illustrated trade books. Query.

ACADEMIC PRESS, INC. (Subsidiary of *Harcourt Brace Jovanovich, Inc.*)—111 Fifth Ave., New York, NY 10003.
Scientific, technical, medical, behavioral and social science books. Query.

ACADEMY PRESS, LTD.—360 North Michigan Ave., Chicago, IL 60601. Jordan Miller and Anita Miller, Publishers.
Feminist and general nonfiction. Pays on royalty basis.

ACROPOLIS BOOKS LTD.—Colortone Bldg., 2400 17th St. N.W., Washington, DC 20009.
Family nonfiction; how-to books; professional books on elementary education; books on leisure-time activities. Pays on royalty basis. Query.

ADDISON-WESLEY PUBLISHING CO.—Reading, MA 01867. Ann Dilworth, Executive Editor; Kathleen Leverich, Children's Book Editor.
Juvenile fiction; contemporary, historical, fantasy, mystery, adventure; juvenile nonfiction. Adult nonfiction: social issues, biographies, cookbooks, sports, popular psychology, self-help. Query first on adult manuscripts. Pays on royalty basis.

AERO PUBLISHERS, INC.—329 West Aviation Rd., Fallbrook, CA 92028.
Illustrated nonfiction on aviation and space. Pays on royalty basis. Query.

ALLYN & BACON, INC.—470 Atlantic Ave., Boston, MA 02210. Richard Carroll, Vice-President, Elementary-High School Texts; Wayne Barcomb, Vice-President, College Texts; John Gilman, Director, Professional Books.
Textbooks for kindergarten through college. Professional books on education, business, drama and computer science. Pays on royalty basis.

AMERICAN BOOK COMPANY (Division of *Litton Educational Publishing, Inc.*)—450 West 33rd St., New York, NY 10001.
Textbooks and educational material for elementary and secondary schools. Pays on royalty basis.

AMERICAN WEST PUBLISHING COMPANY (Division of *Crown Publishers, Inc.*)—One Park Ave., New York, NY 10016.
Specialized nonfiction on the West: history, natural history. Pays on royalty basis. Query.

AMPHOTO *(American Photographic Book Publishing Co., Inc.)*—750 Zeckendorf Blvd., Garden City, NY 11530.
Books on photography. Pays on royalty basis. Query.

ARBOR HOUSE PUBLISHING COMPANY, INC.—641 Lexington Ave., New York, NY 10022.
General fiction and nonfiction. Query.

ARCO PUBLISHING COMPANY—219 Park Ave. South, New York, NY 10003. David Goodnough, Editor.
Books on business, sports, hobbies, health and nutrition, horses, pets, tests and testing; how-to books; general nonfiction. Pays on royalty basis or by outright purchase. Query with outline.

ARKHAM HOUSE PUBLISHERS, INC.—Sauk City, WI 53583.
Supernatural/macabre fiction and verse. Pays on royalty basis. Query.

ARLINGTON HOUSE, INC.—165 Huguenot St., New Rochelle, NY 10801. Richard E. Band, Editor.
Self-help books; nostalgia on 1920-1960 era; books on conservative politics. Pays on royalty basis. Query.

ASSOCIATION PRESS—291 Broadway, New York, NY 10007. Robert W. Hill, Director.
General nonfiction: recreation, sports, social and behavioral sciences, family life and marriage, adult education, sex education, religious and ethical subjects. Pays on royalty basis. Query.

ATHENEUM PUBLISHERS—122 East 42nd St., New York, NY 10017. Alfred Knopf, Jr., Chairman of the Board; Herman Gollob, Vice-President and Editor-in-Chief.
Fiction; nonfiction: biography, history, current affairs, belles-lettres; juveniles. Quality paperback reprints. Pays on royalty basis.

THE ATLANTIC MONTHLY PRESS—8 Arlington St., Boston, MA 02116. Peter Davison, Director.
Fiction, biography, history, belles-lettres, poetry, general nonfiction, juveniles. Pays on royalty basis. Query. (Publishing in association with *Little, Brown*)

AUGSBURG PUBLISHING HOUSE—426 South Fifth St., Minneapolis, MN 55415. Roland Seboldt, Director of Book Development.
Fiction and nonfiction on Christian themes; juveniles. Pays on royalty basis.

BAKER BOOK HOUSE—1019 Wealthy St. S.E., Grand Rapids, MI 49506. Daniel Van't Kerkhoff, Editor.
Nonfiction, 30,000 to 60,000 words; Bible study aids, homiletic literature; Bible quizzes and puzzles; short manuscripts on marriage, birthday, etc. Pays on royalty basis for full-length manuscripts.

BARLENMIR HOUSE, PUBLISHERS—413 City Island Ave., New York, NY 10064. Address The Editorial Board.
Books on psychology, gourmet cooking, art, music; self-help and general nonfiction. Pays on royalty basis.

A. S. BARNES & COMPANY, INC.—Box 421, Cranbury, NJ 08512.
Books on sports, outdoors, cinema, art, crafts, horses, recreation; general nonfiction. Pays on a royalty basis. Query.

BARONET PUBLISHING COMPANY—509 Madison Ave., New York, NY 10022. Norman Goldfind, Publisher.
General nonfiction: self-help, health and nutrition, historicals, cookbooks. Fiction: family sagas, science fiction. Pays on royalty basis. Query.

BASIC BOOKS, INC., PUBLISHERS—10 East 53rd St., New York, NY 10022.
Books on behavioral and social sciences; belles-lettres; history; general nonfiction. Query.

THE BEACON PRESS—25 Beacon St., Boston, MA 02108.
General nonfiction on current events and major social issues. Scholarly works on contemporary affairs; liberal religious books. Pays on royalty basis. Query.

BENZIGER, BRUCE & GLENCOE, INC. (Subsidiary of *MacMillan Inc.*)—17337 Ventura Blvd., Encino, CA 91316.
Elementary, secondary, junior college texts, professional books; Catholic education and liturgical books. Pays on royalty basis. Query.

THE BETHANY PRESS—Box 179, St. Louis, MO 63166. Sherman R. Hanson, Editor.
Well-researched books on Protestant religious and humanitarian themes. Pays on royalty basis. Query.

BETTER HOMES AND GARDEN BOOKS—See *Meredith Corporation.*

BINFORD & MORT—2536 S.E. 11th Ave., Portland, OR 97202. L. K. Phillips, Editor.
Nonfiction, around 70,000 words, on Pacific Northwest. Pays on royalty basis.

BLOCH PUBLISHING COMPANY, INC.—915 Broadway, New York, NY 10010. Charles E. Bloch, President.
Books on Jewish subjects. Query.

THE BOBBS-MERRILL COMPANY, INC.—4 West 58th St., New York, NY 10019. Daniel Moses, Editor-in-Chief; Barbara Norville, Mystery Line; Evelyn Gendel, Craftsline.
Novels, mystery and suspense fiction, biography, autobiography, popular science, history, crafts. Juvenile fiction and nonfiction. Pays on royalty basis. Query; no unsolicited manuscripts accepted.

THOMAS BOUREGY & COMPANY, INC.—22 East 60th St., New York, NY 10022. Debra Manette, Editor.
Light, wholesome romances, modern Gothics, westerns, 50,000 to 55,000 words. Pays on royalty basis.

BOWMAR—4563 Colorado Blvd., Los Angeles, CA 90039.
Educational books on elementary school subjects. Pays on royalty basis or by outright purchase. Query.

BRADBURY PRESS, INC.—2 Overhill Rd., Scarsdale, NY 10583. Richard Jackson, Editor.
Juvenile fiction and nonfiction. Pays on royalty basis.

GEORGE BRAZILLER, INC.—One Park Ave., New York, NY 10016.
Literature, history, philosophy, science, art, social science; fiction. Query.

BROADMAN PRESS—127 Ninth Ave. North, Nashville, TN 37234. Johnnie Godwin, Supervisor.
Religious and inspirational fiction and nonfiction. Usually pays on royalty basis. Query.

CAHNERS BOOKS—See *CBI Publishing.*

CANFIELD PRESS (Division of *Harper & Row*)—1700 Montgomery St., San Francisco, CA 94111.
High school and junior college textbooks. Pays on royalty basis. Query.

CAREER PUBLISHING, INC.—928 South Main St., Orange, CA 92667. S. Michele McFadden, Editor.

Vocational textbooks on jobs and careers, for adults who read at 8th grade level. Pays on royalty basis. Query with outline and sample chapters.

THE CAXTON PRINTERS, LTD.—Box 700, Caldwell, ID 83605.
Authentic Americana, preferably on frontier and the West. Pays on royalty basis. Query.

CBI PUBLISHING (formerly *Cahners Books*)—51 Sleeper St., Boston, MA 02210.
Books for business and industry; vocational books; cookbooks. Pays on royalty basis.

CELESTIAL ARTS—231 Adrian Rd., Millbrae, CA 94030. David Morris, Editor.
General nonfiction; poetry; popular psychology, occult; cookbooks, self-help and how-to books. Pays on royalty basis.

THE CHATHAM PRESS—143 Sound Beach Ave., Old Greenwich, CT 06870. Devin A. Garrity, Editor.
Illustrated nonfiction on nature and outdoor recreation. Pays on royalty basis. Query with outline and sample chapter.

CHILDRENS PRESS—1224 West Van Buren St., Chicago, IL 60607. Joan Downing, Managing Editor.
Juvenile fiction and nonfiction, 50 to 1,000 words, for supplementary use in classrooms. Picture books, 50 to 10,000 words. Pays on royalty basis or by outright purchase.

CHILTON BOOK COMPANY—201 King of Prussia Rd., Radnor, PA 19089. Glen Ruh, Associate Editorial Director; Lydia Driscoll, Senior Editor, Arts and Crafts; Steve Davis, Assistant Managing Editor, Automotive.
General nonfiction: how-to, biography, history, popular music, sports, nature, travel, popular science, business, arts and crafts, automotive, popular psychology, sociology, the occult. Pays on royalty basis. Query with outline and sample chapter.

CHRISTIAN HERALD HOUSE—40 Overlook Dr., Chappaqua, NY 10514. Gary Sledge, Editor.
Nonfiction on religious themes, nature, animals, nostalgia. Fiction for family audience; autobiography. Pays on royalty basis.

CITADEL PRESS—120 Enterprise Ave., Secaucus, NJ 07094. Allan J. Wilson, Editor.
General nonfiction; fiction. Pays on royalty basis.

CLARION BOOKS—See *The Seabury Press.*

CONCORDIA PUBLISHING HOUSE—3558 South Jefferson Ave., St. Louis, MO 63118.
Fiction and nonfiction, with moral or religious tone; juveniles. Pays on royalty basis.

CONTEMPORARY BOOKS (formerly *Henry Regnery Co.*)—180 North Michigan Ave., Chicago, IL 60601.
General non-fiction, sports, etc. Query.

CONTINUUM BOOKS—See *Seabury Press.*

CORNELL MARITIME PRESS, INC.—Cambridge, MD 21613. Mary Jane Cornell, Editor.
Maritime technical, professional and how-to books. *Tidewater Publishers:* books on Chesapeake Bay, Maryland and Delmarva Peninsula. Pays on royalty basis. Query with outline.

COWARD, McCANN & GEOGHEGAN—200 Madison Ave., New York, NY 10016. John J. Geoghegan, President and Publisher.
Fiction and quality suspense; general nonfiction. Juvenile fiction and nonfiction, preschool through young adult. Pays on royalty basis. Query.

CREATIVE BOOK COMPANY—P.O. Box 214998, Sacramento, CA 95821.

How-to manuals, 10 to 30 pages, on professional and personal growth, community organization, development and promotion. Pays $100 to $300, by outright purchase.

THOMAS Y. CROWELL COMPANY—666 Fifth Ave., New York, NY 10019.
Fiction and nonfiction; reference books; juveniles. College and secondary school texts. Pays on royalty basis. Query. (Incorporating *Intext Press, Inc.*)

CROWN PUBLISHERS, INC.—One Park Ave., New York, NY 10016. Herbert Michelman, Editor-in-Chief; Lawrence Freundlich, Executive Editor; Norma Jean Sawicki, Children's Books Editor.
Fiction and general nonfiction: cookbooks, craft books, how-to contemporary politics, history, biography. Juveniles. Pays on royalty basis. Query for nonfiction.

THE DARTNELL CORPORATION—4660 Ravenswood Ave., Chicago, IL 60640.
Manuals, 60,000 to 100,000 words, on business topics. Pays on royalty basis.

JOHN DE GRAFF, INC.—Clinton Corners, NY 12514.
Nonfiction on pleasure boating. Pays on royalty basis. Query.

DELACORTE PRESS—One Dag Hammarskjold Plaza, 245 East 47th St., New York, NY 10017. Address Saul Cohen, Executive Managing Editor.
General fiction and nonfiction. Pays on royalty basis. Query; no unsolicited manuscripts accepted.

THE DEVIN-ADAIR COMPANY—143 Sound Beach Ave., Old Greenwich, CT 06870.
Serious nonfiction on politically conservative subjects, popular health, Irish-interest topics. Pays on royalty basis. Query.

THE DIAL PRESS—One Dag Hammarskjold Plaza, 245 East 47th St., New York, NY 10017. Juris Jurjevics, Editor-in-Chief; Phyllis Fogelman, Editor, Children's Books.
General fiction and nonfiction. No mysteries, westerns, verse, romances or technical material. Pays on royalty basis. Query or send sample chapter.

DIMENSION BOOKS, INC.—P.O. Box 811, Denville, NJ 07834. Thomas Coffey, Editor.
Catholic nonfiction. Pays on royalty basis.

DODD, MEAD & COMPANY—79 Madison Ave., New York, NY 10016.
General fiction and nonfiction: biography, history, belles-lettres, travel. Juveniles. Pays on royalty basis. Query.

DOUBLEDAY & COMPANY, INC.—245 Park Ave., New York, NY 10017.
General fiction and nonfiction. Complete manuscripts for science fiction, mysteries; submit outline with background of author for westerns; address appropriate department. For other types, send for "How to Submit Your Book to Doubleday," including return envelope. Pays on royalty basis.

DOW JONES-IRWIN, INC.—1818 Ridge Rd., Homewood, IL 60430. Ralph Rieves, Editor.
Business books. Pays on royalty basis.

DRAKE PUBLISHERS, INC.—801 Second Ave., New York, NY 10017.
General nonfiction, 50,000 to 90,000 words: hobby, crafts, biography, history. Pays on royalty basis or by outright purchase. Query with outline and table of contents.

E. P. DUTTON & COMPANY, INC.—201 Park Ave. South, New York, NY 10003.
General nonfiction: biography, adventure, history, travel. Fiction; mysteries; juveniles. Query first with outline. Pays on royalty basis.

WM. B. EERDMANS PUBLISHING COMPANY, INC.—255 Jefferson Ave. S.E., Grand Rapids, MI 49503.
Protestant theological nonfiction; Great Lakes regional books; fiction, juveniles. Pays on royalty basis.

ELK GROVE PRESS (Division of *Childrens Press, Inc.*)—P.O. Box 1637, Whittier, CA 90609. Ruth Shaw Radlauer, Editor.
Juvenile fiction and nonfiction: preschool concept books, to 1,000 words; middle grades and up, to 10,000 words. Pays on royalty basis or by outright purchase. Query, stating length and reading level.

EMERSON BOOKS, INC.—Reynolds Lane, Buchanan, NY 10511.
Nonfiction: self-help, crafts, martial arts, how-to, etc. Pays on royalty basis.

EPM PUBLICATIONS, INC.—Box 442, McLean, VA 22101. Jane M. Currier, Editor.
Specialized nonfiction: Americana, photography, social sciences, recreation. Pays on royalty basis. Query.

PAUL S. ERIKSSON—Battell Bldg., Middlebury, VT 05753.
Adult fiction, general nonfiction, biography, etc. Pays on royalty basis. Query.

M. EVANS & COMPANY, INC.—216 East 49th St., New York, NY 10017.
General fiction, nonfiction, juveniles. Query. Return envelope required for reply.

FARRAR, STRAUS & GIROUX—19 Union Sq. West, New York, NY 10003.
General fiction, nonfiction, juveniles. Query. (Incorporating *Noonday Press*, paperback publishers)

FREDERICK FELL PUBLISHERS, INC.—386 Park Ave. South, New York, NY 10016. Charles G. Nurnberg, Vice-President.
Nonfiction: business, crafts and hobbies, physical and mental health, the occult, how-to, self-help. Pays on royalty basis. Query with outline and sample chapters.

FLEET PRESS CORPORATION—160 Fifth Ave., New York, NY 10010. S. Nueckel, Editor.
General nonfiction; sports and how-to books. Pays on royalty basis. Query; no unsolicited manuscripts accepted.

FOLLETT PUBLISHING COMPANY—1010 West Washington Blvd., Chicago, IL 60607. Marci Ridlon Carafoli, Children's Books Editor; Elaine Goldberg, Adult Trade Editor.
Juvenile fiction and nonfiction. General nonfiction: sports, self-help, how-to, reference. Query for adult nonfiction; no unsolicited manuscripts accepted by Adult Trade Division.

FORTRESS PRESS—2900 Queen Ln., Philadelphia, PA 19129. Norman A. Hjelm, Director and Senior Editor.
Books on theology and general religion for lay readers, students, ministers, scholars. Pays on royalty basis.

FOUR WINDS PRESS—Scholastic Magazines, Inc., 50 West 44th St., New York, NY 10036.
Juvenile and young-adult fiction and nonfiction; adult nonfiction. Overstocked.

THE FREE PRESS (Division of *Macmillan Publishing Co., Inc.*)—866 Third Ave., New York, NY 10022. Edward W. Barry, President.
College-level texts and professional books in social sciences and humanities. Pays on royalty basis.

FUNK & WAGNALLS PUBLISHING COMPANY, INC.—666 Fifth Ave., New York, NY 10019. Address Trade Editorial Department.
Adult nonfiction: reference, current affairs, science, biography, how-to. Pays on royalty basis. Query with outline.

BERNARD GEIS ASSOCIATES—128 East 56th St., New York, NY 10022.
General fiction and nonfiction. Pays on royalty basis. Query.

THE K.S. GINIGER COMPANY, INC.—235 Park Ave. South, Suite 407, New York, NY 10003.

General nonfiction; reference and religious books; juveniles. Pays on royalty basis. Query; no unsolicited manuscripts accepted.

GOLDEN BOOKS—See *Western Publishing Company, Inc.*

GOLDEN PRESS (Division of *Western Publishing Co., Inc.*)—850 Third Ave., New York, NY 10022.
Juvenile fiction and nonfiction; reference books; adult nonfiction.

THE STEPHEN GREENE PRESS—Box 1000, Brattleboro, VT 05301.
General nonfiction; Americana with New England interest; history and social commentary; books on country living and individual outdoor sports. Pays on royalty basis. Query with outline and sample chapters.

GROSSET & DUNLAP, INC.—51 Madison Ave., New York, NY 10010.
History, biography, literature, science, fine arts; self-help, cookbooks, reference books; general adult nonfiction. Query; no unsolicited manuscripts accepted.

GROVE PRESS, INC.—196 West Houston St., New York, NY 10014. Address C.A. Umbach.
General fiction and nonfiction. Pays on royalty basis. Query.

HAMMOND, INC.—Maplewood, NJ 07040. Frank Brady, Editorial Director, Trade Division.
Nonfiction on travel, leisure, psychology, how-to, cookery, photography, nostalgia. Query with outline. Pays on royalty basis or outright purchase.

HARCOURT BRACE JOVANOVICH, INC.—757 Third Ave., New York, NY 10017.
Kathy Robbins, Director, Trade Division; Barbara Lucas, Juvenile Editor.
Juvenile fiction and nonfiction, 5,000 to 60,000 words, for beginning readers through young teens. Pays on royalty basis. No unsolicited manuscripts accepted by Adult Trade Division. (Incorporating *Jove/HBJ*. See under Paperback Publishers.)

HARPER & ROW—10 East 53rd St., New York, NY 10022.
Fiction, nonfiction, biography, economics, etc.; address Trade Department. College texts; address College Department. Juvenile fiction, science fiction, fantasy and nonfiction, preschool through young adult; address Junior Books Department. Books on religion, theology, etc.; address Religious Books Department. Paperback originals; address Paperback Department. Pays on royalty basis.

HART PUBLISHING COMPANY, INC.—15 West Fourth St., New York, NY 10012.
Adult nonfiction. Pays on royalty basis. Query.

HARVEY HOUSE, INC.—20 Waterside Plaza, New York, NY 10010. L. F. Reeves, Publisher.
Picture books, fiction and nonfiction. Books on science and social studies for kindergarten through junior high. Pays on royalty basis or by outright purchase.

HASTINGS HOUSE, PUBLISHERS, INC.—10 East 40th St., New York, NY 10016.
Walter Frese, Editor. Judy Donnolly, Juvenile Editor.
General nonfiction, Americana, biography, books on travel, cooking, communication arts, visual arts; juveniles. Pays on royalty basis.

HAWTHORN BOOKS—260 Madison Ave., New York, NY 10016. Anne Harrison, Editorial Department.
General nonfiction. No unsolicited manuscripts accepted.

D. C. HEATH & COMPANY—125 Spring St., Lexington, MA 02173.
Text books, audio-visual material for schools and colleges. Professional books for *Lexington Books* Division. Query.

HILL & WANG (Division of *Farrar, Straus & Giroux*)—19 Union Sq. West, New York,

NY 10003. Arthur W. Wang, Editor-in-Chief.
Nonfiction; history, social history; drama. Pays on royalty basis. Query.

HOBBS/CONTEXT CORPORATION—Room 1505, 52 Vanderbilt Ave., New York, NY
10017.
Educational texts and supplementary reading; technical reports; how-to material;
instructional cassettes. Pays on royalty basis. Query.

HOLIDAY HOUSE—18 East 53rd St., New York, NY 10022. Margery Cuyler, Editor.
General juvenile books; science and nature books, preschool through young adult.
Pays on royalty basis.

HOLT, RINEHART AND WINSTON, INC.—383 Madison Ave., New York, NY 10017.
Address General Book Division.
General fiction and nonfiction; juveniles. Pays on royalty basis. Query with outline
and sample chapters.

HOPKINSON AND BLAKE—185 Madison Ave., New York, NY 10016. Barbara
Habenstreit, Editor.
General nonfiction: cookbooks, self-help; special interest in cinema. Pays advance
against royalties. Query Len Karlin.

HORIZON PRESS—156 Fifth Ave., New York, NY 10010. Ben Raeburn, Editor.
General nonfiction; art, architecture, science and reference books; fiction. Pays on
royalty basis.

HOUGHTON MIFFLIN COMPANY—2 Park St., Boston, MA 02107. David Harris,
Managing Editor.
Contemporary fiction; historical and suspense novels. Nonfiction: history, natural
history, biography, reference, cookbooks, craft books. Juveniles; poetry. Pays on
royalty basis. Query.

HOWELL BOOK HOUSE, INC.—730 Fifth Ave., New York, NY 10019.
Nonfiction on dogs and dog care. Pays on royalty basis. Query.

HOWELL-NORTH BOOKS—1050 Parker St., Berkeley, CA 94710. F. D. North, Editor.
Railroad histories, western Americana, pictorials. Pays on royalty basis (no advance).
Query.

H. P. BOOKS—P.O. Box 5367, Tucson, AZ 85703. Carl N. Shipman, Managing Editor.
Illustrated how-to books, 50,000 to 80,000 words, on cooking, motorcycles and
automobiles, etc.; books on photography and travel. Pays on royalty basis. Query.

HUMANITIES PRESS—Atlantic Highlands, NJ 07716.
Scholarly books on academic subjects. Pays on royalty basis. Query.

INDEPENDENCE PRESS (Division of *Herald House*)—Drawer HH, 3225 South Noland
Rd., Independence, MO 64055. Paul A. Wellington, Editor.
Juvenile fiction, 150 to 200 pages. Nonfiction, 150 to 200 pages; self-help, autobiog-
raphy, biography. Pays on royalty basis. Query with outline.

INTERNATIONAL MARINE PUBLISHING COMPANY—21 Elm St., Camden, ME
04843. Peter Spectre, Editor.
Books on marine subjects: pleasure boating, boat building, etc. Pays on royalty basis.
Query.

INTEXT PRESS—See *Thomas Y. Crowell Co.*

JEWISH PUBLICATION SOCIETY—1528 Walnut St., Philadelphia, PA 19102. Maier
Deshell, Editor.
Nonfiction, fiction and juveniles, related to Jewish life, literature, etc. Translations.
Pays on royalty basis. Query.

JOHNSON PUBLISHING COMPANY—820 South Michigan Ave., Chicago, IL 60605.
Nonfiction, scholarly books, juveniles, primarily about black people. Query. Stamped, self-addressed envelope required for return of manuscript.

JONATHAN DAVID PUBLISHERS, INC.—68-22 Eliot Ave., Middle Village, NY 11379. Alfred J. Kolatch, Editor-in-Chief.
General nonfiction. Pays on royalty basis or by outright purchase. Query with detailed outline and sample chapter.

JOSSEY-BASS, INC., PUBLISHERS—615 Montgomery St., San Francisco, CA 94111. Professional trade and textbooks in the social and behavioral sciences. Pays on royalty basis. Query.

JUDSON PRESS—Valley Forge, PA 19481. Harold L. Twiss, Editor.
Religious books on current moral and social issues; inspirational and devotional material. Pays on royalty basis.

KEATS PUBLISHING, INC.—36 Grove St., Box 876, New Canaan, CT 06840. An Keats, Editor.
Nonfiction: health, inspiration, how-to. Pays on royalty basis. Query.

ROBERT R. KNAPP, PUBLISHER/EDITS—Box 7234, San Diego, CA 92107.
Professional reference and textbooks in the humanities and social sciences, especially education, psychology, psychiatry and statistics. Pays on royalty basis. Query.

ALFRED A. KNOPF, INC.—201 East 50th St., New York, NY 10022. Ashbel Green, Vice-President and Senior Editor; Pat Ross, Juvenile Editor.
Distinguished fiction and general nonfiction. College texts in the humanities and social sciences. Juvenile fiction and nonfiction; picture books, 3,000 to 5,000 words. Pays on royalty basis. Query.

JOHN KNOX PRESS—341 Ponce de Leon Ave. N.E., Atlanta, GA 30308. Richard A. Ray, Director.
Books on religion, biblical studies, counseling; inspirational material. Pays on royalty basis. Query with outline or sample chapter.

LANTERN PRESS—354 Hussey Rd., Mt. Vernon, NY 10552.
Juvenile fiction and nonfiction; adult nonfiction. Pays on royalty basis or by outright purchase. Query.

SEYMOUR LAWRENCE, INC.—90 Beacon St., Boston, MA 02108.
Fiction; books on child development; juveniles. Pays on royalty basis. Query on nonfiction.

LION BOOKS—111 East 39th St., New York, NY 10016. Harriet Ross, Editor-in-Chief.
Young-adult nonfiction: sports, history, personality, diet and nature. Pays on royalty or by outright purchase.

J. B. LIPPINCOTT COMPANY—521 Fifth Ave., New York, NY 10017. Edward L. Burlingame, Editor-in-Chief. Dorothy Briley, Editor, Books for Young Readers.
Adult and juvenile fiction and nonfiction. Pays on royalty basis. No unsolicited manuscripts; requires a descriptive letter or outline and one or two sample chapters.

LITTLE, BROWN & COMPANY—34 Beacon St., Boston, MA 02106. Roger Donald, Editor-in-Chief. John G. Keller, Children's Book Editor.
Fiction, general nonfiction, sports books, juveniles; law, medical and college texts.

LITTLE GOLDEN BOOKS®—See *Western Publishing Company, Inc.*

LOTHROP, LEE & SHEPARD COMPANY—See *William Morrow & Co.*

ROBERT B. LUCE, INC.—2000 N St. N.W., Washington, DC 20036. Allison C. Gilbert, Assistant Editor.

Nonfiction on public affairs; fiction. Pays on royalty basis.

McGRAW-HILL BOOK COMPANY–General Trade Book Division, 1221 Ave. of the
Americas, New York, NY 10020. Frederic Hills, Editor-in-Chief; Eleanor Nichols,
Editor-in-Chief, Juvenile Department.
Fiction; general nonfiction: biography, history, education, popular science, business,
reference. Juvenile fiction and nonfiction, biography, etc. Pays on royalty basis.
Query with outline for adult books.

DAVID McKAY COMPANY, INC.–750 Third Ave., New York, NY 10017. Alan
Tucker, Manager, General Book Division.
Mysteries, Gothics, romantic suspense. Nonfiction: human behavior, popular history,
social commentary, etc. How-to books on gardening, cooking, outdoors; books by
experts. Mature fiction and nonfiction for young adults. Complete manuscript preferred. Pays on royalty basis. (Incorporating *Charterhouse, Peter Wyden* and
Weybright and Talley)

MACMILLAN PUBLISHING COMPANY, INC.–866 Third Ave., New York, NY 10022.
Address Trade Department or Children's Book Department.
Fiction, mystery and suspense; general nonfiction: how-to, self-help, history, biog-
raphy; juveniles; religious, medical, business and technical books.

MACRAE SMITH COMPANY–225 South 15th St., Philadelphia, PA 19102. Ruth
Miner, Editor.
Adult fiction and nonfiction; reference. Juvenile and young-adult books. Pays on
royalty basis.

MEREDITH CORPORATION, BOOK DIVISION (*Better Homes and Gardens Books*)–
1716 Locust St., Des Moines, IA 50336. Don Dooley, Editorial Director. Address
The Editors.
Books on gardening, crafts, health, decorating, do-it-yourself projects, etc. Pays on
royalty basis or by outright purchase. Query with outline and sample chapter.

JULIAN MESSNER (Division of *Simon & Schuster*)–1230 Ave. of the Americas, New
York, NY 10020. Lee M. Hoffman, Executive Editor.
Nonfiction, 52,000 words, for 12- to 15-year-olds. Curriculum-oriented nonfiction,
5,000 to 15,000 words, for 3rd to 6th graders, on social studies, science, sports,
nature, the environment, contemporary affairs, crafts; plays.

MOODY PRESS–820 North LaSalle St., Chicago, IL 60610. Mr. Leslie H. Stobbe,
Editor.
Evangelical publishing house associated with Moody Bible Institute. Conservative
religious fiction and nonfiction. Pays on royalty basis.

MOREHOUSE-BARLOW COMPANY, INC.–78 Danbury Rd., Wilton, CT 06897.
Nonfiction, curriculum-oriented texts; adult and juvenile religious books. Pays on
royalty basis or by outright purchase. Query with outline and sample chapter.

WILLIAM MORROW AND COMPANY, INC.–105 Madison Ave., New York, NY
10016. John C. Willey, Editor-in-Chief.
Adult and juvenile fiction and nonfiction. *Morrow Junior Books:* Constance C.
Epstein, Editor. Junior books for all ages except preschool. *Greenwillow Books:*
Susan C. Hirschman, Editor-in-Chief. Fiction for middle grades and up. *Lothrop, Lee
& Shepard Company:* Juvenile fiction and nonfiction. Pays on royalty basis. Query.

NASH PUBLISHING–One Dupont St., Plainview, NY 11803. Cynthia Swan. Editor.
Nonfiction on controversial current issues; how-to; self-help; psychology. Royalty or
outright purchase. Query.

THOMAS NELSON, INC.—30 East 42nd St., New York, NY 10017. Gloria R. Mosesson, Editor.
Adult and juvenile fiction and nonfiction.

NELSON-HALL PUBLISHERS—325 West Jackson Blvd., Chicago, IL 60606. V. Peter Ferrara, Editor.
Nonfiction trade books, on applied psychology, sociology, anthropology. Scholarly books in the behavioral sciences, by authorities in the field. Pays on royalty basis. Query with outline.

NEW VIEWPOINTS (Division of *Franklin Watts, Inc.*)—730 Fifth Ave., New York, NY 10019. Will Davison, Editor.
College-level nonfiction, expecially on history and social sciences. Pays on royalty basis. Query.

NEW YORK GRAPHIC SOCIETY—11 Beacon St., Boston, MA 02108.
Books on fine arts, film, Americana, crafts and general adult topics. Query with outline or proposal and vita.

W. W. NORTON & COMPANY, INC.—500 Fifth Ave., New York, NY 10036.
Fiction and nonfiction. Pays on royalty basis.

OCEANA PUBLICATIONS, INC.—75 Main St., Dobbs Ferry, NY 10522. W. W. Cowan, Managing Editor.
Books on law and public policy. Pays on royalty basis or by outright purchase. Query.

ODDO PUBLISHING, INC.—Storybook Acres, Beauregard Blvd., Fayetteville, GA 30214. Paul C. Oddo, President.
Juveniles and remedial-reading school books. Royalty or outright purchase. Query.

OHARA PUBLICATIONS, INC.—1847 West Empire Ave., Burbank, CA 91504. Han Kim, Publisher.
Nonfiction on the Pacific, the Orient; fiction. Pays on royalty basis. Query with synopsis and vita.

101 PRODUCTIONS—834 Mission St., San Francisco, CA 94103. Jacqueline Killeen, Editor.
Nonfiction on cooking, gardening, domestic arts. Pays on royalty basis.

OPEN COURT PUBLISHING COMPANY—Box 599, La Salle, IL 61301. Thomas G. Anderson, Editor.
Scholarly books on philosophy, mathematics, comparative religion, history, political science, economics, etc. Elementary textbooks. Pays on royalty basis. Query.

OXFORD UNIVERSITY PRESS—200 Madison Ave., New York, NY 10016.
Authoritative books on literature, history, religion, philosophy, biography, etc.; college textbooks, medical, reference and art books; paperbacks. Pays on royalty basis. Query.

OXMOOR HOUSE, INC.—Box 2262, Birmingham, AL 35202. Ann H. Harvey, Managing Editor.
Nonfiction on cooking, gardening, home improvement, travel, crafts, art, antiques, sewing, nature, sports, southern history. Pays on royalty basis.

PANTHEON BOOKS (Division of *Random House*)—201 East 50th St., New York, NY 10022. Address Wendy Wolf.
Nonfiction: academic trade books on history, political science, sociology, etc. Pays on royalty basis. Query; no unsolicited manuscripts accepted.

PARENTS' MAGAZINE PRESS—52 Vanderbilt Ave., New York, NY 10017. Selma Lanes, Editor.

Picture books, 500 to 2,500 words, for 4- to 8-year-olds. Pays on royalty basis.

PARKER PUBLISHING COMPANY, INC.—West Nyack, NY 10994.
Self-help and how-to books, 65,000 words: popular health, the occult, inspiration, in-service teaching and education, secretarial, selling, personal and business self-improvement, money opportunities, speech and letter writing, coaching and electronics. Pays on royalty basis.

PARNASSUS PRESS—4080 Halleck St., Emeryville, CA 94608.
Juvenile fiction and nonfiction, pre-school through young adult. Pays on royalty basis. Query.

PAULIST PRESS—1865 Broadway, New York, NY 10023. Kevin A. Lynch, C.S.P., Editor.
Books on Catholic theology, philosophy, liturgy, religious education. Pays on royalty basis.

PELICAN PUBLISHING COMPANY, INC.—630 Burmaster St., Gretna, LA 70053. James L. Calhoun, Executive Editor.
General nonfiction; Americana, regional-interest books, architecture, tour guides. Pays on royalty basis.

S. G. PHILLIPS, INC.—305 West 86th St., New York, NY 10024. Sidney Phillips, Editor.
Juvenile fiction and nonfiction for all age groups: biography, history, anthropology, contemporary fiction. Pays on royalty basis. Query; no unsolicited manuscripts accepted.

PILGRIM PRESS (formerly *United Church Press*)—287 Park Ave. South, New York NY 10010.
Nonfiction: religion, theology, ethics; social sciences, humanities, current affairs. Pays on royalty basis. Query with outline and sample chapters.

PLATT & MUNK—1055 Bronx River Ave., Bronx, NY 10472. Kate Klimo, Editor.
Mass-market juveniles for 1- to 10-year-olds. Outright purchase.

PLAYBOY PRESS—747 Third Ave., New York, NY 10017. Robert Gleason, Executive Editor.
Fiction and nonfiction. Query.

CLARKSON N. POTTER, INC.—One Park Ave., New York, NY 10016. Jane West, Editor-in-Chief.
General trade books, especially on Americana, science, art, antiques, folk art. Pays on royalty basis. Query.

PRAEGER PUBLISHERS, INC.—200 Park Ave., New York, NY 10017.
Nonfiction: international relations, history, social sciences, economics, reference, urban affairs. Pays on royalty basis. Query.

PRENTICE-HALL, INC.—Englewood Cliffs, NJ 07632. John Grayson Kirk, Editor-in-Chief, Trade Books Division.
Fiction; nonfiction: biography, history, politics, sports. Juveniles; college books; educational textbooks; business and professional books. Pays on royalty basis. Query.

PRINCE PUBLISHERS—349 East Northfield Rd., Livingston, NJ 07039. Dick Atkins, Editor.
Popular fiction, from 30,000 words, and general nonfiction, from 40,000 words, preferably on movies, TV, crime, gambling, politics. Pays on royalty basis. Query with outline for nonfiction, with synopsis and sample chapter for fiction.

PRUETT PUBLISHING COMPANY—3235K Prairie Ave., Boulder, CO 80301. Gerald Keenan, Managing Editor.
Nonfiction on history and development of American West, railroad, Rockies region; special education materials; college texts. Pays on royalty basis. Query.

PUBLIC AFFAIRS PRESS—419 New Jersey Ave., S.E., Washington, DC 20003.
Nonfiction on current affairs and social sciences. Payment varies.

G. P. PUTNAM'S SONS—200 Madison Ave., New York, NY 10016. Judith Wederholt, Editor, Charles Mercer, Margaret Frith, Co-Directors, Juvenile Department.
Adult and juvenile fiction and nonfiction. Pays on royalty basis. Query; no unsolicited manuscripts accepted.

QUADRANGLE/THE NEW YORK TIMES BOOK COMPANY—3 Park Ave., New York, NY 10016. Roger Jellinek, Editor-in-Chief.
Nonfiction. Query with outline.

RAINTREE PUBLISHERS LTD. (formerly *Advanced Learning Concepts*)—205 West Highland Ave., Milwaukee, WI 53203.
Juvenile fiction and nonfiction: mystery and adventure, science fiction, biography, how-to, easy-to-read stories. Pays on royalty basis or by outright purchase.

RAND McNALLY & COMPANY—Box 7600, Chicago, IL 60680. Address the Editorial Department, Trade Publishing Division.
Adult nonfiction on exploration, adventure, travel, Americana, history, nature, etc. Juvenile fiction and nonfiction. Query.

RANDOM HOUSE, INC.—201 East 50th St., New York, NY 10022. Jason Epstein, Editorial Director, Walter Retan, Editor-in-Chief, Random House Juvenile Books; Jess Stein, Vice-President, Reference Books.
General fiction and nonfiction; reference and college textbooks; juvenile fiction and nonfiction, picture books, easy-to-read material. Pays on royalty basis. Query. (Incorporating *Vintage Books,* paperback publishers.)

HENRY REGNERY CO.—See *Contemporary Books.*

FLEMING H. REVELL COMPANY—Old Tappan, NJ 07675. Richard Baltzell, Editorial Director.
Inspirational and devotional religious books; self-help, biography. Pays on royalty basis.

THE WARD RITCHIE PRESS—474 South Arroyo Pkwy., Pasadena, CA 91105. William Chleboun, Editor.
General nonfiction; cookbooks; Americana; fiction. Pays on royalty basis. Query.

RODALE PRESS—33 East Minor St., Emmaus, PA 18049. Carol Hupping Stoner, Executive Editor.
Nonfiction books for children and adults on gardening, farming, wild foods, nature, crafts, natural foods, health, livestock, alternative energy systems. Pays on royalty basis.

THE RONALD PRESS COMPANY—79 Madison Ave., New York, NY 10016.
General information books; reference; handbooks; college texts. Payment varies. Query.

RICHARDS ROSEN PRESS, INC.—29 East 21st St., New York, NY 10010. Ruth C. Rosen, Editor.
Young-adult books, to 40,000 words, on guidance, journalism, theater, social problems. Payment varies.

ROY PUBLISHERS, INC.—30 East 47th St., New York, NY 10021. Hanna Kister, Editor.
General fiction, nonfiction and juveniles, with emphasis on international interests. Pays on royalty basis. Query; no unsolicited manuscripts accepted.

RUTLEDGE BOOKS—25 West 43rd St., New York, NY 10036. Jeanne McClow, Editor-in-Chief.
Unusual adult nonfiction; cookbooks; sports books. Pays on royalty basis. Query with outline.

SAGE BOOKS (Division of *Swallow Press*)–811 West Junior Terrace, Chicago, IL 60613.
Nonfiction on the West. Pays on royalty basis.

ST. MARTIN'S PRESS, INC.–175 Fifth Ave., New York, NY 10010. Marcia Markland, Associate Editor.
Fiction; general nonfiction: history, political science, biography, music; reference books; college textbooks. Pays on royalty basis.

SANTILLANA PUBLISHING COMPANY, INC.–575 Lexington Ave., New York, NY 10022. Sam Laredo, Vice-President, Trade Publications.
Young-adult and juvenile fiction and nonfiction. Pays on royalty basis.

SCHOCKEN BOOKS–200 Madison Ave., New York, NY 10016. Leon King, Editor.
Nonfiction: history, education, sociology, religious thought, Judaica, women's studies. Pays on royalty basis. Query.

CHARLES SCRIBNER'S SONS–597 Fifth Ave., New York, NY 10017. Jacek K. Galazka, Editor.
Fiction, general nonfiction, juveniles. Query.

SCRIMSHAW PRESS–6040 Claremont Ave., Oakland, CA 94618. Frederick Mitchell, Editor.
Nonfiction, usually illustrated. Pays on royalty basis.

THE SEABURY PRESS–815 Second Ave., New York, NY 10017.
Continuum Books: Justus George Lawler, Senior Editor. General-interest books on literature, behavior, education, etc. *Crossroad Books:* Religious books. *Clarion Books:* James C. Giblin, Editor-in-Chief. Juveniles, preschool through young adult. Pays on royalty basis. Query.

SHEED, ANDREWS & McMEEL, INC. (formerly *Sheed and Ward*)–6700 Squibb Rd., Mission, KS 66202. James F. Andrews, Editor-in-Chief.
General fiction and nonfiction; philosophy, theology, psychology, history, with religious emphasis.

SIERRA CLUB BOOKS–530 Bush St., San Francisco, CA 94108.
Books on conservation, environment, natural history, science, alternative technology; guidebooks. Query.

SILVER BURDETT–250 James St., Morristown, NJ 07960. Barbara Thompson Howell, Vice-President and Editor-in-Chief.
Educational books for preschool, elementary, secondary, college and professional readers. Pays on royalty basis or by outright purchase. Query.

SIMON & SCHUSTER–1230 Ave. of the Americas, New York, NY 10020. Michael V. Korda, Editor-in-Chief; Jonathan Dolger, Managing Editor.
General nonfiction; occult, popular science; regional books. Fiction: mysteries, suspense, Gothics, historical romance; mainstream novels. Query. Manuscripts not requested and not addressed to an editor by name will be returned unread. Pays on royalty basis.

STACKPOLE BOOKS–Cameron and Kelker Sts., Harrisburg, PA 17105.
Nonfiction on outdoors, Americana, ecology, crafts and hobbies, health and nutrition, and the future. Pays on royalty basis. Query.

STECK-VAUGHN COMPANY–Box 2028, Austin, TX 78767. Paul C. Craig, Vice-President, Product Development.
Textbooks; educational material. Pays on royalty basis.

STEIN & DAY–Scarborough House, Briarcliff Manor, NY 10510.

General fiction and nonfiction. Pays on royalty basis. Query with summary or outline and sample chapter for nonfiction, with first chapter for fiction. No unsolicited manuscripts accepted.

STERLING PUBLISHING COMPANY—419 Park Ave. South, New York, NY 10016. Burton Hobson, Editorial Director.
How-to, general information, hobby and sports books. Pays on royalty basis or by outright purchase. Query.

SUMMIT BOOKS—Simon and Schuster Bldg., 1230 Ave. of the Americas, New York, NY 10020. Christine Steinmetz, Senior Editor.
General trade fiction and nonfiction. Overstocked; no manuscripts requested until further notice.

SUNSTONE PRESS—Box 2321, Santa Fe, NM 87501.
Southwestern nonfiction; fiction; poetry; craft and cookbooks. Pays on royalty basis. Query.

SWALLOW PRESS—811 West Junior Terrace, Chicago, IL 60613. Durrett Wagner, Editor.
General nonfiction. Pays on royalty basis. Query.

TAB BOOKS—Blue Ridge Summit, PA 17214. Pete Deksnis, Editor.
Nonfiction, 80,000 words, with illustrations: how-to, craft and hobby, automotive, servicing and repair, broadcasting, etc. Pays on royalty basis or by outright purchase. Query.

J. P. TARCHER, INC.—9110 Sunset Blvd., Los Angeles, CA 90069.
General nonfiction: psychology, social science, science, self-help, current biography, medicine, cooking, gardening, California guides. Pays on royalty basis. Query with outline and sample chapter.

TIDEWATER PUBLISHERS—See *Cornell Maritime Press.*

FREDERICK UNGAR PUBLISHING COMPANY, INC.—250 Park Ave. South, New York, NY 10003.
Reference, nonfiction; literary translations and criticism. Pays on royalty basis. Query.

UNION OF AMERICAN HEBREW CONGREGATIONS—838 Fifth Ave., New York, NY 10021. Daniel Syme, Director of Education.
Texts and instructional material, for students and teachers, on Jewish concerns and experiences. Pays on royalty basis. Query with outline and samples.

UNITED CHURCH PRESS—See *Pilgrim Press.*

THE VANGUARD PRESS, INC.—424 Madison Ave., New York, NY 10017. Bernice Woll, Editor. Address Editor, Manuscript Department.
Adult fiction and nonfiction. Juvenile fiction and nonfiction, especially in new fields. Pays on royalty basis. Query with sample chapters.

VAN NOSTRAND REINHOLD COMPANY—450 West 33rd St., New York, NY 10001.
Adult nonfiction. Pays on royalty basis.

THE VIKING PRESS, INC.—625 Madison Ave., New York, NY 10022.
Novels; biography; history, science, sociology. *Studio Books:* Art and travel. *Junior Books:* Older juveniles. *Viking Compass Books, Viking Seafarer Books, Viking Portable Library:* Paperbacks. *Puffin Books:* Juvenile paperbacks. Pays on royalty basis: Query.

HENRY Z. WALCK, INC. (Division of *David McKay Co.*)—750 Third Ave., New York, NY 10017. Alexandra Whitney, Manager.
Juveniles. Pays on royalty basis.

WALKER AND COMPANY—720 Fifth Ave., New York, NY 10019.
Nonfiction; fiction, mystery. Pays on royalty basis. Query with synopsis.

FREDERICK WARNE & COMPANY, INC.—101 Fifth Ave., New York, NY 10003.
Juvenile and young-adult books.

WATSON-GUPTILL PUBLICATIONS—1515 Broadway, New York, NY 10036.
How-to books for artists, art teachers, students and hobbyists. Pays on royalty basis.

FRANKLIN WATTS, INC.—730 Fifth Ave., New York, NY 10019. Jeanne Vestal, Editor-in-Chief.
Juvenile and young-adult fiction on contemporary themes and nonfiction. Query.

WESTERN PUBLISHING COMPANY, INC.—Juvenile Picture-storybook Division, 1220 Mound Ave., Racine, WI 53404. Betty Ren Wright, Managing Editor.
Picture-storybooks, to 800 words; childhood experiences, early learning concepts, mechanical subjects; humor. Novels, from 35,000 words, for preteen and early-teen readers. Pays by outright purchase. Query with synopsis for novels. (Incorporating *Whitman Tell-a-Tale®* books and novels, *Little Golden Books®* and *Golden Books*)

THE WESTMINSTER PRESS—902 Witherspoon Bldg., Philadelphia, PA 19107. Barbara Bates, Children's Book Editor.
Juvenile fiction and nonfiction for 9-year-olds and older. Pays on royalty basis.

WEYBRIGHT AND TALLEY—876 Park Ave., New York, NY 10021. Truman M. Talley, President.
Nonfiction on business, Wall Street and Washington subjects for general public, politics, nature, scientific explorations. Query with outline or table of contents and sample chapter.

ALBERT WHITMAN & COMPANY—560 West Lake St., Chicago, IL 60606. Caroline Rubin, Editor.
Juveniles. Payment varies. Overstocked.

WHITMAN TELL-A-TALE® BOOKS—See *Western Publishing.*

WHITMORE PUBLISHING COMPANY—35 Cricket Terrace, Ardmore, PA 19003. Linda Peacock, Managing Editor.
Nonfiction: education, politics, economics, science, health, psychology, career planning; fiction, poetry on these themes. Pays on royalty basis.

WILDERNESS PRESS—2440 Bancroft Way, Berkeley, CA 94704. Thomas Winnett, Editor.
Guides to western outdoor areas, hiking, etc. Pays on royalty basis. Query.

JOHN WILEY & SONS, INC.—605 Third Ave., New York, NY 10016. Robert B. Polhemus, Publisher, Physical Life Sciences and Engineering; Walter Maythem, Publisher, Social Sciences; Robert C. Douglas, Vice-President and General Manager, College Division.
Technical, scientific and business books. Pays on royalty basis. Query. (Incorporating *Xerox College Publishing*)

WINCHESTER PRESS—205 East 42nd St., New York, NY 10017. Jock Bartlett, Managing Editor.
Nonfiction: how-to; sports, outdoors, conservation. Pays on royalty basis. Query.

WORD BOOKS—4800 West Waco Dr., Waco, TX 76703. Floyd W. Thatcher, Editor.
Religious nonfiction. Pays on royalty basis.

WORKMAN PUBLISHING COMPANY—231 East 51st St., New York, NY 10022. Sally Kovalchick, Editor.
General nonfiction; crafts, gardening, family activities. Pays on royalty basis.

WYDEN BOOKS—Box 151, Ridgefield, CT 06877.
General nonfiction. Pays on royalty basis. Query.

XEROX COLLEGE PUBLISHING—See *John Wiley & Sons, Inc.*

ZONDERVAN PUBLISHING HOUSE—1415 Lake Dr. S.E., Grand Rapids, MI 49506. James E. Ruark, Managing Editor.
Books on Protestant religious subjects, inspirational and devotional themes, psychology; biography, autobiography. Pays on royalty basis.

PAPERBACK BOOK PUBLISHERS

ACE BOOKS—360 Park Ave. South, New York, NY 10010. Address Editorial Dept.
Science fiction, westerns, nurse romances, women's historical novels, gothics, nonfiction, self-help. Query with outline and sample chapters. Pays on royalty basis.

ANCHOR PRESS/DOUBLEDAY—245 Park Ave., New York, NY 10017. Loretta Barrett, Editorial Director.
Adult trade books in sociology, modern life styles and philosophy, psychology, parapsychology, etc., for sophisticated readers. Query.

ARCO BOOKS, INC.—219 Park Ave. South, New York, NY 10003. David Goodnough, Editor.
Nonfiction originals and reprints, from 50,000 words. Pays on royalty basis or by outright purchase.

AVON BOOKS—959 Eighth Ave., New York, NY 10019. Walter W. Meade, Editorial Director.
Modern fiction with commercial slant; educational nonfiction, 60,000 to 200,000 words. Pays on royalty basis. Query.

AWARD BOOKS—See *Charter Books.*

BALLANTINE BOOKS, INC.—201 East 50th St., New York, NY 10022.
General fiction and nonfiction; male-oriented suspense novels. Science fiction-fantasy. Query. No unsolicited manuscripts accepted. Pays on royalty basis.

BANTAM BOOKS, INC.—666 Fifth Ave., New York, NY 10019.
Popular fiction, nonfiction (novels, westerns, cookbooks, romances, etc.). Accepts material through agents primarily. Query. Pays on royalty basis.

BELMONT TOWER BOOKS—Tower Publications, Inc., 2 Park Ave., New York, NY 10016. Peter McCurtin, Editor-in-Chief.
Historical romance, westerns, Gothics, modern novels, series packages. Pays on royalty basis. Query with outline and sample chapter.

BERKLEY PUBLISHING CORPORATION—200 Madison Ave., New York, NY 10016. Page Cuddy, Editor-in-Chief.
Science fiction, mysteries, suspense and espionage novels, general-interest fiction and nonfiction. Payment varies. Query.

CAMELOT BOOKS (Division of *Avon Books*)—959 Eighth Ave., New York, NY 10019. Nancy Coffey, Editor.
Fiction and nonfiction for 8- to 18-year-olds. Payment varies. Query.

CHARTER BOOKS (formerly *Award Books*)—1120 Ave. of the Americas, New York, NY 10036. Sybil Pincus, Senior Editor.

Fiction: adventure, espionage, suspense. Nonfiction: self-help, diet, and health, reference; hobbies, antiques; modern history; and do-it-yourself and how-to books. Pays on royalty basis. Query with outline. Stamped, self-addressed envelope required for return of manuscript.

CHRONICLE BOOKS—870 Market St., San Francisco, CA 94102.
General nonfiction: outdoor adventure, architecture, guide books, illustrated books. Pays on royalty basis.

COLLIER BOOKS—866 Third Ave., New York, NY 10022.
General nonfiction. Pays on royalty basis. Query.

CORNERSTONE LIBRARY, INC.—630 Fifth Ave., New York, NY 10020.
Books on chess, tennis, golf, bridge, etc.; guide books; how-to books. Pays on royalty basis.

DALE BOOKS—Davis Publications, Inc., 229 Park Ave. South, New York, NY 10003. Ted Maass, Director of Publications.
Fiction and nonfiction: puzzles, science-fiction, women's fiction, westerns, mysteries and sports. Reprints.

DAW BOOKS, INC.—1301 Ave. of the Americas, New York, NY 10019. Donald A. Wollheim, Publisher and Editor.
Science fiction and fantasy, 50,000 to 70,000 words. Pays on royalty basis.

DELL BOOKS—One Dag Hammarskjold Plaza, 245 East 47th St., New York, NY 10017. Saul Cohen, Executive Managing Editor.
Fiction and nonfiction. Query. (Incorporating *Laurel Editions, Laurel Leaf Library, Yearling Books, Delta Books*)

DELTA BOOKS—Dell Publishing Co., One Dag Hammarskjold Plaza, 245 East 47th St., New York, NY 10017. Martha M. Kinney, Editor-in-Chief.
Nonfiction of general and academic interest, in history, psychology, science, literature, etc. Query.

FAWCETT WORLD LIBRARY—1515 Broadway, New York, NY 10036. Leona Nevler, Publisher.
Gold Medal Books (Joseph Elder, Editor): Original fiction, nonfiction for mass market. *Fawcett Crest Books* (Arlene Friedman, Editor-in-Chief): Fiction and nonfiction reprints. Pays on royalty basis. Query.

GARDEN WAY PUBLISHING COMPANY—Charlotte, VT 05445. Roger M. Griffith, Editor.
How-to books on gardening, cooking, homesteading, animal husbandry, energy conservation, building and other county crafts. Pays on royalty basis or by outright purchase. Query with outline and sample chapter.

GOLD MEDAL BOOKS—See *Fawcett World Library*.

GROSSET "SPECIALS" (Division of *Grosset & Dunlap, Inc.*)—51 Madison Ave., New York, NY 10010.
Mass-market nonfiction. No unsolicited manuscripts accepted.

HARLEQUIN BOOKS LTD.—240 Duncan Mill Rd., Don Mills, Ont., Canada M3B 1Z4.
Harlequin Romances and *Harlequin Presents:* Contemporary romance novels. Pays on royalty basis.

JOVE BOOKS (Formerly *Pyramid Publications;* division of *Harcourt Brace Jovanovich, Inc.*)—757 Third Ave., New York, NY 10017. Marie R. Reno, Jeanne Glass, Editors.
Fiction: sagas, historical romance, suspense, adventure, contemporary novels, science fiction; general nonfiction. Pays on royalty basis.

LAUREL EDITIONS—Dell Publishing Co., One Dag Hammarskjold Plaza, 245 East 47th St., New York, NY 10017. Chris Kuppig, Senior Editor.
Nonfiction of general and academic interest, in history, psychology, science, literature, philosophy, etc. Query.

LAUREL LEAF LIBRARY—See *Dell Books*.

LEISURE BOOKS—2 Park Ave., New York, NY 10016.
Fiction; nonfiction.

MAJOR BOOKS—21335 Roscoe Blvd., Canoga Park, CA 91304. John Mitchell, Senior Editor.
Popular fiction, mysteries, Gothics, romantic-suspense, espionage, Westerns, science-fiction; nonfiction—how-to, self-help, the occult, inspirationals, cookbooks. Length, 60,000 words. Pays on royalty basis.

MANOR BOOKS—432 Park Ave. South, New York, NY 10016.
Reprints and originals, fiction and nonfiction. Queries only, with outlines and sample chapters. No unsolicited manuscripts. Pays on royalty basis or by outright purchase. Send queries to Editorial Department.

NEW AMERICAN LIBRARY—1301 Ave. of the Americas, New York, NY 10019. Elaine Geiger, Editor-in-Chief.
Signet Books: Commercial fiction, emphasizing romantic melodrama. Nonfiction: self-help, how-to, etc. *Plume Books:* Nonfiction: hobbies, crafts, gardening, outdoor life, etc. *Mentor Books:* Nonfiction originals for high school and college market. *Meridian Books:* Supplementary material for undergraduate college texts. Pays on royalty basis. Query with outline and sample chapters for nonfiction.

NOONDAY PRESS—See *Farrar, Straus & Giroux* (hardcover publisher).

PENGUIN BOOKS, INC.—625 Madison Ave., New York, NY 10022.
Adult nonfiction; no poetry or juveniles. Query; no unsolicited manuscripts accepted.

PINNACLE BOOKS, INC.—One Century Pl., 2029 Century Park East, Los Angeles, CA 90067. Andrew Ettinger, Editor.
General nonfiction; popular, commercial fiction: escape reading, adventure, espionage, historical intrigue and romance. Pays on royalty basis. Query; no unsolicited manuscripts accepted.

PLUME BOOKS—See *New American Library*.

POCKET BOOKS (Division of *Simon & Schuster*)—1230 Ave. of the Americas, New York, NY 10020. Address Editorial Department.
Reprints; some originals (science fiction). Query.

POPULAR LIBRARY, FAWCETT BOOKS GROUP, CBS PUBLICATIONS—600 Third Ave., New York, NY 10016. Patrick O'Connor, Editor-in-Chief.
General fiction, Gothics, westerns, science fiction. Pays on royalty basis. Query.

PUFFIN BOOKS—See *The Viking Press, Inc.* (hardcover publisher).

PYRAMID PUBLICATIONS—See *Jove Books*.

REWARD BOOKS (Subsidiary of *Prentice-Hall, Inc.*)—Englewood Cliffs, NJ 07632. William Costello, Editor-in-Chief.
Nonfiction: self-help, inspiration, the occult, money opportunity, popular health, dieting, beauty, folk remedies, sports, popular psychology. Pays on royalty basis.

ST. ANTHONY MESSENGER PRESS—1615 Republic St., Cincinnati, OH 45210. Jeremy Harrington, O.F.M., Editor.
Catholic nonfiction. Pays on royalty basis.

SALTAIRE PUBLISHING LTD.– P.O. Box 910, Victoria, B.C., Canada V8W 2R9. John Hicks, Managing Editor.
Original paperbacks on outdoor themes, especially how-to books on hunting, fishing, camping, related subjects, regional or national. Pays on royalty basis. Query with sample chapters.

SIGNET BOOKS–See *New American Library.*

TEMPO BOOKS–1120 Ave. of the Americas, New York, NY 10036. Harriet McDougal, Editor-in-Chief.
Adult and young-adult fiction; nonfiction: sports, the occult; puzzles. Pays on royalty basis (by outright purchase for puzzles). Query with outline.

TOWER PUBLICATIONS–See *Belmont Tower Books.*

TROUBADOR PRESS–385 Freemont St., San Francisco, CA 94105. Address Milo Schaaf.
Adult and juvenile nonfiction; coloring books, cookbooks, cut-out and puzzle books, illustrated trade paperbacks. Pays on royalty basis or by outright purchase. Query with outline.

VINTAGE BOOKS–See *Random House, Inc.* (hardcover publisher).

WARNER BOOKS–75 Rockefeller Pl., New York, NY 10019. Bernard Shir-Cliff, Editor-in-Chief.
Fiction: historical romance, contemporary women's fiction. Controversial nonfiction. Pays on royalty basis. Query with sample chapters.

WASHINGTON SQUARE PRESS (Division of *Simon & Schuster, Inc.*)–630 Fifth Ave., New York, NY 10020.
Educational nonfiction and anthologies for high school market and general public. Query.

WILSHIRE BOOK COMPANY–12015 Sherman Rd., North Hollywood, CA 91650. Melvin Powers, Editor.
Specialized nonfiction: inspirational; psychological self-help; feminism; tennis, horseback riding, pet care, etc. Pays on royalty basis. Query with synopsis or outline.

YEARLING BOOKS–See *Dell Books.*

UNIVERSITY PRESSES

University presses generally publish books of a scholarly nature or of specialized interest by authorities in a given field. Many publish only a handful of titles a year. Always query first. Do not send any manuscripts until you have been invited to do so by the editor.

BRIGHAM YOUNG UNIVERSITY PRESS–209 University Press Bldg., Provo, UT 84602.

BROWN UNIVERSITY PRESS–Alumnae Hall, 194 Meeting St., Providence, RI 02912.

BUCKNELL UNIVERSITY PRESS–Lewisburg, PA 17837.

CAMBRIDGE UNIVERSITY PRESS–32 East 57th St., New York, NY 10022.

THE CATHOLIC UNIVERSITY OF AMERICA PRESS–620 Michigan Ave., N.E., Washington, DC 20064.

COLORADO ASSOCIATED UNIVERSITY PRESS–University of Colorado, 1424 15th St., Boulder, CO 80302.

COLUMBIA UNIVERSITY PRESS—562 West 113th St., New York, NY 10025.

CORNELL UNIVERSITY PRESS—124 Roberts Pl., Ithaca, NY 14850.

DUKE UNIVERSITY PRESS—Box 6697, College Station, Durham, NC 27708.

DUQUESNE UNIVERSITY PRESS—101 Administration Bldg., Pittsburgh, PA 15219.

FAIRLEIGH DICKINSON UNIVERSITY PRESS—Rutherford, NJ 07070.

FORDHAM UNIVERSITY PRESS—Box L, Bronx, NY 10458.

GEORGIA STATE UNIVERSITY, SCHOOL OF BUSINESS ADMINISTRATION, PUBLISHING SERVICES DIVISION—University Plaza, Atlanta, GA 30303.

HARVARD UNIVERSITY PRESS—79 Garden St., Cambridge, MA 02138.

HOWARD UNIVERSITY PRESS—2935 Upton St. N.W., Washington, DC 20008.

INDIANA UNIVERSITY PRESS—10th and Morton Sts., Bloomington, IN 47401.

IOWA STATE UNIVERSITY PRESS—Ames, IA 50010.

THE JOHNS HOPKINS UNIVERSITY PRESS—Baltimore, MD 21218.

KENT STATE UNIVERSITY PRESS—Kent, OH 44242.

LOUISIANA STATE UNIVERSITY PRESS—Baton Rouge, LA 70803.

LOYOLA UNIVERSITY PRESS—3441 North Ashland Ave., Chicago, IL 60657.

MEMPHIS STATE UNIVERSITY PRESS—Memphis, TN 38152.

THE M.I.T. PRESS—28 Carleton St., Cambridge, MA 02142.

MICHIGAN STATE UNIVERSITY PRESS—1405 South Harrison Rd., East Lansing, MI 48824.

NEW YORK UNIVERSITY PRESS—21 West 4th St., New York, NY 10003.

OHIO STATE UNIVERSITY PRESS—Hitchcock Hall, Rm. 316, 2070 Neil Ave., Columbus, OH 43210.

OHIO UNIVERSITY PRESS—Administration Annex, Athens, OH 45701.

OREGON STATE UNIVERSITY PRESS—Box 689, Corvallis, OR 97331.

OXFORD UNIVERSITY PRESS—200 Madison Ave., New York, NY 10016.

THE PENNSYLVANIA STATE UNIVERSITY PRESS—215 Wagner Bldg., University Park, PA 16802.

PRINCETON UNIVERSITY PRESS—Princeton, NJ 08540.

RUTGERS UNIVERSITY PRESS—30 College Ave., New Brunswick, NJ 08903.

ST. JOHN'S UNIVERSITY PRESS—Grand Central and Utopia Parkways, Jamaica, NY 11439.

SOUTHERN ILLINOIS UNIVERSITY PRESS—Box 3697, Carbondale, IL 62901.

SOUTHERN METHODIST UNIVERSITY PRESS—Dallas, TX 75275.

STANFORD UNIVERSITY PRESS—Stanford, CA 94305.

STATE UNIVERSITY OF NEW YORK PRESS—99 Washington Ave., Albany, NY 12246.

SYRACUSE UNIVERSITY PRESS—1011 East Water St., Syracuse, NY 13210.

TEMPLE UNIVERSITY PRESS—Philadelphia, PA 19122.

UNIVERSITY OF ALABAMA PRESS—Drawer 2877, University, AL 35486.

UNIVERSITY OF ARIZONA PRESS—Box 3398, College Station, Tucson, AZ 85722.

UNIVERSITY OF CALIFORNIA PRESS—2223 Fulton St., Berkeley, CA 94720.

UNIVERSITY OF CHICAGO PRESS—5801 Ellis Ave., Chicago, IL 60637.

UNIVERSITY OF GEORGIA PRESS—Athens, GA 30601.

UNIVERSITY OF ILLINOIS PRESS—Urbana, IL 61801.

UNIVERSITY OF IOWA PRESS—Iowa City, IA 52242.

UNIVERSITY OF MASSACHUSETTS PRESS—Munson Hall, Amherst, MA 01002.

UNIVERSITY OF MICHIGAN PRESS—Ann Arbor, MI 48106.

UNIVERSITY OF MINNESOTA PRESS—2037 University Ave., S.E., Minneapolis, MN 55455.

UNIVERSITY OF MISSOURI PRESS—107 Swallow Hall, Columbia, MO 65201.

UNIVERSITY OF NEBRASKA PRESS—901 North 17th St., Lincoln, NE 68588.

UNIVERSITY OF NEW MEXICO PRESS—Albuquerque, NM 87131.

UNIVERSITY OF NORTH CAROLINA PRESS—Box 2288, Chapel Hill, NC 27515.

UNIVERSITY OF NOTRE DAME PRESS—Notre Dame, IN 46556.

UNIVERSITY OF OKLAHOMA PRESS—1005 Asp Ave., Norman, OK 73019.

UNIVERSITY OF PENNSYLVANIA PRESS—3933 Walnut St., Philadelphia, PA 19174.

UNIVERSITY OF PITTSBURGH PRESS—127 North Bellefield Ave., Pittsburgh, PA 15260.

UNIVERSITY OF SOUTH CAROLINA PRESS—USC Campus, Columbia, SC 29208.

UNIVERSITY OF TENNESSEE PRESS—Communications Bldg., Knoxville, TN 37916.

UNIVERSITY OF TEXAS PRESS—Box 7819, University Station, Austin, TX 78712.

UNIVERSITY OF UTAH PRESS—Bldg. 513, Salt Lake City, UT 84112.

UNIVERSITY OF WASHINGTON PRESS—Seattle, WA 98195.

UNIVERSITY OF WISCONSIN PRESS—Box 1379, Madison, WI 53701.

THE UNIVERSITY PRESS OF HAWAII—2840 Kolowalu St., Honolulu, HI 96822.

THE UNIVERSITY PRESS OF KANSAS—366 Watson Library, Lawrence, KS 66045.

THE UNIVERSITY PRESS OF KENTUCKY—Lafferty Hall, Lexington, KY 40506.

UNIVERSITY PRESS OF MISSISSIPPI—3825 Ridgewood Rd., Jackson, MS 39211.

THE UNIVERSITY PRESS OF NEW ENGLAND—Box 979, Hanover, NH 03755.

THE UNIVERSITY PRESS OF VIRGINIA—Box 3608, University Sta., Charlottesville, VA 22903.

THE UNIVERSITY PRESS OF WASHINGTON, D.C.—University Press Bldg., Dellbrook Campus, C.A.S., Riverton, VA 22651.

THE UNIVERSITY PRESSES OF FLORIDA—15 N.W. 15th St., Gainesville, FL 32601.

WAYNE STATE UNIVERSITY PRESS—5980 Cass, Detroit, MI 48202.

WESLEYAN UNIVERSITY PRESS—55 High Street., Middletown, CT 06457.

YALE UNIVERSITY PRESS—302 Temple St., New Haven, CT 06511.

SYNDICATES

Syndicates are business organizations that publish nothing themselves, but buy material from writers, artists, etc., to sell to newspapers all over the country and the world. Authors are paid a percentage of the gross proceeds or, in some cases, an outright fee.

Features by people well known in their fields, of course, have the best chance of being syndicated. In general, syndicates want columns that have been popular in a local newspaper, perhaps, or magazine. Since most syndicated fiction has been published previously in magazines or books, beginning fiction writers should try to sell their stories to magazines before submitting them to syndicates.

The following list includes the major syndicates in the market for free-lance material. For a complete list, see the *Editor & Publisher Annual Directory of Snydicated Features,* available from *Editor & Publisher,* 850 Third Ave., New York, NY 10022. It is always best to query syndicates before sending manuscripts—their needs change frequently.

B P SINGER FEATURES, INC.–3164 West Tyler Ave., Anaheim, CA 92801. Jane Sherrod, Editor.

Fiction, all lengths, previously published and on universal themes; biography and women's interest material, all lengths. Illustrated columns and short humor. Books for foreign reprint. Color transparencies, cartoons, comic strips. Pays on percentage basis or by outright purchase.

CONTEMPORARY FEATURES SYNDICATE–P.O. Box 1258, Jackson, TN 38301. Lloyd Russell, Editor.

Articles, 1,000 to 3,000 words, on human-interest topics: how-to, back-to-nature, etc. Pays $25 to $50, on acceptance.

ENTERPRISE SCIENCE NEWS–Newspaper Enterprise Assn., 230 Park Ave., New York, 10017. David Hendin, Editor.

Science feature material, 800 to 1,000 words, with photos, by experienced science and medical writers. Pays from $75, on publication.

FIELD NEWSPAPER SYNDICATE (formerly *Publishers-Hall Syndicate*)–401 North Wabash Ave., Chicago, IL 60611. Richard Sherry, President; Christian Chenoweth, Executive Editor.

Columns, comic strips, panel cartoons, serials.

GLOBAL COMMUNICATIONS–303 Fifth Ave., Suite 1306, New York, NY 10016. Timothy Green Beckley, President.

Fiction and nonfiction for weekly tabloids and men's magazines; interviews and personality pieces for U.S. and overseas markets; well-researched pieces on psychic experiences and U.F.O.s. Pays to $1,500, on publication.

THE HOLLYWOOD INFORMER SYNDICATE–Box 49957, Los Angeles, CA 90049. John Austin, Director.

Feature material, 1,000 to 1,500 words, on TV and motion picture personalities. Story ideas for 3-part serials on major personalities. Pays on percentage basis for features, negotiated rates for ideas, on acceptance.

KING FEATURES SYNDICATE–235 East 45th St., New York, NY 10077. Allan Priaulx, Executive Editor.

Columns, comics, features of all types, photos. Most contributors are on contract. Pays varying rates.

LOS ANGELES TIMES SYNDICATE–Times Mirror Square, Los Angeles, CA 90053. Thomas B. Dorsey, Editor.

Query; no unsolicited manuscripts accepted.

NATIONAL CATHOLIC NEWS SERVICE–1312 Massachusetts Ave. N.W., Washington,

DC 20005. Thomas N. Lorsung, Managing Editor; Angela Schreiber, Feature Editor; Robert A. Strawn, Photo Editor.
Services Catholic diocesan weekly newspapers. Articles on Catholic church and Catholic issues; photos. Pays to 5¢ a word, after publication.

NEWSPAPER ENTERPRISE ASSOCIATION, INC.—230 Park Ave., New York, NY 10017. Robert Cochnar, Editorial Director.
Current news features. Limited free-lance market.

NORTH AMERICAN NEWSPAPER ALLIANCE—200 Park Ave., New York, NY 10017. Sheldon Engelmayer, Editor.
General-interest news and feature stories, to 750 words. Special Sunday articles, to 1,500 words. Series, 2 to 5 parts. Pays from $25, immediately after distribution.

THE REGISTER AND TRIBUNE SYNDICATE—715 Locust St., Des Moines, IA 50304. Dennis R. Allen, President.
Ideas for regular newspaper columns, comic strips and any continuing features. Pays on percentage basis. Query with outline.

RELIGIOUS NEWS SERVICE—43 West 57th St., New York, NY 10019. Lillian R. Block, Managing Editor.
Religious news stories and features. Photos on religious subjects. Pays 2¢ a word, from $5 for photos, on acceptance.

TRANSWORLD FEATURE SYNDICATE, INC.—141 East 44th St., New York, NY 10077. Mary Taylor Schilling, International Manager; Elsa H. Zion, U.S. Manager.
Feature material for overseas and North American markets. Query.

UNITED FEATURE SYNDICATE—200 Park Ave., New York, NY 10017. Sidney Goldberg, Managing Editor.
Comics, columns, occasional special series of articles. Pays on percentage basis.

UNIVERSAL TRADE PRESS SYNDICATE—85 South St., New York, NY 10038. Paul S. Gruberg, Director.
Services trade papers. Spot news and feature articles. Pays on percentage basis. Query with 50-word synopsis.

THE WASHINGTON STAR SYNDICATE—444 Madison Ave., New York, NY 10022. Harry Elmlark, Editor.
Features. Limited free-lance market.

WOMENS' NEWS SERVICE—200 Park Ave., New York, NY 10017. Sid Goldberg, Editor.
Trendy articles, 300 to 700 words, with photos, on style or leisure; interviews with newsmakers; new features of national interest. Pays $25 to $50, after acceptance.

LITERARY PRIZE OFFERS, GRANTS AND FELLOWSHIPS

Each year many important prize contests are open to free-lance writers. Some of these are conducted regularly. Others are one-time competitions, and writers should watch the newspapers and magazines, including "Prize Offers and Awards" column in *The Writer*, for announcements of these special contests.

The short summaries given below are intended merely as guides. Closing dates, requirements, and rules are tentative. No manuscript should be submitted to any competition unless the writer has first checked with the Contest Editor and received complete information about a particular contest.

Also included here are a number of fellowships and grants available to free-lance writers. Authors should write to the addresses given for complete details for making application.

Send stamped, self-addressed envelope with all requests for contest rules and application forms.

ACADEMY OF AMERICAN POETS–1078 Madison Ave., New York, NY 10028.
Offers the Walt Whitman Award of $1,000 and publication of a book of poetry by a poet who has not had a book of poems published. Closes in November.

THE ATLANTIC–8 Arlington St., Boston, MA 02116.
Offers continuing awards for "*Atlantic* Firsts," outstanding stories by new writers, 2,000 to 10,000 words. These stories are purchased at the magazine's top rates, and judged at the end of the year for a first prize of $750 and a second prize of $250.

CAROLINA QUARTERLY–P.O. Box 1117, Chapel Hill, NC 27514.
Annual Fiction and Poetry Contests, open to writers who have not had a book published in the field of entry. Closes in February.

COLORADO QUARTERLY–Hellems 134, University of Colorado, Boulder, CO 80309.
Offers the Colorado Quarterly Award of $1,000 for an unpublished, 40,000-word fiction or nonfiction manuscript. Closes in December.

COLUMBIA TRANSLATION CENTER–307A Mathematics, Columbia University, New York, NY 10027.
Offers one-year fellowships of $10,000 to young American writers for the study of difficult or neglected language. No closing date.

COMMUNITY CHILDREN'S THEATRE OF KANSAS CITY–c/o Mrs. Thomas Woodbury, 1015 West 55th St., Kansas City, MO 64114.
Playwriting for Children Award of $500 for a children's play. Closes in January.

COUNCIL ON INTERRACIAL BOOKS FOR CHILDREN–1841 Broadway, New York, NY 10023.
Offers five prizes of $500 each for children's book manuscripts by previously unpublished African American, Chicano, Puerto Rican, American Indian and Asian American writers. Closes in December.

CREATIVE ARTISTS PUBLIC SERVICE PROGRAM–250 West 57th St., New York, NY 10019.
Gives fellowships ranging from $3,500 to $10,000 to creative writers who are residents of New York State. Deadline for applications is in June.

E.P. DUTTON & CO., INC.–201 Park Ave. South, New York, NY 10003.
Offers the Dutton Man in His Environment Book Award for a full-length nonfiction work dealing with the past, present or future of man in his environment. The award is a $10,000 advance against royalties. Closes in December.
Also offers the Dutton Animal Book Award for an adult fiction or nonfiction book relating to animals. The award is a $15,000 advance against royalties. Closes in December.

EUGENE V. DEBS FOUNDATION–P.O. Box 843, Terre Haute, IN 47808.
Offers the Edwin Markham Poetry Prize of $500 for a poem on a theme of social protest. Closes in April.

HARPER & ROW PUBLISHERS–10 East 53rd St., New York, NY 10022.
Offers the Harper-Saxton Fellowship to aid talented new writers. The fellowship consists of $7,500, of which $5,000 is an advance against royalties, and $2,500 is an outright grant. No closing date.

HOUGHTON MIFFLIN CO.–2 Park St., Boston, MA 02107.
Offers the Houghton Mifflin Literary Fellowships to help promising authors who need financial assistance to complete literary projects in fiction and nonfiction. The

award is $10,000, of which $7,500 is an advance against royalties, and $2,500 is an outright grant. No closing date.

ILLINOIS ARTS COUNCIL–111 North Wabash, Chicago, IL 60602.
Offers Project Completion Grants of up to $500 for Illinois creative artists.

IOWA SHORT FICTION AWARD–English–Philosophy Bldg., The University of Iowa, Iowa City, IA 52240.
Offers $1,000 plus publication for a book-length collection of short fiction by a writer who has not published a volume of fiction. Opens in August and closes at the end of September.

JACKSONVILLE UNIVERSITY–College of Fine Arts, Jacksonville University, Jacksonville, FL 32211.
Annual Playwriting Contest is conducted for full-length, previously unproduced plays. A prize of $2,000 is awarded, and the winning play is produced. Closes in January.

THE MACDOWELL COLONY–Peterborough, NH 03458.
Offers fellowships for room and board for one to four months to provide professionals in the arts freedom to concentrate upon creative work. Apply four months in advance.

MADEMOISELLE MAGAZINE–350 Madison Ave., New York, NY 10017.
Conducts College Writing Competitions in Fiction and Poetry, open to college undergraduates. Cash prizes and publication in the magazine are awarded to the winning works. Contests usually close in January.

MASSACHUSETTS ARTS AND HUMANITIES FOUNDATION–14 Beacon, Boston, MA 02108.
Offers $3,500 Artists Fellowships to Massachusetts writers, in the categories of poetry, fiction and drama. Closes in March.

NATIONAL ENDOWMENT FOR THE ARTS–Literature Program, Washington, DC 20506.
Offers fellowships for published writers of exceptional talent to enable them to advance their careers. Guidelines available in summer; applications taken in fall.

NEW ENGLAND THEATRE CONFERENCE–50 Exchange St., Waltham, MA 02154.
Offers the John Gassner Memorial Playwriting Awards of $200 and $100 for unpublished, unproduced one-act plays. Open to New England playwrights. Closes in April.

NEW YORK POETRY FORUM–c/o Dorothea Neale, Director, 3064 Albany Crescent, Apt. 54, Bronx, NY 10463.
Offers annual poetry contests with awards totaling $550. Closes in November.

O'NEILL FOUNDATION AWARDS–O'Neill Theatre Center, 1860 Broadway, New York, NY 10023.
Stipend of $150, plus production of winning plays at the annual National Playwrights Conference in Waterford, CT. Open to unproduced plays only. Opens in September and closes in December.

OPEN CIRCLE THEATRE–Goucher College, Towson, MD 21204.
Playwrights Prize of $200 and production for an original, unproduced full-length play. Half the parts should be for women. Closes in December.

PARIS REVIEW–541 East 72nd St., New York, NY 10021.
Offers the Aga Khan Fiction Prize of $500 for an outstanding piece of fiction. Closes in May.

POETRY SOCIETY OF AMERICA–15 Gramercy Park, New York, NY 10003.
Offers a number of awards for unpublished poems in various forms: John Masefield

Memorial Award ($500) for a narrative poem in any form to 200 lines; Celia B. Wagner Memorial Award ($250) for the best poem worthy of the tradition of the art; Elias Lieberman Student Poetry Award ($100) for a poem by a high school or preparatory school student. Contests close in December.

REDBOOK—230 Park Ave., New York, NY 10017.
Offers the annual Young Writers' Contest, which carries an award of $500 plus publication for a short story by a writer 18 to 28 years of age. In addition *Redbook* buys the winning story for $1,000 and publishes it. Closes in December.

MARY ROBERTS RINEHART FOUNDATION—Room 504, 516 Fifth Ave., New York, NY 10036.
Offers grants-in-aid to provide financial assistance to help creative writers complete work definitely projected. No closing date.

SAN FRANCISCO FOUNDATION—425 California St., Rm. 1602, San Francisco, CA 94104.
Offers the Phelan Award of $2,000 for an unpublished work by a California native, ages 20 to 35, and the Jackson Award of $2,000, which is a grant-in-aid to a Northern California or Nevada resident. Closes in January.

SEVENTEEN—850 Third Ave., New York, NY 10022.
Offers prizes of up to $500 for short stories by teen-agers. Closes in July.

SOUTHWEST THEATRE CONFERENCE—c/o Dr. David Rush, Dept. of Drama, Southwest Texas State University, San Marcos, TX 78666.
Offers a cash award of $1,000 for a new, previously unproduced play by a present or former resident of the Southwest. Closes in August.

SYRACUSE UNIVERSITY—Syracuse University Press, 1011 East Water St., Syracuse, NY 13210.
Offers the John Ben Snow Prize for an unpublished, book-length manuscript on New York State. An award of $1,000 as an advance against royalties is given, plus publication. Closes in December.

THEATRE AMERICANA—Box 245, Altadena, CA 91001.
Offers the C. Brooks Fry Award of $300 for the best full-length play of those chosen for production during the season. Closes in April.

UNICO MAGAZINE—Unico National, 72 Burroughs Pl., Bloomfield, NJ 07003.
Offers seven literary awards totaling $3,000 for original, unpublished short stories and articles by Italian-American writers between the ages of 18 and 35. Closes in June.

UNIVERSITY OF CHICAGO THEATRE—5706 South University Ave., Chicago, IL 60637.
Offers the Sergel Drama Prize for an original, unproduced play. Award consists of $1,500 and production. Closes in July.

UNIVERSITY OF SOUTH ALABAMA—307 University Blvd., Mobile, AL 36688.
Playwright's Theatre Project offers a $500 prize and production by Theatre USA for an original, unproduced play with a small cast. Closes in January.

VIRGINIA QUARTERLY REVIEW—One West Range, Charlottesville, VA 22903.
Offers Emily Clark Balch Awards of $500 each to the best short story and poem published in the magazine during the calendar year. Manuscripts first accepted for publication and purchased at regular rates, then eligible for awards.

WAGNER COLLEGE—Staten Island, NY 10301.
Offers the Stanley Drama Award of $800 for an original full-length play or musical that has not been professionally produced or published. Recommendation by a teacher, critic or playwright is required. Closes in June.

WILMETTE CHILDREN'S THEATRE–1200 Wilmette Ave., Wilmette, IL 60091.
Sponsors annual playwriting contest for plays for children. Two prizes ($300 and $200) plus production are awarded annually. Closes in May.

YALE UNIVERSITY PRESS–Box 92A, Yale Station, New Haven, CT 06520.
Offers the Yale Series of Younger Poets Award, consisting of publication for a book-length poetry manuscript. Open to American writers under 40 who have not had a volume of verse published. Closes in February. Entry fee, $5.00.

YANKEE–Dublin, NH 03444. Deborah Stone, Fiction Editor.
Offers a prize of $600 for the best short story published in the magazine during the year. Closes in February.

ORGANIZATIONS FOR WRITERS

AMERICAN MEDICAL WRITERS ASSOCIATION
5272 River Rd., Suite 290
Bethesda, MD 20016
Lillian A. Sablack, *Executive Secretary*
The American Medical Writers Association is an international society whose members are engaged in communication about medicine and its applied professions, in all media. One of the association's main objectives is to offer guidance in the art and techniques of medical communication and to develop courses and workshops for these purposes. The association also publishes an official journal, *Medical Communications,* a national *News-letter,* and a membership directory.

Any person actively interested in or professionally associated with any medium of medical communication is eligible for membership. The annual dues for Active-Members are $30.00. Student Member dues are $10.00 annually.

AMERICAN SOCIETY OF JOURNALISTS AND AUTHORS
123 West 43rd St.
New York, NY 10036
Holly Redell, *Administrative Secretary*
The American Society of Journalists and Authors (formerly the Society of Magazine Writers) attempts to secure for the free lancer a respected place in American letters, and has over 450 members, who meet exacting standards of achievement in nonfiction writing. It has established a recommended rate schedule and a code of ethics and good practices for writers and editors. Other services for members include: monthly news-letter; monthly dinner meetings with speakers; Dial-a-Writer Referral Service; all-day workshops and craft sessions.

Membership is open to qualified professional free-lance writers of nonfiction; qualifications of applicants are judged by the Membership Committee. Initiation fee is $25 and annual dues range from $45 to $60, depending upon location.

AMERICAN TRANSLATORS ASSOCIATION
Box 129
Croton-on-Hudson,
NY 10520
Rosemary Malia, *Staff Administrator*
American Translators Association is a professional society concerned with the interests of practicing translators. It serves as a forum and clearing house to advance the standards of the profession and to promote the intellectual and material interests of translators and interpreters in the United States. Its publications contain material useful to professionals and to aspirants for a career as translators.

Membership is open to any person actively engaged in translating, interpreting, or professionally related work *(Active Member),* or to any person or organization interested in the objectives of the Association *(Associate Member)*. Dues for individuals are $20 annually.

THE AUTHORS LEAGUE OF AMERICA, INC.
(Authors Guild and Dramatists Guild)
234 West 44th St.
New York, NY 10036

The Authors League of America is a national organization of over 7,500 authors and dramatists, representing them on matters of joint concern, such as copyright, taxes, and freedom of expression. Since reorganization in 1964, an author or dramatist automatically becomes a member of the League upon joining The Authors Guild, Inc., or The Dramatists Guild, Inc., which are themselves corporate members of the League, but are concerned with the protection and promotion of the professional interest of their respective memberships, including contract terms.

Who is eligible to join The Authors Guild? By resolution of The Authors Guild Council, any author who shall have had a book published by a reputable American publisher within seven years prior to his application; or any author who shall have had three works, fiction or nonfiction, published by a magazine or magazines of general circulation, either national or local, within eighteen months prior to his application; or any author whose professional standing, in the opinion of the Membership Committee, shall entitle him to membership whether or not he shall have had work published as defined above, shall be eligible to join The Authors Guild as an *active* member with voting rights.

The Authors Guild Council has also provided that the Membership Committee may give permission to an author with work in progress but not yet meeting the specifications for active membership to enroll as an *associate* member with all rights except voting rights. The circumstances of such permissions are left to the discretion of the Membership Committee. Many authors become associate members when they are offered a contract by a publisher for their first book.

Both active and associate members pay annual dues of $35.

THE DRAMATISTS GUILD, INC.
234 West 44th St.
New York, NY 10036
Patricia Prince, *Administrative Secretary*

The Dramatists Guild exists to protect and promote the professional interests of authors of dramatic and dramatico-musical works, to protect their rights in such works, and to improve the conditions under which their works are created and produced. It also has as its purpose to formulate types of production contracts with respect to dramatic and dramatico-musical works.

Anyone who has written one full-length play may apply to the Dramatists Guild for Associate Membership, but the membership committee must vote upon the application. Associate membership dues are $20 for the first year. Payment of Dramatists Guild dues covers membership in The Authors League of America, and Dramatists Guild members automatically become members of The Authors League.

MYSTERY WRITERS OF AMERICA, INC.
105 East 19th St.
New York, NY 10003
Gloria Amoury, *Executive Secretary*

Mystery Writers of America, Inc., exists for the purpose of raising the prestige of mystery and detective writing, and of defending the rights and increasing the income of all writers in the field of mystery, detection, and fact crime.

There are five chapters of the MWA in the United States: New York, New England, Midwest, Northern California and Southern California, and an At Large membership for those living in the United States but not conveniently near one of the chapters. As of 1977, membership totaled approximately 800.

There are four classifications of membership in MWA: 1) *Active*—for anyone who has made a single sale in the field of mystery, suspense, or crime writing (book, magazine, newspaper, motion picture, radio, television). Only *Active* members may vote or hold office. 2) *Associate*—for non-writers who are allied to the mystery field—editors, publishers, critics, literary agents, motion picture, radio or television producers. 3) *Corresponding*—for writers living outside the United States. *Corresponding* members do not need to be American citizens. 4) *Affiliate*—for new writers who have not as yet made a sale, or non-writers who are mystery enthusiasts.

Annual dues for *Active* members are $30; for *Associate* members, $35; for *Corresponding* members, $10; and for *Affiliate* members, $35.

NATIONAL ASSOCIATION OF SCIENCE WRITERS, INC.
Box H
Sea Cliff, NY 11579
Rosemary Arctander, *Administrative Secretary*

The National Association of Science Writers exists to "foster the dissemination of accurate information regarding science through all media normally devoted to informing the public," according to a statement by its founders, and the association conducts a varied program to increase the flow of news from scientists, to improve the quality of its presentation, and to communicate its meaning and importance to the reading public.

The NASW sponsors briefings and meetings for its members with newsworthy scientists, offers a job placement service, and maintains a Free Lance Committee which deals with the special problems of members who free lance, and also publishes a guidebook of free-lance procedures and a directory of members who are available for free-lance assignments.

Anyone who is actively engaged in the dissemination of science information, and has two years or more of experience in this field, is eligible to apply for membership. Active members must be principally engaged in reporting science through newspapers, magazines, television, or other media that reach the public directly. Associate members report science through limited-circulation publications, and other special media. Annual membership dues are $35.

P.E.N. AMERICAN CENTER
156 Fifth Ave.
New York, NY 10010
Mel Mendelssohn, *Executive Secretary*

P.E.N. American Center is an independent association of writers—poets, playwrights, essayists, editors and novelists—that promotes and maintains intellectual cooperation among men and women of letters in the United States and abroad in the interest of literature, exchange of ideas, freedom of expression, and good will.

The P.E.N. American Center sponsors literary symposiums, panels, and workshops; grants literary prizes; provides services and aid for imprisoned writers; operates an extensive program for translators, including conferences and prizes, and publishes a directory of grants and awards available to writers.

The criteria for membership are the publication of two books of literary merit in the United States, and nomination by a P.E.N. member. There are three classifications for dues, although no special privileges go with the higher amounts, which simply constitute contributions to P.E.N. *Regular:* $20 per year; *Contributing:* $35 per year; *Sustaining:* $50 and up per year.

THE POETRY SOCIETY OF AMERICA
15 Gramercy Park
New York, NY 10003
Charles A. Wagner, *Executive Secretary*

The purpose of The Poetry Society of America is to secure fuller recognition for poetry, to kindle a fuller and more intelligent appreciation of poetry, especially of the work of living American poets, and to encourage and foster American poetry and aid and assist American poets.

Members of the Society are elected by the Executive Board. Persons in sympathy with the general purposes of the Society, including poets and students and lovers of poetry, are eligible for membership. Members are divided into three classes: *Members, Associate* members, and *Honorary* members, all of whom are qualified to vote in the elections of officers and of members of the Executive Board or upon a proposed amendment to the Constitution of the Society.

To qualify as *Members,* applicants must submit five short poems, published or unpublished. Poets of standing qualify for membership without the need to submit work. *Associate* membership includes critics, educators, librarians, teachers of English, etc. All such individuals qualify automatically. *Honorary* membership is strictly limited to outstanding poets by invitation of the Executive Board.

Dues for all classes of membership are the same—$18 annually.

SCIENCE FICTION WRITERS OF AMERICA
Peter D. Pautz, *Executive Secretary*
68 Countryside Apts.
Hackettstown, NJ 07840

The purpose of the Science Fiction Writers of America, a professional organization of science-fiction writers whose works have been published in the United States, is to foster and further the interests of writers of science fiction and fantasy.

The Science Fiction Writers of America presents the Nebula Awards annually for excellence in the field, and publishes the *Bulletin* and *Forum* for its members.

Any writer who has had a work of science fiction published, performed or broadcast is eligible for membership in the Science Fiction Writers of America, either as an active or associate member. For membership information and applications, writers should apply to the Membership Chairman at the above address. Dues are $20.00 per year, plus $12.50 installation fee for new members.

SOCIETY OF AMERICAN TRAVEL WRITERS
1120 Connecticut Ave., Suite 940
Washington, DC 20036
Ken Fischer, *Administrative Coordinator*

The Society of American Travel Writers is a professional association of writers, photographers, editors, broadcasters, and public relations representatives with an ultimate aim to serve the traveling public. Through magazine and newspaper articles, travel books and guides, and radio and television programs, its members strive to provide travelers with accurate reports on destinations, facilities and services.

Membership in the Society of American Travel Writers is by invitation of the Board of Directors. Active Membership is limited to salaried travel editors, writers, broadcasters, or photographers; and to those who are employed as free lancers in any of the above areas and with a sufficient steady volume of published or distributed work about travel to satisfy the Board of Directors. Associate Membership is open to persons regularly engaged in public relations within the travel industry. Initiation fee for Active members is $50, for Associate members, $100. Annual dues for Active members are $50, for Associate members, $90.

SOCIETY OF CHILDREN'S BOOK WRITERS
P.O. Box 296
Los Angeles, CA 90066
Lin Oliver, *Executive Director*

The Society of Children's Book Writers is a national organization of authors, editors, publishers, illustrators, librarians, educators and agents, that offers a variety of services to people who write for or share an interest in children's literature.

The functions of the Society of Children's Book Writers are (1) to serve as a network for the exchange of knowledge—providing, through its publications, market, workshop, contest, grant, and scholarship information; (2) to serve as a voice for its membership, aiding writers of children's books to effect necessary changes within the fields; (3) to stimulate, through sponsorship of conferences, workshops and awards, creation of the finest books for young people.

Full memberships are open to those who have had at least one children's book or story published within the last six years. Associate memberships are open to all those with an interest in children's literature, whether or not they have published. Yearly dues are $25 for both full and associate members.

SOCIETY FOR TECHNICAL COMMUNICATION
1010 Vermont Ave., N.W.
Washington, DC 20005
Curtis T. Youngblood, *Executive Director*

The Society for Technical Communication is a professional organization dedicated to the advancement of the theory and practice of technical communication in all media. The membership represents virtually every discipline associated with technical communication, including technical writers and editors, publishers, artists and draftsmen, researchers, educators, and audio-visual specialists. There are about 50 chapters in the United States and Canada.

There are four classifications of membership: *Senior Member, Member, Affiliate Member,* and *Student Member.* Each grade requires certain experiences in some phase of technical communication.

Annual dues are $20 (Student Members, $10).

WESTERN WRITERS OF AMERICA, INC.
1050 West D Street
North Platte, Nebraska 69101
Nellie Yost, *Secretary-Treasurer*

Western Writers of America, Inc., is a non-profit organization of professional writers of fiction and nonfiction pertaining to the traditions, legends, development and history of the American West. Its chief purpose is to promote a more widespread distribution, readership and appreciation of the literature of the West.

Awards of merit—WWA Spur Awards—are given each year to the authors of the best Western material in five categories published during the past year.

There are two types of membership: *Active* and *Associate.* To be eligible for an *Active* membership, a writer must have either three Western books published, or twenty-five Western short stories or articles sold and published, or have credit for twenty original Western teleplays or five original Western screenplays actually produced and presented. Only active members can hold office or vote for officials or changes in the constitution. *Associate* membership is open to writers with one published Western book or five magazine stories or articles. *Associate* membership may also be granted to other persons active in the field of Western literature, such as editors, publishers, literary agents, literary critics, and motion picture and television producers and directors. Dues are $25 a year.

WRITERS GUILD OF AMERICA, EAST, INC.
22 West 48th St.
New York, NY 10036
Leonard Wasser, *Executive Director*

The Writers Guild of America (East and West) represents writers in the fields of radio, television, and motion pictures. For jurisdictional purposes, there are two separate corporations—Writers Guild of America, East, Inc., and Writers Guild of America, West, Inc. (see below). However, in actual operations, as far as contracts, dues, membership, etc., are concerned, the two corporations function together to create a national organization.

The purpose of the Guild is to promote and protect the professional interest of all creators and adaptors of literary, dramatic, and musical material in the radio, television, and motion picture industries, and to represent its members for the purpose of collective bargaining.

In order to qualify for membership, a writer must be presently employed in one of the three fields or have had material produced in one of these three fields within the past two years.

The basic dues are $12.50 a quarter. In addition there are quarterly dues based on a percentage of the writer's earnings in any of these fields over which the Guild has jurisdiction. The initiation fee is $400 ($500 as of September 1978).

The Writers Guild has basic agreements with the producers and employers in all of these fields covering free lance writers and also, in some instances, staff writers.

WRITERS GUILD OF AMERICA, WEST, INC.
8955 Beverly Blvd.
Los Angeles, California 90048
Michael H. Franklin, *Executive Director*

The Writers Guild of America, West, Inc., represents all screen, television and radio writers in Hollywood (some 4,200 of them) with respect to their contractual relationship with producers, agents and their fellow writers.

The writer's remuneration, rights, and working conditions are all of concern to the Guild, which seeks always to spell them out by legal agreement, and also to further the writer's general ascendancy in the industry. Contracts are held by the Guild with practically every producer in Hollywood in all three media.

For this service the writer pays to the Guild $40 annual basic dues and 1% of his earnings.

Entrance requirements for membership are sale of original literary material to radio, screen, or television within the preceding two-year period, or employment as a writer, in any one of these three fields during the same period of time.

Writers Guild of America, West, is affiliated with the Writers Guild of America, East, which performs the same functions under the same conditions of membership requirements and dues for screen, television, and radio writers east of the Mississippi.

AMERICAN LITERARY AGENTS

Most literary agents do not usually accept new writers as clients. Since the agent's only income is a percentage—usually 10%—of the amount he receives from the sales he makes for his clients, he must have as clients writers who are selling fairly regularly to good markets. Always query an agent first. Do not send any manuscripts until the agent has asked you to do so. The following list is only a partial selection of representative agents. Addresses given are in New York City. (Zip codes are given in parentheses.)

Maxwell Aley Associates, 145 East 35th Street (10016)
American Play Company, Inc., 52 Vanderbilt Avenue (10017)
Julian Bach Literary Agency, Inc., 3 East 48th Street (10017)
Bill Berger Associates, Inc., 444 East 58th Street (10022)
Lurton Blassingame, 60 East 42nd Street (10017)
Georges Borchardt, Inc., 136 East 57th St., New York, NY (10022)
Brandt & Brandt, 101 Park Avenue (10017)
The Helen Brann Agency, 14 Sutton Place South (10022)
Curtis Brown, Ltd., 575 Madison Avenue (10022)
James Brown Associates, Inc. 22 East 60th Street (10022)
John Cushman Associates, Inc. 25 West 43rd Street (10036)
Joan Daves, 515 Madison Avenue (10022)

Anita Diamant, 51 East 42nd Street (10017)
Candida Donadio & Associates, Inc., 111 West 57th Street (10019)
Ann Elmo Agency, Inc., 52 Vanderbilt Avenue (10017)
Barthold Fles Literary Agency, 507 Fifth Avenue (10017)
Harold Freedman, Brandt & Brandt Dramatic Dept., Inc., 101 Park Avenue (10017)
Samuel French, Inc., 25 West 45th Street (10036)
Sanford J. Greenburger Associates, Inc., 757 Third Avenue (10017)
Blanche C. Gregory, Inc., 2 Tudor City Place (10017)
Harvey & Hutto, 110 West 57th Street (10019)
International Creative Management, 40 West 57th Street (10019)
Lucy Kroll Agency, 390 West End Avenue (10024)
The Lantz Office, Inc., 114 East 55th Street (10022)
Lenniger Literary Agency, Inc., 437 Fifth Avenue (10016)
Robert Lescher Literary Agency, 155 East 81st Street (10021)
The Sterling Lord Agency, 660 Madison Avenue (10021)
McIntosh, McKee & Dodds, Inc., 22 East 40th Street (10016)
McIntosh & Otis, 475 Fifth Avenue (10017)
Harold Matson Company, Inc., 22 East 40th Street (10016)
William Morris Agency, Inc., 1350 Avenue of the Americas (10019)
Harold Ober Associates, Inc., 40 East 49th Street (10017)
Paul R. Reynolds, Inc., 12 East 41st Street (10017)
Flora Roberts, Inc., 65 East 55th Street (10022)
Marie Rodell—Frances Collin, 141 East 55th Street (10022)
Russell & Volkening, Inc., 551 Fifth Avenue (10017)
Gloria Safier, Inc., 667 Madison Avenue (10021)
John Schaffner, 425 East 51st Street (10022)
Ad Schulberg Agency, 300 East 57th Street (10022)
James Seligmann Agency, 280 Madison Avenue (10016)
Gunther Stuhlman, 65 Irving Place (10003)
A. Watkins, Inc., 77 Park Avenue (10016)
WB Agency, Inc., 156 East 52nd Street (10022)
Mary Yost Associates, 141 East 55th Street (10022)

INDEX TO MARKETS